The ANC and the Liberation Struggle in South Africa

The history of the ANC, which is the oldest liberation movement on the African continent, is one that has generated a great deal of interest amongst historians in recent years. Gone are the days when the history of African nationalism could be relegated to the margins of the study of the South African past. Instead, with the ANC having ascended to the helm of political power, a position it has maintained for over twenty years, there can be no question that its history occupies an important and permanent place in the history of the nation.

This volume gathers together some of the most important contributions to the literature on the ANC's role in South Africa's struggle for liberation. Besides important themes such as gender, ethnicity, and healthcare, contributions from leading historians also address why the ANC decided to engage in armed struggle; what role the South African Communist Party played in making this decision; how the ANC External Mission contributed to the upsurge of mass protest in South Africa in the 1970s and 1980s; and the ANC's contribution, relative to the other components of the liberation struggle, in ensuring the eventual demise of the old racial order. The chapters in this book were originally published in the *South African Historical Journal*, the *Journal of Southern African Studies,* and *African Studies.*

Thula Simpson is a Senior Lecturer in the Department of History at the University of Pretoria, South Africa. He has published extensively on the ANC's armed struggle and the organisation's relationship with popular protest movements in South Africa. He is the author of *Umkhonto we Sizwe: The ANC's Armed Struggle* (2016).

The ANC and the Liberation Struggle in South Africa

Essential writings

Edited by
Thula Simpson

Routledge
Taylor & Francis Group

LONDON AND NEW YORK

First published 2017
by Routledge
2 Park Square, Milton Park, Abingdon, Oxon, OX14 4RN, UK

and by Routledge
711 Third Avenue, New York, NY 10017, USA

Routledge is an imprint of the Taylor & Francis Group, an informa business

British Library Cataloguing in Publication Data
A catalogue record for this book is available from the British Library

ISBN 13: 978-1-138-20826-1

Typeset in Times New Roman
by RefineCatch Limited, Bungay, Suffolk

Publisher's Note
The publisher accepts responsibility for any inconsistencies that may have
arisen during the conversion of this book from journal articles to book chapters,
namely the possible inclusion of journal terminology.

Disclaimer
Every effort has been made to contact copyright holders for their permission to
reprint material in this book. The publishers would be grateful to hear from any
copyright holder who is not here acknowledged and will undertake to rectify
any errors or omissions in future editions of this book.

Contents

CONTENTS

Citation Information

The chapters in this book were originally published in various issues of the *South African Historical Journal,* the *Journal of Southern African Studies,* and *African Studies.* When citing this material, please use the original page numbering for each article, as follows:

Chapter 1
Dialectical Dances: Exploring John Dube's Public Life
Heather A. Hughes
South African Historical Journal, volume 64, issue 3 (September 2012) pp. 418–433

Chapter 2
'A Member of the Race': Dr Modiri Molema's Intellectual Engagement with the Popular History of South Africa, 1912–1921
Jane Starfield
South African Historical Journal, volume 64, issue 3 (September 2012) pp. 434–449

Chapter 3
Women and the Problem of Family in Early African Nationalist History and Historiography
Meghan Healy-Clancy
South African Historical Journal, volume 64, issue 3 (September 2012) pp. 450–471

Chapter 4
The African National Congress in the Western Transvaal/Northern Cape Platteland, c.1910–1964: Patterns of Diffusion and Support for Congress in a Rural Setting
Andrew Hayden Manson and Bernard Mbenga
South African Historical Journal, volume 64, issue 3 (September 2012) pp. 472–493

Chapter 5
The Lasting Legacy: The Soviet Theory of the National-Democratic Revolution and South Africa
Irina Filatova
South African Historical Journal, volume 64, issue 3 (September 2012) pp. 507–537

Chapter 6
The Genesis of the ANC's Armed Struggle in South Africa 1948–1961
Stephen Ellis
Journal of Southern African Studies, volume 37, issue 4 (December 2011) pp. 657–676

Chapter 16

'Umkhonto we Sizwe, We are Waiting for You': The ANC and the Township Uprising,
September 1984 – September 1985
Thula Simpson
South African Historical Journal, volume 61, issue 1 (January 2009) pp. 158–177

Chapter 17

Sex in a Time of Exile: An Examination of Sexual Health, AIDS, Gender, and the ANC,
1980–1990
Carla Tsampiras
South African Historical Journal, volume 64, issue 3 (September 2012) pp. 637–663

For any permission-related enquiries please visit:
http://www.tandfonline.com/page/help/permissions

Notes on Contributors

Melissa Armstrong is a Ph.D. candidate in the Department of History at Carleton University, Ottawa, Canada. Her doctoral research project concerns the provision of health care by the African National Congress and its military wing, Umkhonto weSizwe, during the struggle against apartheid in South Africa between 1963 and 1990.

Garth Benneyworth is a Research Associate of the McGregor Museum, Kimberley, South Africa, and a former councillor of the Nelson Mandela National Museum. His work is in the field of military history, with a particular focus on the Boer War, and 20th century conflict in South Africa.

Scott Everett Couper is the Development Manager at the historic Inanda Seminary in South Africa, and an ordained minister of the United Church of Christ, based in KwaZulu-Natal. He is the author of *Albert Luthuli: Bound by Faith* (2010). He also teaches at the University of KwaZulu-Natal and at Seth Mokitimi Methodist Seminary.

Stephen Ellis was a Senior Researcher at the Afrika-Studiecentrum, Leiden, The Netherlands, and Professor in the Department of Social and Cultural Anthropology at the Vrije Universiteit Amsterdam, The Netherlands. He worked on – and was an activist on – human rights, and published on development, on violence, and on religion. He was the author of several books, including *The Criminalization of the State in Africa* (with Jean-François Bayart and Béatrice Hibou, 1999).

Irina Filatova is Professor of the State University, High School of Economics in Moscow, Russia, and Professor Emeritus of the University of KwaZulu-Natal, South Africa. She specialises in African and Russian history and is the author of *The Russians and the Anglo-Boer War* (with Apollon Davidson, 1998) and *The Hidden Thread: Russia and South Africa in the Soviet Era* (with Apollon Davidson, 2013).

Meghan Healy-Clancy is Assistant Professor of History at Bridgewater State University, USA, and a non-resident Fellow at the Du Bois Institute at Harvard University's Hutchins Centre for African and African American Research. She researches gender, race, and the politics of culture in South Africa. She is the author of *A World of Their Own: A History of South African Women's Education* (2014).

Heather A. Hughes is Professor of Southern African Studies at the University of Lincoln, UK. Her research specialises in Southern Africa, nationalism, biography, heritage, and mobility. She is the author of *First president: a life of John L. Dube, founding president of the ANC* (2011).

Paul S. Landau is Professor of History at the University of Maryland, USA. His field of study is southern Africa, and he is currently writing about violence and revolutionary ferment in

South Africa in 1960–3. His most recent books are *Popular Politics in the History of South Africa, 1400–1948* (2010), which was a finalist for the Herskovits prize; and *Images and Empires: Visuality in Colonial and Postcolonial Africa* (co-edited with Deborah Kaspin, 2002).

Arianna Lissoni is a researcher in the History Workshop at the University of the Witwatersrand, Johannesburg, South Africa. She is one of the editors of the *South African Historical Journal*. Her research interests are South African liberation history and politics.

Tom Lodge is Professor of Peace and Conflict Studies in the Department of Politics and Public Administration, and Dean of the Faculty of Arts, Humanities and Social Sciences, at the University of Limerick, Republic of Ireland. His most recent books are *Mandela: A Critical Life* (2006) and *Sharpeville: An Apartheid Massacre and its Consequences* (2011).

Andrew Hayden Manson is a Research Professor in History and Politics at North-West University, Mafikeng Campus, South Africa. He is the author of *"People of the Dew": A History of the Bafokeng of Phokeng/Rustenberg Region, South Africa, From Early Times to 2000* (with B. Mbenga, 2010). He has researched widely in the field of Batswana history, the formation of the Bechuanaland Frontier, western Transvaal rural history, and aspects of the Bophuthatswana homeland.

Bernard Mbenga is a History Professor at North-West University, Mafikeng Campus, South Africa. Among other books, he has co-authored *New History of South Africa; The Cambridge History of South Africa, Vol. I, From Early Times to 1885* and *A History of the ANC in the North-West Province of South Africa Since 1909.*

Thula Simpson is a Senior Lecturer in the Department of History at the University of Pretoria, South Africa. He has published extensively on the ANC's armed struggle and the organisation's relationship with popular protest movements in South Africa. He is the author of *Umkhonto we Sizwe: The ANC's Armed Struggle* (2016).

Jane Starfield is Senior Lecturer in the Department of English at the University of Johannesburg, South Africa. Her research field encompasses South African (and African) literature, with a particular focus on Dr Modiri Molema, on whom she has published a variety of scholarly articles.

Raymond Suttner is part-time Professor at Rhodes University and Emeritus Professor at the University of South Africa. A scholar and a social and political activist, he was actively involved in the liberation struggle against apartheid. He is the author of several books, including *Inside Apartheid's Prison* (2001), *The ANC Underground* (2008), *50 Years of the Freedom Charter* (2006), and *Recovering Democracy in South Africa* (2015). His book, *30 Years of the Freedom Charter* (1986, with Jeremy Cronin), was banned by the apartheid government.

Carla Tsampiras is Senior Lecturer in Medical Humanities at the University of Cape Town, South Africa. Her work is concerned with understanding how constructions of 'race', gender, sexuality, and class influence understandings of, and responses to, health concerns. Her other areas of interest include gender, violence and slavery in South Africa, the global crises, and Health and Medical Humanities.

Preface

The essays in this book form part of an important turn in South African historiography. The reasons for the shift are twofold, and both have their origins in the political transition of the 1990s. The first is that the post-1994 dispensation highlighted the significance of a number of events and themes from within the country's African nationalist tradition that had previously been neglected by most historians of South Africa. But one of the causes of this neglect was that the resources necessary for the study of those topics were not available to researchers during the apartheid years. An important feature of the post-1994 period has been the emergence of a number of archival collections relevant to the liberation struggle.

These are the two factors that have fostered the emergence of the new literature. In the early 2000s they converged, and it is since then that the study of the ANC and the liberation struggle has come into its own. I have been fortunate enough to be both a witness and a contributor to this process. During my research on the ANC's armed struggle, I often felt the need for a companion general *History of South Africa* that could place the events I was considering within the context of broader developments in the country. It is a need that I have tried to address in my work, as is reflected in my two contributions to this volume, which focus respectively on the role of the ANC underground during the 1976 Soweto Uprising and the township rebellion of the mid-1980s.

I believe this volume as a whole will perform a similar integrative function, and that it raises a number of important issues that must be considered in any future history of South Africa.

The long period between the formation of the ANC and the negotiated settlement of the 1990s meanwhile indicates just how complex and protracted the liberation struggle was. One manifestation of this complexity is the remarkable diversity of the *forms* of resistance that the ANC felt compelled to adopt during its course. This diversity is well represented in this volume.

The first chapter is by Heather A. Hughes, a biographer of John Dube,[1] who was the first president of the ANC. In her chapter she discusses the ways in which Dube's life was interpreted and reinterpreted by succeeding generations of ANC members. She describes how these re-evaluations were crucially influenced by the changing imperatives of the struggle, and she shows that this process has continued into the new South Africa, where his reputation and visibility have grown as a consequence of the post-apartheid government according him a prominent place in the nationalist canon.

Jane Starfield meanwhile reflects on the writings of one-time ANC National Executive Committee member Dr Modiri Molema, focusing particularly on his contributions in the fields of history and ethnography, which, she notes, had been 'until then powerful discursive tools in the armoury of colonial domination'. She discusses how Molema, with his nationalist ambitions, sought to reclaim them as instruments that could be utilised in the struggle for liberation.

---

[1] H. Hughes, *First President: A Life of John Dube, Founding President of the ANC* (Auckland Park: Jacana, 2011).

Meghan Healy-Clancy offers a gendered perspective of the ANC's early years. Focusing particularly on the 1930s, she describes the ways in which women made a variety of political contributions as participants, documenters and theoreticians of the struggle. Whilst noting that they typically premised their activism on their roles as mothers, wives, sisters, and daughters, she seeks to challenge the notion that in doing so they functioned as either a stabilising or a conservative influence. She argues that they were deeply 'concerned to create a new sort of African family – both capable of protecting its privacy and [of serving as] a model for new forms of public life – that could nurture an African nationalist body politic' capable of challenging the racial order.

Andrew Manson and Bernard Mbenga consider the ANC's strength on the ground in the Western Transvaal/Northern Cape platteland between 1910 and 1964. They argue that there existed a close correlation between levels of ANC support in the area, and attempts by the state to impose segregationist and apartheid policies. They argue that the last of the attempted impositions that they discuss, namely the enforcement of the Bantustan policy in the 1950s, served to establish the area as an ANC stronghold in the long term, and one that would make an important contribution at various stages of the struggle, beginning with its role as a 'pipeline' out of the country into neighbouring Bechuanaland in the early 1960s.

The next cluster of chapters considers the radicalisation of the ANC in the years immediately following the Second World War. Irina Filatova explores the 'National Democratic Revolution' (NDR), which has been the cornerstone of ANC policy since the 1960s. She traces the genealogy of the doctrine and shows that after its initial development in the Soviet Union, it was transmitted to the ANC through the South African Communist Party (SACP) in the 1950s. She also discusses its career within the ANC from the 1960s onwards, pointing out that it not only survived the fall of the Berlin Wall, but it also outlived the collapse of apartheid in such a way that it may yet represent the country's future.

Stephen Ellis discusses the ANC's move to armed struggle, a process that culminated in the establishment of Umkhonto we Sizwe (MK), which became the ANC's military wing. His essay advances three main points: firstly, that it was the SACP and not the ANC which took the first step towards violence; that Nelson Mandela was in fact acting as a disciplined SACP member when he formed MK and served as its first commander-in-chief; and that these factors combined with the external support rendered to MK by the Soviet Union meant that the armed struggle was in fact 'inscribed in the politics of the Cold War' from its birth.

Of Raymond Suttner's two articles, the first deals with the ANC's response to the growing threat of legal proscription in the 1950s. He explains that the movement's counter-strategy centred on the so-called 'M-Plan', which was devised early in the decade to enable it to continue operating underground if the need arose. He argues that the plan's impact on the ANC has been more profound than historians have previously acknowledged, and that some aspects of the movement's political culture, such as its tendency towards hierarchical top-down forms of organisation, should be traced to the 1950s and the implementation of the plan, rather than to the exile period from the 1960s onwards, as has often been claimed. Suttner's second essay considers Chief Albert Luthuli's attitude towards the formation of MK. Based on an analysis of Luthuli's speeches, he argues that they indicate that his stance was one of 'possible pragmatism' on the question of violence.

In making this point, Suttner is responding above all to the works of Scott Everett Couper, a biographer of Luthuli,[2] who has argued that the former ANC president remained implacably opposed to the adoption of armed struggle in South Africa until the end of his life. Couper's

---

[2] S. Couper, *Albert Luthuli: Bound by Faith* (Scottsville: University of KwaZulu-Natal Press, 2010).

chapter in this volume is a rejoinder to Suttner in which he reiterates his basic argument. Referring to the fact that Luthuli received the Nobel Peace Prize within a week of Umkhonto we Sizwe's launch in December 1961, he says it is a 'historiographic oxymoron' to contend that Luthuli accepted the award 'for his unambiguous advocacy of strict non-violent methods to fight Apartheid and the next week supported the launch of the armed struggle'.

Paul Landau also considers the move to armed struggle, revisiting the issue of the role of the SACP in the establishment of MK. He focuses particularly on the interaction between African and non-African Party members. Perhaps his principal area of disagreement with Stephen Ellis and others who have written before him, is that rather than seeing the SACP as acting as a unified, cohesive political force during the late fifties and early sixties, he feels that there was much more competition *between* Party members than has previously been acknowledged, and he makes that the focus of his analysis.

Tom Lodge touches on some of the same questions in his chapter, which focuses on the history of the SACP in the decade following its banning in 1950. Two issues in particular receive his attention: the first concerns the Party's reconstitution as an underground organisation in the years following its prohibition; whilst the second relates to the role played by its members within the wider liberation movement during the same period. Whilst concurring with Ellis that many communists acceded to command positions in the ANC, he echoes Landau in arguing that to extrapolate from this a 'picture of the party in command is too simple', for it fails to capture the complexity of the ANC's internal political dynamics.

Garth Benneyworth considers the first phase of the armed struggle, discussing Nelson Mandela's African tour of 1962, in which the MK commander's mission was to mobilise continental support for the newly formed military organ. In his article Benneyworth considers the links Mandela formed with freedom fighters and military personnel from across the continent; the training he received whilst abroad; and his activities in South Africa upon his return. In the process he revisits an unsolved mystery of South African history, namely the fate of the gun that Mandela received during his African tour and later deposited at Liliesleaf Farm in Rivonia, but which has never been recovered.

Arianna Lissoni discusses the history of the ANC's External Mission between 1960 and 1969, a period stretching from the Sharpeville Massacre to the Morogoro Conference. She details the difficulties that Oliver Tambo and his colleagues faced in establishing and consolidating the movement's position in Africa. She shows that the principal challenges they faced were the need to overcome hostility both within and beyond the ANC's ranks towards the reconstitution of what had been an Africans-only organisation in South Africa in the fifties into a 'unitary, non-racial liberation front' in exile; as well as the problem of adjusting MK and its often restless cadres to a new, and much more adverse strategic environment.

For all the stresses and strains that the movement encountered during the decade, those years proved to be crucial in the struggle, because by 1969 the External Mission had ensured that the ANC would survive what had been a determined and nearly successful attempt to secure its annihilation.

Melissa Armstrong explores the issue of the provision of health care within the ANC between 1964 and 1989. She argues that the needs of MK cadres, who formed the single largest component of the exile community, served as the principal influence guiding the evolution of the ANC's medical section. She points out that the health section began its existence as a small clinic in MK's camp in Kongwa, Tanzania in the 1960s, while she identifies the mid-1970s, when the ranks of the ANC were swelled by a new generation of exiles, as the key period in the creation of what became an institutional (and indeed a bureaucratic) Health Department. She argues that the efforts of this medical sector during the exile years proved to be 'critical for the survival' not only of MK's cadres, but the movement as a whole.

Armstrong's contribution is complemented by an article by Carla Tsampiras, which discusses perhaps the greatest challenge the Health Department faced during its existence, namely the threat of AIDS. Focusing initially on the AIDS education that the ANC offered to its members, she expands to discuss pregnancies and sexually transmitted infections generally, before reflecting on what her findings suggest regarding the sexual practices and healthcare needs that existed in the movement in the years leading up to its legalisation in 1990.

Clearly, whatever one feels about the issues that are raised – and the chapters show that there already exists strong disagreement about a number of them – there can be little doubt regarding the importance of their role in creating the new South Africa and determining some of its most salient characteristics. Previously the articles existed in widely dispersed publications. Yet their influence has been such that their basic arguments will in many cases be widely known, invariably second hand via other publications, and often with their original provenance remaining unacknowledged. This volume is offered in the hope that the task of gathering these works into a single collection will be useful to the general reader in providing an introduction to the basic literature on the ANC and the liberation struggle, whilst also serving as a resource for those specialists interested in taking the next step in the development of the field.

Thula Simpson
Hatfield, Pretoria
December 2016

Acknowledgements

The chapters in this book by Heather A. Hughes, Jane Starfield, Meghan Healy-Clancy, Andrew Hayden Manson and Bernard Mbenga, Irina Filatova, Scott Everett Couper, Paul S. Landau and Carla Tsampiras, were first published in a special issue of the *South African Historical Journal* (SAHJ) in September 2012 (Volume 64, Number 3) that commemorated the ANC's centennial. The chapters by Raymond Suttner, Tom Lodge, Garth Benneyworth and Melissa Armstrong, as well as Thula Simpson's essay on the ANC and the township uprising, all appeared in other issues of the SAHJ.

Thula Simpson's article on the ANC underground in Johannesburg during the Soweto Uprising was first published as an article in *African Studies* in 2011.

The chapters by Arianna Lissoni and Stephen Ellis were first published as articles in the *Journal of Southern African Studies* in 2009 and 2011 respectively.

I would like to thank the authors and the journals concerned for permitting the inclusion of these works in this volume.

I would also like to express my gratitude to Nicholas Barclay, Oscar Masinyana and Jenny Guildford from Routledge, Taylor and Francis, for their help and encouragement in seeing this book through to publication.

Lastly, I would like to dedicate this volume to the memory of Angela Gumede Simpson.

Thula Simpson
Pretoria

Dialectical Dances: Exploring John Dube's Public Life

HEATHER A. HUGHES

University of Lincoln, Lincoln, UK

Abstract

This article investigates the relationship between biographical subject and author. By using the example of John Dube, it traces the changing fortunes of the 'the life' at the hands of various writers, during his life but more particularly after his death. It culminates with a discussion of the recently-published first full-length biography of Dube.

Introduction

John Langalibalele Dube, the founding president of the South African Native National Congress one hundred years ago, has only recently become the subject of a full-length biography. Yet he has by no means been neglected in the historiography of twentieth-century African nationalism in South Africa. Several competing images of him emerge. One – perhaps the most striking – posits a clear trajectory to his public life: that he started out with a radical mission, upsetting colonial officials and missionaries in the process, but along the way made compromises and ended his career politically emasculated and a supporter of segregation. Another version, by contrast, stresses his consistency as a moderate voice; yet another finds his ambiguity, his multiple voices, most in evidence.

Eric Hobsbawm devised the notion of a 'dialectical dance' as a way of characterising those who, in times of profound change, had neither a vested interest in maintaining the status quo nor in completely overthrowing it.[1] At various times they danced between different ideologues and extremists; on balance, they tended to be politically moderate. Early twentieth-century South Africa was possibly such a setting: in the aftermath of the South African War, there were sharply competing ideas as to who should be included in and excluded from a state-building project that sought to consolidate the interests of a

An earlier version of this paper was presented to the Southern African Historical Society Conference: 'The Past and its Possibilities: Perspectives of Southern Africa', 23rd Biennial Conference, University of KwaZulu-Natal, Durban, 27–29 June 2011. Grateful thanks to Muzi Hadebe, Mwelela Cele, Brian Willan, Jacob Dlamini, Thula Simpson, Meghan Healey and Jeff Guy for comments.
1.   E. Hobsbawm, *The Age of Revolution 1789–1848* (New York: Mentor, 1962), 84–85.

modernising industrial economy, whose leaders were themselves divided into squabbling factions. Was someone like John Dube one of these dialectical dancers, balanced awkwardly as a moderate,[2] or else unable to hold a position, swayed by his own constituency as well as those keen to minimise his influence?

The notion of a dialectical dance simultaneously brings the relationship between subject and scholarship into focus: it may be the case that it is choreographed not so much *through* a public life as *outside* of it and/or *afterwards*, as different writers survey the evidence and come to their own various conclusions. Marks alluded to this phenomenon with specific reference to Dube: 'On the whole, American scholars have heard the voice of Booker T. Washington, British liberals that of Victorian liberalism.'[3] The theme of this article, then, is the ways in which Dube's public life has been understood and interpreted in the historical/biographical record. It draws inspiration from the work of Lucy Riall, who made a strong case for the need to understand how 'a life' is constructed in retrospect and over time, in her study of the Italian nationalist Giuseppe Garibaldi.[4]

In terms of the sources that have been drawn upon, written sketches and more discursive treatments in which Dube is the clear subject are the most important. Reference is also made to selected historical texts which have shaped our image of him, despite the fact that he plays only a bit part in them. Discussion concentrates on published texts, although it should be noted that at least two of Dube's contemporaries, G.G. Nxaba and R.R.R. Dhlomo, both had intentions of producing biographies and had begun to make sketch notes which survive in the archival record;[5] likewise, there are unpublished theses that have exerted an important influence and merit inclusion for this reason. In addition, reference is made to a certain amount of oral evidence, where this has had some influence in shaping perceptions about Dube's life.

2. We should, however, note Campbell's caution that 'the dichotomy between "moderates" and "radicals" is grossly inadequate for disentangling the web of association' within the African middle classes. He was referring specifically to the interwar years but the point holds more generally. J. Campbell, 'T.D. Mweli Skota and the Making and Unmaking of a Black Elite', paper presented at the University of the Witwatersrand History Workshop, 1987, 20.

3. S. Marks, *The Ambiguities of Dependence: Class, Nationalism, and the State in Twentieth-century Natal.* (Johannesburg: Ravan Press, 1986), 69.

4. L. Riall, 'The Shallow End of History? The Substance and Future of Political Biography', *Journal of Interdisciplinary History*, 40, 3 (2010), 375–397.

5. G.G. Nxaba's 11-page manuscript is in the American Board Papers, Houghton Library, Harvard. Although difficult to date, it was likely written before 1917, the year in which Dube's first wife, Nokutela Mdima, died. Nxaba was related to Dube through this marriage. Its focus is on the early years of Ohlange and the struggles of the staff under the Dubes' leadership to establish the institution. It also recounts details of Dube's family background to emphasise his prominence – for example, that his father James had once loaned the sum of £1,000 to a white man – and is the only known source to list all of John Dube's siblings. R.R.R. Dhlomo edited *Ilanga* for nearly 30 years; in his retirement, he was attempting to write a biography of Dube, but struggling under difficult circumstances: 'no typewriter, and by candle light', as he told Tom Karis, who interviewed him in 1964 (University of KwaZulu-Natal Malherbe Library, Karis-Carter Microfilm Collection, Reel 9A, Dube section). Both Nxaba and Dhlomo wished to convey a sense of the adversity against which Dube had had to struggle (which they keenly felt themselves), as well as the considerable material accomplishments of his parents.

The making of John Dube's reputation to 1946

By the time of his death in 1946, John Dube had acquired a towering reputation as a leader of his generation. He had of course enjoyed considerable prominence in public life, most notably as founder of Ohlange (1901) and *Ilanga* (1903), and then as inaugural president of the African National Congress (1912–1917), but three decades had passed since the last of these achievements. Moreover, half of his presidential incumbency has been marked by inactivity, and he had had to relinquish control of both Ohlange and *Ilanga* in the 1920s. While he had remained active at the helm of nationalist politics in Natal and Zululand, he had fallen out with detractors both within and outside Congress and his acceptance of a position on the Natives Representative Council in 1937 divided opinion. How, then, had his unrivalled stature been established?

The tireless efforts of his remarkable mentor, William Wilcox, are of some significance. Wilcox often enters the story of Dube's life as the missionary under whose auspices the young John Dube travelled to America to study in the late 1880s, but then as often departs from it, never to reappear. In fact the two men stayed closely in touch, collaborating on issues as diverse as orthography, mission station rents and the launch a self-help scheme (the Zulu Industrial Improvement Company). In 1909, in order to assist Dube with a fundraising mission abroad, Wilcox wrote an article for the *Missionary Review of the World*.[6] Entitled 'John L. Dube, the Booker Washington of the Zulus', it stressed Dube's Christian duty and achievements at Ohlange. Wilcox and his wife were forced to return to the States in 1918, penniless and defeated in their independent endeavours to set up self-help Christian communities in South Africa.[7] Yet they never gave up their support for Dube. Wilcox produced another article on Dube's work in 1927, just months before he died. This time, Dube had been elevated: 'The story of John Dube, the Booker Washington of South Africa'. Again, it was written to assist his protégé on a mission abroad to raise funds for a trades building at Ohlange; again, it was certain to attract attention in one of the most widely-read Christian magazines of the time.[8]

Wilcox's 1927 article, written when its subject was 55, contains an outline biographical narrative, beginning with Dube's struggle with faith and conversion to Christianity at school; his pleading with Wilcox to be allowed to travel to America; the hardship he faced there in his attempts to be educated; his breakthrough as a public speaker and early success on the fundraising circuit; his return to Natal and founding of Ohlange and *Ilanga* and his fortitude in keeping them afloat, despite a severe lack of resources; his presidency of the African National Congress; and his continuing power as a public speaker before numerous influential audiences. The youthful episodes in this account,

---

6. In *Missionary Review of the World*, 32 (1909), 917–919.
7. The Wilcoxes' missionary endeavours in southern Africa are recounted in Cherif Keita's documentary, *Cemetery Stories: A Rebel Missionary in South Africa* (Carleton College, 2009).
8. W. Wilcox, 'The Story of John Dube, the Booker Washington of South Africa', *Congregationalist* 10 March 1937; University of KwaZulu-Natal Campbell Collections, Killie Campbell Cuttings Book 4, 131. By the time Dube took this trip, he had relinquished his total control of Ohlange but continued to support it in a number of ways.

presented in minutely-detailed direct speech, feature far more prominently than the later adult life.

> 'Well, John', I asked him, 'what troubles you?'
> 'Nothing much', he replied, 'only I want to be a Christian, and you asked us all to come and have a talk with you.'[9]

Wilcox's own sense of achievement was intimately bound up with Dube's, particularly his role in setting the young man on the path that led to subsequent greatness. He thus presented his narrative as a heroic battle with, and eventual conquest of, darkness and adversity, and of fame well-earned. It is an account, moreover, that carries the stamp of great authority, given the closeness of the two men. Lastly, since it recounts Dube's early years in such detail, it has been one of the most important sources of information about this youthful period in his life ever since.

It is of interest that apart from the title, there is no other mention of Booker Washington in this article. By the time of his death in 1915, Washington had become a byword for responsible African American accommodation within the status quo. Dube had sought Washington's endorsement for his work in South Africa as early as 1898; this had finally been conferred in 1910. Although both Dube and Wilcox had tended to rub against the grain far more than Washington had ever done, they undoubtedly admired his achievements (and since both had been bitterly thwarted in their endeavours for want of cash, were perhaps even a little envious of the resources he was able to command). In any event, they were clearly prepared to ally themselves with his memory for present and future purposes.

Whoever penned Dube's entry just a few years later for *The African Yearly Register* (possibly the general editor himself, T.D. Mweli Skota, or another prolific contributor, H.I.E. Dhlomo)[10] did not refer to him in these terms at all. The *Register* is interesting as an example of how the biographical sketch can be used not merely to convey 'factoids' of information about the subject but also to present that subject as he (and in a few rare examples, she) was viewed by contemporaries. Manganyi saw the historical significance of the *Register* as the first attempt by black South Africans to exploit the biographical form for purposes of declaiming a new identity, 'part and parcel of the attempt at creating the New African'. This was an intellectual non-starter for him, because the concept of the 'New African' embraced the ideology of the coloniser and denied the possibility of what he called 'cultural improvisation'.[11] Nevertheless, the only two editions of the *Register* that ever appeared, in 1930 and 1932, together sold 12,000 copies:[12] it was both popular and influential in its own time and has been an important source of information for scholars of modern southern African history ever since.

9. Wilcox, 'The Story of John Dube'. Two years previously, Wilcox had published his memoirs of his first attempts to establish mission work among the Tonga at Inhambane in the 1880s; it is couched in the same immediate style. See his *The Man from the African Jungle* (New York: Macmillan Press, 1925)

10. Couzens discusses the matter of authorship in his *The New African. A Study of the Life and Work of H.I.E. Dhlomo* (Johannesburg: Ravan Press, 1985), 1.

11. N.C. Manganyi, 'Biography: The Black South African Connection', in A.M. Friedson, ed., *New Directions in Biography*. (Honolulu: University of Hawaii Press, 1981), 55–57.

12. Campbell, 'T.D. Mweli Skota', 2.

In the *Register,* Dube's pre-eminence is established in several ways.[13] A double-page spread is devoted to him, consisting of a photograph on the left and text on the right. Of the nearly 300 entries in the 'living' section, 37 are accorded this honour of two-page spreads (in only one case, that of Mangena Mokone, this stretches to four), 23 of them from South Africa and neighbouring territories and the rest from other parts of Africa. The photograph shows a commanding close-up portrait of Dube, impeccably attired, sporting handle-bar moustaches, and looking confidently just past the camera, as if acknowledging an appreciative audience. In his bearing he is every bit the respected leader. The word 'founder' occurs three times in the opening paragraph: this is clearly a source of Dube's great stature, being the *originator* of so much that defined the African middle class: a newspaper, a school, and a political organisation. Importantly, all three were still in existence at the time of publication, unlike countless other efforts that had spluttered into life and failed for lack of resources, something of which Skota himself was all too aware.

The main part of the entry focuses on Dube's tenure as president of Congress, particularly on the delegation he led to Britain in 1914 to protest the passing of the Natives Land Act. In this version, the mission ended because of the declaration of war in August and statements by British politicians that they would continue to press for the rights of Africans – in other words, due to circumstances beyond the control of the delegation. The narrative continues that some time later (date unspecified), Dube resigned from the presidency, a careful formulation leaving his reputation intact. Several subsequent accounts claimed that he had been pushed, rather than had jumped (and it was an episode that Wilcox had misremembered in his contribution, declaring that Dube had served two terms in office).

The final paragraph begins by noting that he has continued to play a leading role in education and politics in Natal. His talents as an orator are recounted, as are his popularity 'with all sections of the community' and his fame among chiefs across the subcontinent. These last points indicate in the *Register*'s discourse that Dube had played an important role in reducing ethnic and linguistic divisions and in fostering the nationalist (or even Pan-African) vision so vital to Skota. Interestingly, the description 'progressive' is not used in relation to Dube. Since it acts as 'the ideological touchstone or keyword of the whole book',[14] omission is possibly as suggestive as commission, indicating a certain ambivalence towards him.

The making of John Dube's reputation after 1946

Some writers argue strongly that biography can properly be undertaken only after the death of the subject. This is not merely due to the important matter of defamation and the threat of legal proceedings that might prevent the publication of anything that could potentially be construed as slanderous while the subject is alive. It is also about perspective and the need to assess lasting influence, particularly in the case of well-known or

---

13. For Dube's entry, see T.D. Mweli Skota, ed. and comp., *The African Yearly Register. Being an Illustrated National Biographical Dictionary (Who's Who) of Black Folks in Africa* (Johannesburg: R.L. Esson and Co. and The Orange Press, 1932), 144–145.
14. Couzens, *The New African*, 7.

controversial figures.[15] If this last-mentioned point is any guide, then Dube's prospects in the following two decades were not promising. While he emerged a giant from the press coverage immediately after his death, what little was added to the published record thereafter served to question, rather than reinforce, the image of greatness that had been so carefully crafted through his life.

On his death in February 1946, Dube's achievements were extensively recounted in both print and funeral eulogy. However, an observation about funeral eulogy can equally apply to print recollection at the time of death, that it will tend by its very nature to "'celebrate, commemorate, honour, dedicate, mourn" and thus *praise* the life of the deceased'.[16] Since this is a widely-accepted convention – whatever one feels about the life, this is not the appropriate time for any sort of dispassionate appraisal – the contribution of eulogy to the making of a posthumous legacy needs to be treated with great caution. In Dube's case, his supporters used the occasion for a concerted attempt at establishing a reputation of heroic, even epic, proportions.

Although most newspapers carried stories about Dube's passing, *Ilanga* (as one would expect) led the tributes, and several pages were given over to praise for his achievements, in editorials, letters, reports of speeches, songs and sonnets. It was not only the amount of space devoted to such praise, but also the prominence of the contributors that was important. Senator Edgar Brookes and H.I.E. Dhlomo headed a long list, Dhlomo setting the tone:

> It is the practice in this country to judge the achievements of Africans in a condescending spirit by making a special tape-measure for the blackman. His work is assessed and valuated not according to absolute standards but according to the theory that he belongs to a child race – and thus certain allowances and considerations have to be made for him. This attitude, this practice, has done much injury to African endeavour in art, music, and other spheres. The life and achievements of Dr Dube are above this.[17]

Dhlomo then turned to the theme of Dube's greatness, pointing to the many ways in which he had faced up to and conquered adversity, emerging stronger each time. Both Booker Washington and Dube had 'led their people out of the Egypt of oppression and despair' to the Canaan of 'Hope, Solidarity, Self Help, self-realisation and expression'. But whereas Washington had confined his achievements to education, Dube's could be measured across a broad terrain, as 'an educationist, a politician, a publicist, editor, artist'. The difficult task of unifying Africans, which Dube had tackled with great energy, was also something unknown to Washington. Dube was clearly the greater leader.[18]

The young Jordan Ngubane's contribution for *Inkundla yaBantu* in June 1946 probably helped to make Dube's life and work more accessible to his own generation. His assessment

15. On the effects of defamation laws, see P. Alexander, 'The Art of the Impossible: Problems of Literary Biography', lecture presented to Christ's College, Cambridge, November 2003. On this same issue as well as on that of perspective, see H. Lee, *Biography: A Very Brief Introduction* (Oxford: Oxford University Press, 2009), 9–10.

16. D. Ochs, cited in A.D. Kunkel and M.R. Dennis, 'Grief Consolation in Eulogy Rhetoric: An Integrative Framework' in *Death Studies*, 27, 1 (2003), 3; emphasis added.

17. *Ilanga*, 23 February, 1946.

18. *Ibid*.

was mixed, even equivocal, already demonstrating a willingness to question the *Ilanga* image. While Dube had been considered a radical at the time of the Bhambatha Rebellion, Ngubane's verdict was definite: he 'was not a revolutionary or a radical. Even his style of writing and angle of approach were not remarkable for their aggressiveness. He wrote in somewhat plaintive and moderate tones in pleading the case of his people'. As his influence grew in white circles, continued Ngubane, so it waned in African ones; he had also been 'chased around' by the ICU. Yet he possessed qualities which made him an impressive figure: 'His enemies said he was stubborn and sometimes capricious. His friends admired his patience, ability to negotiate through difficult situations and his refusal to take defeat.' Above all, 'he was against racial nomination of any sort... whether we agree with him or not, he was a distinguished nation-builder'.[19] Here was Dube presented as the flawed hero.

Just two years later, a highly influential work appeared, Edward Roux's *Time Longer than Rope*.[20] Roux, who was active in leftwing politics, knew Dube and had taught at Ohlange, and in this sense he spoke with some authority. He pointed out that 'in his youth [Dube] appears to have been rather more of a radical' than when we encounter him in the heat of the Durban anti-pass protests of 1929. On this occasion, he is described as a 'good boy', watching the unfolding events from the safety his Chevrolet, the protesters taking no notice of him. Later in the narrative, Dube re-appears as a 'traitor' for allegedly supporting the Hertzog Bills. 'But who cared for Dube? He was known to be a Government man', Roux adds.[21] These were fleeting if memorable anecdotes, without serious analytical support or documentary evidence. Yet here was the earliest articulation of that perception that would reappear: Dube had been radical in his youth and had danced rather a long way rightwards through his political career.[22]

R.V. Selope Thema's 'How Congress Began', which appeared in *Drum* in 1953, failed to make any mention at all of Dube, choosing instead to focus on Pixley kaIsaka Seme, who had lately passed away. Given the title of the piece, this seems distinctly odd. Selope Thema had been closely involved in Dube's exit from the presidency in 1917, and may have had his own motives for airbrushing him from his recollections. Nevertheless, this article has been influential as an eyewitness account and has helped to boost Seme's reputation as having founded Congress almost single-handedly.

In *The African Patriots*, published in 1963, Mary Benson portrayed Dube (whom, like Roux and Thema, she knew) in a more charitable light, despite the fact that the ANC had recently embarked on an armed struggle from exile, and the old, 'polite' political methods of the early generation of nationalists were by then heavily under attack. She described Dube on the eve of his assumption of the Congress presidency as 'a determined and practical visionary' who had been moved by the Natal government's failure to provide schooling for Africans. His vision extended to the founding of *Ilanga* and a couple of years

19. J.K. Ngubane, 'Three Famous Journalists I Knew: John Langalibalele Dube', in *Inkundla yaBantu*, 9, 121, Second fortnight, June 1946.

20. E. Roux, *Time Longer Than Rope: The Black Man's Struggle for Freedom in South Africa* (London: Gollancz, 1948). This work was reissued by the University of Wisconsin Press in 1964. Page references are from the later edition.

21. Roux, *Time Longer Than Rope*, 100, 250 and 288.

22. An observation also noted by R. Hunt Davis in his 'John L. Dube: a South African Exponent of Booker T. Washington', *Journal of African Studies*, 2, 4 (1975/6), 511.

later he 'had courted arrest by protesting outspokenly against the execution of Zulus during the Bambata rebellion of 1906'. Anticipating a theme of later scholarship, Benson claimed that even in 1912, 'first and foremost Dube was a Zulu patriot...[this] was both a virtue and a disadvantage; however, for the time being the Native National Congress saw only his virtue'. By the 1920s, she continued, Dube had become a 'moderate', though with strong words against government policy.[23]

Benson's work was part of a wave of emerging Africanist scholarship, whose primary impetus was the achievement of statehood across the continent. Nationalism and the nature of resistance to colonial rule were prominent, linked themes in this literature[24] and served as the context for the first sustained evaluations of Dube's career, by Shula Marks in the United Kingdom and Manning Marable and R. Hunt Davis in America. Marks's *Reluctant Rebellion: The 1906–8 Disturbances in Natal* was published in 1970; her interest in Dube's role was developed in an article in the new *Journal of Southern African Studies* and subsequently in a series of interlinked essays on African leadership in Natal.[25] Marable's doctoral thesis for the University of Maryland was submitted in 1976; it was never published, although shorter contributions, partially based on it, were.[26] Davis's study appeared as an article in another recently-established periodical, the *Journal of African Studies,* in 1975/6.[27] Marks's first article in part positioned itself against Davis's work, which in turn drew substantially on Marable's work in progress. Thus, although it was the last in this trilogy actually to appear, Marable's contribution is dealt with first.

Marable's thesis is notable for several reasons. As an African American, he brought an important 'subaltern' perspective to his work. In addition, he interviewed a number of people who had worked with and known Dube, such as Gideon Mvakwendlu Sivetye and William Ireland. Although he was also constrained in the amount of research he was able to complete in South Africa, he concentrated his attention on hitherto-unexplored documentary sources in America (at least for this subject matter), and as a result those chapters tracing Dube's American years and connections are the strongest. His work had little to say about Dube's involvement in Congress, focusing as it did on his educational endeavours.

Marable stressed the formative influences of Booker Washington and a philosophy that involved subscribing to 'a pragmatic alliance with white paternalists'.[28] He then traced

---

23. M. Benson, *The African Patriots. The Story of the African National Congress of South Africa* (Chicago, New York and London: Encyclopaedia Britannica Press, 1963), 29 and 61.

24. Seminal contributions include G. Shepperson and T. Price, *Independent African. John Chilembwe and the Nyasaland Uprising of 1915* (Edinburgh: The University Press, 1958); T. Hodgkin, *African Nationalism in Colonial Africa* (London: Frederick Muller, 1956); B. Davidson, *Africa in Modern History: The Search for a New Society* (Harmondsworth: Penguin, 1978), and P. Walshe, *The Rise of African Nationalism and South Africa: The African National Congress 1912–1952* (London: C. Hurst, 1970).

25. S. Marks, 'The Ambiguities of Dependence: John L. Dube of Natal', *Journal of Southern African Studies,* 1, 2 (1975), 162–180; Marks, 'The Ambiguities of Dependence'.

26. M. Marable, 'African Nationalist: The Life of John Langalibalele Dube' (Phd thesis, University of Maryland, 1976); M. Marable, 'A Black School in South Africa', *Negro History Bulletin,* 34, 4 (1974), 258–261; and M. Marable, 'Booker T. Washington and African Nationalism', *Phylon,* 35, 4 (1974), 398–406. It is of interest that this last-mentioned work was Marable's first exploration of biography, to which he returned much later: his biography of Malcolm X was published just days after his death in March 2011.

27. Davis, 'John L. Dube', 497–528.

28. Marable, 'Booker T. Washington', 401.

Dube's attempts to establish Ohlange and keep it running with the help of his American Committee and various other American philanthropists. His judgement of Dube's legacy was a harsh one: he was 'leader of the conservative Black nationalist movement... due in large measure to his own limited social vision and lack of independent economic funds'. In embracing a cautious, pro-capitalist ideology and rejecting Gandhian passive resistance, Dube encouraged his followers to accept segregation. Thus, 'the tactics of Natal's small Black middle class helped to create the anti-humane regime in Southern Africa'.[29] There had been redeeming features to Dube's early position – in America in the 1890s, his rhetoric had often been virulently anti-colonial, for example – but ultimately Dube sold out. Marable was thus adding weight to the 'Roux view'.

Davis, like Marable, saw Washington as a major influence on Dube. Indeed, his study was designed around two related questions, why such a passionate Washingtonian exponent came from Natal, and why that individual was John Dube. He saw parallels in the two men's lives and emphasised the American origins of the African National Congress, in part explaining in these terms what he considered its early moderation and responsibility. He argued strongly that Dube must be seen 'primarily as an educator whose political activities formed an extension of a social philosophy founded on education'. In contrast to Marable, Davis concluded that he 'demonstrated a remarkable consistency throughout his public life... that can best be understood when considered in the context of his conscious adoption of Booker T. Washington's philosophy, strategy and tactics'.[30] (It is worth noting that Peter Walshe was probably the first to query the contradiction in such an argument: 'although Dube was... an admirer of Washington, the very formation of Congress as a permanent organisation to defend African interests was more in keeping with Du Bois's methods'.[31])

Marks's study of Dube was less concerned with positing an American connection than with situating Dube in the changing political economy of South Africa, something that neither Marable nor Davis had attempted. She introduced what became the influential concept of 'the ambiguities of dependence', in order to characterise what she saw as apparent contradictions not only in Dube's publicly-declared position, but in those of other twentieth-century Natal/Zululand leaders as well. As far as Dube was concerned, her verdict differed greatly from all the foregoing writers: he was remarkably consistent, not in his moderation and attachment to Washington but in demanding racial equality and pressing for African unity, both of these 'revolutionary' aspirations in the early twentieth century and sounding distinctly outspoken even in the 1940s.[32]

Yet his structural location as a 'powerless and dependant "intercalary leader" mediating between two unequal societies'[33] was what underlay his apparent shifts between defiance and acquiescence. Rejecting the somewhat literal reading of documentary evidence to be

29. Marable, 'African Nationalist', 183 and iii.
30. Davis, 'John L. Dube', 513 and 527. It may be noted that Davis also surveys a number of works discussing Dube.
31. Walshe, *The Rise of African Nationalism*, 13. Recent scholars have cautioned against drawing too bold a distinction between what were often tendencies, rather than oppositions, in African American thought: see W.J. Moses, *Creative Conflict in African American Thought* (Cambridge: Cambridge University Press, 2004).
32. Marks, 'The Ambiguities of Dependence', 166.
33. *Ibid.*, 167; she drew the concept of 'intercalary leader' from the work of Donovan Williams.

found in both Marable's and Davis's work, she instead presented a complex analysis of Dube's adherence to Washington's philosophy (in particular the need for industrial education), arguing that while this was engrained in his make-up, it was also a 'mask' he employed in order to push the bounds, striking out independently of state control at Ohlange and on *Ilanga lase Natal*. Nowhere was this more evident than in his assumption of the presidency of the South African Native National Congress, when in his acceptance address he spoke with 'two voices to his two different audiences', whites and Africans. To the former, he stressed his adherence to Washington and his cautious approach to change, while to the latter he stressed the urgency of political emancipation.[34]

In her later work, Marks explored further this idea of speaking to different audiences, relating it not only to Dube's politics but to the vested interests of different scholars, as noted above. She also added a further dimension, linking back to Mary Benson's observations: Dube's vacillation between a broadly-based *African* nationalism and a narrowly-based *Zulu* nationalism, a product of the increasingly restrictive policies of the state and his casting-about for modernising allies.[35] Her overall conclusion was that it was the world, rather than the individual, that had changed: Dube straddled two distinct eras of South African history, one rooted in a slow-paced agrarian past and the other in an aggressively industrialising one. Under such circumstances, 'his strategy and ideology were outflanked by the times'.[36] Marks's argument is that the structural ambiguity that Dube exhibited (as well as A.W.G. Champion, Solomon kaDinuzulu and M.G. Buthelezi, her other subjects) is located in society, rather than the individual. One can therefore observe that her concept of ambiguity and Hobsbawm's of 'dialectical dance' both share the sense of a tension between opposing positions – Marks uses the notion of a 'tightrope' to convey this – but with one difference: while Marks tends slightly toward privileging structure over agency, Hobsbawm tends toward privileging agency over structure.

The years from the mid-1980s were a period of considerable deceleration in Africanist scholarship, as the phase of optimism about independence gave way to a more sombre period of reflection on the 'failure of development'. It was also one which saw an intensification of the liberation struggle within South Africa and the onset of negotiations with the exiled ANC; Rassool's observation that 'there is always a struggle for control over the story of a life' holds for any act of biography, but is especially apt for these years, in two respects.[37] First, as Lodge noted, the early 1990s witnessed 'the birth of a new genre of iconographic literature devoted to the lives and achievements of great black South Africans', an important development in view of the fact that (book length) political biography in South Africa up to that point had remained almost exclusively white.[38] Brian Willan's detailed and insightful study of Solomon Plaatje, published in 1984, was then virtually the only exception.[39] Among those subjected to biographical treatment – sometimes only by way

34. Marks, 'The Ambiguities of Dependence', 175.
35. Marks, 'The Ambiguities of Dependence', 68–73.
36. Marks, 'The Ambiguities of Dependence', 165.
37. C.S. Rassool, 'The Individual, Auto/Biography and History in South Africa' (Phd thesis, University of the Western Cape, 2004), 46.
38. T. Lodge, 'Paper Monuments: Political Biography in the New South Africa', *South African Historical Journal*, 28 (1993), 249.
39. B. Willan, *Solomon Plaatje: A Biography* (Johannesburg: Ravan Press, 1984).

of a preface to collected speeches or writings – were Monty Naicker, Yusuf Dadoo, Nelson Mandela and Oliver Tambo. Notably, all were post-World War II leaders of the Congress Alliance: earlier generations of leadership were barely mentioned.

Yet when they were (and this is the second observation on Rassool's point), it was to claim them as emblems of a more recent struggle. In Dube's case, examples included the contributions of Herbert Mnguni and E.S. Reddy. Mnguni drew explicit lessons from Dube's life for the cause of Black Liberation (the need for education in preparation for taking control of the country, the need for a voice in the media, the need to be courageous in the face of oppression)[40]. E.S. Reddy wrote extensively on the role that Indian nationalists had played in the South African struggle. In one article, he argued that a 'close friendship and mutual respect' had developed between Dube and Gandhi during the latter's time in South Africa. He teased out the parallels in their lives, born within a couple of years of each other; travelling abroad to study; founding settlements, newspapers and political movements; and admiring Booker Washington. These parallels, in Reddy's work, supported something more:

> There was frequent social contact between the inmates of the Phoenix Settlement and the Ohlange Institute, as well as the mission at Inanda. Zulus and whites used to attend Gandhiji's prayer meetings at Phoenix. He was often seen playing with Indian and Zulu children.[41]

Whatever its historical accuracy, Dube was being called upon as an ally in promoting the nonracialism that was so vital an ideological position at a time when the ANC was embarking on negotiations with the South African government.

Such political claims did not go uncontested. As the struggle between the United Democratic Front and Chief Gatsha Buthelezi's Inkatha movement intensified through the 1980s, especially in Natal, so Inkatha too made concerted efforts to claim Dube (and other early ANC leaders) as an ally. In many of his speeches, Buthelezi used Dube's life and achievements as a measure of his own, simultaneously claiming the 'old ANC' as Inkatha's forerunner. Nowhere was this clearer than on the occasion of Inkatha assuming ownership of *Ilanga* in 1987:

> [*Ilanga's*] founder was the Revered Dr John Dube... The Black heroes of those times came together, and in 1912 established the African National Congress... Our John Dube was elected President in that historical event.
> Right from the outset of Black politics in modern South Africa the heroes of our past set their eyes on gaining a rightful place for the sons and daughters of Africa in the land of their birth. The old ANC drew everybody together and committed itself to waging the struggle for liberation on every possible front... We must take that struggle everywhere, to every point. Black newspapers must follow that struggle wherever it goes. I struggle in the KwaZulu Legislative Assembly. I struggle in the KwaZulu/Natal Indaba. I struggle in the white universities. I struggle against the captains of industry...[42]

40. H.M. Mnguni, 'Dr John Langalibalele Dube', *Matatu*, 3/4, 2 (1988), 149–156.
41. E.S. Reddy, 'Mahatma Gandhi and John Dube', *The Leader*, 5 June 1992, and then as chapter 4 of E.S. Reddy, *Gandhiji's Vision of a Free South Africa* (New Delhi: Sanchar Publishing House, 1995).
42. 'A Few Remarks Announcing Inkatha's take-over of *Ilanga*', address by Mangosuthu G. Buthelezi, Chief Minister of KwaZulu, President of Inkatha and Chairman, The South African Black Alliance, 15 April 1987. University of KwaZulu-Natal, Durban: Natal Collection. A larger-scale attempt to situate Dube in a

Images of Dube after 1994

As the party of which he was the inaugural president swept to power in 1994, Dube's reputation was bound to grow, alongside his visibility. In the historic elections of that year, Nelson Mandela chose to vote at Ohlange, a moment inscribed in his autobiography:

> I voted at Ohlange High School in Inanda, a green and hilly township just north of Durban, for it was there that John Dube, the first president of the ANC, was buried. This African patriot had helped found the organisation in 1912, and casting my vote near his graveside brought history full circle, for the mission he began eighty-two years before was about to be achieved.
>
> As I stood over his grave, on a rise above the small school below, I thought not of the present but of the past...[43]

John Dube's name began appearing everywhere: in speeches (for election victories, for Youth Day, at the inauguration of the African Union, in commemorations of the 90th anniversary of the ANC),[44] in the press[45] and as it mushroomed exponentially, on the internet. His cyber-presence became firmly established on sites as diverse as Wikipedia (where we are still thoughtfully warned that 'this article may require clean up...'), the ANC's John Dube page, Oberlin University (where a project was run to publicise this suddenly-famous alumnus), the Dictionary of African Christian Biography, South African History Online, the New African Movement and KwaZulu-Natal Literary Tourism, as he was brought into service to promote the development of a new form of cultural/heritage

tradition leading up to Inkatha can be found in E.D. Gasa, 'John L. Dube, his *Ilanga lase Natali* and the Natal African Administration, 1903–1910' (Phd thesis, University of Zululand, 1999). Gasa, who had earlier tried unsuccessfully to submit his work to the University of Natal, asserted that Dube was 'very instrumental in resuscitation by the Zulu royal family of traditional forms and active collaboration by all educated Africans in traditional and cultural activities, to which many present entities including Zulu Cultural Council or Inkatha owe their origin' (323). This contest to claim a legitimate pedigree of nationalist history for Inkatha was part of a wider one: see S. Klopper, '"He Is My King, but He Is Also My Child": Inkatha, the African National Congress and the Struggle for Control of Zulu Cultural Symbols', *Oxford Art Journal*, 19, 1 (1996), 53–66.

43.   N. Mandela, *Long Walk to Freedom* (Johannesburg: Macdonald Purnell,1994), 610.

44.   See for example Mandela's Election Victory Speech, 4 May 1994, at http://www/sas.upenn.edu/african_ Studies/Articles_Gen/Election_Victory_15727.html ; 'Letter from the President: African Union will see the Dawning of a Brighter Day', ANC Today 5 July 2002, at http://lists.anc.org.za/pipermial/anctoday/2002/ 000056.html ; 'Speech by Popo Molefe on Youth Day' Issued by NorthWest Communication Service at http://polity.org.za/html/govdocs/speeches/1995/sp0616a.html; Pallo Jordan, 'How an oak tree grew from a tiny acorn planted early last century (ANC 90th anniversary)', *Sunday Times* online edition, 6 January 2002 at http://www.suntimes.co.za/2002/01/06/anc/anc01.asp; all accessed 23 June 2003. (Of course over the period since 2003, internet addresses have changed and material has been rearranged or has disappeared. I have printouts as evidence for these examples.)

45.   See for example T. Lodge, 'John Langalibalele Dube, a Pioneer Visionary', *Financial Mail Millennium Issue*, 17 December 1999, at http://secure.financialmail.co.za/report/millenium/cc.htm, accessed 21 January 2012; T. Masemola, 'The Man who "woke up" a Nation', *Natal Witness Archive*, at http://www.pmb history.co.za/portal/witnesshistory/custom_modules/TheWayWeWere/The%20man%20who%20'woke%20up'% 20a%20nation.pdf, accessed 21 January 2012. Profile: John Dube. *Metrobeat*, 49 (2003), 20.

tourism.[46] With the notable exception of the Oberlin material (which uses primary sources and relies heavily on Marable), the content of these sites is heavily derivative and makes little attempt at evaluation, preferring to present the 'factual' outlines of Dube's life.

The new government also set about the task of creating its own canon of 'great and good' by instituting an awards system which included the Order of Luthuli, for contributions to the achievement of 'democracy, human rights, nation building, justice and peace, and resolution of conflict'. In 2005, in the third batch of annual awards, Dube was posthumously awarded the Order of Luthuli in Gold.[47] His reinstatement as the heroic nation-builder seemed complete.

One scholarly treatment that appeared in 2001 paid no attention to any of this new-found celebrity status, choosing instead to focus on one incident in Dube's life before he was famous: his attempt to become pastor of the Inanda Congregational Church in 1895, despite the fact that he was not ordained. Its intent was to show that alliances and divisions at Inanda were far more complex than along the expected 'Christian-traditionalist' lines; Dube had the backing of the local chief in his attempts to assert his authority, while his rival favoured the maintenance of white mission control.[48]

Whether treating Dube as a biographical subject or as a historical one (that is, as a representative of a class and/or race and an age), the writers and speakers discussed thus far have focused more or less exclusively on Dube's public record. Yet Tom Lodge's observation in the preface to his *Mandela: A Critical Life*, that 'Mandela's domestic or private life cannot easily be separated or compartmentalised from his political or public career'[49] surely has wider application than to this most charismatic of leaders; it certainly has particular relevance in the case of John Dube. However, it also masks the point that conventions in biography-writing have changed. (Marable, for example, noted certain details of Dube's private life but dismissed them as entirely unimportant.) Lodge's statement could only have been made in more recent times, as Hamilton makes clear:

> In Western multicultural societies embracing new technologies such as the Internet, biographical curiosity and information drove or accompanied every advance in the 1990s, humanizing portraiture to an extent inconceivable a century before, when prominent people were depicted as matchstick men.[50]

46. For Wikipedia, see http://en.wikipedia.org/wiki/John_Langalibalele_Dube; for Oberlin, see http://www. oberlin.edu/external/EOG/Dube/Dube.htm; for the entry in the Dictionary of African Christian Biography, see http://www.dacb.org/stories/southafrica/dube_john.html; for the ANC's John Dube Page, see http://www.anc.org.za/showpeople.php?p=31; for Dube at The New African Movement, see Miranda Perry at http://pzacad.pitzer.edu/NAM/general/student-essays/perry.htm, and for KwaZulu-Natal Literary Tourism see http://www.literarytourism.co.za/index.php?option=com_content&view=article&id=55: john-dube&catid=13:authors&Itemid=28. All of these were accessed 12 January 2012. (As above, internet addresses have changed and material has been rearranged or has disappeared; while I have printouts as evidence for these examples, the most recent addresses are given here.)

47. On the Order of Luthuli, see http://www.thepresidency.gov.za/pebble.asp?relid=774, accessed 17 January 2012; Dube's full citation is at http://dev.absol.co.za/Presidency/orders_list.asp?show=489, accessed 17 December 2011.

48. H. Hughes, 'Doubly Elite: Exploring the Life of John Langalibalele Dube', *Journal of Southern African Studies*, 27, 3 (2001), 445–458.

49. T. Lodge, *Mandela: A Critical Life* (Oxford: Oxford University Press, 2007), xi.

50. N. Hamilton, *Biography, a Brief History.* (Cambridge, MA: Harvard University Press, 2007), 237–238.

This trend began before the 1990s, reflecting a change in our attitudes to privacy, and perhaps a more sceptical attitude to authority, so that biography ceased to perform the function of instructing others as to how to live their lives. It would not be far wrong to claim that it is now *de rigueur* in biography-writing to present subjects' private lives as well as their public achievements for scrutiny: failure to do so leaves a sense of a task incompletely done.

In Dube's case, connecting public and private lives has particular significance, a proposition that is at the centre of the new biography, *First President*.[51] It argues that many of his public achievements rested on significant aspects of his personal life, to the extent that it would not be possible to tell the story of the one without referring to the other. An early example is his conversion to Christianity, a pivotal moment. It was already well established that he had been born into a second-generation Christian family in Inanda; his father James was one of the earliest ordained African Congregational ministers. Yet in that church, great emphasis was placed on personal commitment, not merely on background. Conversion thus took on very profound importance. Mokoena shows clearly in her study of Magema Fuze[52] that conversion was an intellectual as well as a religious turning point: it changed one's entire orientation. Dube's conversion occurred before he had even left high school years; they are in consequence recounted in some detail in *First President*.[53]

Most of the scholarly literature on the history of African Christian communities still conveys the impression that they were very largely cut off from traditionalist society. Again, John Dube's own family history questions this interpretation. His father James was known by another name (Ukakonina) because he was related to the Qadi chief, Mqhawe, and accepted as a leading member of the chiefly inner circle. Moreover, John Dube's elder brother, the first-born of the family, dropped out of school and reverted to traditionalism, establishing a homestead at Inanda and in time became an *induna* of Mqhawe's successor, Mandlakayise. Prophetically perhaps, his name was Africa. *First President* argues that the relationship between the brothers was critical at the time of the Bhambatha Rebellion in 1906. The old chief Mqhawe showed strong signs of supporting the rebellion; even though Dube sympathised with the rebels, he knew that if Mqhawe did come out in support, his new school and his new newspaper would be doomed. He and Africa together helped to persuade Mqhawe to pull back.[54] It has often been claimed that the Dube family was the exception that proved the rule about Christians and traditionalists. It is more likely to be the case that this family is (currently) better-documented, and that if our gaze is directed to both domestic as well as public evidence in the historical record, many more such instances will be discovered.

There is a further example from *First President* that is probably of greater significance. The ending of Dube's period of office as Congress president in 1917 has been always been surrounded by a certain puzzlement in the literature, whether he was ousted or resigned, and over precisely what issue, organisational laxity or supposed support for the principle of

51. H. Hughes, *First President. A Life of John L. Dube, Founding President of the ANC* (Johannesburg: Jacana Press, 2011).

52. H. Mokoena, *Magema Fuze, the Making of a* Kholwa *Intellectual* (Pietermaritzburg: University of KwaZulu-Natal Press, 2011).

53. Hughes, *First President*, 31–40.

54. *Ibid.*, 124–125.

segregation. *First President* attempts a different explanation, positing a combination of public failure (the costly and fruitless delegation that Dube had led to Britain in 1914, followed by three years of inactivity caused largely by Congress's undertaking that it would cease agitation for rights while the war was on) and personal disgrace. He and his wife Nokutela (whose contribution to the 'redemptive mission' represented by Ohlange and *Ilanga* is told here for the first time) had been unable to have children; the pressures of social and private expectation proved too great for Dube, who caused a local scandal by making a school girl pregnant. While the baby died and Dube was absolved of any wrongdoing by a school investigative committee, it meant the end of the Dubes' marriage. Nokutela Dube lived out her remaining days in the Eastern Transvaal, until her death in early 1917. The argument in *First President* is that she had been well known and liked in Congress circles, and her death crystallised a great deal of dissatisfaction with Dube (not least a lingering distaste for his moral lapse, which of course at that time would not have been aired in public, but of which his colleagues would have been well aware). Thus, at the critical Congress meeting in February 1917, he was given no option other than to resign, and not necessarily for reasons to do with his stance on segregation, which was consistent with what it had been and remained all his life: he rejected it, unless South Africa could be split into two equal halves (which he knew to be impossible).[55]

Thus, key political moments in Dube's career (or at least it is argued in *First President*) can be explained not so much in terms of a dialectical dance between contending political positions as between public and private constraints and possibilities. Ohlange was in many ways a casualty of Dube's transgression and by the time he married Angelina Khumalo in 1920, he knew that he would have to relinquish control of the school, a defining moment of bitterness for him. Yet even through the long 'post' period of his life (post-president, post-head of Ohlange) which is most usually thought of as his 'conservative' period (participation in state-sponsored structures and in the Joint Councils; acceptance of an honorary PhD from UNISA), Dube was unwavering in his calls for a colour-blind franchise – not for different, racially exclusive organs of government but for the House of Assembly and the Senate of South Africa. Conversely, even from his younger, supposedly 'radical' years, one can find somewhat conservative views, on women's 'place' and on racial mixing, for example. What thus emerges is a 'mix of defiance and compliance, radicalism and moderation, broadness and narrowness of vision'[56] throughout his life. E.P. Thompson's observation on Thomas Carlyle seems particularly appropriate to Dube: 'it was within the social dialectic of this time that progressive human feelings might keep company in the same man with reactionary thought'.[57] This was a complex dance indeed.

Conclusion

A figure like John Dube himself represents a critical part of the process by which biography becomes possible in southern Africa: the spread of literacy (he was a newspaper editor as well as a highly respected author), the teachings of missionaries (he was an ordained

---

55.   *Ibid.,* 189–197.
56.   *Ibid.,* 259.
57.   E.P. Thompson, *William Morris, Romantic to Revolutionary* (New York: Pantheon, 1976), 30.

minister), the very disaggregation of societies into 'individual beings' (he was a biographer himself, producing the first life of Isaiah Shembe, not long after the appearance of the Skota's *Register*).[58] As subject himself of 'biographical work', Dube became a figure of heroic proportion in his lifetime. The critical scholarship after 1946 sometimes portrayed him as either flawed hero or even anti-hero, although much of it was more intent on analysing how history had made him, rather than the other way around. Even before 1994, however, his memory was once more being put to political use, culminating in his full reinstatement as nation-builder in the New South Africa.

What does *First President* add to all this? In attempting to present a fuller view of Dube's life, perhaps what it does is to show 'the capacity of even a flawed man to struggle nobly against the misfortunes of life'[59] – for arguably that is what Dube was, and that is what he did. Yet in appearing to add to our understanding by including the dimension of the private life, biography can also appear 'to be omitting nothing [and yet] has emerged from a process of choices'.[60] The point is that in reality, biography is always provisional, and for that reason, Dube's reputation will go on being made and remade.

58.   J. Dube, *uShembe* (Pietermaritzburg: Shuter and Shooter, 1936).
59.   Richard Holmes's comment on what he considered Samuel Johnson's central purpose of biography to be. R. Holmes, *Dr Johnson and Mr Savage* (London: Harper Perennial, 2005), 194.
60.   Lee, *Biography*, 10.

'A Member of the Race': Dr Modiri Molema's Intellectual Engagement with the Popular History of South Africa, 1912–1921

JANE STARFIELD

University of Johannesburg

Abstract

This paper offers a prelude to the reconsideration of the writing life and contribution of an African intellectual and nationalist who, studiously and courageously, subjected the concepts of race, culture and nationalism to critical evaluation. Molema's engagement with popular politics began after his return from years of studying medicine at Glasgow University. However, from 1912 to 1921, he engaged with the history of South Africa intellectually, only later producing essays and speeches for more popular audiences. His study of black South Africans, *The Bantu Past and Present* (1920) challenged racist interpretations of the past, while also taking subtle aim at racism in Scotland during and after World War I. The text is multi-layered, moving from first- to third-person narration, which suggests that the author's own identity was subtly entangled with this project. In the Preface, the young writer defines his writing identity, revealing that the book's purpose is historical, ethnographical and, implicitly, nationalist. This paper examines the Preface's crucial role in defining the author's writing identity as nationalist and intellectual. Molema used his standpoint knowledge as 'a member of the race' whose story he 'unfold[ed] to the world' to begin the task of carefully reclaiming black history from the margins of South African cultural life.

The position of the writer and the possibility of new engagements after 1910

In 1920, Modiri Molema, a Motswana[1] doctor from Mafikeng, a small town on the outskirts of the British Empire, once site of a memorable siege in the South African War, began his first book with these words: '[t]his work is no production of art. It purports to be

---

1. This aspect of Dr Molema's ethnic identity is important to this account. The linguistic and cultural group to which he belonged at Mafikeng was the Barolong boo RaTshidi [henceforth, Tshidi Rolong] speakers of a dialect of Setswana: Serolong. For more on Setswana and the Serolong variant, respectively, see D. Jones, *Selected Works*, vol. 7, ed. B. Collins and I. Mees (London: Routledge, 2002), 47 and 61.

a simple portrayal of the life of the Bantu (or Native Peoples of South Africa)'.[2] Using terminology a little in advance of the official parlance of the day, he called it *The Bantu Past and Present*.[3] This humble statement belied the narrative complexity of the 400-page work it prefaced. *The Bantu* (henceforth) is a work of remarkable vision and design, through which Molema sought entry into two highly problematic discourses that represented Africans to the world – history and ethnography. He also hoped that his work would serve as a popular account of African history and culture. However, while he imagined a coherent historical account of black South Africans, and suggested ways in which the segregated nature of the post-Union state might be challenged and changed, his thinking was powerfully infiltrated and shaped by European notions of Enlightenment, democracy, race and civilisation.

In the white-dominated power dispensation that the shapers of the Union of South Africa created, black intellectuals struggled to write and then publish their views, whether in financially besieged newspapers or in texts that sought entry into established intellectual disciplines. However, the circumstances in which black intellectuals in South Africa endeavoured to develop their thinking were severely limited by the dialectics of nation, time, language and space, as this article shows. Interestingly, in the early twentieth century, writing *about* the 'nation' often occurred – or at least began – *outside* that nation. Several black intellectuals elaborated their ideas during periods of temporary exile, but their writing was deeply influenced by the double liminality of their position: firstly, being away from, yet belonging to, the people being described and, secondly, being *of* the people included within the geographical boundaries of the (incipient) 'nation', yet deliberately excluded from its body politic. The grounds of exclusion overlapped with that intransigent boundary between colonist and colonised.[4]

One of the first published texts in which a black author presents a discursive treatment of history, culture, self and community, *The Bantu* is an important articulation of the difficulties that black intellectuals encountered in attempting to analyse the position of black people in the state imagined by white South Africans and British colonial powers. In the ensuing decade, Glasgow-educated Dr Seetsele Modiri Molema began a remarkable alternative career as historian, ethnographer and biographer, fully realising that these

---

2. S.M. Molema, *The Bantu Past and Present* (Edinburgh: W.E. Green & Son, 1920 & 1963), vii. (*The Bantu*, henceforth.) For his account of the Siege, see S.M. Molema, 'Fifty Years Ago' [1949] (Draft), 6. Unisa Archives, ACC142, Molema Varia, Essays: '[o]n the 17th May 1900 the relieving force arrived. Col Mahon with a flying column of 1,000 men from Kimberley joined Col Plumer with his force from the north [...] forced the besiegers to withdraw eastward from whence they had come. Thus ended the siege which [...] was celebrated in London with untrammelled enthusiasm which added the word 'mafficking' to the English language'.

3. In official and popular terminology, African South Africans were termed 'Natives' during this period.

4. Few Cape black property owners could vote (until 1936), among them Dr Molema, his father and uncle. Ironically, however, the Representation of Natives Act (1936) *removed* African voters from the Voters' Roll. Molema attended the formation of the All Africa Convention (Bloemfontein, 1935), an organisation formed to protest against the increasing marginalisation of Africans from public life. See W. Beinart, *Twentieth-Century South Africa* (Oxford: Oxford University Press, 1994), 118, and P. Walshe, *The Rise of African Nationalism in South Africa* (Johannesburg: A.D. Donker, 1970 and 1987), 111–118, 128.

forms of representing the past were – largely – the preserve of white colonial writers.[5] They were colonial in belonging either to the country's white settler community or to the assemblage of historians and ethnographers who traversed Africa, helping to define its boundaries and indigenous peoples and, thereby, to entrench ethnic and racial differences in the early twentieth-century world. Molema had not only to 'write the histories of suppressed groups', but also to 'construct a narrative of a group or class that [had] not left its own [written] sources'.[6]

Entangled as he was in the cultures of African and colonial societies in South Africa and later in Scotland, where he studied medicine, Molema ostensibly set out to tackle the ways in which existing historical and ethnographical writings represented black people. However, the problematic, not to say troubling, relationship of the author to his text should give us pause. That relationship is broached in the Preface, a two-page paratext that establishes the generic complexity of *The Bantu*.

The prefatorial revelations of Molema

Although Molema entitled the first part of *The Bantu* 'A Revelation', it was the Preface that would prove most self-revelatory. A preface, according to Gérard Genette, consists of 'a discourse produced on the subject of the text that follows or precedes it', yet identifying the 'sender' of a preface may be more difficult.[7] Were Molema's text an autobiography, one might term his Preface 'actorial', where the 'author of the preface may be one of the characters in the action'.[8] However, Molema's liminal position as author of a text that is *autoethnographic* makes his prefatory claim to write as 'a member of the race' challenge the reader to question the narrative personae he creates to narrate both preface (first-person) and main text (pp. 1–388 and appendices).

This article proposes that part of the difficulty that readers and critics have encountered with *The Bantu* lies in the underexplored relationship between its author and his text, which, he claims, is *his* history as well as that of his people. His race, the Preface emphasises, is vital: it authenticates his account of the people whose history he writes because he is one of them. Race is not the sole focus of his work; he is concerned, *as* a writer, with the act of writing and with the construction of the disciplines in which he writes. Layering the history of his people from past to future has personal meaning for him, as the allegorical four-part structure of the main text reveals. It is implicitly divided into two 'testaments'. Parts I and II ('The Revelation' and 'The Past') form an 'Old Testament', chiefly concerned with migration and the establishment of well-developed (if

5. Jack Goody cogently discusses the 'take-over of history by the west' in *The Theft of History* (Cambridge: Cambridge University Press), 1. Conceptions of time, space and periodisation have been profoundly influenced by western models.

6. D. Chakrabarty, *Provincializing Europe: Postcolonial Thought and Historical Difference* (Princeton University Press, 2008), 98. Molema held strong views on the important of written history. See S.M. Molema, *Chief Moroka: His Life, His Times, His Country and His People* (Cape Town: Acacia, 1951), 188–189.

7. G. Genette, *Paratexts: Thresholds of Interpretation* (Cambridge: Cambridge University Press, 1987 and 1997), 161, 194.

8. *Ibid.*, 179.

Figure 1. Dr S.M. Molema – frontispiece to *Montshiwa* (Johannesburg: Struik, 1966).

conflicting and competing) settled cultures in southern Africa. His New Testament (Parts III, 'The Present', and IV, 'Possibilities and Impossibilities') hailed the new faith which, he ardently believed, transcended the subcontinent's old ways. He celebrated what he saw as the benefits of European culture: the arrival of missionaries, literacy, humanism, modernity and – more cautiously – industrialisation in southern Africa, and the futures that black South Africans might enjoy if not prevented by governments and racism (Europe's harmful bequests).

The chronicling of time occupied his mind and, Genette reminds us, time is important in determining the nature of the preface and the attitude its writer ('sender') conveys in it.[9] Molema states that the time at which he wrote was significant at least in part because he was a young black South African seeking to explain the participation of black troops from the colonies in the armies of both 'sides', 'but particularly on the Allied side'.[10] Also significant, but not described in this 'incipit',[11] is the intense period during which he wrote *The Bantu*, when, temporarily exiled from home, he studied medicine in Glasgow and Dublin. The details of his experience are largely sublimated in the main text, with very few references to self after the Preface and opening chapter. Instead, his argument about the need for an explanatory text such as his moves from the particular (self) to the general (community):

9. *Ibid.*, 174 ff.
10. Molema, *The Bantu*, vii. The footnote on p. vii states that he had written the book by 1917 and that his publishers had wanted to publish it the following year, but that wartime paper shortages prevented them. He revised it before its publication in 1920.
11. Genette, *Paratexts*, 168.

PREFACE [1]

THIS work is no production of art. It purports to be a simple portrayal of the life of the Bantu (or Native Peoples of South Africa).

The Great War is quoted to explain everything. It may be quoted as a reason for this work also. There are black races participating on both sides, but particularly on the Allied side. Among these latter are the Bantu, on behalf of Great Britain. So I have hoped that my presenting to the public some facts about my people, the Bantu, would not.be out of place, and that it might increase the public interest in them.

To the scientist, inquiry into the life and usages of backward races affords a vivid illustration of the primitive conditions of the more advanced races, and of the ascent of nations from this condition. It explains also some of those apparently arbitrary customs that persist even in the most highly-civilised peoples.

To members of the governing race, some knowledge of the governed race, their mind and manners, seems necessary. For, knowing with whom one has to deal often decides how to deal. Much of the misunderstanding and contempt between nationalities, too, is largely due to want of acquaintance with each other. In such cases, of course, the weaker nation suffers.

This, then, is a story designed for the average English-speaking person, without any great acquaintance with South African people and affairs.

To members of the Bantu race I hope this small book may be an incentive to many to collect and record the history of their people.

[1] This book was written in 1917 and was actually in the press in the early part of 1918, but its publication was stopped by the paper difficulties arising from the war. It has been brought up to date.

vii

Figure 2. S.M. Molema, Preface to *The Bantu Past and Present* (1920) (Johannesburg: Struik, 1963).

So I have hoped that my presenting to the public some facts about my people, the Bantu, would not be out of place, and that it might increase the public interest in them.[12]

Artless as this may sound, his complex narrative strategy revealed the way in which the young intellectual, who later managed three careers (doctor, writer and politician) simultaneously, offered the reading public an account, at once popular and academic, of past, present and future. Before considering other implications of the Preface, we should consider not only the time at which Molema wrote it, but also the place of his book in the history of South African writing.

The Bantu marks an important stage in the history of the book, as one of the earliest discursive texts by a black South African intellectual, also remarkable for being published outside the country of its author's birth, by W.E. Green & Son, Edinburgh, in 1920. Four years earlier, P.S. King (London) published his mentor, Sol Plaatje's *Native Life in South Africa*,[13] and a year later, W.E.B. du Bois's newspaper, *The Crisis* would republish *Native Life* in America.[14] Both texts have, over the years, enjoyed somewhat more public exposure than the cultural writing of Eastern Cape minister of religion, journalist and politician, Walter Benson Rubusana: *Zemk' Inkomo Magwalandini* ('There go your Cattle, you cowards' [1906 and 1911]), a collection of Xhosa writings and 'a peerless collection of praise poems'.[15] It seems that his period in London overseeing the publication of the Xhosa Bible may have afforded him time to write a book concerned with the preservation of historical culture.[16] Conserving popular memory was the intention of all three writers.[17]

Each of these three writers may have conceived his work in South Africa, but took time to write it while in temporary exile. While, on 20 June 1913, the 'South African Native' had awakened to find himself 'not actually a slave, but a pariah in the land of his birth', the period of enforced exile that Plaatje spent in London from 1914 to 1916 gave him the freedom to protest this fact with rhetorical cogency.[18] How much longer was Molema's temporary exile in Glasgow from April 1914 to early 1921, a period of fascinated engagement with his medical studies and passionate longing for home, as letters to his

---

12. Molema, *The Bantu*, vii.
13. Green received Molema's book proposal on 24 September 1917 and expressed their interest in a reply on 26 September, University of the Witwatersrand, Historical Papers, *Silas T. Molema and Solomon T. Plaatje Papers* (henceforth MPP), A979, Ad4, 26 Sep 1917, C.E. Green, Edinburgh, to S.M.M., Glasgow.
14. N. Parsons, 'Introduction', *Native Life in South Africa* [electronic text] (University of Botswana, 1999) http://www.thuto.org/ubh/etext/nlisa/nl-np.htm, accessed 10 May 2011.
15. The dating this source provides seems unreliable. Potgieter asserts that Rubusana accompanied King Dalindyebo to Edward VII's coronation in 1904, whereas this event took place on 9 August 1902! D.J. Potgieter *et al.*, eds, *Standard Encyclopaedia of Southern Africa*, vol. 3 (NASOU: Cape Town, 1971), 620. S. Lee, *King Edward VII: A Biography, Part 2* (Whitefish, MT: Kessinger, 1925), 158. However, Opland states more reliably that Rubusana printed his anthology independently in 1906: J. Opland, 'The Image of the Book in Xhosa Oral Poetry', in D. Brown, ed., *Oral Literature and Performance in Southern Africa* (London: James Currey, 1999), 64. Lovedale Press reissued *Zemk' Inkomo Magwalandini* in 1964 and New Africa Books' newer edition appeared in 2002, edited by Professor Sizwe Satyo.
16. See B.W. Andrzejewski, S. Pilaszewicz, and W. Tyloch, *Literature in African Languages: Theoretical Issues and Sample Surveys* (Cambridge: Cambridge University Press, 2010), 603.
17. See S.T. Plaatje, *Sechuana Proverbs with Literal translations and their European Equivalents* (London: Routledge, 1916), 1: '[t]he object of this book is save from oblivion...the proverbial expressions of the Bechuana people...'.
18. S.T. Plaatje, *Native Life in South Africa* (Johannesburg: Ravan, 1916 and 1982), 21.

father and siblings confirm.[19] While he could have tried to return after graduating (4 April 1919), passages for civilians were limited, as the demobilisation of the troops took priority. So, World War 1 and his desire to specialise in surgery and obstetrics after graduating kept him on Clydeside and in Dublin, and made him a writer in exile.[20]

McClennan argues that '[e]xile either causes creative freedom and reflects a global aesthetic or it results in heightened provincialism and literary regionalism. Exile writing is either global or it is national'.[21] Much more problematic are the practices of writing in temporary exile, when – for a time – the only links with home are letters (rendered more sporadic by erratic postage during warfare), occasional newspaper articles and infrequent visits from friends.[22] McClennan argues that exile writing is multifaceted:

> the literature of exiles contains a series of dialectic tensions revolving around central components of the exile's cultural identity: nation, time, language, and space. Understanding the exile's experience of nation as dialectical allows us to account for the tensions between nationalism, transnationalism, globalization, counternationalism, and anti-nationalism present in exile texts.[23]

It is argued here that, for the writer in temporary exile, the same dialectical components remain in tension within his cultural identity, yet are influenced in particular ways by plans to return home to re-shape the world along 'modern' lines. Thus, the writer acts as agent and analyst of emergent nationalism in his own country, and through his own experience of living abroad, is able to link it to similar processes around the world.

Aspects of Molema's identity emanated from a relationship with Europe (or rather an implied and, as Chakrabarty puts it, 'provincialized' Europe) that began long before his

---

19. MPP A979 Ad1, 11 Apr 1919, S.M.M., Manchester, to STM, Maf. This correspondence is housed in the Molema-Plaatje Papers. Modiri Molema was the first-born son of Chief Silas Thelesho Molema, himself the fifth son of Chief Molema of the Tshidi Rolong. See J.V. Starfield, 'Dr S. Modiri Molema (1891–1965): The Making of an Historian' (PhD dissertation, University of the Witwatersrand, 2007), chs 1 and 2, for biographical accounts of the two chiefs' lives.

20. See G.U.A. 32166, 4 April 1919, Dr S.M. Molema's MB & ChB Degrees. Having registered in the summer term of 1914, he had completed his degree in under five years. Also MPP A979 Ad1, 1 Sep 1919, S.M.M., Dublin, to Silas Thelesho Molema (S.T.M.), Mafikeng, in which he tries to convince his father he should stay on in Britain to study further. In MPP A979 Ad1, 16 May 1920, S.M.M., Glasgow, to S.T.M., Mafikeng, uses interesting terminology to thank his father for educating him and his siblings: 'I can safely say that no son loves and honours his father more than I love and honour you, and I shall ever be deeply thankful to Providence for such a father, and to you for the excellent and rare education you have given me – *education which makes me today one of the foremost men of my race and one of the best educated among black and white in South Africa*' (my emphasis).

21. S. McClennen, *The Dialectics of Exile: Nation, Time, Language, and Space in Hispanic Literatures* (West Lafayette, IN: Purdue University Press, 2004), 2.

22. During his time in Glasgow, Molema received occasional letters, parcels and visits from Plaatje: see MPP A979 Da6.1, 11 July 1920, Plaatje, London, to S.M.M., Glasgow, commenting on *The Bantu*. In Ad1, 30 Nov 1919, S.M.M., Dublin, to S.T.M., Mafikeng: Modiri said he planned to meet Plaatje in Glasgow in January 1920. Plaatje, in London with the second South African Natives National Congress Delegation to Britain, had already sent Modiri a parcel of clothes from the Molemas. Ad1, 18 June 1920, S.M.M., Glasgow, to S.T.M., Mafikeng, reported that he and Plaatje visited Edinburgh together in May.

23. McClennan, *Dialectics of Exile*, 2–3.

arrival at Southampton in 1914.[24] This 'provincialised' (or imagined) Europe was implicitly present in many aspects of Mafikeng home life: in the family's religious observance at the Methodist Church his grandfather had founded; in his father's dedication to educating the rising generation of Molemas at missionary institutions, and in the notional Scotland of his Presbyterian education at Lovedale. The history that Modiri wrote while exiled in the 'second city of Empire' was guided by Enlightenment philosophy, and his Methodist and missionary upbringing.[25] This implicit 'Europe' both mingled and contrasted with the 'inner domain of cultural identity' – his Setswana and African culture – and found expression in *The Bantu*.[26]

Molema's representations of 'nation, time, language, and space' are further moderated by his hope that the 'implied readership' of *The Bantu* will be multicultural, yet defined by language: '[t]his, then, is a story designed for the average English-speaking person, without any great acquaintance with South African people and affairs'. The book would, he trusted, cross the racial divide to appeal to black (specifically 'Bantu') readers: 'To members of the Bantu race I hope this small book may be an incentive to many to collect and record the history of their people'.[27] A linguistic, historical and geographical definition of the term 'Bantu' appears in Chapter 1 of the book.

Why write a history and ethnography while studying towards one of the most time-consuming and challenging (intellectually and physically) courses in the Glasgow University repertoire?[28] His letters home offer no answer to this question, so it is to the Preface that one looks for his motivation and his identity as the writer of this text:

> The Great War is quoted to explain everything. It may be quoted as a reason for this work also. There are black races participating on both sides, but particularly on the Allied side. Among these latter are the Bantu, on behalf of Great Britain. So I have hoped that my presenting to the public some facts about my people, the Bantu, would not be out of place, and that it might increase the public interest in them.[29]

He uses these words assertively, claiming a rightful space for Africans in a war that would change the political face of Europe. This observation also reflected a *post*-colonial turn in which a member of a colonised race seized the power of narrating African history and

24. Chakrabarty, *Provincializing Europe*, ix–xiii. This section draws on Chakrabarty's personalised reflections in the Preface to the 2007 edition of this text. On Modiri's journey to Britain, see MPP A979 Ad1, 18 March 1914, copy of typed letter from S.T.M. to S.M.S. on board the Armadale Castle (Union Castle Co, Ludgate Circus, London). Also Passenger List for Armadale Castle, 24 March 1914, S. Molema, aged 23, Student, http://search.ancestry.com/Browse/view.aspx?dbid=1518&path=Southampton%2c+England. 1914.03.Armadale+Castle.8&sid=&gskw, accessed 2.

25. J. Starfield, Interviews with Professor Isaac Schapera, London, December 1991. On Glasgow's status in the British Empire, see F. Driver and D. Gilbert, *Imperial Cities: Landscape, Display and Identity*. (Manchester: Manchester University Press), 12.

26. P. Chatterjee, *The Nation and its Fragments: Colonial and Postcolonial Histories* (Princeton: Princeton University Press, 1993), 7.

27. Molema, *The Bantu*, vii.

28. Modiri's letters home (MPP, A979, Ad1) refer repeatedly to the taxing curriculum, set out *in toto* in the transcript of his degree: G.U.A. 32166, 4 April 1919, Dr S.M. Molema's MB & ChB Degrees, Glasgow University.

29. Molema, *The Bantu*, vii.

culture and tried (not always successfully) to drag it from the grasp of negative interpretation.[30]

Time, space, nation and history meet in this statement. The prolonged experience of World War I brought ordinary British citizens into contact with members of the peoples colonised, either as workers or students in their own towns or through photographs, newspapers or early newsreels. While colonial troops were known to serve in active or in auxiliary roles, 'European views of colonial troops shaped how and where those troops were used during the war, and colonial peoples in turn came into contact with a world much broader than most had previously known'.[31]

Encounters with people from the colonies – particularly black or Indian people – were, Molema observed, unusual in Glasgow, despite its being a city that had long played host to medical students from abroad.[32] In August 1915, he wrote to his father, Chief Silas, that the only time he and James Moroka (future ANC president) heard 'their Tswana language [was] when we meet as we are the only two Batswana here in Scotland'.[33] Attempting to explain the origins and culture of black people was, in a sense, an attempt to explain his own strangeness, his singularity as a smallish, unenlisted, light-skinned black man in a city of white people. His first letter home in 1914 noted that he was one of just seven 'coloured' students in the whole university (presumably his own calculation).[34]

He was not the only black person receiving cold glances. Antipathy to the presence of foreign sailors and dockworkers in Glasgow became violent in the months after Armistice: 'hostile crowds of white working class people abused and attacked black, Arab, Chinese and South Asian workers, predominantly British colonial sailors.'[35] What began on Clydeside escalated into a general strike as engineers, miners and shipbuilders downed tools in working-class solidarity. Supposedly left-wing union leaders roused British Merchant Seamen and other white workers by emphasising 'the "unfair" competition provided by overseas labour'.[36] Although the riots in late January and June 1919 occurred in the docks and city centre, word spread to the University and the middle-class African Races Association of Glasgow (ARA) – of which Molema was a past president – protested

---

30. C. Saunders, *The Making of the South African Past* (Cape Town: David Philip, 1988), 108, correctly establishes Theal's influence on Molema's work, but does not note his critique of Theal in *The Bantu* (357) and later works (*Chief Moroka*, 50–51).

31. T. Dowling, *World War 1*, vol. 1 (Santa Barbara, CA: ABC–CLIO, 2006), 55.

32. See K. Collins, *Go and Learn: The International Story of Jews and Medicine in Scotland* (Aberdeen: Aberdeen University Press, 1988), 15, 18, 23, 28; Jenkinson suggests that black-white encounters were more common in shipping and industry at this time. J. Jenkinson, 'Black Sailors on Red Clydeside: Rioting, Reactionary Trade Unionism and Conflicting Notions of "Britishness" following the First World War', 2008, http://ruskin.academia.edu/BessieSmith/Papers/984158/Black_Sailors_on_Red_Clydeside_rioting_reactionary_trade_unionism_and_conflicting_notions_of_Britishness_following_the_First_World_War, accessed 10 February 2012.

33. MPP, A979 Ad1, 27 Aug 1915, S.M.M., Glasgow, to S.T.M., Maf. Plaatje's newspaper, *Tsala ya Batho* (The People's Friend), (22 Nov 1913), noted that 'Mr James Moroka [...] sailed for England a couple of years back after studying some years in Lovedale. He passed the Matriculation Examination in October and [...] entered the Medical College in Edinburgh as a medical student. It would have taken him five years to matriculate in this country, which shows that there is something wrong with native education out here'.

34. MPP A979 Ad1, 24 Apr 1914, S.M.M., Glasgow, to S.T.M., Maf.

35. Jenkinson, 'Black Sailors', 2.

36. *Ibid.*

in a letter to the *Daily Record and Mail* on 25 June 1919: 'Did not some of these men fight on the same battlefields with white men to defeat the enemy and make secure the British Empire?'[37] This plea that the contribution of black, 'coloured' and Asian workers and servicemen to the war effort be acknowledged conveys a sentiment – and an outrage – almost identical to Molema's: '[t]here are black races participating on both sides...'.[38] Evidence shows that Modiri was an active ARA member from 1917, when he presented a version of Chapter 27 of *The Bantu* to its members.[39] Importantly, Molema's presence in Glasgow during the industrial upheaval and his decision to cite the participation of 'black races' in the war as the impetus for writing the book links his intellectual endeavour to the conflicted issue of race in Britain at this time.

Such information helps to explain the assertion, in the Preface, of his authority to write on the subject:

> Finally, *I* may say that *I* am *a member of the race* whose life *I* have described in the following pages, *kith and kin* of the people whose story *I* am unfolding to the world. This has given *me* the advantage, as it were, of telling the story of *my own life*, relying much on *my personal observation and experience*, and more correctly interpreting the psychological touches which must be unfathomable to a foreigner.[40]

Molema features in three ways in this extract: implicitly, as the writer, and then as the Prefatorial 'I' (instances one, three and four), linking his identity to the significance of his narration; he is also the 'I' of 'a member of the race', and so a character in this account – an object of narration. At this juncture, the writer allows his textual self a brief appearance, before using the phrase 'kith and kin' to merge him into the ethnic and racial identities later explained in *The Bantu*. 'Kith and kin' are 'country and kinsfolk', those to whom one is related, one's friends and countrymen.[41] The merging of self into a communal and, indeed, national, identity also precipitates the fusion of character and narrator. Although he pronounces the ensuing text 'the story of *my* own life' (my emphasis) and other personal pronouns underscore this claim, 'I', 'me' and 'my' retreat at the end of the Preface to make way for the more authoritative third-person narrator of history and autoethnography. In this genre, the third person resembles a theatrical mask, shielding the liminal self that

---

37. *Ibid.*, 33. This letter was signed by the African Canadian secretary of the ARA, Leo W. Daniels. In 1922, Daniels penned a letter to W.E.B. du Bois on the prejudice against black people in the colonial world. University of Massachussetts, W.E.B. Du Bois Archives, 3147/49–56, 'Letter from Leo W. Daniels to W.E.B. Du Bois, December 25, 1922', http://oubliette.library.umass.edu/view/pageturn/mums312-b019-i145/#page/7/mode/1up, accessed 13 February 2012.

38. The full quotation appears on page 8.

39. Molema, *The Bantu*, 322, fn. 1. See J. Starfield, 'A Dance with the Empire: Modiri Molema's Glasgow Years, 1914–1921', *Journal of Southern African Studies*, 27, 3 (2001), 479–503 for discussion of the ARA.

40. Molema, *The Bantu*, viii (my emphasis).

41. Molema's used an English that some readers may find old-fashioned. Even his friend and colleague, Victor Mapanya, would later make this observation: Victor Mapanya, Interview with Jane Starfield, 1992. Mapanya made particularly reference to Molema's last published work, *Montshiwa, Barolong Chief and Patriot* (Johannesburg: Struik), which he said was invaluable as a cultural document, but written in English that was beyond the 1960s generation. The *OED* links are http://0-www.oed.com.ujlink.uj.ac.za/view/Entry/103759?rskey = y9UxQj&result = 1&isAdvanced = false#eid and <http://0-www.oed.com.ujlink.uj.ac.za/view/Entry/103433?rskey = 3m4QoJ&result = 1&isAdvanced = false#eid, accessed 30 January 2012.

hovers 'in the wings of the first-person' ('*les coulisses de la première personne*'), never quite appearing in his own right.[42]

In his writing, he was no longer the lone Motswana of cloisters and lecture halls, lodging houses, or the Byres and Dumbarton Roads bordering the Gilmorehill campus. This individual, he asserted – the first-person 'I' – was bound through the powerful term 'race' and strong ties of kinship to a social structure that, he claimed repeatedly in *The Bantu*, was analogous to societies found in contemporary and historical Europe.

In oblique reference to the War, he cites, in Chapter 15, the depiction of German savagery in the days of Roman historian Tacitus (retold in Gibbon's *Decline and Fall of the Roman Empire*) to illustrate the possibility that a people deemed 'savage' and 'primitive' could develop – over some centuries – into opponents who could almost outmatch the British Empire.[43] To draw this parallel, he momentarily suspends 'linear time' in his history of Africa, to impose a periodisation of his own for a dual purpose. One may criticise his comparative historical example of ethnic evolution for relying heavily on Social Darwinist notions of the 'primitive' and the 'civilised', but this reconstruction should not be read too literally. This instance from Gibbon becomes an allegory of survival, part of the larger narrative of African ('Bantu') potential that he builds into his text.[44]

Re-imagining a national past

A period of exile, however temporary, may invite the writer to re-imagine his or her relationship to time in his or her country of origin. As McClennen observes:

> Regarding time, writing about exile experience reflects the fact that the exile has been cast out of the present of his or her nation's historical time. This causes a series of dialectic tensions between different versions of linear/progressive/historical time and the experience that exile is a suspension of linear time.[45]

The case of Modiri Molema suggests that in this 'suspension of linear time', the writer is assailed by the desire to recapture his nation's historical time, or by writing a narrative with a teleological purpose, to suture together the disparate histories of the African peoples of South Africa to form one national narrative. To understand the process of writing, one must imagine the young Molema in one of his three Glasgow lodging houses, in the university library or even in the Students' Union, escaping from the 'real time' of medical

42. P. Lejeune, *Je est un autre* (Paris: Éditions du Seuil, 1980), 7. Genette, *Paratexts*, 198, 200, and Starfield, 'Dr. S. Modiri Molema (1891–1965)', 18.

43. Molema, *The Bantu*, 201, cited E. Gibbon, *The History of the Decline and Fall of the Roman Empire* (New York: Harper & Brothers, 1840), vol. 2, 434, 439. As the Bibliography of *The Bantu* does not state which version Molema used, I have traced the segment he cited (p. 201) to Chapter 34.

44. J. Clifford, and G.E. Marcus, eds, *Writing Culture: The Poetics and Politics of Ethnography* (Berkeley, CA: University of California Press, 1986), 98, comment on the importance of allegory: 'I treat ethnography itself as a performance emplotted by powerful stories. Embodied in written reports, these stories simultaneously describe real cultural events and make additional moral, ideological and cosmological statements. Ethnographic writing is allegorical at the level of both its content (what it says about cultures and their histories) and of its form (what is implied about its mode of textualisation)'.

45. McClennen, *Dialectics of Exile*, 2.

studies or ward rounds at the Western Infirmary, into the imagined history of the homeland he missed so much.[46]

The tension between historical time and linear time is evident in Molema's reference to cultural and philosophical debates. He frequently invokes European philosophy as one of *The Bantu*'s several metanarratives: he upholds Machiavelli (on government) and Montesquieu and Rousseau (on freedom and the equality of humankind) as universal or transhistorical standards. He appears to place the ideas they advance, together with the Christian principles he invokes as a form of eternal time in which their moral force has enduring value. Narrating history and ethnography in transhistorical mode become what Clifford terms an 'allegory of salvage', in itself a highly problematic idealisation of the past, indeed, an 'ethnographic pastoral'.[4] Like the writing of exile, ethnographic pastoral may lament the vanishing past in ways that idealise and romanticise its social organisation. Thus, Molema elegantly paraphrases the Bantu people into Rousseau's *The Social Contract*:

> '*Each of* the Bantu *puts his person and all his power in common under the supreme direction of the general will, and*[,] *in their corporate capacity*[,] they recognise *each member as an indivisible part of the whole*' ... Anyone acquainted with the Bantu social state will be struck by its approximation to Rousseau's conception of the ideal social compact.[48] (Rousseau's words appear in italics in the original)

Here, as in much of *The Bantu*'s narrative strategy, Molema relies on parallelism or the use of equivalents, giving equal value to the Rousseauian state and precolonial Bantu polities. The use of the eternal present tense suggests nostalgia for the politics and moral values of the precolonial period. One tendency in writing the pastoral is to characterise the present (especially an urban present) as dystopic, whereas the timeless past is cast as a pastoral utopia, as this quotation implies. Implicit here is *dis*-ease with the colonial, capitalist and modernist values that have disrupted African society. As Chakrabarty states so evocatively: 'How can one sing to the ever-changing tunes of capitalist modernization and retain at the same time a comfortable sense of being at home in it?'[49]

While Molema re-imagines aspects of the past nostalgically, his critical and intrinsically violent depiction of Zulu and Ndebele communities serve as a counterpoint: 'Whole tribes were exterminated on one side by Tshaka's Zulu impis, and on the other by Moselekatse's Matabele hordes'.[50] Tempting as it may be to dismiss this essentialist division of African 'tribes' into the militant (more masculine) Nguni and the peaceable (more feminine) Sotho-Tswana as the influence of conservative historian George McCall Theal, another autoethnographic element appears to govern Molema's interpretation, as it did Plaatje's in *Mhudi*. As Stephen Clingman states, it is vital to see the intrinsic interconnectedness of 'identity (the inner) and the social (the outer)', and to question the relationship between

---

46. Molema (1891–1966) would have been 23 on arrival in Glasgow and 29 on leaving.
47. Clifford, *Writing Culture*, 114–115.
48. Molema, *The Bantu*, 134, cited J.-J. Rousseau, *The Social Contract*. I have used the J.M. Dent edition (London, 1762 and 1941), Book I, Ch. 6, 14: the passages in regular type show Molema's adaptations from the original: 'Each of us' and 'they recognize'. Commas in the original are inserted in square parentheses.
49. Chakrabarty, *Provincializing Europe*, 182.
50. Molema, *The Bantu*, 58. He preferred the Setswana spelling of 'Shaka' and 'Mzilikazi'.

"self" and a "concept of the "nation"".[51] Molema's identity was subtly calibrated: not only was he a 'member of the race', but – closer to home – he was a Morolong, descendant of the royal house of the Barolong boo RaTshidi, one component of the Batswana community. While African nationalist leaders encouraged groups like the Rolong, Tswana, Zulu and Xhosa to subsume their ethnic identities into the larger term 'African', in exile Molema wrote at some distance from this nationalist impetus and often felt the competing pull of ethnic allegiance.[52] This is particularly clear in Chapter 5, Part 1, on the Batswana, where he devoted substantial space to the intricate history of the Rolong. Here, he offered a rare autobiographical insight, by introducing Chief Molema, first Christian leader of the Tshidi Rolong, and also considered the first African evangelist in the country's interior:

> Molema was the grandfather of the author, and perhaps the reader will pardon us if we say one or two words about him. It is not, however, solely from the feelings of loyalty and love due to one's forebears that we make a slight digression, but also and mainly because Molema was, and his sons after him have been, are, the corner-stone of the Barolong, as anybody, black or white, who knows aught of Mafeking will tell.[53]

'The author' is as close as he comes to saying 'I' outside the Preface, gracefully alluding to his inner identity (Clingman), but deflecting the reader to his authorial self. Yet, he creates a genealogy for himself and with it, again, the authority to write as one with an indigenous knowledge of Africa that, he suggests, exists *outside* the many published sources woven into the fabric of the text. While he claims particular knowledge of Africa because of his standpoint as an African, he does not fall into the essentialism of some proponents of Standpoint Theory, which 'assumes that identity is somehow 'there' before experience'.[54]

Thus, historical time, overlaid with personal/linear time, and his desire to represent 'the birth of a nation' unite in his desire to create a history that is at once intellectual and also, in intention, popular and 'usable'. In the oscillation between writing about 'the nation now' (post-1910) and describing the pasts of its constituent communities 'then,' there is an implicit 'identification here of country...and realm...[as] permanent and indivisible. This means that although at several times there may be several kingdoms and kings, there is in truth always only one realm which is coextensive with the country....'.[55] This conception of history, asserts Partha Chatterjee, is decidedly nationalist and provides insight into Molema's project. Initially, he views southern Africa as a geographical space whose history is known (or memorised) through the names, characters, feats and rivalries of its chiefs: historical time is measured as one chief succeeds another, or defeats another (witness the *difaqane/mfecane* and the Shakan period). These histories of chiefdoms are part of the narrative thread of the emergent 'nation', the term around which his text revolves; it occurs

51. S. Clingman, 'Bram Fischer and the Question of Identity', *Current Writing* 16, 1 (2004), 65.
52. Plaatje wrote in a 1913 article: 'Tribalism and clan[n]ishness is melting away under the heat of our bungling misgovernment, and a bond of sympathy and co-operation is being automatically weaved amongst the coloured races of South Africa'. S.T. Plaatje, 'Along the Colour Line', 23 December 1913, in B. Willan, ed., *Sol Plaatje: Selected Writings* (Johannesburg: Witwatersrand University Press, 1996), 168.
53. Molema, *The Bantu*, 43.
54. A. Gray, *Research Practice for Cultural Studies: Ethnographic Methods and Lived Cultures* (London: Sage, 2003), 183.
55. Chatterjee, *The Nation and its Fragments*, 95.

342 times in *The Bantu*'s 398 pages. Its meaning is layered and problematised: 'nation', much like 'tribe', signifies for Molema, a distinct ethnic group: the Basuto 'a new nation of very recent formation', while 'the Zulu-Xosa nations are decidedly more aggressive and warlike' and the 'Fingoes' [Ama-Fengu], include the largest number of 'educated men...[of] any single Bantu nation'.[56] While, to some extent, he finds that national characteristics may be intrinsic, he holds the liberal view that they may change in relation to education and opportunity:

> The presumption then is, according to these views, that if from the beginning of things the blacks had lived under the same or similar physical and economic conditions as the whites, they would have been in every way equal to them, or, in other words, all things being equal, nationalities would react similarly to the same environmental stimuli.

However, from 1910, 'nation' refers to South Africa as both country and realm. The 'national' differences between colonists of British and Boer descent in this conflict-ridden new state are nothing in comparison to those between black and white:

> If such intolerance can exist between civilised members of the same stock, how much greater must it be between two nations of dissimilar stock such as the blacks and the whites? – nations, too, in South Africa at any rate, between which there yawns a wide intellectual gulf, two nations differing as much as any two can differ in colour, character, temperament and strength.[57]

When discussing 'the birth of a nation' in and after 1910, he was one of the first black intellectuals to state very clearly in a historical work that the struggle over nationhood was racial – and by that, he meant 'between black and white'.[58] He remembered how, during the South African War, and, later, the run-up to the first national elections, 'the cry "South Africa for the Boers [was] heard"' and the struggle to control the nascent state seemingly took place between Afrikaners and English citizens.[59] In the next statement, he joins the Prefatory claim to write 'as a member of the race' to the increasingly organised struggle for the inclusion of black people within the body politic and against 'race prejudice':

> The Union is supposed to have been the birth of a new nationality, the amalgamation of Boer and Briton, to work for the common end of white South Africa. So far for the first part of the South African racial struggle. Now we turn to consider the second part, which we call a colour problem, to signify that it is a struggle between the white and the black, and not merely between two nationalities like the Dutch and the British.[60]

---

56. Molema, *The Bantu*, 58, 95, 79. To an extent, he does undercut these ethnic stereotypes: 'It must, however, not be imagined that the Zulu-Xosa coast tribes were quite devoid of all knowledge of these peaceful arts, any more than the Bechuana-Basuto tribes of the interior were without a vestige of military spirit' (95).
57. *Ibid.*, 260.
58. *Ibid.*, 6. I do not know whether Molema managed to see D.W. Griffiths' *The Birth of a Nation* (1915), though two phrases 'the birth of the nation' (6) and 'the birth of a new nationality' (259) suggest that he may have. Plaatje certainly saw it in 1915 (see Willan, *Sol Plaatje*).
59. Molema, *The Bantu*, 259.
60. *Ibid.*, 259.

For Molema, race and its visual manifestation, colour, were the vital elements of personal and community identity. From this passage on, his tone shifts from the politeness used up to this point to a strategically rationed rhetorical anger. Yet his engagement with popular politics remained thoughtfully intellectual. Not for him the volcanic eruptions of R.V. Selope Thema, journalist and South African Native National Congress (later ANC) official, who wrote in the Congress newspaper *Abantu Batho* in February 1920:

> [t]he Caucasian has no Divine right or mandate from heaven, to keep us in slavery or subjection. We have a distinct place . . . in God's Scheme of Creation. Consequently we cannot allow ourselves to be exploited for the enrichment of the European Capitalists without invoking the wrath of Heaven upon us.[61]

Molema's anger was less polemical; he diverted his anger into formal rejections of what he regarded as Boer 'racialism': 'Generally . . . the British imitate the Dutch as little as possible, and because racialism is the atmosphere in which the Boer breathes, the British try to be as little prejudiced as possible'.[62] In the latter chapters of *The Bantu*, the rhetoric of anger mounts, as the narrative voice transmutes into the plural and personal, speaking on behalf of the African 'nation' he imagines as united in their opposition to Boer domination:

> We have shown how the Boers have won for themselves among the blacks a *notoriety* for *repression*, *inhumanity*, and *injustice*. How, from first to last, *the Bantu have shunned* the Boer overtures as they would *pestilence* . . . Altogether it may be summed up in a few words the Bantu have lost all respect for the Boers (if ever they acquired any). *Perhaps the Boers did not think it counted, whether gaining or losing the respect of such an ignoble folk*; but cruel deeds as well as noble deeds, even to such a folk, have far-reaching effects.[63] (My emphasis)

In the first sentence, the italicised terms contain a version of 'double-voicing', in Bakhtinian terms, in which the 'persuasive discourse' of African nationalism is heard in the barely veiled violence of verbs, nouns and epithets in Molema's text.[64] The first-person (plural) narrator appears to speak on behalf of the irate Bantu, thus affirming the ties that this intellectual sought to cement with the increasingly popular ideology of nationalism. Still dealing in the generalised ethnicities that nationalism encourages, the narrative persona briefly inhabits the consciousness of the 'Boers'. The dramatic irony of the italicised third sentence is that Molema is a member of the 'ignoble folk' by whom this set of colonial masters would not mind being despised. The irony reverberated beyond the pages of the text, as in 1920, the white, largely 'Boer' government of Louis Botha and Jan Smuts had limited knowledge of the powerful African intellectuals who were articulating an oppositional discourse against their rule.[65]

Again, unlike the more populist wing of the Congress, Molema was trying to synthesise an inclusive account of the African past that might help to overcome ethnic divisions

---

61. J.V. Starfield, ' "Not Quite History": The Autobiographical Writings of R.V. Selope Thema and H. Selby Msimang', *Social Dynamics*, 14, 2 (1988), 18.
62. Molema, *The Bantu*, 271.
63. *Ibid.*, 359.
64. M.M. Bakhtin, *The Dialogic Imagination* (Austin, TX: University of Texas Press 1981 and 2004), 348.
65. While Botha read *Native Life*, it is not known whether he lent the copy Georgiana Solomon sent him to Smuts – or whether either general ever read *The Bantu*. See Willan, *Sol Plaatje*, 198–99.

among black South Africans. Like Rubusana and Plaatje before him, he wanted to preserve an African account of a past that was rapidly being overwritten, literally by the urbanisation and industrialisation, and figuratively, in the narratives of settler and colonial historians and ethnographers.[66] This aspect of his endeavour was achieved only in part, as Saunders and Smith have observed. Like most historians (professional and amateur) writing in the 1920s, Molema relied extensively yet not exclusively on the work of conservative Settler historians, but began distancing himself from Theal towards the end of *The Bantu*.[67] One should not minimise Theal's presence in Molema's work, but it as well to remember that he also employed a considerable array of sources, from Herodotus to W.E.B. du Bois and Plaatje (with Hume, Herbert Spencer and Nietzsche in between).

'*Go bua gase go dira*': The preface to an engagement[68]

In focusing largely on the Preface to *The Bantu*, this paper has explored the role that Molema defined for himself at the outset of his literary career. By identifying himself as an African writer of a history and ethnography – until then powerful discursive tools in the armoury of colonial domination – he was making a statement that not only introduced his first work, *The Bantu*, but that would also preface a remarkable political and cultural engagement that endured until the last day of his life (see author interview with Mapanya).[69] In terms of the former, he pursued a political career in the local Mafikeng ANC, and represented his community on many local bodies. In December 1949, he was elected onto the executive of the national ANC and served under his old friend James Moroka, as Treasurer-General until 1952. In these busy years, he wrote prolifically, publishing two biographies, while other manuscripts remained unpublished at the time of his death. His many essays are now mostly archived at the University of South Africa.

By making the courageous decision to identify his writing self as 'a member of the race', he assumed an authority to write about his black countrymen that he believed other historians of South Africa did not have. This enabled him to create what is regarded as the first full-length history and ethnography of Black people in South Africa by an African writer. He wished to make it a history that would have relevance for the emergent nationalist movement, and joined Plaatje's *Native Life* in opening a vein of sustained rhetorical anger against racial oppression in South Africa. This study has also gone some way to examining the effect that writing in exile may have had on this and other works by African nationalist writers during this period of fascinating engagements between intellectuals and popular politics in early twentieth-century southern Africa.

66. C. Saunders, *Making of the South African Past*, 108; K. Smith, *The Changing Past: Trends in South African Historical Writing* (Johannesburg: Southern, 1988), 132; J.V. Starfield 'Dr. S. Modiri Molema (1891–1965)', 3.

67. Molema (*The Bantu*, 357) labelled Theal, 'the champion of the Boers'. His antipathy towards Theal deepened in his later biography, *Chief Moroka* (1951, 286), He charged that Theal (*History of South Africa, 1828–1846* [1888]) 'and many others before and after him, have wasted much ink and time in trying to belittle the African contribution' to the 1837 defeat of the AmaNdebele. The Rolong contribution to this defeat was often ignored.

68. Plaatje, *Sechuana Proverbs*, 38, Proverb 176: the literal translation is 'To speak is not to act'.

69. See Starfield, Interview with Mapanya.

Women and the Problem of Family in Early African Nationalist History and Historiography

MEGHAN HEALY-CLANCY

Harvard University, USA

Abstract

Women played critical roles in making African nationalism ideologically and practically possible in South Africa. They not only participated in organisations, institutions, and campaigns that were well-documented by contemporaries. Some also documented themselves – inscribing their ideals of nation, race, and citizenship in speeches, portraits, and writing. These women travelled around the country and, in a few influential cases, around the world – theorising African women's struggles in South Africa with reference to struggles elsewhere, especially across the black Atlantic. Yet they generally authorised their public engagements in terms of their commitments as mothers, wives, sisters, and daughters – proclaiming an interest in 'social' rather than 'political' work. Women's familial modes of public engagement led South Africa's first wave of feminist historians to see them as marginal influences on the making of an essentially patriarchal nationalism. But a survey of rich journalistic sources from the 1930s suggests that nationalist women were not uncritically defending patriarchy when they organised around domestic concerns. Rather, they were concerned to create a new sort of African family – both capable of protecting its privacy and a model for new forms of public life – that could nurture an African nationalist body politic.

Women's contributions to the ideological and practical development of African nationalism in South Africa have received scant analytical attention. In the growing literature on the evolution of African nationalism between the 1912 formation of the South African Native National Congress and the advent of apartheid in 1948, neither biographies of

Thank you to all of the participants in the June 2011 Southern African Historical Society conference panel on 'Exceptional Women in South African History and Historiography' (particularly our chair, Catherine Burns, and my co-panellists Eva Jackson, Lauren Jarvis, and Jill Kelly), Diana Wylie, Leslie Hadfield, and Duana Fullwiley for their insights on a previous version of this paper.

prominent women nor in-depth analyses of key women's groups figure.[1] This lacuna is remarkable when contrasted with women's public engagements during this period, as reflected in the growing vibrancy of writing by and about women in the African-oriented press.

This article makes a preliminary attempt to rethink the goals, actors, achievements, and constraints of early African nationalism from a gendered perspective.[2] After a critical review of scholarly depictions of women as marginal to politics during this period, it traces the emergence of a women's 'welfare' group, the Daughters of Africa, in the pages of *The Bantu World* during the 1930s. Drawing upon this sample of rich journalistic sources, the article explores how, in a nadir of male-led political organisation, women's discussions of home, family, race, and nation attained prominence in public culture. These sources suggest that women performed integral roles in the construction of an African nationalist body politic: a constituency that saw itself as a nation. As Peter Limb has recently shown, this constituency shared a broad tent: nationalism then encompassed 'the various ideological currents circulating among Africans who experienced common political oppression and articulated a countrywide striving for unity'.[3] His emphasis on the *articulation* of 'a countrywide striving for unity' is critical: early African nationalism was about constructing a unifying public culture, as a prerequisite to mobilisation on a national level.

The women involved in creating a nationalist body politic often spoke of their public engagements as expressions of their concerns about 'welfare', as 'social clubs', or as 'self-help' groups. We can recognise these terms from the footnotes of texts on women's roles in the sorts of organisations with which progressive historians, particularly those writing during the anti-apartheid struggle, were more comfortable: male-led political congresses or conventions and trade unions. Therein lay the power of groups like the Bantu Women's League, the National Council of African Women, the Daughters of Africa, Zenzele, and the early African National Congress Women's League: just as historians have generally dismissed these groups as essentially stabilising and conservative influences, so too did officials of the segregationist state. To white officials, women's organisations and discourse

---

1. Prominent women make appearances as colleagues and kin in scholarship on powerful men and male-dominated political organisations. But women, women's groups, and family life have generally remained peripheral to scholars' discussions of the institutional and ideological development of African nationalism. Peter Limb's pioneering recent work on the early ANC is typical, although as I show below he recognises the need for more research on women and gender: see P. Limb, *The ANC's Early Years: Nation, Class and Place in South Africa before 1940* (Pretoria: Unisa, 2010). Heather Hughes' recent biography of John Dube suggests that Dube's successes as a politician and educator would have been limited without the private and public efforts of his first wife Nokutela and second wife Angeline: see H. Hughes, *First President: A Life of John L. Dube, Founding President of the ANC* (Auckland Park: Jacana, 2011), especially 259–260. Her reconstructive work on Nokutela is particularly impressive. Steven Gish also acknowledges the importance of Alfred and Madie Hall Xuma as 'the unofficial "first family" of black South African political life': see S. Gish, *Alfred B. Xuma: African, American, South African* (New York: New York University Press, 2000), 117. But no published study moves past acknowledgment of the presence of women in prominent men's homes and in public culture to *theorize* what that presence meant for the development of African nationalism.
2. This is the first publication coming out of ongoing research, from which I intend eventually to write a book.
3. Limb, *The ANC's Early Years*, 11.

seemed docile – banal as bathwater, and as soothing to potential radicals. At best, as one official put it hopefully in the early 1920s, women might exert 'a steadying influence over more unstable elements' in their homes and communities.[4] At worst, it seemed that women's groups were simply fora for idle talk: the Johannesburg Native Commissioner fretted of the Daughters of Africa in 1943, 'It is very easy to have a constitution published & to put into it all sorts of wonderful things, but it is quite a different thing to have a real virile body doing useful work'.[5]

If we conceive early African nationalism not just as a series of failed campaigns – against which the African National Congress Youth League heroically rose – but as a foundational period of building a body politic and public culture – in which post-war radicals came of age – we can see the richness of women's early contributions more clearly. Through a loose stitch in the '"patchwork quilt" of patriarchies' that was segregationist South Africa, African women's political marginality in the eyes of officials gave them space to think, talk, and write about nation, race, and unity.[6] They deployed kinship publicly not simply to carve out space for themselves in a male-dominated society. Rather, they used discourses of home and family to envision, and to enact, new forms of national and racial allegiance.

Women promoted an empowering racial consciousness, predicated on the idealised familial rights and obligations of what I term a 'New African family': a domestic unit that both sought to protect its *privacy* from the racist state and self-consciously modelled new forms of proudly racial *public life*. Members of New African families shared a commitment to individual and racial progress through education and public health; empowerment through entrepreneurship and collective economic efforts; and community through the proliferation of political congresses or conventions, trade unions, and social welfare organisations. In a classic 1945 statement, public intellectual Herbert Dhlomo described 'the New African' as a politically assertive man, demanding through strikes and boycotts

4.   Natal's Chief Native Commissioner, C.A. Wheelwright, at an event at the Inanda Seminary for African girls in 1922. See 'Inanda Seminary: New Dormitory Opened, by Chief Commissioner', *Natal Mercury* (22 April 1922). Clipping in Campbell Collections, University of KwaZulu-Natal, Durban (CC), Inanda Seminary Papers (ISP), File 2a. On the multivalent gendered allure of 'welfare', see also S. Marks, *Not Either an Experimental Doll: The Separate Worlds of Three South African Women* (Bloomington: Indiana University Press, 1987), 30–39; and M.E. Healy, '"A World of Their Own": African Women's Schooling and the Politics of Social Reproduction in South Africa, 1869 to Recent Times' (PhD thesis, Harvard University, 2011). Catherine Higgs' work on Zenzele clubs in the Eastern Cape also emphasises official disinterest in interfering with the working of those 'self-help' groups, which unlike their counterparts elsewhere in colonial Africa did not identify as 'political' organisations. See C. Higgs, 'African Women's Self-Help Organizations in South Africa, 1927–1998', *African Studies Review* 47, 3 (December 2004), 119–141; and C. Higgs, 'Helping Ourselves: Black Women and Grassroots Activism in Segregated South Africa, 1922–1952', in C. Higgs, B.A. Moss, and E.R. Ferguson, eds, *Stepping Forward: Black Women in Africa and the Americas* (Athens: Ohio University Press, 2002), 59–72.

5.   Handwritten note by Native Commissioner J.M. Brink on the pamphlet, 'The General National Conference of the Daughters of Africa, to be held in the Bantu Men's Social Centre, Johannesburg, Friday, Saturday, Sunday, December 17th, 18th, 19th, 1943', National Archives of South Africa, Pretoria (SAB), Depot TAB, Source KJB, Volume 411, Reference N1/14/3. 'Useful work', Brink suggested in this note, included raising contributions to the British war funds.

6.   For this term, see B. Bozzoli, 'Marxism, Feminism, and South African Studies', *Journal of Southern African Studies* 9, 2 (1983), 139–171.

'a social order where every South African will be free to express himself and his personality fully, live and breathe freely, and have a part in shaping the destiny of his country'.[7] But Dhlomo and his male and female peers argued forcefully in *The Bantu World* that sociopolitical transformation *began* at home: through the agency of mothers, wives, sisters, and daughters.

Early African nationalist public culture as a domain of female exclusion in feminist historiography

The first scholars to consider the gendered dimensions of early African nationalism were feminist historians and anti-apartheid activists of the 1980s and 1990s. They were concerned to situate the histories of South African women within a common analytical frame, which emphasised the underlying principle of patriarchal power in a racialised, capitalist state.

These scholars emphasised women's exclusion from the early African National Congress (ANC), and apparent acquiescence in this exclusion, as natural extensions of the broader patriarchal society in which they lived. As Judy Kimble and Elaine Unterhalter held in 1982,

> Before the 1950s, there was little discussion of 'women's emancipation' as such, either by the ANC or its women's organisations. In general, moreover, this was not a question raised by women in South Africa at this time, with the exception of the white Women's Enfranchisement Association of the Union.[8]

Cherryl Walker concurred in her landmark study:

> The public sphere of politics and political parties was a male domain ... Conservative men, reared in a strongly patriarchal tradition, the early ANC leaders aspired to full partnership within a parliamentary democracy with the whites. They had embraced the system of values of the dominant group within society, the white middle class. In the process they adopted without questioning its view on the subordinate place of women, views which did not conflict with their own patriarchal tradition. Right up to the 1950s and beyond, the ANC continued to see women primarily as mothers and wives. This view conditioned the outlook of its female members as well. Politics in the early twentieth century was thus a male-defined occupation.[9]

Walker saw women's exclusion from full membership in the ANC as effectively entailing their utter estrangement from politics. Women did participate in the ANC's female auxiliary, the Bantu Women's League, founded by Charlotte Manye Maxeke in 1918. But, as Walker said dismissively,

> The function of the Women's League during this period was to provide the catering and organise the entertainment at meetings and conferences – the community interests of African men and women

7.   H.D. Dhlomo, 'African Attitudes to the European', *The Democrat* (1 December 1945), 21 and 24.
8.   J. Kimble and E. Unterhalter, '"We Opened the Road for You, You Must Go Forward": ANC Women's Struggles, 1912–1982', *Feminist Review* 12 (1982), 11–35; 28.
9.   C. Walker, *Women and Resistance in South Africa* (Cape Town: David Philip, 1982; 1991), 26.

did not extend to the kitchen. There was, at that stage, little effort to broaden established views on women's role on the part of either the men or the women of the ANC.[10]

Walker stressed that Maxeke – who became the first black southern African woman to receive a university degree when she earned her bachelors of science from Ohio's Wilberforce University in 1901 – had a career which was 'far removed from that of the average black woman at the time'.[11] But even Maxeke 'did not question the assumption that women's primary function was a domestic one'.[12] Her 'major concerns were social rather than political, and centered on the church. In this she differed little from many socially active white women'.[13] Walker concluded that Maxeke and her colleagues in the Bantu Women's League 'were not seeking radical change in established patterns of relationships with men and their families'.[14]

Frene Ginwala took issue with Walker's characterisation of the ANC's marginalisation of women in an essay in 1990, published just before Ginwala helped to re-establish the ANC Women's League in South Africa. She concurred with Kimble, Unterhalter, and Walker that women's long exclusion from formal membership in the ANC was a product of the alignment of settler and indigenous patriarchies, neither 'surprising nor exceptional for the time'. But, she insisted, 'The absence of women from political institutions does not necessarily lead to their absence in the political arena'.[15] Ginwala stressed that although the Bantu Women's League had been initiated largely to 'provide suitable shelter and entertainment' for activist men, it immediately took on a life of its own. Not only did Maxeke assume national prominence by representing women's concerns to officials, but also local branches organised official appeals in response to 'grassroots' concerns such as high rents and the exploitation of farm workers. Women attended and spoke in the ANC's annual conferences, representing branches of the Bantu Women's League or 'affiliated women's groups such as the Daughters of Africa or Zenzele'.[16] In short, Ginwala stressed that women were there, and that their political strategies were not dissimilar to those of men. Women, she suggested, even tended to be more attentive to popular concerns and therefore more radical than their male peers in the 1910s and 1920s. In the 1930s, however, she maintained that women's political vitality declined, along with that of the ANC. The Bantu Women's League fell into quiescence as Maxeke's health deteriorated; upon her 1939 death, the League had been succeeded by the National Council of African Women, which 'did not regard itself as primarily a political organisation but rather one involved in "non-european welfare." Most of its members were teachers or nurses. It took up issues of teachers' salaries, education, provision of crèches, widows rights of inheritance, delinquent children, etc'.[17] Ginwala, like Walker, seemed unsympathetic toward this move toward 'welfare' in the 1930s, emphasising white liberal domination in the transition.[18]

10. Walker, *Women and Resistance in South Africa*, 33.
11. *Ibid.*, 38.
12. *Ibid.*, 39.
13. *Ibid.*, 37.
14. *Ibid.*, 40.
15. F. Ginwala, 'Women and the African National Congress, 1912–1943', *Agenda* 8 (1990), 77–93; 78.
16. *Ibid.*, 87.
17. *Ibid.*, 88.
18. *Ibid.*, 89.

Ultimately, then, Ginwala's characterisation differed from that of Kimble, Unterhalter, and Walker in degree, rather than in kind. She agreed that nationalist public culture was a domain of female marginalisation, but she argued that some women pushed their way into male-dominated political fora at an early stage.

Common to all of these analyses remains a narrow conception of nationalist public culture that valorises women's presence in the spaces where they were in fact least common – the halls of the male-led ANC. All evince a striking disinterest in women's engagements in the social welfare organisations in which they predominated – thereby neglecting the ideological and practical implications of women's attention to African families, bodies, homes, and communities for the creation of an African body politic.[19] If we instead see women's familial concerns as public and political matters, a more complex gendered history of nationalism emerges.

A derogation of familial concerns as only tenuously political (or even as public) particularly pervaded Julia Wells' 1990s work on women's anti-pass law mobilisations.[20] Wells asserted that when African women mobilised politically before the Second World War, they tended to do so on the basis of their maternal responsibilities. With evident uneasiness, she suggested that these responsibilities did not fuel sustained engagement in militant protest:

'The women who participated in the resistance movements had to transcend social norms which limited women's activities to the sphere of home and family. The conservative nature of both African and Western custom at those times militated heavily against women stepping beyond the bounds of the household into the sphere of public and political life', Wells contended. Women's anti-pass protests, she claimed, were limited, single-issue campaigns. 'Each of the episodes centered on a conservative goal – to retain a known social order rather than create a new one'.[21] Wells remained adamant that 'maternal politics are clearly not to be confused with feminism', and that mobilisations in which women come together on the basis of their nurturing roles 'should not be mistaken for political maturity'.[22] She shared this critique of 'maternal thinking' or 'social feminism' with

---

19. An exception to this disinterest in welfare is Deborah Gaitskell, who has been producing fascinating work on Christian women's social organising for the over three decades. As early as 1983 she referred to 'social welfare and community projects' as 'activist spheres' for mission-educated 'black liberal women': see D. Gaitskell, 'Introduction', *Journal of Southern African Studies* 10, 1 (Special Issue on Women in Southern Africa, October 1983), 1–16; 6. But her analytical interest has been more in the 'politics of the personal' amongst Christian women (black and white) than in the role of these women in nation-building projects.

20. See J. Wells, *We Now Demand! The History of Women's Resistance to Pass Laws in South Africa* (Johannesburg: Witwatersrand University Press, 1993). See also J. Wells, 'The History of Black Women's Struggle against Pass Laws in South Africa, 1900–1960' (PhD thesis, Columbia University, 1982); 'Why Women Rebel: A Comparative Study of South African Women's Resistance in Bloemfontein (1913) and Johannesburg (1958)', *Journal of Southern African Studies* 10, 1 (1983), 55–70; and 'The Rise and Fall of Motherism as a Force in Black Women's Resistance Movements', paper presented at the Conference on Women and Gender in Southern Africa, University of Natal, 1991.

21. Wells, *We Now Demand!*, 139.

22. J. Wells, 'Maternal Politics in Organizing Black South African Women: The Historical Lesson', in O. Nnaemeka, ed., *Sisterhood, Feminisms, and Power: From Africa to the Diaspora* (Trenton: Africa World Press, 1998), 251–262; 253.

American feminist scholars who dismissed a politics predicated on motherhood as particularist at best and essentialising at worst.[23]

But as Cherryl Walker suggested in the 1990s, sensitive historical accounts of women's political engagements might step back from normative evaluations of how protofeminist movements were, to understand more fully what these movements meant to their participants and what they in fact achieved. Walker retreated from a critique of the nurturing bases of women's politics, drawing upon the profusion of studies on South African women's public culture that had followed her pioneering work.[24] Significant among them was her anthology *Women and Gender in Southern Africa to 1945*, in which she suggested that 'historically motherhood in African society cannot be equated with submission and passivity'.[25] She concluded that it was

> inadequate to categorise a women's politics constructed around the maternal and familial role as inherently conservative and leave it at that. This labeling seems to rest on an uncritical acceptance of conventional views (which one might describe as masculinist) of what the domain of the political is, with its corresponding designation of the domestic as the realm of the personal and therefore, by definition, the apolitical.[26]

She insisted that 'women invest in motherhood (and the family) and this needs to be recognised and understood – understood not simply as the product of their socialisation or patriarchal ideology but as something mediated by their own experience of this role'.[27]

---

23. Sara Ruddick advocated 'maternal thinking' and Jean Bethke Elshtain advocated 'social feminism' as modes of 'pro-family' feminism in the early 1980s, sparking a sharp critique from Mary G. Dietz. See S. Ruddick, 'Maternal Thinking', *Feminist Studies* 6, 2 (Summer 1980), 342–367; J.B. Elshtain, *Public Man, Private Woman* (Princeton: Princeton University Press, 1981); and M.G. Dietz, 'Citizenship with a Feminist Face: The Problem with Maternal Thinking', *Political Theory* 13, 1 (February 1985), 19–37. While feminists debated maternalist politics as a normative strategy in the United States, scholars of women's organisation in Latin America and Africa have emphasised that motherhood carried different political valences in different contexts. For southern African discussions, see S. Meintjes, 'The Woman's Struggle for Equality during South Africa's Transition to Democracy', *Transformation*, 30 (1996), 47–64; G. Fester, 'Women's Organisations in the Western Cape: Vehicles for Gender Struggle or Instruments of Subordination?' *Agenda*, 34 (1997), 45–61; G. Fester, 'Merely Mothers Perpetuating Patriarchy? Women's Grassroots Organizations in the Western Cape 1980 to 1990', in A. Gouws, ed., *(Un)Thinking Citizenship: Feminist Debates in Contemporary South Africa* (Burlington, VT: Ashgate, 2005), 199–219; and M. Epprecht, 'Women's "Conservatism" and the Politics of Gender in Late-Colonial Lesotho', *The Journal of African History* 36, 1 (1995), 29–56.
24. Besides Wells' scholarship, important work included Helen Bradford's research on women in the Industrial and Commercial Workers Union and Deborah Gaitskell's work on *manyanos*. See H. Bradford, '"We Are Now the Men": Women's Beer Protests in the Natal Countryside, 1929', in B. Bozzoli, ed., *Class, Community, and Conflict: Southern African Perspectives* (Johannesburg: Ravan Press, 1987); and D. Gaitskell, '"Wailing for Purity": Prayer Unions, African Mothers, and Adolescent Daughters, 1912–1940', in S. Marks and R. Rathbone, eds, *Industrialisation and Social Change in South Africa* (London: Longman, 1982), 338–357.
25. Walker, 'Preface to the Second Edition', *Women and Resistance in South Africa*, xx. See also C. Walker, ed., *Women and Gender in Southern Africa to 1945* (Cape Town: David Phillip, 1990).
26. Walker, *Women and Resistance in South Africa*, xxi–xxii.
27. *Ibid.*, xxii. See also C. Walker, 'Conceptualising Motherhood in Twentieth Century South Africa', *Journal of Southern African Studies* 21, 3 (September 1995), 417–437.

Walker suggested a new agenda, in which 'the contribution of black women historians who are alive to the subtleties of South African languages and culture would be particularly valuable',[28] to deconstruct the historical specificities of maternalism. We might ask:

> What set of relationships and interests was at stake for women when they rallied in defence of 'motherhood' and 'the family' in the anti-pass campaign and how might these have differed for different groups of women? What did 'mother' mean, and why did the term resonate so deeply with women, that 'women' and 'mother' could be used interchangeably? How might the meaning have varied according to class, religious affiliation and age and between urban and rural dwellers? Are motherhood and its defence necessarily incompatible with progressive politics and especially a feminist politics, as Wells' formulation suggests?[29]

Remarkably, these bold questions have yet to be taken up in any sustained way. Historians took a hiatus from serious consideration of women in early nationalist politics for the next decade, as many turned to a more urgent set of issues in the transition to democracy.[30] But that is not to say that this history was entirely absent from scholarly discussion. In her canonical work on gender and nationalism, literary scholar Anne McClintock suggested almost in passing that in the 'first thirty years of the ANC', African nationalist 'women's potential militancy was muted and their political agency domesticated by the language of familial service and subordination'.[31] She made this claim on the basis of the South African Native National Congress' constitutional clause making wives auxiliary members and ANC President Pixley ka Isaka Seme's call that 'no national movement can be strong unless the women volunteers come forward and offer their services to the nation' – neglecting to ask, following Walker, what women themselves might have been doing with familial discourses and relationships.[32] When Natasha Erlank returned to the topic of women and early African nationalism in 2003, she turned from earlier debates about women's early strategies of engagement to explore in detail the discourses by which African men justified their nationalist leadership in a racialised and gendered state. This move was in line with the recent trend toward analysis of masculinity, influential in gender

---

28. This issue of language and its cultural nuances is critical, as language training continues to be a weakness for non-African scholars. I am beginning with the large corpus of English articles that I have assembled, but I am embarking on a major translation project of African language texts (beginning with isiZulu, which I have studied for several years but of which I am not a native speaker). See footnote 62.
29. Walker, *Women and Resistance in South Africa*, xx.
30. For example, Walker embarked on a project about land claims and post-apartheid restitution. But debates about the future of a women's movement within and outside of the ANC continued: see S. Hassim, *Women's Organizations and Democracy in South Africa: Contesting Authority* (Madison: University of Wisconsin Press, 2006). This retreat also may have been related to the racially divisive Conference on Women and Gender in Southern Africa at the University of Natal, Durban, in 1991: see P. Heatherington, 'Women in South Africa: The Historiography in English', *The International Journal of African Historical Studies*, 26, 2 (1993), 241–269; and T. Barnes, 'Owning What We Know: Racial Controversies in South African Feminism, 1991–1998', in Higgs, Moss, and Ferguson, *Stepping Forward*, 245–256.
31. See A. McClintock, *Imperial Leather: Race, Gender, and Sexuality in the Colonial Contest* (New York: Routledge, 1995), 380. See also an earlier version of this piece, A. McClintock, 'Family Feuds: Gender, Nationalism, and the Family', *Feminist Review*, 44 (Summer 1993), 61–80.
32. McClintock, *Imperial Leather*, 80; She does not provide a date or source for Seme's quote.

studies across Africa and elsewhere.[33] Erlank concluded that nationalist men's exclusion of women from formal membership was integral to their 'fraternal' appeals to white men, as their self-consciously modern equals:

> According to them, a modern family life marked our their status as members of a civilized middle class eligible for European rights and privileges. Black nationalist activity, therefore, was not only premised on the exclusion of women, but also relied on the exclusion of women for its own legitimation.[34]

When Nomboniso Gasa released her *Women in South African History* in 2007, she thus wrote against Walker and Wells, whose work she still considered 'seminal'.[35] But while Gasa acknowledged that Walker's 1990s self-criticism had reflected 'growth', she maintained that neither Walker nor Wells had ever been able to see black women's struggles from an intersectional viewpoint.[36] 'Why the Berlin Wall between blackness and liberation struggle on one hand and feminism on the other?' she asked.

> These are the kinds of binaries that are completely unnecessary and do not make sense of black women's experiences ... At the heart of the earlier struggles is the fact that African women were homeless by state design ... Their struggle against the pass laws, which were a tangible way of infringing their rights, was, in fact a struggle to be in the public domain at the same time as a struggle for free movement.[37]

Gasa importantly maintains that debates over how 'feminist' early African nationalist women were distract from our ability to see how their complex positions as black women shaped their political engagements.

Yet Gasa does not draw out what seem to me the most interesting of her claims: that women's struggles in defence of their families and homes were struggles to make space for Africans in a white supremacist state that not only restricted their access to urban spaces that whites considered 'public', but also allowed them no familial spaces that really felt 'private'. Africans were 'homeless' because their domestic realms were not secluded from

---

33. On African masculinities, see L. Chrisman, 'Fathering the Black Nation of South Africa', *Social Dynamics*, 23 (1997), 57–73; R. Morrell, ed., *Changing Men in Southern Africa* (Pietermaritzburg: University of Natal Press, 2001); L. Lindsay and S. Miescher, eds, *Men and Masculinities in Modern Africa* (Portsmouth, NH: Heinemann, 2003); and L. Ouzgane and R. Morrell, eds, *African Masculinities: Men in Africa from the Late Nineteenth Century to the Present* (Pietermaritzburg: University of KwaZulu-Natal Press, 2005).

34. N. Erlank, 'Gender and Masculinity in South African Nationalist Discourse, 1912–1950', *Feminist Studies*, 29, 3 (Autumn 2003), 653–67; 668. See also C. Pateman, *The Sexual Contract* (Cambridge: Polity Press, 1988), 77–78, on whose theoretical framework she draws. Erlank usefully roots her exploration of gendered leadership dynamics in the private and public lives of a family (ANC President Alfred Xuma and his African American clubwoman wife, the ANCWL President Madie Hall Xuma). Her discussion draws upon I. Berger, 'An African American 'Mother of the Nation': Madie Hall Xuma in South Africa, 1940–1963', *Journal of Southern African Studies*, 27, 3 (September 2001), 547–566.

35. N. Gasa, "Let Them Build More Gaols", in Gasa, ed., *Women in South African History: Basus'iimbokodo, bawel'imilambo/They Remove Boulders and Cross Rivers* (Cape Town: HSRC, 2007), 129–152; 129.

36. N. Gasa, 'Feminism, Motherisms, Patriarchies and Women's Voices in the 1950s', in Gasa, *Women in South African History*, 207–229; 213.

37. *Ibid.*, 214.

state intrusion.[38] This claim suggests that women's theorising and organisation around domestic issues – in their avowedly 'social' as well as expressly 'political' activities – were integral parts of public culture. But although Gasa rejects the analytic binary between 'feminism' and 'nationalism', she continues to valorise women's presence in male-dominated political fora and in organised expressions of political protest. She neglects groups like the Daughters of Africa and Zenzele entirely, building instead on Walker's and Wells' attention to moments of militant expression – even as she urges us to take black women's 'multiple voices and multiple forms of self-representation' more seriously.[39]

The time is ripe for serious reinvestigation of women's roles in early African nationalism. The ANC's centenary has sparked popular and scholarly debate on its elite roots, history of male domination, and capacity for transformational policy-making in a post-apartheid society wrought by gendered, as well as race and class-based, inequalities.[40] As Limb has pointed out,

> One of the great unknowns of South African historiography remains the intersection of women with early ANC politics. Women are largely absent from early ANC history, largely due to the paucity of sources but also because the organisation did not facilitate direct female membership until the 1940s, limiting women's potential involvement.[41]

Yet Limb suspects that scholars might take *manyanos* (prayer unions) and 'clubs and self-help organisations' seriously as sites in which 'women also used culture in political ways and developed women's cultures of resistance' – citing ANC activist Fatima Meer's insistence that *manyanos* were 'the most authentic African women's organisation', which both enabled everyday resilience and nurtured the 'potential for quick politicisation'.[42] Like male-dominated political groups, women's groups were generally led by members of the tiny black educated elite – a class whose values and aspirations Daughters of Africa founder Cecilia Lillian Tshabalala embodied. But this class was neither as financially secure nor as distant from the masses as the term 'elite' suggests.[43] Moreover, the membership of

---

38.   This reminds me of feminist political philosopher Nancy Fraser's injunction: 'Not everyone stands in the same relation to privacy and publicity; some have more power than others to draw the line'. Quoted in J.B. Landes, 'Introduction', in Landes, ed., *Feminism, the Public and the Private* (New York: Oxford University Press, 1998), 1–17; 3.
39.   Gasa, 'Let Them Build More Gaols', 131.
40.   The call for papers and conference programme of 'One Hundred Years of the ANC: Debating Liberation Histories and Democracy Today', Johannesburg, September 2011, reveal the sharp salience of the ANC's past.
41.   Limb, *The ANC's Early Years*, 30.
42.   Limb, *The ANC's Early Years*, 119–120. See also W. Beinart, 'Amafeladwonye (The Diehards)', in Beinart and C. Bundy, eds, *Hidden Struggles in Rural South Africa* (Berkeley: University of California Press, 1987), 233–240; W. Beinart, 'Women in Rural Politics: Hershel District in the 1920s and 1930s', in B. Bozzoli, ed., *Class, Community, and Conflict: South African Perspectives* (Johannesburg: Ravan, 1987), 324–357; and M. Epprecht, 'Domesticity and Piety in Colonial Lesotho: The Private Politics of Basotho Women's Pious Associations', *Journal of Southern African Studies*, 19, 2 (1993), 202–224.
43.   As Limb has reminded us, 'With some African primary teachers earning less than factory workers, the mere accretion of literacy does not guarantee membership of a privileged elite'. See Limb, *The ANC's Early Years*, 12–13.

the Daughters of Africa – which one member estimated at 5,000 at its height – was diverse, comprised of women in trades from teaching to domestic work.[44]

Limb also suggested, quite in passing, something that my research strongly supports: such groups kept female activists going through the 1930s, as ANC President Pixley ka Isaka Seme was accused of 'culpable inertia' amidst a raft of disfranchising measures.[45] Drawing upon oral historical and journalistic sources, Limb noted that

> Bertha Mkhize, a working tailor, took part in ANC pass protests in 1931 and 1936. It is unclear how she first encountered the ANC, but she was active in the Daughters of Africa, founded in 1937 by Lil[l]ian Tshabalala of Driefontein and the Durban Bantu Women's Society with the support of Angeline Dube to promote female economic uplifting. Thus, activists found ways around the torpor induced by Seme.[46]

Limb's observation asserts the salience of social groups to nationalist public culture and reveals the extent of their historiographic neglect: press sources show that the Daughters of Africa was founded five years earlier than Limb claims – preceding Mkhize's entry into anti-pass activism, and possibly structuring it. Indeed, Mkhize claimed that her engagement in Durban anti-pass protests in the 1930s came out of her discussions with other members of the Daughters of Africa. 'They all decided that it was a very bad thing; we must try and fight it. How are we going to fight it? It wasn't Congress, it had nothing to do with Congress', Mkhize recalled.[47] Departing from Mkhize's provocative suggestion, the rest of this article illuminates some of the manifold things that African women's centrality to 'welfare' enabled them to do.

Women and political kinship in early African nationalist public culture

In November 1935, readers of *The Bantu World* encountered the Johannesburg newspaper's new 'women's supplement'. The insert 'Marching Forward' offered news about women of African descent – under the banner of a radiant black woman in a Western dress, leaning forward and smiling broadly (see Figure 1).

Reportage on women's progress was not wholly new: under banners like 'Bantu Women in the Home' and 'Page of Interest to Women of the Race', the paper had already published numerous articles boasting of women's educational, professional, and personal successes.[48] Amongst these were articles that made the banner 'Bantu Women in the Home' quite

44. Angeline Dube, interviewed at Ohlange Institute by A. Manson, D. Collins, and A. Mngomezulu, 8 March 1979, CC, Killie Campbell Oral History Programme (KCOHP), Killie Campbell Audio Visual Collection (KCAV) 116. This figure was likely too high. But even if the Daughters of Africa had boasted half as many members, they would have been not far from the size of the ANC, which had no more than 4,000 paid-up members in the 1930s. See Limb, *The ANC's Early Years*, 361.

45. See R. Rive, 'The Early Years', in R. Rive and T. Couzens, eds, *Seme: The Founder of the ANC* (Braamfontein, South Africa: Skotaville, 1991), 9–35; 12.

46. Limb, *The ANC's Early Years*, 367–368.

47. Bertha Mkhize, interviewed at her home in Inanda by A. Manson and D. Collins, 14 and 22 August 1979, CC, KCOHP, KCAV 151.

48. See, for example, 'Educated Bantu Women Alive to the Urgent Needs of Their People', *The Bantu World* (31 December 1932), 16; 'Married Nurses Should Work', *The Bantu World* (5 August 1933), 10; and 'Mrs. Z.K. Mathews Brings Honour to Her People By Her Work', *The Bantu World* (9 June 1934), 10.

Figure 1. 'Marching Forward' banner, *The Bantu World* (23 November 1935), 9.

ironic. In one, Mrs. R.W. Msimang, a district nurse in Orlando township, Johannesburg, opined,

> I hope my husband will do everything in his power to help me in the pursuit of my career, broadening of my experience, the development of personality. Whatever other accusations I may be in a position to lure at my husband's head, I shall not be able to accuse him of being a tyrant, chaining me all day long to our home's front door. I shall belong to myself, not him, nor to my home, nor again my children, but entirely and absolutely to myself. I shall be free.[49]

Pumla Ngozwana, an early graduate of the South African Native College at Fort Hare, gave an address entitled 'The Emancipation of Women' to high school girls at the Inanda Seminary outside of Durban in 1935, which the paper reprinted in its entirety.[50] Despite these debates, women's eventual marriage and responsibility for maintaining their homes and children was assumed, as strong homes were seen as imperative to the welfare of 'the nation'.[51] Mrs E.B. Morake, who became the first black South African woman to receive a Masters of Arts when she graduated from Teachers College, Columbia University, in 1932, thus emphasised her domestic science training as the key model for other African women to emulate: 'At this period of transition, the race need women who are well equipped for the management of the home', she advised.[52] Angeline Dube, wife of founding ANC member

49. Mrs R.W. Msimang, Orlando District Nurse, 'Husbands Should Encourage Their Wives to Take Interest In Life', *The Bantu World* (20 May 1933), 10.
50. P.E. Ngozwana, BA, 'Emancipation of Women', *The Bantu World* (18 May 1935), 13. Transcript of speech continued in *The Bantu World* (25 May 1935), 13; and *The Bantu World* (1 June 1935), 12. Ngozwana married a Ugandan man in 1939; she spent the rest of her career working in Ugandan women's social welfare groups and in national and international politics: see 'Kisosonkole, Pumla Ellen Ngozwana', in K.E. Sheldon, *Historical Dictionary of Women in Sub-Saharan Africa* (Lanham, MD: Scarecrow, 2005), 120.
51. See, for instance, 'Girls Should Aim Very High In Life: Women of Character are a Blessing to the Race', *The Bantu World* (8 April 1933), 11.
52. 'Ability of Bantu Women Proved: Mrs. EB Morake Returns Home with Honours', *The Bantu World* (28 January 1933), 1.

John Dube, was praised as 'passionately devoted to the many arduous duties of her husband' and central to the operations of the Dubes' school, the Ohlange Institute.[53]

But as the 'Editress' complained two months into publication of 'Marching Forward', still too few women were eager to narrate their own stories of personal and racial progress:

> Most of them decline to say something because 'we have nothing to say' or because 'what we do is not worth mentioning'. Now this is modesty gone astray ... When they say they do nothing worth mentioning they forget that their critics mention every little bit they do that reflects on them. These critics watch for every false step a woman makes and then rush to print condemning women as 'bad'... These articles, therefore, are not published just to interest you, but are published to help you do likewise; to encourage you and to silence our 'bursting' critics. That is why you should cast aside wrong modesty and tell us about yourself, your aims and aspirations. Somewhere, in this big country, there is another woman, placed as you are, who would find comfort in your life sketch. If you neglect this opportunity of proving yourself, remember that those who look down on women will never neglect an opportunity of blaming all women for the weaknesses of others. Now come out of your shells, sisters, and tell us what you're doing in your part of the country.[54]

At first glance, this editorial appears empowering. It calls for women to write themselves into public life through a script of their own making, in which their words and actions would be mutually constitutive: positive female images would provide female readers with an example to emulate, while reassuring 'hard-boiled male critics' that women were not losing their moral compass amidst economic and social flux.[55] But the context of the production of this 'women's section' reveals a more complex dynamic.

First, the Editress was a man: Rolfes Robert Reginald Dhlomo. The descendent of early African Christian converts, older brother of nationalist intellectual Herbert Dhlomo, and graduate of the pioneering African educationalist and activist John Dube's Ohlange Institute and the elite American Board Mission institution Adams College, Dhlomo was in his early 30s when he assumed a female *nom de plume*.[56] Unlike the satirical commentary on political and social affairs that he penned under his other major alias, 'R. Roamer Esq.', his persona as the Editress was strictly didactic. Amidst *The Bantu World*'s first beauty pageant, in which editors invited female readers from around the country to submit their best self-portraits and elect 'Miss Africa', the Editress had made a name for herself as a strident critic of cosmetics, warning women that make-up conferred 'the impression of cheapness'.[57] As Lynn Thomas has pointed out, powder was particularly suspect, as Dhlomo charged that women sought 'to turn themselves white' and should embrace 'the beauty of their natural coloring'.[58]

---

53. 'Prominent Woman Encourages Others to Live Full Lives', *The Bantu World* (4 February 1933), 10.
54. The Editress, 'Women's Critics', *The Bantu World* (25 January 1936), 7.
55. *Ibid.*
56. T. Couzens, *The New African: A Study of the Life and Work of H.I.E. Dhlomo* (Ravan: Johannesburg, 1985), 42–61; and 'Pseudonyms in Black South African Writing, 1920–1950', *Research in African Literatures* 6, 2 (1975), 226–231.
57. The Editress, 'Disappointing Make-Ups', *The Bantu World* (23 June 1934), 12.
58. See L. Thomas, 'The Modern Girl and Racial Respectability in 1930s South Africa', in A.E. Weinbaum, L.M. Thomas, P. Ramamurthy, U.G. Poiger, M.Y. Dong, and T.E. Barlow, eds, *The Modern Girl Around the World: Consumption, Modernity, and Globalization* (Durham: Duke University Press, 2008), 96–119; 108; Miss Roamer, 'Beautiful Bantu Women Need No Lipstick or Powder to Aid Nature', *Bantu World* (4 March 1933), 10; and R.R.R.D., 'True Beauty', *The Bantu World* (29 September 1934), 12.

Second, the public sphere into which Dhlomo encouraged women to write themselves was contradictory. *The Bantu World* had been founded in 1932 by white ad man Bertram Paver, eager to generate new revenue through a nationally-circulating weekly targeting the African market.[59] The ranks of literate Africans, with money to spend on the consumer goods that *The Bantu World* hawked, were small: 12 per cent of the national African population of 6,500,000 were literate in the mid-1930s.[60] But these literate Africans were eager for a national platform on which to share their achievements and thus shape the agenda for what they called 'racial uplift'. By the mid-1940s, some 24,000 copies of *The Bantu World* sold each week; its staff claimed that at least five people read each issue and that they shared its contents with countless illiterate people.[61] *The Bantu World* published the majority of its content in English, the language of mission high schools, although it also published articles in Zulu, Xhosa, Sotho, Tswana, Venda, Tsonga, and Afrikaans (some which were translations of the English articles, others which were original). The women's section, from which most of the articles on which I draw here come, was published predominantly in English.[62] While older African-oriented papers had come out of school printing presses and had targeted regional markets, *The Bantu World* was uniquely national and commercial. The scope of its reportage resembled that of African American newspapers with national audiences (like the *Chicago Defender*); while it centred on news of interest to Bantu-language speakers in South Africa, it gestured toward a broader black world, with some news from across the continent and the diaspora. But *The Bantu World* possessed a constrained cosmopolitanism, working within what Les Switzer has termed a 'captive African commercial press' beholden to the concerns of white advertisers and oriented toward an audience of white liberal-segregationists – 'friends of the native' who were both allies in a context of black disfranchisement and moralising critics of African conduct.[63]

The Bantu World, then, was predicated on fictions of racial and gendered autonomy. While at first glance it looked like the Editress was an assertive black woman, she was a he – inciting female discourse in order to shore up what Thomas has termed 'racial respectability' in the context of 1930s South Africa, and what Evelyn Brooks Higginbotham has more famously called a 'politics of respectability' in the late nineteenth and early twentieth century United States. 'Racial respectability refers to people's desires and efforts to claim positive recognition in contexts powerfully structured by racism, contexts in which respectability was framed through racial categories and appearances

59.   Thomas, 'The Modern Girl and Racial Respectability', 97.
60.   *Ibid.*
61.   L. Switzer, '*Bantu World* and the Origins of a Captive African Commercial Press', in L. Switzer, ed., *South Africa's Alternative Press: Voices of Protest and Resistance, 1880s–1960s* (New York: Cambridge University Press, 1997), 189–212; 190.
62.   As part of the broader project of which this article is a preliminary part, I am working on translating *The Bantu World*'s African language articles (beginning with isiZulu, which I have studied, and later including other languages, with assistance) authored by women or dealing with women's issues. I have also assembled a collection of isiZulu articles from *Ilanga Lase Natal,* and I am beginning research in other newspaper archives over the next year. My understanding of the meanings of home, family, and politics will doubtless be deepened considerably with this further research.
63.   Switzer, '*Bantu World* and the Origins of a Captive African Commercial Press', 190.

were of the gravest importance', as Thomas has explained.[64] African male journalists, particularly Rolfes and Herbert Dhlomo, took their responsibilities as gatekeepers of racial respectability seriously. And they believed that women, due to the profound influence they possessed as mothers, would determine the substance of the race. Thus the Editress wrote in her next column,

> The world looks up to women to-day; for they play an important part in the moulding of future generations and in the security of homes. Once women get off the rails of decency the whole social structure of a people tumbles in ruins. We want our womenfolk to realise this, so that they do not pull their menfolk down.[65]

Writing under the pseudonym 'X.Y.Z'. in 1939, Rolfes Dhlomo emphasised that

> the whole future, the whole form and destiny to which a race must be shaped lies, NOT in the hands of our politicians, NOT in the hands of our teachers and NOT in the powers of our ministers, but in the hands of the women of the race.[66]

Women's centrality to social reproduction meant that their poor conduct bore dire racial consequences: 'For women to conduct themselves in an unseemly manner knowing well how, in virtue of their natural responsibility over their offspring and race, they have an unalterable influence, is, to put it straight, an open crime of "murder" against human society'.[67] Herbert Dhlomo, although he seemed less fond of apocalyptic language than his brother, emphasised that women's new forms of public presence, particularly in urban areas, entailed new challenges to respectability. 'Liberation means responsibility', Herbert Dhlomo had insisted in 1930. 'In her old state of bondage and subjection, woman was kept pure and virtuous by prohibition; in her new position of freedom and equality she must keep pure and virtuous by inhibition'.[68] By inciting women to talk about themselves positively, the Dhlomos apparently aimed to inspire a virtuous cycle of respectability in the African elite public sphere, the forum in which key tenets of racial pride and nationalism were nurtured. But of course, political discourse within this 'captive' press could not take turns too radical for white advertisers and readers. In this contradictory space, women's social welfare organisations bore great appeal. By organising around domestic concerns, women could stage public critiques of white supremacy.

Indeed, two of the first women the Editress featured after this plaintive call were the paradigmatic 'social welfare' leaders Sibusisiwe Makhanya and Cecilia Lillian Tshabalala. Makhanya had trained in social work at Teachers College, Columbia University, before

---

64. Thomas, 'The Modern Girl and Racial Respectability', 98; see also E.B. Higginbotham, *Righteous Discontent: The Women's Movement in the Black Baptist Church, 1880–1920* (Cambridge: Harvard University Press, 1993), 185–229.
65. The Editress, 'Disturbing Conduct', *The Bantu World* (1 February 1936), 7.
66. X.Y.Z., 'Women and Their Responsibility', *The Bantu World* (30 September 1939), 9.
67. X.Y.Z., 'Failure of Responsibility', *The Bantu World* (14 October 1939), 9. On the similar stakes of urban women's respectability in colonial Zimbabwe, see T. Barnes, *'We Women Worked So Hard': Gender, Urbanization, and Social Reproduction in Colonial Harare, Zimbabwe,1930–1956* (Portsmouth: Heinemann, 1999).
68. H.I.E. Dhlomo, 'Bantu Womanhood', *Umteteli wa Bantu* (10 May 1930), http://pzacad.pitzer.edu/NAM/newafrre/writers/hdhlomo/umteteli/10_5_30.gif, accessed 19 February 2011.

returning to her birthplace in Umbumbulu, Natal, to operate a community health centre and coordinate the Bantu Youth League, a group aimed at cultivating health and a Christian sense of 'citizenship' in young people.[69] Tshabalala fit a similar profile: she was doing 'outstanding work in the Driefontein area, Natal', upgrading the schools as the administrator of a state grant and organising the Daughters of Africa. 'In this Daughters of Africa movement, Miss Tshabalala teaches the African women of the different communities – how to run a home and she gives demonstration lessons in cookery and some other matters affecting the African race', readers learnt. Thanks to lessons on nutrition, agricultural techniques, and business and savings strategies, members 'now have fine vegetable gardens, and flower gardens. They now begin to realise what business means. They sell their eggs, fowls, vegetables in town . . . These are the type of women we want who will uplift the African race'.[70]

Tshabalala was also more cosmopolitan than the typical Zulu country girl. After her schooling at the Ohlange Institute, Tshabalala

> left for America. In America, after completing her studies, she was offered a teaching post; not only that, she was also a Sunday school teacher, teaching Negroes. Miss Tshabalala was not only interested in her teaching but also in social work. She stayed in America for eighteen (18) years. She returned to South Africa in 1930 together with Miss Sibusisiwe Makanya.[71]

She spent much of her time in the United States in Hartford, Connecticut, where she worked at the Colored Congregational Church. She secured her initial connections there through connections with American Zulu Mission missionaries, some of whom were nonplussed by her: one dismissed her as 'either by birth or education a Zulu aristocrat [who] cannot ever think of herself as a member of the crowd or any considerable group'.[72] Tshabalala also spent over two years as a missionary to the Gold Coast, with the African

69. The Editress, 'Miss Violet Sibusisiwe Makanya', *The Bantu World* (1 February 1936), 9. She spelled her name 'Makhanya' later in life, following changed isiZulu orthography; I follow that spelling. On Makhanya, see 'Resumé of Sibusisiwe Makhanya (Fifi) – her life and activities', CC, Sibusisiwe Makhanya Papers (SMP), File 4; U. Khan, 'A Critical Study of the Life of Sibusisiwe Makanya and Her Work as Educator and Social Worker in the Umbumbulu District of Natal, 1894–1971' (MA thesis, University of Natal, 1995); S. Marks, *Not Either an Experimental Doll: The Separate Worlds of Three South African Women* (Bloomington: Indiana University Press, 1987), 30–42; and R.H. Davis, Jr., 'Producing the "Good African": South Carolina's Penn School as a Guide for African Education in South Africa', in A.T. Mugomba and M. Nyaggah, eds, *Independence without Freedom: The Political Economy of Colonial Education in Southern Africa* (Santa Barbara, CA: ABC-Clio, 1980), 83–103.
70. Viyella, 'Miss C.L. Tshabalala's Career', *The Bantu World* (14 March 1936), 10. From extant information, I cannot ascertain the identity of 'Viyella', but I know that the prose in this article is simpler than either of the Dhlomo brothers' typical stylings.
71. Viyella, 'Miss C.L. Tshabalala's Career', 10.
72. C.H.P., Boston, to Clara Bridgman, Johannesburg, 10 August 1927, Houghton Library, Harvard University, American Board of Commissioners for Foreign Missions: African Mission Records 15.4, Volume 40. She worked with the Bridgman/Cowles missionary family. See also J. Nauright, '"I Am with You as Never Before": Women in Urban Protest Movements, Alexandra Township, South Africa, 1912–1945', in K. Sheldon, ed., *Courtyards, Markets, City Streets: Urban Women in Africa* (Boulder: Westview, 1996), 259–283; 276.

Figure 2.   Lillian Tshabalala, Photos in Viyella, 'Miss C.L. Tshabalala's Career', *The Bantu World* (14 March 1936), 10; Tshabalala, 'The Message for the New Year', *The Bantu World* (13 February 1937), 11.

Methodist Episcopal Church.[73] Her association with the impressive Makhanya likely paled in comparison to her association with African Americans, who appeared as impossibly glamorous, accomplished figures in *The Bantu World*.[74] Tshabalala had not just been part of an African American community, but had garnered sufficient respect to teach them about God. Upon her return she rejected a teaching post at Adams College, the elite American Board institution on Natal's South Coast, because 'she wished to serve her own people – the Africans. So she left Durban for her place, "Kwa Zamowake" (Kleinfontein), just three miles from Driefontein'.[75]

Soon after this profile, Tshabalala seized *The Bantu World* as a platform for an incitement to female discourse and organisation of her own. In 'What is the Club Woman?' Tshabalala described a domestic geography in which women's concerns about their families demanded action on behalf of the race:

> The typical club woman is a home woman who has found that she cannot isolate her home from her community, government and social [life], and that health conditions also invade its sanctuary, and that in order to protect her brood she must go out from its walls for part of her time and do her best to make government and social order and physical conditions as fine as possible, that they may upbuild and not destroy. In a few words her motive power is to keep African ideals in Home, in School, in Government, in Human Relations.[76]

73.   *Ibid.*
74.   See, for example, R. Marta, 'Miss Rilda Marta's Trip to the United States Full of Excitement', *The Bantu World* (29 June 1935), 12.
75.   Viyella, 'Miss C.L. Tshabalala's Career', 10.
76.   C.L. Tshabalala, 'What is the Club Woman?' *The Bantu World* (4 April 1936), 12.

A 'home woman', Tshabalala suggested, would recognise that her ostensible 'sanctuary' was no such thing. She would know that African domestic spaces were permeated by not only the reach of the state, but also 'health conditions' – the tuberculosis and sexually transmitted infections that migrant men brought back from the mines, the persistent ailments that accompanied poverty, and widespread malnutrition for many Africans in rural 'reserves' and in the overcrowded urban slums to which most urban families were confined.[77]

The 'home woman' must therefore become a 'club woman' to ensure the social and cultural reproduction of African families in a white supremacist state. The 'African ideals' that Tshabalala delineated were vague: 'The club movement when it learns its strength becomes an invincible power working for health, happiness, righteousness and humanity in these provinces of ours and in all other nations with which we should and shall have international relation in the future', she suggested. But her certainty that 'club women' would define the contours of a proud African race in the Union of South Africa and beyond was clear:

> We want communications that are extensive of the home, where we shall be friends with each other, with people of all races and creeds, where good schools, high standard of living and public health, recreation, beauty and the moral atmosphere shall tempt the finest type. We cannot get these things unless we work together: we must put them into daily intercourse and into politics.

When a 'home woman' became a 'club woman', Tshabalala assured her readers, 'you have helped to make your race one hundred per cent African'. She presented the Daughters of Africa, then entering its fourth year, as a 'self cultural body standing for progress', a model for readers to emulate. 'The typical self cultural club to-day should regard itself as a small training school, to link up knowledge and wisdom with the world that lies about it'.[78]

The aims of a 'club woman' were national and worldly – but rendered in gendered idioms of home and family that resonated intimately. Participation in 'cultural clubs', Tshabalala suggested in a subsequent article, was like 'cultivating the ground, getting it ready for bringing out crops. Culture makes soil fertile. Culture of human beings ought to do the same thing'. Here she invoked African women's historic productive and reproductive centrality to encourage them to form clubs that would nurture representative racial leadership.

> Every club should be the center of a true democracy, and as our Women's Federation is made up of individual clubs, here we should find a large circle of African Daughters radiating great principles of life – freedom of thought and speech, tolerance, sincerity and justice, service and cooperation.[79]

77. See R.M. Packard, *White Plague, Black Labor: Tuberculosis and the Political Economy of Health and Disease in South Africa* (Berkeley: University of California Press, 1989); and D. Wylie, *Starving on a Full Stomach: Hunger and the Triumph of Cultural Racism in Modern South Africa* (Charlottesville: University Press of Virginia, 2001).
78. C.L. Tshabalala, 'What is the Club Woman?'
79. C.L. Tshabalala, 'Arise, O Ye Daughters!' *The Bantu World* (27 June 1936), 11.

As they sang in a hymnal at a 1936 branch meeting, the Daughters of Africa saw themselves as *'iziseko ze sizwe'* – the rocks that sharpened and bolstered the nation.[80]

But as grand as the scale of their ambitions may have been, Tshabalala reminded her readers that the Daughters of Africa's work remained preliminary. 'A baby race we are, therefore of necessity our clubs are getting together meetings where we learn how to get acquainted', she contended. 'Let us get started and continue to crawl until we can walk like other women'.[81] The women who were 'walking', she made clear in a 1937 address to the Daughters of Africa, reprinted in its entirety in *The Bantu World*, were the American women whose extensive club movements Tshabalala had encountered during her time in the United States. On one hand, she presented an idyllic vision of American interracial cooperation and gendered unity, which South African clubwomen ought to emulate. White American women may have pioneered women's clubs, but

> the Negro woman in the States has also followed the example of her older sister with haste unequalled. They have all types of fraternal organisations to build and consolidate their race as a whole educationally, socially and otherwise. Whatever financial assistance the Negro receives from her beneficiaries (the whites) only adds to her steady but honest labours, her continuous effort to stand on her own for it's a bird that uses her wings daily that will fly unassisted tomorrow.

On the other hand, she used her account of a 1927 clubwomen's conference that she had attended in Chautauqua, New York, to suggest that white women had not begun to assist black women's groups out of the goodness of their hearts. White women had 'resolved more emphatically to help and emancipate the NEGRO in their midst, and to befriend foreigners in their country and to suppress their natural Nordic pride and also master their superiority complex', only after a discussion of the effect of American racism on the reception of American missionaries to countries like Japan and India.

> The Orient could not very well understand Christian workers coming from a country where human beings like NEGROES are still lynched and burnt at the stake; where human cuts and joints are kept as souvenirs and could not help wondering as to whether the West has Christianity worth while to be really exported.[82]

The global dimensions of the women's club movement thus seemed to offer new openings for the globalisation of anti-racist struggle, in an increasingly desperate context. 'Abyssinia the only independent Ethiopian State has been instantly wiped off the map of the world ... we are ascending the steep hill harder and higher and becoming more prejudiced against European races inspite of our good nature characteristic to the African peoples', Tshabalala acknowledged.

> We are also feeling the old sting in the last war of our young country men who were sunk, giving their lives and their services for humanity's sake. Stung and bitten because we are at this late [stage] entering the dark doors of segregation and colour line opened as well as created by the new legislature in the land of our birth.

80. A. Xaba, 'Isililo Sama Dodakazi Ase Kleinfontein [Meeting of the Daughters at Kleinfontein]', *The Bantu World* (1 August 1936), 7.
81. Tshabalala, 'Arise, O Ye Daughters!'
82. 'Miss C.L. Tshabalala's Address: Other Women', *The Bantu World* (15 January 1938), 11.

Yet she concluded her address by encouraging women to address the national and global scourge of racism by tending to their bodies and minds, and those of their children. 'Avoid all foods that will stunt your growth physically, mentally, morally, intellectually and spiritually', she urged in closing.[83]

Tshabalala's movement between global, national, local, and bodily sites of racial progress and anti-racist struggle may appear jarring – a distraction from the more straightforwardly political moments of women's organisation for which historians have conventionally searched. But Tshabalala's capacious conception of the spaces of African women's politics enabled the Daughters of Africa to build a wide national tent – under which members of local groups found space to think their way out of segregationist South Africa and to articulate a new model of African identity that enabled fundamental *resilience*, as well as moments of more recognisable resistance. In a state that categorically denied Africans control over their homes or families, struggles for domestic health and well-being were waged in a public culture in which 'family' and 'home' were powerful idioms that enabled women to talk about 'race' and 'nation', as well as political spaces in which women and men alike fervently believed that women might shape their racial and national future. By caring for African bodies and minds, female social welfare activists could create a new body politic.

Conclusion: Rethinking the links between male- and female-dominated nationalist groups

At a national level, Tshabalala asserted her group's solidarity with such male-dominated political groups as the ANC and the All African Convention – the federation of African nationalist groups that had first convened in 1935 in opposition to the pending removal of men in the Cape from the franchise, and the deepening restrictions on African access to land and rights to mobility throughout the Union. At a Daughters of Africa meeting at Inanda in early 1938, for example, Tshabalala spoke of their work 'pressing forward to join hands with the SONS OF AFRICA known as THE ALL AFRICAN CONVENTION, fraternally walking hand in hand with the DAUGHTERS OF AFRICA, standing together in friendship and mutual confidence'.[84] The timing of her appeal for gendered unity was critical: At that time, the All African Convention was in a state of utter internal crisis and division, and its members had formally invited affiliates from black educational, religious, and commercial organisations to extend its organisational power. Tshabalala suggested that the Daughters might parlay their social authority into a unifying national influence. In the early 1940s, the Daughters of Africa worked out a constitution that espoused ambitious core goals:

> The objects of this organisation shall be to correlate the African women's organizations or clubs into one compact body for the purpose of supporting all that improves our homes, our communities, our race, and our nation as a whole in whatever way possible. To help our clubs to satisfy both personal and public needs, the cultural club to enrich the inner life, and the civic club to serve its community and the departmental club to unite while giving individual

83. 'Miss C.L. Tshabalala's Address: Other Women', *The Bantu World* (15 January 1938), 11.
84. 'Address Given by Miss C.L. Tshabalala to "Daughters of Africa" in Conference at Inanda M.S.', *The Bantu World* (22 January 1938), 11.

scope ... The membership of this organisation shall be unlimited since its purpose touches all phases of Community, State, and National Welfare.[85]

From 1940, the group also attained an actual national presence, forming branches around Johannesburg and Pretoria. Tshabalala moved to Alexandra, Johannesburg, to run an office there. The Alexandra-based secretary, significantly, was 'live wire' Josie Palmer (who also went by the name Josie Mpama): an outspoken member of the Communist Party of South Africa since 1928.[86] Palmer remained a prominent member of the group between at least 1941 and 1943.[87] Julia Wells, who interviewed Palmer toward the end of her life, noted that 'Miss Palmer was a member of the Daughters of Africa, but felt there was nothing in it, just meetings and conferences. She couldn't remember them ever having organised any demonstrations. She couldn't tolerate this so she left the organization, probably in the early forties'.[88] But her presence, and leadership role, in the group for at least three years suggests that these 'meetings and conferences' offered the radical *something*. Moreover, Tshabalala herself grew 'radicalized' during her time in Alexandra, leading her to join the leftist African Democratic Party in 1943, as John Nauright has pointed out. In Alexandra, the Daughters of Africa quickly became 'crucial to the creation of networks of working women', and these networks sustained the 1943–1944 Alexandra bus boycotts.[89]

Yet even as at least some of the Daughters of Africa engaged in more radical public projects, they continued to discuss how to create empowering homes. As teacher Mrs W.M.J. Nhlapo, BA, reminded members at a 1942 Johannesburg meeting,

> One of the first tasks to which the African woman and her organisation should devote their energy, is that of emancipating herself from the age-long inferiority complex born of the age-long idea to which she has for long and in divers ways, been schooled that her place is that of remaining and toiling in the home. Another task is that of seeing in the home, not an institution of a menial character, but the anvil on which men and women are to be shaped. Destroy the homes, you have destroyed the very life of a people.[90]

Most critically, the group's status as a social organisation with a 'self-help' agenda enabled it to evade official opprobrium. An account of the 1942 Daughters of Africa conference noted that the Native Commissioner of Johannesburg had made a 'stirring

85. C.L. Tshabalala, "The Simple Form of the Draft Constitutions of the Daughters of Africa Association of the Transvaal Province: Condensed," n.d. but c. 1941, SAB, Depot TAB, Source KJB, Volume 411, Reference N1/14/3.

86. See 'Alexandra News', *The Bantu World* (4 January 1941), 12.

87. See *Ibid.*; J.W. Palmer, Assistant Secretary, '"Daughters of Africa" Federation (Tvl)', *The Bantu World* (16 May 1942), 8; W.M.B. Nhlapo, 'Daughters of Africa: 3rd Annual Federation at Orlando', *The Bantu World* (28 November 1942), 5; and 'The General National Conference of the Daughters of Africa, to be held in the Bantu Men's Social Centre, Johannesburg, Friday, Saturday, Sunday, December 17th, 18th, 19th, 1943', SAB, Depot TAB, Source KJB, Volume 411, Reference N1/14/3.

88. J. Wells, notes from interview with Josie Palmer, 19 October 1977, Historical Papers Collection, University of the Witwatersrand, Johannesburg, File AD2088.

89. Nauright, '"I Am with You as Never Before"', 277; J.M. Brink, 'Meeting re: Alexandra Township Buses in Mayor's Parlour', 1 January 1945, SAB, Depot SAB, Source NTS, Volume 9693, Reference 717/400.

90. 'African Women and Organisation', *The Bantu World* (1 August 1942), 8.

speech' at the event, congratulating 'the African women on raising from their erstwhile inferior position in Bantu society' and praising their contribution to the War Funds.[91] As an elderly woman, Albertina Mnguni similarly recalled that she and other Daughters of Africa in Natal were once 'summoned to come and explain what this association of ours was. I took this Constitution [of the Daughters of Africa] ... They read it very carefully, and decided that it was in fact a welfare organisation, and we were released'.[92]

The national influence of the Daughters of Africa began to diminish after the 1943 formation of the ANC Women's League under Madie Hall Xuma – an African American clubwoman for whom ideals of national and global racial progress were also intertwined with ideals of personal and familial development.[93] But these sources suggest that the Daughters of Africa was a *foundational* group, which left a lasting intellectual imprint on its members and on nationalist public culture that scholars should take more seriously. As Mnguni summarised the significance of the Daughters of Africa, 'We wanted our nation to know one another'.[94] At this moment of conceptualising the future of African nationalism and gendered relations in South Africa, historians should take heed of the personal, familial, national, and transnational strategies by which women first came to 'know one another' and to define the contours of their 'nation'.

91. 'Daughters of Africa Conference', *The Bantu World* (7 February 1942), 8.
92. Albertina Mzimela/Mnguni, interviewed at her home in Umlazi by Simeon Zulu, 23 September 1980, CC, KCOHP, KCAV 329.
93. See Berger, *An African American 'Mother of the Nation'*.
94. Mnguni, CC, KCOHP, KCAV 329.

The African National Congress in the Western Transvaal/Northern Cape Platteland, c. 1910–1964: Patterns of Diffusion and Support for Congress in a Rural Setting

ANDREW HAYDEN MANSON AND BERNARD MBENGA

North-West University, Mafikeng Campus, South Africa

Abstract

This article examines the nature and trajectory of ANC engagement with the predominantly rural inhabitants of the former western Transvaal/northern Cape, the region of the present-day North-West province. Even before the formal launching of the ANC, a number of influential figures in the region, in particular members of the Molema family in Mafikeng, provided an intellectual framework for the founding of an African nationalist movement. From its inception then the organisation gained significant support in the rural districts, both because the Molema's were an important chiefly family, and because the Batswana rural elites saw in the ANC an instrument for countering the impact of the 1913 Native Land Act. In the 1920s the ANC was able to sustain its initial success by the formation of ANC branches in most of the small dorps (towns) in the western Transvaal platteland. By the end of the decade however, the ANC's influence waned, and the South African Communist Party and the Industrial and Commercial Workers' Union of Africa (ICU), were able to mobilise African political opinion and activity more effectively. The situation began to change in the 1950s as the state began increasingly to direct its attention to controlling the lives of rural Africans and taking control of traditional authorities. The 1957 'Hurutshe Revolt' was the catalyst for a wider regional resistance to the carrying of passes for women specifically, and state intervention in general. The article traces the genesis of this resistance, and through the recent availability of source materials, the role of the ANC in the affair. Support for the ANC quickened after this, and the Zeerust became to key to ANC strategy as the period of exile began.

Introduction

The purpose of this paper is to explore ANC activities specifically and African response and resistance generally to dispossession and discrimination in this region, during the years that the organisation operated 'above ground'. There has been little focus in the various ANC histories and narratives on this part of the country, South Africa's western Highveld platteland (countryside) and we hope therefore to provide some of the missing pieces of the organisation's attempts to penetrate into what is largely a rural and conservative landscape. Indeed the evidence is sketchy and limited, but it is possible to document some of the activities and patterns of ANC presence in the region, which now makes up the North-West Province.

We should begin by noting that some significant figures in the founding of the ANC resided in Mafikeng, now the capital of the North West province, which had until Union, been part of the Cape Colony. Foremost of course were members of the Molema family and Sol Plaatje, who lived in the town from 1898 to 1910 when he left for Kimberley. The significance of this fact is not just symbolic, for both Seetsele Modiri Molema and Plaatje retained an enduring interest in events in the wider region, as will be outlined later. Silas Thelesho Molema, a councillor of the Tshidi-Barolong *kgosi* (chief) Montshiwa, and later his private secretary, represented the Barolong at the South African Native Convention in Bloemfontein in 1909, which resolved to request the British government to extend the Cape qualified franchise for Africans to those who would become part of the Union of South Africa.[1] He also supported the founding of the South African National Native Congress (SANNC, later ANC), and was invited by Pixley ka-Isaka Seme to help draft the SANNC's first constitution.[2] He also raised funds for the delegations of 1914 and 1919 to travel to Great Britain to protest against the provisions of the Native Land Act of 1913. Shortly before his death in September 1927 he successfully led a deputation to the government to protest against discriminatory provisions contained in the Native Administration Act. He was also instrumental in supporting Plaatje to launch the Setswana newspaper, *Koranta ea Becoana*.[3]

Thelesho's son, the medical doctor, Modiri Molema, was a significant and long-time member and office bearer in the ANC. He became active in politics from 1936 after the passing of the Hertzog Bills, and his involvement was extended further in 1940 when A.B. Xuma assumed leadership. He was National Treasurer of the ANC from 1949 until 1953. Arrested for civil disobedience in the 1952 Defiance Campaign, he was forced to resign his position as a member and office bearer of the ANC in September 1953 in terms of the Suppression of Communism Act of 1950.[4] Significantly he played a notable role in the affairs of the Barolong, and exerted a considerable influence on the various chiefs based in

1. B. Willan, *Sol Plaatje, South African Nationalist, 1876–1932* (London: Heinemann, 1984), 140.
2. University of Witwatersrand (hereafter UW), William Cullen Library, (hereafter WCL), Historical and Literary Papers Collection (hereafter HLPC), Silas Molema Collection, Microfilm Cc9, P. Ka-Isaka Seme to Silas Molema, 3 November 1911.
3. This sketch is taken from the 'Introduction to the Inventory of the Silas T. Molema Collection and the Solomon T. Plaatje Papers', WCL, UW.
4. The Notice is contained in UW, WCL, HLPC, Microfilm Cc 9, 'Proclamation in Terms of the Suppression of Communism Act...' Minister of Justice, C.J. Swart, 11 September 1953.

Mafikeng. As Jane Starfield has observed, 'leadership of the Tshidi [Barolong] at Mafikeng was of prime importance to three generations of Molemas and led Modiri to play a leading role on more committees than most people can manage in their lives'.[5] Despite being isolated from the larger cities of the country, Molema, often at short notice, attempted to attend most of the ANC's Executive or Working Committee meetings, particularly in Johannesburg. Though involved in the higher echelons of the organisation, he kept an eye on local affairs as well.

The chiefs (*Dikgosi*)

Even before the formation of the ANC, chiefs were considered to be an important cornerstone in spreading its message and influence. As Walshe notes, 'Congress had anticipated incorporating the chiefs, hoping in this way to extend its influence from the educated elite and urban areas to tribal Africans and hence the whole nation'.[6] Congress was therefore concerned to establish branches of the ANC in rural districts and to grant traditional leaders symbolic importance in the ANC through representation in a Council of Chiefs who sat behind the National Executive during conference; a kind of parliamentary 'upper House'. The close ties between the Barolong in Mafikeng and the SANNC were not only maintained through the Molema family but also through the ruling Montshiwa lineage. John L. Dube, the SANNC's first President, called upon the financial assistance of chief Lekoko Montshiwa of the Barolong in funding expenses incurred by Plaatje in carrying out work for the SANNC. This applied in particular to the 1912 Deputation by the SANNC to discuss a range of issues with the government in Cape Town.[7] Plaatje was considered to be a 'special representative' of the Barolong by Dube.

Several chiefs had been present at the formation of the ANC and 'virtually all of those of any significance had at least sent representatives',[8] Lekoko Montshiwa for example sending Silas Molema and T.J. Tawana another of his 'sub-chiefs'. In addition, they provided significant financial support and added weight to various representative protest delegations to government. The leadership of the ANC from about 1913 to the mid-1920s wanted the ANC to provide a platform for 'progressive' chiefs to play an active role in the organisation's political and cultural activities. The groundswell of support for the ANC up to about the mid-1920s, can thus be attributed to these objectives, coupled with the hope among rural Africans (and their leaders) that the ANC might be able to reverse the damaging consequences of the 1913 Land Act. When it became apparent that the organisation could do little to alter the deleterious effects that resulted, support seemed to wane. In addition, it should be remembered that the Native Affairs Department (NAD) began to conceive of a more active role for chiefs as agents in controlling the African rural

5. J. Starfield, 'Dr Modiri S. Molema, (1891–1965), The Making of a Historian', PhD thesis, University of the Witwatersrand, 2008, 43. A complete history of Molema's political life awaits writing.
6. P. Walshe, *The Rise of African Nationalism in South Africa, 1912–1953*, (Los Angeles: C. Hurst, 1970).
7. UW, WCL, HLPC, Silas Molema Collection, Cc 9, Dube to Lekoko Montshiwa, 3 November 1911.
8. Walshe , *Rise of African Nationalism*, 210.

population from the 1930s.[9] A consequence of this essentially paternalistic policy was that it placed considerable pressure on chiefs from adopting too forthright a defence of ANC activities. We intend to cast some light on how these specific patterns of ANC/chiefly relations played themselves out on the western Highveld platteland, and to account for a revival of ANC fortunes from the late 1940s in this region.

The Dikgosi and the Congress movement in the western Transvaal Platteland

It should be noted that even before the founding of the SANNC, chiefs other than those individuals representing the Barolong in the former western Transvaal were in the forefront of protests against the Act of Union, which essentially wrote the majority of Africans out of any political representation and in the newly crafted state. The Transvaal Native Union (TNU) took a decision in June 1909, to send a delegation to England to put forward the claims and views of Africans regarding the impending Union to the Secretary of State for the Colonies. A Petition from the TNU was also forwarded to the Governor. However, due to insufficient funds, the intention of sending the men failed.[10] The TNU consequently embarked on an effort to collect funds for this visit. The delegation comprised three chiefs, two of them, J.O.M. Mamogale and August Mokgatle, to whom we also refer below, were from the Rustenburg region. In addition to this much of the money that was collected also came from their adherents and other Africans in the vicinity.[11] This sense of outrage over the Union is captured in a report by the missionary to the baFokeng, Ernst Penzhorn, who reported in 1911 that 'the presently false striving for independence by blacks and their mistrust of whites, now running the country, causes difficulties to arise for the mission work'.[12]

In the Hurutshe reserve, the chiefs were reported by the missionary Jensen, of the Hermannsburg Missionary Society, to be indignant and dissatisfied by the passing of the Land Act in 1913 and pressed Jensen to give evidence on their behalf to the Beaumont Commission appointed to investigate the possibility of setting aside more land for African occupation. Jensen wrote that all the baHurutshe leaders, as well as most African *dikgosi* in the western Transvaal, had joined the South African Native Congress which was coordinating opposition to the legislation. What this indicated, Jensen added, was that 'the natives here are slowly but surely waking up, and they are not prepared to accept everything the white population is doing to them'.[13]

The Transvaal Native Congress (TNC), an affiliate of the ANC, was a mainly urban organisation, but one that managed to retain some contact with rural constituents and was able to penetrate the rural localities of the former Western Transvaal. In 1914 it

9. S. Dubow, '"Holding a Just Balance Between Black and White": The Native Affairs Department in South Africa, c1920–1933,' *Journal of Southern African Studies*, vol. 12 (1986), 217–239.
10. Secretary for Native Affairs (SNA), vol. 433, NA 1900/09. Native Commissioner, Rustenburg to Secretary for Native Affairs, 17 August 1909.
11. See correspondence in SNA 433, NA 1900/09.
12. Mission Reports of the Hermansburg Missionary Society, *Hermansburger Missionsblatt*, (*HMB*) University of South Africa (hereafter UNISA) Archives, 11 January 1911, no. 1, Reports From Our Bechuana Mission, Saron.
13. UNISA Archives, *HMB*, 1915, Report by Jensen for 1913, p. 83.

attempted to launch a body known as the Transvaal Native Chiefs Council, one of whose leading lights was the Bakwena ba Mogopa chief, John Mamogale.[14] But its ability to have some impact on the lives of rural people is illustrated by an event that took place in 1917, and which in fact belies the notion that it was unconcerned with developments in the rural districts. It also unmistakably shows the kind of attention that Congress was receiving from the side of chiefs in the Rustenberg region, and suggests quite a high level of militancy among them. In July the TNC held a meeting in Phokeng in the Rustenburg district. Two police informers, Paul Mokgatle and Pitsoe Magano, attended the meeting and submitted reports to their police contact, Police Constable Freddy Hicks. Both informers noted the presence of a number of chiefs from the district including August Mokgatle, (baFokeng) Diederick Mogale, (baKwena ba Mogopa) Hermon Selon, (baKwena ba Modimosana be Mmatau) and Chief Mosume of the Pelle Location, J.O.M. Mamogale and Abraham Mamogale of Hebron as well as representatives of Chiefs Mabe and Motsatsi. They noted too the presence of none other than Sol Plaatje and S.M. Magato at the time President of the SANNC at the meeting. According to Simpson, 'the main focus of discussion at this meeting was the 1913 Land Act and the voicing of objections to the unfair division of land'.[15] The reports of the two informers differ in respect to the tone of the meeting. Paul Mokgatle quoted Chief Mogale as saying,

> if we cannot get our land back we must be ready to die, not I alone but all the chiefs must hear the word, life or death ... I hope there is no informer amongst us ... we must not let any outsider know.[16]

He also called for the collection of funds 'so that when trouble comes we will be ready'. The other man (Magano) focused more on the fact that the Land Act would effectively emasculate the chiefs as 'all our rights are being taken away and we are being left with nothing at all'.[17]

Another meeting was called for by the TNC for the 7 August 1917 in Hammanskraal. Between 300 and 500 people attended including a number of additional chiefs from various districts in the Transvaal. Kgosi Mokgatle cited one Botomana Manoshi, a court interpreter for the NAD, as saying that 'We will fight against the government, against the man who has government buttons and has got a big stomach, and we will cut his belly open and take out the fat for the hardship he has imposed on us'.[18] The next day a further meeting was held Leeuwkraal, in the Pilanesberg district, which, according to Mokgatle was attended by 900 people. Most of the chiefs from the Rustenburg district were in attendance, as were several from other parts of the Transvaal. At this meeting, Magato railed against the Land Act and the fact that Africans had been forced to fight in the First World War. He ended by saying,

14.   State Archives Pretoria (hereafter SAP), Native Affairs Files (hereafter NTS), vol. 108, r 897/14/f, NC Rustenburg to Secretary for Native Affairs, 13 October 1914.
15.   G. Simpson, 'Peasants and Politics in the Western Transvaal, 1920–1940', MA Thesis, University of the Witwatersrand, 1985, 176.
16.   From Native Affairs Files, Transvaal Archives, Pretoria (NTS) vol. 7661, 123/332. Native Unrest, Rustenburg, 1917–1924. Paul Mokgatle, Sworn Statement.
17.   *Ibid.*
18.   Cited in Simpson, 'Peasants and Politics', 178, from SAP, NTS vol. 7661, Native Unrest, Rustenburg.

You chiefs must know that the English government did not make these laws but that big-stomached man ... the boer ... we have no rifles and nothing ready. We must all understand that every man in South Africa who is black, if we unite or work together our dust is enough to suffocate them all to death [loud cheering and enthusiasm].[19]

The authorities, in particular Hicks, took the reports seriously, especially as Mokgatle was the secretary for *Kgosi* August Mokgatle's *lekgotla* (council) and was both educated and well informed. Hicks was of the view that 'the natives are talking war and saying if the boers can rebel [in the 1914 Rebellion] they can also. There can be no doubt that all the natives mean to rise and murder the white people of the country'.[20] In view of the TNC's opposition to the 1913 Land Act Hicks claimed it was the white landowners who soon would be subject to physical attack. White fears were furthermore fuelled by rumours that Africans in the Saulspoort district were purchasing guns and ammunition from the premises of a Jewish storekeeper. This reached a further level of hysteria with reports that the Africans were being assisted by both the Boers and Germans in the Pilanesberg (mountain range), but perhaps understandable in the context of both the world war and the recent Boer rebellion of 1914. This led to a spate of letter writing by concerned English and some Afrikaner farmers to the NAD, the police and even the Prime Minister, General Botha, requesting protection.[21] These alarmist reports soon found their way into the local press.[22]

As a consequence of all this the SAP decided that it should take some action. The 'Jew's shop' was raided, but only one shotgun and revolver were found, for which the owner had a license. 'Chief Mamogale was interviewed by none other than the Prime Minister and reportedly laughed at rumours of an uprising'.[23] Though it was believed by the Rustenburg Native Commissioner, after thorough investigation that 'whites' were the source of all the stories, Hicks and his informant Paul Mokgatle continued well into 1918 to submit reports that the chiefs of the district, in cahoots with TNC leaders were planning an armed rebellion. In fact the situation was probably somewhere between these two polarities.

In conclusion the TNC showed, on this occasion at least, that it was capable of responding to the concerns of rural people. Yet Simpson describes the influence of the TNC in the Rustenburg region at least, as being, 'sporadic and haphazard',[24] and that the relationship waned after about 1917. This would seem to be a fair assessment and can be ascribed either to the radicalisation of the TNC after 1920 which alienated a conservative chiefly constituency,[25] and/or a realisation by them that the TNC had little to offer in way of tangible support. Thus, in 1919 when the TNC was 'supporting a campaign against passes, chiefs Mamogale and Mokgatle [the very chiefs who had

19. Cited in Simpson, 'Peasants and Politics', 179.
20. SAP, NTS vol. 7661, Native Unrest, Rustenburg, Statement of PC F. Hicks.
21. Simpson, 'Peasants and Politics', 181–182.
22. *Sunday Times*, 28 October 1917.
23. *Ibid.*, 184.
24. Simpson, 'Peasants and Politics', 183.
25. P. Bonner, 'The Transvaal Native Congress 1917–1920: The Radicalisation of the Black Petit Bourgeoisie on the Rand', in S. Marks and R. Rathbone, *Industrialisation and Social Change in South Africa: Class Formation, Culture and Consciousness* (New York: Longman, 1982), 113–134.

attended the TNC meetings in 1917] urged the government to enforce the Pass Laws and arrest the ringleaders of the 'pass strike'.[26] Of course this sudden volte face may have been to curry favour with the NAD which was attempting to buttress the authority of chiefs as a means of ensuring control in rural areas-a tactic that did not always bear fruit, as chiefs were not as readily compliant as they may have hoped. Naboth Mokgatle, the Fokeng author and ANC supporter from Phokeng, also presented the TNC as a phenomenon of the towns.[27] In giving evidence to the Native Economic Commission in 1930, the local long-serving missionary in Phokeng, Ernst Penzhorn similarly presented the 'Native Organisations' as urban; 'het almal ontstaan in die dorpe locasies en dit is die ding wat baaie moeilikhede veroorsaak'[28] (they all existed in the town locations and that is the cause of a lot of the problems). He went on to state that the relationship between black and white people in the Rustenburg region was good, and the 'chiefs will not have anything to do with these Native Congresses ... when they [Congress people] come here they send them away ... the ICU will never come here. The chiefs would not allow them for one minute'.[29] While there may have been a waning of chiefly interest in the ANC, it did not mean that all their adherents followed suit. Walshe refers to an incident in 1924 when, 'in the Rustenburg district of the Transvaal Natives "openly defied their chiefs" and proposed to set up their own organ of government-a state of affairs that had to be checked by the NAD'.[30] This, he goes on to state, was an indication of 'the alienation of rural people from their chiefs'. Broadly speaking however, we can find no indications of sustained interest in the specifically the ANC from the early 1920s to the late 1940s, when, we argue, there were quite specific reasons why this was to change.

The ANC in the Dorps

We turn now to an examination of the ANC in the towns of the region under scrutiny. Trawling through the official records there is evidence of TNC branches in several of towns and districts. It had in 1919–1920 a branch in Ventersdorp. It is difficult to assess how active it was, and it was certainly moderate in its demands. It passed a number of resolutions in 1919–1920 which were forwarded to the Magistrate in Ventersdorp, who passed them on to the Secretary for Native Affairs in Pretoria. For example, it called for the Education Department to establish 'free and compulsory education for African children in Ventersdorp, along the same lines as the Klipspruit government school', requested that that the Poll Tax in the Transvaal be 'brought into line with that paid by other Africans in South Africa', and complained over 'shooting' of Africans in the vicinity of Ventersdorp.[31] It is not clear if these were generalised grievances or specific to Africans in the town. It is apparent from the correspondence that there was contact between the TNC in Johannesburg

26. Simpson, 'Peasants and Politics', 183.
27. N. Mokgatle, *The Autobiography of an Unknown South African* (Berkley: University of California Press, 1971).
28. Cited in Simpson, 'Peasants and Politics', 184 from SABAK/26, Penzhorn to Native Economic Commission (NEC).
29. *Ibid.*
30. Walshe, *Rise of African Nationalism*, 212, cited in *Umteteli*, 26 April 1924.
31. SAP, NTS vol. 108, r.5211 /12/101/3, SNA to S. M. Magatho, 10 September 1919.

and the rural peripheries, for in September 1919 J.S. Makgatho visited the town to meet with the local branch. The SNA gave his approval and accordingly 'advised the local officers [of the Native Affairs Department] and the S.A. Police' of his impending visit.[32]

There was also a branch in Lichtenburg, and at Delareyville and Rooijantjesfontein in 1920. The Chairman and Secretary respectively were D.P. Molamu and R.O. Mokoto. The branches took up a number of moderate concerns, for example requesting intervention from the Native Affairs Department to ensure that mail at the local Post Office did not get lost and complaining that the 'Native Pass Offices' in the Lichtenburg/Potchefstroom region were in a poor state.[33] There was also a branch of the TNC in Zeerust, that was concerned to voice its opposition to the effects that the Marico Bosveld Irrigation Scheme would have on African agriculture.[34]

This does at least point to some sort of activity in these regions of the western Transvaal, but not over any sustained period of time. Much like their rural kinsfolk, the ANC in the towns of the region seems to have become relatively moribund after about 1920.

Sol Plaatje and S.M. Molema

If this was the case from the side of the African populace of the western Highveld *platteland*, it was not so in respect of these two figures. It is an interesting but little known fact that both Molema and Plaatje in particular, maintained an interest in and concern for developments in the countryside, despite their other many commitments.

Our first indication of this comes in the form of a 'revolt' in 1924 by members of the baFokeng against the *kgosi* August Mokgatle. The conflict between 1921–1924 was mainly over access to and control over, two farms, Welbekend and Kookfontein which had been purchased by the baFokeng. A group of 'rebels' most of whom were actually members of the royal family or 'councillors, headmen and followers' of Mokgatle himself challenged the way the chief was attempting to privatise these farms.[35] The dispute impacted deeply on the baFokeng and culminated in a legal challenge to August, which reached the Supreme Court in Bloemfontein. Significantly the legal representatives for the 'rebels' enlisted the support of Sol Plaatje, former Chairperson of the SANNC. Plaatje's evidence focused on the role and significance of the *lekgotla* in traditional communities. In the course of giving evidence however, he made a strong plea for the 'democratisation of the system of chiefly authority'.[36] Plaatje argued two points, firstly that 'native government' was naturally democratic but had become warped and disfigured as a result of colonial rule, and that 'educated' Africans were now beginning to clamour for a more democratic dispensation:

> As the young man gets educated and comes into contact with modern development of the white man ... the young man wants his chief to rule his people so [they] can have a say and elect their representatives. That is the tendency.[37]

32. *Ibid.*
33. NTS, vol. 108, r. 5211/12/2.
34. NTS vol.3602, r. 942/308.
35. Cited in Simpson, 'Peasants and Politics', 202, from NTS 3451, SNC to SNA, 16 August 1922.
36. Simpson, 'Peasants and Politics', 248.
37. NTS vol. 316, 15/55 Daniel Mokgatle versus Hertzog, Evidence of Sol Plaatje, 149–172.

The two Judges were deeply impressed by Plaajte's evidence, coming as it did, from a 'civilised and educated native'.[38] It did not stop them however from ruling in favour of August Mokgatle and implicitly against the democratisation of customary law and rule for which Plaatje advocated.

Interestingly Godley the SNA chose to blame the SANNC for much of the trouble. 'To what may be termed the general Native Congress spirit which pervades a more enlightened section of the tribe, may be attributed all the trouble',[39] he wrote. It presumably was to this 'enlightened' section that Plaatje was appealing in his attempts to 'democratise' political attitudes and actions in rural situations.

The second example of their (this time, combined) intervention came the following year. Plaatje and Modiri Molema were called to give evidence in another case, in this instance involving the baKwena ba Mogopa in Hebron. The background to this case is as follows. By the 1920s the baKwena were a divided community, having separated into five segments, the main ones being at Bethanie (Rustenburg district) and Hebron and Jericho (Hammanskraal district). The *kgosi* was J.O.M. Mamogale at Bethanie, but he was not recognised by the other two factions, who were attempting to assert their independence. The opportunity to formally do so came in 1925 when they refused to pay levies on a farm (Elandsfontein) that Mamogale had purchased, They argued that they would derive no material benefit from the farm, which would be utilised predominantly by the Bethanie people. The Hebron baKwena then took Mamogale and the white owner, John Reid, to have to sale of Elandsfontein set aside. The case rested on the interpretation of customary law, as it had done in the baFokeng case, specifically whether Mamogale should have called a general *pitso* of *all* members the chiefdom before embarking on the purchase.

The legal team for the plaintiffs enlisted the support of Plaatje (again) and Modiri Molema, both introduced as being 'civilised and politically minded'.[40] In his evidence Dr Molema was somewhat brief, asserting that in customary law the chief would not go against the will of the people and that he was not 'above the law of the tribe'. Plaatje, however, was far more detailed and set forth a similar view to that he had expressed in the baFokeng case, namely that African customary law was fundamentally democratic, and that current disputes were arising as a consequence of general colonial policy which was encouraging 'growing individualism'.[41] This was to be seen in the growing privatisation of land by Africans, an anomalous situation that occurred in the former western Transvaal despite the provisions in the 1913 Land Act. Though expressing a possibly romanticised view of customary law, Plaatje was once again trying to align Tswana law and custom with a growing yearning among Africans for democracy. He thus concluded that the plaintiffs were attempting to undermine the authority of Mamogale per se, but that their action was

38. SAP, NTS vol. 316, 15/55, Judgement of Justice Kotze in the case of *Daniel Mokgatle and Others versus Minister of Native Affairs*, 29 September 1924.
39. NTS, 316, 15/55, Godley, Memo, 31 January 1924.
40. SAP, NTS 15/55, *Daniel Mokgatle and Others versus J.B.M. Hertzog*, Judgement of Justice J. Tindall, p. 13.
41. Simpson, 'Peasants and Politics', 252.

reflective of a 'tendency to democracy', which was inherent in customary law in its original and pristine form.[42] To his chagrin no doubt the judge ruled in favour of Mamogale, thus upholding the right of chiefs to enter into contractual agreements on behalf of the 'tribe' without entering into full consultation.

While these two figures were thus attentive to the concerns of the rural Batswana of the western Highveld, the general trend among the occupants of the region points to decreasing enthusiasm for the ANC, and its affiliates and representatives. Significantly the Industrial and Commercial Workers' Union (ICU) did make inroads, though not enormous, especially among the farm workers in the 'maize triangle' of the south-western Transvaal, whose attachment to the land was an overriding preoccupation. The first meeting of the ICU in Bloemhof in late 1928 was 'huge' though it did not translate into a significant number of members for the branch.[43] There was also a 'thriving' branch at Makwassie, and at Ventersdorp Clements Kadalie, National Secretary of the ICU, 'inspired blacks there to throw away their passes'.[44] Branches were also formed 'in the heart' of the Lichtenburg diamond fields among the African tenants and diggers in 1928.[45] However, the ICU had limited organisational appeal among the reserve-based black population to the north in the bushveld region of the northwest Transvaal. While Africans there had land in the reserves and had expanded landholdings by making 'communal' purchases for farms, they were possessed of fewer material concerns which the ICU or the ANC could directly articulate.

The Communist Party of South Africa (CPSA) likewise made some inroads at the expense of the ANC, notably in Potchefstroom, where Bradford estimates 'almost all the township residents' of Potchefstroom were communist supporters.[46] Here, Josie Mpama (also Palmer) who was born in the town in 1903, and was the first woman to join the CPSA in 1925, became secretary of the Potchefstroom branch in 1927. The charismatic Mpama mobilised people against the proposed Native Services Contract Bill and the Urban Areas Bill. Her account of her experiences has thrown light on the activities and motives of women involved in the anti-pass campaign in Potchefstroom. Under the direction of a especially established strike committee, the women of the town brought Potchefstroom virtually to a standstill. In December 1929, she was on the stage during a meeting of the CPSA in Potchefstroom, at which the Party leaders J.B. Marks and Edwin Mofutsanyana were present, when it was disrupted by a group of white extremists. A friend and comrade were killed. Together with other communists, she called a protest meeting to coincide with the trial of the perpetrators of the crime.[47]

42. See NTS 325, Rathibe and others versus J.O.M. Mamogale, February 1926, and Simpson, 'Peasants and Politics', 300–307.

43. H. Bradford, 'A Taste of Freedom': The ICU in rural South Africa, 1924–1930 (New Haven: Yale University Press, 1987), 163.

44. Ibid., 164.

45. Ibid., 165.

46. Ibid., 164.

47. See J. Wells, We Now Demand: The History of Women's Resistance to Pass Laws in South Africa (Johannesburg: University of Witwatersrand Press, 1994).

Revival

The fortunes of the ANC in the western Transvaal, northern Cape, were to rise however, with the declining capacity of the reserves, and the imposition of a more regulated and segregated order for Africans, which gained pace with the advent of the National Party to power. The contention that this revival begins in the late 1940s to the early 1950s, coinciding it would seem, with the end of the conservative presidency of Dr Pixley ka Seme.[48]

Perhaps some early sign of this comes in a report that an active ANC committee had been formed 'amongst the Bakwena-ba-Mogopa, and the re-establishment of an ANC presence in the Rustenburg area of the Transvaal' which Walshe identifies as one 'further example of the renewed interest [in the ANC] in the rural areas'.[49] Furthermore, of 58 important local personalities identified as Congress sympathisers in the Rustenburg district, 24 were teachers, 12 chiefs, five farmers, five craftsmen, two interpreters, two agricultural demonstrators and a butcher.

There is also some evidence from the Mafikeng region to support the view that the ANC was reviving in the western Transvaal platteland. This is based on information gleaned from Chief J. T. Seatlholo of the Rapulana Barolong in Rietfontein, (Lothlakane) who in September 1952 approached the Chief Native Commissioner in Potchefstroom

> for assistance with regard to the actions of the African National Congress. They will spoil the Native Law and Custom and the Institution of our chieftainship. I have discussed the matter with Chief Montsioa [of the Tshidi- baRolong in Mafikeng] and asked him to state that I agree with his views (sic). We request that the Department should endeavour to ban this movement from out Native area because it interfered in our tribal administration and the performances of our duties and functions imposed upon us by the government.[50]

Seathlolo took up his complaint again the following year. This prompted the NC in Mafikeng to express the opinion that 'as a result of the African National Congress activities in this district, many natives have lately taken up the attitude that the chiefs in the local reserves no longer have any say over them', and 'they turn more to Congress now than ever'.[51] However, Seathlolo could not really substantiate any of the complaints he had levelled against ANC members, and no action was taken. It does provide some evidence for a shift in attitudes among reserve-based Africans, however.

It was further reported on 27 March 1952 that the ANC held a meeting in the Barolong stadt in Mafikeng which was followed up by another on 6 April on the 'Native Football Ground'. The latter was addressed by amongst others, Rex Molema, the Commissioner's Court Messenger and Tax Collector, who addressed a crowd of about 200, many of whom were reported to be 'young girls'. The police were on duty at this meeting, and though no 'excitatory speeches were delivered', the Mafikeng NC saw this as further evidence for interest in the ANC locally.[52]

48.   T. Karis and G. Gerhart, *From Protest to Challenge, A Documentary History of African Politics in South Africa, 1882–1990*, vol. 2 (Pretoria: UNISA Press, 1997), 81–92.
49.   Walshe, *Rise of African Nationalism*, 387.
50.   HKW 1/1/383, File (32) N1/9/3. NC Mafeking to Chief NC Potchefstroom, 25 September 1952.
51.   HKW 1/1/383, NC Mafeking to Chief NC Potchefstroom, 14 September 1953.
52.   HKW 1/1/383 File (32) n1/9/3/1, NC Mafikeng to Chief NC Potchefstroom, 25 April 1952.

At the 45th Annual Conference of the ANC in Orlando, 1957, the Report from the Transvaal makes reference to the fact that 'more branches have been created in the reserves. Organising teams have gone out to practically every part of the Transvaal'. It refers specifically to Lichtenburg 'where the Seleka women were sentenced to 12 months or a fine of 100 pounds in the fight against the increase in rent, deportations of people [and] removals'.[53]

Ruth Mompati, who was a teacher in Vryburg, describes some of her activities as a clandestine ANC member in the district during the 1950s, which further points to the ANC's re-animation. ANC members from Mafikeng, in particular Thenjiwe Mathimba, came to Vryburg, a distance of some 170 km, to recruit members and help to organise activities. As a teacher she was prohibited from engaging in politics, but remembers during the 1952 Defiance Campaign, that 'the ANC was selling stamps all over the country' and 'Thenjiwe brought them to Vryburg, so we sold them to raise funds for the ANC in Mafikeng'.[54]

After Mompati had relocated to Johannesburg and was working for the legal firm of Nelson Mandela and Oliver Tambo in the mid-1950s, she continued with ANC activity. She would often return to her own hometown, Vryburg, where she would hold meetings with women to raise their awareness about the possible impact of their having to carry passes. Mompati states that after she had spoken to them about the negative impact passes would have upon their lives, 'they all refused to carry passes' and when passes for women finally became a reality, 'it took a lot of coercion from the police to get the women in Vryburg to carry passes. I admired them because it's a small town and the police are vicious'.[55]

The Zeerust resistance

However, the surest indication of a resurgence of support in the ANC comes from the Zeerust district in 1957–1958. In these years a majority of the residents in Moiloa's Reserve, allocated to the baHurutshe in the 1940s, both men and women mounted one of the most sustained acts of defiance among rural people to the South African government's apartheid policy, a telling event in the history of the country's rural resistance to white rule. The generally accepted view is that it was the attempt to force African women to carry passes that triggered the resistance, and rightly the event forms a significant component of the history of women's resistance to the carrying of passes in South Africa. It has been argued that the Hurutshe Revolt was not primarily an issue of pass resistance, but was about retaining access to vital resources in the baHurutshe reserve.[56] In this sense it bears a strong resemblance to the perhaps better known revolt in Sekhukhuneland which broke out

53. UW, WCL, HLPC, South African Institute of Race Relations (SAIRR) Collection, Molema Microfilms, Report of 45th Annual ANC Conference, 10.
54. Interview with Ruth Mompati by Sifiso Ndlovu and Bernard Magubane, Vryburg, 15 August 2001, cited in SADET Oral History Project, in *The Road To Democracy: South Africans Telling Their Stories, Vol. I, 1950 – 1970* (Hollywood: South African Democracy Education Trust & Tsei, 1980), 309.
55. Interview with Ruth Mompati.
56. See J. Drummond and A. Manson, 'The Rise and Demise of African Agriculture in Dinokana, Bophuthatswana, 1918–1992', *Canadian Journal of African History*, vol. 4 (1994), 84–103.

shortly thereafter. Similarly, the full impact of this incident can only be comprehended by an analysis of the subsequent course of events over the ensuing years.

The revolt has been recorded in an excellent account by the Rev. Charles Hooper, who was the Anglican priest in Zeerust, and who witnessed the events as they unfolded.[57] He personally intervened to assist the baHurutshe, for which he was finally deported from South Africa. Other commentators have examined specific aspects of the event, focusing for example on the role of the African National Congress (ANC), and the extent of political consciousness exhibited by the women in the Reserve.[58]

We can only offer here only a brief summary of the actual events that occurred in the reserve in 1957.[59] In March 1957, *Kgosi* Abram Ramotshere Pogiso Moiloa, the ruling *kgosi* of the baHurutshe based in Dinokana was instructed by Carl Richter, the Native Commissioner in Zeerust, to inform the women of Dinokana to present themselves at the *kgotla* to collect their reference books. By this date, the issuing of the passes had been strongly resisted by both urban and rural women throughout South Africa.[60] Ramotshere reacted by first summoning his councillors and then directing a woman's representative from each ward to meet with him so he could discuss the issue. According to informants, in the course of this meeting he decided to reject the reference books and simply ignored the order from Richter who seized the opportunity to depose him as *kgosi.* [61]

Ramotshere did not move out of the reserve as Richter had allegedly ordered him to do, but went into hiding in Dinokana. A pass-issuing unit then set up business in the shop of a white trader, but according to one of the participants in the event, only 80 out of the approximately 8,000 women in the Dinokana area took out passes.[62] On 6 April a delegation of women came from Johannesburg and encouraged others not to accept the passes. And on the 13 April, a group of men from the Witwatersrand who had formed a support group known as the baHurutshe Association, chartered two buses and returned to the reserve to investigate the situation. Events now took a more violent turn. Enraged by the deposition of *kgosi* Ramotshere, his supporters now encouraged by the support of the Hurutshe Association, burnt the houses of known or suspected collaborators. Four men, among them, one Michael Moiloa, were seen as the key collaborators and were blamed (somewhat unfairly) for the state's repressive antics. In nearby Gopane, *kgosi* Albert Gopane was forced to flee to Botswana after townsfolk condemned him for his refusal to oppose the taking of passes.

From its side the state acted quickly to quell the disturbances. The returning buses (of the Hurutshe Association) were stopped and a number of people arrested. Postal and transport services in the reserve were withdrawn, and resisting women were denied access

57. See C. Hooper, *Brief Authority* (London: Penguin, 1960).
58. See A. Manson, 'The Hurutshe Resistance in the Zeerust District of the Western Transvaal, 1954–1959, *Africa Perspective*, 22 (1983), 62–79; J. Yawitch, 'The Zeerust Revolt', unpublished seminar paper, University of Witwatersrand, Johannesburg, 1982.
59. This is drawn from most of the available sources, in particular Hooper's *Brief Authority*, Fairburn's article in *Africa South*, South African Institute of Race Relations, *Survey of Race Relations, 1957–58*, and various newspapers (*New Age, Fighting Talk* and *Drum*).
60. C. Walker, *Women and Resistance in South Africa* (New York: Monthly Review Press, 1982).
61. See Interview with Mrs M. Keebine, South African Institute of Race Relations Oral Archive, Interview by A. Manson, 4 December 1982.
62. *New Age*, 28 November 1957, from Evidence given to the Commission of Enquiry.

to medical treatment. These intimidatory tactics were soon backed up by brute force. By mid-April a Mobile Column, under the command of one Police Sergeant van Rooyen roamed the reserve, seeking women who had refused or burnt passes. In time it was able to locate and arrest 'offenders', mostly women, who suffered severe beatings at the hands of the police and their sympathisers.

The round-up continued for several months, with the state hoping to enforce acceptance of the passes through legal action. It was not particularly successful. By October, 474 people had been arrested, but only 39 convictions obtained. This was principally because the baHurutshe had engaged the services of Advocate George Bizos, later a stalwart of the legal battle against the apartheid policies of the National Party government. Abraham, during this period, was still in hiding, and attempts by Richter to appoint another *kgosi* had come to naught. In addition, as the women of Gopane had shown by their refusal *en masse* to take up passes, this tactic was quite effective in an area where there were few policemen and limited prison accommodation. In October the Native Affairs Department (NAD) then appointed a Commission, the only one up until then to be appointed to investigate a rural trouble spot in South Africa. In the same month a Proclamation in the Government Gazette banned gatherings of more than ten people in the reserve. Presumably this was the pretext, on 15 October, for sealing off the road from Dinokana to Zeerust, to assault men walking to attend the Commission's hearings, and for Harvard aircraft to swoop down on the area in intimidatory fashion. Apart from the extraordinary brevity between the gazetting of the Commission and its sitting, it was unusual in other ways. There was no agenda, there was nobody to lead evidence, and Advocate Bizos was not allowed to cross-examine witnesses.

Up to this point the resistance had been confined to the villages of Dinokana, but after November it spread to the villages of Braklaagte, Witkleigat, Motswedi and Leeuwfontein, encompassing virtually the entire reserve. Resistance was strongest where the local *dikgosi* had supported the state, such as Lucas Mangope in Motswedi and Edward Lencoe in Witkleigat. Although their cooperation with the police may have been tactical (to avoid the obvious harmful consequences), it led to a spiral of violence and counter resistance. The Mobile Column moved into the new trouble spots in late 1957 to lend assistance to the compliant *digosi* and their local bodyguards.

The real backlash came, of all days, on Christmas day itself. The Mobile Column was off-duty and many men of the baHurutshe Association were home for the holiday period. Apparently under the organisation of the baHurutshe Association, *kgosi* Lencoe's house and car were burnt, his wife was assaulted, and he was forced to flee to Botswana on horseback. Thirty-six houses belonging to alleged government supporters were burnt in Witkleigat and 15 in Leeuwfontein. Lencoe's right-hand man was killed during these disturbances. In Motswedi, *kgosi* Mangope suffered an attack on his house and person, and his household was forced to open fire on a mob of enraged villagers.

The police responded quickly. Witkleigat was sealed off and the search for the perpetrators was launched. At Motswedi, a specially constructed court was surrounded by police while Mangope (still suffering the effects of his attack) appeared in a dressing gown to impose fines for pass-burning and arson. In Gopane, the newspaper *New Age* reported that, 'public trials and confession are the order of the day. Men are made to apologise for being [African National] Congress-ites, and then enrolled as the Chief's forces'.[63] A number of other chiefs were also attacked for being alleged supporters of the government, but it is difficult to determine with absolute certainly if this was the case. Thus the event took on the form of the classic collaborator-resister dichotomy, though there were no doubt a range of intermediate positions that people adopted in between these two extremes. Matters reached a bloody climax on 25 January 1958 when four people were shot dead in Gopane. It seems that investigating policemen were mobbed and during the panic shots were exchanged. Those killed may have been innocent bystanders.

The shootings shocked the inhabitants and resistance at this point came to an end. Mass arrests were made and in all about 200 people were charged with murder. By September, five had been convicted of assault, 58 of public violence, and the remainder was acquitted. According to Bizos, most of the women charged with pass burning were acquitted, 'because the prosecutor was unqualified and inexperienced, because the police work was sloppy, and because of the lack of sophistication of the elderly magistrate'.[64] In the climate of uncertainty and fear prevailing between December 1958 and February 1959 many fled their homes, up to a thousand of them crossing over to Botswana (then still the Bechuanaland Protectorate) where they were fed and clothed by the British High Commission office for eight months. Many of these people never returned to South Africa. *Kgosi* Ramotshere Moiloa was banished to the District of Victoria East in the Cape, on 26 February 1958, but he crossed into Botswana in late January 1958 and to have sought protection for himself and a number of his followers from the bamaNgwato paramount Tshekedi Kgama at Pilikwe.[65]

The shootings and Moiloa's flight to Botswana undoubtedly had a demoralising effect on the entire reserve, but they were not the only reasons for the collapse of the revolt. First, the state took an even firmer hand in matters by resorting to banishment and deportation of the supposed leaders of the resistance, by sealing off the reserve, by holding cases in other parts of the Transvaal (cutting off the accused from financial and moral support) and, under Proclamation 607 of March 1958, by banning the ANC in the African areas of the Marico/ Zeerust districts. In Johannesburg, police moved against the Hurutshe Association, rounding up 'troublemakers' and questioning and threatening them with detention. In addition, as summer approached many people wanted to get back to normality-to return home to plant and later harvest their crops, and to tend their cattle herds.

Information about events after April 1958 is scarce. Charles Hooper and Sheila his wife, who throughout the crisis had been materially and morally supportive of the victims and simultaneously critical of the state's attitude and actions, were deported from Zeerust. No reporters were allowed into the reserve. However, in August 1959 on a Trust farm about 40 miles north of Zeerust, the BaHurutshe Regional Authority was proclaimed. The first of its kind in the Transvaal, this body represented a critical stage in the establishment of 'Bantu Authorities', which were a cornerstone of the Bantustan policy of 'Grand Apartheid' – the division of land and (in theory) political control between black and white in South Africa. An uncle of Ramotshere Moiloa, Israel Moiloa, was installed as

63. *New Age*, 13 February 1958.
64. G. Bizos, *Odyssey to Freedom* (New York: Random House, 2007), 113.
65. A. Lissoni, 'The Bahurutshe Chieftaincy and Bophuthatswana', unpublished paper, University of the Witwatersrand, Johannesburg, 2010, 8. He remained in exile for 15 years, and died on 28 May 1982.

kgosi in Dinokana, but the ceremony was presided over by Lucas Mangope, who on this occasion delighted his critics by 'imploring the Minister of Bantu Administration to "lead us and we shall try to crawl"'.[66] This was to be a significant milestone in the career of Mangope; it established him (in the eyes of the government) as the most important traditional leader in the reserve and a likely collaborator in the developing Bantustan policy. He went on to become the first and only President of the ill-fated Bophuthatswana homeland, George Bizos 'was invited to become an honorary member of the [baHurutshe] tribe'.[67]

Another interesting aspects which commentators have noted, is the importance of the urban/rural link provided by the BaHurutshe Association, and the role of the ANC. The part played by the BaHurutshe Association in the revolt, bears striking similarities to that of migrants in Sekhukhuneland, who 'forged networks linking urban and rural areas'...[and] kept their home communities abreast of developments'.[68] Walter Sisulu, elder statesman of the ANC, has described the Sekhukhuneland resistance as 'the first well organised [rural] movement in the history of the ANC',[69] yet events in Zeerust preceded those in the then northern Transvaal, and there is evidence that the Sekhukhune-land migrants drew on the experiences of the BaHurutshe Association. Though perhaps the role of the Association was not as widespread or forceful as that of the men of Sekhukhuneland, it should nevertheless be given due recognition.

As far as the ANC is concerned, Hooper, and some other observers, played down the extent of the organisation's activity. This may have been to protect the baHurutshe against the state's frequent assertion that they were mere docile dupes in the hands of ANC instigators. Others have used the Zeerust revolt to suggest that the ANC's presence in rural areas was limited, and that it failed to adequately deal with the land issues that were central to the concerns of rural people. In an interview in 1983 conducted with Kenneth Mosenyi, he explained how he organised a branch of the ANC in Dinokana, and played a leading role in the affair.[70] The branch had 20 members, in addition to which there was a smaller branch in nearby Gopane. Mosenyi averred that 'it was believed, I can tell you that, I was behind the whole thing'; According to Mosenyi, the people still (in 1983) called him 'Tsotsi Nyenye'.[71] This was in reference to a well known tree under which people hatched their plans for resisting.

The availability of new documentary evidence from the perspective of the state however, and oral recollections now provided without fear of recrimination, confirm this and show the extent of his activity, and that of other residents of the Reserve, in particular Nimrod Moagi. Mosenyi and probably Moagi were paid full-time ANC officials. Mosenyi was a committed and courageous ANC organiser whose contribution has received

66. This is according to Lodge, *Black Politics in South Africa Since 1950* (Johannesburg: Raven, 1983), from the *Cape Times*, 8 August 1959.
67. See Bizos, *Odyssey*, 117.
68. P. Delius, *'A Lion Among the Cattle': Reconstruction and Resistance in the Northern Transvaal*, (Johannesburg: Ravan, 1996), 83, 113.
69. Cited in Delius. *'A Lion Among the Cattle'*, 103.
70. Interview with Kenneth Mosenyi, with Andrew Manson, 18 January 1983. SAIRR Oral Archive, William Cullen Library, University of Witwatersrand, 18 January 1982, UW, WCL, HLPC, SAIRR Oral Archive Collection.
71. SAIRR Oral History Archive interview 18 January 1983.

insufficient recognition. Born on the 15 February 1915, he began his political life as Secretary of the African Furniture, Mattress and Bedding Workers Union in Johannesburg in 1948. Subsequently he became an Executive member of the Council of Non-European Trade Unions. In October 1950 he was elected Secretary of the Orlando branch of the ANC. He was friends with J.B. Marks and D.J. du Plessis, and had strong communist sympathies. Police surveillance puts him at an ANC meeting in Springs in 1950, in February 1951 at a mass ANC/Transvaal Indian Congress (TIC) protest at Newtown, and as attending the ANC Conference in Johannesburg in April as well as Dr Dadoo's birthday celebrations in September 1951![72]

Nimrod Moagi was also a long standing member of the ANC. Born in 1912 he was a photographer by trade. He worked closely with Mosenyi and according to police informers he 'abused the conflict between Moiloa and the missionary [Meyer] to get the "Kaptyn" (chief) on their side'.[73] In 1953 Mosenyi returned to his home in Dinokana, and apparently very soon came to influence Ramotshere Moiloa. He surfaced to the attention of the security police again in 1955, when he led opposition to the Lutheran Church, in particular to Rev Meyer, in Dinokana. From his interview it emerges that this was caused by the Church imposing 'fees' on the congregation.[74] In addition to these men, Boas Moiloa, the chief's uncle, was said to have been 'in close co-operation with the "African National Congress" even long before Abram was deposed'.[75] Simon Molifi, 'a known agitator of unknown status', was apparently tasked with assuming responsibility for 'propogating (sic) communistic ideas should Kenneth Mosenye be prevented to (sic) continue with his undermining activities in Dinokana',[76] and another leading Bahurutshe councilor, David Moiloa was identified as 'n genoemde kummunis'.[77]

Significantly, Mosenyi it seems introduced Moiloa to the ANC. The Security Police records reveal that it was 'under his [Mosenyi's] influence the old Kaptyn Moiloa travelled with him to attend meetings with the ANC', clandestinely in Johannesburg.[78] The culmination of Moiloa's politicisation and identification with the ANC came when he sent a letter of support to the Congress of the People convention in Kliptown in 1954. Unfortunately from him, the letter was intercepted by the police.[79]

Interviewed in 1983, two of the leading figures among the women of the Hurutshe reserve, Joanna Pule and Paulina Keebine, recalled that a number of Women's League office holders in particular Lillian Ngoyi, 'we are saying publicly, was our leader'.[80] The women of Moiloa's Reserve were familiar with the growing national anti-pass movement. In Johannesburg, a number of baHurutshe women were members of the ANC Women's

72. See NTS vol. 326, r 40/55, Memorandum: Kenneth Benjamin Mosenyi.
73. SAP, NTS, vol. 326, r40/55, Memorandum: Nimrod Moagi.
74. NTS vol. 326, r40/55 Memorandum: Nimrod Moagi.
75. SAP, NTS, vol. 362, r 71/57, Native Commissioner, Zeerust to Chief Native Commissioner, Potchefstroom, 14 September, 1957, Confidential.
76. NTS vol. 326, r 40/55, NC Zeerust to Chief NC, Potchefstroom, 14 September 1957.
77. 'A named Communist', NTS vol. 326, r 40/55, Senior Investigator, South African Police to Chief NC, Potchefstroom.
78. *Ibid*. Memorandum on Mosenye.
79. *Ibid*.
80. SAIRR Oral History Archive, Interview with Johanna Pule, with Andrew Manson and Tebogo Kubine, 3 March 1983.

League, and urged women in the reserve to refuse the passes and to adopt the boycott tactics (as adopted in the recent Rand bus boycotts). Moreover, once the resistance gained momentum the ANC acted fairly speedily. Shulamith Miller spent many days in Zeerust after legal assistance had been sought, and Nelson Mandela himself visited prisoners awaiting trial in Zeerust gaol.[81]

As part of the preparations for the anti-pass march to Pretoria planned for 1956, Mompati and other ANC women would go to various places, organising women for the coming march. Mompati used to come to Zeerust and she still remembers:

> We used to get into trains, go to places like Zeerust. You would get a train in the evening from Johannesburg and you'd arrive at midnight in Zeerust. You would do about three meetings with women, and then in the afternoon you would catch a train back to Johannesburg. It was your own money you would use. Women used to do that. And then on the 9 August 1956, we marched to Pretoria. I was in the National Executive of the Women's League then.[82]

The recent elevation of Ramotshere Abram Moiloa to the status to a 'struggle hero' by the post-apartheid ANC government (he has a municipality in the Zeerust district named after him) is thus a legitimate distinction. Not only did he expose himself to the dangers inherent in resisting the all powerful white regime, before and during the revolt itself, but after he went into exile in Bechuanaland he made contact with the ANC after it had been banned in South Africa. He had a connection to number of recruits from Dinokana who served in the celebrated Luthuli Brigade. These men recall encountering him both in Botswana and in Dar-es- Salaam, Tanzania, in the late 1960s.[83]

The crucial question arises: what provoked such a determined response from the residents of this fairly remote Reserve, and the women in particular? It has been argued elsewhere,[84] that there was a steady decline in the productive capacity of Moiloa's Reserve from the mid-1930s. However, by the 1950s this situation was changing, and by 1955 the Reserve exhibited all the hallmarks of collapse-uneconomic landholdings, low levels of production and environmental decline.

A study of Moiloa's Reserve from the 1930s to 1950s reveals in addition a pattern of state intervention to bolster the fortunes of a 'progressive' class of commercialised farmers. The formation of the Moiloa Reserve Local Council in the late 1920s became a 'useful body through which the 'progressives' advanced their interests'.[85] As modern methods of soil conservation and efficient agricultural techniques were introduced so Moiloa's Reserve was earmarked in 1936 to become a 'model Native Area'.[86] Ramotshere Moiloa assumed office in 1933 at the height of these developments. Thus, it has been argued, the 'simmering tensions between the "progressives" and the traditional leadership created the conditions

---

81. These facts are set out in Manson, 'The Hurutshe Resistance', 72–75.
82. Interview with Ruth Mompati.
83. Personal communication, Arianna Lissoni. Department of History, History Workshop, University of Witwatersrand, 7 April 2011. Lissoni has interviewed a number of these men.
84. J. Drummond and A. Manson, ' The Rise and Demise of African Agricultural Production in Dinokana Village, *Canadian Journal of African Affairs*, vol. 27, no. 3 (1993), 77–94.
85. *Ibid.*, 46.
86. NTS vol. 8537, NC, Zeerust to Secretary for Lands, Pretoria, 8 July 1932.

for the [1957] revolt'.[87] As women in particular felt the pinch of rural marginalisation and displacement, so they looked to Ramotshere for assistance in halting this deteriorating situation. As Bundy and Beinart have argued for the Transkei, the institution of chieftaincy thus 'served as a powerful ideological force when rural resources or political structures came under threat'.[88]

From its side, the state had decided to get rid of the chief from as early as mid-1956, over a year before the troubles over passes occurred. Specifically it was believed that he 'would mobilise people against the Betterment Policy in the Reserve'.[89] Surrounded by hostile government officials on one side and a growingly confident group of Reserve-based progressive producers on the other, Moiloa sought the support of the ANC. 'It is clear' wrote the Zeerust Native Commissioner in May 1955, 'that he is under the control of Mosinyi and Nimrod Moagi, instead of experienced men like Michael Moiloa', the self-professed leader of the 'progressives' whose house was burnt to the ground during the disturbances. Coming on the back of these tensions, the demand for women to take passes was the straw that broke the camel's back, and helps to explain the intensity of the resistance in the baHurutshe Reserve.

Thus it was declining access to productive resources in the reserve, coupled with what Delius has characterised as 'the state's increasingly interventionist role in the countryside in the 1950s'[90] in general, that revived support for the ANC in this part of the former western Transvaal. How wide this conclusion has applicability in other parts of our region is hard to accurately determine, but it is probable that similar developments were taking place elsewhere, as in the Molopo Reserve in the northern Cape.

Mosenyi and Moagi's role in the Zeerust area was not confined to the baHurutshe Reserve. They were also involved in resistance in the nearby villages of Leeufontein and Braklaagte. These two villages had been under the threat of removal for over a decade, as they were 'black spots' amidst white farmland. The residents were baHurutshe people, though outside the Reserve itself. The government had manipulated the chieftaincy to install a man who was prepared to comply with the state's plans. The NC in Zeerust reported that Mosenyi

> became actively involved in the [matter of] the relocation of the tribes in Braklaagte and Leeufontein, and it was because of him and others who instigated the trouble that the tribes refused to be moved. They were previously peaceful. Because they refused, though peaceful, they had conflict with the police.[91]

As a consequence of their actions Mosenyi, Moagi, David Moiloa, Boas Moiloa and another man, Ramidida Mokgatle, were all banished. Mosenyi's ban was lifted in 1962 but he only returned to Dinokana in 1969, where he continued to eke out a living. He was not able to resume his farming work, and those who had supported the government in the 57–58 incidents were in the ascendency.[92]

87.   Drummond and Manson, 'The Rise and Demise of African Agriculture', 47.
88.   W. Beinart and C. Bundy, 'State Intervention and Rural Resistance: The Transkei, 1900–1965', in M. Klein, ed., *Peasants in Africa, Historical Contemporary Perspectives* (Beverly Hills: Sage, 1980), 271–315.
89.   NTS, vol. 432, NC Zeerust, to Magistrate, Zeerust, 19 May 1956.
90.   P. Delius, 'A Lion Among the Cattle', 76.
91.   NTS vol. 326, r40/55 'Memorandum on Kenneth Mosenye' (sic).
92.   Interview with Kenneth Mosenyi, 9.

It should be noted however, that there was an alternative legacy in regard to the 'Zeerust Revolt'. Many of the early recruits to Umkhonto we Sizwe, and into the political and intelligence structures of the ANC in exile came from this region. Among them were several men who went on to become members of the Luthuli Brigade and currently reside in Dinokana and its vicinity.[93] Ramotshere Moiloa was said to have been the catalyst for the many men who went into exile from this region.

For example, William Senna, based in Gopane, who was a branch executive member of the ANC in the area, and had been active in the 1957–1958 uprising was one of those who managed to escape into Botswana. For a while, until the early 1960s, Senna would visit the village only at night to avoid detection by the police. The leadership in the ANC Executive of the Transvaal intervened in the situation. Through an emissary, notably one Jonas Matlou, the Transvaal leadership established contact with both those who had fled into Botswana and those that remained in the village 'to collect information in order to enable them to handle the situation' and also 'to facilitate the court proceedings on behalf of the villagers who were arrested'.[94]

By the time of the formation of MK and the launch of the armed struggle in 1961, the situation in Gopane had returned to normality once again, enabling Senna to relocate back to the village. Senna revived his political activism. Senna's relative, John Rantao, who was based in Johannesburg but travelled regularly between the two, became the link person between the ANC Transvaal Executive and Senna in Gopane. Senna's son, Simon, then in higher primary school, recalls as follows:

> It was during this period that became involved in ferrying people out of the country to Botswana. My father started organising the machinery to link with Botswana in order to ferry the people outside the country. People would travel from Johannesburg, through Zeerust and then into Botswana. My father would [sometimes] pick them up in Johannesburg. The ANC at the time was very organised so that they were in the position to avoid infiltration of this machinery. They were using families. For instance, Rantao was related to my father. So even if the police saw him in our village, they thought he was visiting family. And during those visits he delivered messages indicating what was expected of us in the area and so on.[95]

Simon Senna and John Rantao, however, soon realised that the police were monitoring their activities. Therefore to avoid the risk of arrest, they withdrew into the background and brought in younger activists. Many such younger cadres in the Zeerust area belonged to families that were either related or knew one another intimately. Thus in the network of ANC activity in the area, the question of trust was of crucial importance, 'to avoid infiltration by the enemy. And that is why we suffered very few casualties; not more than 15 people were arrested in the area. Although 15 is too high; even 5 is too high'.[96]

93. A. Lissoni, 'Married to the ANC: the Tanzanian Women of Lehurutshe and their Experiences as Wives of MK Veterans', paper presented at 'One Hundred Years of the ANC: Debating Liberation Histories and Democracy Today', University of the Witwatersrand, 22 September 2011.

94. Interview with Simon Senna, conducted by Sifiso Ndlovu, 10 March 2002, Zeerust, SADET Oral History Project, in *The Road To Democracy: South Africans Telling Their Stories, Vol. I, 1950–1970* (Hollywood: South African Democracy Education Trust & Tsehai, 2008), 425.

95. Interview with Simon Senna.

96. *Ibid.*

The support of the local population, and ANC members in particular in assisting activists to cross the border into Botswana was crucial. Lawrence Phakanoka (nom de guerre Peter Tladi) was one such activist. He was from Sekhukhuneland in the Middleburg District and had studied at Fort Hare where he became active in the ANC which he had joined early in 1960. In May 1963, when there were mass arrests of activist students in the country, he had not yet completed his physics degree study at Fort Hare, but was just about to be arrested by the police, when he decided to leave the country and join the ANC in exile. In July 1963, he and other students took a bus from Roodepoort to Zeerust where 'the ANC had firmly established itself'; Phokanoka relates as follows:

> It [i.e. the ANC] created machineries there, making Zeerust a gateway to leave the country for people from as far as the Cape and Natal as well. For instance, a certain Nene from Natal was with us when we went out [to Zeerust]. We went through Zeerust with help from the underground machinery there on 8 July 1963. You went by bus to a certain point. They knew where it was. Then you jumped off. There was a way to identify the contact. You would be wearing a white handkerchief on your head. He wore his. Eventually we made contact. The main contact was Simon Senna from Zeerust. After we made contact, Senna took us to his home, where we met his father. His father was the one arranging networks there. They used bicycles and also travelled on foot. And it was the father who eventually took us to the crossing point on the same evening we arrived ... From there they took us to some other house where we had some food. We were then taken to another house, from where we were taken to the border fence. We went along a footpath, and came to the fence. At one point it had a stepladder over it. We used this to jump over, and once were on the other side they told us that we were not in South Africa anymore. That was the first time I was outside South Africa and I had such a strange feeling. A pass meant nothing from then onwards and so on... And then we got to Lobatse, where we found some comrades.[97]

Another *modus operandi* employed to secrete political activists out of the country through Zeerust, as Simon Senna recollects, was to meet them at the Zeerust Railway Station on a pre-arranged date and time. After identifying one another at the station, Simon would take them to his father's house where they were given food and accommodation. The following day, Senne, who knew all the secret footpaths from Zeerust across the Botswana border, would lead the group of activists across the border into Botswana. Sometimes a group of young people going into exile in Botswana through Zeerust would attempt the venture on their own and get lost in the process. Senne recalls that 'they would be given directions to the village [i.e. Gopane] and then the villagers would hide them' and very early the following morning they would be spirited out of the country.[98]

The radicalisation of the baHurutshe manifested itself in internal political resistance to the regime as well. In 1960 it was reported that 'people in the Hurutshe reserve had rallied in support of Africans in Zeerust town who were protesting against the relocation of the local township'.[99] It is also significant that in later years many military

97. Interview with Lawrence Phokanoka, conducted by Siphamandla Zondi on 1 July 2001, Ga-Mankopane, SADET Oral History Project, in *The Road to Democracy: South Africans Telling, Their Stories Vol. 1, 1950–1970* (Hollywood: South African Democracy Education Trust & Tshai, 2008), 416.
98. Interview with Simon Senna.
99. Cited in Manson, 'The Hurutshe Resistance', from *Society of Young Africa Bulletin* (1960), Non-European Unity Movement Collection, SAIRR Archive, Historical and Literary Papers Collection, William CullenLibrary. University of the Witwatersrand.

encounters took place in that part of the country in subsequent years-during the 1980s in particular.[100]

Conclusion

ANC activism and agitation in the former western Transvaal/northern Cape from its inception to the mid-1960s, was initially quite marked. This was due to the first wave of enthusiasm among the chiefs who saw in the movement a vehicle for leading opposition to the 1913 Land Act. From its side ANC organisers and office bearers such as Plaatje and Molema, attempted to harness this discontent, realising that the *dikgosi* had the means to draw many supporters into the ranks of the ANC. The realisation that the Land Act could not be undone or reversed, led to reduced support in the rural areas for Congress actions. From this time the NAD also intervened more decisively in supporting chiefs, demanding their loyalty to the state in a time when some of their adherents were mounting challenges to chiefly authority. ANC branches also did operate in the towns of the plattelend region, such as Rustenburg, Ventersdorp and Vryburg, but enthusiasm again appeared to wane from the early 1920s. The ICU and the CPSA seem to have made greater strides in building up a mass following in some parts of the platteland during these years. In the Reserves where production remained quite buoyant during the middle decades of the century, the relative material security of Africans meant there few concerns which the ANC could directly articulate. This was to change by the early 1950s with declining capacity in the reserves and more pronounced state intervention to re-order relations in the countryside as segregation transmogrified into apartheid.

Nowhere is this best illustrated as in the Zeerust region where large numbers of rural dwellers, and especially women, unwaveringly resisted the state's impositions, an event now etched into ANC resistance history. A re-evaluation of the evidence, especially of that made recently available, affirms this representation. We show how deteriorating conditions in the Bahurutshe reserve *before* the revolt created the seeds of frustration and anger for the resistance, which the ANC was able to harness to mount resistance to the pass issue. An assessment of developments in the Lehurutshe district *after* this incident took place, further illustrates that it became a crucial support base for the ANC in the long term and a 'pipeline' for recruits to leave the country, among whom were included all three of South Africa's post-democracy Presidents.[101] This appears to have been matched in the more western reaches of the western platteland, particularly in the African reserves around Mafikeng.

100. See A. Manson and B. Mbenga, 'Bophuthatswana in the 1980s, and the UDF in the western Transvaal', South African Democracy Education Trust, *The Road to Democracy in South Africa*, vol. 4, (Pretoria: UNISA Press, 2010), 669–706.
101. N. Parsons, 'The "Pipeline": Botswana's Reception of Refugees', *Social Dynamics*, 34 (2008), 17–22.

The Lasting Legacy: The Soviet Theory of the National-Democratic Revolution and South Africa

IRINA FILATOVA

Professor, National Research University Higher School of Economics, Moscow, Russia and Professor Emeritus, University of KwaZulu-Natal, Durban, South Africa

Abstract

In this article I look into the Soviet roots of the official policy and ideology of the African National Congress (ANC) – the National Democratic Revolution. The article deals with the evolution of the Soviet theory of the national liberation movement, with the history of its adoption first by the South African Communist Party (SACP) and then by the ANC and with the way this theory has been playing itself out in South African politics after the ANC's coming to power. It offers a historical perspective which helps to understand the ANC's present policy and politics and the thinking of its leadership. The article is based on documents from both the South African and Russian archives, interviews with participants of events, Russian contemporary publications and a wide range of other published material.

For three decades, from 1960 until 1991, the Soviet Union was the closest and the most important ally of the African National Congress (ANC). The USSR supplied the ANC's military wing, Umkhonto we Sizwe, with arms, ammunition, military and other equipment, transport and food, it trained Umkhonto and ANC cadres, rendered logistical, financial and political support and assisted in creating and maintaining the international anti-apartheid movement. Taken together, all this meant that for three decades the Soviet Union provided the ANC and the South African Communist Party (SACP) with a safety net which could not, of course, protect their cadres from the hardship and dangers of exile and struggle, but helped both organisations to survive and triumph – a fact that was widely recognised by the ANC leaders at the time.

But the Soviet Union was much more than simply a friend and a donor. Looking back, Jeremy Cronin, the SACP's deputy general secretary, wrote in 2011:

> In the 20th century we were not alone ... We had a sense of being a part of shaping world history. Individually, many of us might not survive, but, so it seemed, we were on the side of history in the struggle for a better future.[1]

Although Cronin had some reservations about 'communists in power', at the time for many parties on the left, the SACP and the ANC among them, it was the USSR that created the feeling that they 'were not alone'. The Soviet Union was at the head of that struggle for the better future, and for the older generation of the SACP and the ANC leadership and cadres – just as for the leadership of many other communist and national liberation organisations all over the world – it was the embodiment of progress and justice, a symbol of the bright future of humanity and the model for a future South Africa – South Africa after the ANC's victory.

It was not surprising therefore that there was a lot of admiration for the Soviet Union – its achievements, its ideology and its policy. Its experience was perceived as a clear pointer to a better future and as a measure of the correctness of South Africa's liberation movement route to it. Garth Strachan, a communist and an MK veteran said in one interview:

> Although it has become popular not to admit this now, at the time – at least in the circles where I moved and up to the mid or late 1980s – the reality was that in ANC ... there was a kind of pro-Soviet hysteria.[2]

'Hysteria' may be too strong a word, but songs were sung and poetry composed about the Soviet people, support was expressed for Soviet initiatives and policy moves. Messages of appreciation and gratitude were read at various Soviet gatherings where ANC and SACP delegations were invariably present. Lenin was a household name among the leadership of both organisations, and the experience of the CPSU was thoroughly and passionately studied and discussed.

After the collapse of the Soviet Union – the event that was perceived as the greatest historical and personal tragedy by many ANC cadres – much of this influence became merely a historical memory. However, one aspect of it is still very much alive and is playing itself out in the South African political arena in the second decade of the twenty-first century. This aspect is the Soviet theory of the national democratic revolution (NDR).

The legacy of the classics

The Soviet theory of the national liberation revolution was first formulated by V. I. Lenin in his *Draft Theses on the National and the Colonial Question* for the Second Congress of the Communist International (the Comintern) in 1920 and in the *Report of the Commission on the National and Colonial Question* to that Congress. It was later developed in his article, '"Left-Wing" Communism – an Infantile Disorder', in his speech to the Second All-Union

1.   *The Sunday Times*, Johannesburg, 31 July 2011.
2.   http://www.liberationafrica.se/intervstories/interviews/strachan/?by-name = 1, accessed 3 February 2012.

Congress of Communist Organisations and Peoples of the East, and in his speeches and reports to the Third and Fourth Congresses of the Comintern.

Lenin's theory as expressed in the *Report of the Commission on the National and the Colonial Questions* (written on the basis of Lenin's *Draft Thesis*) to the Second Congress of the Comintern contained five main points.

1. The world consists of oppressing and oppressed nations [i.e. not just classes – I.F.]; the former are a small minority; the latter, a huge majority.
2. After the First World War 'relations between nations ... are defined by the struggle of a small group of imperialist nations against the Soviet movement and Soviet states with Soviet Russia at their head'.
3. 'Any national movement can only be bourgeois-democratic by nature, for the main mass of the population of backward countries consists of the peasantry ...'. The Commission on the National and Colonial Question to which the *Draft Theses* were presented, substituted the term 'national-revolutionary' for 'bourgeois-democratic' and added that communists could support 'bourgeois liberation movements in colonial countries' only when these movements were 'truly revolutionary, when their representatives will not prevent us from educating and organizing the peasantry and the broad exploited masses in the spirit of revolution'.
4. In pre-capitalist conditions, in the absence of a proletariat, the experience of peasant 'soviets' – councils which emerged during the Russian revolution – should be applied. It was thought that peasants would understand this 'form of communist tactics', but that 'the proletariat of the advanced countries' 'should help the backward toiling masses'.
5. The capitalist stage of development was not inevitable for 'the backward people who get their freedom now', for 'the victorious proletariat' will wage propaganda among them, and Soviet governments[3] 'will render them assistance with all means at their disposal'.[4]

All these points seem clear enough, except the second one: what did Russia's position in the international arena have to do with the colonial question? In fact, this was the crux of Lenin's approach: although Russia did not fit into the category of oppressed nations, it was a victim of the same few but powerful oppressing nations. The main idea of the *Theses* was that socialist Russia and anti-colonial movements were natural allies (despite the bourgeois nature of anti-colonial movements), and as such they should act together in a united front against imperialism. This was because (a) bourgeois movements in the colonies could be national-revolutionary if they allowed communists 'to educate' the masses and lead them; and (b) under the leadership of communists in the colonies and communist parties in the metropolitan powers and, first and foremost, of the communists of Soviet Russia, the most

3. Before the creation of the Soviet Union in 1924, several independent states with Soviets at their head emerged on the territory of the former Russian Empire, as well as e.g. in Hungary and Bavaria.
4. V.I. Lenin, 'Doklad komissii po natsionalnomu i kolonialnomu voprosam, 26 iiulia [Report of the Commission on the National and the Colonial Questions, 26 July]', in V.I. Lenin, *Sobraniie sochinenii [Collected Works]*, 4th ed., vol. 31 (Moscow: State Publishers of Political Literature, 1950), 215–220.

'backward' colonial peoples, i.e. those that had not reached the capitalist stage of development, might avoid having to go through it.

By the mid-1920s Lenin's theses had undergone substantial change. While Lenin stressed the possibility and even the desirability of an alliance with the local bourgeoisie, as long as it did not hamper communist propaganda, the Fifth Congress of the Comintern in 1924 rejected the idea that this bourgeoisie could have any anti-colonial potential. Moreover, even socialists who agreed to support colonial reform rather than an outright revolution in the colonies, were now called 'national reformists'. Soon those who wholeheartedly supported anti-colonial revolutions but not under the banners of the Comintern were to be denounced as the worst enemies of all – 'Trotskyists'.

These changes were initiated at the very top. After Lenin's death the Party's nationality policy was defined by J.V. Stalin who had begun his ascent to the Party leadership by authoring an article on this very topic. Stalin did distinguish between the bourgeoisie of the metropolitan powers and the 'national bourgeoisie' of colonial and dependent countries – as did Lenin. The latter, Stalin wrote, 'could support a revolutionary movement against imperialism in their countries at a certain stage and for a certain time'.[5] However, as a matter of principle he did not trust any alliances with bourgeois parties and movements, even temporary ones, and even in the colonies. Already in his first article on the national question, *Marxism and the National Question* published in 1913, Stalin declared that 'generally the proletariat does not support the so-called "national-liberation" movements because until now all such movements have acted in the interests of the bourgeoisie and have corrupted and confused the class consciousness of the proletariat'.[6]

Unlike Lenin, Stalin also did not believe that in the course of anti-colonial struggle pre–capitalist colonial societies could transfer to socialism, by-passing the capitalist stage of development. In 1927, for example, he told Chinese revolutionaries that it was 'a mistake to speak about the possibility of the peaceful development of a bourgeois-democratic revolution into a proletarian one'.[7]

As national revolutions were capitalist by nature, only capitalist societies could emerge out of them, particularly if they were led by the bourgeoisie. So Stalin thought that the only way avoid this would be 'to achieve the hegemony of the proletariat in the bourgeois-democratic revolution' – which was the main task of communist parties in anti-colonial and national-liberation revolutions. In 1927, on Stalin's insistence (criticised by many in the Party, Leon Trotsky among them) the young Chinese Communist Party attempted to act against the 'right-wing forces' within the Kuomintang, Sun Yat–sen's nationalist movement. Stalin insisted that the right-wingers should be 'isolated inside the Kuomintang and

---

5.   J.V. Stalin, 'Mezhdunarodnoie polozheniie i oborona SSSR. Rech, 1 avgusta. Ob'edinennyj Plenum TsK i TsKK VKP(b) 29 iiulia–9 avgusta 1927 g. [The International Situation and the Defence of the USSR. Speech of 1 August. Combined Plenary Session of the Central Committee and the Central Control Committee of the All–Union Communist Party (Bolshevik)]', in Stalin, *Sochineniia (Works)*, vol. 10 (Moscow: State Publishers of Political Literature, 1949), 11.

6.   J.V. Stalin, 'Kak ponimaiet sotsial–demokratiia natsionalnyi vopros? [How Does Social Democracy Understand the Nationality Question?]', in Stalin, *Sochineniia (Works)*, vol. 1 (Moscow: State Publishers of Political Literature, 1946), 49.

7.   J.V. Stalin, 'Beseda so studentami Universiteta imeni Sun' Yatsena [A Conversation with the Students of the Sun Yat–sen University]', in Stalin, *Sochineniia (Works)*, vol. 9 (Moscow: State Publishers of Political Literature, 1948), 252.

used for the purposes of the revolution' and then 'decisively evicted from the Kuomintang and decisively fought against until they are completely politically destroyed.'[8] 'What is required now of the Chinese Communist Party if it really wants to be independent', he explained, 'is not to leave the Koumintang, but to achieve the leading role of the Communist Party both in the Koumintang, and outside it'.[9]

In fact, it was the Nationalists under Chiang Kai-shek, Sun Yat–sen's successor, who turned against the Communists, nearly annihilating them. Stalin, however, never changed his approach. In the 1930s he still insisted on the idea of the hegemony of the proletariat in the national-liberation struggle. In his article, *The International Character of the October Revolution*, he wrote: 'The era of liberation revolutions in colonies and dependent countries has come – the era of the awakening of the proletariat of these countries, the era of its hegemony in the revolution.'[10]

Whatever further convolutions the Soviet theory of the national-liberation revolution went through, the idea of the hegemony of the proletariat (i.e. the leading role of communists) in such a revolution remained its permanent and crucially important aspect.

The rise and fall of 'the independent native republic'

The Communist Party of South Africa (CPSA), the predecessor of the SACP, joined the Comintern in 1921, but it was only in 1927 that this international communist organisation centred in Moscow became directly involved in South African affairs. James La Guma, one of the leaders of the CPSA, visited Moscow twice during that year. The first time he came in March and then returned in November, together with Josiah Gumede, president of the then small and ineffective ANC, to participate in the celebrations of the tenth anniversary of the Russian revolution. During these visits La Guma met Comintern leaders and discussed the general political line of the CPSA with them.

After several meetings with La Guma, the Comintern's Executive offered its own vision of the line, first formulated by its chairman, Nikolai Bukharin. The final version of this proposal was adopted by the Comintern's Sixth Congress in late 1928. It was decreed that,

> the Communist Party of South Africa must combine the fight against all anti-native laws with the general political slogan in the fight against British domination, the slogan of an independent native South African Republic as a stage towards a workers' and peasants' republic with full rights for all races, black, coloured and white.[11]

8. J.V. Stalin, 'Voprosy kitaiskoi revoliutsii [Questions of the Chinese Revoluton]', in Stalin, *Sochineniia (Works)*, vol. 9, 226–227.
9. Stalin, 'Beseda', 266.
10. J.V. Stalin, 'Mezhdunarodnyi kharakter Oktiabr'skoi revoliutsii [The International Character of the October Revolution Sochineniia]', in Stalin, *Sochineniia (Works)*, vol. 10, 245.
11. A. Davidson, I. Filatova, V. Gorodnov and S. Johns, eds, *South Africa and the Communist International: A Documentary History (1919–1939)*, vol. I (London: Frank Cass Publishers, 2003), 155, 194.

The idea of a two-stage revolution, the first stage for democracy and the second one for socialism, was first formulated by Lenin in 1905.[12] For South Africa the first stage was adapted to include the national liberation of Africans. The second stage remained unchanged, though the 'full rights' of 'all races' were stressed. The definition of the 'independent native republic' was far from clear (for example, it did not explain its class nature) and the new line met steep opposition within the CPSA. The Party finally accepted it under huge pressure from the Comintern, which simply imposed the slogan on its South African branch,[13] but only after prolonged and vicious infighting which nearly obliterated the organisation.

Despite this the slogan of the independent native republic was to have a profound and lasting effect on theoretical thinking and debate within the Party and the ANC. Even decades later much of the dissent in the liberation movement centred on the interpretation of the two stages of the revolution and the correlation between race and class in each of them. The historical importance of this slogan is fully realised by South African communists today. Dominic Tweedie, host of the SACP's 'Communist University' site, wrote:

> It is possible to make out a clear list of texts from the 1920s, approximately one per decade, and to demonstrate that the argument built up through these texts has determined South Africa's history ... This list could start with the Comintern's "Black Republic Resolution of 1928".[14]

In 1935 the Seventh Comintern Congress cancelled the slogan of the independent native republic as abruptly and as harshly as it had introduced it. The advance of fascism and Nazism forced the Soviet leaders to look for allies, and the creation of a united people's front was proclaimed as the immediate task of every communist party. This did not mean that either the idea of national liberation itself, or of the two-stage struggle were put on the backburner. The draft resolution that the Comintern's Executive prepared for adoption by the Ninth Congress of the CPSA in February 1936 specifically mentioned that the changing situation 'has made it inexpedient ... to further advance the slogan of the "Independent Native Republic"', because 'for the fascists ... it facilitates their work in igniting nationalism and race hatred, primarily between the Natives and the whites'. But at the same time the resolution also stated 'the erroneousness of mechanically identifying the task of the national liberation struggle with the tasks of the revolutionary-democratic dictatorship of the workers and farmers',[15] since

> the Native peoples can today be mobilised against imperialism but the mass of Native toilers have not yet matured to the point of raising the struggle against the chiefs of their tribes. They will mature for the solution of this second task first and foremost in the struggle against imperialism.[16]

12. V.I. Lenin, 'Dve taktiki sotsial–democratii v democraticheskoi revoliutsii [Two Tactics of Social Democracy in a Democratic Revolution]', in Lenin, *Sobraniie sochinenii (Collected Works)*, 4th ed., vol. 9 (Moscow: State Publishers of Political Literature, 1947), 3–119.
13. The official name of the CPSA was 'Communist Party of South Africa – Branch of the Communist International'.
14. DomzaNet, Communist University, http://groups.google.com/group/Communist-University, accessed 27 March 2007.
15. Presumably 'farmers' here meant 'peasants'. The authors of the document obviously had little, if any, knowledge of South Africa's realities.
16. Davidson, Filatova, Gorodnov and Johns, *South Africa*, vol. II, 173–175.

The CPSA was also told that the Boers were one of the oppressed nations who had also fought against the British. The Party was accused of not paying enough attention to them, as well as to such 'non-revolutionary' organisations as the ANC and the Industrial and Commercial Workers' Union (ICU) – South Africa's first black trade union. This, in the view of the authors, prevented the creation of a wide people's front in the country. The new slogan offered to the Party was 'For Independent South African Republics!', i.e. one republic for each of the oppressed peoples.[17] Apartheid's creators would have been stunned had they realised that the idea of separate states for separate nations in South Africa had first occurred to the strategists of the Communist International.

From 1935 on the Comintern's leadership demanded that the Party concentrate on the struggle for workers' everyday needs and on the work with and within trade unions. The struggle for the interests of the oppressed 'native masses' became a part of the struggle for the everyday needs of the working class as a whole.[18] The close connection between the Communist Party and the trade unions in South Africa was there to stay as part of the Soviet theoretical legacy. The somewhat diminished role of the struggle for national liberation was soon to be reversed and to occupy centre stage in Soviet theoretical thinking.

The shifting perspective

The changes in the international situation in the wake of the Second World War transformed the Soviet approach towards anti-colonialism. But the new perspective did not emerge overnight. So much so that during the peace negotiations with its wartime allies the USSR demanded some of the former Italian colonies for itself, so as to show the world what 'a socialist colony' could be.[19] This did not work out, and a new approach to the 'colonial issue' had to be found.

In the first post-war years there were no official documents on this subject: the Comintern was dissolved in 1943, and Party congresses were not convened. In his Report to the Meeting of several communist parties in 1947 in Poland A.A. Zhdanov, Secretary of the Central Committee of the Soviet Communist Party, mentioned only that 'attempts to suppress the national-liberation movement by force ... meet the growing armed resistance of colonial peoples'. And the Declaration, passed by the Meeting, instructed communists 'to lead resistance to plans for imperialist expansion and aggression'.[20]

---

17. *Ibid.*
18. See, for example, Davidson, Filatova, Gorodnov and Johns, *South Africa*, vol. II, 186–187, 200–210.
19. A. Davidson and S. Mazov, eds, *Rossia i Afrika. Dokumenty I materially. XVIIIv. –1960. [Russia and Africa. Documents and Materials.* Vol. II (Moscow: Institute of General History, Russian Academy of Sciences, 1999), 135–138; A. Davidson, S. Mazov and G. Tsypkin, *SSSR i Afrika. Dokumentirovannaia istoriia vzaimootnoshenij [The USSR and Africa: Documentary History of Relations]* (Moscow: Institute of General History, Russian Academy of Sciences 2002), 117–124; S. Mazov. 'The USSR and the Former Italian Colonies, 1945–1950', *Cold War History*, 3, 3 (2003), 49–78.
20. *Informatsionnoie soveshchaniie predstavitelei nekotorykh kompartii v Pol'she v kontse sentiqbriia1947 [Information Meeting of Representatives of Some Communist Parties in Poland in Late September 1947]* (Moscow: State Publishers of Political Literature, 1948), 10, 17.

But from the late 1940s, when one colony after another became free, it became necessary to interpret this new phenomenon and to integrate it into existing theoretical constructions, as well as to define the nature of Soviet relations with the new countries. China's experience once again had a decisive influence on Soviet thinking. In 1949 the Chinese Communists, having defeated the Kuomintang, emerged victorious from the civil war, as if to confirm that Stalin's 1927 line on communist leadership in a revolution for national liberation was, after all, correct. Stalin greeted these developments and encouraged his Chinese colleagues to work in other Asian colonies. The Chinese way was, then, the correct one: only an armed revolutionary struggle led by communists could bring real independence. The Chinese communists' victory was the only reference made to the national-liberation movement at the 1949 Meeting of the Communist and Workers' Parties in Hungary in 1949.[21]

But the anti-colonial struggle did not always follow the Chinese example or Soviet theoretical scenarios. It was impossible to admit that something was wrong with the theory – something had to be wrong with the newly independent countries themselves. If a bourgeois party, and not the working class, had led a colony towards its independence, such independence was proclaimed 'formal' or 'illusory'. And independence granted to colonies by former colonial powers was described as a 'manoeuvre' aimed at 'perpetuating' their colonial status or at least keeping them within the sphere of influence of the former colonial powers. 'Colonial status, i.e. above all the economic enslavement of a country by imperialism', wrote the historian Ye. M. Zhukov 'is fully compatible with its formal equality and even with 'independence'.[22] Burma and India were given as examples of such 'illusory' independence. The independence of Indonesia and Vietnam, on the contrary, were both considered genuine, because they had been won by armed struggle.

The armed struggle was the preferred form of anti-colonialism because it was thought to be more 'revolutionary' and ultimately to lead the newly independent countries into the socialist camp.[23] Despite many examples of the opposite, this belief remained a part of Soviet thinking up to the mid 1980s. In 1976 Georgi Mirski, a Soviet academic and one of the top advisers of the CPSU's Central Committee on problems of the national-liberation movement was quoted as saying that while the radicalisation of Third World regimes did not necessarily depend on their coming to power through armed struggle, 'the majority of radical countries' have nevertheless gone through 'a protracted period of armed struggle'. According to him, in the process revolutionary parties became stronger, and 'bourgeois elements' departed from the field of action.[24]

From the mid-1950s on some of these underlying principles had to be reconsidered and reinterpreted in the context of the new political situation. The pace, and in some countries

21.   *Soveshchaniie Informatsionnogo biuro kommunistiheskix partii v Vengrii vo vtoroi polovine noiabria 1949 g. [Meeting of the Information Bureau of Communist Parties in Hungary in late November 1949]* (Moscow: State Publishers of Political Literature, 1949), 46, 48.

22.   Ye.M. Zhukov. 'Obostreniie krizisa kolonialnoi sistemy posle vtoroi mirovoi voiny [The Aggravation of the Crisis of the Colonial System after the Second World War]', in Ye.M. Zhukov, ed., *Krizis kolonialnoi sistemy [The Crisis of the Colonial System]* (Leningrad: Publishing House of the Academy of Sciences of the USSR, 1949), 21.

23.   See, for example, I.M. Lemin, *Obostreniie krizisa Britanskoi imperii posle vtoroi mirovoi voiny [The Aggravation of the Crisis of the British Empire after the Second World War]* (Moscow: Publishing House of the Academy of Sciences of the USSR, 1951), 9.

24.   *The International Herald Tribune*, 30 September 1976.

the radical nature of decolonisation, the fact that many politicians of the newly independent countries were captivated by communist ideology, the founding of the non-aligned movement, the success of Khrushchev's visit to India, Burma and Afghanistan in 1955 – all these factors combined led the Soviet leadership to the conclusion that the anti-colonial process as a whole, irrespective of its character in each country, could become an important ally of the Soviet Union in its struggle against imperialism. In essence this was a return to Lenin's idea that national-liberation movements were natural allies of socialist countries and that the newly independent countries could move to socialism straight from pre-capitalist modes of production, bypassing the capitalist stage.

Moreover, in the situation of the Cold War Moscow began to see the decolonisation process as a precursor of the collapse of the capitalist system – the beginning of the same world revolution that had failed to materialise in the developed countries of Europe and America, but was now advancing from the East and South. At the CPSU's 20th Congress in 1956 Khrushchev for the first time spoke about the collapse of the colonial system and of the emergence of newly independent countries as one of the manifestations of the general crisis of capitalism. He also said, for the first time too, that with the emergence of the socialist camp, civil wars and violent upheavals were no longer a necessary stage of struggle for socialism and that now 'conditions could be created for radical political and economic transformation by peaceful means'.[25]

As far as Africa was concerned, the new line found its clear expression in a secret decree *On the Broadening of Cultural and Public Ties with Negro Peoples of Africa and Strengthening of Soviet Influence on these Peoples*, issued by the CPSU's Central Committee on 20 January 1960.[26]

The NDR and socialist orientation

In the late 1950s the CPSU's Central Committee formed a special group of advisers to work on the theoretical problems of national liberation movements. It was ultimately led by Karen N. Brutents, one of the deputy heads of the CC's International Department, and it was under him, in the 1970s, that the theory was fully developed. The group produced drafts of official party documents and speeches for the party leaders on national liberation. The drafts were sent to the CC's Secretariat and edited there. The texts that emerged as a result became the official party line and were reproduced as its official documents. Several academic research institutes worked on the interpretation of Soviet national liberation theory and studied the ways it was applied and worked in practice. Hundreds of books, thousands of theses and innumerable articles were written on various aspects of this topic.

The theory ran as follows. In the new international dispensation, when socialism had become the most important political factor, young independent states could bypass capitalism, moving straight from pre-capitalist modes of production to socialism. The authors of the theory thought that although in some countries the socioeconomic base was

25.   Otchetnyi doklad of the TsK KPSS XX s'ezdu KPSS (Report of the CPSU's CC to the 20th Congress of the CPSU. 14 February, 1956, http://www.hrono.ru/dokum/195_dok/1956sezd20.php, accessed 3 February 2012.

26.   Davidson and Mazov, *Rossia i Afrika*, 165.

not ripe for socialism, the revolutionary super-structure (i.e. the state), directed by the local working class and assisted by the 'world proletariat' could 'pull the base up' to the necessary level by a certain set of measures. After such a preparatory period a peaceful transition to socialism could follow. The theory operated with several interconnected notions: the national democratic revolution; the national democratic state; revolutionary democracy; and the non-capitalist way of development or socialist orientation.

The notion of the national democratic revolution was the cornerstone of the theory. It emerged in the Soviet political vocabulary of the late 1950s. According to Brutents, it was first put forward by the CPSU and was then 'widely accepted' by the international communist movement, used in the documents and platforms of communist parties, and was 'extensively used at the 1969 International Meeting of Communist and Workers' Parties'.[27]

Brutents explained that:

> the introduction by the Communist parties ... of the category of "national democratic revolution" into their militant political vocabulary, and – what is most important – the use of its socio-economic and political content as an important starting point for elaborating strategy and tactics resulted from the generalisation of the new features of national liberation revolutions in our day. What are the distinctive features of national democratic revolutions? These revolutions which lead to the elimination of colonial and semi–colonial oppression and are also latent with anti–capitalist tendency ... They not only weaken the imperialist system ... When [their] leadership comes from political forces representing the interests of the proletariat, these revolutions ... grow directly into socialist revolutions. When leadership comes from non-proletarian democratic forces ... these revolutions produce, alongside important anti-imperialist and anti-feudal changes, anti-capitalist transformations, paving the way for the transition to socialist reconstruction ... The national democratic tendency of development in the revolution can gain the upper hand either at the first or at the second phase of the revolution.[28]

So, according to the Soviet theory, there was only one possible outcome of the NDR – socialism, which could emerge in one of two ways, either directly from anti-colonialism, or through transformation during a transition period. Such a period was called 'non-capitalist development'.

The idea of 'non-capitalist development' was first formulated by the authoritative International Meeting of Communist and Workers' Parties held in Moscow in 1960, in which 81 parties participated. It was then affirmed in the Programme of the CPSU, adopted by the 22nd Congress of the CPSU in 1961, and used at another International Meeting of Communist and Workers' Parties in 1969. From 1967 the term 'socialist orientation' was introduced, as a 'more precise' alternative to 'non-capitalist' development. The documents of the 1969 International Meeting of the Communist and Workers' parties used both terms interchangeably. Official party documents never provided a definition of socialist orientation, but all interpretations described it as a transitional stage which pre-capitalist societies had to go through if they wanted to move to socialism. The *Africa Encyclopaedia*, for example, gave the following definition:

27. K.N. Brutents, *National Liberation Revolutions Today. Some Questions of Theory.* Part I (Moscow: Progress Publishers, 1977), 146–147.
28. Brutents, *National Liberation,* 148–149.

The socialist orientation or non–capitalist way of development is the initial stage of social progress towards socialism in the countries where the people reject capitalism as a system, but conditions for a socialist revolution do not yet exist.[29]

The 1960 Meeting of Communist and Workers' Parties defined the class basis of the non-capitalist path as 'the united national democratic front of all patriotic forces of the nation', based on the union between the working class and peasants.[30] This front, or 'bloc' was called 'revolutionary democracy'. The authors of the collective monograph, *Africa: Problems of Socialist Orientation*, defined revolutionary democracy as a social group that expressed 'anti-imperialist, anti-feudal, democratic and socialist ideals and the aspirations of different strata of the working people' in countries which found themselves 'at the pre-capitalist and early-capitalist stages of development'.[31]

The 1960 Meeting of Communist and Workers' parties declared that the 'political form of the activity of the revolutionary democracy is the national democratic state'. This was

the state that consistently upholds its political and economic independence, fights against imperialism and its military blocs, against military bases on its territory; fights against the new forms of colonialism and the penetration of imperialist capital; rejects dictatorial and despotic methods of government; ensures the people's broad democratic rights and freedoms (freedom of the press, speech, assembly, demonstration, establishment of political parties and social organisations) and the opportunity of working for the enactment of agrarian reform and other domestic and social changes, and for participation of the people in shaping government policy.[32]

The authors of *Africa: Problems of Socialist Orientation* gave a shorter definition: 'the national democratic state is the transitional state towards the state of the socialist type'.[33]

Long or short, these definitions were so vague that they could be stretched in any direction. Clearly, there were no tangible criteria for a government to be recognised as a revolutionary democracy, and for a country to be considered a national democratic state. But the slogans were attractive and this was what mattered.

---

29. *Afrika. Entsiklpedicheskii spravochnik [Africa. Encyclopaedia]*, vol. 2 (Moscow: Sovetskaia Entsiklopediia, 1987), 389.

30. *Dokumenty Soveshchaniia predstavitelej kommunisticheskikh I rabochikh partii [Documents of the Meeting of Representatives of Communist and Workers' Parties]* (Moscow: State Publishers of Political Literature, 1960), 37.

31. G.B. Starushenko, ed., *Africa: problemy sotsialisticheskoi oriientatsii [Africa: Problems of Socialist Orientation]* (Moscow: Nauka, 1976), 27.

32. *Programmnyie dokumenty borby za mir, demokratiiu i sotsialism. Dokumenty Soveshchanii predstavitelei kommunisticheskikh i rabochikh partii, sostoiavshikhsia v Moskve v noiabre 1957 g., v Bukhareste v iiune 1960 g., v Moskve v noiabre 1960 g [Programme Documents of the Struggle for Peace, Democracy and Socialism. Documents of the Meetings of Representatives of Communist and Workers' Parties, which took place in Moscow in November 1957, in Bucharest in June 1960, and in Moscow in November 1960]* (Moscow: State Publishers of Political Literature, 1961), 67–68. The English translation of this definition comes from the 1962 Programme of the SACP (see below). It was most probably copied from the original Soviet translation handed to the delegates.

33. Starushenko, *Africa: problemy*, 38.

A fluid theory – and its downfall

Soviet theoreticians did not agree on the class composition of revolutionary democracy. Thus, *Africa: Problems of Socialist Orientation* listed 'the revolutionary elements of the national bourgeoisie' among the forces that constituted the class base of the national democratic state, together with the proletariat and the peasantry.[34] R.A. Ulianovski, a Soviet theoretician of the national liberation movement and another deputy head of the Central Committee's International Department, held a similar view. 'It is correct to define the national-democratic state', he wrote,

> as the political power of a broad social bloc of the working people, among whom are the growing proletariat, the urban and rural petty bourgeois strata and the elements of the national bourgeoisie that come out in favour of a progressive social development from an anti-imperialist position.[35]

Brutents, however, wrote that having introduced 'representatives of national entrepreneurship' into their 'social coalition base', revolutionary democrats often began to pursue a policy in the interests of the bourgeoisie.[36] Official documents did not help to clarify the issue. The 1969 International Meeting of Communist and Worker's Parties mentioned the process of 'internal social stratification' in the former colonies, characterised by contradictions between the 'toiling masses' and the 'upper layers of the national bourgeoisie'. The rest of the bourgeoisie was simply not mentioned.[37]

The list of concrete reforms which were thought necessary in order to achieve socialism was also the object of a lively debate.[38] 'A speedy, revolutionary creation of the material, technical, scientific, social and political prerequisites for socialist construction constitutes the essence of non-capitalist development', *Africa: Problems of Socialist Orientation* explained.[39] The authors of the Soviet encyclopaedia of Africa thought that countries of socialist orientation

> take the course toward the elimination of the economic and political domination of imperialist monopolies and trans-national corporations, as well as of internal reaction – feudal landlords, tribal nobility and the pro-imperialist bourgeoisie; strengthen the state sector – the economic basis of socialist orientation; encourage co-operative movements in the rural areas; implement progressive agricultural reforms, aimed at the elimination of feudal property and at the creation of a rural public sector.

34. Starushenko, *Africa: problemy*, 31–32.
35. R.A. Ulianovskii, *Sotsializm i osvobodivshiiesia strany [Socialism and the Liberated Countries]* (Moscow: State Publishers of Political Literature, 1972), 484.
36. K.N. Brutents, *Sovremennyie natsionalno–osvoboditelnyie revoliutsii [Contemporary National-Liberation Revolutions]* (Moscow: State Publishers of Political Literature, 1974), 333–334.
37. *Mezhdunarodnoie soveshchaniie kommunisticheskikh i rabochikh partij. Dokumenty i materially. Moskva, 5–17 iiunia 1969 g [International Meeting of Communist and Worker's Parties. Documents and Materials. Moscow, 5–17 June 1969]* (Moscow: State Publishers of Political Literature, 1969), 61–62.
38. Such debates about interpretations of concrete issues within the theory were, of course, possible, particularly as the authors themselves disagreed on some points. However, the core of the theory, as formulated in the official documents, was never under discussion.
39. Starushenko, *Africa: problemy*, 18.

'The state sector which emerges as a result of the nationalisation of the property of the former colonial administration, foreign monopolies and the big local bourgeoisie', they wrote,

> is the basis for the struggle against the domination of foreign capital and for the development of productive forces and the industrialisation of the economy. In the interests of the development of the productive forces the private sector of the economy (both national and foreign) is also widely used, together with the public sector, under the control of the state and to the extent and in the forms which are defined for every concrete period of social development. Gradually state planning is introduced, as well as the other institutions of a socialist economy.[40]

Other authors added the 'systematic improvement of the standards of life of working people', or 'the creation of a reliable mechanism of defence of revolutionary achievements from external and internal enemies' to the list.[41] An 'independent foreign policy' and simultaneously 'economic, political and cultural cooperation with socialist countries' were among the most important characteristics of a socialist orientation.[42] All theoretical works and official party documents on socialist orientation stressed the importance of the 'leading role of the proletariat' in it, as well as the cooperation with socialist countries.[43]

In reality the reforms (if any) undertaken in each country of socialist orientation were far removed from the wish lists of Soviet theoreticians. It seems that what mattered for these countries to be recognised as non-capitalist by the Soviet bloc was their willingness to proclaim socialism as their goal, to introduce some form of state control over their economy and to support the Soviet Union in the international arena. According to the disingenuous admission of the authors of *Africa: Problems of Socialist Orientation*, the recognition of a state as a country of socialist orientation was similar to diplomatic recognition of a country.[44] In other words, in practice such recognition was a matter of political expediency, rather than theory. The most important factor defining the Soviet policy towards each newly independent country was the degree of its closeness to the Soviet Union, and not its revolutionary history or the quality of its reforms.

Soviet academics looked into every possible theoretical aspect of the transition of former colonies to socialism through socialist orientation, but attempts to verify theory against reality each time resulted either in adjustments of the reality to make it fit the theory, or in ignoring the reality altogether. Ever more sophisticated works on the theory of socialist orientation were published up till the late 1980s, but some were disenchanted with it as early as the late 1970s. Even those who created the theory could not fail to notice that, having come to power, 'national democrats' were often not in any hurry to build socialism in their countries, and that they often got rid of their communist allies. Other attempted to follow the theory but in such a way that could only compromise Soviet propaganda about their 'achievements' (Mengistu Haile Mariam's Ethiopia being only one example). Besides this, by the late 1970s it became clear that Soviet military interventions in support of the

40.   *Africa. Encyclopaedia*, 389.
41.   P.I. Manchkha. *Aktualnyie problemy sovremennoi Afriki [Current Problems of Contemporary Africa]* (Moscow: State Publishers of Political Literature, 1979), 32–33.
42.   For example, Starushenko, *Africa: problemy*, 18–19.
43.   For example, *Mezhdunarodnoie soveshchaniie*, 62–63; Razvivaiushchiiesia strany, 28, 141, *et al*.
44.   Starushenko, *Africa: problemy*.

national-liberation movements seriously threatened détente and the possibility of peaceful coexistence with the West – and the USSR was not ready for a big war.

Doubts about the theory came earliest to its main creators. According to O.A. Westad, author of a definitive history of the cold war in the Third World, in 1979 Karen Brutents sent many a 'devastating memoranda' to B.N. Ponomarev, head of the International Department of the CPSU's Central Committee. He wrote that the building of socialism in the Third World had become too much of a Soviet project, and that the local contribution remained minimal. The reason for this he saw in the petit-bourgeois nature of 'national democrats'.[45] There were sceptics among communists from developing countries and liberation movements too. Among them was one of the leaders of the South African Communist Party, Joe Slovo, who did not believe in the socialist potential of national democracy.[46] But these doubts did not bring any major changes in Soviet policy and they were not made known to the broader public.

The collapse of the Soviet Union brought the theory to an abrupt end. Today it is neither discussed, nor even mentioned, and even those of its authors who survived it were among the most disillusioned about it. G.I. Mirski wrote in his memoirs:

> In 1963–64 we were at the Staraia Ploshchad[47] for months, working on the *Theses of the CPSU's CC on Problems of the National Liberation Movement* ... Enormous time was spent on working out subtle nuances and definitions, such as "people's democratic" and "national democratic" forces and parties, revolutionary democracy and people's democracy, etc. Now, re-reading the surviving drafts of these materials, I am amazed at how much time and energy was wasted on compiling these at best banal, and more often simply false texts, which nobody needed and which bore no relevance to what was going on in Asia, Africa and Latin America! All our prognoses proved wrong, everything happened not as we thought it would ... Very few among the local Marxists could read all that and believe that our recommendations were correct (and if they followed them, it was to the detriment of their countries). Our Soviet public? It was indifferent to these problems. Whole institutes with huge staffs wasted a lot of money on a completely useless cause.[48]

But Mirski was wrong. Soviet theoreticians found more than a few followers, and South African communists and the African National Congress have been, perhaps, the most consistent among them. In the later years of the anti-apartheid struggle the leaders of the SACP and the ANC thought that the national-democratic stage of their revolution could evolve straight into the socialist stage (one of the two possibilities, mentioned by Brutents). The *Africa. Encyclopaedia* noted that

---

45. O.A. Westad, *The Global Cold War. Third World Interventions and the Making of Our Time* (Cambridge: Cambridge University Press, 2005), 284–285.

46. See, for example, J. Slovo. 'A Critical Appraisal of the Noncapitalist Path and the National Democratic State in Africa', *Marxism Today*, 18, 6 (1974), 181, 186. This did not mean that Slovo argued against the two-stage revolution. His idea was that the first stage, the national-democratic revolution, could only succeed if led by the working class, not the 'national democrats'. In his important work, *South Africa – No Middle Road*, he referred to Lenin in this connection: 'Lenin's theoretical commitment to a bourgeois democratic phase in pre–February Russia was bound up with the slogan of a 'revolutionary democratic dictatorship of workers and peasants' and not that of bourgeoisie'. (J. Slovo, *South Africa – No Middle Road* (N.p., n.d. [1976]), 45.

47. Staraia Ploshchad – the square where the building of the CPSU's Central Committee was situated.

48. G.I. Mirski, *Zhizn v trekh epokhakh [Life in Three Eras]* (Moscow: Letnii Sad, 2001), 179–182.

of all countries on the continent [Africa] the transition to socialism directly through a socialist revolution, by-passing or shortening to the minimum the stage of the national democratic revolution and socialist orientation (according to African communists) is only possible in South Africa, where employed labour constitutes more than half of the economically active population ... and where the proletariat led by the SACP numbers more than 2 million. But even here a transitional period is not excluded.[49]

It should be stressed that despite this sentiment, nowhere in their official documents or writing did South African communists mention the possibility of deliberately skipping the first stage and thus starting a socialist revolution right away. The idea was that apartheid and capitalism were so inextricably connected that once the former was gone, the latter would, more or less, collapse on its own.

Many in South Africa think that the socialist revolution did not take place only because the ANC came to power as a result of a negotiated settlement, not a military victory. But the NDR goes marching on in South Africa today, long after the theory was abandoned by its authors. It constitutes the basis of the ANC's official policy, and from the mid-1990s the debate on the left of South Africa's political spectrum is defined by the questions of how it should be implemented and at what pace, not about whether it should or should not be implemented at all.

But how did the NDR get to South Africa in the first place?

For radical reorganisation and racial equality

The Programme of the SACP's predecessor, the CPSA, adopted in 1944 and supplemented in 1947 and 1949, did not mention either the national democratic revolution, or even the national liberation struggle. The party proclaimed its goal as 'the establishment of a Socialist Republic, based on common ownership of the means of production and the rule of the working class and providing equal rights and opportunities for all racial and national groups'. The Programme stated that the reason for the poverty of millions of South Africans was the fact that the 'mines, factories and farms are owned by a small minority which controls the State in their own interests', but it did not so much as mention the race of either the poor or of the minority controlling the mines and farms. The Programme also demanded equal political and economic rights for all groups of the population, although simultaneously it mentioned the need for the 'industrial development of African reserves'. Among its political goals was

the establishment of an independent, democratic Republic in which all adults, regardless of race, colour or sex, shall have the right to vote for and be elected to Parliamentary, Provincial, Municipal and other representative bodies.[50]

Having buried the slogan of the independent native republic, the Comintern instead directed the party towards the every-day problems of workers of all races. National liberation had to be tackled not as a separate issue but within the parameters of workers'

49. *Africa. Encyclopaedia*, 389.
50. *Constitution and Programme. Communist Party of South Africa* (N.p., n.d. [1949]), 26–29.

rights in general. The CPSA followed this line until its dissolution in 1950 – long after the dissolution of the Comintern.

The Manifesto of the ANC Youth League written in the same year as the CPSA programme, 1944, on the contrary, had a lot to say about the colonial invasion of Africa, about land occupation, racial oppression and of the need for Africans to unite on the basis of race for the purpose of 'racial liberation'. The document spoke of the ANC as 'the national liberation movement', although it criticised the organisation for its lack of activity. However, the document did not give any details of what it understood as 'national' or 'racial' liberation. Neither capitalism, nor socialism were mentioned in it. Moreover, clearly hinting at communists, the authors stated that they rejected 'foreign leadership of Africa' and 'the wholesale importation of foreign ideologies into Africa', although they had no objection to borrowing useful elements from these ideologies.[51]

The radical Programme of Action, adopted by the ANC under the influence of its Youth League in 1949 contained the demand for self-determination and proclaimed 'national freedom' as its main principle. 'By national freedom', continued the document, 'we mean freedom from White domination and the attainment of political independence'. However, when the document turned to what 'freedom' and other radical demands implied, it became clear that in effect it was the incorporation of Africans into the existing state structure on the basis of full equality, the improvement of their system of education, the creation of institutions for their cultural self-expression, the economic development of the reserves and other African areas, etc.[52] 'Liberation' for the authors meant granting the Africans the same rights as the whites enjoyed, without any major transformation of the socioeconomic or political structure of South African society.

In 1955 the Congress of the People, organised by the ANC and its allies, adopted the Freedom Charter, which later became the over-arching official programme of the ANC and has not lost this status to this day. Political debate and major political cleavages in today's South Africa develop around different interpretations of the Freedom Charter, not around its validity as a programme of action for a ruling political party.

The Charter was a manifesto for a radical political and socioeconomic transformation of the country by means of the nationalisation and redistribution of the main means of production and of establishing state control over other spheres of the economy. It ran:

> The mineral wealth beneath the soil, the Banks and monopoly industry shall be transferred to the ownership of the people as a whole; All other industry and trade shall be controlled to assist the well-being of the people; ... and all the land re-divided amongst those who work it to banish famine and land hunger; The state shall help the peasants with implements, seed, tractors and dams ... All shall have the right to occupy land wherever they choose; ... Unused housing space to be made available to the people; Rent and prices shall be lowered; Free medical service and hospitalisation will be available to all.[53]

---

51. *ANC Youth League Manifesto, 1944*, http://www.anc.org.za/show.php?id = 4439&t = The%20Early% 20Years, accessed 3 February 2012.

52. *Programme of Action: Statement of Policy Adopted at the ANC Annual Conference 17 December 1949*, http://www.anc.org.za/show.php?id = 4472&t = The%20Early%20Years, accessed 3 February 2012.

53. *The Freedom Charter. Adopted at the Congress of the People, Kliptown, on 26 June 1955*, www.anc.org.za/ show.php?id = 72, accessed 3 February 2012.

In effect the Charter demanded full equality for all racial groups – not just political and social equality, but economic equality too, defined and managed by the state. This, of course, could come only *after* the nationalisation of all big property, redistribution of land and the establishment of state control over the rest of industry and trade.

When the organisers of the conference were charged in the Treason Trial, the State built its case on the assertion that the Charter was a communist document and thus breached the Suppression of Communism Act of 1950. The defendants insisted that although the Charter did mention some socialist measures, it did not call for the nationalisation of the whole economy, and thus was not a communist document.[54] Nelson Mandela, one of the defendants, argued that: 'Under socialism the workers hold state power. They and the peasants own the means of production, the land, the factories and the mills. All production is for use and not for profit.' The Charter, he continued,

> visualises the transfer of power not to any single social class but to all the people of this country be they workers, peasants, professional men or petty-bourgeoisie. It is true that in demanding the nationalisation of the banks, the gold mines and the land the Charter strikes a fatal blow at the financial and gold-mining monopolies and farming interests that have for centuries plundered the country and condemned its people to servitude. But such a step is absolutely imperative and necessary because the realisation of the Charter is inconceivable, in fact impossible, unless and until these monopolies are first smashed up and the national wealth of the country turned over to the people ... For the first time in the history of this country the Non-European bourgeoisie will have the opportunity to own in their own name and right mills and factories, and trade and private enterprise will boom and flourish as never before.[55]

It is difficult to imagine that Mandela did not know that workers, peasants, professionals and petty bourgeoisie did not constitute 'all the people' of the country (particularly since according to Marxist definitions 'petty bourgeoisie' actually means peasants[56]) and even in the USSR there was some small private property. We shall never know whether he wrote the article with all these ideas out of conviction or with conspiratorial purposes. But the court, which doubtless knew much less about socialist theory and practice than Mandela, accepted his logic, and the defendants walked free.

Many later publications both by the ANC and SACP pointed to the fact the programme outlined in the Charter far exceeded the framework not only of 'bourgeois democracy', but

---

54. See, for example, *The New Age*, 17 November 1957.

55. N. Mandela, 'In our Lifetime', *Liberation*, 19 June 1956.

56. This point surprised several pre-publication readers of this article. Here is the definition of 'petit bourgeoisie' from the Great Soviet Encyclopaedia (Marxist to the core): 'Petit Bourgeoisie, the class of small urban and rural property owners who live exclusively or mainly by their labour. Under capitalism they occupy an intermediary position between two main classes, the proletariat and the bourgeoisie ... Irrespective of the material conditions of a petit bourgeois he differs from a proletarian by virtue of having the means of production in his private ownership. However negligible in size this property may be, it constitutes the main source of income of a petit bourgeois. The class position of a petit bourgeois is defined by the fact that in the capitalist market he sells not his labour but his services or the goods that he had produced ... The rural petit bourgeoisie comprises the overwhelming majority of agricultural producers – small and middle peasants and farmers. The urban petit bourgeoisie is represented by artisans, small traders, etc., owners of small urban enterprises. *Bolshaia Sovetskaia Entsiklopedia [Great Soviet Encyclopaedia]*, 3rd ed., vol. 16 (Moscow: Sovetskaia entsiklopedia, 1974), 47.

also of 'national democracy'. One Sisa Majola (obviously, a pseudonym) wrote in the *African Communist* in 1987:

> the Freedom Charter is a programme of people's democracy ... [57] a democratic republic founded on its basis will extend beyond the framework of the classical understanding of 'bourgeois democracy' ... There are two basic reasons for this. Firstly, it is the working class that will be the leading force in the new state, and will use its strategic position so that the revolution will be to its advantage, rather then that of the bourgeoisie. Already the Freedom Charter expresses this notion when it promises to control all other industries for the benefit of the people. In this way, the Freedom Charter curtails the right of the bourgeoisie to manufacturing and trade in whatever manner they choose, it puts a condition to this right, and that clearly expresses the political will of those who till now have been victims of bourgeois exploitation. Secondly, the successful implementation of the whole democratic programme and the stability of the new republic will depend on the skilful combination of pressure by the armed working class on the government both from above and from below, with the aim of putting further revolutionary transformation into effect.[58]

A prominent SACP leader, Ben Turok, admitted that he was the author of the economic part of the Charter.[59] But even if one believes in the correctness of the apartheid court's verdict that the Charter was, indeed, not a communist document, one would have to believe the *African Communist* too and to recognise the fact that it was not quite a capitalist document either. Mandela may have sincerely imagined that black private enterprise would blossom under the conditions of state ownership of the commanding heights of the economy, state control of the rest of it and the lack of security of private property, but no businessman, black or white, would find such an environment conducive to success.

In fact, the contents of the Charter are closer to the 1944 programme of the CPSA than to any other (earlier or later) document of the ANC. Neither of the two programmes mentioned the national liberation struggle or national liberation; neither spoke of South Africa as a colony or of the ANC as a national-liberation movement, but both declared that full equality of all racial groups could only be achieved on the basis of a radical and revolutionary reconstruction of South African society. The difference was that the CPSA programme envisaged a radical reorganisation that would be socialist in character, and the Charter demanded a radical reorganisation that would lead to the state ownership of a major part of the economy and the state control of the other part – whatever such a reorganisation might be called.

Colonialism of a special type and the South African National Democratic Revolution

The new programme of the SACP – the underground successor of the banned CPSA – appeared in 1962. Both in character and contents this document drastically differed from

57. Within the framework of Soviet theory the term 'people's democracy' referred to the governments that based their policy on 'scientific Marxism'. It was usually applied to the countries of the East European socialist bloc, and sometimes to the governments of the countries of 'socialist orientation of the second generation'.

58. S. Majola, 'The Two Stages of our Revolution', *The African Communist*, 110 (1987), 46.

59. B. Turok, 'Calm Down. The ANC Is Not About to Seize Mines', *The Times*, 18 July 2009. See also: B. Turok, *From the Freedom Charter to Polokwane: The Evolution of ANC Economic Policy* (Johannesburg: Institute for African Alternatives and the Africa Institute, 2008).

all previous programme documents of both the CPSA and the ANC. Already its title was indicative – 'the Road to South African Freedom', and the very first sentence declared that South Africa was a colony, although of a 'special kind'. 'As its immediate and foremost task', continued the document, 'the South African Communist Party works for a united front of national liberation.[60]

The authors stressed that Africans' struggle against colonialism and imperialism was the basis of the African national democratic revolution. The document suggested that 'in most parts of Africa, the needs of the people will best be met at the present time by the formation of the states of the national democracy,[61] as a transitional stage to socialism'. The programme stated that 'The minimum essentials for the state of national democracy as indicated in the declaration of 81 Marxist Parties in December 1960', are that it 'consistently upholds its political and economic independence, fights against imperialism and its military blocs,' etc. The authors continued to reproduce the definition of the national democratic state as adopted by the 1960 International Meeting of Communist and Workers' Parties quoted earlier. 'Such a state', they concluded, 'will provide the most favourable condition for advance, along non-capitalist lines, to socialism'.[62]

South Africa's place in the African revolution was specific, because its colonialism was also special. The notion of 'colonialism of a special type' appeared in this programme for the first time. In such a state, the programme ran, 'the oppressing White nation occupied the same territory as the oppressed people themselves and lived side by side with them'.[63] However, the struggle against this special colonialism, was to be the same: the national democratic revolution that will end the white rule and establish the national democratic state. 'The main content of this Revolution', the programme stated,

> will be the national liberation of the African people ... The revolution will restore the land and the wealth of the country to the people, and guarantee democracy, freedom and equality of rights, and opportunities to all ... The destruction of colonialism and the winning of national freedom is the essential condition and the key for future advance to the supreme aim of the Communist Party: the establishment of a socialist South Africa, laying the foundations of a classless, communist society.[64]

The authors of the document thought that only 'the class of African workers alone' which 'constitutes the core of the African National Congress and the Communist Party is capable, in alliance with the masses of rural people, of leading a victorious struggle to end White domination and exploitation'.[65]

The programme declared that 'the Communist Party considers that the slogan of 'non-violence' is harmful to the cause of the democratic national revolution' and that 'patriots and democrats will take up arms to defend themselves, organise guerrilla armies and

60. 'The Road to South African Freedom. Programme of the South African Communist Party', *The African Communist*, 2, 2 (1963), 24.
61. 'States of national democracy' should have been 'national democratic states' (a Russoism in the original).
62. 'The Road to South African Freedom', 37–38.
63. *Ibid.*, 43.
64. *Ibid.*, 24, 26–27.
65. *Ibid.*, 52, 62.

undertake various acts of armed resistance, culminating in a mass insurrection against White domination'. 'Individual' terror, however, was denounced.[66]

The document stated that the ANC was a national-liberation organisation and that, together with the SACP, it was part of the national-liberation alliance. It also pledged the party's 'unqualified support for the Freedom Charter' which it considered to be 'suitable as a general statement of the aims of a state of national democracy'. The Charter, the document ran, 'is not a programme for socialism', but it

> necessarily and realistically calls for profound economic changes ... which will answer the pressing and immediate needs of the people and lay the indispensable basis for the advance of our country along non–capitalist lines to a communist and socialist future.[67]

Many statements in this programme were either quotations from, or a verbatim rendition of, the documents of the 1960 Meeting of Communist and Workers' Parties. Some repeat well-known Soviet approaches to various political phenomena, for example, to the armed struggle. The only exception was the idea of 'colonialism of a special type'.

The origins of this thesis are not entirely clear. The South African historian David Everatt traced this idea to the debates within the South African left in the early 1950s and attributed its emergence to the leading communists, Michael Harmel, Rusty Bernstein and Jack Simons.[68] But Jack Simons himself traced it back to the slogan of the independent native republic. In his correspondence with another communist, John Pule Motshabi, the connection between these two notions was taken for granted.[69] Eddy Maloka, the only South African historian to work with the SACP's London archives before they disappeared, also connected the idea of 'colonialism of a special kind' directly with the 'native republic'. He wrote, however, that this idea was not simply an elaboration of the Comintern resolution, but also 'a response to the relationship that the Party, especially in the Transvaal, had developed with the nationalist movement during the course of the struggles of the 1940s and 1950s'. Maloka also mentioned Harmel and Rusty Bernstein as the most prominent protagonists of this theory.[70]

But the idea of colonialism of a special kind could have more than one origin. In his sensational book, *The Black Man's Burden*, published in 1944, Leopold Marquard, South Africa's prominent liberal and president of the Council of the South African Institute of Race Relations, described 'white' South Africa as a colonial power, and South Africa's African reserves as colonies.[71] This idea may well have contributed to the Communist thinking.

The Report of the CPSA's Central Committee to the last legal national conference of the Party in January 1950 also stated that 'the distinguishing feature of South Africa is that it combines the characteristics of both an imperialist state and a colony within a single,

66. *Ibid.*, 63.
67. *Ibid.*, 62, 64.
68. D. Everatt, 'Alliance Politics of a Special Type: The Roots of the ANC/SACP Alliance, 1950–1954', *Journal of Southern African Studies*, 18, 1 (March 1991), 19–39.
69. UCT Archives and Maniscripts Department. The Simons Collection. BC 1081/5.1
70. E. Maloka. *The South African Communist Party. 1963-1990* (Pretoria: Africa Institute of South Africa. Research Paper No. 65, 2002), 3.
71. J. Burger (L. Marquard), *The Black Man's Burden* (London: Victor Golancz, 1944), 250–252.

indivisible, geographical, political and economic entity'. But the conclusion from this point was different: as 'in South Africa, the Non–European population, while reduced to the status of a colonial people, has no territory of its own, no independent existence, but is almost wholly integrated in the political and economic institutions of the ruling class', its liberation could be achieved only through socialist revolution – not the national one. And the authors of the Report never used the term 'colonialism of a special type'.[72]

It was only in the 1962 programme of the SACP that the thesis of colonialism of a special type was formulated in its entirety and connected to the NDR, thus presuming the revolutionary overthrow of the coloniser. The seemingly insignificant modification of the thesis was to have profound consequences. Linking the notion of South Africa being a colony of a special type with the national democratic revolution was of crucial importance. Before this link was established South Africa was perceived as a 'common society'; after this the struggle was not for equality within such a common society – whether socialist or capitalist; it was not for getting rid of the colour bar, but for vanquishing one part of that society, the 'colonisers' who were defined by their skin colour only.

The introduction of the thesis of the 'colonialism of a special type' and the adoption of the Charter as the programme for the national democratic revolution connected the SACP and the ANC into a simple scheme: the ANC, as a national liberation movement, implements the national-democratic revolution, and the SACP supports and directs it from the vantage position of the 'vanguard' of the working class. It does so by the power of its ideology and by virtue of its members playing the leading role in the NDR, i.e. occupying the leading positions in the liberation movement. After the ideals of the NDR, as formulated in the Charter, are implemented, the SACP builds socialism. Ever since then the notion of the NDR has remained indissolubly connected with the socialist perspective in the minds not only of the SACP and many ANC members but of even broader circles on the left.

In practical terms this thesis meant that the UN Declaration on the Granting of Independence to Colonial Countries and Peoples could in principle be applied to South Africa. In March 1966 in his letter to U Thant, the UN secretary-general, the Soviet permanent representative to the UN, Nikolai Fedorenko, wrote that

> the Soviet Union supports the use of the most determined measures, including force, against the South African government in order to compel it to apply the principles of the UN Declaration on the Granting of Independence to Colonial Countries and Peoples to South-West Africa.[73]

If South Africa was not only a colonial power but also a colony, the Declaration could be applied not just to South-West Africa, but to South Africa itself too.

The theory's road to South Africa

South African communists and the CPSU did not have direct relations with one another after the late 1930s, when the Comintern's commission of enquiry into the affairs of the

72. *South African Communists Speak. Documents from the History of the South African Communist Party. 1915–1980* (London: Inkululeko, 1981), 201, *et al.*
73. *The Soviet News*, 25 March 1966.

CPSA decreed that the small and troublesome South African party should be supervised by the larger and more experienced Communist Party of Great Britain. The closure, in 1956, of the Soviet consulates in South Africa opened during the Second World War, cut whatever unofficial or covert ties there had been. Several South African communists visited the Soviet Union after the war, but they were invited by various cultural organisations and seem to have had no official meetings with CPSU representatives.

The situation started to change only in 1960. The first official delegation of the underground SACP – its chairman, Yusuf Dadoo, and its representative in Europe, Vella Pillay – visited the USSR in July 1960. They presented a report on the South African situation to their hosts, appealed for financial assistance and received it.[74] The second delegation came later in the same year. It participated both in the celebrations of the Anniversary of the October 1917 Revolution and took part in the International Meeting of Communist and Workers' Parties. This time Dadoo and Pillay were accompanied by Michael Harmel and Joe Matthews, members of the SACP's Central Committee, who, unlike Dadoo and Pillay, came straight from South Africa. From the point of view of theoretical discussions, this was certainly a very important visit. The group first travelled to China, spent a long time in the USSR and was received by N.A. Mukhiddinov, secretary and Presidium member of the CPSU's Central Committee. V.G. Shubin, author of the most authoritative study of the ties between the SACP and CPSU in the 1960s–1980s, mentions a few problems that the delegation discussed in Moscow: the trade boycott of South Africa by the USSR, the opening of Radio Moscow broadcasting to South Africa, the purchase and distribution of the *African Communist* in the USSR, etc.[75] However, Joe Matthews later recalled 'putting forward the policy of armed struggle' and discussing it with representatives of other communist parties.[76]

According to Matthews, he and Harmel spent 'several months' in the USSR. They visited Kiev and Leningrad, but spent most of the time in Moscow, mostly at what had been Stalin's 'nearby dacha',[77] where from the late 1950s on the CPSU received representatives of 'fraternal parties', particularly those that were illegal in their own countries. Matthews recalled that the South Africans met representatives of several other parties at the dacha, and that they all talked all the time about the theory, practice and forms of struggle. He also remembered that sometimes officials of the CPSU's Central Committee and representatives of the Soviet military were present at such discussions. At their hosts' request the South Africans wrote memoranda on the situation in their country, historical essays and memoirs.[78]

Theoretical issues were also discussed during the visit to Moscow of Dadoo and Moses Kotane, the party's general secretary, in late 1961. They came to participate in the CPSU's 22nd Congress, and on 18 November met B.N. Ponomarev, a secretary of the Central Committee and head of its International Department. According to Shubin, the three most

74. V. Shubin, *ANC. A View from Moscow* (Cape Town: Mayibuye Books–UWC, 1999), 34–37.
75. *Ibid.*, 37–40.
76. B. Magubane, P. Bonner, J. Sithole, P. Delius, J. Cherry, P. Gibbs and T. April. 'The Turn to Armed Struggle', in *The Road to Democracy in South Africa. Vol. 1 (1960–1970)* (Cape Town: South African Democracy Education Trust, 2004), 81.
77. Stalin's country house in Volynskoie close to Moscow.
78. B. Magubane, *et al.*, 'The Turn', 81; I. Filatova, Interview with Joe Matthews, Cape Town, 4 November 2004.

important problems discussed at this meeting were: how open the activity of the SACP should be; the correlation between different forms of struggle; and what – which kind of state – should be the goal of the struggle at the time. Ponomarev thought that people of South Africa should know about the existence of the Party, but that it would be possible to turn it into a mass organisation only at the next stage of the struggle – for socialism. The goal of the first stage, the national democratic revolution, was to be the creation of a 'national democratic state' – according to the scenario offered by the 1960 International Meeting of Communist and Workers' Parties. As for the armed struggle, Ponomarev reported this question to the CPSU's leadership. He wrote that the representatives of the SACP asked the opinion of the CPSU Central Committee on whether this course was correct and, if so, requested assistance with the training of 'several military instructors'. The answer to both questions was positive.[79]

According to Shubin, before the project of the 1962 programme was adopted South African communists discussed it with the CPSU's Central Committee.[80] The archives, on which Shubin's information was based, were later closed, so for the time being there is no possibility to verifying this. It is obvious, however, that the main ideas of the programme could only emerge within the context of the Soviet NDR theory.[81] It is also obvious that the programme emerged after the renewal of direct contact between the CPSU and the SACP in 1960–1961 and after the SACP's delegation participated in the 1960 Moscow Meeting of Communist and Workers' Parties and in the protracted discussions with other participating communists and representatives of the CPSU.

This does not mean that any of these ideas were imposed on the SACP. Without exception, all memoirs or books published by the ANC and SACP leaders in the last two decades stress that the Soviet Communist Party never dictated a particular political line to the ANC or to the SACP. This was, obviously, true, at least in the 1960s to 1980s (the situation was different during the Comintern era). There was no need to dictate: the CPSU, the SACP and the ANC were all led by like-minded people, and their vision of the world and of their course in it were extremely close. South African and Soviet communists saw themselves as colleagues and comrades, fighting for a common cause. Harold Strachan, a veteran of Umkhonto we Sizwe, the ANC's military wing, said, correctly: 'Your [Soviet] leadership and ours had the same ideas. They were the same bunch of people'.[82]

South African communists were not told what to think. They made their own choices and drew their own conclusions. Moreover, they themselves contributed to the creation of the NDR theory. After the 1960 Meeting of the Communist and Workers' Parties the South African delegation proudly reported to its party that it 'played a not unimportant part ... It addressed the plenary session twice, first on general questions ... and the second time on the special question of factional activities, basing itself on our own experiences'.[83] In *Marxism Today* Joe Slovo discussed – critically – the particulars of the notion of non-capitalist development and the criteria for defining a country (in this case, Ghana) as a

79.   Shubin, *ANC. A View*, 40–43.
80.   Conversation with V.G. Shubin, Cape Town, 6 September 2008.
81.   *The African Communist* called colonialism of a special type 'a revolutionary theory rooted in Marxism-Leninism': *The African Communist*, 113 (1988), 60.
82.   I. Filatova, Interview with Harold Strachan, Durban, 23 December 1998.
83.   Shubin, *ANC. A View*, 39.

national democratic state.[84] He was later quoted by Soviet academics as an expert,[85] but, according to Shubin, his critique was at first badly received by powerful promoters of the theory of 'socialist orientation' in Moscow.[86]

But, of course, the relationship of the SACP and the ANC with the CPSU was not that of equal partners. The scope for debate was limited and strictly defined, and while Soviet assistance was a lifeline for the SACP and the ANC, South Africa was not in any way a priority for Soviet policymakers. Besides that for those, who saw the socialist system as their ideal, Soviet authority in all questions of theory and practice, strategy and tactics, international relations and everything else, was enormous. And the historical experience of the Soviet Party and the scale of Soviet support for national liberation movements certainly increased the weight of its theoretical arguments.

The 1962 SACP programme became the foundation of all theoretical constructions which guided the SACP and to a very large extent the ANC during nearly three decades of struggle against apartheid, and which guide these organisations even today. The next SACP programme, adopted 27 years later, noted that

> the 1962 programme has made an indelible contribution to the scientific analysis of the situation in South Africa, and to practical revolutionary work for national liberation. It has proved to be a major guiding light over more than a quarter of a century of struggle, inspiring the work of party and non-party militants alike.[87]

The meaning of this document did not escape the South African government. In February 1964 South Africa's Foreign Affairs Department received a summary of the programme from the country's ambassador in Washington, to whom it had been leaked by the CIA. The summary was sent as a 'secret' document, although by then it had, of course, been published by the SACP itself. The Department recommended that selected parts of this summary be published, stressing in particular the document's arguments in favour of the creation of 'people's armed forces' and its proclaimed goal of 'the formation of national democracy as a transitional stage' to socialism.[88]

The NDR and the ANC

In June 1969 the next International Meeting of Communist and Workers' Parties took place in Moscow. It affirmed and strengthened the main points of the Soviet theory. The SACP was represented by Dadoo, Harmel, J.B. Marks (the party's chairman) and

84. J. Slovo, 'A Critique of the Non-capitalist Path and the National Democratic State in Africa', *Marxism Today*, 18, 6 (June 1974), 178–186.

85. See, for example, *Razvivaiushchiiesia strany v sovremnnom mire. Puti revoliutsionnogo protsessa [Developing Countries in the Contemporary World. The Ways of the Revolutionary Process]* (Moscow: Nauka, 1986), 142, 148.

86. Conversation with V.G. Shubin, Cape Town, 6 September 2008. See also V.G. Shubin, *Afrikanskij natsionalnyj congress v gody podpolia i vooruzhennoj borby [The African National Congress during the Years of Underground and the Armed Struggle]* (Moscow: Africa Institute, 1999), 301.

87. 'The Path to Power. Programme of the South African Communist Party adopted at the 7th Congress, 1989', *The African Communist*, 118 (1989), 73–74.

88. Department of Foreign Affairs Archives, 123/1, vol. 10.

'J. Jabulani', that is, the party's rising star, Thabo Mbeki.[89] After the Meeting its materials were published in full in a special supplement to the *African Communist*,[90] but the draft documents were circulated among the leadership of participating parties many months before then and discussed and commented on.[91] So the contents of these documents were known to at least some members of the ANC leadership by the time when the South African version of the NDR theory had been adopted by the ANC at its conference in Morogoro, in Tanzania.

The conference – the first one in exile – was held, in April–May 1969. It passed a resolution, in fact, a programme, *Strategy and Tactics of the ANC*. The document opened with the following words:

> The struggle of the oppressed people of South Africa is taking place within an international context of transition to the Socialist system, of the breakdown of the colonial system as a result of national liberation and socialist revolutions, and the fight for social and economic progress by the people of the whole world. We in South Africa are part of the zone[92] in which national liberation is the chief content of the struggle.[93]

The influence of the SACP's thinking and documents on this first *Strategy and Tactics* was there for everyone to see. 'South Africa's social and economic structure and the relationships which it generates', the document went on,

> are perhaps unique. It is not a colony, yet it has, in regard to the overwhelming majority of its people, most of the features of the classical colonial structures. Conquest and domination by an alien people, a system of discrimination and exploitation based on race, technique of indirect rule; these and more are the traditional trappings of the classical colonial framework ... What makes the structure unique and adds to it complexity is that the exploiting nation is not, as in the classical imperialist relationships, situated in a geographically distinct mother country, but is settled within the borders.

The Morogoro resolution stated that 'the main content of the present stage of the South African revolution is the national liberation of the largest and most oppressed group – the African people', but that this national struggle was

> happening in a new kind of world – a world which is no longer monopolised by the imperialist world system; a world in which the existence of the powerful socialist system and a significant sector of newly liberated areas has altered the balance of forces; a world in which the horizons liberated from foreign oppression extend beyond mere formal political control and encompass the element which makes such control meaningful – economic emancipation.

89.   M. Gevisser. *Thabo Mbeki. The Dream Deferred* (Johannesburg & Cape Town: Jonathan Ball, 2007), 277.
90.   'Materials from the International Communist Meeting. Moscow, June 5–17, 1969', *The African Communist*, (38) 1969, Special Supplement.
91.   Mayibuye Centre, Yusuf Dadoo Collection, 2.3.6.
92.   This odd expression, 'the zone of national liberation', was used in the English edition of Brutents's book. See, for example, Brutents, *National Liberation*, 146.
93.   'Strategy and Tactics of the ANC, adopted by the Morogoro Conference of the ANC, Tanzania, 25 April – 1 May 1969', http://www.marxists.org/subject/africa/anc/1969/strategy-tactics.htm, accessed 3 February 2012. The long quotations in the next few paragraphs are also taken from this document, as indicated in the text.

'In the last resort', concluded the resolution,

> it is only the success of the national democratic revolution which – destroying the existing social and economic relationship – will bring with it a correction of the historical injustices perpetrated against the indigenous majority and thus lay the basis for a new – and deeper internationalist – approach.

The document further states:

> It is ... a fundamental feature of our strategy that victory must embrace more than formal political democracy ... This perspective of a speedy progression from formal liberation to genuine and lasting emancipation is made more real by the existence in our country of a large and growing working class whose class consciousness complements national consciousness.

Those who are familiar with Marxist terminology know that 'economic emancipation' or 'genuine and lasting emancipation' can never be achieved under capitalism. And this is exactly how the ANC cadres, even those who were not communists, saw it. Tambo openly came out in favour of socialism in his address to the 24th CPSU's congress in 1971, when he said that the ANC was leading the masses towards revolution for the overthrow of the fascist regime, the seizure of power and the building of a 'socialist society'.[94] In his article in *World Marxist Review* Tambo wrote:

> It is important that the world opinion should understand the true nature of the people's movement in our country. Some people are still inclined to think that the struggle of the black population is a struggle for civil rights. But this obscures the national liberation character of our movement. Perhaps this is partly due to the over-emphasis at certain times on the struggle against apartheid, instead of the struggle against the entire system of national and class oppression ...[95]

According to Shubin, 'on several other occasions' Tambo

> made his Moscow interlocutors understand that his intentions went beyond the eradication of apartheid. During his last visit to the Kremlin in March 1989 Tambo spoke about the struggle for a national democratic revolution, the goal of which was political power, non-racialism and an end to exploitation.

'There are long-term goals as well', he said, but added: 'we are not pushing them'.[96] If this was the message of the non-communist leader of the ANC, it is not difficult to imagine the perceptions of the rank and file in the organisation. In fact, one does not need to imagine. This is what, in 1976, Tokyo Sexwale, at that time an Umkhonto operative, was telling three SASO-inclined youths, whom he was teaching the basics of armed struggle, as well as the ANC's ideology:

> I told them that the ANC works hand in hand with the South African Communist Party, and that some members of the ANC are also members of the SAC Party. [And] that the ANC and the SAC

---

94.   *24 s'ezd KPSS (SPCU's 24th Congress). Bulletin no 10* (Moscow: Pravda, 1971), 54.
95.   *World Marxist Review*, December 1975.
96.   Shubin, *ANC. A View*, 361–362.

Party are ideological allies, since they both believe in the nationalisation of the means of production.[97]

The Morogoro resolution asserted that the armed struggle was 'the only method left open to us' and that a the goal of this struggle 'in the first phase' was 'the complete political and economic emancipation of all our people and the constitution of a society which accords with the basic provisions of our programme – the Freedom Charter'.[98]

Essentially the Morogoro resolution was a re-wording of the main elements of the 1962 SACP programme: the national democratic revolution with the goal of achieving more than just a 'formal' political independence; the two-stage revolution; economic emancipation as a result of a radical restructuring of the socioeconomic system and the redistribution of the country's wealth; racial equality promised after this has been achieved; the Freedom Charter as the programme of the national democratic revolution; and the black proletariat as its leading force.

There were some differences between the two programmes. It seems that the Morogoro resolution offered racial equality only to a portion of the white proletariat, while the *Road to Freedom* envisaged that a slightly broader spectrum of white society could benefit from it. And since it was a programme for the first, national democratic stage of the revolution, the Morogoro document never mentions socialism or communism as such as its ultimate or direct goal – which the SACP programme does. However, interestingly enough, the Morogoro resolution insisted on 'economic emancipation' already during the first stage, which *The Road to Freedom* did not. The reason for this could be that by 1969 the theoreticians of South Africa's NDR had come to the conclusion that, in the concrete conditions of their country, this transitional stage could only be very short or, indeed, non-existent, and that South Africa would move to the second stage almost right away. This belief was widely discussed in left academic circles, close to the ANC, and it found its way into the Soviet *Africa. Encyclopaedia*, quoted earlier.

The next programme of the SACP was adopted 27 years later, in 1989, but neither the essence, nor the wording of the theory changed. It offered a more nuanced characterisation of some of its aspects, particularly of the class content of colonialism of a special type, and introduced a section on the crisis of this sort of colonialism. It confidently spoke of the 'seizure of power' – this at a time when some of the party's top leaders were already deeply involved in 'negotiations about negotiations' with various representatives of the Nationalist government. It also discussed in detail the moves that the party and the working class as a whole would have to undertake in order to achieve the transition to socialism after the seizure of power.[99]

The NDR theory with 'colonialism of a special type' was transplanted virtually whole into the ANC's Morogoro programme and then repeated without change in the new SACP programme. It ran through every aspect of ANC thinking. This is, for example, how, in the shortest possible form, it was incorporated in the Umkhonto confidential training pamphlet which circulated illegally (it was not supposed to be written) in various versions

97. T.M. Sexwale, 'Legal Deposition Made to South African Police. December 1976', Rhodes House Library, Oxford, Research Papers of Howard Barrell. MSS Afr. s. 2151, A 14.
98. 'Strategy and Tactics of the ANC, adopted by the Morogoro'.
99. 'The Path to Power'.

since the late 1970s, and was finally standardised by several ANC military leaders in the late 1980s. The definition of the NDR was the very first, opening paragraph of the document. It ran:

- The National Democratic Revolution unites all classes among the oppressed – all the progressive, patriotic forces – behind the pursuit of democracy and self-determination.
- National democracy in South Africa will mean: a united S.A. which is run – politically, economically & socially – by the will of the majority, exercised on the basis of one person, one vote – i.e. – power will be in the hands of the masses.
- The back of White Monopoly Capitalism will be broken.
- The redistribution of wealth, of land and other means of production – which will dramatically improve the living and working standards of the oppressed.
- The implementation of the Freedom Charter with its programme of profound agrarian transformation & socialisation of those sectors of the economy in the grip of Monopoly Capitalism – i.e. – the destruction of the Colonial State.[100]

In this shortened and crystallised form the NDR remained entrenched in the mass consciousness of the ANC and survived intact all the way into the new democratic South Africa.

'... But his soul goes marching on'

The negotiated settlement of 1990–1994 meant that there has been no seizure of power, that nationalisation had to be forfeited at least for some time, and that the socialist perspective had to be postponed. The collapse of the Soviet Union and of the socialist order in Easter Europe and Russia have certainly contributed to these developments. But was this a complete change of heart?

Some in South Africa believe that it was. with the Cold War's end liberation movements in that region dropped their socialist rhetoric of the Soviet kind and adopted the principles of mixed economy and liberal democracy.

It is difficult to agree with this. The NDR has certainly not gone away. It remains the official policy of the ANC, it survives in the perceptions and expectations of its rank and file and it continues to shape and define South Africa's public debate. What is debated is the pace and ways of implementing it, the interpretation, not the principles and the expected results – these, for the ANC and its allies, remain indisputable truths.

The 1997 ANC National Conference, which elected Thabo Mbeki to the presidency of the party, adopted a new *Strategy and Tactics of the ANC*. Once again the document referred to the ANC as a national liberation movement and affirmed the need for it to continue the national democratic revolution – this after more than three years of the party being in power. It stated, that

100. [R. Kasrils, W. Anderson and Others], 'MCW (ANC confidential training leaflet). Circa 1988–89, Lusaka', Rhodes House Library, Oxford. Research Papers of Howard Barrell. MSS Afr. s. 2151, A 21.

the symbiotic link between capitalism and national oppression in our country, and the stupendous concentration of wealth in the hands of a few monopolies ... render trite the vainglorious declaration that national oppression and its social consequences can be resolved by formal democracy underpinned by market forces ...[101]

However, this document mentioned neither the Freedom Charter nor nationalisation, nor state control. Not only the African middle class, but even the black bourgeoisie appeared among the 'forces of transformation'. Moreover, the authors declared the development of the African bourgeoisie as one of the tasks of the national-democratic revolution. The explanation given was that this would help to separate the notions of race and class.[102]

So there was no nationalisation for the time being – but the government went on with other forms of redistribution. Such understandable measures as the Africanisation of the public sector, black economic empowerment in the private sector and social grants for the poorest sections of the population were just the beginning of this process. Mbeki's leadership saw the centralisation of the presidency's grip on power, the tightening of government control over all spheres of the economy and the greatly increased regulation of the private sector. In fact, the new mining legislation was challenged in court, for it was perceived that it undermined property rights entrenched in South Africa's constitution. And the drive for the privatisation of the parastatals, started by Mandela's government of national unity, soon ran out of steam: indeed, it was obvious from the start that this idea was not popular among the ANC leadership and particularly among the ANC's allies – the SACP and the Congress of South African Trade Unions (COSATU). Control by encroachment, not by seizure, seemed to be the core of Mbeki's policy, and the purpose of this control lay in the government's power and ability to redistribute as it saw fit. But socialism was no longer on the agenda in the foreseeable future – at least not socialism of the Soviet type.

The new version of the *Strategy and Tactics*, adopted by the ANC in 2007, stated this openly. The aim of the NDR was now a 'national democratic society', which was to be 'social democratic' in nature. The 'revolution' – an ongoing process – was this time to have not just the black bourgeoisie, but also some sections of the white population among its 'motive forces'. The contents of the revolution also changed. 'The liberation of Africans in particular and Blacks in general from political and socio-economic bondage' remained its main goal, but the document for the first time mentioned 'uplifting the quality of life of all South Africans' – although 'especially the poor, the majority of whom are African and female'.

'Colonialism of a special type' was mentioned only in the past, as was 'the apartheid capitalist system'. The need for redistribution, however, remained. The document still insisted that 'such was the symbiosis between political oppression and the apartheid capitalist system that, if decisive action is not taken to deal with economic subjugation and exclusion, the essence of apartheid will remain'. And in this line it was this document that mentioned 'nationalisation of land' as official policy for the first time. However, 'The

---

101. '*Strategy and Tactics As amended at the 50th National Conference, December 1997*', http://www.anc.org.za/show.php?id = 2424, accessed 3 February 2012.
102. *Ibid.*

relationship between the national democratic state and private capital in general' was defined as 'one of 'unity and struggle', co-operation and contestation' – a far cry from the NDR as it was seen in the past. Moreover, the document pledged as one of the goals of the ANC the encouragement of a common 'national identity' and the use of the state 'as an instrument of social cohesion'.[103] It would seem that at least in theory the ANC was returning to the notion of South Africa as a common society, although in practice its policy remained deeply racially divisive. But one thing was certain: the 2007 *Strategy and Tactics* was the death knell for the NDR of the kind that was conceived in the USSR at the height of its power and influence.

However, that socialist-orientated NDR was not allowed to die. The ANC documents, adopted by its conferences during the decade of 1997–2007 were mainly associated with the section of its leadership close to Thabo Mbeki, its president at the time, and in 1999–2008, the president of the country. Many in the SACP and COSATU sharply criticised these documents because, the critics said, not only was the pace of reforms too slow, but the country was generally heading in the wrong direction. Their rallying cry was the return of the ANC to the ideals of the Freedom Charter and 'the spirit of Morogoro'. According to Blade Nzimande, the SACP's Secretary General, at its November 2006 Augmented meeting the party's Central Committee came to the conclusion that 'the NDR requires some serious socialist type measures ... with a state that decisively intervenes in the economy and seeks to re-direct the massive resources in the hands of the capitalist class towards significant developmental projects'.[104] At its 9th Congress in September 2006 COSATU was even more outspoken. Its political resolution defined 'the political economy of the NDR in the current epoch as articulated in the Freedom Charter' and adopted 'an official position that rejects the separation of the NDR from socialism and asserts that the dictatorship of the proletariat is the only guarantee that there will be a transition from NDR to socialism'.[105]

The left's attack on the 2007 *Strategy and Tactics* was particularly vehement. The leaders of both the SACP and COSATU denounced it in the media, and a popular SACP *Communist University* site called it 'fascist' and entitled an article about it 'No Passaran'.[106] In the end the document was passed by the 2007 ANC's National Conference in Polokwane, but Mbeki and his followers – the document's authors and main movers – suffered a severe defeat at the hands of the team headed by his deputy, Jacob Zuma. This could not have been achieved without the support, rendered to him by the left, who were hoping that Zuma would correct Mbeki's 'deviations'.

It is impossible to say why Mbeki, a former communist and, for many years, a member of the SACP's Central Committee, chose a course which seemed to lead the country away

---

103. '*Strategy and Tactics of the ANC. Building A National Democratic Society. As adopted by the 52nd National Conference of the African National Congress, 16–20 December 2007, Polokwane, Limpopo*', http://www.anc. org.za/show.php?id=2535, accessed 3 February 2012.

104. B. Nzimande, 'The Motive Forces of the National Democratic Revolution', *Umsebenzi Online*, 6, 4 (7 March 2007). The wording of the declaration of the CC meeting is more cogent than that of Nzimande's report about it. See: *SACP, Statement of the Augmented Central Committee*. South African Communist Party, Media Release, 26 November 2006.

105. *Resolutions of the 9th COSATU National Congress*, 1.4 The National Democratic Revolution (NDR) and Socialism. N.d. [September 2006]. Besides other things, the resolution was an open recognition of the fact that the Charter *was* a socialist document, at least in the eyes of trade unionists.

106. DomzaNet, Communist-University@googlegro.com, accessed 6 April 2007.

from the prospect of socialism. Perhaps he had a change of heart, as happened to many of his Soviet colleagues. It may also have been that Mbeki – in the late 1960s a star student of Moscow's Lenin School – understood better than the SACP's present leadership, that without massive infusions of Soviet aid the socialist-orientated NDR could only be achieved through major economic and social upheavals. He certainly knew that the Soviet theoreticians of the NDR had unanimously and continuously stressed that the existence of the USSR was the main pre-condition and basis of building socialism through the NDR. And Mbeki's reading of the NDR in general and in the new global situation in particular may have been different from that of the SACP leaders: he may have believed that the NDR should first create a 'normal' racially mixed capitalist society, where race would not coincide with class, and later, when the conditions were ripe, move to a socialist transition. There is, after all, no doubt, that both nationally and internationally Mbeki followed an 'anti-imperialist' line, aligning his government with anti-Western forces, wherever and in whichever way possible.

After the 2009 national elections Zuma become the president of the country and rewarded the SACP and COSATU leadership with cabinet positions and the creation of a Planning Commission, whose main task was to redefine the country's economic policy. A new land bill began to make its way slowly through the legislature. But four years after the left's epochal victory at Polokwane, there was no real sign of dramatic change – and certainly not of a new, socialist NDR. Zuma had stressed that he just wanted business as usual – and thus it was.

It was at this stage that Julius Malema, the firebrand head of the ANC Youth League, which in 2007 was Zuma's most ardent supporter, demanded that the government nationalise the mines, banks and land. Malema constantly referred to the Freedom Charter, reminding the mother body that nationalisation was the underlying principle of this main policy document of the organisation. Malema 'stole' the drive for nationalisation from the SACP and COSATU, accusing them of unwillingness and an inability to act, and even suggested that the Youth League would from now on lead the struggles of the working class. This greatly upset the SACP and COSATU, and even the ANC leadership under Zuma and provoked indignation among those who had traditionally considered the demand for nationalisation and socialism as their political domain.

Malema was expelled from the ANC for indiscipline. But the slogan of nationalisation could not but seem appealing to the impoverished, unemployed and unemployable, mostly young population of South Africa. Malema may have been defeated but he has put the socialist-orientated NDR back on the South African political agenda, and the ANC leadership had to react.

Thus the conflict between the two visions of the NDR is still playing itself out on South African soil. The Soviet theoretical legacy is not going away.

The Genesis of the ANC's Armed Struggle in South Africa 1948–1961*

STEPHEN ELLIS

(Afrika-Studiecentrum, Leiden and Vrije Universiteit, Amsterdam)

Revelations made by veterans of the period, and the opening of various archives, have thrown significant new light on the origins of Umkhonto we Sizwe. It is now clear that the South African Communist Party (SACP) was the first component of the congress alliance to decide to launch an armed struggle against the apartheid state, in late 1960, having consulted the Chinese leader Mao Zedong in person. Only later was the issue debated in the senior organs of the African National Congress and other allied organisations. It has also become apparent that the first commander of Umkhonto we Sizwe, Nelson Mandela, was a member of the SACP. The main thrust of these observations is to demonstrate the degree to which the start of the armed struggle in South Africa was inscribed in the politics of the Cold War.

On 16 December 2011, South Africa commemorates the 50th anniversary of the start of hostilities by Umkhonto we Sizwe. The sixteenth of December 1961 is generally regarded as the formal beginning of the armed struggle that was to culminate in the 1994 election of South Africa's first majority government, led by the African National Congress (ANC). The month following the commemoration, January 2012, marks the centenary of the ANC's own foundation. The coincidence of these two anniversaries will be the occasion for much official celebration in South Africa and among friends of the ANC elsewhere.

Umkhonto we Sizwe was originally described by its leaders as an autonomous body formed by members of the ANC and members of the South African Communist Party (SACP) working in parallel. Key ANC leaders recognised Umkhonto we Sizwe as the ANC's armed wing within months of its creation, as this article will briefly describe. These days, Umkhonto we Sizwe – often known as MK for short – enjoys a prestigious position in official discourses on South Africa's liberation as the unit at the sharp edge of the long struggle against the apartheid state from which the ANC derives its historical legitimacy. Yet the story of Umkhonto we Sizwe's creation that emerges from recent research made possible by the opening of previously inaccessible archives, by interviews with key participants,[1] and by a spate of biographies and autobiographies,[2] differs significantly from the version of events that was popularised by the ANC itself over decades.[3] The most notable insights of new research

---

* Stephen Ellis is grateful to Paul Trewhela and to two anonymous readers for comments on a draft of this article. He is also grateful to Maxi Schoeman and her colleagues in the Department of Political Sciences at the University of Pretoria for providing him with a visiting fellowship in 2010.

1 B. Magubane, P. Bonner, J. Sithole, P. Delius, J. Cherry, P. Gibbs and T. April, 'The Turn to Armed Struggle', in South African Democracy Education Trust (SADET), *The Road to Democracy in South Africa: Volume 1 (1960–70)* (Cape Town, Zebra Press, 2004), pp. 53–145, may be regarded as the most complete account, and can also be considered as semi-official.

2 These are too numerous to list, but several are cited elsewhere in this article.

3 For example, F. Meli, *South Africa Belongs to Us: A History of the ANC* (London, James Currey, 1989), pp. 146–7.

concern the leading role played by the SACP in the creation of Umkhonto we Sizwe and the influence of the Cold War context of the early 1960s more generally.

The accounts of Umkhonto we Sizwe's origin that have received the widest circulation reflect the version of events given by the organisation's first commander,[4] Nelson Mandela, in his famous speech from the dock on 20 April 1964 during his trial by the Supreme Court in Pretoria. This oration is a modern classic of political rhetoric.[5] At its core is a reasoned justification, by a man expecting to be sentenced to death, of his choice to adopt a policy of violence against a state that denied voting rights to the majority of the population and a government that had refused time and again to respond to appeals for dialogue made by the ANC and others. In the course of his speech, Mandela gave a brief account of the formation of Umkhonto we Sizwe. His first-hand version of events, given under such dramatic circumstances, was for many years used by the ANC to argue for the justice of its recourse to arms. Mandela's own legal training had taught him that a speech from the dock was not made under oath and was not subject to cross-examination in court. The value of his testimony as evidence therefore remained untested.[6]

Mandela implied that the decision to turn to armed struggle arose from discussions in the second quarter of 1961 that culminated in a decision taken by himself and others 'at the beginning of June 1961', when he and some colleagues 'came to the conclusion that as violence in this country was inevitable, it would be unrealistic and wrong for African leaders to continue preaching peace and non-violence'.[7] The result was the establishment of Umkhonto we Sizwe, whose existence was announced to the South African public on 16 December of the same year. This was a highly symbolic date since 16 December figured in the ideology of the ruling National Party as Dingaan's Day or the Day of the Covenant, commemorating the 1838 Battle of Blood River, prior to which a party of *voortrekkers* preparing to confront a Zulu army had taken a public vow.

It has now become clear that Mandela's statement in his 1964 'I am prepared to die' speech did not do justice to the role played in the inception of the armed struggle by the SACP, which had received promises of support from the two Communist superpowers of the time, the Union of Soviet Socialist Republics (USSR) and China. Related to this omission, it is now possible to establish beyond reasonable doubt that Mandela himself was a member of the Communist Party for a period in the early 1960s, notwithstanding his own denials or evasions both then and subsequently.[8] This throws significant new light on the recent history of South Africa. Accordingly, this article reconstructs the main outlines of how key figures in the congress alliance, the opposition formation that included both the ANC and the SACP, arrived at their momentous decision to found Umkhonto we Sizwe and to take up arms against the South African state.

The Origins of South Africa's Armed Struggle

The drift towards armed struggle in South Africa may be traced back to the late 1940s,[9] when the end of the Second World War and the unexpected election of a National Party government

---

4 Noted by J. Slovo, *Slovo: The Unfinished Autobiography of ANC Leader Joe Slovo* (Melbourne, Ocean Press, 1997), p. 176.

5 N. Mandela, *I Am Prepared to Die* (London, International Defence and Aid Fund for Southern Africa, 1979), pp. 28–48.

6 C.J.B. Le Roux, 'Umkhonto we Sizwe: Its Role in the ANC's Onslaught against White Domination in South Africa, 1961–1988' (Ph.D. thesis, University of Pretoria, 1992), p. 47.

7 Mandela, *I Am Prepared to Die*, p. 33.

8 N. Mandela, *Long Walk to Freedom: The Autobiography of Nelson Mandela* (London, Abacus, 1995), p. 86.

9 Le Roux, 'Umkhonto we Sizwe', p. 1. Raymond Mhlaba, a key participant in the armed struggle, makes a similar assessment in *Personal Memoirs: Reminiscing from Rwanda and Uganda, Narrated to Thembeka Mufamadi* (Pretoria, Human Sciences Research Council and Robben Island Museum, 2001), pp. 56–7.

in 1948 transformed South African politics. In 1950, the Communist Party of South Africa (CPSA), threatened with legal suppression by a ferociously anti-communist government, chose to dissolve itself. Many activists of other persuasions feared that similarly draconian measures would soon be used against them. This, and the radical nature of the National Party's policy of apartheid more generally, caused some opponents of the government to wonder whether organised violence may not emerge as a real option within the foreseeable future. In 1952, Nelson Mandela, then beginning his legal career in Johannesburg, discussed the likelihood of a turn to armed struggle at some future date with his close friend Walter Sisulu.[10] Both men were already leading officials of the ANC: Sisulu having served as secretary-general since 1949 and Mandela being president of the movement's Transvaal section. Like many other former members of the ANC Youth League, who in earlier days had taken strongly 'Africanist' positions opposed to the influence of the Communist Party and other organisations that they thought to be dominated by minority ethnic groups, Mandela and Sisulu had come to appreciate the need for all who were opposed to apartheid to co-operate in their common interest. Both were leaders of the defiance campaign that provided the ANC with its first experience of mass, non-violent resistance and that received support from others in the emerging congress alliance.

As a consequence of working closely with activists outside the ANC, Walter Sisulu in particular moved closer to the Congress of Democrats, a body of white leftists that included many Communists in search of new outlets for their political activities following the dissolution of their party. In 1953, the same year that the small band of Communists secretly re-established the Party, this time under the name the South African Communist Party, Sisulu's contacts in the Congress of Democrats provided him with funds emanating from the World Federation of Democratic Youth, a Soviet front organisation, that enabled him to embark on a lengthy trip overseas with others including his ANC colleagues Duma Nokwe and Henry 'Squire' Makgothi. It was while Sisulu was preparing for this journey, which was to take him among other places to Romania, Poland, Russia and China, that Mandela again raised the question of violence, 'ask[ing] him to discuss the possibility of armed struggle with the Chinese'.[11] This Sisulu duly did, putting the idea to members of the central committee of the Chinese Communist Party whom he met during his stay in Beijing. His Chinese hosts are said to have responded in a non-committal way, commenting only that '[y]ou have to do it when the conditions are right'.[12]

Nor were Sisulu and Mandela alone in speculating about the eventual necessity for armed struggle. Oliver Tambo, who succeeded Sisulu as ANC secretary-general in 1955, later recalled that in that same year 'the question of violence was raised but deferred because of [the] situation'.[13] It was also around this time, according to Raymond Mhlaba, a member of both the ANC and the SACP, that '[s]ome of us even suggested the need to take up arms and engage the Boers militarily'.[14] Mhlaba recalled discussing the matter with Mandela and in the mid-to-late 1950s he made a series of proposals on these lines at meetings of the underground Communist Party.[15] Other people urging armed resistance at this time included what some authors term 'semi-gangster elements', among whom Sisulu placed the Sophiatown organiser of the ANC Youth League, Joe Modise.[16]

---

10 E. Sisulu, *Walter and Albertina Sisulu: In Our Lifetime* (Cape Town, David Philip, 2002), p. 146; Mandela, *Long Walk to Freedom*, p. 320.

11 Sisulu, *Walter and Albertina Sisulu*, p. 112.

12 Magubane *et al.*, 'The Turn to Armed Struggle', p. 54.

13 ANC minutes of Inkatha/ANC consultative meeting, London, 29–30 October 1979, 31 pp. Copy in Archive for Contemporary Affairs, University of the Free State, Bloemfontein, H.J. Coetsee Papers, PV357, 1/A1/5.

14 Mhlaba, *Personal Memoirs*, p. 107.

15 *Ibid.*

16 Magubane *et al.*, 'The Turn to Armed Struggle', p. 55.

Various accounts, then, suggest that by the mid-1950s a significant number of ANC leaders of the younger generation considered that a policy of armed struggle would have to be adopted at some future point even if it was inopportune at present. The most authoritative study of the matter concludes that some of them, including Sisulu and Mandela, regarded an armed struggle as inevitable.[17]

At this juncture, in 1956 the National Party government, reacting to the radicalism of the defiance campaign and to the emergence of a block of organisations allied in opposition to apartheid, indicted 156 people associated with the ANC and other organisations on charges of treason. Looking back many years later, a leading Communist, Lionel 'Rusty' Bernstein, described the treason trial as 'the great underestimated factor in the history of the South African movement'.[18] It brought anti-apartheid militants of various persuasions into closer contact than ever before as they sat together in the dock facing long prison sentences.

Other events and currents both inside and outside the country were also leading to a growing radicalisation of opinion within the ANC and some other sectors of the extra-parliamentary opposition in South Africa. The emancipation of the colonised and subjugated peoples of what was then becoming known as the Third World was emerging as a key theme of international affairs. Elsewhere in Africa, Algerian nationalists were fighting against France. In 1957 Ghana became the first colonial territory south of the Sahara to receive independence, and its prime minister and later president, Kwame Nkrumah, proclaimed himself the leader of a pan-African movement against colonial rule. Becoming steadily more militant during the course of his presidency, Nkrumah developed a close relationship with the People's Republic of China, which in time provided him with instructors for a training centre for guerrilla warfare where radicals from all over Africa could receive instruction.[19] Egypt's Gamal Abdel Nasser, apostle of Arab unity and anti-colonialism, was another radical African hero of the period. The veteran general secretary of the SACP, Moses Kotane, who also sat on the ANC's national executive, met some of the heroes of the anticolonial left, including Nasser, the Indian Prime Minister Jawarhalal Nehru and the Chinese foreign minister Zhou Enlai, at the Bandung conference in Indonesia in 1955.[20] The 1959 overthrow of the Batista government in Cuba by a guerrilla force led by Fidel Castro was an inspiration to militants of the left worldwide.

Within South Africa itself, violent disturbances in the rural areas of Zeerust and Sekhukhuneland engaged the attention of the most militant ANC and SACP members, who were able to connect to local activists in those areas.[21] The most important of this series of rural risings was an armed revolt by peasants in Pondoland, which 'profoundly influenced the whole orientation of the ANC leadership', in Bernstein's words, leading it to confront seriously the question of armed struggle, 'because there was the beginnings of an armed resistance movement'.[22] According to Mhlaba,[23] some activists in the radical ANC stronghold of the Eastern Cape at this time formed a group of volunteers dedicated to armed struggle apparently without seeking permission from their national leadership.

In this changing climate, advocates of armed struggle gained a more respectful hearing than in previous years. 'It was only later, towards the end of the 1950s, that Rusty Bernstein

---

17 *Ibid.*, p. 54.
18 R. Bernstein, 'Comments on Francis Meli's Manuscript? History of the ANC', South African Historical Papers, Cullen Library, University of the Witwatersrand, Johannesburg, Bernstein Papers AL 3051, R4.1–4.4.
19 *Nkrumah's Subversion in Africa* (Accra, Ministry of Information, no date [1966]).
20 B. Bunting, *Moses Kotane: South African Revolutionary* (London, Inkululeko Publications, 1986, rev. edn), Chapter 12.
21 Le Roux, 'Umkhonto we Sizwe', pp. 49–51.
22 Bernstein, 'Comments on Francis Meli's Manuscript? History of the ANC'.
23 Quoted in J. Buthelezi, 'The Struggle for Liberation Still Continues', undated MS [c.1971]. ANC archives, University of Fort Hare, Lusaka papers, additional material, box 53, folder 7.

asked why my question was not taken seriously within the new Communist Party', Mhlaba recalled in old age. 'From then on we discussed the issue of orchestrating an armed struggle. We discussed the recruitment and training of soldiers, how to obtain assistance from abroad and how to acquire weapons and explosives'.[24] Within the ranks of the 450 to 500[25] members that the SACP had at the end of the 1950s, two specific streams of militancy emerged, one among the black trade unionists who had been a special target for recruitment by the Party since the 1940s, the other among white veterans of the Second World War. One Communist militant, Arthur Goldreich, had experience of underground warfare with a Zionist group in Israel. Perhaps the most militant of all the combat veterans was Jack Hodgson, whose work as a miner had left him with an expert knowledge of explosives and whose wartime service had included front-line experience in North Africa. Hodgson not only began experimenting with bomb-making equipment but even, his widow later recalled, suggested that 'we should be robbing banks to raise money for our revolution'.[26]

On 21 March 1960, a demonstration in front of the police station in the township of Sharpeville led to the police shooting an estimated 69 people, leading to worldwide condemnation. The government responded by proclaiming a state of emergency and banning several organisations including the ANC. Some of those detained during the state of emergency that lasted from March to August 1960 are said to have discussed the prospect of armed struggle even while they were behind bars.[27] Among the 300 or so SACP members still at liberty, a handful of the Johannesburg comrades discussed armed resistance as they moved from one safe house to another to escape detention in April and May 1960. According to one participant, the leading SACP theoretician Michael Harmel made a presentation to his comrades suggesting that 'peaceful methods of struggle were over; that one had to now look at alternatives; and that the alternative was armed struggle – violence. And [the presentation] set this in the context of Marxist theory and communist theory, and revolutionary practice'.[28] In August 1960, Harmel proceeded to circulate a draft paper on armed struggle among a select group of Party members. This was subsequently adopted by the SACP central committee in the form of a document entitled 'South Africa: What Next?'[29]

As the authoritative chapter published in 2004 by the South African Democracy Education Trust (SADET) states, there is 'a good deal of evidence' that the SACP embraced a policy of armed struggle before any other body.[30] This finding, however, requires elaboration.

International Support

While the SACP was moving towards a policy of armed struggle, some of its leading members were able to discuss the issue extensively in Moscow, the home of international communism, and in Beijing, increasingly an alternative pole of influence in the communist world.

In July 1960, for the first time since the establishment of the SACP as an underground party seven years earlier, a delegation of South African Communists visited Moscow for talks with officials of the Communist Party of the Soviet Union (CPSU). SACP chairman Yusuf

---

24 Mhlaba, *Personal Memoirs*, p. 107.

25 V. Shubin, *ANC: A View from Moscow* (Johannesburg, Jacana, 2008, 2nd rev. edn), p. 5.

26 Rica Hodgson in an undated interview with Julie Frederikse: South African Historical Archive, Cullen Library, University of the Witwatersrand, Johannesburg, Frederikse collection, AL 2460.

27 Magubane *et al.*, 'The Turn to Armed Struggle', p. 71.

28 B. Turok, quoted in 'Umkhonto we Sizwe – The Formation of the MK', South African History Online, available at http://www.sahistory.org.za/pages/governance-projects/organisations/MK/MKframeset.htm, retrieved on 30 December 2010.

29 Shubin, *ANC*, p. 12.

30 Magubane *et al.*, 'The Turn to Armed Struggle', p. 80.

Dadoo and European representative Vella Pillay had a first round of meetings on their own.[31] Thereafter, these two were joined by Harmel and Joe Matthews, who came directly from South Africa before the end of August[32] with a view to attending a congress of Communist and workers' parties that was scheduled for November 1960. Before the start of their conference the South African delegates[33] took the opportunity to visit Beijing – inferior to the Soviet Union in prestige in the communist world but increasingly asserting its political and ideological independence. The South African delegation was received by no less than Chairman Mao Zedong in person. Chinese officials are said to have lectured the South Africans on the errors of Soviet thinking, while Mao listened to Dadoo's views on armed struggle without comment.[34] The South Africans also discussed the armed struggle with Deng Xiaoping, Mao's deputy and eventual successor, to whom they made a request for military training.[35] It is not clear precisely what Deng's answer was, but subsequent events suggest that it was far more positive than when Sisulu had raised the matter for the first time in Beijing seven years earlier.

After the Chinese interlude, the South Africans returned to Moscow where they duly participated in the November congress of Communist and workers' parties and had more talks with government and party officials. Joe Matthews later recalled 'putting forward the policy of armed struggle' during this period.[36] According to Matthews, he and Harmel spent several months in the USSR and had extensive talks with Soviet officials and military officers at Stalin's former dacha outside Moscow, used by the CPSU to receive representatives of 'fraternal parties', especially clandestine ones.[37] However, Vladimir Shubin, the author of the most detailed study of relations between the South African and Soviet communist parties and himself formerly a senior official working on related matters, makes no mention of this. He refers to several of the matters discussed by the South African delegation with their Soviet counterparts, including notably an agreement by the CPSU to give financial aid to the South African party (that amounted to $30,000 before the end of 1960), but writes that the SACP raised the question of armed struggle with its Soviet counterpart 'for the first time' only a year later, on 21 October 1961.[38] The talks referred to by Joe Matthews thus appear to have gone undocumented, at least in the archives consulted by Shubin.

The South Africans' discussions on armed struggle in Moscow and Beijing in the second half of 1960 occurred at a time when Soviet perspectives on issues of national liberation were changing fast in response to world events. The CPSU central committee had recently appointed a group of advisors to work on theoretical issues concerning national liberation.[39] In late 1960, an Africa section was formed within the central committee's international department[40] in recognition of the continent's enhanced political importance as a result of its decolonisation. The convening of the 1960 conference of Communist and workers' parties from all over the world was itself a reflection of a growing conviction among the USSR's

---

31 Shubin, *ANC*, pp. 25–6.
32 Magubane *et al.*, 'The Turn to Armed Struggle', p. 81, state that they arrived in Moscow in July 1960.
33 I. Filatova, 'The Lasting Legacy: The Soviet Theory of the National-Liberation Movement and South Africa', paper presented to the Liberation Struggles in Southern Africa workshop, University of Cape Town, 4–6 September 2008, p. 16, suggests that the whole group travelled to China. Shubin, *ANC*, p. 26, suggests that Dadoo went alone.
34 Information contained in an unpublished manuscript by Essop Pahad quoted in Shubin, *ANC*, pp. 26–7. In searching for the original manuscript in the ANC archive at the Mayibuye Centre, University of the Western Cape, Bellville, in February 2011, I was informed that it had been removed by ANC personnel.
35 Magubane *et al.*, 'The Turn to Armed Struggle', p. 81, where Deng's name is written as Dang Tsia-Ping.
36 *Ibid.*
37 Filatova, 'The Lasting Legacy', p. 16.
38 Shubin, *ANC*, p. 29.
39 Filatova, 'The Lasting Legacy', p. 7.
40 Shubin, *ANC*, p. 24.

rulers that the decolonisation movement in Asia and Africa was a precursor to the collapse of the capitalist system worldwide.[41]

In developing a new perspective on African nationalist movements with a view to determining their suitability as allies, Marxist-Leninist theoreticians were able to draw on views expressed by Lenin himself and on ideas about a two-stage revolution that went as far back as the earliest debates within the Russian Social Democratic Party, the forerunner of the CPSU. In a series of speeches and articles starting with his contributions at the second congress of the Communist International, or Comintern, in 1920, Lenin had argued that national liberation movements could be allies of the Soviet Communist Party.[42] In 1928, this line of argument was adopted by the CPSA after the Comintern's sixth congress had instructed South African delegates present in Moscow to campaign for the establishment of an 'independent native republic' in conformity with current thinking in the motherland of international communism. The decision caused consternation among the many CPSA members who had previously regarded South Africa's white proletariat rather than its black population as their main focus of action. In 1935, however, at its next congress, the Comintern withdrew the independent native republic slogan as abruptly as it had introduced it.[43] Obedient to direction from Moscow, the CPSA then turned its attention away from black political emancipation to the struggle for workers' immediate interests, concentrating on work with trade unions. After the Soviet Union's entry into the Second World War on the same side as the South African government in 1941 the CPSA had even less strategic interest in encouraging nationalist activity among the country's black population. Accordingly, the CPSA's official programme published in 1944, and supplemented in 1947 and 1949, made no mention of a national liberation struggle. It proclaimed its goal to be 'the establishment of a Socialist Republic based on the common ownership of the means of production and the rule of the working class and providing equal rights and opportunities for all racial and national groups'. Nor did it make any substantial mention of race.[44]

Only after the election of the National Party and the implementation of its apartheid policy did the CPSA once again begin to explore the idea of an alliance with black nationalists. At the CPSA's January 1950 conference, its last before its dissolution, discussion of an alliance between Communists and bourgeois proponents of a national-democratic revolution is said to have been greeted 'with great acclamation'.[45] Thereafter, the CPSA's underground successor, the SACP, was impelled to work with the ANC and other anti-apartheid organisations even in the absence of any clear ideological or strategic framework. Some Party members wanted to pursue an idea already apparent in the report of the CPSA central committee to the 1950 Party conference, namely that South Africa was itself a colonial power of sorts.[46] This notion was also being developed by the liberal thinker Leo Marquard, president of the South African Institute of Race Relations, who argued that South Africa was by nature a colonial power, the country's African areas being its colonies.[47]

---

41 Filatova, 'The Lasting Legacy', p. 7.
42 *Ibid.*, p. 2.
43 B. Hirson, 'Bukharin, Bunting and the "Native Republic" Slogan', *Searchlight South Africa*, 3 (July 1989), pp. 51–65.
44 'Programme of the Communist Party of South Africa Adopted at the National Conference in Johannesburg in January 1944', Document 82 in *South African Communists Speak: Documents from the History of the South African Communist Party 1915–1980* (London, Inkululeko Publications, 1981), p. 188.
45 University of Cape Town, Simons Papers, BC1081, 0.1, Jack Simons to Dirk Kotzé, 20 April 1991.
46 Filatova, 'The Lasting Legacy', p. 17. For a substantial extract from the report, see 'Nationalism and the Class Struggle', Document 91 in *South African Communists Speak*, pp. 200–11.
47 Simons papers, 0.4, letter from Jack Simons to the editor of the *Cape Times*, 23 July 1993; Filatova, 'The Lasting Legacy', p. 17, notes that Marquard's 1957 presidential address to the SAIRR was devoted to this subject.

Given the direction taken by their own Party over several years, therefore, the South African Communists who visited Moscow in 1960 were delighted to find an atmosphere in which national liberation was so clearly in vogue in the very home of their movement. The new theories on nationalism emanating from advisers of the CPSU central committee offered South African Communists a way of resolving the contradiction between their aspiration to bring about a socialist revolution and their efforts to resist the white minority government in partnership with others who were not committed to the same ultimate goal. It meant that South African revolutionaries could concentrate in the first instance on the task of liberating the black national majority, as in colonies elsewhere in Africa, in the knowledge that this was in conformity with Marxist revolutionary science. SACP theoreticians duly determined that South Africa was the site of a colonialism of a special type, remarkable for the fact that coloniser and colonised lived in the same national territory. This was to become the key analytical concept in the SACP's 1962 programme, *The Road to South African Freedom*.[48] Many statements in this manifesto were actually quotations from the documents of the meeting of Communist and workers' parties that Dadoo and his colleagues had attended in Moscow two years previously.[49] In order to be sure that its analysis was a correct one, the SACP sent the draft of its 1962 programme to the central committee of the CPSU for perusal before it was passed.[50]

In short, it appears that towards the end of 1960, some leaders of the SACP had decided in principle to adopt a policy of armed struggle. They had raised the issue, officially or unofficially, with leading figures in both the Soviet Union and China, including in personal meetings with Mao Zedong and Deng Xiaoping, senior members of the Chinese Communist Party. Thereafter, the SACP seems to have moved quickly to endorse the new policy formally, adopting it at a Party conference at the end of 1960, when Harmel was still in Moscow. Rusty Bernstein recalled that discussion on the issue was short,[51] no doubt since it had already been extensively debated beforehand and was known to have at least the unofficial approval of the CPSU. Ben Turok has also provided a description of this meeting, which took place 'towards the end of 1960'. He recalls Bernstein reading a draft resolution on armed struggle. After it was approved, Bernstein burned the document.[52]

To be precise, the Party conference that took the momentous decision to launch an armed struggle is reported to have 'instructed its Central Committee to devise a Plan of Action that would involve the use of economic sabotage'.[53]

The Formation of Umkhonto we Sizwe

Even before March 1960, South Africans of various backgrounds had gone beyond debating whether they should take up arms against the government to actually organising small groups for the task, although they were pitifully ill-equipped. Andrew Masondo, an academic who was later to be a leading member of both the SACP and the ANC, recalled that 'the idea of the [congress] movement moving away from its non-violent stance was discussed within youth circles even earlier than 1960. I remember that a group of us at Fort Hare actually formed a

---

48 Document 115 in *South African Communists Speak*, pp. 284–320.
49 Filatova, 'The Lasting Legacy', p. 15.
50 According to Vladimir Shubin, cited in Filatova, 'The Lasting Legacy', p. 18.
51 L. Bernstein, *Memory Against Forgetting: Memoirs from a Life in South African Politics, 1938–1964* (London, Viking, 1999), p. 225.
52 B. Turok, *Nothing But the Truth: Behind the ANC's Struggle Politics* (Johannesburg, Jonathan Ball, 2003), pp. 122–3.
53 J.N. Lazerson, *Against the Tide: Whites in the Struggle against Apartheid* (Boulder, CO, Westview Press, 1994), p. 230.

group to prepare for the eventuality of an armed struggle taking place'.[54] This did not last, though, 'because we were not a homogenous group ideologically'.[55] Radical young ANC members like these became particularly impatient with their organisation's policy of non-violence after a split in 1958–9, when an Africanist wing broke away to form the rival Pan-Africanist Congress (PAC), threatening to outbid the ANC in radicalism.

After the Sharpeville massacre, South Africans of many persuasions were actively planning violent attacks in opposition to apartheid. On 9 April 1960, the day after the banning of the ANC and the PAC, a white farmer tried to murder Prime Minister Hendrik Verwoerd, firing two shots into his face. Mandela, as a leading ANC militant, was keenly aware of the upsurge of subversive activity. According to police sources, in May 1960 he persuaded some people who had been preparing to launch acts of sabotage to postpone their plans in favour of a co-ordinated approach.[56] This is perhaps a reference to the existing body of ANC volunteers in the Eastern Cape who had been 'able to go underground with the whole force still intact' after the ANC's banning.[57] There was a notable increase in radical activity after the lifting of the state of emergency in August 1960 had released thousands of militants back onto the streets. By this time, some ANC radicals were making common cause with other networks to form *ad hoc* sabotage groups. The Trotskyite socialist Baruch Hirson recalled the rivalry of the time in his memoirs, writing that '[w]e could see the possibility of one of these movements outstripping everyone else, leaving people like us behind'. He went on to recollect how 'the only way to prevent our eclipse was to seize the moment'.[58] Some ANC radicals took initiatives of their own, such as the former ANC Youth League activist Joe Modise, who joined a small group that tried to blow up the railway line between Soweto and Johannesburg in May 1961.[59] The PAC was advocating a style of radical populism that threatened to unleash a race war. Monty Berman, a Communist Party member who wanted to establish a broad front of anti-apartheid forces, worked with John Lang of the Liberal Party to set up a National Committee for Liberation (NCL). The NCL soon merged with yet another group to become the African Resistance Movement (ARM);[60] Berman, piqued at being excluded from any leading role in the Communist Party's own incipient sabotage network,[61] threw himself into this alternative. Although the ARM is generally said to have been established only in 1964, the Truth and Reconciliation Commission of the 1990s reports that it existed already in 1961.[62] A state intelligence file also claims that a predecessor of the ARM, known only as 'the group', existed in 1961.[63] Masondo recalled that ANC militants frustrated by their own organisation's official policy of non-violence were attracted by the ARM.[64] Together, these reports suggest that many of the rather bewildering number of subversive organisations founded in the early 1960s had a rather weak institutional identity. Many are probably better described as networks than organisations, arising from within a fairly limited pool of activists.

---

54 A. Masondo, 'Sawing Electric Pylons', *Dawn*, souvenir issue (1986), pp. 21–3.
55 *Ibid.*
56 'Kampanje vir die vrijlating van Nelson Mandela', 'uiters geheim' memorandum, c.1981, H.J. Coetsee Papers, PV 357, 1/M1/48.
57 Mhlaba, quoted in Buthelezi, 'The Struggle for Liberation Still Continues'.
58 B. Hirson, *Revolutions in My Life* (Johannesburg, Witwatersrand University Press, 1995), p. 301.
59 J. Modise, 'The Happiest Moment in My Life', *Dawn*, souvenir issue (1986), p.10.
60 C. Vermaak, *The Red Trap: Communism and Violence in South Africa* (Johannesburg, A.P.B. Publishers, 1966), pp. 55–6.
61 Slovo, *Slovo*, p. 152.
62 *Truth and Reconciliation Commission of South Africa Report* (Pretoria, TRC/Department of Justice, 1998), Volume 2, p. 10.
63 South African National Defence Force Documentation Centre, Pretoria, MID/MI group 6, L/04, African Resistance Movement.
64 Masondo, 'Sawing Electric Pylons', p. 21.

The government, meanwhile, faced the post-Sharpeville crisis with a show of bravado. Prime Minister Verwoerd, stung by a public warning from his British counterpart, Harold Macmillan, about the wind of change sweeping through Africa, rather than offer any concession that might be construed as weakness, began to prepare South Africa's departure from the Commonwealth and a declaration of its new status as a republic. He did not deign to consult any organised body of opinion outside the white community. In 1961 he appointed to the Justice ministry the right-winger John Vorster, once a general of the paramilitary Ossewabrandwag. Vorster proceeded to introduce laws permitting detention without trial. Yet it seems that neither the South African government nor any of the disparate groups and networks plotting campaigns of violence had any idea that before the end of 1960 the SACP had already had talks with senior officials of two superpowers on the opening of an armed struggle against the apartheid state.

The SACP's international connections were not the only asset it enjoyed, despite its small size. The Party had a discipline that no rival organisation could match. Its members had a ready guide to conspiratorial work in the form of texts by Lenin and other Marxist theoreticians of struggle. Like some of the white militants in rival groups, there were SACP members with combat experience, while others were professional engineers, such as David Kitson and Dennis Goldberg, or had other skills that could be used for bomb-making.

So, reassured by Soviet theoreticians of the suitability of a nationalist alliance, the SACP set about preparing to launch its campaign. It was clear that it would need to prepare public opinion and, more specifically, that it would require some sort of arrangement with the ANC. This had to be achieved at a time when both organisations were outlawed and many individuals were subject to various legal restrictions. Furthermore, the ANC's president, Albert Luthuli, remained committed to a strategy of non-violence. He, too, almost certainly was uninformed of the talks in the USSR and China.

The only ANC members who definitely knew of the progress being made by the SACP towards organising armed resistance were those who were also senior members of the Party. Since ANC membership was formally open to black South Africans only, this meant that a crucial position was occupied by the handful of senior black Communists who were also ANC members. These included most notably Moses Kotane, who was the general secretary of the SACP as well as being an influential member of the ANC's national executive committee. Of the 15 people elected to the SACP central committee in 1958,[65] five were also members of the ANC. Other than Kotane, these included Sisulu and Mhlaba, long-term advocates of armed struggle. It is notable that one of four other people co-opted to the SACP central committee in mid-1960 was ANC member Joe Matthews,[66] who was to participate in the meetings in Moscow and Beijing later that year that were so crucial to the decision to launch an armed struggle.

According to Matthews, another prominent ANC militant was also co-opted by the Party's central committee at this time – Nelson Mandela. Near the end of his life Matthews stated that Mandela had sat on the Party's central committee at the same time as himself.[67]

The police often suspected Mandela of being a SACP member. The prosecution at his trial in 1964 produced as an exhibit a 62-page manuscript entitled 'How to be a Good Communist', written in Mandela's own hand, one of the hundreds of documents found by police in their raid on Umkhonto we Sizwe and SACP headquarters at Lilliesleaf Farm,

---

65 Shubin, *ANC*, p. 7.
66 *Ibid.*
67 In an interview with Irina Filatova on 4 November 2004, quoted in A. Davidson and I. Filatova, *Rossiia I Yuzhnaia Africa: Tri veka sviazej, 1960–2010 (Russia and South Africa: Three Centuries of Contacts. Part Two: 1960–2010)* (Moscow, Publishing House of the Higher School of Economics, forthcoming), Chapter 3.

Rivonia, in July 1963. This four-part text appears to have been largely a translation of an original by Liu Shao-chi,[68] the president of the People's Republic of China from 1959 to 1968 who was eventually purged by Chairman Mao and died in prison. Mandela had apparently acquired it from Joe Matthews[69] or Rusty Bernstein.[70] When asked to explain this document, Mandela claimed that he had been asked to edit 'How to be a Good Communist' to improve its readability.[71] Whenever he was asked whether he was ever a communist, Mandela was somewhat evasive. 'Well I don't know if I did become a Communist', he replied to a leading question from his own attorney towards the end of the marathon treason trial in 1960. 'If by Communist you mean a member of the Communist Party and a person who believes in the theory of Marx, Engels, Lenin, and Stalin, and who adheres strictly to the discipline of the party, I did not become a Communist'.[72] From prison in 1966 he wrote to the Department of Justice to 'emphatically deny that I was a member of the CPSA'[73] – a telling formulation, since he well knew that the CPSA had been extinct since 1950.

One of the historic leaders of the SACP, Joe Slovo, described in his autobiography his impression of Mandela in 1961. He noted that '[i]deologically [Mandela] had taken giant strides since we confronted one another in the corridors of the University during the early 1950s on the role of the Party in the struggle. His keen intelligence taught him to grasp the class basis of national oppression'.[74]

We can interpret Slovo's remark as a rather coy way of saying that Mandela had become a Communist, as at least three other prominent members of the SACP, including Matthews, have testified to Mandela's Party membership, and others have hinted at it. Vital documentary testimony is contained in the minutes of a regular Party meeting in 1982 which record former central committee member John Pule Motshabi recalling that Mandela had been recruited at the time J.B. Marks was campaigning for chairmanship of the Party, in other words before 1962.[75] Another leading Party member, Hilda Bernstein, interviewed years later, was adamant on the question of Mandela's Party membership. 'Mandela denies that he was ever a member of the party but I can tell you that he was a member of the party for a period', she stated in 2004,[76] and the same interviewer also received confirmation from Brian Bunting.[77] Two senior Party members arrested by the police told their interrogators that Mandela had attended a SACP meeting in 1961 and a central committee meeting in 1962.[78]

In light of this evidence it seems most likely that Nelson Mandela joined the Party in the late 1950s or in 1960 and that he was co-opted to the central committee in the latter year, the same year as Joe Matthews. That Mandela's name does not figure in the central committee membership list quoted by Shubin from his research in Soviet as well as South African archives[79] is by no means strong counter-evidence since, as the former SACP activist Ben

---

68 A. Sampson, *Mandela: The Authorized Biography* (New York, Alfred A. Knopf, 1999), p. 189.
69 Magubane *et al.*, 'The Turn to Armed Struggle', p. 55.
70 Sampson, *Mandela*, p. 189.
71 Police file on Nelson Mandela, confidential source. See also Shubin, *ANC*, p. 44.
72 S. Johns and R.H. Davis, Jr. (eds), *Mandela, Tambo and the African National Congress: The Struggle Against Apartheid, 1948–1990: A Documentary Survey* (New York, Oxford University Press, 1991), p. 71.
73 Sampson, *Mandela*, p. 136.
74 Slovo, *Slovo*, pp. 175–6.
75 Simons papers, BC1081, 0.7.2, Minutes of SACP Africa Group Meeting, 13 May 1982.
76 H. Bernstein, interview with P. O'Malley, 25 August 2004, *O'Malley: The Heart of Hope*, available at http://www.nelsonmandela.org/omalley/index.php/site/q/03lv00017/04lv00344/05lv01461/06lv01476.htm, retrieved on 23 October 2010.
77 P. O'Malley, *Shades of Difference: Mac Maharaj and the Struggle for South Africa* (New York, Viking Penguin, 2007), p. 63, noting that other sources are embargoed until 2030.
78 Testimony by Piet Beyleveld (1964) and Fred Carneson (1966), quoted in 'Kampanje vir die vrijlating van Nelson Mandela', Coetsee Papers, PV 357, 1/M1/48.
79 Shubin, *ANC*, p. 7.

Turok writes, 'few, if anyone, knew the entire membership'[80] of a Party that had organised itself in a series of hermetic cells to avoid detection and that operated on a need-to-know basis.

The fact of Mandela's Party membership throws an interesting light on the sequence of events after the SACP had taken its formal decision to begin an armed struggle in the last weeks of 1960. In early 1961 Mandela took the lead in a public campaign urging the government to convene a national convention that would be a last chance to talk to the extra-parliamentary opposition. A close analysis of the campaign for a national convention concludes that this initiative was primarily intended to provide proponents of armed struggle with a paper trail that would justify their forthcoming change of policy.[81] In other words, the SACP, having decided to organise a campaign of armed resistance and knowing that the government remained closed to dialogue, was concerned to present matters in the best possible light for public and international consumption. Mandela was the best person for this job.

The Party also looked to Mandela to bring the ANC round to the idea of armed struggle. For while the ANC had for years been home to militants in favour of taking up arms, its president, Chief Luthuli, was an advocate of non-violence, as were other leading lights of the multilateral congress alliance that constituted the broad nationalist movement that the SACP saw as its partner in struggle. Some leaders of the South African Indian Congress had learned methods of non-violent resistance from none other than Gandhi himself during the many years the Mahatma lived in South Africa.

It was in order to deal with the position of allied organisations that in mid-1961 the main advocates of armed struggle within the ANC, led by Nelson Mandela, set up a series of meetings within the decision-making organs of the ANC and its partners in the congress alliance. These were the meetings that Mandela referred to in his 1964 'I am prepared to die' speech as the pivotal moment in the decision to launch an armed struggle. Thus, after consulting Sisulu, Mandela convened a meeting of the ANC working committee in June 1961, where he presented the proposal for the formation of a military organisation.[82] This meeting was secret, like all meetings of the banned ANC at that time.

It is most striking that one of the senior ANC members present at the working committee meeting who argued most strongly against the proposal to adopt a policy of armed struggle was Moses Kotane, who spoke in favour of continuing with non-violent protest. Kotane's reasoning was simply that the advocates of armed struggle were unprepared for the consequences. His stance is surprising because he was the general secretary of the SACP as well as being a member of the ANC's governing body. How could he argue against a policy of armed struggle within the councils of the ANC when the Communist Party had already decided in favour, especially when the practice of democratic centralism required that once the Party's senior organ had decided on a policy, all members must concur? It seems unlikely that Kotane was stating a view he did not actually espouse in order to lay a false trail regarding the Party's role. The most probable answer is that Kotane managed the problem posed by dual membership by reasoning that he spoke within ANC fora as an ANC member, and was therefore entitled to articulate his personal view rather than that of his Party.[83] If so, this was a measure both of the depth of Kotane's conviction concerning the folly of armed struggle at this juncture and of his standing within the SACP, as his action carried the risk of

---

80 Turok, *Nothing But the Truth*, p. 49. Slovo, *Slovo*, p. 130, describes the ultra-secretive method of election to the central committee.
81 Le Roux, 'Umkhonto we Sizwe', pp. 94–5.
82 Mandela, *Long Walk to Freedom*, p. 320.
83 Magubane *et al.*, 'The Turn to Armed Struggle', p. 88.

his being stripped of his office. But despite his opposition to armed struggle, Kotane told Mandela in private that he could agree to the issue being raised with the movement's highest authority, the national executive.[84] This led to a subsequent meeting, also in Durban, the following week.

Today, the ANC national executive committee meeting of June 1961, held in secret, at night, is presented in popular histories as the most dramatic of all those at which the issue of armed struggle was debated, not least because of the presence of Luthuli.[85] Luthuli, recognising that there was a substantial current of opinion inside the movement in favour of taking up arms, accepted that a military organisation could be formed provided that it was separate from and independent of the ANC. The national executive committee agreed to this formula.[86] This meant that as from June 1961, the ANC remained formally committed to non-violence even though some of its leading members were engaged in preparing violent activities on behalf of another organisation, soon to be dubbed Umkhonto we Sizwe, Zulu and Xhosa for the Spear of the Nation.

The decision of the ANC's national executive to turn a blind eye to the formation of a new militant organisation paved the way for a further discussion to be held by the joint executive of the entire congress alliance, which met just a day later, also in Durban. This included representatives not only of the ANC but also the Indian Congress, the Coloured People's Congress, the South African Congress of Trade Unions and the Congress of Democrats. All of these organisations included members of the clandestine SACP in their ranks. This meeting too was a dramatic affair, although less momentous than that of the previous day as the congress alliance's governing body generally accepted ANC decisions in deference to the ANC's superior size and weight. According to Mandela's account, Chief Luthuli opened proceedings by saying that even though the ANC had endorsed the decision on the formation of a military unit, it remained a matter of such gravity that those present should consider the issue afresh. Once again Nelson Mandela made the case in favour and, after a night of discussion, he received a mandate from the organisations represented at this meeting.[87] The way was now open for militants to assemble the people and the resources to initiate a campaign of sabotage, secure in the knowledge that they had substantial backing within organisations that had a popular base far wider than that of the tiny SACP.

In a speech in 2010, President Jacob Zuma claimed not only that Luthuli supported the foundation of Umkhonto we Sizwe, but that he was actually the one who gave it its name.[88] Yet a study of Luthuli's writings concludes that he never renounced his personal commitment to non-violent methods, on account of which he was awarded a Nobel peace prize in 1961, and that he never underwent a conversion to the cause of armed struggle.[89] It is possible that both versions are accurate in the sense that Luthuli remained a partisan of non-violence while wishing to remain informed of events affecting the movement of which he remained the nominal president until his death in 1967. He continued to attend meetings that tracked the progress of the ANC abroad, without questioning the creation of Umkhonto we Sizwe.[90] Joe Slovo confirmed the strength of the support for non-violence within the ANC and allied movements when he stated that the main reason for making Umkhonto we Sizwe independent

84 Mandela, *Long Walk to Freedom*, p. 321.
85 'Umkhonto we Sizwe – The Formation of the MK'. See also Mandela, *Long Walk to Freedom*, pp. 321–2.
86 Mandela, *Long Walk to Freedom*, p. 322.
87 *Ibid.*, pp. 323–4.
88 'Zuma Praises Albert Luthuli', 25 November 2010, *News 24*, available at http://www.news24.com/SouthAfrica/Politics/Zuma-praises-Albert-Luthuli-20101124, retrieved on 15 March 2011.
89 S.E. Couper, '"An Embarrassment to the Congresses?": The Silencing of Chief Albert Luthuli and the Production of ANC History', *Journal of Southern African Studies*, 35, 2 (June 2009), pp. 331–48.
90 R. Kasrils, *Armed and Dangerous: My Undercover Struggle Against Apartheid* (Oxford, Heinemann, 1993), pp. 49–50.

was 'that we had just emerged from a phase when the whole congress movement had not officially broken with old policies', the Indian congresses being especially deeply committed to non-violence.[91] What is clear, however, is that once leading members of the ANC had committed themselves to a policy of violence, albeit under the flag of the nominally autonomous organisation called Umkhonto we Sizwe, the authority of Luthuli, banned by the government and presiding over a movement that was proceeding on a different path, drained away. Luthuli played little further role in ANC decision-making, which passed swiftly into the hands of members who went into exile.[92]

The Durban Communist Rowley Arenstein interpreted the adoption of armed struggle by the ANC as 'the act of the Johannesburg SACP clique – a hijacking!'[93] In this regard it is telling to note the key role played by the ANC's working collective in Johannesburg, which 'took the plunge into the new phase of revolutionary violence' in partnership with the SACP's central committee and piloted the decision through the ANC's structures.[94] The ANC's working collective in Johannesburg included Kotane, J.B. Marks, Mandela, Sisulu and Duma Nokwe,[95] all of whom may now be seen to have been prominent SACP members. In other words, the Party had control over the decision-making process that led to the creation of Umkhonto we Sizwe both through its own organs and through the presence of Party members within a key committee of the ANC.

'Luthuli was simply brushed aside', Arenstein told an interviewer. 'He was told that MK was separate from the ANC, that the ANC should stay committed to non-violence but that he shouldn't expel individual ANC members who participated in MK'.[96] There is contemporary evidence to support the contention that the creation of Umkhonto we Sizwe as a nominally autonomous organisation was a purely tactical manoeuvre, as, in May 1962, Mandela, together with two leaders of the ANC's external wing, Oliver Tambo and Robert Resha, wrote a memorandum to the government of Ghana describing Umkhonto we Sizwe as 'an armed organization formed by the A.N.C. to carry out planned attacks'.[97] Later in the year, after Resha had stated publicly in London that Umkhonto we Sizwe was the ANC's armed wing,[98] the ANC dropped the line that it was not committed to violence.

Joe Slovo subsequently explained the mechanics of creating the new organisation in pursuit of the agreements reached in mid-1961. 'To constitute the [Umkhonto we Sizwe] High Command the ANC appointed Mandela and the Party appointed me',[99] he wrote. Since, in fact, Mandela was also a senior member of the Party, this joint division of labour with the ANC was a mere form of words that disguised the degree of the Party's influence. Soon, few people remembered the legalistic contortion that the ANC remained committed to non-violence in spite of the fact that some of its leading members were also the commanders of a guerrilla force, and Umkhonto we Sizwe became regarded simply as the ANC's army. The bulk of ANC members never knew, then or subsequently, how their organisation had been bounced into adopting the armed struggle.

---

91 J. Slovo, 'The Sabotage Campaign', *Dawn*, souvenir issue (1986), p. 24.
92 Couper, "An Embarrassment to the Congresses?".
93 Attributed to Rowley Arenstein by Professor Colin Bundy, panel discussion of the history of the SACP, University of the Western Cape, 18 January 1991, Simons Papers, 0.1.
94 Slovo, *Slovo*, p. 173.
95 *Ibid.*
96 Interview with R.W. Johnson in *London Review of Books*, 13, 4 (21 February 1991), pp. 22–3.
97 'Memorandum Presented to the Government of the Republic of Ghana by the African National Congress of South Africa', 10 May 1962, Padmore Library, Accra. I am grateful to Jan-Bart Gewald for supplying a copy of this document.
98 Slovo, *Slovo*, p. 177.
99 Slovo, 'The Sabotage Campaign', p. 24.

Members of the SACP were adept at backroom politics of this type. The Party was, as Rusty Bernstein put it, 'a sect'.[100] Since the original Communist Party had been banned by law in 1950, its members had adopted the practice of joining other organisations through which they could exercise their self-appointed role in the vanguard of revolutionary change. These were circumstances to which Leninist techniques of political organisation were perfectly adapted. Turok was later to recall 'how easy it was for a small group like ours to exert much influence in the mass movement without giving away our existence'.[101] In the many cases where Party members were also members of another organisation, such as the ANC or the Congress of Democrats, internal Party discipline required that 'at all times, the first loyalty of Party members is to their Party',[102] the very rule that Kotane flouted in 1961 when he argued in ANC meetings against adopting a policy of armed struggle.

The Armed Struggle in Cold War Context

Armed with a mandate from the round of ANC meetings in June 1961, Slovo and Mandela led the effort to form Umkhonto we Sizwe into a real organisation. Within six months the new outfit had some 250 members[103] drawn from both the ANC and the SACP. SACP member Mac Maharaj, at that time studying in England, had been 'approached ... to go for training' as early as March 1961, and was sent to East Germany to train originally as a printer, and subsequently in sabotage.[104] Joe Modise, whose militancy had already led him to carry out sabotage actions, was enlisted by Communist Party members Duma Nokwe and Walter Sisulu.[105]

Rival networks were also making their mark, with Monty Berman's group carrying out an arson attack in September 1961.[106] Tambo, Mandela and Resha claimed in their memorandum to the Ghanaian government that Umkhonto we Sizwe's first act of sabotage was an attack on Johannesburg's phone system in October 1961,[107] which in fact was almost certainly the work of one of the liberal groups that fused to form the ARM. Straining to impose its own authority over the emerging sabotage campaign, the SACP infiltrated some of its own people into these networks.[108] The PAC was organising militant networks that were soon to result in the emergence of Poqo.[109]

The SACP central committee now implemented the plans for foreign training that it had been preparing since the visits to Moscow and Beijing by leading members the previous year. It gave highest priority to the training of those earmarked as future officers of Umkhonto we Sizwe, later referred to as the high command. In October 1961, the central committee sent a coded message to Raymond Mhlaba instructing him to leave for military training abroad. He slipped out of the country in company with Andrew Mlangeni.[110] Travelling via Tanzania,

---

100 Bernstein papers, AL3051, R4.1–4.4, notes for an autobiography.
101 Turok, *Nothing But the Truth*, p. 44.
102 South African Study Group, North-West London, 'On the Communist Party', 1959, 12pp. typescript, Simons Papers, 0.1.
103 Le Roux, 'Umkhonto we Sizwe', p. 126.
104 M. Maharaj interviewed by H. Bernstein in 1991, available at http://www.nelsonmandela.org/omalley/index.php/site/q/03lv03445/04lv03996/05lv04011.htm, retrieved on 28 December 2010.
105 Modise, 'The Happiest Moment in My Life', p. 10.
106 T. Karis and G. Gerhart, *From Protest to Challenge: A Documentary History of African Politics in South Africa, 1882-1990, Vol. 5, Nadir and Resistance, 1964–1979* (Pretoria, Unisa Press, 1997), p. 22.
107 'Memorandum Presented to the Government of the Republic of Ghana'.
108 Vermaak, *The Red Trap*, p. 57.
109 B.B. Maaba, 'The PAC's War Against the State, 1960-1963', in SADET, *The Road to Democracy*, Vol. 1, pp. 257–97.
110 Mhlaba, *Personal Memoirs*, pp. 111–12; Slovo, *Slovo*, p. 173, gives the date as September 1961.

Ghana and the USSR to his final destination in China, Mhlaba met others sent for military training in the same country. They were Joe Gqabi, Wilton Mkwayi, Patrick Mthembu and Steve Naidoo, the latter coming from London, where he had been living for some years.

After arriving in China the trainees were divided into two groups, one sent to Shen-Yon military academy, the other stationed in Nanjing.[111] They were visited by Chairman Mao Zedong in person, Mhlaba recalled.[112] In addition to seeking the South Africans' opinions on Sino-Soviet issues, Mao is said to have questioned them about class conditions in their region, about the terrain, and about the degree of military experience of opponents of the South African regime. Mao 'urged his listeners not to follow blindly the experience of the Chinese Red Army. He suggested to them that the experience of the FLN [Front de libération nationale] in opposition to French colonial rule in Algeria might be more relevant', according to Paul Trewhela,[113] a Party member who gleaned information from key members of the underground. It is astonishing that this personal contact with such a senior Communist leader went undetected by the South African police, did not emerge at subsequent trials, and remained unknown outside a tiny circle until the present century.

So secret was the Chinese training that even senior ANC officer-holders remained uninformed. On his way back from Nanjing to rejoin his comrades in South Africa, Mhlaba passed through Tanzania where he met Oliver Tambo, leader of the ANC's external mission, soon to take over the effective leadership of the ANC as its internal structures crumbled in the face of government repression. Tambo 'did not know about our military training in China', Mhlaba noted.[114] Most early military trainees, however, were sent to African countries. In June 1962, some 32 recruits left South Africa for this purpose,[115] and a further 135 fighters from camps in Tanzania were sent to various countries for training in the half-year from September 1962,[116] with larger groups to follow.

At the outset, Umkhonto we Sizwe's strategic thinking was based on the supposition that the apartheid state was brittle enough for a determined offensive to inspire a wider insurrection that would overwhelm it. This optimism was sustained by a Marxist-Leninist analysis that South Africa was just another colonial state, albeit of a special type, as proclaimed in the SACP's 1962 manifesto, and that the decolonisation of the European colonial empires marked an incipient collapse of capitalism more widely. One internal Party document stated that the 'African Revolution' spelled 'the certain doom of apartheid in the near future'.[117] Another maintained that Umkhonto we Sizwe 'provides the basis for the rapid establishment of a people's liberation army, should such a step become necessary in the future'.[118] SACP leaders were inspired in particular by the recent Cuban revolution, which came about after a small body of guerrillas had been able to set up bases in the countryside from which it raised the population in support. Similarly, the aim of Umkhonto we Sizwe's commanders was for trained guerrillas to return to South Africa within the near future with a view to setting up bases in remote areas, especially of the rural Transkei, from which they could launch attacks and train others.

---

111 S.M. Ndlovu, 'The ANC in Exile, 1960-1970', in SADET, *The Road to Democracy*, Volume 1, p. 454.

112 Mhlaba, *Personal Memoirs*, p. 115.

113 P. Trewhela, 'Raymond Mhlaba: ANC Leader Imprisoned with Mandela', *Independent*, 23 February 2005, available at http://www.independent.co.uk/news/obituaries/raymond-mhlaba-484366.html, retrieved on 20 May 2011.

114 Mhlaba, *Personal Memoirs*, p. 117.

115 E. Mtshali, 'December Sixteen', '61 in Durban', *Dawn*, souvenir issue (1986), p. 13.

116 Shubin, *ANC*, p. 20.

117 'Some Problems Before Us – A Discussion Document', SACP document, no date [August 1961?], Simons Papers, 0.7.2.

118 'The New Year – Some Tasks and Perspectives', SACP document, no date [December 1961?], Simons Papers, 0.7.1.

By the second half of 1961, Umkhonto we Sizwe was ready for its launch. There was one premature attack on 15 December, but the campaign began in earnest the next day with a wave of bomb attacks on symbolic targets and on property. The fact that militants from other networks 'struck simultaneously' on 16 December[119] and remained active makes it difficult to gauge the relative size of MK's campaign. According to a later chief of security police intelligence, there were in total some 400 acts of sabotage by various groups in the years 1961 to 1963.[120] In March 1966, the police chief, Lieutenant-General J.M. Keevy, stated that there had been 409 acts of sabotage in South Africa since 16 December 1961.[121]

The launch of an armed insurrection in which Communists played a prominent role could not fail to cause concern in various capitalist countries, including notably Britain and the USA. Although no outside intelligence agencies seem to have been aware of the SACP's requests for support in Moscow and Beijing, it was not difficult for them to detect communist influence in the growing agitation in South Africa. Just as hard evidence of the SACP's precise relationship to its Communist superpower sponsors has emerged only over time, so too has documentation concerning the efforts made by capitalist powers to influence the course of events.

Following its rise to power in 1948, the National Party had brought its own people into the police special branch, but it remained beholden to the British intelligence services for international contacts.[122] Many of the Ossewabrandwag radicals who had advocated paramilitary action during the Second World War years and who had favoured a German victory now joined the National Party and became prominent on its right wing. Their influence inside the National Party increased during the crisis after Sharpeville. After the appointment of Vorster to the Justice ministry in 1961, another Ossewabrandwag veteran, H.J. van den Bergh, with whom Vorster had once been interned, received rapid promotion in the police to become head of the security branch in 1963.

From the start of his career in state security, Van den Bergh, a prominent Anglophobe as well as an anti-communist, looked for support particularly from the US Central Intelligence Agency. In time, he formed a particularly close bond with the equally anti-communist CIA chief of counter-intelligence James Jesus Angleton.[123] Only later, after Van den Bergh had set up the Bureau for State Security (BOSS), South Africa's first modern intelligence service, did one of his staff unravel the details of CIA relationships with some of the liberal activists who had sustained sabotage networks in the early 1960s. Some of these connections appeared to implicate British intelligence as well, and many ARM activists became convinced that a dashing war veteran who trained them in sabotage techniques was a British agent.[124] The BOSS analyst Piet Swanepoel produced a voluminous report showing in detail how, from roughly mid-1960, a CIA front organisation provided funding to John Lang and others to finance a national convention movement and a number of other groups founded by them thereafter.[125] Some of this money may have found its way to the ARM, whose John Harris

119 Bernstein, *Memory Against Forgetting*, p. 234.
120 H.D. Stadler, *The Other Side of the Story: A True Perspective* (Pretoria, Contact Publishers, 1997, 2nd edn), p. 26.
121 Vermaak, *The Red Trap*, p. 43.
122 J. Sanders, *Apartheid's Friends: The Rise and Fall of South Africa's Secret Service* (London, John Murray, 2006), pp. 9-17.
123 Author's interview with former BOSS operative, Pretoria, 15 October 2010.
124 M. Brokensha and R. Knowles, *The Fourth of July Raids* (Cape Town, Simondium, 1965), pp. 11-12.
125 'Kampanje vir die vrijlating van Nelson Mandela', Coetsee Papers, PV 357, 1/M1/48. The information contained in this memorandum was based on research subsequently published in P.C. Swanepoel, *Really Inside BOSS: A Tale of South Africa's Late Intelligence Service (and Something about the CIA)* (Pretoria, private publication, 2008), pp. 138-87.

planted a bomb at Johannesburg station in July 1964, killing an elderly woman, on account of which Harris was convicted and hanged.

Since the CIA also had a close relationship to the leading PAC militant Potlake Leballo,[126] the US intelligence organisation in effect had at least three parallel lines of influence in South Africa, one aiding the state to improve its security apparatus, a second in the form of a connection to the radical-populist PAC, and the third a sophisticated strategy to develop influence inside the liberal-radical opposition to apartheid. The common denominator between all of these was, needless to say, anti-communism.

An appreciation of the extent and sophistication of the CIA's interest in South Africa throws some light on the persistent rumour that Nelson Mandela's arrest in August 1962 after his return from a trip abroad to raise support for Umkhonto we Sizwe was made possible by information provided to the South African police by the US intelligence agency. Gerard Ludi, a South African intelligence agent who succeeded in penetrating the SACP central committee, in later years claimed that Millard Shirley, the chief CIA operative in the country, had agents in the ANC and SACP at that time. Nevertheless, Ludi said that he did not know whether the CIA had actually tipped off the South African police about Mandela's whereabouts.[127] Some reports suggest that Ludi eventually became more explicit about Shirley's role.[128] Ludi was a credible source as he and Shirley were so close that they later went into business together. According to one newspaper investigation carried out after Mandela's eventual release, CIA officers at the time of his arrest considered it one of their 'greatest coups'.[129] The US government has contested the story of CIA involvement, but more than one former South African security officer recalls Van den Bergh admitting that the CIA gave information leading to Mandela's arrest.[130] Three decades after Mandela's arrest, the story of a CIA tip-off was regarded as accurate by former diplomats who had served at the US embassy during that period.[131]

Conclusion

'This is one part of our history that is not known', Eric Mtshali, SACP and ANC member and founder-member of Umkhonto we Sizwe told an interviewer for the SADET project, which has sponsored pioneering work in this area. '[T]hat is that the South African Communist Party arrived at the decision [to commence an armed struggle] ahead of the ANC'.[132] Joe Slovo also hinted at the Party's leading role when he wrote that '[t]here was perhaps no other period in our history when the Party played such a seminal role in the unfolding of the struggle as in the years between 1960 and 1963'.[133] The SACP central committee is reported to have claimed the decision to introduce armed resistance as its own achievement in an internal Party document adopted in 1977.[134]

---

126 Author's interview with former BOSS operative, Pretoria, 15 October 2010. This relationship has been widely reported by others also.
127 'CIA Linked to Mandela's 1962 Arrest', *Washington Post*, 11 June 1990.
128 J. Stein, 'Our Man in South Africa', *Salon*, available at www.salon.com/news/news961114.html,retrieved on 23 October 2010.
129 J. Albright and M. Kunstel, 'CIA Tip Led to '62 Arrest of Mandela: Ex-Official Tells of U.S. "Coup" to Aid South Africa', *Atlanta Constitution*, 10 June 1990, p. A14; P.J. Schraeder, *United States Foreign Policy Toward Africa: Incrementalism, Crisis and Change* (Cambridge, Cambridge University Press, 1994), p. 202; Sanders, *Apartheid's Friends*, pp. 17–20.
130 Author's interview with former BOSS official, Pretoria, 15 Oct. 2010; Sanders, *Apartheid's Friends*, pp. 19–20.
131 Letter from former US diplomat to the author, 14 March 1997.
132 Magubane *et al.*, 'The Turn to Armed Struggle', p. 82.
133 Slovo, *Slovo*, p. 170.
134 J. Grobler, *A Decisive Clash? A Short History of Black Protest Politics in South Africa, 1875–1976* (Pretoria, Acacia, 1988), p. 156.

In formal terms, the decision to adopt a policy of armed struggle seems to have been taken by an extended meeting of the central committee of the SACP, having the status of a Party conference, probably in December 1960, and was implemented during the course of the following year.[135] This conference appears to have been a small group of people, fewer than twenty. In present circumstances, it is not possible to verify the issue by reference to the minutes of relevant Party meetings, as the archives of the SACP have not been made public.[136]

As Magubane and others noted in their review of the literature concerning the respective roles of the ANC and the SACP in the adoption of armed struggle, a 'common ploy is to aver that both did so "at about the same time"'.[137] The demonstration that Nelson Mandela was a prominent Party member in the early 1960s should cause us to reject the oft-told story of MK's emergence from ANC and SACP activists working more or less in parallel. In fact, it is clear that the Party took the decision first and then influenced the ANC, with Mandela playing a prominent intermediary role.

The Party was able to influence the ANC, not least by the very effective use of its own particular style of legalism. Party members were bound by the discipline imposed by the rules of their organisation and the decisions of their own governing body. While they were also encouraged to join other organisations, including the ANC, they were at all times bound to uphold their loyalty to the Party.[138] At the same time, they made a careful distinction between actions undertaken on the formal instructions of the Party and those carried out in an informal capacity or while acting as a member of another organisation, in which case the Party as an institution could take its distance.

A good example is provided by another speech from the dock, this one by the former SACP chairman, Bram Fischer, during his trial in 1966. Fischer, like Mandela a highly principled man, stated that 'it was not until 1963 that I knew that Slovo was a member' of Umkhonto we Sizwe. He went on to claim that 'there was no question of Umkhonto having to report to the Central Committee or of instructions being given by the Central Committee to Umkhonto'.[139] At first sight these assertions appear hard to credit, not least as they are contradicted by Slovo's own statements concerning 'the important role which the Party played in the creation and building of MK'.[140] Closer inspection suggests this to be an example of the Party's formal legalism – it is indeed possible that Fischer was not officially informed, in his capacity as a Party functionary, of Slovo's work with MK until 1963, even though he must have been made informally aware of it much earlier, as he conceded elsewhere in his trial statement. In the same way, it is quite possible that the SACP central committee did not formally receive reports from the high command of Umkhonto we Sizwe since the latter was technically an independent body and not a Party organ. However, this did not preclude individual members of the high command, every single one of whom was a SACP member, with the exception of the co-opted member Modise, from communicating with SACP colleagues informally, and nor did it prevent the central committee from discussing the armed struggle.

135 Magubane et al., 'The Turn to Armed Struggle', pp. 82–3.
136 E. Maloka, The South African Communist Party in Exile, 1963–1990 (Pretoria, Africa Institute of South Africa, 2002, Research Paper no. 65) is based on a study of SACP archives. It is unclear what has become of these papers subsequent to their examination by Maloka.
137 Magubane et al., 'The Turn to Armed Struggle', p. 80.
138 See note 102.
139 Statement at his trial by Bram Fischer, Mayibuye Centre, Yusuf Dadoo papers, Box 2, File 4.
140 Slovo, Slovo, p. 177.

Coda

During his years in prison, Fischer often recalled Moses Kotane's words: 'if you throw a stone into the window of a man's house, you must be prepared for him to come out and chase you',[141] uttered as a warning to comrades who wanted to raise the public profile of the underground SACP in defiance of the law. 'The backlash will be fantastic', Kotane had said. 'The police will go mad'.[142] His prediction was still more applicable in the face of an organised campaign of sabotage.

Kotane, from a peasant family, with little formal education, in the end analysed the situation more accurately than the Communist Party's intellectual heavyweights.

---

141 E-mail from Paul Trewhela, 14 October 2010. Kotane's warning is also recorded as 'when you throw a stone at people they are going to come back and break your windows', quoted in Magubane *et al.*, 'The Turn to Armed Struggle', p. 73.

142 Quoted in Magubane *et al.*, 'The Turn to Armed Struggle', p. 73.

The African National Congress (ANC) Underground:
From the M-Plan to Rivonia*

RAYMOND SUTTNER

University of South Africa

Introduction

Existing scholarship on African National Congress (ANC) underground organisation suffers from an over-reliance on documentary resources, which has tended to conceal its texture, complexity and detail. This article covers an early part of that experience, reinterpreting some literature on the ANC's M-Plan as well as using oral evidence to throw light on its meaning and impact. The historiography is given a different interpretation mainly because this contribution places more weight on the Plan than is usually given. Its impact was far wider than most scholars suggest. In particular, it formed the basis for establishing the ANC underground immediately after its banning.

Another feature that emerges is that many of the traits conventionally attributed to the exile experience can also be found in the period when the M-Plan was adopted. It is fairly common to refer to the exile experience in contrast to that of the 1950s and 1980s as manifesting top-down, hierarchical forms of politics.[1] Yet, this article shows that from the early days of preparation for underground organisation, there was a similar emphasis. Marxist influence, often attributed to training in the Soviet Union or political education in MK (Umkhonto we Sizwe, the ANC's armed wing), can also be found on a large scale in the political education associated with the M-Plan in the 1950s.

*   I am grateful to the Nordic Africa Institute in Uppsala and SIDA for funding this research project, to South African Breweries for supplementary funding, and to the Centre for Policy Studies (CPS), Johannesburg, for hosting me in a hospitable environment. I am indebted to Claire Kruger of the CPS information unit for bibliographical assistance and Soneni Ncube, Portia Santho and Martin Ngobeni for endless photocopying. More recently, I have been attached to the University of South Africa, where I have benefited from the encouragement and advice of Greg Cuthbertson, head of the History Department. Gail Gerhart, Tom Karis, Irina Filatova, Peter Limb, Phil Bonner, Michael Neocosmos, Vladimir Shubin and Janet Cherry have provided encouragement, incisive comment and criticism, as have anonymous reviewers of the *South African Historical Journal*. The responsibility for the product as it stands lies with the author alone.

'Rivonia' in the title refers to the Rivonia trial, named after the underground hideout of the top leadership of the ANC and South African Communist Party (SACP). The trial led to the life imprisonment of Nelson Mandela, Walter Sisulu and others.

1.   See R. Suttner, 'Culture(s) of the African National Congress of South Africa: Imprint of Exile Experiences', *Journal of Contemporary African Studies*, 21, 2 (May 2003), 303–20.

Methodological Questions

Studying underground political activity presents special problems to the researcher. The underground political operative has to be invisible in order to achieve success. This is one of the reasons why it was so easy for writers to conclude that the ANC was absent during the period of crackdown on opposition after Rivonia. Unlike organisations with a public presence, an underground one would obviously not have made itself known or its operatives 'available for interviews' by historians.

Even today this presents problems. Many of those who worked underground are no longer alive and even if they are, they cannot easily be located because there may be few people who know that they were working secretly during the 'difficult times'. Also, there may well be an opposite tendency – an element of fiction against which one has to guard, a tendency for people to claim they worked underground or exaggerate exploits, given that it is hard to check. The difficulty is greatest in covering the earlier periods, when memories may have faded or events are recalled in a selective or distorted manner. Where there are few if any survivors of a particular period, it is hard to test one's sources.

The literature on underground activity in South Africa is very limited: mainly pages or chapters of biographies or autobiographies, usually of leaders.[2] There is a limited range of writings of underground workers below the level of national leadership.[3] There is also very little record of underground activity in the rural areas.[4]

Certainly underground work presented special and distinct problems for high profile and easily recognisable figures such as Nelson Mandela and Walter Sisulu. It was obviously more difficult for them to make the transition from legal activity on one day to illegality the next. But while some of this has been documented, there is little that has been written about the experiences of rank-and-file ANC underground workers. The documented sources generally relate to what is visible through media or court records. And those which have received attention have tended to be high-profile cases. What still needs to be properly studied is the large number convicted of 'furthering the aims' of the ANC in the early 1960s and other less-publicised cases.[5] There is also a body of archival data, only recently made available, that needs to be consulted in order to throw further light on some activities.[6]

Before one can draw conclusions about the impact of underground activity within the ANC experience, more primary research needs to be undertaken. At this point we need to uncover

2.	See, for example, N. Mandela, *Long Walk to Freedom: The Autobiography of Nelson Mandela* (Randburg, 1994); J. Slovo (with an introduction by H. Dolny), *Slovo: The Unfinished Autobiography* (Randburg and London, 1995); E. Sisulu, *Walter and Albertina Sisulu: In Our Lifetime* (Claremont, 2002); A. Sampson, *Mandela: The Authorised Biography* (London, 1999); R. Bernstein, *Memory Against Forgetting: Memoirs from a Life in South African Politics* (London, 1999).

3.	See, for example, J. Middleton, *Convictions: A Woman Political Prisoner Remembers* (Randburg, 1998); R. Suttner, *Inside Apartheid's Prison* (Melbourne, New York and Pietermaritzburg, 2001); Sisulu, *Walter and Albertina Sisulu*, when writing of the Sisulu children; A. Sibeko [Zola Zembe], with J. Leeson, *Freedom in our Lifetime* (Durban and Bellville, 1996), though he became a leadership figure later.

4.	But see P. Delius, *A Lion Amongst the Cattle: Reconstruction and Resistance in the Northern Transvaal* (Portsmouth, NH, Johannesburg and Oxford, 1996); Suttner 'Culture(s)', 308–10; Interviews with Victor Moche, Johannesburg, 23 July 2002; Noloyiso Gasa, Johannesburg, 23 Dec. 2002; John Nkadimeng, Johannesburg, 2 Jan. 2003; Radilori Moumakwa, Mafikeng, 15 May 2003.

5.	E. Feit, *Urban Revolt in South Africa, 1960–1964: A Case Study* (Amherst, Mass., 1971) did some limited work of this kind. See also interview, Joe Matthews, Johannesburg, 20 Feb. 2003.

6.	See V. Shubin, 'Digging in the Gold Mine: The Mayibuye Centre Archive as a Source on the History of the South African Liberation Movement', *Comparative Studies of South Asia, Africa and the Middle East*, 19, 1 (1999), 46–52.

precisely what that underground organisation was – including its extent and character and the many variations within it. The scale of such activity may have been large or small. Sometimes conditions did not allow for more than a presence. That may have been without any public impact for some time, as in the case of the more repressive bantustans such as the Transkei.[7] Such an embryonic presence was nevertheless important in situations of illegality and especially in moments of extreme repression. These pockets of resistance or potential resistance were also significant because they may have been important bases for the later emergence of more substantial manifestations of ANC support.

Other periods and experiences have been more thoroughly documented on the basis of written and oral sources.[8] Only three years ago Jeremy Seekings referred to the absence of any literature on the ANC or SACP (South African Communist Party) underground.[9] To understand underground activity, recourse to oral evidence is most important, though it is extremely limited, with the possible exception of the testimony collected by the South African Democracy Education Trust project on the history of the liberation struggle, whose sources are not yet publicly available, and in the work of Howard Barrell on MK and David Everatt on the SACP.[10]

In this type of enquiry it is impossible to operate with notions like a 'representative sample', in the sense that one cannot start with a clear idea of what the extent of the phenomenon being studied may be. One has to work with a 'snowball sample', while being aware that certain categories of participants may be neglected unless one consciously seeks them out, in particular, women participants and those who have for one or other reason fallen into disfavour.

What Do We Mean by Underground Political Activity?

Underground work is political activity that is not open or openly declared for what it is. Under the cover of doing one thing, one may in fact also be performing an activity below the surface and not visibly. Essential to underground action is that while something happens at the surface or nothing surfaces, the politically significant activity happens below the surface.

Where one is in complete hiding, one does not surface at all. Everything that happens is invisible. Alternatively one may have a public face, but that is quite distinct from the underground one

7.   See interview, Noloysio Gasa, 23 Dec. 2002.
8.   In the case of exile there are books of interviews: for example, H. Bernstein, *The Rift. The Exile Experience of South Africans* (London, 1994), as well as archived transcripts of unpublished interviews, housed mainly at Mayibuye Centre in the University of the Western Cape. There is also a great deal of official documentation at Mayibuye Centre and other sites: see also Shubin, 'Digging in the Gold Mine'. MK has received attention in, for example, H. Barrell, *MK: The ANC's Armed Struggle* (Johannesburg, 1990) and H. Barrell, 'Conscripts to their Age: African National Congress Operational Strategy, 1976–1986' (DPhil thesis, Oxford University, 1993). The period of the 1980s has received much attention: for example, J. Seekings, *The UDF: A History of the United Democratic Front in South Africa, 1983–1991* (Cape Town, Oxford and Athens, 2000); I. van Kessel, *'Beyond Our Wildest Dreams': The United Democratic Front and the Transformation of South Africa.* (Charlottesville and London, 2000); T. Lodge and B. Nasson, *All, Here, And Now: Black Politics in South Africa in the 1980s* (Cape Town, 1991). Prison experiences have been dealt with extensively in Fran Buntman's book, *Robben Island and Prisoner Resistance to Apartheid* (Cambridge, 2003), as well as many archived transcripts of interviews, and collections.
9.   Seekings, *UDF.*
10.   Barrell, 'Conscripts to their Age'; D. Everatt, 'The Politics of Nonracialism: White Opposition to Apartheid, 1945–1960' (DPhil thesis, Oxford University, 1990); D. Everatt, 'Alliance Politics of a Special Type: The Roots of the ANC/SACP Alliance, 1950–1954', *Journal of Southern African Studies*, 18, 1 (1991), 19–39; D. Everatt, 'The Banning and Reconstitution of the Communist Party: 1945–1955', in C. Bundy, ed., *The History of the South African Communist Party* (Rondebosch, 1991), 33–51.

that will not be revealed publicly and will only be revealed in disguised form or to a restricted range of people.

Underground activity is not necessarily illegal because in some situations where one has rights or apparent freedom of political activity, one may nevertheless be under surveillance. For one or other reason it may be important that what one is doing is not observed by the police. In some situations the activity may be illegal but the organisation may not have been banned, as was the case in the 1980s when the United Democratic Front (UDF) and its affiliated organisations were generally still legal, but the state of emergency prohibited certain activities.[11] Continuing these activities underground was not generally seen as a prelude to permanent underground and illegal existence.

Furthermore, illegal underground activity often coexists with quite legal activities at the same time, though the manner of coexistence was substantially different in various periods. This was the case when the Communist Party was reconstituted as an illegal organisation, but its members simultaneously participated quite legally in the Congress Alliance.[12] Likewise, in the 1970s and 1980s, some activists participated in legal organisations, including UDF affiliates, while simultaneously performing illegal underground activity for the ANC and SACP.[13]

A final question that arises, though it becomes more of a factor with the establishment of the ANC in exile, is what are the boundaries of underground activities? This relates to both place and time. Does one classify an activity as underground by the time and place in which it is finally executed, or are the preparatory phases part of the underground work, even if these were much earlier and in another country? In my view, one cannot treat preparatory work in a much earlier period and undertaken in London, Angola, Swaziland or anywhere else, as unconnected to the final execution of underground activity. The concept of underground work should include training and other preparations that might have taken place in such areas.[14] In fact, preparatory phases for entering the country often involved great danger and the establishment of a wide range of logistical arrangements.[15]

Origins of Underground Activity in South Africa

There are some activists who envisaged the possibility of illegal action long before it became necessary. Ray Alexander Simons,[16] in preparing to emigrate to South Africa in 1929, was trained by Latvian Communists for underground work. They believed that while the Communist Party of South Africa (CPSA, as it was then called) was a legal organisation, there had to be

11. The United Democratic Front was launched in Cape Town in 1983 and embraced some 600 affiliates of various types, representing millions of members. It offered a powerful, open and mass challenge to the apartheid regime, contributing significantly to the unbanning of ANC and resolution of the apartheid conflict.
12. The Congress Alliance refers to the alliance formed in the 1950s between the ANC, South African Indian Congress, Congress of Democrats, Coloured People's Congress and the South African Congress of Trade Unions (SACTU). On the establishment of the SACP underground, see Everatt, 'The Politics of Nonracialism', and R. Suttner, 'The Reconstitution of the South African Communist Party as an Underground Organisation', *Journal of Contemporary African Studies*, 22, 1 (forthcoming Jan. 2004).
13. Interviews with Steward Ngwenya, Johannesburg, 4 Dec. 2002; Paul Mashatile, Johannesburg, 22 Apr. 2003; Pravin Gordhan, Pretoria, 13 Apr. 2003; Robbie Potenza, Johannesburg, 13 May 2003. Others planned their legal activity in a manner that coincided with the overall strategic goals of the ANC: interview with Amos Masondo, Johannesburg, 10 March 2003.
14. I am indebted to Professor Irina Filatova for raising this question with me.
15. Interview with Totsie Memela, Pretoria, 20 Aug. 2003.
16. Ray Alexander Simons's *Autobiography*, forthcoming.

preparation for the possibility of illegality. In addition, about 14 South African Communists were educated in Comintern schools or universities, where there was a distinct and compulsory course on the underground.[17] Among those trained were leading ANC/SACP figures such as Moses Kotane, J.B. Marks and Communist trade unionist, Betty du Toit.[18] At various times there were travels to and from the Comintern, Comintern representatives visiting South Africa and interacting with South African Communists, as well as South African Communists visiting the Comintern to consult, attend meetings or study. All of these activities were to a large extent secret, underground operations.[19]

On various occasions, the Comintern urged the CPSA to prepare for underground.[20] Possibly because of the disarray within the organisation, resulting from various fissions at the time,[21] no serious consideration seems to have been given to this advice. Consequently, there was no experience of underground activity or any preparations of a substantial kind before the 1950s, by organisations as opposed to individually trained cadres.

While the ANC was declared illegal in 1960, there was extensive experience in underground activity inside and outside that organisation (in the reconstitution of the SACP) during the 1950s. It is necessary to revisit plans for underground like the M-Plan, which have generally been characterised as having an essentially limited impact.[22] This evaluation derives from the narrow character of the focus, which looks mainly at only one phase of ANC and the M-Plan's history – the moment of its first attempted implementation. By expanding the focus, it will be found that the M-Plan was one of the more substantial sources on which the ANC underground drew in establishing itself after banning in 1960. At the same time, having a plan was insufficient for successful implementation. Without the organisational muscle of the SACP, then already enjoying some experience in underground organisation, the ANC underground may have taken off with much greater difficulty.[23]

M-Plan

There are claims that the ideas embraced in the M-Plan were first advanced by A.P. Mda.[24] Some people in the Pan Africanist Congress (PAC) claimed that the M in the M-Plan referred to Mda

---

17. See I. Filatova, 'Indoctrination or Scholarship? Education of Africans at the Communist University of the Toilers of the East in the Soviet Union, 1923–1937', *Paedagogica Historica: International Journal of the History of Education*, 35, 1 (1999), 54–5, and information found in A. Davidson, I. Filatova, V. Gorodnov and S. Johns, eds, *The Communist International and South Africa: Documentary History*, vol. 1 (London, 2003), 6. The Communist International (Comintern) was a worldwide organisation of Communist parties, located in Moscow from 1919 until its dissolution in 1943. During its existence every Communist Party was described as a 'section' of the Communist International. On various occasions the Comintern intervened in the affairs of Communist parties of various countries, including that of South Africa.

18. *Ibid.*, 6.

19. For various examples of such activity, see *ibid.*, 8ff, and Ray Alexander Simons, *Autobiography* (unpublished).

20. Davidson *et al., The Communist International*, vol. 2, document 34, 107ff.

21. J. and R. Simons, *Class and Colour in South Africa*, (London, [1969] 1983), ch. 19.

22. For example, T. Lodge, *Black Politics in South Africa since 1945* (Johannesburg, 1983); Mandela, *Long Walk*; Sampson, *Mandela*.

23. Eric Mtshali argues that it would not have succeeded without Communist Party involvement: interview, Johannesburg, 8 Feb. 2003. This is contested by Ahmed Kathrada: interview, Cape Town, 18 Feb. 2003, and Vladimir Shubin, personal communication by e-mail, 3 June 2003.

24. G.M. Gerhart, *Black Power in South Africa: The Evolution of an Ideology* (Berkeley, Los Angeles and London, 1978), 131–2, note 9. See also T. Karis and G.M. Carter, eds, *From Protest to Challenge: A Documentary History of African Politics in South Africa 1882–1964*, vol. 3; T. Karis and G.M. Gerhart, *Challenge and Violence 1953–1964* (Stanford, 1977), 36.

and not Mandela.[25] It may well be true that Mda thought of these ideas first, but it was the later conceptualisation, associated with Mandela, that achieved the organisational significance that is considered here.

The M-Plan was conceived as a moment of transition or rupture within the decade of mass struggle of the 1950s.[26] The Defiance campaign was also conceived that way by people like Walter Sisulu, referring particularly to volunteers in the Eastern Cape as *Amadela Kufa*, 'defiers of death'. He argues that 'a revolutionary situation was emerging'.[27] If these tendencies are correct, then the rupture between mass democratic politics of the 1950s and underground and ANC revolutionary politics started earlier than 1960, however uneven the character of this break may have been.

As with the question of armed struggle – under discussion long before formation of MK – underground organisation was not only a 'last resort', forced on the ANC, but was under consideration and to some extent in preparation, long before illegality and the formation of MK.[28] The first plans for underground, in the M-Plan, were elaborated some seven years before the banning, almost at the same time as the reconstitution of the SACP and around the time when Mandela urged Sisulu to seek arms from the Chinese when visiting the People's Republic.[29]

Our interest here is not simply how successfully the M-Plan was implemented between 1953 and 1955. The ANC National Executive Committee in 1955 pointed to its general lack of implementation.[30] The question being asked is how lasting was the impact of the M-Plan, and whether it simply petered out in the 1950s after some success mainly in the Eastern Cape, as its conventional treatment appears to suggest? And in what ways did it help constitute the ANC underground in later periods in a number of parts of the country,[31] and indeed impacted on the UDF people's power period?[32] To what extent were the ideas of the M-Plan embedded in organisational consciousness after the period of its initial attempted implementation, and with what consequences?

What was the Essential Quality of the M-Plan?

The M-Plan was prompted by a belief that political conditions were becoming more repressive. This was evident in the banning of the Communist Party and restrictions on many leading figures in the Congress movement. The ANC had to organise itself in a way that adapted to these new conditions. The assumption that everything it did could be achieved through public activity,

25. Personal communication, Gail Gerhart, e-mail, 17 Dec. 2002, a claim, which Joe Matthews, in interview, met with great scepticism.
26. N. Mandela, *The Struggle is My Life* (London, 1990), 40, 134ff; Karis and Gerhart, *Challenge and Violence*, 35ff; Sampson, *Mandela*, 81–2; Lodge, *Black Politics*, 75–6; E. Feit, *African Opposition in South Africa: The Failure of Passive Resistance* (Stanford, 1967), 72–5; W. Sisulu, in conversation with G.M. Houser and H. Shore, *I Will Go Singing: Walter Sisulu Speaks of His Life and the Struggle for Freedom in South Africa* (Cape Town and New York, c. 2001), 80–1; G. Mbeki, *The Struggle for Liberation in South Africa: A Short History* (Cape Town, 1992), 74.
27. Sisulu, *I Will Go Singing*, 79.
28. Mandela, *Long Walk*, 146. See Delius, *Lion amongst Cattle*, 131ff; R. Mhlaba, *Raymond Mhlaba's Personal Memoirs: Reminiscing from Rwanda and Uganda* (Pretoria and Robben Island, 2001), 116.
29. Mandela, *Long Walk*, 134–5.
30. Lodge, *Black Politics*, 75. See also Feit, *African Opposition*, 75.
31. Sampson, *Mandela*, 81; Eric Mtshali interview; Noloyiso Gasa interview.
32. J. Cherry, 'Traditions and Transitions: African Political Participation in Port Elizabeth', in J. Hyslop, ed., *African Democracy in the Era of Globalisation* (Johannesburg, 1999), 404.

especially huge rallies and very large branches, had to be changed. Greater sensitivity to questions of security was needed, on the assumption that there could be a clampdown and that the ANC might be banned. It also had to prepare and immediately institute measures to communicate in smaller units and with a greater degree of secrecy.[33] In January 1953, Joe Matthews, then a young ANC leader, wrote to his father, Professor Z.K. Matthews, then Cape leader of the ANC, about 'a secret meeting . . . of the top leaders of both the SAIC [South African Indian Congress] & ANC, half of whom were banned'. They had planned the future with 'cold-blooded realism', preparing for the organisation to continue 'under conditions of illegality by organising on the basis of the cell system'.[34] Matthews recalls that meeting, over 50 years later, saying, 'there were very strong feelings that sooner or later the organisation would be banned and that certain preparations should be made'. But the expected scale of repression that was anticipated, did not immediately follow:

> Gradually after the Defiance campaign, things returned to what one might call 'South African normality'. Meetings began again, conferences were held. . . . The campaign for the Congress of the People proceeded. So the declaration of banning of ANC occurred much later but they had sort of prepared for it.[35]

Mandela confirms that the NEC had instructed him to draw up a plan that would enable the organisation to operate from underground'.[36] The M-Plan embraced a number of elements. On the one hand, it may have been conceived simply as a preparation for a future underground existence of the organisation as a whole. It may have also had a more limited purpose – greater security to prevent falling victim to the increasing repression, manifested in careless use of sensitive documents.[37] But it was also the extension of modes of operation that were already in existence. Many in the leadership, despite being subjected to heavy banning orders, were already carrying out Congress activities in secret, meeting among themselves and with those who were still allowed to operate legally.[38] Walter Sisulu said that the M-Plan was 'actually intended to go into effect when banning orders began to take place'.[39] After his restriction, the Security Police noted:

> his public activities decreased to such an extent that he no longer came into the limelight . . . However he has dug himself in (established his position) and there is plenty of evidence from utterly reliable and delicate sources that he is, in secret and behind the scenes, as busy as before with advice and guidance and instigation among the non-whites.[40]

Oliver Tambo was made Secretary-General in 1955, but because of his work as a lawyer, he could not manage the full-time organisational work. Consequently, Sisulu continued to work in a full-time capacity underground, with Tambo having the power to veto anything he did. In effect, Sisulu remained *de facto* SecretaryGeneral.[41]

The M-Plan was not a classic conception for a tightly knit vanguard-type underground. Despite the greater security involved, the plan also envisaged expansion of the membership and

33. Karis and Carter, *Challenge and Violence*, 38–9; Mandela, *The Struggle is My Life*, 40; Mandela, *Long Walk*, 134ff; Lodge, *Black Politics*, 75–6; Feit, *African Opposition*, 72–5.
34. Karis and Carter, *Challenge and Violence*, 35–6.
35. Interview, Joe Matthews.
36. Mandela, *Long Walk*, 134.
37. Karis and Carter, *Challenge and Violence*, 39.
38. Mandela, *Long Walk*, 136.
39. Sisulu, *I Will Go Singing*, 80.
40. Walter Sisulu, Ministry of Justice files, quoted by Elinor Sisulu, *Walter and Albertina Sisulu*, 121.
41. *Ibid.*

organisation.[42] One of the key distinctions between the Communist and ANC underground, despite the deep involvement of Communists in the ANC, was that the Communist underground was modelled on Leninist vanguard strategies, albeit operating in a situation where much Communist effort went into building the ANC.[43] The ANC underground, by contrast, was envisaged as a way of enabling a mass organisation to operate in underground conditions.[44] While that may have been the original intention, in the long run it proved unsustainable.

Top-Down 'Transmission' and Elements of Local Initiative

As with all plans for underground, the M-Plan embraced a hierarchical structure, with very clear 'top down' manifestations. Thus Mandela writes that '[t]he ... organisational machinery ... would allow the ANC to take decisions at the highest level, which could then be swiftly transmitted to the organisation as a whole without calling a meeting ...'.[45] 'Press statements' and 'printed circulars' would be unnecessary.[46] The same emphasis can be found in the description of the operation of the M-Plan in East London, given by Johnson Malcomess Mgabela:

> Going from house to house we spoke with the people *and gave them some orders*, trying to bring political understanding of what the ANC were doing. We had to organise small meetings because the government declared any meeting of more than ten people an illegal gathering. So we used the Mandela Plan: going to a house; staying there with ten people; giving them an understanding of what the ANC was doing; *giving them orders*; going to the next house. We tried to give people a message of what the ANC stood for and what its plans of actions were. You would tell people here, tell people there. You would even go to a public place like a shebeen or stand with a few people on a street corner ... All of this was to be done underground. No name must be written down. Everything must be kept in secret. From the national level the *instructions came to us* through the leadership of the region. We had to *take these instructions to the branches; the branches had to take it to the area committees and the area committees had to take it to the street committees.*[47]

At the same time, the plan had important elements promoting local initiative and participation, that was an inspiration during the 1980s People's Power period, especially in Kwazakele in Port Elizabeth.[48] This can be seen in Mandela's elaboration of the aims, again showing its conception to be quite different from a vanguardist approach. He speaks of building local branches as 'local Congresses' and extending and strengthening 'the ties between Congress and the people and to consolidate Congress leadership'.[49]

These steps were seen as part of the consolidation of 'the Congress machinery',[50] and are elaborated in Mandela's autobiography:

42. Mandela, *Long Walk*, 134–5; Sampson, *Mandela*, 81; Feit, *African Opposition*, 72–5.
43. SACP (South African Communist Party), *The Road to South African Freedom. Programme Adopted at the Fifth National Conference of the Party Held Inside the Country. In South African Communists Speak. Documents from the History of the South African Communist Party. 1915–1980* (London, [1962] 1981); Kathrada interview; interview with Brian Bunting, Cape Town, 18 Feb. 2003. It is interesting to note, however, that the Comintern 'instruction' to the Communist Party, to prepare for underground, mentioned above, includes advising that the 'mass character' of the Party should be safeguarded.
44. See V. Shubin, *The ANC: A View from Moscow* (Bellville, 1999) 11.
45. Mandela, *Long Walk*, 134.
46. Mandela, *The Struggle is My Life*, 40; see also Sampson, *Mandela*, 81.
47. J.K. Coetzee, L. Gilfillan, and O. Hulec, *Fallen Walls: Voices from the Cells that Held Mandela and Havel* (Robben Island, 2002), 60, my emphasis.
48. Cherry, 'Traditions and Transitions', 404.
49. Mandela, *The Struggle is My Life*, 40.
50. *Ibid.*

The smallest unit was the cell, which in urban townships consisted of roughly ten houses on a street. A cell steward would be in charge of each of these units. If a street had more than ten houses, a street steward would take charge and the cell stewards would report to him. A group of streets formed a zone directed by a chief steward, who was in turn responsible to the secretariat of the local branch of the ANC. The secretariat was a subcommittee of the branch executive, which reported to the provincial secretary. My notion was that every cell and street steward should know every person and family in his area, so that he would be trusted by the people and would know whom to trust. The cell steward arranged meetings, organised political classes and collected dues. He was the linchpin of the plan.[51]

Thembeka Orie describes the role of the steward in the Port Elizabeth area:

Each street had its own steward whose task was to recruit within the street. The steward had to inform on the types of people in each street, whether there were for example policemen. The most important task for the steward was to know everything happening within the street, be it a social event like a funeral, an initiation ceremony or a fight.

Theses duties were crucial because when it came to organising meetings, the ANC could not risk holding a meeting of more than ten people in one street knowing that there were police in the neighbourhood. Social functions like African traditional ceremonies (initiation) or funerals for instance, were used by the ANC to advance its political goals. The street stewards therefore had to be always on the alert in order to organise properly and thereby utilise such occasions effectively.[52]

The use of the concept 'steward' appears to have its etymological origins in the church, especially the Methodist church.[53] Joe Matthews confirms this likelihood:

There was a very strong church influence in New Brighton. There was a very strong religious bent in that branch and it was Methodist and it was drawn from people like Gladstone Tshume, [who] was a Communist but he never missed a church service. . . . It came from that idea of a steward who not only is responsible for organisation but also for collecting the subscriptions and that of course is one of the jobs of the steward in the church. It's making sure that people are paying their quarterly subscriptions.[54]

At this point, the term was not widespread within the union movement in South Africa. Eddie Webster writes:

Shop-stewards were introduced into trade unions in South Africa in the late 19th century by British craft workers. However, they operated rather weakly until the 1970s when, influenced by the growth of a shop-steward movement in Britain, the emerging industrial unions placed central emphasis on building a working class leadership based on the shop-floor . . .[55]

If this is correct, it is another illustration of the continuity of experiences, and influences, in this case Christian and trade-union ones, from one phase of African nationalism to a quite different one.[56]

51. Mandela, *Long Walk*, 135; see also Feit, *African Opposition*, 72–3.
52. T. Orie, 'Raymond Mhlaba and the Genesis of the Congress Alliance: A Political Biography' (MA thesis, University of Cape Town, 1993), 102–3.
53. *Shorter Oxford English Dictionary*, vol. 2 (3rd ed., Oxford, 1986); and personal communication from Greg Cuthbertson, e-mail, 31 Jan. 2003, who writes that the word 'steward' is 'still used in Methodism to designate the function of material custodian in church affairs. Of course, Primitive Methodism and to a lesser extent Wesleyan Methodism were significant feeders of the trade union movement in Britain, and Methodism in its many forms in SA, including the AME [African Methodist Episcopal] tradition, has also played a part in liberation movements.'
54. Interview, Joe Matthews.
55. E. Webster, 'Introduction', in S.M. Pityana and M. Orkin, eds, *Beyond the Factory Floor: A Survey of COSATU Shop-Stewards* (Johannesburg, 1992), 7. A similar view is expressed by Sakhela Buhlungu, personal communication by e-mail, 15 July 2003.
56. See P. Walshe, *The Rise of African Nationalism in South Africa: The African National Congress, 1912–1952* (London, 1970).

Political Education

Considerable weight was placed on political education, in motivating the plan[57] and indeed throughout the 1950s.[58] Many people appear to have gone through some form of internal education where a common understanding of Congress politics was developed, through lectures and discussion. Those who participated at one level were expected to give the lectures at another.[59] Mandela explains:

> As part of the M-plan, the ANC introduced an elementary course of political lectures for its members throughout the country. These lectures were meant not only to educate but to hold the organisation together. They were given in secret by branch leaders. Those members in attendance would in turn give the same lectures to others in their homes and communities. In the beginning, the lectures were not systematised, but within a number of months there was a set curriculum.

> The lecturers were mostly banned members, and I myself frequently gave lectures in the evening. This arrangement had the virtue of keeping banned individuals active as well as keeping the membership in touch with these leaders.[60]

Inside and outside these structures and within this overall perspective, many cadres saw political education as their key task during this period. Elias Motsoaledi recalls:

> We took those who understood into a house and continued with political classes in order to give the movement its impetus; you must have real members not only paper members. People did not know the history of the ANC so we had to impart this knowledge to them. Secondly, they needed to know the day-to-day issues which affected them; to make him understand exactly why he was treated the way he was treated. I had so many people from all over Soweto who came to me for political classes . . .[61]

An important element of these processes that appears to have been neglected thus far, is that they not only inducted members into the Congress movement, but also created a body of organic intellectuals, a category of individuals who would be equipped to make sense of the world people lived in, and advance and explain changing strategies and tactics of the organisation. Obviously this would be an important asset in difficult times, when results seemed few and somewhere in an unknown future. This was something that would happen in a number of other structures – in the Communist Party, in the MK camps, in the trade unions, on Robben Island and in the UDF.

Using Gramsci's approach, an intellectual is not defined purely by the qualifications that he or she has obtained, but by the functions that the person performs – the role played in relation to others.[62] In the case of the South African struggle, these internal courses saw people learning one day and becoming teachers the next.[63] Many had little, if any, formal education, yet they carried out an intellectual function.

57. Mandela, *Long Walk*, 135.
58. Anon., 'Internal Education in the Congress Alliance', *Africa Perspective*, 24 (1984), 99–111; Mtshali interview; interview with Billy Nair, Cape Town, 21 Feb. 2003; R.V. Lambert, 'Political Unionism in South Africa: The South African Congress of Trade Unions, 1955–1965' (PhD thesis, University of the Witwatersrand, 1988); Everatt, 'Politics of Nonracialism'.
59. Mandela, *Long Walk*, 135.
60. *Ibid.*
61. Quoted by Philip Bonner and Lauren Segal, *Soweto: A History* (Cape Town, 1998), 50.
62. Q. Hoare and G. Nowell-Smith, eds, *Selections from the Prison Notebooks of Antonio Gramsci* (London, 1971), 3–23.
63. Eric Mtshali describes receiving such lectures and Cleopas Ndlovu later reports on receiving lectures from Mtshali: Mtshali interview; interview with Cleopas Ndlovu, Durban, 30 June 2003.

One significant aspect of the political education is that much of its content was informed by Marxism.[64] Generally, the widespread diffusion of Marxist thinking within the ANC today tends to be attributed to the exile experience, when some cadres were sent to Party schools and much of the political education was Marxist.[65] But these Congress Alliance courses indicate that the modes of analysis were already within that paradigm long before the period of exile. Even before the establishment of the Congress Alliance and SACTU in particular, this was happening within the trade unions in Natal where many Communists were placed.[66]

This also raises an interesting contemporary question. Given this Marxist orientation during the 1950s and the apparent popularity of socialism during the exile period and within the country in the 1980s, what has happened to that tradition within the ANC in the present period? Has it simply been obliterated from peoples' minds and if so, how was that achieved, or does it mean that the conviction and training was in fact very superficial?[67] Alternatively, is this orientation in abeyance, yet a potential basis of socialist support? If so, under what conditions can it be mobilised? Or, is Marxism now primarily a rhetorical device within the ANC, used to defend sometimes conservative macroeconomic policies and deployed against the left?[68]

Extent of Initial Success and Failure of the M-Plan

Accounts of the implementation of the M-Plan generally refer to its success being mainly in the Eastern Cape, particularly in Port Elizabeth, though Lodge refers to some degree of implementation in Cato Manor, but no source is given.[69] Feit refers to limited attempts in a number of areas in Eastern Cape, Natal and Transvaal.[70] Mtshali refers to implementation in the whole of Durban.[71] There was also considerable success in parts of East London.[72]

Archie Sibeko indicates implementation in the Western Cape:

> The regime had unintentionally made this easier by concentrating Africans in townships . . . [B]ranches were quickly divided into wards, zones and cells, each with its own leadership.

> This structure enabled regional and branch leaders to communicate very quickly to all members. We could call a branch meeting on a Sunday morning within 30 minutes, or mobilise people to deliver leaflets to every household in the township in a short space of time.[73]

Mtshali describes implementation of the M-Plan in Durban:

64. Anon, 'Internal Education'; interviews with Mtshali, Nair and Ndlovu. Some of the actual lectures, including those referred to by Mandela, can be found in archival collections, including the University of the Witwatersrand Cullen Library, A 84/2, DA14: 45/2 ANC G'52, 'Notes for Lecturers. Elementary Course on Politics & Economics' and A 84/2, DA14: 45/3, 'The World We Live In'.
65. For that influence, see interview with Serache, Johannesburg, 31 Aug. 2002; M. Sparg, J. Schreiner and G. Ansell, eds, *Comrade Jack: The Political Lectures and Diary of Jack Simons, Novo Catengue* (Johannesburg, 2001). See also Suttner 'Culture(s) of the ANC'.
66. Nair interview.
67. Interview with Petros 'Shoes' Mashigo, Pretoria, 12 Apr. 2003, who indicates some of the limitations.
68. J. Moleketi and J. Jele, *Two Strategies of the National Liberation Movement in the Struggle for the Victory of the National Democratic Revolution* (Johannesburg, 2002).
69. Lodge, *Black Politics*, 75–6; Mandela, *Long Walk*, 136; Sisulu, *I Will Go Singing*, 81.
70. Feit, *African Opposition*, 75.
71. Mtshali interview.
72. Interviews with Mgabela and Monde Colin Mkunqwana in Coetzee *et al.*, *Fallen Walls*, 60, 77–8.
73. Sibeko, *Freedom*, 49–50.

> We were told about the M-Plan, in the Party and the ANC. In fact, the people who implemented the M-Plan in Durban, were mainly members of the Communist Party
>
> Q. In what parts of Durban was it implemented to your knowledge?
> A: In fact the whole of Durban, and that including the townships.
> Q: By saying it was implemented you mean people established cell structures?
> A: Yes cell structures, but at the time M-Plan did not work effectively because ANC was legal.
> Q: It was premature?
> A: It only worked effectively when ANC was banned . . .[74]

John Nkadimeng also claims that the implementation of the M-Plan at an early stage after its inception (as well as later, as a plan for underground when the ANC was illegal), was much wider than the areas conventionally named.[75] He claims that it was implemented in a number of areas of the then Transvaal and had a role in the Pondoland and Sekhukhuneland risings, though this needs further investigation and clarification.[76]

But the success of the M-Plan should not be measured purely or mainly by the extent to which it was implemented at its inception, which seems to be the main emphasis in Karis and Gerhart[77] and other works. For various reasons related to a lack of resources as well as resistance to changes that did not seem immediately necessary, and fears of centralisation, many members were reluctant to make the organisational shift at the time.[78] Others did not consider it necessary to take the precautions when an immediate clampdown was imminent. This recalls Moses Kotane's statement when asked why the Communist Party had not prepared for underground before its banning:

> 'It is very easy to say we should,' he said later. 'But no person can react to non-existent conditions. Many romantic people say we could have made preparations, but I dispute this. You don't walk looking over your shoulder when there is nothing to look back at. Theoretically you can train people to be pilots when there are no aeroplanes. But the realities have to be there.'[79]

In the same way, many ANC people found it abstract to organise for illegality while the organisation was unbanned.[80] But once it was declared illegal it became a necessity.

Revival/Implementation of M-Plan after Banning

There is some evidence that conceptions of the M-Plan, even if unevenly implemented in an earlier moment, were embedded in people's consciousness and formed the basis of organising underground units after banning.[81]

Noloyiso Gasa's parents were leading Western Cape ANC figures, Vulindlela [Welcome] Zihlangu and Dorothy Zihlangu. Gasa reports on the implementation of the M-Plan after banning:

74. Mtshali interview.
75. Nkadimeng interview.
76. This assertion is confirmed by interview with Henry Makgothi, Johannesburg, 3 Mar. 2003.
77. Karis and Gerhart, *Challenge and Violence*.
78. Mandela, *Long Walk*, 135–6; Lodge, *Black Politics*, 76; Sampson, *Mandela*, 81–2.
79. B. Bunting, *Moses Kotane, South African Revolutionary: A Political Biography*, 3rd ed. (Bellville, 1998), 179.
80. Mtshali interview.
81. Noloyiso Gasa interview; Sampson, *Mandela*, 80; F. Meli, *South Africa Belongs to Us: A History of the ANC* (Harare, 1988), 153; Benson, *Nelson Mandela*, 76, 91–2; Nkadimeng interview; Mtshali interview; Makgothi interview.

I only heard about that [M-Plan] after the organisation was banned. And then people were told not to meet in large numbers . . . When we used to ask why are the general meetings not there any more, because we used to enjoy them, they would say the securities have forced people not to meet in large numbers again. But we could see that people were meeting and you would gather from them that there was a plan that was proposed that people should meet in tens in separate venues. That is how I got to know about it.

Q: So you are saying the way they organised when the ANC was banned was based on that earlier M-Plan?

A: Yes . . .

People were in prisons, they were detained and after their detention they came back and they said they could not meet in large numbers any more so they met separately in tens. When you asked how did they work, they only met in separate venues but they discussed the same agendas. That is how we came to know about it, but I was never in those meetings.

Q: So this was really the organisation operating underground?

A: I should think so.[82]

Frances Baard confirms this interpretation of the M-Plan forming the basis of underground, in Port Elizabeth.[83] This became an explicit decision at the Lobatse conference held in Bechuanaland in 1962. The final resolutions instructed all organs and units 'as a matter of urgency . . . to ensure the full implementation of the 'M' plan . . . and its rapid extension to every area in South Africa . . .'.[84]

At the same time, habits of organisation from the phase of legality were carried over into the period of underground. Given that the model of a good branch chair from the Xuma/Calata period[85] may have been one who kept records and other documents in good order, Welcome Zihlangu continued this practice after banning, though taking care to hide the records. Gasa reports:

In fact when people were detained and they started meeting in tens I was not involved at all except when I wrote notes for my father after he came back from meetings. He could write but he had a bad handwriting.

Q: So he wanted it neat. But why did he want it in writing if it was illegal?

A: I don't know. Maybe to remind themselves

Q: Did he hide it then?

A: Yes at home we had a trapdoor where he used to hide these things

Q: What did you hide there?

A: Books, their membership cards, their minutes

Q: So they had records . . . But they did it secretly?

A: I should think so, my father was a chairman of a branch and he used to bring these things home . . .[86]

Similar practices can be found elsewhere. Photographs taken by Nat Serache in Dinokana, a village outside Zeerust, show a woman indicating where she used to hide ANC membership cards during the period of banning. There are other instances involving both ANC and CPSA

---

82.   Noloyiso Gasa interview.

83.   F. Baard, *My Spirit is Not Banned* (Harare 1986), 71. See also confirmation by Eric Mtshali that the substantial implementation of the M-Plan was after the banning of the ANC: Mtshali interview.

84.   Meli, *South Africa*, 153.

85.   Walshe, *Rise of African Nationalism*, 389ff. Dr A.B Xuma and Rev (later Canon) James Calata, as President and Secretary-General, tried to build structures of the organisation on a sound financial and administrative footing.

86.   Noloyiso Gasa interview.

membership cards. Many members wanted to retain the cards in a safe place.[87] It was possibly a symbol of their continued commitment to the organisation.

ANC is Banned: Development of ANC Underground

The reconstitution of the Communist Party of South Africa as the South African Communist Party has importance for the later development of the ANC as an underground organisation.[88] It appears that the ANC drew on the experience and some of the facilities of the SACP in developing its own organisational capacity as an underground organisation.[89] By the time the ANC was banned, the SACP had already had seven years of experience underground. It operated for 10 years before taking its first loss.[90] Many of the leading figures in the ANC underground were also members of the Communist underground. All but one of the Rivonia accused (Mandela being the exception), are now known to have been members of the SACP, most in the leadership of the organisation.

When the ANC was banned many of its leaders were in prison together, held under the State of Emergency. But a meeting of the National Executive of the ANC was held – by those outside of prison – at which the decision to declare a day of mourning was taken. It was also resolved that in the event of the government banning the ANC, it would not dissolve.[91] On 1 April 1960, a statement was issued by the 'Emergency Committee of the African National Congress' (chaired by Kotane[92]) declaring, *inter alia*,

> We do not recognise the validity of this law, and we shall not submit to it. The African National Congress will carry on in its own name to give leadership and organisation to our people until freedom has been won and every trace of the scourge of racial discrimination has been banished from our country.[93]

A defiant statement in *African National Congress Voice: An Occasional Bulletin*, No 1, April 1960, also carried advice to those holding illegal literature. Such suggestions for security would become characteristic of underground publications in later years. It declared:

> We shall continue to work Underground until the unjust and immoral ban suppressing the ANC has been repealed.
>
> This bulletin, 'Congress Voice,' will be issued from time to time. Read it. Study it. Pass it on. But do not be caught with it, or tell anyone where you got it.[94]

The new situation of illegality presented a challenge to the activists who had escaped arrest. The organisation's structure had to be changed to meet the new situation. Michael Dingake describes the atmosphere:

> The abnormal times called for 'the suspension of normal procedures and practices. The democratic elections gave way to executive appointments in a hierarchical order. The task of operating the ANC underground was formidable after years of above ground existence . . .[95]

87. Everatt, 'The Politics of Nonracialism', 93.
88. See Suttner, 'Reconstitution of the South African Communist Party'.
89. Sampson, *Mandela*, 138; Nkadimeng, Mtshali, Matthews, Makgothi interviews.
90. Bernstein, *Memory against Forgetting*, 132, 185; Kathrada interview.
91. Mbeki, *The Struggle for Liberation*, 86.
92. Shubin, *ANC*, 12.
93. Karis and Gerhart, *Challenge and Violence*, 572.
94. *Ibid.*, 574, capitalisation in original.
95. M. Dingake, *My Fight Against Apartheid* (London, 1987), 58–9.

> Annual conferences or any other conference as provided for in the constitution of the organisation were suspended . . . It was part of the new spirit of discipline to accept the suspension of this crucial concept of the freedom struggle without reservations . . . It was not easy and the morale of the masses was ailing . . .[96]

The state of mind of many of the members was, however, not conducive to this transition. Dingake indicates the difficulty in communicating with and coordinating the membership:

> Within the liberation movement there was much confusion . . . Loyal members of the organisation, lacking close contact and guidance, swayed with the wind . . .

> The general euphoria of the pre-State of Emergency had been interrupted . . . The experience was sobering to some of us who, for the first time, lived and worked practically under conditions of illegality. The task of organising and maintaining underground machinery was an uphill battle. Activists had to learn new methods and acquire different techniques of operation. Not only that, we had to change ourselves to adapt to new conditions.

> There was an element of demoralisation induced by the state of emergency. While the 'liberation struggle had not been crushed . . . [t]he ban and the State of Emergency undermined the mood of enthusiasm, disrupted the trend of mass political involvement in the fight against oppression and triggered minds in search of novel solutions to the political problem of the country.[97]

Pointing to what would re-emerge as a greater challenge to the ANC during the Black Consciousness period and the later rise of Inkatha, Dingake remarked that 'Black organisations which had not been banned and others who claimed to represent the interests of the oppressed tried to cash in and fill the vacuum left by the ban on the PAC and the ANC'.[98] Ian Mkhize, a former member of the Pietermaritzburg ANC branch recalls:

> I must say, it seemed for a while that the ANC had a demise – it seemed like it was virtually dead . . . It was in 1963 that I joined the Liberal Party. It certainly, was, in my own view, going the same way as ANC at that moment . . . They were the only alternative that was available. I would have taken a stand against them being anti-communist, but we had no option. Somehow we had to get a political platform.[99]

Dingake puts a rather optimistic interpretation on this trend:

> What was interesting was that the majority of ANC members who joined other organisations did not do so out of disillusionment or rejection of the ANC. They regarded working through other avenues without prejudice. On investigating further, one invariably came up against the disinclination of people to operate underground. It is natural. Underground work is hard, demanding and pregnant with hazards. Only the truly dedicated, selfless and disciplined cadres are suitable for the underground.[100]

Cleopas Ndlovu observes a similar phenomenon. Many members of branches were reluctant to stop wearing Congress uniforms and recognise that their legal rights had been curtailed. Nevertheless, in his experience, substantial numbers still worked in the underground organisation. By his estimation this amounted to about sixty per cent of the membership of the branches with which he was acquainted.[101] While the SACP was then fairly seasoned in underground work, the ANC had not made serious preparations. Successful transition of a mass organisation

96.   *Ibid.*, 64.
97.   *Ibid.*, 62.
98.   *Ibid.*, 59.
99.   J. Frederikse, *The Unbreakable Thread: Non-Racialism in South Africa* (Johannesburg and Harare, 1990), 93.
100.   See Mtshali interview for similar comments below.

to underground structures was very complicated. Obviously, not every ANC member joined an underground unit. But the scale was much greater and the security consequences more problematic than in the case of the SACP.

The expertise and facilities of the SACP appear to have been crucial. Communists were very active in building the ANC as an allied underground force. But there was some suspicion of the Communists. Mtshali says 'it was difficult to change ANC comrades, to adapt to underground conditions. Many of them left the ANC at that time because underground work was a foreign animal to them and many of them suspected that it was the Communist Party doing work.'[102] While facilities were sometimes shared, as was the case with Rivonia, there was never a merger of the ANC and SACP underground. The SACP retained its vanguard and tightly knit, small-scale character.[103] Mtshali speaks of the Party 'playing its vanguard role in the mass movement'.[104]

Tasks of the ANC Underground

The first task of the ANC underground in this period was to ensure survival of the organisation under conditions of illegality. Mtshali explains the situation in Durban, where SACTU continued to function legally, though with many of its members in detention or under restriction. The space it occupied was used partly by the ANC to create a platform for advancing its positions.

> The Party's big task was . . . [building] the ANC branches, using our experiences to build the ANC underground, also using SACTU, because SACTU was not banned and the leadership of SACTU were mainly Communists in almost all provinces. So we effectively used our experience, but we were not masquerading as members, because we were trade union organisers (and ANC members).[105]

> Q: You established quite a few ANC underground units?
> A: We applied the M-Plan, from street to street from area to area.
> Q: Did you encounter a lot of fear on the part of the people or were you able to get quite a lot of people to do it?
> A: No we were able to get a few people to do it.

They first had to 'make sure that ANC does not die'. They also had to distribute whatever literature was produced 'on time and widely'.

While the ANC was illegal it had to try to exert influence both from the underground, but also through influencing organisations that were still legal. Mtshali recalls how the ANC in Natal tried to ensure the development of and influence residents' associations in townships.[106] They had to 'work with them and say the same things that we were saying when we were ANC. But this time not as ANC but as members of the Residents' Associations and Ratepayers associations or as members of the unions.'[107]

101. *Ibid.*
102. *Ibid.*
103. Kathrada and Bunting interviews; A. Lerumo [Michael Harmel], *Fifty Fighting Years: The South African Communist Party 1921–1971* (London, 1971), 88.
104. Mtshali interview.
105. E. Feit, *Workers Without Weapons* (Hamden, Connecticut, 1975), ch. 8.
106. Mtshali interview.
107. *Ibid.*

Much of the work of the underground was of a welfare nature, finding and providing aid to relatives of detainees, organising legal defence and fines for those charged.[108] This would continue to be one of the roles, alongside the building of organisational structures, throughout most of the years of the ANC's underground period.[109] In addition, these structures facilitated recruitment to MK, exit from and entry to the country,[110] though their capacity was initially very limited.

ANC Underground Organisation and Rivonia

The establishment of the ANC underground organisation was almost simultaneous with the creation of MK, though the first acts of MK were only a year later. The establishment of MK as an organisation independent of the ANC represented a compromise, which Joe Matthews claims, created its own problems. Being outside constitutional structures meant the absence of normal checks on who was recruited and that MK acted on its own, sometimes leading to serious security problems. According to Cleopas Ndlovu, however, this is 'nonsense'. Structures of the ANC were in fact involved.[111] He claims that Matthews, then based in Basutoland (now Lesotho) was not conversant with the process. This question deserves further investigation, since the potential for the problems Matthews claims occurred must have been there if MK was independent of ANC structures.[112] The extent to which the issue did arise may relate to the extent to which there was a *de facto* overlap between ANC and MK structures.

After a shaky start, the ANC underground organisation began to function reasonably well, consolidating its structures and work. MK performed well and, according to Michael Dingake, its call for volunteers led to an 'unprecedented' response from the youth, the organisation being 'inundated' with applications for training abroad.[113] But there were serious lapses of security:

> The successful sabotage operations of 1962–3 created extreme over-confidence with its dangerous corollaries of recklessness and complacency. Regions, areas, streets and cells, through tbeir structures, exhorted the membership to observe some elementary rules of security: change venues of meetings, be punctual at meetings, don't discuss your role in the organisation with other members of the organisation who are not working directly with you, be careful whom you talk to and what you say, etc. These elementary principles were broken daily . . . It was all the result of emotional fervour overwhelming common sense and mutual trust generated among the membership by the wave of spectacular achievements of MK. The optimistic side of the mood was good. The incipient complacency and recklessness produced by such a mood however was dangerous.[114]

Important logistical measures, such as transport of MK recruits out of the country, were not always undertaken with proper security, with drivers sometimes shouting on the streets that they would be making such a journey.[115] On other occasions, unscheduled accommodation of MK recruits would be imposed on cadres, endangering security of a wide range of people.[116] Sobizana

108. Dingake, *My Fight*, 59–60.
109. Sisulu, *Walter and Albertina Sisulu*, 244. See also interview with Phumla Tshabalala, Johannesburg, 13 July 2003.
110. Interviews Phumla Tshabalala and also Ralph Mgijima, Johannesburg, 15 July 2003.
111. Matthews and Ndlovu interviews.
112. Phil Bonner believes, from research he has been conducting, that Matthews' point may well be valid.
113. Dingake, *My Fight*, 68–9.
114. *Ibid.*, 75–6.
115. *Ibid.*, 77.
116. *Ibid.*, 77–8.

Mngqikana, on returning to his home city, East London, from Fort Hare, was recruited into ANC underground structures. These instances flouted basic rules of conspiracy and clandestine work, leading

> to calamitous disaster, as we were to witness. For example, one of our leaders would boast to some non-ANC acquaintances that he had been reinforced by intellectuals in his organisation. This meant us ex-Fort Harians. We would be confronted by individuals claiming to know our political affiliations and activities. Sometimes we felt honoured by this, not appreciating the grave consequences that could arise. Sometimes we had fundraising parties where freedom songs were sung.

At one point, as a member of the Border Regional Command Secretariat, Mngqikana experienced the reprimand of more seasoned revolutionaries. The Border committee had instructed him to write without sensitivity to the changed conditions, demanding a report back on the ANC conference in Lobatse:

> In response to our demand a delegation comprising Vuyisile Mini [a trade union leader and composer of famous freedom songs, later to be hanged by the apartheid regime in 1964] and [Caleb] Mayekiso came to East London. The meeting lasted from 8 p.m. to 5 a.m. the following day. The four-room house in which we held the meeting was discreetly guarded and secured by MK cadres. Before we could delve into the main part of the meeting, Mini, in tears, expressed dismay at the uncomradely letter we had written. 'Did we know the implications of the resort to armed struggle', he asked? 'Did we appreciate that blood is going to flow and that lives are going to be lost?' At some stage he couldn't continue as tears rolled down his cheeks. Mayekiso, I remember, mildly reproached him: 'Vuyisile, Vuyisile stop this, stop this!' After a while he cooled down and proceeded to give a report of the Lobatse conference and the expectations that the leadership had of us . . .
>
> I felt sad and guilty during and after Mini's intervention for . . . I was the author of the uncomradely letter Mini was referring to. I realised then and afterwards the gravity of armed struggle.[117]

This dressing down did not, however, ensure that the sense of gravity and need for security was generally appreciated:

> Later a group of some of us underground activists were summoned to a meeting where we were told about MK tasks and asked to join. Here again lack of underground discipline was to surface among MK cadres. You would get cadres berating people at bus ranks for not joining the struggle . . .
>
> Disaster was to strike in early 1963. Some MK comrades started test-shooting revolvers at night, not far from the public location bus rank. One of them left the revolver at his uncle's place, not very far from the testing site. And the police got wind of this . . .[118]

Conclusion

Writings about early ANC preparations for underground organisation may too readily have written off the significance of the M-Plan, which seems to have had a widespread influence, though not necessarily at its time of initial implementation. Also, the tendency to use epithets such as 'amateurish' to describe the first phase of illegal organisation and MK activity after

117. Interview, Sobizana Mngqikana, Stockholm, 2 Feb. 2001. This intervention of Mini, one of the most famous revolutionary martyrs, is also interesting in showing that what some have described as the 'masculine' character of the ANC may take a variety of forms, not necessarily that of the macho hero.
118. Sobizana Mngqikana interview.

banning, underestimates the difficulties under which the ANC had to operate. Without the elapse of time between illegality and underground organisation, enjoyed by the Communists, the tasks were much more difficult for the ANC. Of necessity, the underground had then to be immediately built, in the main, by those who were known as ANC supporters from their previous above-ground, legal work. Furthermore, there are probably very few examples of a mass movement, as opposed to a vanguard organisation or small numbers of units, trying to establish structures underground. The ANC's sizw produced special problems of coordination and security, whether established over a short or longer period.

In addition, what emerges from this study is that the 1950s were not only a period of mass democratic upsurge, but also a decade when top-down transmission, hierarchical organisation and widespread diffusion of Marxist doctrine took place within the ANC. The tendency to counterpose the exile experience with allegedly more democratic and grassroots phases of the 1950s and 1980s has tended to ignore the presence of similar elements found, in varying degrees, in all phases. It may be better to see every phase of ANC history after the 1950s as containing to a greater or lesser extent both democratic and undemocratic elements, hierarchical and 'bottom up' aspects, and that none deserves romanticism or any form of blanket characterisation.

'The Road to Freedom is via the Cross':
'Just Means' in Chief Albert Luthuli's Life

RAYMOND SUTTNER

University of South Africa

Abstract

This article deals with the ambiguities relating to the use of violence on the part of Chief Albert Luthuli, president of the African National Congress (ANC) until his death in 1967, the first African to be awarded the Nobel Peace Prize. The article examines what Luthuli said and did and what are argued to be multiple meanings attached to these. The article does not set out a definitive reading but uses statements of Luthuli and others to probe ambiguity and symbolism, which point to the possibility that much of his work may have opened up debate on the apparent fruitlessness of non-violence against an intransigent regime. Whether adoption of violence was Luthuli's desire is not argued, but he appears to have come to terms with it. The counter-arguments that stress absolute opposition to violence are not rebutted on a point-by-point basis to argue Luthuli's preference for violence, rather than possible pragmatism.

Chief Albert John Luthuli[1] was announced as Africa's first Nobel Peace Prize winner 50 years ago, in 1960. Revisiting his life is necessary, not purely because of neglect, much as one uncovers an archaeological relic of the South African past. We are, instead, examining the legacy of a figure who may well provide inspiration and guidance on the issues that confront South Africa now and in the future.

Many find it difficult to articulate questions pertaining to morality and ethics. There is a sense that a person who speaks about these matters is being precious or claiming special subjective qualities for him or herself, and that this belongs to the clergy who are not in any case always taken seriously. Words connoting the moral or ethical content of our actions have lost currency. This seems to have been particularly so in the political world, possibly going back to the post-1990 or 1994 period, or even earlier.

One of the reasons why Luthuli's life is important to revisit is that it fuses ethics, especially personal commitment to the values of his religion and to his political beliefs and actions. There is a sense in dealing with Luthuli that we are not merely addressing cold political issues where

---

1.   Luthuli preferred the spelling Lutuli, but I follow that of his descendants, who use Luthuli.

our judgement is required, although he has clear direction. But that direction is also informed by his religious beliefs which converge with the way he acts out his political life. How he represents these presupposes that he has made a choice, the undertaking of which requires political and religious examination.

There is no one in current South African politics as far as I know, who bears these values in this way and yet it is more necessary now than ever before. We are in a time when we need to turn, without blindness to the faults they may have or have had, to the lessons of exemplary leaders and reconsider what it is that we can learn and transmit to others. We need to build on this in order to inform our politics in a different way from that which currently prevails. There is of course a danger in notions like 'exemplary leadership' and one must be conscious of the need to avoid idealisation and this is not always easy to observe when one becomes absorbed in such work.

Unfortunately, the legacy of Chief Luthuli has been relatively neglected compared with others. As Dr Albertinah Luthuli (his eldest daughter, 'Ntombazana') remarked, I (the author) want to bring him up from '6 feet under'[2] into public view. Most of the major leaders have had substantial biographies written about them, which is not the case with Luthuli. There has only been a short biography by Mary Benson and that is not a substantial or careful scrutiny of his life.[3] This paper is intended to take Chief Luthuli seriously not merely as an event (as often happens in memorial lectures) where we talk about something else but link it to Luthuli. This legacy is revisited in its own right, attempting to achieve the rigour that it requires. This entails probing the legacy and his choices in order to understand them properly, but also in certain cases to examine concepts he uses and ideas he expresses and ask whether he has treated them in a manner that is the only meaning that can be given. It is asked whether these words can bear another and possibly more dynamic and changing content, one that is more emancipatory. While that may not have been his interpretation 60 years ago, the re-reading is quite compatible with Luthuli's life view and constantly enquiring spirit.

We will only discharge our duty properly if we do not turn such exercises into romanticism and assume that everything that the Chief said or did was correct for all time. He was a child of his time, and many of the beliefs that he held or interpretations offered by him may well have been revisited[4] had he not died in so tragic and unresolved a manner, struck by a goods train.[5] Elements of Luthuli's life are discussed not merely in appreciation of his qualities, but also to engage with them critically and argue that some of his views were mistaken or are now known to be inapplicable or wrong. This disagreement is a sign of the importance attached to Luthuli, that he still 'lives' and is not merely a figure to which we accord periodic heroic or other noble allusions. It is not merely by repeating what he said that we honour him. It is by engaging in a robust manner with his legacy that we examine his contemporary relevance.

It will also be argued that Luthuli's life was full of ambiguities, as was his thinking. This is an indication of complexity and nuance and that he was a man who was willing to learn

2.   Interview conducted by the author, Ballito, 21 July 2009.
3.   M. Benson, *Chief Albert Lutuli of South Africa* (London: Oxford University Press, 1963).
4.   Where his views are likely to have changed include his notions of civilisation and 'copying from others' certain other cultural and identity-related questions. See for example, G. Pillay, ed., *Voices of Liberation, Volume 1: Albert Lutuli* (Pretoria: HSRC Press, 1993), 43.
5.   That an apartheid-era inquest found no foul play does not close the matter, as with most other inquests of that time. I need to go no further than to record that it is open to question, but I cannot pursue that topic here.

when confronting situations that changed. Mahatma Gandhi, when confronted by much greater inconsistency in his thinking, did not contest this assessment, but said 'judge me by my actions'.[6] With Luthuli I am arguing not that there was a weakness in ambiguity, but that while he wanted to address a particular issue, he sometimes opened up debate going well beyond that and allowing for conclusions that may well not have been originally intended. I do not see Luthuli as seeking any final answers, but asking questions repeatedly and openly with a willingness to learn.

Luthuli found violence repugnant. Most of the generation from the 1960s onwards when confronted by the demand that they renounce violence, were in fact called upon to renounce the armed struggle of the African National Congress (ANC).[7] This became a condition for release from prison or detention in the 1980s, rejected by most and accepted, for a range of reasons, by some.[8] As with most people in their normal life, Luthuli abhorred the harm wreaked by violence, the power of one imposed on an unwilling other. Like Gandhi, he was not a pacifist and all his statements on violence have an element of conditionality attached, related to the practicality of implementing *the principle* at a specific moment. Violence at an abstract level could do no good. At a concrete level, the violence of the oppressors could force the oppressed to depart from the principle of non-violence and to have recourse to methods, like armed struggle, more appropriate to the situation. Violence was never a principle with the national liberation movement, while peace is. The final part of the Freedom Charter reads: 'There Shall be Peace and Friendship'.[9] Armed struggle may have been heroic at specific times, but it was never a principle of the ANC.

Consequently, when dealing with his attitude towards violence, it is not argued that Luthuli wanted violence, but that there is room to see his stance as opening a debate and even an element of *conditional* support[10] (as with Gandhi), that is, allowing it to be ethically correct under certain circumstances (which support could also have been withdrawn with a change in such conditions). In other words, the departure from the principle of non-violence was an aberration, while non-violence was the norm. Gandhi expresses an example of the reasons behind conditional departure from non-violence in 1947:

6.   Quoted in N. Sen, ed., *Wit and Wisdom of Mahatma Gandhi* (New Delhi: New Book Society, 1995), 44.
7.   The ANC is the oldest existing liberation movement, formed in 1912 (as the South African Native National Congress and is now in government), on the African continent. Initially it was open to African men only. This raises the complicated issue of terminology, which has considerable ideological significance as a result of apartheid naming and dividing. In this paper the South African population is described as comprising whites (at one stage called 'Europeans') and blacks (at one stage called non-Europeans, and still called non-whites by some). The word black supplanted non-white with the rise of the Black Consciousness Movement in the late 1960s, amongst many of those who supported the anti-apartheid struggle, in order to stress the unity of all black (previously non-white) people. The black people however comprise groupings subjected to different levels of oppression under apartheid: Africans, coloureds (of mixed race) and Indians. It is true that all South Africans are 'Africans' in a sense of belonging and other existential or geographical reasons, but the term used here specifically refers to that section which had been subjected to the most intensive oppression under apartheid.
8.   It is not my intention to condemn those who signed such declarations. There is a range of factors that impact on these decisions, including lengthy terms served in relative isolation or simple and honest acknowledgement that no more of that life could be endured.
9.   See R. Suttner and J. Cronin, *50 Years of the Freedom Charter* (Pretoria: UNISA Press, 2006), 266 and commentary, 189ff.
10. Since first writing this very qualified sentence, I have interviewed all his daughters, a son-in-law and other informants who are very clear that he supported the armed struggle. Interviews: Dr Albertinah Luthuli and Thembekile Luthuli Ngobese, Kwa Mashu, 29 August 2009; Thandeka Luthuli-Gcabashe, Umhlanga Rocks, 28 August 2009; and Thulani Gcabashe, Edendale, 29 September 2009.

... The violence we see today is the violence of cowards. There is also such a thing as the violence of the brave. If four or five men enter into a fight and die by the sword, there is a violence in it but it is the violence of the brave. But when ten thousand armed men attack a village of unarmed people and slaughter them along with their wives and children it is the violence of cowards. America unleashed its atom bomb over Japan. That was the violence of the cowards. The non-violence of the brave is a thing worth seeing. I want to see that non-violence before I die.[11]

Chief Luthuli was not one to suppress debate no matter how strongly he felt about a subject. But in opening up questions early in his presidency of the ANC in 1952, he risked that the resultant discussion would lead to conclusions quite different from those which he initially advocated. This, as indicated, was not to say that his initial premise of commitment to non-violence would not again become hegemonic, given a change of conditions, as has happened in post-1994 South Africa. In other words, violence may be an exception which is conditionally accepted, but once the conditions no longer exist, the respect for non-violence as a general approach returns. As a principle of social coexistence it is always necessary, even if temporarily in abeyance. Alternatively, having acquired the skills or special tools for practising violent acts it is within the realms of possibility that these may again be retrieved and threaten democracy. That is part of the climate of present-day South Africa, where violence is often treated as a virtue, rather than, as Luthuli did, seen as a necessity under special conditions.[12]

Just Means and Just Ends

Chief Luthuli's conception of justice in the sense of what he strove for may not be a subject of great contestation in the sense that it derives from broadly agreed ideas such as those found in the Universal Declaration of Human Rights and the Freedom Charter,[13] supported and informed by his own Christian outlook, drawn from the Old and New Testament. This is not extensively developed in his writings, but may be generally uncontentious. But the question of what means may be employed to realise just ends under a very unjust order is an issue of debate and disagreement. This is part of a wider discussion over whether any means are justifiable if one's goal is worthy. Chief Luthuli, like many others, believed the means that the ANC employed should be worthy of its just cause, that it should not act in a manner that devalued that cause; and though he often adds the notion of practicality, he associates a just means with non-violent activity. In this respect he was in line with the thinking of Gandhi, though both were not pacifists.[14] The implication that his line of principle was conditional, being dependent on actions of the oppressor, can be found in his ANC presidential address of 1953, where he says, '[w]e can assure the world that it is our

11.   G. Gandhi, ed., *The Oxford India Gandhi: Essential Writings* (New Delhi: Oxford University Press, 2008), 649.
12.   See R. Suttner, 'The Zuma Era – its Historical Context and the Future', *African Historical Review*, 41, 3 (2009), 28–59; and 'Violence: Necessity or Virtue', *Mail & Guardian* (Johannesburg), 14–20 May 2010, 33.
13.   Although not directly mentioned, these principles infuse the address delivered on receiving the Nobel Prize in 1961. See Pillay, *Voices*, 130–145.
14.   Pillay, *Voices*, 157, citing Treason Trial (1956–61) testimony; N. Mandela, *Long Walk to Freedom: The Autobiography of Nelson Mandela* (Randburg: Macdonald Purnell, 1994), 260; I. Meer, *A Fortunate Man* (Cape Town: Zebra Press, 2002), 224; Benson, *Chief Lutuli*, 65. See also Mahatma Gandhi, above.

intention to keep on the non-violent plane. We would earnestly request the powers that be *to make it possible for us to keep our people in this mood*'.[15]

What is explored are the implications of this stance in Luthuli's life and the complexity in attempting to achieve this aspiration. It will be argued that to decide what is an appropriate or just means in every situation, whether as a Christian, a Communist, and/or an international human rights activist, is not simple. It will be contended that Chief Luthuli's own beliefs on the matter are open to more than one interpretation; or he opened a debate on a potential for more than one interpretation.[16] In fact, recent interviews and discussions with his three surviving daughters, a son and one son-in-law, take the question into another realm. They indicate a broader degree of support for armed resistance as 'intransigence' intensified. But this was provided the masses were properly trained and not used as cannon fodder.[17]

At the time when Chief Luthuli became national president of the ANC there was already much talk about 'taking up the gun' and 'fighting back'. Walter Sisulu in concert with Nelson Mandela, without any organisational mandate, had in fact enquired of the Chinese – without success – whether they would provide support in the event of an armed struggle.[18] These leaders who were moving towards taking up arms were in fact acting in line with the sentiments of many of the rank and file.[19] Many later 'jumped the gun' and started burning sugar cane fields in Natal province in the late 1950s, before the question of armed action had been formally placed on the ANC's agenda.[20]

While there were these currents tending towards a military option, others counselled caution. Chief Luthuli is reputed to have been slow to approve of any violent action – on principle. Mandela argues that the Chief, while inclined towards non-violence did not stand in the way of armed struggle.[21] This will not go unchallenged and is likely to remain controversial amongst historians (despite what I have quoted from his children).[22] Moses Kotane, the South African Communist Party (SACP) general secretary, who had become a close confidant of the Chief during the Treason Trial of 1956–61, while not opposed to violence on principle, initially considered resort to arms as being reckless on the revolutionary basis that one should not risk lives until all other options have been fully exhausted.[23] In this respect, there is a degree of convergence with the non-ethical reference of Luthuli to practical reasons for non-violence, and

---

15. E. Reddy, compiler, *Luthuli: Speeches of Chief Albert John Luthuli* (Durban and Bellville: Madiba Publishers and UWC Historical and Cultural Centre, 1991), 57. Italics inserted.

16. But see S. Couper, 'My People Let Go: A Historical Examination of Chief Albert Luthuli and his Position on the Use of Violence as a Means to Achieve South Africa's Liberation from Apartheid', *International Congregational Journal*, 5, 1 (2005), 102, 106 and discussion below. Couper says this but comes to quite different conclusions from mine. Rev. Couper was the priest serving the Groutville Congregational community until recently. See also for distinct interpretations: B. Bunting, *Moses Kotane: South African Revolutionary* (Bellville: Mayibuye Books, 1998), 229ff; Pillay, 'Introduction', Voices, 3–33.

17. Interview, Albertinah Luthuli; discussion with Thembekile Ngobese; and interview, Thandeka Luthuli-Gcabashe.

18. While this was not the first or last time Mandela acted outside of the collective (for example his apparent call for violent resistance in the Sophiatown removals of the 1950s, and later his unilateral initiation of negotiations), it is unusual for Sisulu's political life.

19. South African Democracy Education Trust (SADET), *The Road to Democracy in South Africa, Volume 1* (Cape Town: Zebra Press, 2004), 53–146.

20. *Ibid.*, 62ff.

21. Mandela, *Long Walk to Freedom*, 260; Meer, *A Fortunate Man*, 224.

22. SADET, *Road to Democracy*, 89–90; and for opposing views, see Couper, 'My People Let Go'.

23. Mandela, *Long Walk to Freedom*, chapter 41; Bunting, *Moses Kotane*, 73–74.

the oral evidence of the qualifications he placed on support for armed action. For both there was a conditionality that made non-violence viable, longer than it did for Mandela.

Kotane had great influence on the ANC leadership. It required an all-night discussion with Mandela chiding him with the example of the Cuban Communist Party having fallen behind the popular organisations by its tardiness to take up arms in the Cuban revolution, to contain Kotane's negative sentiments. Kotane agreed not to oppose Mandela and be silent in the ANC National Executive Committee (NEC), that is, not necessarily signifying that he approved, without qualification.[24] It should be noted, however, that the formation of MK (mKhonto we Sizwe, the Spear of the Nation, as the ANC's military wing) was on an ambiguous basis. In order to protect ordinary ANC members and leaders who were not engaged in MK, it was established as a separate body. Consequently, although Mandela repeatedly reported to the Chief on MK and was in fact arrested on return from one of these visits,[25] formally it was not an ANC organisation at the time of its establishment. This created various problems of accountability and in the recruitment process.[26]

Perhaps we have tended to draw too sharp a line between the peaceful and armed struggle, and this can be illustrated in the actions and words of Chief Luthuli, around which there remain controversy.

The announcement of the Nobel Prize award to Chief Luthuli was made in 1960. He received the prize in 1961. It is said that the formation of MK and its initiation of sabotage was postponed to avoid embarrassing Luthuli while receiving this award and also casting doubts on the longstanding peaceful campaigns of the organisation that he led. The proximity in time was nevertheless acknowledged by Mandela to have been unfortunate.[27]

But any embarrassment must be qualified and the potential of using violence could have been foreseen. Even in his earlier non-violent statements, Luthuli gives indications of the ultimate fruitlessness of these efforts. Indeed, in one of his most famous speeches 'The Road to Freedom is via the Cross', after the government deposed him as a chief, he reflected in 1952:

> Who can deny that 30 years of my life have been spent knocking in vain, patiently, moderately and modestly, at a closed and barred door? What have been the fruits of my many years of moderation? Has there been any reciprocal tolerance or moderation from the government? No! On the contrary, the past 30 years have seen the greatest number of laws restricting our rights and progress, until today we have reached a stage where we have almost no rights at all.[28]

What conclusion is the listener or reader to draw from this statement? It is a statement of failure of non-violent peaceful activities. Not one to run away from unpleasant facts, he put on record that non-violence had not succeeded. For the person who followed Luthuli, could this not have been seen as an invitation or encouragement to debate the matter further? Luthuli believed

24. Mandela, *Long Walk to Freedom*, 258–260.
25. On the separation of ANC and MK, see Mandela, *Long Walk to Freedom*, 260–261. On repeated consultation between Mandela and Luthuli, see interviews with Thembekile Ngobese, Albertinah Luthuli and Thandeka Luthuli-Gcabashe above.
26. J. Matthews, interview, SADET, *The Road to Democracy: South Africans Telling their Stories, Volume 1, 1955–1970* (Houghton: Mutloatse Publishers, 2008), 19–20; R. Suttner, *The ANC Underground in South Africa* (Jacana: Johannesburg, 2008), 34–35.
27. Mandela, *Long Walk to Freedom*, 273.
28. Pillay, *Voices*, 47. The speech was delivered in November 1952 (see Reddy, *Luthuli*, 41), not after the Treason Trial, as stated by Couper, 'My People Let Go', 104. This trial only began in 1956.

strongly in non-violence, but in many of his statements, as indicated, he suggests that it was not only a good in itself but the most *practical* course to follow. But in this declaration he concedes that the approach had not brought results. As an open-minded person, was he not inviting others to question that course or debate its validity, or consider pursuing it with greater vigour and imagination? The reference to knocking on the door for 30 years without results quickly became part of the repertoire of struggle songs, demanding an opening:

Open Malan, we are knocking: (four times)
Wake up Luthuli, Luthuli of Africa (twice)
You will never refuse when you are sent (twice)
Let God be praised (four times)
What has the black person done?
Let Africa return! (four times)[29]

The refrain is ambiguous, because it is not calling for something beyond 'knocking', even though Luthuli had concluded that this had not succeeded. But again, knocking may itself be more or less aggressive and does not necessarily connote polite petitioning, given that the ANC was already engaged in acts of defiance. On the connotation of knocking, many activists will testify to the anxiety and fear induced by the loud knocking of the police. There is, however, no denying that one of the interpretations to which Luthuli's own words are open, is that the results of non-violence were very limited. The time for armed struggle may have arrived, or have been near; at the very least, it needed to be considered. It does not worry me greatly whether or not Luthuli fervently supported or gave qualified support or was simply silent on the armed struggle and the formation of MK. All that is indicated is that within his non-violent stance, he himself voiced frustration at the results it had yielded and provided the foundation on which an armed struggle could be debated or justified.

This differs from Couper, who while referring to Luthuli's 'complex and ambiguous' stance, insists on his steadfast adherence to non-violence.[30] That cannot be without qualification, nor can it be said that he supported armed struggle without caveats. My refuge is in the notion of ambiguity, the sign of an unresolved question, which seems to best capture the state of mind of the Chief. This is to be read together with the abovementioned reference to conditionality. Equally, if Couper, as indicated above, sees much of Luthuli's statements being suffused with ambiguity, why should he state that this passage was 'certainly not intended by him to be used to justify the armed struggle'?[31] Surely the Chief could not have discounted such an interpretation, which was part of the basis for many people's resort to arms in later times?[32]

In his statement after the Rivonia trial verdict, Luthuli said:

The African National Congress … held consistently to a policy of using militant, non-violent means of struggle … But finally all avenues of resistance were closed. The African National Congress and other organisations were made illegal; their leaders jailed, exiled or forced underground.[33]

29. Translation from the Zulu version, in L. Kuper, *Passive Resistance in South Africa* (New Haven: Yale University Press, 1957), 14–15.
30. Couper, 'My People Let Go', 106, 107.
31. *Ibid.*, 113.
32. See Mandela's statement from the dock, in N. Mandela, *The Struggle is My Life* (London: IDAF, 1990), 163.
33. T. Karis and G. Gerhart, *From Protest to Challenge: A Documentary History of African Politics in South Africa 1882–1964, Volume 3: Challenge and Violence, 1953–1964* (Stanford: Stanford University Press, 1977), 798–799.

Like Mandela in his court statement in the Rivonia trial,[34] he referred to the need to contain spontaneous acts of violent resistance in the face of intensified apartheid repression. '[S]poradic acts of uncontrolled violence were increasing throughout the country. At first in one place, then in another, there were spontaneous eruptions against intolerable conditions; many of these acts increasingly assumed a racial character.' Luthuli continues:

> The African National Congress *never abandoned its method of a militant, non-violent struggle*, and of creating in the process a spirit of militancy in the people. However, *in the face of the uncompromising white refusal to abandon a policy which denies the African and other oppressed South Africans their rightful heritage – freedom – no one can blame brave just men for seeking justice by the use of violent methods;* nor could they be blamed if they tried to create an organized force in order to ultimately establish peace and racial harmony. [35]

This is a statement that should not be hurriedly unpacked. It is first and foremost an affirmation of opposition to violence as an undesirable means for dealing with disputes. It signals that non-violence has not yielded results and is in itself another qualification on his allegedly absolutist position on violence. Logically, what Luthuli recounts as the result of his moderate knocking on closed and barred doors is that it had seen a worsening of the situation. Is it not implicit, or a very legitimate conclusion, that more aggressive steps could follow and that he, Luthuli, could not condemn those who had taken this route? None of this detracted from the commitment to non-violence where circumstances allowed. That is obviously not the only inference that can be drawn, especially given the time, for some have said that non-violent resistance was not pursued with sufficient vigour. It was not non-violence that had failed but as J.N. Singh put it, 'we have failed non-violence'.[36] Indeed Luthuli may then have thought that the ANC had not done so with sufficient imagination, though he did not voice this. But then 'finally', as he puts it, 'all avenues of resistance were closed'. To avert random violence, an organised force was created. Without volunteering to join or saying he actively supported it, he makes it clear that those who chose to take up arms were 'just men … seeking justice by the use of violent methods …'[37]

I am reading into what Luthuli said, elaborating more than he ever did in his public statements,[38] because while condemning violence – in principle – we should not fetishise or esssentialise the difference between violence and non-violence in ANC history. ANC history manifests continuities which repeatedly contain ruptures and likewise ruptures bear within them elements of continuity. That is why even in the words of one of the main proponents of non-violence one can read an argument for changing tack, towards armed struggle, amongst other possibilities.[39]

Couper, while noting the complex and ambiguous nature of Luthuli's positions,[40] and that there can be many understandings,[41] (though the position advanced here is not any of the 10 listed), but relying on Luthuli's Nobel Prize speech, comes down for a more or less unqualified

34. Mandela, *The Struggle*, 165ff; Mandela, *Long Walk to Freedom*, 260.
35. Karis and Gerhart, *Challenge and Violence*, 798–799. Emphasis inserted.
36. Quoted in Mandela, *Long Walk to Freedom*, 261; and in Meer, *A Fortunate Man*, 224.
37. Karis and Gerhart, *Challenge and Violence*, 789–799.
38. As indicated above, the oral evidence accessed thus far does point to his having accepted armed struggle.
39. Lyn Graybill notes caveats to this effect in his Nobel Prize speech. See L.Graybill., *Religion and Resistance Politics in South Africa* (Westport: Praeger, 1995), 38.
40. Couper, 'My People Let Go', 106.
41. *Ibid.*, 108.

support for non-violence.[42] But after citing a rather garbled rendition of ANC history by Pillay,[43] and his own textual analysis of words in Luthuli's Rivonia statement, an analysis that seems to 'protest too much', he again reiterates a *preference* for non-violence.[44]

That preference was there. It is not intended to suggest that violence was in the Chief's mind from early on, certainly not for him, but only that it is a legitimate and possible inference, which experience had forced upon his thinking. It is important that we understand that in practice no approach was irreversible nor displacing all others.

Indian Political and Cultural Influence: Oaths and Dress as Signifiers of Embryonic Violence[45]

In the early 1950s, we have noted on the part of some of the leading cadres as well as regional leaders, anticipation of conflict and the day when the African people would again be soldiers. We have thus far only the testimony of males, and it may be that there was similar talk amongst the women, but we do not know, insofar as available evidence is concerned. This is also a period where the most dedicated, the 'voluntiyas' (volunteers), wore a specific uniform, distinguishing themselves as cadres of the liberation movement, willing to make unlimited sacrifices. The uniform marked them off as a special group of highly disciplined and not merely casual members or followers of the ANC. There does not appear to be any evidence to suggest an African or other black people having influenced the form of this uniform, apart from the use of the 'Gandhi cap'. Luli Callinicos[46] has suggested that the jacket derives from the shirts Nehru used to wear. There is an undoubted similarity, but the Nehru shirt was multi-coloured and of soft fabric, while the voluntiyas only wore tough khaki jackets, usually with nothing underneath, in the photographs I have seen. (Nehru often wore a shirt or vest under the shirt.) It seems most likely that it was an adaptation of the uniforms worn during the World Wars, although nothing I have read or anyone with whom I have spoken has been able to point to the precise origins.

The volunteers also swore an oath to undertake to operate within the discipline of the organisation.[47] Significantly, Gandhi also placed great weight on oaths and vows, using these in the early recruitment of Indian volunteer protesters in South Africa, notably in a great 'bonfire' of registration certificates in 1908. They could foster unity not only within the self but also be of use in the structures of the organisation. The oath is also related to *psychological preparedness for sacrifice*, on which more is said below.[48] Gandhi had specifically chosen the cap or had it adapted from the Kashmiri hat as an emblem of the Indian struggle and nation to be.[49] In a sense, this sets up a tension between the uniform carrying potential military connotations and the cap, bearing the imagery of Gandhism and non-violence. On the other hand, while armed struggle was adopted, the ANC never renounced peaceful, legal struggle where it was feasible. This can

42.   *Ibid.*, 119.
43.   Pillay, *Voices*, 30.
44.   Couper, 'My People Let Go', 122.
45.   This argument is developed more substantially in R. Suttner, 'Dress, Gestures and Other Cultural Representations and Manifestations and Indian Influence on the Formation of ANC Masculinities', *Historia*, 54, 1 (2009), 51–91.
46.   Personal communication, 4 July 2009.
47.   M. Benson, *South Africa: The Struggle for a Birthright* (London: IDAF, 1985), 143–146.
48.   M. Chatterjee, *Gandhi's Diagnostic Approach Rethought: Exploring a Perspective on his Life and Work* (New Delhi: Promilla, 2007), chapter 4.
49.   E. Tarlo, *Clothing Matters: Dress and Identity in India* (Chicago: University of Chicago Press, 1996), 70.

be seen in the eagerness with which openings of the late 1970s and 1980s were encouraged for mass activities.

Interestingly, amongst the contemporary interpretations running counter to some of the implications I have raised, was Helen Joseph being very impressed and seeing the uniforms as signifying 'peace volunteers' at her first attendance of an ANC conference in 1954.[50]

In accepting the Nobel Prize, Luthuli again raises military connotations through his attire, wearing the headdress, necklace and other elements of the apparel of his chieftaincy. Luthuli was acting in line with what the ANC would do throughout its existence, joining the struggles of the day to its heritage, by some wearing the insignia of chieftaincy or other signifiers identifying them with their clan or chiefdom. The ambiguities that this may have evoked were part of the ambiguities that the ANC always carried.

What Luthuli wears around his neck appears to be *iminqwamba*, which is associated with medicinal powers[51] and it is made of hawks' claws.[52] The history of association of medicinal powers with both curing individuals and preparation for war,[53] and the hawk representing aggression, increase the ambiguity around Luthuli's identity and the potential associations which can be drawn.

'Ramshackle Home', Nobel Prize Money and Swazi Farms

Chief Luthuli was a remarkable man, but in his home there were tendencies and issues of disagreement that one finds in many others. The children were not immune to the aspirations of young people for the good things of life. According to Albertinah Luthuli (Ntombazana), some of the daughters felt somewhat ashamed of their home, compared with others. When they approached the Chief, they told him that he was a man who was visited by important people from all over the world and he should host them in a better house. He should find a way of earning more money to do this. The Chief was not convinced that there was anything wrong with the house. He was quite happy with it.

When the news of the Nobel Prize reached the family, the elder sisters started to imagine the home they would buy, one that would make them the envy of the rest of Groutville. Their imaginations came to a halt when almost all the money was spent on buying farms in Swaziland, because, the Chief explained, people might have to leave the country and the ANC could make use of them. Nokukhanya, MaBhengu, Luthuli's wife would tend these farms from time to time, in order to ensure that they were not seen by the Swazis as unoccupied. According to Thulani Gcabashe, her son-in-law, during the 1960s there were MK cadres or recruits being tended for by MaBhengu and he also worked on the farms. In the 1960s they were also able to take a lot of produce back to Groutville, although the farms collapsed in the 1970s.[54]

---

50.   E-mail communication with 1950s veteran, Norman Levy, 15 July 2009.
51.   E-mail communication with John Wright, 4 August 2008.
52.   Personal communication, Luthuli's grandson, Nkululeko Luthuli, 4 June 2008.
53.   See J. Guy, *The Maphumulo Uprising: War, Law and Ritual in the Zulu Rebellion* (Pietermaritzburg: UK-ZN Press, 2005). See similar evidence prior to the Wankie campaign of 1967, in Suttner, *ANC Underground*, chapter 4. The detachment was named after Luthuli. This is the ANC's representation, but in the interview, Albertinah Luthuli referred to this specifically as indicating the Chief's identification with armed struggle.
54.   Interviews Thulani Gcabashe and Albertinah Luthuli. Earlier telephonic conversation with Thembekile Ngobese, 14 April 2009, where the use of the farms as ANC transit camps was confirmed. See also P. Rule, with M. Aitken and J. van Dyk, *Nokukhanya: Mother of Light* (Johannesburg: Grail Press, 1993), 131ff.

The only part of the money that was used by the family was for the purchase of a flat to be shared by sisters Albertinah and Thandeka in the event of their finding themselves without a home.[55] The family lifestyle in their house in Groutville remained unaltered until the death of the Chief.

In many of the interviews conducted with individuals who left the country, these relate that they were met in Swaziland by ANC veterans like John Nkadimeng and stayed at some unknown place.[56] The weight of evidence leads one to conclude that there is little doubt that the Chief, whatever his initial reservations may have been, decided to contribute practically to the success of MK through such logistical support.

Couper seems to support the likelihood that these were ANC transit camps though their objective was not clear. My starting point is that armed activity is not merely carrying a gun but also includes a range of logistical support assisting exit and entry into the country. Without this, a particular underground or armed action would not have been possible. Clearly, accommodation and meals was part of such ancillary support.[57] Couper indicates that this may have been what happened:

> One would need to determine what kind of 'refugees' these farms were intended to serve. It is true that the lines between a 'combatant' refugee and a 'political refugee' were very blurred during the struggle. Perhaps the distinction was not even attempted as regards the use of the farms. Second, were the farms utilised as 'safehouses', or as launching pads for military operations across the border? Either case is very doubtful. The answer to these questions would point to whether the farms in exile suggest Luthuli's support of the ANC's change of strategy.[58]

This quotation shows that it is not clear from the written record what the precise terms of Luthuli's engagement with the ANC armed struggle became. As Couper suggests, there is a version that may provide the answer. Luthuli is reported, apart from the oral evidence above, to have told Moses Kotane: 'When my son decides to sleep with a girl, he does not ask for my permission, but just does it. It is only afterwards when the girl is pregnant and the parents make a case that he brings his troubles home'.[59] One thing is clear and that is that transit houses, whether for political, combatants, safehouses or military operations, are all actions in support of MK or other underground work.[60]

One possible additional document which supports the notion that Luthuli probably did come to terms with armed struggle during this period, is the view expressed by Professor Z.K. Matthews, who was very like-minded with Luthuli in many of these matters. He is reported to have had a similar stance to Luthuli at the NEC meeting deciding on the formation of MK.[61] In a World Council of Churches speech in 1964, he said, *inter alia*:

> It is clear that Mandela and his colleagues *were still inspired by the spirit of non-violence. They reluctantly recognised that violence was inevitable*, but they were convinced that if it did come, it

---

55. Interview Albertinah Luthuli.
56. Suttner, *The ANC Underground*, for example, chapter 4. See also H. Bernstein, *The Rift: The Exile Experience of South Africans* (London: Jonathan Cape, 1994), for many such accounts scattered within her interview material.
57. See Suttner, *ANC Underground*, chapter 6, regarding women performing logistical tasks.
58. Couper, 'My People Let Go', 116.
59. Bunting, *Moses Kotane*, 274.
60. See Suttner, *ANC Underground*, chapter 6, on the erroneous notion of logistical support treated as non-combatant work.
61. Joe Matthews interview in SADET, *South Africans Telling their Stories*, 19–20.

was their duty as responsible leaders of the people, to take certain steps about it, namely, to ensure (1) that such a movement should be *under the guidance of responsible leaders like themselves imbued with the spirit of non-violence*; (2) that it should be carried out without any loss of life, but should be directed against installations which did not involve danger to life.[62]

This is a significant confirmation of the continuity within the rupture that MK comprised, that Matthews sees it as an action taken by those who were committed to non-violent struggle. Then he concludes by asking:

When the flower of African youth ... are being sentenced to long terms of imprisonment during peace time, for fighting for their legitimate rights in what they believe to be the only ways open to them, can we say that the Christian thing to do is to advise them to acquiesce in their present situation and wait, Micawber-like, for something to turn up?[63]

In a small way, the oral record in the interviews and reports on discussions held have provided the likelihood of an answer that narrows the ambiguities.

In Choosing the Road to Freedom, be Prepared to Do What you Advocate and Suffer

Gandhi was very clear that he himself should be prepared to do whatever he advocated.[64] Mandela in facing the death penalty indicates that when one says one is prepared to die, one must have prepared oneself for that and be sure that this is in fact the case.[65] Luthuli stressed that anyone who took an action should be certain that s/he was ready for the consequences. The Natal region of the ANC had not been properly informed of the impending Defiance Campaign by the previous president, A.W.G. Champion, and consequently delayed their entry. At the moment of decision, Chief Luthuli, the new Natal president said: 'Look, we will be calling upon people to make very important demonstrations and unless we are sure of the road and prepared to travel along it ourselves we have no right to call other people along it.' M.B. Yengwa, who had just become secretary of Natal, described what happened after that: 'We all said we were prepared and he said he too was prepared and he asked us to pray. We gave our pledge and we prayed'.[66] Yengwa is reported as saying that this was the turning point in Luthuli's life. He had decided, not irresponsibly, to damn the consequences, as long as he was advancing the cause of the movement.[67]

One of the reasons I find myself drawn to a leader, the details of whose life are sketchy compared to those of others whose biographies have been written, is the character of his statements. They are words from which it is hard to retreat; they put his body on the line. They do not speak purely of the current situation and strategies but what he, Albert Luthuli, chose to do. He speaks of the sacrifices and potential dangers to which he committed himself to face. The

---

62. Z.K. Matthews, 'The Road from Non-violence to Violence', Speech at a conference in Kitwe, sponsored by the World Council of Churches, May 1964: see T. Karis and G. Gerhart, eds, *From Protest to Challenge: A Documentary History of African Politics in South Africa, 1882–1990, Volume 5: Nadir and Resurgence, 1964–1979* (Pretoria: UNISA Press, 1997), 354. Italics inserted. The reference to avoiding 'loss of life' refers to the earliest days of MK, later superseded, although civilians were not supposed to be targets.

63. *Ibid.*, 356.

64. Chatterjee, *Gandhi's Diagnostic Approach*, chapter 4.

65. Mandela, *Long Walk to Freedom*, 360.

66. Benson, *The Struggle for a Birthright*, 144–145.

67. *Ibid.*, 145.

statements unequivocally and publicly say he is prepared to open himself to great injury in order to realise what is required. The road to freedom is via the cross and that is a road that is full of pain. The cross itself may be ambiguous, a cross of thorns, rather than the noble result desired. This is captured in Matthew's Gospel, where the governor's soldiers 'twisted together a crown of thorns and set it on His head'. They then mocked Him before crucifixion[68] (see below).

In the same speech ('The Road to Freedom'), Luthuli, in choosing to remain in the liberation struggle even if deposed as a chief, stares directly into the dangerous future that lay before him and gives us a glimpse of his process of thinking:

> As for myself, with a full sense of responsibility and a clear conviction, I decided to remain in the struggle for extending democratic rights and responsibilities of all sections of the South African community. I have embraced the non-violent passive resistance technique in fighting for freedom because I am convinced it is the only non-revolutionary, legitimate and humane way that could be used by people denied, as we are, effective constitutional means to further our aspirations.
>
> The wisdom or foolishness of this decision I place in the hands of the Almighty.
>
> What the future has in store for me I do not know. It might be ridicule, imprisonment, a concentration camp, flogging, banishment and even death. I only pray to the Almighty to strengthen my resolve so that none of these grim possibilities may deter me from striving, for the sake of the good name of our beloved country ... to make it a true democracy and a true union in form and spirit of all the communities in the land.
>
> My only painful concern at times is for the welfare of my family but I try even in this regard, in a spirit of trust and surrender to God's will as I see it to say: 'God will provide.'
>
> It is inevitable that in working for freedom some individuals and some families have to take the lead and suffer: The road to freedom is via the cross.[69]

Before interpreting the main part of the speech, the conditionality attached to the methods employed is again evident when Luthuli says 'denied, as we are, effective constitutional means to further our aspirations'. This obviously indicates the crossing of a threshold of legality and invites the question whether the struggle should adopt non-constitutional means and how far this interpretation can be taken.[70] At the same time, it remains an affirmation of non-violence and legality so long as conditions permit.

My general interpretation of this part of his speech, 'The Road to Freedom', is Luthuli unpacking what he understands his life's choice to mean. He interrogates what his commitment to freedom implies for a human being who has chosen that path. In so doing I read out of what is there and I read into it, perhaps, what is implicit or symbolic.

Should we read anything into his saying that the wisdom or foolishness of this decision is placed in the hands of the Almighty? Luthuli has made his decision. He may have prayed for guidance. But this invocation of the Almighty is to 'strengthen my resolve', in the decision he has himself made, so that he is not deterred by some of the grim consequences. In other words, he is not speaking of a situation where he surrenders to the Almighty. His own agency initiates some events, which the Almighty may, however, consider wise or foolish.

68. Matthew, 27: 27–31.
69. Pillay, *Voices*, 50; Reddy, *Luthuli*, 43–44.
70. See Couper, 'My People Let Go', for a different interpretation to mine.

The cross is a guide but also requires a specific choice, a purpose in one's life that needs dedication to that goal. The way to freedom is via the cross may mean that that is the way you must act but it also means that the cross is the goal, an unfolding goal as freedom is a dynamic concept that is not finalised once and for all.[71]

What follows appears to envisage what the costs may be and in this he has a cross to bear. He asks the Almighty to empower him to carry out what he has decided to do, even if he bears these costs, in carrying the cross on his shoulder. *He does not ask the Almighty to avert any such mishap from occurring. He is ready to face the potential dangers and damage. That is his choice as a free human being, connected to the Almighty insofar as he draws strength in his resolve. He asks for no mercy. He is ready to endure the consequences of his choice, which he feels is taken as a Christian, but being fallible, the Almighty might well show him one day that he has been wrong.*

When he relies on God to provide for his family in the sense of there being a way for those who tread a righteous path, not that they will be 'rewarded' but that he believes the Almighty will guide him in finding the means to survive.

The final passage of the Luthuli quotation seems to carry three meanings:

- The way to freedom is that of the cross – it is the route to follow and it coincides with the freedom struggle.
- It is a painful path in that bearing the cross is a burden in a physical or other non-spiritual sense or also entailing a constant spiritual test.
- The third meaning is potentially not surviving, martyrdom.

In a speech at the 44th Congress of the ANC in 1955, he exhorts the members to be willing to serve and sacrifice:

> But for all this we cannot claim to have prosecuted our campaigns with any semblance of military efficiency and technique. We cannot say that the Africans are accepting fast enough the gospel of service and sacrifice for the general and large good without expecting personal and at that immediate reward. They have not accepted fully the basic truth enshrined in the saying no cross, no crown.[72]

I see this as joining a call for sacrifice as necessary for freedom and that no suffering, means no freedom. Now the use of the word 'cross' again means nothing as simple as accepting Christian beliefs or following the way of the Lord, it is suggested, but an understanding that one has taken a course that can entail hardship. This can mean jail, flogging, death, but also willingness to act without thought of reward. In a sense that initial stress is to speak to the other side of our current problem in South Africa, the need for greed to be satisfied instead of serving the needs of others through our efforts.[73]

Here Luthuli is adding to the earlier statement the need to make sacrifices and eschew

71. J. Hoffman, *Gender and Sovereignty: Feminism, the State and International Relations* (Aldershot: Palgrave, 2001), 6ff, 23ff; A. Arblaster, *Democracy* (Philadelphia: Open University Press, 2002), 3, 6–9 and 15–16. As indicated below, it can also suffer reversals, as history has shown repeatedly.

72. Pillay, *Voices*, 89–90. Note the use of the words 'military efficiency and technique'. This is a significant change in discourse, though it does not in itself suggest support for or acceptance of military activity.

73. On E News International (a South African television station) on 22 March 2009, ANC Youth League leader, Julius Malema (in contrast) said that those who left the ANC to join the then new opposition party, Congress of the People (COPE), were 'now poor: you can only prosper in the ANC'.

selfishness, and this may be 'rewarded' perhaps with flogging and other forms of punishment, but even though that is not certain, those who are dedicated must prepare themselves for such possibilities.

This was a choice and we must not assume that it came to Luthuli, or anyone else, easily. It is said that Jesus hesitated. At the Mount of Olives, according to Luke, and at Gethsemane, according to Matthew, faced with death on the cross, He became sorrowful and troubled, even to death. Because of this He prayed that this cup pass,[74] or be removed from Him.[75] But, Jesus said, not my will but Your will be done. No one, no human being really wants to go the way of the cross, is how I read this, not even Jesus, who counselled others to do so.

Greg Cuthbertson argues, in addition, that this interpretation being offered is represented in Luthuli's mind as an extension of Christ's redemptive act on a cross. The powerful imagery of the cross is present in Luthuli's religious and political experiences; there is a symmetry that sets up a continuum between the material and the metaphysical. He does not separate religion and struggle.[76]

The reference to the crown as related to the cross, has a pathos because 'cross' signifies reward, but could in Christian terms also refer to the 'crown of thorns'. There is therefore an ambiguity which points to victory and crown on the one hand, and the cross of suffering and a crown of humiliation, on the other. Luthuli speaks of 'ridicule, concentration camps, banishment and death', so he is clearly aware of this ambiguity. The 'road to freedom is via the cross' which spells terrible suffering and even the 'crown' could be more humiliation. But the hope of the Christian, in his optimism, is that 'victory and the crown is also a possibility'.

> His vivid portrayal of 'being in the hands of the Almighty' is a reference to Christ's suffering even to death. He speaks of 'surrender to God's will' as the price to pay for freedom which he equates with salvation, which was to find an echo in the liberation theology of the 1960s.[77]

Luthuli was likely to have drawn on a range of texts in the New Testament, such as St Matthew's Gospel,[78] which says that 'no one is worthy of me who does not take up his cross and follow me'. This is Jesus's injunction: 'Anyone who wishes to be a follower of mine must renounce self; he must take up his cross and follow me. Whoever wants to save his life will lose it, but whoever loses his life for my sake will find it'.[79]

Walter Sisulu in stressing the revolutionary implications of the ANC's Defiance Campaign referred to a new breed of militants being developed who were prepared to suffer to the limit, being known as 'defiers of death'.[80]

---

74. Matthew, 22: 36–46.
75. Luke, 22: 39–46.
76. Personal communication with Greg Cuthbertson, 4 March 2009. See also A. Nolan, God in South Africa: The Challenge of the Gospel (Cape Town: David Philip, 1988), especially chapter 8.
77. Personal communication, Greg Cuthbertson.
78. Matthew, 10: 38.
79. Matthew, 16: 24–25.
80. W. Sisulu, I Will Go Singing: Walter Sisulu Speaks of his Life and the Struggle for Freedom in South Africa, in conversation with G.M. Houser and H. Shore (Cape Town and New York: Robben Island Museum and the Africa Fund, nd., c. 2001), 79.

Strengthened in One's Choice by Solidarity with Others in Struggle

Albert Nolan addresses the question of how one might draw strength in carrying out one's commitment. He associates the notion of 'liberation struggle' with the ideas of hope of a solution.[81] He notes the importance of singing and dancing, and remarks that they are also a celebration of solidarity or unity in struggle:

> The struggle rescues people from alienation, isolation and individualism. It restores *ubuntu* (humanness) and the experience of being a living member of a living body. Hence the slogan 'an injury to one is an injury to all'.[82] I can only presume that this is derived from the statement of Paul in I Corinthians: 'God has arranged the body … so that each part may be equally concerned for all the others. *If one part is hurt, all parts are hurt with it.* If one part is given honour, all parts enjoy it'.[83] I am also reminded of Jesus saying, 'Whatever you do to the least of my brothers and sisters, you do to me'.[84] …
>
> … To participate fully in the struggle you need something more than commitment, you need heroic *courage* …. [I]t is the struggle that helps them to overcome their natural fears. *The experience of solidarity and support together with the examples of others gradually enables a person to overcome fear and to act with confidence and courage.*[85]

Nolan sees the struggle as embodying a religious aura, celebrating hope, the experience of community, the self-sacrifice, the total commitment, the courage, the discipline and the willingness to live and die. These, he argues, are normally associated with religion.[86]

> When Jesus discovered great faith outside of the system … he exclaimed: 'Nowhere in Israel have I found faith like this'.[87] Would it be an exaggeration to say of the struggle in South Africa today: 'Nowhere in the Church have I found faith like this?' Perhaps we need to dig still deeper to find out whether this is true or not.[88]

The above statement amplifies some of what has been analysed earlier. What we have generally seen is the individual choices that the Chief made. What Nolan argues, speaking for the 1980s, is that individual choice is strengthened; the resolve is buttressed by solidarity with others and not purely the support of the Almighty. That common commitment and association strengthens the ability to withstand the suffering that may be incurred in carrying out the original choice.

Not all concepts have a single meaning, like a stone. In the social sphere there are many concepts that may have a range of meanings, connoting development from one phase, progress or perhaps retrogression and perversion of an idea from what it was at an earlier time. Thus Anthony Arblaster writes that there cannot be one meaning attached to the word 'democracy', because it is contextually defined and mediated by a range of factors that have altered the dominant meaning – which may not be exclusive, at various times.[89] John Hoffman writes of a momentum

---

81.   Nolan, *God in South Africa*, 158.
82.   This is a well-known unionist slogan in South Africa.
83.   Nolan quotes here from I Corinthians, 12: 24–26.
84.   Nolan, *God in South Africa*, 159. His source here is Matthew, 25: 40. Emphasis in original.
85.   Nolan, *God in South Africa*, 160. Initial emphasis in original. Emphasis in last sentence inserted.
86.   *Ibid.*, 160–161.
87.   Nolan's source is Matthew, 8: 10.
88.   Nolan, *God in South Africa*, 161.
89.   Arblaster, *Democracy*, 161.

concept. This connotes a mode of understanding some concepts as always in development and that in fact is never ending in its boundaries; its development may continue to become more or less emancipatory over time.[90]

The struggle is surely also a dynamic concept that may develop in a range of ways that reflect the enhancement of the values that Nolan notes as prevalent 22 years ago. Alternatively, what he, Arblaster and Hoffman speak of, may be reversed or diverted. It is necessary to analyse the contemporary meanings of the struggle and accept what is attributed to that word by Nolan may or may not be valid today.

If we see some sort of reversal or retrogression, it adds relevance to the revisiting of Luthuli's life as apparently an exemplar of struggle through common and individual sacrifice. His life and message is an example required for us to restore what may have been lost.

Conceptual Usage Conditioning Luthuli's Stance on Violence

Subversion and revolution

Luthuli uses concepts in line with their currency in his time and the meanings with which many people still associate them today. It is important that concepts like freedom, revolution, justice, and struggle be understood as not having a limited meaning but a plurality of meanings related to conditions prevailing at any particular moment, and the ideology and subjective perspective of a range of actors, whose location differs. As we have noted above, Luthuli himself indicates that non-violence had a certain conditionality attached to its success, and this had political and a range of other implications. Reference has also been made to evolution and retrogression in the meaning of concepts. Luthuli in 1952 clearly regards some concepts as dynamic, but in the case of certain others he does not allow for their being mediated by a range of factors and their meanings being in flux. He thus tends towards a static conceptualisation of some concepts that may potentially be understood as dynamic. This is first examined in the context of the words revolution and subversion.

In 'The Road to Freedom ...'[91] and other writings, Luthuli is at pains to dissociate the ANC policies, strategy and tactics from revolution and subversion. That interpretation is open to question, allowing as indicated, that Luthuli's thinking was not complete and this is an early speech in a life that was cut short.

Despite variations within various schools, there is a body of thinking that associates revolution with violence and much of the classic Marxist-Leninist and national liberation movement literature has been tied to insurrectionism with one decisive moment where power is seized or control of the state is decisive.[92] This is opposed to evolutionary change which is seen as non-revolutionary, more cautious and less likely to better people's lives. One of the weaknesses of many of the models of revolution is that they rest on this one decisive moment – violent or otherwise – where

90. Hoffman, *Gender and Sovereignty*, 6ff, 23ff.
91. See Pillay, *Voices*, 46–50.
92. V.I. Lenin. *The State and Revolution* (Moscow: Progress Publishers, 1969) favouring seizure; and A. Hunt, 'Introduction', in A. Hunt, *Marxism and Democracy* (London: Lawrence & Wishart, 1980) and B. Kagarlitsky, *The Dialectic of Change* (London and New York: Verso, 1990), placing more weight on cumulative reforms. The position with emphasis on the single decisive act is also found in ANC literature. See ANC, *Strategy and Tactics of the ANC*, 1969, at anc.org.za/history/stratact.html, accessed 28 November 2008.

everything changes. Nothing before that instance can have similar significance. Nor can weight be placed on a series of substantial or 'structural reforms'.[93]

It essentialises revolution in counterposition to evolution. In fact, a series of evolutionary changes over time may transform a society in a revolutionary way, by which I mean that its basic conditions of existence are changed. For classical Marxists, the bourgeoisie should be replaced by a new ruling class, the working class and the dictatorship of the proletariat is instituted.[94] That would mean that the inauguration of democracy in South Africa was not revolutionary. But arguably it was a revolutionary change in that revolution may be a process, whereby there are decisive moments, not just one decisive change. Many or all of these were brought about primarily by non-violent means. None of this means that 'revolutionary moments or phases' great or small will continue. They may be stalled or reversed. What has been described as the 'democratic breakthrough' of 1994 may have suffered a 'democratic setback', through current violence and acts against constitutional rights.[95]

The significance of defiance

Even though the Natal region of the ANC was caught ill-prepared for the Defiance Campaign, Luthuli became a fervent supporter and very many powerful images of him are where he wears the Congress volunteer uniform. In an example of the apparent contradictory or ambiguous element in his statements indicated earlier, Luthuli said at the time: 'I have joined my people in the new spirit that moves them today; *the spirit that revolts openly* and boldly against injustice and expresses itself in a determined and non-violent manner'.[96]

They broke the law, they broke the laws that stated what could and could not be done by a parliament that clamed to be sovereign in South Africa. They challenged the question of allegiance to an authority which was not elected by the majority of South Africans. They asserted the rights of those excluded from lawmaking and voting by saying 'this we will not obey'. It was profoundly radical and by some definitions, such as the statement of Sisulu, an embryonic revolutionism.[97] There are phases or a series of significant moments which may cumulatively comprise a revolution and the notion of violence may or may not be one of these. What is sought to achieve in revolution may well be done without violence.

Like the Defiance Campaign, the burning of passes after Sharpeville made a powerful impact on many people.[98] The image of Luthuli burning his pass is still discussed amongst many of those who later joined MK.

Defiance is not simply passive resistance (the term often used by Luthuli and also Gandhi, despite both criticising it), as Gandhi himself stressed that non-violent disobedience was active resistance or the 'moral equivalent of war'.[99] In some ways by wishing to operate within an environment of civil/citizen's rights, admission to the rights of citizenship within the existing polity, Luthuli was obliged to use a specific language that apparently adhered to the authority of that polity. It was only later (and glimpses of this can be found in early statements by Luthuli) that

93.   See Kagarlitsky, *The Dialectic*, chapter 1.
94.   Lenin, *State and Revolution*. But see Hunt, 'Introduction' and Kagarlitsky, *The Dialectic*.
95.   See Suttner, 'The Zuma Era'.
96.   'The Road to Freedom', in Pillay, *Voices*, 48. Emphasis inserted.
97.   See above.
98.   Interview with Nkadimeng, 7 March 2003, Johannesburg.
99.   Chatterjee, *Gandhi's Diagnostic Approach*, chapter 6.

the ANC advanced a notion of rejection of that goal for their own constitutional order presented in various documents. The Defiance Campaign was an early phase of rejection of the status of that order, a denial of political obligation/allegiance to the authorities of the time.

'Subversive'

Luthuli is at great pains to stress that the Congress was not subversive. He is rebutting the attribution of subversion to those who struggle for human rights. It is also possibly part of a reaction to the wholesale use of the word 'communism' to paint the ANC and other anti-apartheid opponents as 'subversive'. In reality where a state is founded on the denial of human rights, the advocacy of such rights *is* subversive, just as that order subverts the dignity of human beings. Subversion must relate to something and in this case saying: 'I believe in the Universal Declaration of Human Rights or the Freedom Charter' was to advocate subversion in an order founded on denial of rights to the majority of South Africans.

It is argued, therefore, that the notion of subversion is contextual. What is subversive in one place is not that in another. In the context of apartheid South Africa, advocating much of what constituted the Christian and humanistic ethics of the Chief was subversive.

A just cause must be struggled for through organisation

Related to the remarks of Nolan, Luthuli did not rely purely on personal dedication and willingness to sacrifice and determination to reject the unjust order. He knew that individuals had to be organised into structures where their actions could be made effective. Despite being a major and highly impressive figure, later drawing a large following from both black and white,[100] he knew that the Congress had to be organised. In 1949, he addressed this:

> It may at times be necessary that we make known the complaints and needs of the African people either by proclaiming them or by boycotting the ways of the whites … [T]hese should be the views or deeds of the majority of the nation. That is why it is desirable that all Africans, male and female, should be members of the African National Congress. *The current slogan says: 'Speak from strength.'* For the present we members of the Executive regard *as a priority the task of increasing the number of branches* of the African National Congress in Natal.[101]

The difference between organisation and mobilisation is one which is being addressed and tends to be neglected today. Mobilising people for a rally or even an election, does not ensure that they will regard the organisation as an enduring home. The branch and other structures were meant to ensure that whoever spoke for the organisation had this strength backing their words. When the ANC faced hard times an organisation had to be built that could withstand the despondency that arose; the ANC's survival had to be ensured. When Nelson Mandela was freed and later negotiated he had *organisational strength* behind him, not purely personal magnetism.

Non-sectarian/multi- and non-racial struggle

One leader, no matter how great, cannot be credited with achievements of an organisation or set of organisations. But it is significant that Luthuli was very non-sectarian, condemning the

---

100.   Benson, The *Struggle for a Birthright*, chapter 15.
101.   Pillay, *Voices*, 41. My emphasis.

elevation of differences based on 'isms'.[102] As early as 1938, in attending a church conference in India and later passing through Sri Lanka (then Ceylon) he became aware of willingness to suffer on the part of Communists, which he describes.[103] This non-sectarianism and his experiences are part of his openness to what became a very close relationship with Communist leader, Moses Kotane,[104] and also the Congress Alliance, many of whose members in the Congress of Democrats especially were underground Communists.

Although white and black and, amongst black people, Africans, Indians and coloureds were organised separately, they did act together on many occasions and this contributed to the development of non-racialism. Ntombazana (Dr Albertinah Luthuli), while conceding that she did not usually contest what her father said, one day expressed her reservations about non-racialism. Provocatively, she referred to his statement that they should not have boyfriends in secret, but rather bring them home. She asked what his reaction would be if she brought home a white boyfriend. The Chief's response was that he would embrace him. That ended the debate, according to Ntombazana.[105]

What is interesting to reflect upon is that already in the late 1950s and for a short while in 1960 when he was unbanned, Luthuli started to develop a large following amongst white people.[106] This is one of the reasons why he was feared and it is also a reason why mischief may not be excluded in his death, whatever any inquest record may say.

The role of the Indian community in relation to Luthuli, as well as in the struggle in general, needs to be more fully retrieved than has been the case. In the situation of Luthuli, being isolated in Groutville and often banned, sections of the Indian community provided office space and arranged logistics for secret meetings with Kotane and others.[107]

Gender and struggle

The means envisaged by Luthuli included and needed equal participation of men and women in Congress activities. Even in his early days as a chief, Luthuli began to address the question of gender equality (without using those words) in his insistence on women being part of community deliberations, thus entering places women had never been in before.[108] His relationship with Nokukhanya, MaBhengu, is clearly one of equality. There was no such thing as boys' work and girls' work under MaBhengu.[109] Far from Luthuli being the male heroic figure that set out alone to do his mighty deeds, his speeches had to pass through the careful scrutiny of MaBhengu, herself a former teacher, as was the Chief. Ntombazana notes:

> Ubaba's respect for UMama was such that there was nothing he did without consulting her. Every speech he wrote was first presented to her, for her criticism and approval before he presented it to the audience for which he had prepared it. And mother, for her part, would interrupt her work,

102. For example, Pillay, *Voices*, 90.
103. A. Luthuli, *Let My People Go* (Glasgow: Fontana, 1962), 72–73.
104. Bunting, *Moses Kotane*, chapter 14; SADET, *Road to Democracy*, 65.
105. Interview with Albertinah Luthuli.
106. Benson, *The Struggle for a Birthright*, chapter 10.
107. Interviews Albertinah Luthuli, Thembekile Ngobese, amongst other evidence.
108. Luthuli, *Let My People Go*, 56–57.
109. P. Rule, with M. Aitken and J. van Dyk, *Nokukhanya: Mother of Light* (Johannesburg: The Grail Press, 1993), 66–84 and generally.

no matter how urgent, and sit and listen to him, making an input when necessary, and generally strengthening his confidence.[110]

It is also noteworthy that, as male head of the family, he did not act out conventional patriarchal rights with his children. Ntombazana notes: 'Ubaba never imposed his status as family head upon us. Everybody had an equal opportunity to talk and no one was considered too young to have his views respected'.[111]

The relationship between Luthuli and MaBhengu was complex. She was the breadwinner, working the fields from 4 am. But she went to bed early and every evening Luthuli would sit with the children and discuss their problems. When they had finished they would say prayers and sing hymns, then he would write. But if they had to go out to 'release' themselves, he would be the one to take them outside. If some child's blanket fell off, it was the Chief who would gently cover him or her again. In a sense Luthuli played a nurturing role. Thembekile says that when he was at home he was really at home for them. When she thinks back, she does not think of him as not having been there.[112]

Obviously, we cannot read a developed gender consciousness or feminism into Luthuli. But the signs of gender awareness were there from an early stage. In other words, in taking the road of the cross, the road of the oppressed and downtrodden, his call was made to men as well as women.

He placed great weight and sought out the women in the struggle, the views of women who became leaders like Dorothy Nyembe, who worked on the white farms and had special knowledge, important to the ANC. He placed great stress on empowering women leadership figures, like Lilian Ngoyi, who despite limited formal education was rising as a leadership figure in the 1950s.[113]

Conclusion

This contribution makes no pretence of finalising any debate on Luthuli and the use of violence as a means of struggle. Certainly Luthuli is part of the process leading to the taking up of arms through the ideas he evoked in his speech 'The Road to Freedom ...' amongst other contributions. As a man he may be seen as one of the first examples of 'heroic masculinity'[114] in the evolution and intensification of the South African struggle. But his heroism did not connote patriarchal neglect of the home, of which he was very much a part.

Arguing a case for Luthuli's approval of armed struggle has tended to lose sight of the use of violence not merely producing some heroic result, but in fact being a 'tragic necessity' for the ANC.[115]

It is futile to argue as if his stance on the use of violence was a point of law, a series of facts having to be presented and then coming to a decision on a balance of probabilities or beyond reasonable doubt. The meanings of the life of Luthuli just do not allow that. At the same time,

---

110. 'Ubaba: Recollections by Ntombazana', in Reddy, *Lutuli*, 13 at 15.
111. *Ibid.*, 17.
112. Interview with Thembekile Ngobese.
113. *Ibid.*
114. E. Unterhalter, 'The Work of the Nation: Heroic Masculinity in South African Autobiographical Writing of the Anti-Apartheid Struggle', *The European Journal of Developmental Research*, 12, 2 (2000), 157–178; Suttner, *ANC Underground*, chapter 6.
115. Suttner, 'Violence: Necessity or Virtue'.

his daughters assert with no reason to gain or vested interest, that he accepted armed struggle, subject to adequate preparation. This indicates that the notion derived from the written records alone (which would appear to be a minority view) excludes access to vital material. In this case, it appears to change the meaning of Luthuli's stance.[116]

The reason why it may be argued that Luthuli's heritage has a more general importance, initially through speeches like those considered here, is that these raise a subjective moral component in struggle that has tended to be lost in the times we live. In unpacking that component, which is something quite different from being learned and understanding strategy and tactics and various ideologies, one sees the willingness to sacrifice and the preparedness to make that sacrifice no matter how high it may be. This, we have seen, is also present in the ideas of Mandela and Gandhi, amongst others. It is outside the debate of what one is going to do, but a vital component, in that unless one is emotionally and psychologically prepared, one could possibly retreat at a decisive moment, as many have done.

In addition, that choice and the range of sacrifices are strengthened by an array of factors, in the case of Luthuli, drawing on the Almighty and, according to Albert Nolan, faith in Christianity, being in turn strengthened in the solidarity of struggle. Yet we need to periodically revisit the attribution of these subjective qualities to mass activists and objective qualities attached to the struggle, as Nolan does for the 1980s. If these values are no longer found in a substantial way, how are they rebuilt insofar as they are required to infuse our future democratic life with unselfish concern for others and not merely personal enrichment and gratification through various means?

This paper is an attempt to do some justice on one crucial area of his concern to the relatively neglected legacy of a giant figure, whose life embodied important moral values which need to be reinserted into the debates of the day. This work must be taken further, on all fronts of learning – especially and urgently with the old people who may not live much longer. Some of those who may have been valuable sources of information have already left us.

Acknowledgement

The author is indebted to Greg Cuthbertson, Peter Limb, Nomboniso Gasa and anonymous reviewers for valuable comments that have helped to improve this article.

References

ANC, *Strategy and Tactics of the ANC* (1969), available at: anc.org.za/history/stratact.html, accessed 28 November 2008.

Arblaster, A., *Democracy* (Philadelphia: Open University Press, 2002).

Benson, M., *Chief Albert Lutuli of South Africa* (London: Oxford University Press, 1963).

Benson, M., *South Africa: The Struggle for a Birthright* (London: International Defence and Aid Fund for Southern Africa, 1985).

Bernstein, H., *The Rift: The Exile Experience of South Africans* (London: Jonathan Cape, 1994).

Bunting, B., *Moses Kotane: South African Revolutionary* (Bellville: Mayibuye Books, 1998).

Chatterjee, M., *Gandhi's Diagnostic Approach Rethought: Exploring a Perspective on his Life and Work* (New Delhi: Promilla, 2007).

Couper, S., 'An Embarrassment to the Congresses? The Silencing of Chief Albert Luthuli and the Production of ANC History', *Journal of South African Studies*, 35, 2 (2009), 331–348.

116. As in S. Couper, 'An Embarrassment to the Congresses?: The Silencing of Chief Albert Luthuli and the Production of ANC History', *Journal of Southern African Studies*, 35, 2 (2009), 331–348.

Couper, S., 'My People Let Go: A Historical Examination of Chief Albert Luthuli and his Position on the Use of Violence as a Means by Which to Achieve South Africa's Liberation from Apartheid', *International Congregational Journal*, 5, 1 (2005), 101–123.

Gandhi, G., ed., *The Oxford India Gandhi: Essential Writings* (New Delhi: Oxford University Press, 2008).

Graybill, L., *Religion and Resistance Politics in South Africa* (Westport: Praeger, 1995).

Guy, J., *The Maphumulo Uprising: War, Law and Ritual in the Zulu Rebellion* (Pietermaritzburg: UK-ZN Press, 2005).

Hoffman, J., *Gender and Sovereignty: Feminism, the State and International Relations* (Aldershot: Palgrave, 2001).

Hunt, A., 'Introduction', in A. Hunt, *Marxism and Democracy* (London: Lawrence & Wishart, 1980).

Kagarlitsky, B., *The Dialectic of Change* (London and New York: Verso, 1990).

Karis, T. and Gerhart, G., *From Protest to Challenge: A Documentary History of African Politics in South Africa 1882–1964, Volume 3: Challenge and Violence, 1953–1964* (Stanford: Stanford University Press, 1977).

Kuper, L., *Passive Resistance in South Africa* (New Haven: Yale University Press, 1957).

Lenin, V.I., *The State and Revolution* (Moscow: Progress Publishers, 1969).

Luthuli, A., *Let My People Go* (Glasgow: Fontana, 1962).

Mandela, N., *Long Walk to Freedom: The Autobiography of Nelson Mandela* (Randburg: Macdonald Purnell, 1994).

Mandela, N., *The Struggle is My Life* (London: IDAF, 1990).

Matthews, Z.K., 'The Road from Non-Violence to Violence', Speech by Z.K. Matthews, 1964, in Karis, T. and Gerhart, G., *From Protest to Challenge: A Documentary History of African Politics in South Africa, 1882–1990, Volume 5: Nadir and Resurgence, 1964–1979* (Pretoria: UNISA Press, 1997), 347–356.

Meer, I., *A Fortunate Man* (Cape Town: Zebra Press, 2002).

Nolan, A., *God in South Africa: The Challenge of the Gospel* (Cape Town: David Philip, 1988).

Pillay, G., ed., *Voices of Liberation, Volume 1: Albert Lutuli* (Pretoria: HSRC, 1993).

Reddy, E., compiler, *Luthuli: Speeches of Chief Albert John Luthuli* (Durban and Bellville: Madiba Publishers and UWC Historical and Cultural Centre, 1991).

Rule, P., with Aitken, M. and van Dyk, J., *Nokukhanya: Mother of Light* (Johannesburg: The Grail Press, 1993).

Sen, N., ed., *Wit and Wisdom of Mahatma Gandhi* (New Delhi: New Book Society, 1995).

Sisulu, W., *I will Go Singing: Walter Sisulu Speaks of his Life and the Struggle for Freedom in South Africa* (in conversation with G.M. Houser and H. Shore) (Cape Town and New York: Robben Island Museum and the Africa Fund, nd., c. 2001).

South African Democracy Education Trust (SADET), *The Road to Democracy in South Africa, Volume 1* (Cape Town: Zebra Press, 2004).

South African Democracy Education Trust (SADET), *The Road to Democracy: South Africans Telling their Stories, Volume 1, 1955–1970* (Houghton: Mutloatse Publishers, 2008).

Suttner, R. and Cronin, J., *50 Years of the Freedom Charter* (Pretoria: UNISA Press, 2006).

Suttner, R., 'Dress, Gestures and Other Cultural Representations and Manifestations and Indian Influence on the Formation of ANC Masculinities', *Historia*, 54, 1 (2009), 51–91.

Suttner, R., 'The Zuma Era – its Historical Context and the Future', *African Historical Review*, 41, 3 (2009), 28–59.

Suttner, R., 'Violence: Necessity or Virtue', *Mail & Guardian* (Johannesburg), 14–20 May 2010, 33.

Suttner, R., *The ANC Underground in South Africa* (Johannesburg: Jacana, 2008).

Tarlo, E., *Clothing Matters: Dress and Identity in India* (Chicago: The University of Chicago Press, 1996).

Unterhalter, E., 'The Work of the Nation: Heroic Masculinity in South African Autobiographical Writing of the Anti-Apartheid Struggle', *The European Journal of Developmental Research*, 12, 2 (2000), 157–178.

Emasculating Agency: An Unambiguous Assessment of Albert Luthuli's Stance on Violence

SCOTT EVERETT COUPER

KwaZulu-Natal, South Africa

Abstract

The nationalist narrative that Albert Luthuli received in December 1961 the Nobel Peace Prize for his unambiguous advocacy of strict non-violent methods to fight Apartheid and the next week supported the launch of the armed struggle is historographic oxymoron. Nationalist pundits decry that the acknowledgement of such a gross contradiction 'distances Luthuli from his movement'. Or, they confess that 'all nascent countries adopt myth' in the interests of nation building. Or, they simply deny the contradiction exists by introducing 'ambiguity'. The author asserts that Luthuli held and articulated an unambiguous stance against the use of violence within the South African context during the 1950s and 1960s. The author suggests that Nelson Mandela, at best, undermined Luthuli and, at worst, committed insubordination by launching *uMkhonto we Sizwe* without the ANC and Luthuli's knowledge or assent. The author utilises archival evidence to resolve irreconcilable differences in nationalist historiography and seeks to restore Luthuli's agency by resisting his absorption into Mandela's 'cult of personality'.

Introduction

I write this article in response to Raymond Suttner's '"The Road to Freedom Is via the Cross": "Just Means" in Chief Albert Luthuli's Life'.[1] In his article, Suttner inserts 'ambiguity' into the debate regarding Albert Luthuli's stance on violence. Suttner articulates an emphasis on ambiguity twice in the abstract and throughout the article.[2] Suttner accurately iterates that his article 'does not set out a definitive reading'.[3]

1.　R. Suttner, '"The Road to Freedom Is via the Cross": "Just Means" in Chief Albert Luthuli's Life', *South African Historical Journal*, 62, 4 (2010), 693–715.
2.　Suttner, 'The Road to Freedom', 693, 694–695, 699, 702, 704–705, 707.
3.　*Ibid.*, 693.

Of course, the insertion of ambiguity does not constitute an argument.[4] Ambiguity casts doubt on what may be known but does not offer a clear alternative. Suttner acknowledges this when in his abstract he conveys, 'Whether adoption of violence was Luthuli's desire is not argued, but he appears to have come to terms with it'.[5] Terminology such as 'appears' and 'come to terms with' are in themselves ambiguous and, as will be pointed out in the course of this article, reveal that Luthuli's stance on violence is concocted by Suttner, with vague vocabulary and shifting claims, to be nebulous.

Suttner posits: 'The counter-arguments that stress absolute opposition to violence are not rebutted on a point-by-point basis to argue Luthuli's preference for violence, rather than possible pragmatism [sic]'. Yet, argumentation on a 'point-by-point basis' is preferable.[6] More often than not, points rebutted would be Luthuli's own in favour of strict non-violent tactics. The 'counter-arguments that stress [Luthuli's] absolute opposition to violence' are, I presume, mine.[7] However, my arguments do not stress Luthuli's 'absolute opposition to violence', as if he was a pacifist, which he was *not*. Of course, theoretically Luthuli justified violence in extreme circumstances. Luthuli's amanuensis for his 1962 autobiography 'Let My People Go', The Rev. Charles Hooper, once revealed,

> Publicly, [Luthuli] advocated only non-violence and dialogue because they were what he passionately wanted South Africans to believe in; but privately he maintained that Stauffenberg was right in trying to destroy Hitler... [Luthuli's] condemnation of violence was conditional and qualified.[8]

What I argue is: prior to, during and after Nelson Mandela launched *uMkhonto we Sizwe* (MK), Luthuli opposed the use of violence within the South African context and there is little, if any, evidence that he ever came to support it thereafter. Luthuli did not know of, or support, MK's launch. Mandela's launch of the armed struggle can therefore be rendered insubordinate, as all agreed in a July 1961 Joint Congresses' meeting that MK was to be under the suzerainty of the African National Congress (ANC) led by Luthuli who served as President-General.

Despite making 'no pretence of finalising any debate', Suttner 'concludes' that Luthuli acted 'in support of' and 'decided to contribute practically to' MK and therefore the liberation struggle's turn to violence.[9] Of course, the above contradiction is intended to cast doubt on a clear and unambiguous argument that Luthuli did not approve of or

---

4. Exceptions to this are Shula Marks' and Jabulani Sithole and Sibongiseni Mkhize's excellent publications: S. Marks, *The Ambiguities of Dependence: Class, Nationalism and the State in Twentieth Century Natal* (Johannesburg: Ravan, 1986); J. Sithole and S. Mkhize, 'Truth or Lies? Selective Memories, Imagings and Representations of Chief Albert John Luthuli in Recent Political Discourses', *History and Theory*, 39 (2000), 69–85.

5. Suttner, 'The Road to Freedom', 693. Yet, Suttner correctly argues Luthuli did not desire violence: 'That preference [for non-violence] was there. It is not intended to suggest that violence was in the Chief's mind from early on, certainly not for him...' (Suttner, 'The Road to Freedom', 701).

6. Suttner, 'The Road to Freedom', 693.

7. See Suttner, 'The Road to Freedom', 697, fn 16.

8. C. Hooper, *Sechaba*, 'Letter in the S.A. Press', October 1967, 7.

9. Suttner, 'The Road to Freedom', 713, 703.

support the armed struggle. Suttner utilises highly selective statements by Luthuli wherein ambiguity is manufactured to exist rather than selecting or refuting certain views Luthuli articulated in the press and in speeches at the time in question (1960–1964).

I base my arguments on statements made by Luthuli that are self-explanatory and clear rather than conducting interpretive gymnastics to argue for 'multiple meanings' possibly attached to given statements.[10] It is important to note that Suttner's thesis is *not* that Luthuli *intended* his statements to have multiple meanings. Rather, it is suggested that one can *read into* Luthuli's statements multiple meanings, just as Christian apologists read into the Hebrew scriptures the prophesy of Jesus as the Messiah.[11] All this makes for good nationalist ideology in Suttner's case and good theology in Christianity's case. But, neither makes good history.

Basis of agreement

Despite the fact that the first sentence in Suttner's article is factually incorrect, we do not disagree on all things Luthuli.[12] There are many points that Suttner presents throughout his article with which I fully concur. I shall allude to them from time to time in this response, but not dwell on them, as that makes for a poor debate.

Suttner's rationale for examining Luthuli's legacy is excellent. I agree fully with his justification for studying Luthuli. I endorse Suttner's view that Luthuli is relevant for the current South African context. Suttner is correct in declaring Luthuli a source of 'inspiration and guidance' from which we need to learn and which we need to transmit.[13]

I support Suttner's lament of the dearth of scholarship about Luthuli. Suttner highlights that 'There has only been a short biography by Mary Benson...'.[14] To partially remedy this, I published the first substantive biography chronicling Luthuli's entire life three months before the publication of Suttner's article.[15]

Phantom debate

Suttner claims in a hyper-qualified statement, 'that there is room to see [Luthuli's] stance as opening a debate and even an element of *conditional* support ... [for violence] ... that is

10. Suttner, 'The Road to Freedom', 693.
11. Suttner confides, 'I am reading into what Luthuli said, elaborating more than he ever did in his public statements...' ('The Road to Freedom', 700).
12. The Nobel Committee announced Albert Luthuli as the 1960 Nobel Peace Prize winner in October 1961, not 1960. See Suttner, 'The Road to Freedom', 693, 698.
13. Suttner, 'The Road to Freedom', 693.
14. *Ibid.*, 694.
15. S. Couper, *Albert Luthuli: Bound by Faith* (Pietermaritzburg: UKZN Press, 2010). The biography is an edited version of my PhD dissertation: S. Couper, '"Bound by Faith": A Biographic and Ecclesiastic Examination (1898–1967) of Chief Albert Luthuli's Stance on Violence as a Strategy to Liberate South Africa' (PhD thesis, University of KwaZulu-Natal, Durban, 2009).

allowing it to be ethically correct under certain circumstances'.[16] Here in one sentence, there are, one ('room to see'), two ('an element'), three ('conditional support') and four ('under certain circumstances') qualifications regarding Luthuli's stance on the use of violence. As this paper earlier alludes, no one argues that Luthuli was a pacifist; no one argues that Luthuli possessed an 'absolute opposition to violence'.[17]

Suttner's conclusion that for Luthuli 'in practice no approach was irreversible nor displacing all others' is sound.[18] Far from 'fetishising' Luthuli's non-violent position, I assert that he renounced pacifism and therefore, in theory, held a fluid, though predominantly non-violent, position on violence.[19] Nonetheless, *in the South African context* from the first public reference to non-violence in 1948 to his death, Luthuli's position on violence was not ambiguous.[20] Since Luthuli's death in July 1967, the ANC has inaccurately and consistently argued, 'Approached by Mandela, Luthuli agreed to the armed struggle' in July 1961.[21] This is a distortion of the historical record.

If one wishes to argue a theoretical ambiguity into Luthuli's stance on violence during the 1950s and 1960s, dozens of Luthuli's very unambiguous statements strictly advocating non-violent strategies must be confronted to be somehow invalid. Below is a sample of unambiguous statements Luthuli made regarding his position on violence before (1960), during (1961) and after (1962) Mandela launched MK.

> In the circumstances that obtain in the country – I must say this first – I may have indicated that there might be differences of point of view among different members, but as far as the [C]ongress is concerned, in the circumstances that obtain definitely we are for non-violence. When it comes to a personal level, as to whether at any time one would, I would say that if conditions are as they are, I would never be a party to the use of violence because I think it would be almost national suicide, in the circumstances as they are.[22]

> Even for practical reasons non-violence is the only course we can follow. Direct attack by an unarmed public against the fully armed forces of the government would mean suicide. There are no responsible persons among us in the African National Congress who advocate violence as a means of furthering our cause.[23]

> When we strive for the same goal through non-violent methods, the government visits us with more and harsher laws to suppress – if not completely destroy – our liberation efforts. IS THIS NOT INVITING THE OPPRESSED TO DESPERATION? NONETHELESS, I WOULD URGE OUR PEOPLE NOT TO DESPAIR OVER OUR METHODS OF STRUGGLE, THE

16. Suttner, 'The Road to Freedom', 695.
17. *Ibid.*, 693.
18. *Ibid.*, 701.
19. *Ibid.*, 700.
20. Luthuli Museum, A. Luthuli, '[Mahatma Gandhi] Memorial on the Occasion of the Centenary Celebrations of [Howard University]', Washington, DC, United States, original handwritten draft, 1948.
21. University of Fort Hare, Howard Pim Africana Library, ANC Archives, Oliver Tambo Papers (A2561), Folder C 39, O. Tambo, 'July 21', original typed manuscript, July 1967: University of Fort Hare, Howard Pim Africana Library, ANC, Nelson Mandela Foundation, Exhibition, viewed on 9 July 2008.
22. G. Pillay, ed., *Voices of Liberation, Albert Luthuli* (Pretoria: Human Sciences Research Council, 1993), 152, 163.
23. *Rand Daily Mail*, '100 Brave Cold to Greet Luthuli', 12 December 1961. Note that Luthuli made this statement *days* before Mandela launched MK, in retrospect, declaring Mandela irresponsible.

MILITANT, NONVIOLENT TECHNIQUES. SO FAR WE HAVE FAILED THE METHODS – NOT THE METHOD US.[24]

The fabrication of ambiguity, the countering of a phantom absolutist thesis and the decontextualising of Luthuli's views are sophistic tactics. Concocting multivalent meanings to counter a contextualised thesis backed by primary source evidence is only a distraction. An indefinite reading of Luthuli's stance on violence necessitates the avoidance of a point-by-point argument that responds to direct evidence from Luthuli. An ambiguous interpretation of Luthuli's views on the use of violence in the South African context aims to simply muddy the water while not offering any new substantive evidence. However, new interpretations require new evidence.

An unambiguous open-minded democratic leader

Suttner speculates that Luthuli was open-minded about the use of violence (presumably in the South African context):

> With Luthuli, I am arguing not that there was a weakness in ambiguity, but that while he wanted to address a particular issue, he sometimes opened up debate going well beyond that and allowing for conclusions that may well not have been originally intended. I do not see Luthuli as seeking any final answers, but asking questions repeatedly and openly with a willingness to learn.[25]

However, being open-minded does not therefore mean that Luthuli did not take unambiguous and certain stances – for example against Communism or against the use of violence in South Africa's 1961 context. In fact, the best example of Luthuli 'not seeking any final answers' or 'asking questions repeatedly' was his attempt as Chair to revive his position that the ANC remain non-violent. When Mandela and his other lieutenants won initial debates allowing them to form MK during ANC Working and National Executive meetings of June and July 1961, a resolution stating thus was referred to the Joint Congresses. But at the meeting of the Joint Congresses, Luthuli as Chair backtracked and began the discussion afresh, intentionally wiping clean the slate and considering the previous discussion and decision null and void. This upset Mandela; he understood the ANC had finished the discussion and was recommending it to the Joint Congresses for approval. In this instance, by opening up discussion and presenting it again for debate, Luthuli hoped to insert his allies into the debate and bolster his own position against the use of violence. This narrative is found in *A Long Walk to Freedom*. Mandela relates:

> The meeting had an inauspicious beginning. Chief Luthuli, who was presiding, announced that even though the ANC had endorsed a decision on violence, 'it is a matter of such gravity, I would like my colleagues here tonight to consider the issue afresh'. It was apparent that the chief was not fully reconciled to our new course.[26]

24. A. Luthuli, 'Our Way Is Right – We Must Keep On', *Golden City Post*, 25 March 1962 (Luthuli's emphasis).
25. Suttner, 'The Road to Freedom', 695.
26. N. Mandela, *Long Walk to Freedom: The Autobiography of Nelson Mandela* (Boston, New York, Toronto and London: Bay Back Books and Little, Brown and Company, 1994), 273.

Dozens of Luthuli's statements in the press throughout the rest of 1961 and well into 1962 reveal that Luthuli was more than 'not fully reconciled to the new course'. In fact, Luthuli was fundamentally opposed to the new course. The above narrative demonstrates that Luthuli's willingness to consider other options and open up debate is evidence of his *un*ambiguous, not ambiguous, position on violence.

As a leader, Luthuli understood his position, be it Chair of a meeting or as the ANC's President-General, to be one that fosters inclusivity and transparent discussion. Luthuli understood his leadership role to be that of a democrat. That Luthuli performed this role admirably is not a sign that *his* personal perspectives were ambiguous. In respect to violence, Luthuli's positions were certain and clear. Luthuli fulfilled his democratic leadership role by recognising, allowing for and acknowledging as valid or understandable differing positions. Yet, fostering an environment for open discussion or having an open-mind should *not* be mistaken as evidence of Luthuli's personal views, ambiguous or otherwise.

Luthuli's family

The following statements in Suttner's article are problematic for a number of reasons.

> [The children] indicate a broader degree of [Luthuli's] support for armed resistance as 'intransigence' intensified. But this was provided the masses were properly trained and not used as cannon fodder.[27]

> ... his daughters assert with no reason to gain or vested interest, that [Luthuli] accepted the armed struggle, subject to adequate preparation.[28]

> ...the oral evidence accessed thus far does point to [Luthuli] having accepted the armed struggle.[29]

First, the 'oral evidence assessed thus far' is threadbare. It consists only of interviews or discussions via phone with the family. Older evidence from the family casts doubt on the contemporary remembrances introduced. For example, in 1985 Nokukhanya, Albert Luthuli's wife, stated the opposite view her children have in regards to Luthuli's stance on violence. She proclaimed:

> Like my husband, I am sick and tired of violence. Albert worked towards a better South Africa by negotiation, not by the barrel of a gun which is what the ANC of today is doing. I am glad my husband has not lived to see what's happening to the present-day ANC.[30]

In *Bound by Faith*, I cite interviews with Ronald Harrison and Edward Hawley that confirm Luthuli's opposition to violence.[31] For example, Hawley testified that as late as 1964

27. Suttner, 'The Road to Freedom', 697.
28. *Ibid.*, 714.
29. *Ibid.*, 700, fn 38.
30. *Durban Daily News*, '"Albert Would Have Rejected Today's Violence..." Mrs Albert Luthuli', date unknown, 1985, 39.
31. Couper, *Bound by Faith*, 163–164.

Luthuli was against the armed movement but he could not do anything about it as he was not listened to by the younger generation and they were going to do what they were going to do. Hawley remembered:

> His response was, and I can remember this almost verbatim, 'I have never been a violent man. And I could never be one... The young men still come to see me. When they tell me that non-violence has always been met with violence, I have no words left'.[32]

Second, it is difficult to believe that the Luthuli children have no vested interest in whether their father agreed to and supported the MK's formation and launch. There is a vested interest. Albertinah is an ANC member of the national parliament. Thandeka was an ANC appointed ambassador to the Caribbean and Venezuela. The entire family has a stake in the promotion of the memory of Albert Luthuli that is financially subsidised by the national government in which the ANC has a ruling majority. The grandsons are appointed leaders of varying Luthuli foundations and trusts. It is unlikely that they are consciously or unconsciously impartial. I do not imply that the family is lying or adulterating their memory. They are not. The reason why their statements are genuine brings me to my next two points.

Third, the statements by the family above insert a massive qualification that Luthuli accepted or supported the armed movement *subject to adequate preparation*. This qualification renders Suttner's argument based on the family's testimony null and void. Most historians (as have many members of the ANC and MK) understand that adequate preparation was *never* obtained for the armed struggle.[33] Janet Cherry's recent book, *Umkhonto weSizwe,* makes this conclusion brutally clear.[34] For Luthuli, adequate preparation meant knowledge of, agreement to and training for the masses so they were not rendered spectators in the armed movement. Adequate preparation entails the engendering of the means by which to win a violent conflict quickly and decisively so as to minimise damage to both belligerents. MK cadres had little or no military experience. MK operatives were naïve. Not even Mandela, the Commander in Chief, had even learned how to fire a gun before he launched MK.[35] There was little or no preparation to fight a military conflict either before or after Mandela launched MK. Luthuli's qualification for his theoretical support for the use of violence, as per his children's statements, was never met. Luthuli on more than one occasion understood armed conflict with the Apartheid regime to be 'suicide'.[36] Upon hearing of the acts of sabotage, Luthuli unambiguously stated, 'For myself, I regret anything that is violent'.[37] The so-called evidence from Luthuli's children that he 'accepted' the armed struggle was heavily qualified by a hypothetical context that never existed. The children, according to the above, are truthful and accurate. The children's perspectives (unquoted) are not

32. *Ibid.*, 181.
33. *Dawn: Journal of Umkhonto we Sizwe – Souvenir Issue, Twenty-Fifth Anniversary of MK*, ANC, 1986.
34. J. Cherry, *Umkhonto Wesizwe* (Auckland Park: Jacana, 2011).
35. N. Mandela, *Conversations with Myself* (London: Macmillian, 2010), 93–9-4.
36. *Rand Daily Mail*, '100 Brave Cold to Greet Luthuli', 12 December 1961; *Daily Mail*, 'I Go to See the Chief Macmillan Couldn't Visit', by 'Farlie', 10 February 1960; *Daily News*, 'Luthuli Asks: Can't NATS. Start Talking to Us?', 11 February 1960.
37. P. Rule, *Nokukhanya: Mother of Light* (Underberg: Grail, 1993), 130.

evidence for an ambiguous non-argument. The masses were never properly trained. Therefore, the argument for Luthuli's apparent support based on his family's evidence falls away.

Fourth, the children's use of the terms 'supported' and then 'accepted' is a moving of the goal posts, a changing of the debate's terms. Did Luthuli 'support',[38] or had he 'accepted',[39] or had he 'been slow to approve',[40] or did he express 'a broader degree of support for',[41] or did he '[appear] to have' or 'probably' 'come to terms with',[42] or did he 'contribute practically to',[43] or did he simply, as Mandela states, 'not stand in the way of'[44] or did he convey his 'identification with [the] armed struggle'?[45] All can't be argued by constantly changing the goal posts. The eight above phrases have different nuanced meanings. Luthuli was not 'slow to approve'; reliable sources indicated he likely never approved.[46]

Rather than 'supported', 'approved', 'agreed to' or 'contributed practically to', at most, I would argue for the term the family quite rightly used: 'accepted'. An 'acceptance of' is also a 'resigned to'. 'Accepted' could likely mean that he 'came to terms with', as one does with the death of a loved one. Does 'accepting' mean that Luthuli supported or agreed with the death of a loved one? No. He accepted it. He yielded to it. He dealt with it. He had to. He had no choice. I too agree that Luthuli 'came to terms' with the reality that he was now marginalised from the movement since the launch of MK without his knowledge or permission. He related as much to Edward Hawley. In specific reference to the launch of MK, Luthuli confided to Moses Kotane:

> When my son decides to sleep with a girl, he does not ask for my permission, but just does it. It is only afterwards when the girl is pregnant and the parents make a case that he brings his troubles home.[47]

The father must 'come to terms with' the errant child and try to repair the damage. This is not support of or practical contribution to the misdeed; it is only 'coming to terms with' the very unfortunate reality. But, this never meant that Luthuli supported or agreed to the use of violence.

Suttner noted, 'Albertinah Luthuli referred to [the naming of the Wankie Detachment after Luthuli] specifically as indicating the Chief's identification with armed struggle'.[48] I submit that this footnoted oral evidence is suspect. One, it is anachronistic. The ANC

38. Suttner, 'The Road to Freedom', 695, fn 10.
39. *Ibid.*, 696, 714.
40. *Ibid.*, 697.
41. *Ibid.*, 697.
42. *Ibid.*, 693, 703.
43. *Ibid.*, 703.
44. *Ibid.*, 697.
45. *Ibid.*, 702, fn 53.
46. J. Slovo, *An Unfinished Autobiography* (Randburg: Ravan, 1995), 147; South African Democracy Education Trust (SADET), *The Road to Democracy in South Africa, Volume I (1960–1970)* (Cape Town: Zebra Press, 2004), 89.
47. B. Bunting, *Moses Kotane: South African Revolutionary: A Political Biography* (London: Inkululeko, 1975), 274.
48. Suttner, 'The Road to Freedom', 702, fn 53.

named the detachment *after* Luthuli's death, so it could not have been an indication of Luthuli's identification with the armed struggle. The fact that the detachment, or any detachment, was, or could only be, named after Luthuli following his death suggests that it was safe to name it after him without causing offence to or risking rebuff by him. The naming of the detachment was the ANC's means by which to honour Luthuli, not a means by which Luthuli identified with the ANC and its violent tactics.

Fifth, I too have interviewed members of the Luthuli family, including Albertinah, addressing explicitly the issue of violence. None indicated that Luthuli supported the armed struggle despite this being my specific research question. When I interviewed Albertinah and asked about her father's stance on violence, she did not respond specifically to her father's view. She provided the ANC's compelling rationale for turning to armed violence, not Luthuli's. When one speaks with family 50 years after the fact, we are likely looking at nationalist ideology that has been historicised as Luthuli's view.

As pointed out by Naidoo in his book *In the Shadow of Chief Luthuli*, even Luthuli's closest confidants (Goolam Suleman and E.V. Mahomed) would not have been told of sensitive (indicting) information regarding Luthuli due to security concerns.[49] Certainly, Luthuli's children would not be privy to such information about his supposed support for violence given the risk of their arrest and torture. Also, Luthuli's children (at least those named) were away from home, either educated in Swaziland or other boarding schools or training and working in Durban hospitals (McCord and King Edward hospitals). Luthuli's grandsons were not yet born or were too young to know anything of Luthuli's strategic sentiments.

Misuse of Gandhi

In his article, Suttner repeats a mistake that the ANC in *Sechaba* and Nelson Mandela make when they justify the ANC's abandonment of non-violent strategies.[50] Both *Sechaba* and Suttner utilise Gandhi's supposed rationale for using violence in certain contexts. In my PhD dissertation, I explained the flawed nature of Mandela and the ANC's use of Gandhi to justify the ANC's position to abandon non-violent methods.[51]

---

49. L. Naidoo, *In the Shadow of Chief Albert Luthuli: Reflections of Goolam Suleman* (Groutville: Luthuli Museum, 2010), 18–19.

50. See 'From Gandhi to Mandela: In Commemoration of the 75th Anniversary of the Formation of the Natal Indian Congress by Mahatma Gandhi', *Sechaba*, 3, 5 (5 May 1969), 10–12. *Sechaba* cited M. Gandhi, 'Declaration on Question of the Use of Violence in Defense of Rights', *Guardian*, 16 December 1938. N. Mandela, 'Epilogue: Nelson Mandela Looks at Gandhi', in J. Wassermann, ed, *A Man for All Seasons: Mohandas Gandhi* (Pretoria: Voortrekker Museum, n.d.), 22. In this text, Mandela justified the resort to violence when stating: 'Gandhi himself never ruled out violence absolutely and unreservedly. He conceded the necessity of arms in certain situations. He said, "Where a choice is set between cowardice and violence, I would advise violence... I prefer the use of arms in defence of honour rather than remain the vile witness of dishounor...".' Yet, here Gandhi speaks of a hypothetical ultimatum, neither of which extremes Gandhi would choose. Rather, Gandhi and Luthuli would choose 'courageous non-violence'. Of course, if the choice was *only* cowardice or violence, Gandhi would choose the later. But, neither Gandhi nor Luthuli believed these were the only two strategies and certainly cowardice and violence were not the preferred and advocated ones.

51. Couper, 'Bound by Faith', 105–106, 176–178.

Gandhi's statement does not demonstrate that he 'allowed [violence] to be ethically correct under certain circumstances' or provide 'reasons behind conditional departure from non-violence'.[52] In the quotation cited, Gandhi establishes a three tiered hierarchy of ethics. First, according to Gandhi's quote, at the bottom is the 'violence of cowards'. Second, in the middle, Gandhi indicates that 'there is such a thing' as the 'violence of the brave'. Yet, Gandhi offers no endorsement of this tier; it simply exists. Third, at the top of the hierarchy, and thus the preferred option for Gandhi (and Luthuli), is the 'non-violence of the brave' which is endorsed as 'worth seeing'. Suttner, as did the ANC publication *Sechaba*, uses a quotation by Gandhi to substantiate a justification for the ANC's turn to violence despite the fact that Gandhi's quotation conveys the *opposite*. Gandhi's preferred option is the 'non-violence of the brave', not the 'violence of the brave'.

Chronology

Suttner and I agree that 'the formation of MK was on an ambiguous basis'.[53] But here our agreement ends. Suttner repeats an earlier error by stating that the Nobel Committee announced that Luthuli won the Nobel Peace Prize in 1960.[54] It did not. The Committee announced Luthuli as the Peace Prize winner in October 1961. The sequence of events is essential to understanding Luthuli's strategy for liberation and thus his stance on violence in the 1960s South African context.

In July 1961, the ANC and Joint Congresses decided not to discipline Mandela should he *form* an armed movement. In October 1961 the Nobel Committee announced that Luthuli won the Nobel Peace Prize specifically for his and the ANC's non-violent resistance against Apartheid. From October through December 1961, Luthuli's ponderously and vociferously pleaded in the press for his lieutenants not to initiate violence. Luthuli received the Nobel Peace Prize on 10 December. On 16 December, upon Luthuli's return to South Africa from Oslo after receiving the Prize, Mandela *launched* MK without Luthuli's knowledge or sanction. Luthuli's December 1961 statement that 'no responsible persons among us' in the ANC would advocate violence renders Mandela's launch of MK insubordinate. Any historian who fails to engage in the chronology (the sequence of events), and not philosophical musings about interpretive dialectics, can't begin to refute the thesis that Luthuli adamantly opposed the formation and launch of MK.

MK's launch was *not* postponed to avoid embarrassing Luthuli.[55] Arguably, Mandela intended the 'unfortunate' timing of MK's launch to, at most, embarrass, or, at least, render Luthuli politically obsolete. MK began to be formed at the earliest in August 1961. To suggest that MK's launch could have been made *before* December is highly unrealistic. One can't secretly mobilise cadres, train, plan and implement a sabotage campaign in such a short period of time. Mandela likely hurriedly and prematurely launched MK so as to neutralise Luthuli's then increasingly persuasive argument that non-violent strategies had greater efficacy given that Luthuli (and, in Luthuli's eyes, the ANC) won the Nobel Peace

52. Suttner, 'The Road to Freedom', 696.
53. *Ibid.*, 698.
54. *Ibid.*, 693, 698.
55. *Ibid.*, 698.

Prize for his and the ANC's non-violent strategies. Mandela did not postpone MK's launch; he accelerated it. Why else did the Commander in Chief of MK initiate armed action in 1961 before he departed for his own training in 1962?

That Mandela stated that Luthuli 'did not stand in the way of armed struggle' does not convey that he therefore supported it.[56] Furthermore, no one has explained *how* Luthuli would have stood in the way of the armed struggle other than drafting pleas to continue non-violent strategies in the press well into 1962 (which he did and some evidence suggests he was told by his own movement to stop doing this as he was embarrassing it).[57] Luthuli had no power to 'stand in the way' other than to offer his resignation as President-General. There is evidence that he considered this option.[58] Why then argue that a non-obstructionist position is evidence for Luthuli's agreement with or support for MK? Luthuli did all that he could to dissuade. This was the greatest means by which he could 'stand in the way' without 'standing in the way'.

The cross

Suttner inserts ambiguity into Luthuli's stance on violence by claiming that his views were not mature in 1952. For example, Suttner relates:

> In 'The Road to Freedom...' and other writings, Luthuli is at pains to dissociate the ANC policies, strategies and tactics from revolution and subversion. That interpretation is open to question, allowing as indicated, that Luthuli's thinking was not complete and this is an early speech in a life that was cut short.[59]

This statement belittles Luthuli, rendering him an immature political thinker immediately before he became President-General of the ANC. Luthuli wrote 'The Road to Freedom Is via the Cross' when he was about 55 years old. Luthuli's thoughts are quite mature by this point, having been chosen to be a leader in many entities for over 20 years. Luthuli died at close to 70 years of age; so the insinuation that Luthuli was killed before his political thought was mature does not give Luthuli the credit he deserves. If Luthuli 'was at *pains* to dissociate' ANC policies from revolution and subversion, why are these views 'open to question', or reinterpretation? Why insert ambiguity into certainty?

Suttner is correct to interpret the cross as a sign of sacrifice (for a Christian, but not a first century Roman soldier). Suttner's musings on the cross as a sign of sacrificial servanthood are benign, if not altogether agreeable. However, he conveniently neglects that the cross (or, rather, Jesus on it) is intrinsically non-violent in nature. Suttner states:

56.   *Ibid.*, 697.
57.   S. Couper, 'An Embarrassment to the Congresses?': The Silencing of Chief Albert Luthuli and the Production of ANC History', *Journal of Southern African Studies*, 35, 2 (2009), 331–348.
58.   Publication unknown, 'Lutuli Was Stumbling Block to Violence, Witness Says', 22 July 1964; *Newscheck*, 'An Unfulfilled Life', 28 July 1967, 10.
59.   Suttner, 'The Road to Freedom', 709.

the conditionality attached to the methods employed is again evident when Luthuli says 'denied, as we are, effective constitutional means to further our aspirations'. This obviously indicates the crossing threshold of legality and invites the question whether the struggle should adopt non-constitutional means and how far this interpretation can be taken. At the same time, it remains an affirmation of non-violence and legality so long as conditions permit.[60]

First, the qualification 'so long as conditions permit' is a stealthy fabrication. Luthuli speaks of no 'conditionality attached to the methods'... 'so long as conditions permit'. Second, if we read the entire sentence quoted, we see the statement does not at all '[invite] the question' of how far unconstitutional means can be taken, that is, the use of violence. The entire sentence reads:

> Viewing *non-violent passive resistance* as a non-revolutionary and, therefore, a most legitimate and human political pressure technique for a people denied all effective forms of constitutional striving, I saw no conflict in my dual leadership of my people: leader of this tribe as chief and political leader in Congress. (my emphasis)

A people are 'denied all effective forms of constitutional striving'. Because no constitutional means exist to counter oppression, Luthuli advocates 'non-violent passive resistance'. Suttner misreads, when he states, 'This obviously indicates the crossing of a threshold of legality and invites the question whether the struggle should adopt non-constitutional means and how far this interpretation can be taken'. However, the non-violent passive resistance *is* the non-constitutional means Luthuli advocates. There is therefore no '[invitation] to question *whether* the struggle should adopt non-constitutional means and how far this interpretation can be taken' (my emphasis). For Luthuli at the time of writing, there is already a denial of constitutional means available and the tactic therefore should be 'non-violent passive resistance'. My interpretation is validated by Luthuli when he argues, 'I have embraced the non-Violent Passive Resistance technique in fighting for freedom because I am convinced it is the only... way that could be used by people denied, as we are, effective constitutional means to further aspirations'. By quoting only half of Luthuli's clear statement, Luthuli's statement is misunderstood. Ambiguity is invented and it is mistakenly proposed that Luthuli suggested or led to the question of whether violence should be employed.

Suttner argues that Luthuli conveys the 'fruitlessness' of non-violent strategies in 'The Road to Freedom Is via the Cross' statement and one can therefore interpret that he invited or encouraged the consideration to opt for violent strategies.[61] Concerning the question contained in 'The Road to Freedom' statement '...who will deny that thirty years of my life...?', Suttner inquires:

> What conclusion is the listener or reader to draw from this statement? It is a statement of failure of non-violent peaceful activities. Not one to run away from unpleasant facts, he put on the record that non-violence had not succeeded. For the person who followed Luthuli, could this have been seen as an invitation or encouragement to debate the matter further?[62]

60.   *Ibid.*, 705.
61.   *Ibid.*, 698.
62.   *Ibid.*, 698.

The answer is 'No' – unless the reader or hearer only read or heard selective excerpts from the statement and ignored its title. In the statement, Luthuli conveys his view that despite profound disappointment, he and the ANC will continue to pursue the thus far failing non-violent tactics out of obedience and trust that they will in the end succeed; hence he entitles the statement, 'The Road to Freedom Is via the Cross'. The biblical narrative from which Luthuli drew is pregnant with the message of perseverance despite apparent failure.[63] Even in defeat (failure), which is death, success, or 'the Road to Freedom', will result. This is the quintessential meaning of the cross and thus of Christianity: Do not compromise your behaviour, for eventual victory (eternal life) despite temporary defeat (death) will be the result. A fundamental understanding of Christian themes allows one to comprehend these Christocentric motivations. Luthuli can't be properly understood if one does not know or can't understand the theological vantage from which Luthuli made political and ethical decisions.

In a 2008 article, I explain the seminal influence theology had on Luthuli's politics.[64] I cross-referenced a sermon 'A Christian Life: A Constant Adventure' with the 'The Road to Freedom Is via the Cross' statement. Luthuli wrote the sermon a week before the statement. Therefore, the sermon theologically informs the statement. I quote at length from my 2008 article:

> An examination of Luthuli's sermon 'Christian Life a Constant Adventure', an immediate source of material for his statement 'The Road to Freedom Is via the Cross', reveals that contrary to nationalists' histories, the above quote is *not* a rallying call to abandon existing methods of resistance, but rather a call to continue them *despite* their seeming inefficacy. The title and the continuing text of the statement confirm this. Juxtaposed with the sermon, the conclusion that the statement advocates a continuance of non-violent methods becomes irrefutable. A key biblical verse, upon which the sermon and thus the statement rest, relates how despite the apparent futility of previous strategies, they ought to be continued in faith. The scripture of emphasis from which Luthuli preached reads as follows:

> 'When he had finished speaking, [Jesus] said to Simon, "Put out into the deep water and let down your nets for a catch." Simon answered, "Master, we have worked all night long but have caught nothing. Yet if you say so, I will let down the nets"'.

> The biblical texts relates that at the time of Jesus' command, Simon Peter and the disciples were at the 'shore of the lake', cleaning their nets. Jesus calls the disciples to 'put out into the deep water'. This is not a change of tactics, but rather a re-doubling of past efforts. One of Luthuli's themes, as expounded upon above, is that all are called to a 'larger worthy cause', that is an intensification of what is currently being done, for the purpose of establishing the 'kingdom of God'. Simon Peter protests: 'We have been there, done that. And we have nothing to show for it. But, because you are asking, we will continue to do what we believe to be futile. We do so, if not out of faith, then out of obedience'. Luthuli emphasised in his sermon that often humans are 'paralysed or discouraged with our failures' and it is only 'complete obedience' that we are called forward. Understanding this

---

63. Luthuli's autobiography, *Let My People Go*, is the biblical refrain of Moses who out of sheer obedience repeatedly advocates to Pharaoh to release the captives. Moses repeated mantra during the seven plagues is continued no matter the failure of the previous to persuade: A. Luthuli, *Let My People Go: An Autobiography* (London: Collins, 1962).

64. S. Couper, 'When Chief Albert Luthuli Launched "Into the Deep": A Theological Reflection on a Homiletic Resource of Political Significance', *Journal of Theology for Southern Africa*, 130 (2008), 76–89 and 108–115

story as a typological re-enactment, Luthuli understands that he is to 'launch into the deep', from chieftaincy to full-time ANC leader, from local leader to national leader. The sermon emphasises that neither vocation nor methods are being altered, despite past failures. The statement, sourcing the sermon, indicates that only scope, or degree of the vocation and methods, is being increased.[65]

Whenever Luthuli referred to the fruitlessness of non-violent tactics he emphasised that nonetheless or *despite* the fruitlessness, no matter the failures, non-violent strategies must be continued and violence must not be implemented. Especially in 'The Road to Freedom Is via the Cross', Luthuli preaches 'no matter the lack of success, one must continue and persevere in obedience' (not to him, but presumably to biblical tenets or Christ's teachings).

'Who can deny that thirty years of my life. . .?' was not a justification to abandon the non-violent struggle (nor was it a clever means by which Luthuli sought to be intentionally misinterpreted so as to be seen to be vaguely open to a violent struggle). In fact, the rhetorical question as a whole, argues that despite the fact that 'the past thirty years of [his] life have been spent knocking in vain', Luthuli will continue to use non-violent strategies, even to death (the cross). It is historically disingenuous to quote Luthuli's 1952 statement and use it to advocate Luthuli's openness to violence in the 1960s when it advocates precisely the opposite.[66]

Suttner selects one expression of exasperation and, conveniently, other declarations that express a resolve for non-violent strategies are ignored or minimised. For example, Suttner interprets Luthuli's 'Who can deny. . .?' exasperation:

> But in this statement [Luthuli] concedes that the approach had not brought results . . . there is no denying that one of the interpretations to which Luthuli's own words are open, is that the results of non-violence were very limited. The time for armed struggle may have arrived, or have been near; at the very least, it needs to be considered.[67]

These conjectures are the author's and the ANC's – not Luthuli's. Suttner states further, 'As an open minded person. . .surely the Chief could not have discounted such an [ambiguous] interpretation'. Let us assume Suttner is correct: Luthuli predicted others would interpret his statement liberally. Hence, I argue, in order to correct such *misinterpretations*, Luthuli concludes his statement unambiguously:

> I have embraced the Non-Violent Passive Resistance technique in fighting for freedom because I am convinced it is the only non-revolutionary, legitimate and humane way that could be used by people denied, as we are, effective constitutional means to further aspirations.

To this Suttner writes, 'My refuge is in the notion of ambiguity, the sign of an unresolved question, which seems to best capture the state of mind of the Chief'. Yet, Luthuli

---

65. Couper, 'When Chief Albert Luthuli Launched "Into the Deep"', 87–88.
66. 'The Turn to Armed Struggle', the chapter in *The Road to Democracy* co-authored by Bernard Magubane, Philip Bonner, Jabulani Sithole, Peter Delius, Janet Cherry, Pat Gibbs and Thozama April, anachronistically cites Luthuli's 1952 statement in a chapter about the armed struggle (1961): see B. Magubane *et al.*, 'The Turn to Armed Struggle', SADET, *The Road to Democracy*, 53–145.
67. Suttner, 'The Road to Freedom', 699.

emphasised his disappointment with the National Party ('Who can deny that thirty years of my life...?') as a rhetorical means by which to demonstrate that he of all people is justified to opt for violence, but nonetheless does not. Therefore, others such as his younger subordinates should not (and may not?) resort to violence as they have not yet endured thirty years of knocking. Suttner simply inserts his and/or the ANC's ambiguity into Luthuli's certainty. That some misinterpret resolute statements do not render those same statements ambiguous.

Suttner states that 'the cross itself is ambiguous'.[68] Is it? The cross is perhaps the clearest example possible to advocate non-violent strategies.[69] The cross is a call to sacrifice non-violently to the death. For Luthuli, though death and/or failure may be the result, evil will be conquered through the power of the divine through the Christ on the cross. By subjecting himself to the cross, does Jesus at all consider violent methods to resist his oppression and the injustice done to him? No. The cross is not ambiguous. Jesus in action, implements his directive to his disciples not to use the sword in defence of him or of one's self (Matthew 26:52). The title of the statement 'The Road to Freedom Is via the Cross' is a very unambiguous declaration to not resist evil with violence, but with sacrifice, even to death. Suttner acknowledges this to some extent when he states 'The cross is a guide...', the cross suggests the 'way you must act' and 'it is the route to follow'.[70] Therefore, I fail to see how Suttner's three point itemisation of the cross' meaning does not include a non-violent sacrificial response to evil.[71] The carrying or bearing of the cross is an intrinsically non-violent action.

I concur with Suttner when he states that Luthuli's use of the words 'military efficiency and technique' does 'not in itself suggest support for or acceptance of military activity'.[72] I would not have imagined this interpretation. I would re-word 'not in itself suggest' to 'not at all suggest' Luthuli's support for or acceptance of military activity.

The Rivonia statement

I agree with Suttner that Luthuli's Rivonia Statement should not be hurriedly unpacked. In fact, I assert that its careful unpacking reveals the legitimacy of my thesis. A portion of Luthuli's Rivonia Statement reads:

> The African National Congress never abandoned its method of a militant, non-violent struggle, and of creating in the process a spirit of militancy in the people. However, in the face of the uncompromising white refusal to abandon a policy which denies the African and other oppressed South Africans their rightful heritage – freedom – no one can blame brave just men for seeking justice by the use of violent methods...

---

68. *Ibid.*, 705.
69. Of course, this statement is true for Christians and not for first century Roman soldiers who also executed violent robbers and zealots (armed revolutionaries) on crosses.
70. Suttner, 'The Road to Freedom', 706.
71. *Ibid.*. The cross makes Christian non-pacifists, such as myself, uncomfortable.
72. Suttner, 'The Road to Freedom', 706, fn 72.

Suttner argues:

> [The Statement] is first and foremost an affirmation of opposition to violence as an undesirable means for dealing with disputes [sic]. It signals that non-violence has not yielded results and is in itself another qualification on his allegedly absolutist position on violence.[73]

First, as earlier mentioned, there is no 'absolutist position'; this is a phantom debate. Second, Luthuli's statement intentionally begins with the powerful proclamation that the ANC 'never' abandoned its method (singular) of a non-violent struggle.[74] Herein, Luthuli makes a very skilful distinction between the ANC (including he who leads it) and the 'brave just men [who seek] justice by the use of violent methods'. Luthuli states very cleverly that 'no one can blame' *others outside* the ANC's parameter (who are 'brave just men for seeking justice by the use of violent methods'). In fact, Mary Benson records Luthuli using the same rationale and the same words before MK's launch. Benson relates that Luthuli expressed:

> If the oppressed people here ever came to indulge in violent ways that would be in reaction against the policy of Government suppressing them. However, much as you may disagree with them, you cannot blame them. But the leadership stand by the non-violent method.[75]

Luthuli does not say: The ANC never abandoned its method of a militant, non-violent struggle *until* Whites refused to abandon their supremacy. The statement simply articulates that the ANC, of which he is the General-President, never forsook the non-violent struggle.[76] Luthuli states that due to the Nationalist Party's oppressive tactics, no one can blame those who (autonomously) sought justice by violent means. Luthuli's statement is a justification, and not his or the ANC's support, for violent methods. If it was, then everything that Luthuli stated to the world in the days before Mandela launched MK on 16 December 1961 and after in 1962 was deceitful.

To justify something does not imply support. Justification is a term that expresses understanding and even reasonability, but not support. As early as the 1950s Luthuli stated that the Apartheid regime was making it increasingly difficult to avoid violence and its 'intransigence' motivated violence for self-defence and retaliation: 'no one can blame...' is a phrase of justification, not support. In fact, whenever Luthuli made a statement regarding the government's intransigence, he also nonetheless emphasised the use of non-violent methods in the struggle. 'Understanding' with 'justification' combined with 'solidarity' and 'sympathy' can assist with the 'acceptance' of the violent situation – especially when you

---

73. *Ibid.*, 700.
74. Perhaps Luthuli is being legalistic. Luthuli can say this because the ANC was banned and could not formally or within a fully representative body adopt a changed strategy. Such a statement leads one to wonder to what extent the ANC made Luthuli ignorant of the Lobatse Conference in 1962 wherein the ANC unofficially officially accepted MK as the armed wing of the ANC, abandoning what Slovo termed as a 'necessary fiction'.
75. M. Benson, *Chief Albert Lutuli of South Africa* (London: Oxford University, 1963), 65 (emphasis is Benson's and therefore Luthuli's).
76. I do not subscribe to an argument wherein the ANC also claims that it never abandoned non-violent strategies by qualifying that it supported violent *and* nonviolent strategies simultaneously (the 'Four Pillars' mantra).

can do nothing to control it. This is different from a claim that Luthuli indicated 'support' of the armed movement or that he articulated an ambiguous position. In the Rivonia Statement, Luthuli declares that, as the leader of the ANC, he and the ANC never supported the armed movement but nonetheless understand and sympathise with those who have chosen a violent option. The phrase 'no one can blame...' and its explanation for why one can't blame does not constitute support for the use of violence.

Solidarity, as was the case with Archbishop Desmond Tutu toward members of the ANC who resorted to violence, is not synonymous with countenance or agreement with violent tactics. For example, Tutu once clearly articulated Luthuli's non-violence stance and his 'no one can blame...' philosophy:

> We are driven... to invoke a non-violent method which we believe is likely to produce the desired result. If this option is denied us, what then is left? If sanctions should fail there is no other way but to fight. Should the west fail to inspire sanctions it would, in my view, be justifiable for Blacks to try to overthrow an unjust system violently. But I must continue to work to bring an end to the present tyranny by non-violent means. Should this option fail, the low intensity civil war... will escalate into a full-scale war. When that happens, heaven help us all. The Armageddon will have come![77]

Archbishop Tutu's stance on violence echoed Luthuli's.[78] The World Council of Churches (WCC) stance also echoed Luthuli's. The WCC's 1969 Programme to Combat Racism committed funds to liberation movements around the world despite their violent tactics *and* continued to advocate and support only non-violent strategies to combat Apartheid.[79] To provide mercy, comfort, care, solidarity and hospitality to combatants is not an indication of one's support of violent tactics. Such a gesture could be one of solidarity with the oppressed, not an agreement or support for the forms of resistance that they chose. To give aid to an ANC exile, especially within a Christian or humanitarian context, is no indication in and of itself of an agreement with the ANC's turn to violence. Justification and understanding, even an articulation of the armed movement's position, was for Christians an act of solidarity, *not* agreement.

Suttner offers more circumstantial evidence for his ambiguous argument through Z.K. Matthews who 'was very like-minded with Luthuli'.[80] Suttner suggests that statements Matthews made to the WCC in 1964 are evidence 'Luthuli probably did come to terms with armed struggle during this period'.[81] First, Matthew's views in 1964 are at most his views, not Luthuli's. Second, what Matthews offers in his 1964 statement to the WCC (that opposed violence) is an explanation of, not support for, the ANC's position. A typical Christian position, which Matthews, Tutu and Luthuli articulated, stands in solidarity with the oppressed while not necessarily condoning or participating in the oppressed's violent

---

77.　D. Tutu 'Freedom Fighters or Terrorists?', in C. Villa-Vicencio, ed., *Theology & Violence: The South African Debate* (Grand Rapids: William Eerdmans, 1988), 3, 77.

78.　S. Couper, 'Luthuli and Kairos', in *The Nonconformist*, 1 (2007), 32–43.

79.　B. Pityana, 'Tumultuous Response: The Voices of the South African Churches, in P. Webb, ed., *A Long Struggle: The Involvement of the World Council of Churches in South Africa* (Geneva: World Council of Churches Publications, 1994), 84–101.

80.　Suttner, 'The Road to Freedom', 703–704.

81.　*Ibid.*, 703.

acts of desperation. Third, Matthews does not necessarily offer his views, but rather the ANC's views justifying its rationale for resorting to violence. In 1964, Matthews simply regurgitated to the WCC Mandela's rationale given to the ANC Working and Executive committees and Joint Congresses meetings in June and July 1961. Fourth, the qualifications that Luthuli 'probably came to terms' with the turn to violence 'during this period' is a tacit admittance that Luthuli did not support the armed movement prior to 1964 and that therefore Mandela committed insubordination against Luthuli and the ANC in the December 1961 launch of MK, thus unilaterally changing the ANC forever.

Fashion

I am unsure why Suttner breaks into a commentary on fashion in his article.[82] Perhaps suggested is an argument that the Congress' attire conveyed a latent militarism and therefore Luthuli possibly supported the formation and launch of MK. I question this line of argumentation to insert ambiguity in Luthuli's thinking. Be that as it may, I speculate whether the uniforms had an ecclesiastic origin. Within the Congregationalist faith tradition from which Luthuli was born and bred, uniforms are worn by various fellowships: *amaButho*, *amaDodana*, *iziPhika* and *isiLilo*. The former two wear a khaki uniform, including jacket, so as to identify themselves as 'Soldiers of Christ'. Neither the fellowships nor the uniforms carry any violent connotations.

Suttner comments that Luthuli's position on violence is confused because 'Luthuli raises military connotations through his attire [at the Nobel acceptance ceremony] wearing the headdress, necklace and other elements of the apparel of his chieftaincy'.[83] First, and most importantly, these accoutrements were *not* 'apparel of his chieftaincy'. As a chief, Luthuli rarely or never wore traditional attire. He was the chief of the *amaKholwa* community, hence of Christian congregants at the Groutville mission station. Other than in Norway, the only other instance where I have observed Luthuli pose in traditional clothing was for staged photographs taken during his 1948 visit to the USA. Second, I am unclear as to what are the 'other elements' of apparel to which Suttner refers.[84] Other writings comment on Luthuli's 'traditional Zulu warrior's robes' that are 'flowing'.[85] Descriptions of Luthuli's apparel are often hyperbole. When Luthuli accepted the Prize, he simply wore western clothes with a necklace and a headdress of traditional origin, which he had to *borrow*, because they were *not* 'apparel of his chieftaincy'. I have suggested in other writings that Luthuli's Nobel accoutrements had nothing to do with militarism or some stealthy quasi-approval of violence. Luthuli's Nobel speech affirmed non-violent tactics.[86] To suggest that a necklace (made of hawk's claws, and a hawk represents aggression and aggression is

82.   *Ibid.*, 701.
83.   *Ibid.*, 702.
84.   *Ibid.*
85.   Naidoo, *In the Shadow of Chief Albert Luthuli*, 71.
86.   It is true that within his Nobel speech, Luthuli 'tipped his cap' as an affirming recognition that in colonial contexts that were administrative rather than settler, violence was used as a means to establish justice (as the metropoles would not have a decisive military advantage and the functionaries would simply return to the metropoles). For Luthuli, South Africa constituted a radically different context (Exceptionalism) that required the avoidance of violence at all costs.

synonymous with militarism and violence) is evidence for Luthuli's ambiguous stance on violence is weak and does not counter direct and unambiguous statements by Luthuli in his speech to the contrary. The necklace and headdress were likely symbols of pan-African solidarity as Luthuli accepted the Prize on behalf of the African continent (not just the ANC or South Africa) and therefore to acknowledge the then newly emerging African independent states.

Swaziland farms

Suttner concludes that the farms in Swaziland which Luthuli purchased with the Nobel Peace Prize money indicate he supported the turn to violence. There is little evidence to lead to this conclusion. There are a number of means by which the farms could have been used to support the liberation struggle non-violently, all of which have evidence. The most obvious is that the proceeds of food grown on the farm could be sold and donated to the ANC in London. This in fact did happen. The farms could be used as an asset to be sold, the proceeds going to toward the provision of scholarships. This in fact did happen. The farms could serve as a refuge for those in exile escaping arrest in South Africa. This *may* have happened. Nokukhanya recalled:

> Our hope was that when things really got hot inside South Africa, people would escape to these farms and set up camp there. Besides providing refuge for exiles, our purpose was to use the land for farming to make profit which would go toward helping the refugees.[87]

Suttner states that Luthuli's wife tended these farms 'from time to time'.[88] This is an under-exaggeration. Nokukhanya toiled alone for six months at a time for four years until 1966.[89] I have always wondered how it is that the ANC President's wife laboured alone as a farmer, ploughing and reaping, seemingly without any support from the ANC. What organisation allows its President-General's wife to exert alone for half the year, separated from her very ill husband, for years? Does this scenario make sense if the ANC was using this farm as some means by which to prosecute the armed struggle? What, if any, measures did the ANC take to assist Nokukhanya? What measures, if any, did the ANC take to support the viability of these farms? In the end, the farms had to be sold at a loss. The proceeds from the sales established the Luthuli Education Trust, a fund for 'student teachers', not MK cadres.[90] Luthuli wanted the sale of the farms to go towards 'libraries and books', not grenades and AKs.[91]

Suttner states, 'The weight of evidence leads one to conclude that there is little doubt that the chief… decided to contribute practically to the success of MK through such logistical support'.[92] The 'weight' is in fact incredibly light. Nokukhanya reports in her biography that few refugees were harboured at the farms and no indication exists that the

87. Rule, *Nokukhanya*, 131.
88. Suttner, 'The Road to Freedom', 702.
89. Rule, *Nokukhanya*, 130–138.
90. *Ibid.*, 138.
91. *Ibid.*
92. Suttner, 'The Road to Freedom', 703.

farms provided 'logistical support' for MK. John Nkadimeng's evidence is that they stayed 'at some unknown place'.[93] There is no evidence that the 'unknown place' is Luthuli's farm and therefore no indication that he contributed 'practicably to the success of MK'. Even if one acknowledges, as I do, that the Luthulis intended the farms to in part shelter ANC exiles, the evidence from Nokukhanya suggests that the farms were rarely, if ever, used for this purpose.

Only Wilson Conco and Masabalala Yengwa (at the time, non-exiles) checked in and paid visits to Nokukhanya. Though intended for harbouring ANC exiles, there is no indication that the farms were used for 'logisitcal support', as 'transit houses... or [for] military operations' or that any exiles were 'combatants' – these are sexy extrapolations of more benign intentions.[94] Furthermore, if the farms provided refuge for exiles or combatants, this does not at all constitute a practical contribution to the armed struggle or 'actions in support of MK' any more than Gandhi's stretcher brigade supported the slaughter of indigenous peoples by the Natal colonial government during the Bambatha Rebellion.[95] The provision of refuge would constitute Christian humanitarianism.

Luthuli's death

Suttner continues the nationalist and ANC suspicions of Luthuli's death being the result of foul play. Suttner quips:

> What is interesting to reflect upon is that already in the late 1950s and for a short while in 1960 when he was unbanned, Luthuli started to develop a large following amongst white people. This is one of the reasons why he was feared and it is also a reason why mischief may not be excluded in his death, whatever any inquest record may say.[96]

There are five problems with the above reflection. First, the reflection is anachronistic. Luthuli died in 1967, yet referred to are Luthuli's public stature in the 1950s and into 1960 to provide a motive for the Apartheid regime to assassinate him. From 1960 to 1967, the situation had radically changed, for South Africa, the liberation movement and Luthuli. A context in 1960 is not a motivation to assassinate in 1967. By 1967, Luthuli had been almost completely silenced and invisible due to the constraints placed upon him by his own movement not to condemn the armed struggle and by the government's 1962 Sabotage Act which further prevented his words and image from being published.[97] Luthuli received a very harsh banning order in 1964 that rendered him incarcerated in the little hamlet of Groutville. The exiled ANC and Oliver Tambo had long since changed strategies and were in operational control of the liberation movement, or what little was left of it after Rivonia. Luthuli's context in 1959 when he was received rapturously in Cape Town by Whites cannot be the context in 1967 when Luthuli was old, frail, alone, disillusioned and silenced. Luthuli was little or no threat in 1967.

93.   *Ibid.*
94.   *Ibid.*
95.   *Ibid.*
96.   *Ibid.*, 712.
97.   Couper, 'An Embarrassment to the Congresses?', 331–348.

Second, if Luthuli was popular with Whites in 1967 and had to therefore be killed by government, then his non-violence stance would be the primary basis upon which he would be popular with Whites. A link between Luthuli's early popularity with Whites to his 1967 death must be predicated on his continued non-violent resistance to the Apartheid regime. Even moderate Whites would not support a Black leader who advocated for the violent overthrow of the Nationalist Party regime, least of all in the 1960s. This motive as evidence therefore falls away.

Third, no evidence exists to support the conspiracy theory. Dismissed by Suttner is an inquest in which the family and the family's attorney participated and did not at all contest. The family's advocate, Andrew Wilson, cross-examined the informants. Other researchers, after reviewing the evidence and interviewing Wilson, also conclude that the cause of Luthuli's death was 'almost certainly an accident'.[98]

Fourth, Suttner is again fighting a phantom argument by stating 'mischief may not be excluded in his death'. No one excludes mischief as a cause of Luthuli's death, least of all me. However, wishful thinking for a nationalist narrative (or a suspenseful biography) is not sufficient to make historical claims. Evidence must be presented. 'Mischief' has always been included as a possible cause of Luthuli's death. That does not mean that it was the cause, or even that that there is any substantive case for it being the cause.

Fifth, archival evidence presented in my book *Bound by Faith* leads to a reasonable conclusion that the Apartheid government did not murder Luthuli. I speculate with evidence that Luthuli suffered a stroke and this led to a vulnerability to being struck by a train on a narrow footplate on a bridge not designed for pedestrian traffic. In early 1955, Luthuli suffered from a gradually debilitating stroke and a coronary attack. For the next 12 years until his death, Luthuli suffered from chronic high blood pressure. Oliver Tambo was greatly worried about his health in 1961 while they were in Norway. In one 1965 letter to a friend in the United States, Nokukhanya laments 'Of late, my husband's memory is very poor. I do not think he can stand another trip to your country. For recalling persons he is zero'.[99] In January 1966, doctors admitted Luthuli to hospital for hypertension. Nokukhanya returned to Swaziland on account of Luthuli's 'very weak' health.[100] In March 1967, Luthuli drafted his Last Will and Testament. From April 1967, Luthuli was in the hospital for four weeks. He almost had to have a painful blind eye removed. Luthuli's handwriting deteriorated. In July 1967, Swedish journalists described him as 'an old and tired man'.[101] On the night before his death, Nokukhanya stated her husband 'gets so exhausted' and looks 'so tired'.[102] I submit that in evaluating a person's cause of death, no historian can ignore that Luthuli drafted and signed a Last Will and Testament before being admitted for a

98. Charlotte Owen and Peter Corbett produced an audio-visual documentary and investigated Luthuli's death. I. Shevlin, 'The Chief's Voice Is Heard Again', *Sunday Tribune Magazine*, 18 July 1993, 3.
99. Rule, *Nokukhanya*, 135.
100. *Ibid.*, 137.
101. T. Sellström, ed., *Sweden and National Liberation in Southern Africa, Vol. I, Formation of a Popular Opinion 1950–1970* (Uppsala: Nordiska Afrikainstitutet, 2003), 241.
102. Rule, *Nokukhanya*, 140.

month to hospital only three months before his death and that numerous eyewitnesses testified to a deteriorating state of health up until the night before he died.

Conclusion

The conclusion of Suttner's article states:

> It is futile to argue as if [Luthuli's] stance on the use of violence was a point of law, series of facts having to be presented and then coming to a decision on a balance of probabilities or beyond reasonable doubt.[103]

First, the 'point of law' phrase is another indication that Suttner is engaged in a phantom debate. I do not argue Luthuli's stance on violence as a 'point of law'. I examine the chronology, read Luthuli's public statements and draw a conclusion set in a specific time and place. This is what historians do.

A quest to discern Luthuli's stance on violence is 'futile' if one does not read the archives or his repeated statements to the contrary from 1948, through the Defiance Campaign in Durban to the end of his political career when the 1962 Sabotage Act was enforced and he could no longer be quoted in South Africa. If one reads Luthuli's statements in the newspapers (particularly his *Golden City Post* articles in 1960, 1961 and 1962 that are often draconian in their conclusiveness) and if one believes what Luthuli actually says about his stance on violence, then it is not futile to argue Luthuli's stance on violence.

Below is one of dozens of Luthuli quotations from 1961 that begs for an unambiguous interpretation.

> I firmly believe in non-violence. It is the only correct form which our struggle can take in South Africa. Both from the moral and the practical point of view the situation in our country demands it ... To refrain from violence is the sign of the civilised man ... Non-violence gives us a moral superiority ... we pledge ourselves to non-violent activity because our better natures and our consciences demand this of us ... My hope and prayer is that any activity on our part now or in the future time will be on peaceful lines ... If we are to be sincere when we advocate non-violence, we must see to it that we do not create situations where others, rightly or wrongly, for whatever reason, will declare it necessary to use violent methods against us ... let it be remembered that to create situations where violence becomes inevitable makes one a sponsor – intentional or not – of violence.[104]

Jacob Zuma and others violate Suttner's warning not to 'argue as if [Luthuli's] stance on the use of violence was a point of law' when they repeat ANC nationalist historiography that states Mandela and the ANC persuaded Luthuli to embrace the armed struggle.[105]

103. Suttner, 'The Road to Freedom', 713.
104. A. Luthuli, 'Why I Believe in Non-Violence', *Golden City Post*, 28 May 1961.
105. J. Zuma, 'Chief Albert Luthuli Memorial Lecture by His Excellency President Jacob Zuma at Inkosi Albert Luthuli International Convention Centre', Durban, 24 November 2010 found at: http://www.info.gov.za/speech/DynamicAction?pageid_461&sid_14832&tid_24964, accessed 7 February 2011; S. Couper, 'Irony upon Irony upon Irony: The Mythologising of Nationalist History in South Africa', *South African Historical Journal*, 63, 2 (2011), 339–346; S. Khumalo, 'Zuma Slams Luthuli Claims', *The Mercury*, 25 November 2010.

Nationalist versions of Luthuli's stance on violence emasculate him of his agency. His views are simply grafted, morphed and fused into Mandela's and the ANC's. To do such is an injustice to Luthuli, regardless if we disagree with his obstinate regret of the liberation struggle's turn to violence.

Secret Party: South African Communists between 1950 and 1960

TOM LODGE

University of Limerick, Ireland

Abstract

Since 1990 a rich body of autobiographical writing and interview testimony together with freshly available archival materials can support an assessment of the role played by South African communists in anti-apartheid opposition during the 1950s. Numbering only a few hundred, communists were very influential in leadership positions in the Congress Alliance and shaped programmes and actions in accordance with their own strategy of a united front. This article explores the ways on which the party established its own organisational structures as well as considering the extent and impact of its wider concerns.

Introduction

In 1953, South African communists attended the first conference of their clandestine party, three years after the dissolution and prohibition of the Communist Party of South Africa (CPSA). The establishment of the new South African Communist Party (SACP) was preceded by the spread of clandestine networks constituted by former CPSA activists. The new party would remain unannounced until 1960. Members remained visibly active in other organisations until their arrests or exile would lead to the final destruction of its organised structures inside South Africa in 1965.

For a long time, information about the SACP in the 1950s and early 1960s would remain very restricted. The party's own disclosures about its development in the 1950s supplied a most abrupt narrative. An authorised history by Michael Harmel writing under a pseudonym, 'A. Lerumo', became the standard source. In its treatment of this period, Harmel's history mainly recapitulated the mass-based campaigning of the African National Congress (ANC) and its public allies in which 'the Communist Party and its members played a worthy role'.[1]

---

1.   A. Lerumo, *Fifty Fighting Years: The South African Communist Party, 1921–1971*, 3rd ed. (London: Inkululeko, 1987), 82–98.

A little more information became available subsequently from other party publications. A volume of documents noted that the evolution of the 'party line' could be tracked through statements by key individuals published openly through the press during the 1950s.[2] In exile, approved biographies of veteran members would appear periodically and these could supply occasional insights into the party's inner life in the 1950s.[3] Otherwise, though, the other main source of information about the SACP's development during the 1950s was from the trials of Communist Party activists between 1965 and 1966 in which former party members testified as state witnesses.[4] The reliability of such testimony was obviously questionable.

After legal restrictions on the party were lifted in 1990 its members began to speak more freely in interviews and to publish their memoirs which have become progressively more candid. A pioneering essay by Raymond Suttner has reconstructed the way the SACP established its 'underground' from such sources.[5] More recently, archival materials have become accessible in university libraries. Archival sources, memoirs, biographies and oral testimony now illuminate a rich picture of the party's clandestine activities inside South Africa up to the end of 1960 and they help us to understand much better the complexities of its relationship with the Congress Alliance, the larger movement in which its members were so busy. In this article I will sketch out the key features of this hidden history as well as assessing its wider significance in the scholarly interpretation of anti-apartheid resistance in the 1950s.

Reassembly: 1950–1953

A consideration of the state of the Communist Party at the time of its banning is a useful starting point because the new party would initially recruit exclusively from CPSA veterans. The most up to date information about the CPSA's following in 1950 is contained in the national conference report of 1949. At that time it had 2,482 members. Most of these, 1,673, were black. There were 269 white, 428 Coloured and 112 Indian communists. The largest concentration of party membership was around Cape Town, just over a thousand, with nearly another thousand in and around Johannesburg. The report refers to smaller clusters of party activists in Durban, Pretoria, East London and Port Elizabeth and a few more in 'outside areas'. About half the membership was drawn from 'industrial workers', about 450 members were farmworkers, 200 were 'intellectuals' or professionals and the rest housewives and domestics.[6]

This picture was shaped by the information available to the Cape Town-based leadership. In the 1949 report, Port Elizabeth appears as a minor centre of party activity. In fact, as the

2. B. Bunting, ed., *South African Communists Speak: Documents from the History of the South African Communist Party, 1915–1980* (London: Inkululeko, 1981), 217.
3. B. Bunting, *Moses Kotane: South African Revolutionary* (London: Inkululeko, 1975), 224.
4. G. Ludi and B. Grobberlaar, *The Amazing Mr Fischer* (Cape Town: Nasionale Boekhandel, 1966); B. Mtolo, *Umkhonto we Sizwe: The Road to the Left* (Durban: Drakensberg Press, 1966).
5. R. Suttner, 'The Reconstitution of the SACP as an Underground Organisation', *Journal of Contemporary African Studies*, 22, 1, 2004, 43–68.
6. University of Cape Town (UCT), Manuscripts and Archives, Simons Papers, 0.12.3, Report of the District Committee to the Annual District Conference of the CPSA, Cape Town, 23 April 1950.

memoirs of one of the key local leaders, Raymond Mhlaba, suggest, here from 1947 overlapping membership between the party and the ANC, in which party officials assumed leadership roles, helped to extend its influence and to create a habit of local ANC militancy. The party also encouraged trade union members to join and radicalise the ANC branches in their vicinity. In contrast to other regions, here the normally anti-communist Congress Youth League was well before 1950 'leftist' in orientation with Mhlaba himself serving as its propaganda officer and in this capacity conducting Marxist study classes.[7] Also unnoticed in the Party's reports at this time was the expansion of communist recruitment in Johannesburg's migrant worker communities, especially in the Denver and Jeppe hostels. Here too, in response to party policy, hostel-based communists, as well as playing an animated role as trade unionists, also joined the ANC. In the words of one of the Johannesburg party leaders, they brought to each of these agencies – that is the party, the ANC and the unions – 'a very particular style of work that wasn't indigenous to these organisations'.[8]

Despite the predominance of black membership and the movement of African party cadres into the ANC, the party was beset by disagreements over strategy. In January 1950, the Central Committee's report, after noting the CPSA's expanding influence amongst Africans, addressed the issue of how the Party should build its relationship with the ANC. The report was sharply critical of both the ANC and its Youth League, arguing that the leadership of both were 'liberal capitalists' seeking only 'the freedom [...] of squeezing profit out of the people'. Even so, the party should engage more closely with the national movement, with the objective of changing it 'into a revolutionary party [...] distinct from the Communist Party but working closely with it'. In such a transformed party, ideological struggle promoted by the communists would help to ensure that 'class conscious workers and peasants would constitute the main leadership'.[9]

Michael Harmel, one of the party's key thinkers, disagreed with this view. In an unpublished set of notes on the party's history that he wrote in 1960, Harmel maintained that the report 'was strongly criticised' because of its perceived departure 'from the established united front position' and was rejected by the conference. Harmel himself felt the report revealed a 'liquidationist' predisposition and attributed its authorship to Jack Simons, a member of the party's Central Committee through the 1940s, who later refused to join the SACP.[10] United fronts had been prescribed Comintern policy from 1935 and they implied that communist parties should seek the broadest range of alliances with even bourgeois-led groups in the struggle against fascism. In the international communist movement this strategic line had been supplanted in 1947 by Andrei Zhdanov's two camp theory, in which the world was divided into mutually antagonistic capitalist and anti-capitalist forces, and from this

7.   T. Mufamadi, *Raymond Mhlaba's Personal Memoirs: Reminiscing from Rwanda and Uganda* (Pretoria: Human Sciences Research Council, 2001), 35–73.

8.   Lionel ('Rusty') Bernstein, quoted in P. Delius, 'Sebatakgomo and the Zoutpansberg Balemi Assoociation: the ANC, the Communist Party and Rural Organisation', *Journal of African History*, 34 (1993), 310.

9.   'Race Oppression and the Class struggle: Report of the Central Committee to the National Conference of the CPSA, January 1948.' Full text in UCT, Manuscripts and Archives, Simons Papers, 0.12.1. Extract reprinted in Bunting, ed., *South African Communists Speak*, 200–211.

10.   University of the Witwatersrand (Wits), Historical Papers, Ronnie Kasrils Papers, A3345, A6.1.4.2, M. Harmel, 'Some notes on the Communist Party in South Africa'.

perspective, communist parties were supposed to avoid alliances with any bourgeois-led groups even in colonies. [11]

South African communists do not seem to have paid much attention to Zhdanov's ideas, though. CPSA documentation from the late 1940s makes it quite clear that the CPSA was still trying to build a united front against what it perceived as 'fascist' Afrikaner nationalism, not just with black organisations but with white parliamentary parties as well and of course with white labour[12]. As we shall see, within the SACP there would be differences over the degree to which communists should seek to change the ANC, with Michael Harmel amongst those who believed that the ANC should still retain an African 'national' bourgeois element in its leadership and should therefore eschew explicitly socialist politics.

So, on the eve of its dissolution, the CPSA represented a small but effective political organisation, with its African members in one centre at least, Port Elizabeth, beginning to reorganise the ANC as a mass-based militant movement. It leadership, though, was divided by three strategic orientations. First there was a group who saw the party's main future as working in alliance with the ANC. Within this group, though, as we have noted, there were disagreements about the degree to which the party should seek to transform the ANC ideologically and socially. Second, there was a small minority, especially in the Cape, who maintained reservations about any alliance with African nationalism and who argued that the party itself should build a mass African following as well as concentrating on extending the party's work in building African trade unions.[13] Finally, there was a small number who still believed that the party's main mission should be to retain influence within the officially recognised labour movement, that is the registered unions, white, Indian and Coloured, as well as still seeking to influence white politics.[14]

Who took the initiative to reorganise a communist party is an issue over which even insider accounts are at odds with each other. Harmel referred to 'a group of comrades gathered around [...] Moses Kotane [... who] decided to build the Party up on new lines' in late 1950.[15] Raymond Mhlaba remembered Kotane at this time visiting Port Elizabeth to discuss the party's re-establishment.[16] Rusty Bernstein, though, referred to two small groups that 'started embryo parties' that subsequently merged; the more assertive of these, he believed, 'was composed of Wits students headed by Joe Slovo, Ruth First and Harold Wolpe'.[17] Fred Carneson when interviewed remembered a meeting in Cape Town of former Central

---

11.   P. Hudson, 'The Freedom Charter and Socialist Strategy in South Africa', *Politikon*, 13, 1 (1985), 78–81; I. Filatova, 'The Lasting Legacy: The Soviet Theory of National Democratic Revolution and South Africa', *South African Historical Journal*, 64, 3 (2012), 512–513.

12.   For references to fascism and the need for a united front to fight fascism see UCT, Manuscripts and Archives, Simons Papers, 0.12.2, Report of the Central Committee to the National Conference of the CPSA, 8–10 January 1949.

13.   David Everatt quotes an article in *Viewpoints and Perspectives* by a white former CPSA member in Cape Town in early 1953 that advocated the building of cohesive organisation of the industrial working class in alliance with rural workers and peasants. D. Everatt, *The Origins of Non-Racialism: White Opposition to Apartheid in the 1950s* (Johannesburg: Wits University Press, 2009), 84.

14.   R. Hodgson, *Foot Soldier for Freedom* (Johannesburg: Picador Africa, 2013), 62.

15.   Harmel. 'Some notes on the Communist Party'.

16.   Mufamadi, *Raymond Mhlaba's Personal Memoirs*, 95

17.   L. Bernstein, *Memory against Forgetting* (London: Viking, 1999), 125. See also J. Slovo, *Slovo: The Unfinished Autobiography* (Randburg: Ravan Press, 1995), 83.

Committee members in mid-1951 to address the possibility of reconstitution. On this occasion many of the old leaders opposed illegal activity. Jack Simons was among those who opposed the party's re-establishment; in his case, as noted above, he had already argued the case for working to transform the ANC into a revolutionary organisation, a task that did not require a separate organisation. It was at this juncture that the initiative shifted to the Transvaal-based communists.[18] However, independently of the Transvaal groups, in Cape Town would-be underground communists including Albie Sachs, Dennis Goldberg and Ben Turok assembled in the Modern Youth Society and attended Marxist study classes given by Jack Simons.[19] A band of white Modern Youth Society adherents took part in the ANC-led Defiance Campaign, courting arrest by using the 'non-white' entrance in the main post office. Though the Johannesburg-based groups succeeded by late 1952 in bringing most of these networks together, the complexity of the process merits emphasis because it helps to explain the continuation within it of divergent ideological beliefs and strategic predispositions. The party established District Committees in 1952 before holding its first formal national conference in 1953, Michael Harmel's notes record, after a national meeting around Easter 1952 definitively undertook to form a new clandestine organisation. The early formation of separate District groups also helped to build doctrinal diversity into the new party.

The 1953 founding conference adopted the party's new name, endorsed a brief interim programme of aims and instituted two key rules: members should maintain 'total silence' about the party until any decision to announce its existence and any recruitment should be sanctioned by 'unanimous [District] committee decision'.[20] The conference, held on the premises of a Indian-owned trading store in in the Eastern Transvaal, was attended by 25 delegates elected through a procedure in which members of the new organisation's base units, three- to four-member 'groups' would nominate one of themselves and one other person that they guessed might belong to the new party. The District Committee would eliminate wrong guesses and provide a final list, adjusted to ensure racial, geographical and gender balance: in the words of Bernstein, 'not quite Western style democracy, but as far as we dared to go.'[21] Groups were linked to the Committee by only one member and had no lateral contact with each other. The Central Committee elected at the conference was entrusted to co-opt additional members. These principles ensured that lower echelon members, even when elected or co-opted onto District Committees, remained uncertain about the identities of party leaders as well as members in other districts.[22]

Who joined the new party? Brian Bunting told Sylvia Neame that before its prohibition the party 'was full of people who were totally unsuitable for illegal work'.[23] Only a small minority of the old membership was recruited into the clandestine units. Several CPSA veterans refused when they were approached including Edwin Mofutsanyana, Sam Kahn, and, as we

18. Everatt, *The Origins of Non-Racialism*, 80.
19. B. Turok, *Nothing but the Truth: Behind the ANC's Struggle Politics* (Johannesburg: Jonathan Ball, 2003), 30.
20. Bernstein, *Memory against Forgetting*, 129.
21. *Ibid.*
22. Bernstein, *Memory against Forgetting*, 130; Harmel, 'Some notes on the Communist Party'.
23. Bunting, *Moses Kotane*, 173. Wits, Historical Papers, Sylvia Neame Papers, A2729, Folder E1, Brian Bunting, interviewed by Sylvia Neame, London, 14 May 1986.

have noted, Jack Simons.[24] Issy Heymann, who had joined the CPSA in the mid-1930s, was only invited to join the SACP in 1959 after being initially asked by Michael Harmel to allow his business address to be used for secret correspondence: he believed he was being tested 'to see if I was scared or if I would be conscientious about it'.[25] In a report he delivered at a meeting of the Communist Party of the Soviet Union (CPSU), Moses Kotane claimed that by 1961, the SACP had a membership of between 400 and 500 and this was after a recent phase of expansion.[26] Ben Turok suggested that at the end of the 1950s SACP membership was much smaller, around 130.[27] We know that recruitment was selective and vetted by party leadership and at least one well known Indian CPSA member, Ismail Meer, who wanted to join, believed he had been deliberately 'discarded'.[28] Another person keen to join, whose recruitment was delayed for a long time, was Harry Gwala, a former full-time CPSA official, and an energetic trade unionist in his home town of Pietermaritzburg. In anticipation of the party's re-formation, he established a Marxist study group while he continued to build his rubber workers' union. He finally joined the SACP in 1962. In his case, he thought, the reluctance to invite him into the new party may have been due to his own history of disagreements about the 'style of working' in the labour movement. As he told Sylvia Neame in 1989, 'I don't like orders coming from above'.[29]

In the process, certain key constituencies of the old party were either to fall away altogether or would weaken in the new organisation. SACP membership would become increasingly African. African recruitment efforts especially targeted individuals who held local leadership positions – organisers of residents' associations, for example, as well as trade union officials. As Turok observed, in the 1950s the Party was now a vanguard organisation and 'the people we selected were key people, and each one had to be a leader in his or her own right'.[30] The hostel-based migrant grouping in Johannesburg remained within the party: these were manufacturing workers, though the other township-based African members were likely to be engaged in either literate occupations or as small businessmen. Moses Kotane and Walter Sisulu, two of the most important African communists in the 1950s, maintained livelihoods as a furniture dealer and an estate agent respectively, while Govan Mbeki supplemented his salary from *New Age* from the proceeds of his wife's shop in Idutywa in the Transkei. *The Guardian* and its successor, *New Age*, employed several distributors in different centres, all of them African communists, and as Fred Carneson, their manager, noted much later: 'these people were not just newspaper sellers; they were top class political organisers.'[31] Walter Sisulu joined

24. Wits, Historical Papers, Sylvia Neame Papers, A2729, Folder E1, Brian Bunting, interviewed by Sylvia Neame, 14 May 1986.
25. Wits, Historical Papers, David Everatt Papers, A2521, Issy Heymann, interviewed by David Everatt, 31 May 1987, Transcript, 16.
26. Wits, Historical Papers, Ronald Kasrils Papers, A6.1.4.2, Moses Kotane, 'Notes on Aspects of the Political Situation in the Republic of South Africa, 9 November 1961'.
27. Wits, Historical Papers, David Everatt Papers, A2521, Ben Turok, interviewed by David Everatt, 1990. Transcript, 130.
28. Suttner, 'The Reconstitution of the SACP', 50.
29. Wits, Historical Papers, Sylvia Neame Papers, A2729, Folder F2, Harry Gwala, interviewed by Sylvia Neame, Berlin, 29 October 1989.
30. Ben Turok, interviewed by Tom Lodge, London 1985.
31. Wits, Historical Papers, Sylvia Neame Papers, A2729, Folder E2, Fred Carneson, interviewed by Sylvia Neame, 15 May 1986, Transcript, p. 34. Sylvia Neame Papers, A2729, Folder E2.

the party in 1955 while serving as the ANC's secretary general after attending Michael Harmel's Marxist study group and one year later he was co-opted onto the Central Committee.[32] Port Elizabeth's communists were led by Raymond Mhlaba, a dry cleaning worker, though, with his secondary schooling, untypically well-educated. Through the 1950s, a new emphasis on African recruitment would bring university graduates into the fold, what the party perceived to be a prestigious new intelligentsia: the lawyers Joe Matthews and Duma Nokwe were early entrants in this group. Govan Mbeki was a key mentoring influence for several of the Fort Hare students who joined the party around 1960, including Chris Hani and Zola Skweyiya as well as a young mathematics lecturer, Andrew Masondo.[33] This entry of this fresh cohort was a development that prompted some discomfort among the older African working-class membership in Johannesburg.[34] In the late 1950s, African recruitment efforts also began to focus on high schools.[35] Success in enrolling African 'intellectuals' may have encouraged certain recruiters to become additionally restrictive in their selection. Natoo Babenia, who joined Umkhonto we Sizwe (MK) in 1962, was discouraged from joining the party, being told, apparently, that he 'was not sufficiently intellectually adept'.[36] He joined the party later, in prison.

The CPSA's old presence in the white labour movement was not reproduced in the new party: the most conspicuous white trade-unionist in the CPSA, Danie du Plessis, was among those who opposed reconstitution. From the SACP's inception, the Johannesburg-based party leadership seems to have given up any ambition to retain serious influence in the white labour movement. This is clear from Arnold Selby's recollections. Selby joined a unit of the underground party in 1952, before the SACP's formal establishment. This was a unit constituted wholly by trade unionists – Selby himself was at that time National Secretary of the African Textile Workers' Union. Other group members included Lesley Massina, organiser of the African Laundry Workers, Vic Syfret from the (white) Amalgamated Engineering Workers' Union, and Eli Weinberg, the group leader, who worked for the mainly white National Union of Distributive Workers. The group was directed to 'concentrate on the organisation of African workers', especially those who were unorganised workers, particularly those employed in larger scale undertakings, rather than in small factories, and especially those workers in 'key concerns' such as transport and engineering, a shift away from the areas in which African unionism had made its main inroads. To this end, Vic Syfret 'did good work' with the Non-European Railway and Harbour Workers, Selby recalled. Directives about union work were communicated to group members at their weekly meetings through visits by Michael Harmel, and more occasionally, Joe Slovo. In 1954, unit members proposed that they should set up a Workers' Council of Action, a group they hoped would build opposition within the Trades and Labour Council to oppose impending job reservation legislation. This initiative was vetoed by party leadership for, as Joe Slovo told them, 'this work was among existing unions but we should

32. E. Sisulu, *Walter and Albertina Sisulu: In our Lifetime* (Claremont: David Philip, 2002), 123.
33. C. Bundy, *Govan Mbeki* (Auckland Park: Jacana Media, 2012), 103. H. Macmillan, *Chris Hani* (Auckland Park: Jacana Media, 2014), 21.
34. See John Pule Motshabi's remarks about his own and David Bopape's reactions in Simons Papers, 08.1, 'Minutes of Africa Group meeting, 13 May 1982'.
35. See J.J. Jabulani, 'Why I joined the Communist Party', *African Communist*, 44, 1971, 79–81.
36. N. Babenia, *Memoirs of a Saboteur* (Bellville: Mayibuye Books, 1995), 62.

concentrate on organising the unorganised into strong mass industrial unions [...] this was the general line'. After the formation of the South African Congress of Trade Unions (SACTU) in 1955, the trade unionists unit was dissolved and its members were reassigned to other groups. One effect of this was to reduce the chances that trade unionists could function as a collective caucus within the party.[37]

More surprising than its withdrawal from the white labour movement was the cessation of party influence within Indian trade unions in Durban. Indian unions had been a major arena of CPSA activity but 'during the 1950s' according to one veteran of the SACP's Durban base, Rowley Arenstein, 'Indian workers were left in the cold'.[38] This was partly because union officials engaged in this sector who were also CPSA members were among the group that felt that communists should retain a 'class-based' emphasis in organising and concentrate on factory-based labour organisation. It was also the case, though, that through the 1940s the party in Durban shifted its strategic focus among Indians away from workplace concerns in favour of defence of broader rights.[39] Betty du Toit and Mike Muller, key textile worker organisers, were among those who remained at odds with the new party; Du Toit had been involved in disagreements with the Cape CPSA leadership over trade union strategy for much of the 1940s.[40] Pauline Podbrey was another key Indian labour organiser who became disaffected with the party in the early 1950s.[41] Indian workers in Durban were discouraged from undertaking politically-motivated strikes by the threat of their replacement with Africans as indeed happened after the dismissals of 300 Indian workers following a local ANC-led stay away in June 1953.[42]

Whites and Indians were not the only workers left out. In 1955, when busy as an organiser for the Congress of the People, Ben Turok encountered a group of Coloured farmworkers in Kraaifontein who had once constituted a CPSA branch and who had never been contacted by any political activists since the party's dissolution.[43] However, the Western Cape-based mainly Coloured Food and Canning Workers' Union, as well as its African counterpart, were important bases for SACP recruitment through the 1950s, though rather oddly, Ray Alexander, its original secretary, was not on the initial list of former CPSA members asked to join the new party.[44] She was invited and became a member in 1954.[45]

37. All quotations in this paragraph are from this source. Wits, Historical Papers, Sylvia Neame Papers, A2729, Arnold Selby, interviewed by Sylvia Neame, Berlin, 31 May 1985, Transcript, 10–14.

38. Rowley Arenstein, interviewed by Iain Edwards, Durban 1986. I am grateful to Iain Edwards for a copy of this transcript.

39. V. Padayachee, S. Vawda and P. Tichman, *Indian Workers and Trade Unions in Durban, 1930–1950* (Durban: Institute for Social and Economic Research, 1985), 159–167.

40. Bettie du Toit, interviewed by Tom Lodge, London, 29 January 1978. See also B. du Toit, *Ukubamba Amadolo: Workers' Struggles in the South African Textile Industry* (London: Onyx Press, 1978).

41. Wits, Historical Papers, African Studies Institute Oral History Collection, Pauline Podbrey, interviewed by Maureen Tayal, London, 8 August 1983.

42. Bill Freund discusses the reasons for declining Indian worker militancy during the 1950s in *Insiders and Outsiders: The Indian Working Class in Durban* (London: James Currey, 1995), 57–61.

43. Turok, *Nothing but the Truth*, 53–54.

44. Possibly, because her husband Jack Simons had already refused, though this seems unlikely as she was a key CPSA organiser with a longer party history than Jack Simons.

45. Her autobiography makes only occasional references to SACP activity through the 1950s until her departure into exile in 1965 and it is very evident that despite attending meetings trade unions remained her chief commitment. See R. A. Simons (edited by R. Suttner), *All My Life and All My Strength* (Johannesburg: STE, 2004), 196–297.

When interviewed in 1986, Arenstein maintained that in the early 1950s, the new party leadership was rather inclined to be contemptuous of trade unionism viewing it as economistic 'reformism' and that their over-riding preoccupation with alliance with the national liberation movement meant that a low priority was accorded to labour organisation for its own sake. This is quite likely. Moses Kotane, the dominant African communist, and the SACP's general secretary, was by his own admission 'not by nature a trade unionist [... and] more inclined to political things'.[46]

As in the past, active white communists were often drawn from Baltic Jewish immigrants or their children. Of the 33 white communists mentioned in this article who probably constitute the larger share of white South Africans active in the party during the 1950s, at least 19 were either Lithuanian or Latvian born, or the children of parents born in Jewish communities in these countries. However, they were more likely to include well-educated middle-class professionals than had been the case with the CPSA's leadership: the white liberal universities supplied a steady stream of recruits through the 1950s.[47] People from a British-descended working class background, a prominent group in the CPSA's early history, were rarer in the SACP: Fred Carneson, who first became a communist while working in Pietermaritzberg's post office, was unusual in this respect. Another son of working-class English immigrants was Jack Hodgson, an ex-mineworker in both South Africa and Northern Rhodesia where he helped Roy Welensky set up the mineworkers' union.[48]

Despite their mostly middle class status, white members in Johannesburg usually lived in the comparatively modest suburbs, just adjacent to the city centre, Hillbrow's apartment blocks, and small cottages in Bellevue and Yeoville. The lawyers tended to live better and indeed the comparative affluence of Joe Slovo's and Ruth First's household in Roosevelt Park apparently elicited a degree of resentment 'among the lesser mortals of the movement'.[49] The key personalities in the new party's white leadership group were comparatively young, in their late 20s or early 30s, and a significant number had served as soldiers in the Second World War. Several of these army veterans – including Brian Bunting, Joe Slovo, Wolfie Kodesh, Fred Carneson and Lionel Bernstein – had returned home deeply impressed by what they took to be insurrectionary takeovers of Italian towns by communist partisans.[50]

Regional variations in the party's sociology may help to explain the political differences between districts. In Cape Town, Ben Turok, who joined the SACP in 1954, found that in this centre the party 'tended to be sectarian' and 'work in the national movement was hampered by the insistence on class perspectives'. Here too there was an especially 'uncritical identification with Soviet positions'.[51] In general, he thought, communists in Cape Town 'had a

46. UCT, Manuscripts and Archives, Simons Papers, 0.12.1, Minutes of CPSA conference, 1938, p. 27.
47. See for example, B. Hepple, *Young Man with a Red Tie: A Memoir of Mandela and the Failed Revolution, 1960–63* (Auckland Park: Jacana, 2013), 29.
48. Hodgson, *Foot Soldier for Freedom*, 41.
49. Turok, *Nothing but the Truth*, 79.
50. Brian Bunting, interviewed by Tom Lodge, London, 27 February 1985; Wits, Historical Papers, A3299, A8.1, L. Bernstein, *Letter from Italy*, Johannesburg, Communist Party of South Africa; G. Shaw, 'Wolfie Kodesh, Obituary', *The Guardian*, 13 November 2002, Slovo, *Unfinished Autobiography*, 29–30.
51. Turok, *Nothing but the Truth*, 50.

more leftist perspective' than elsewhere.[52] This may have been a consequence of the presence in Cape Town of an alternative Marxist tradition, at that time represented by Trotskyites in the Non-European Unity Movement. Turok's impression of the Cape's ideological fervour was confirmed by Denis Goldberg who also described the local party as 'sectarian', this time referring to the constraints on members' personal lives.[53]

In Johannesburg, it is likely that 'cross pollination between the Communist Party and the national movement' – Bunting's phrase – was most developed, and Moses Kotane's local influence kept in check any propensities for 'seeing the party as a rival to the ANC'.[54] As we shall see, both Kotane and Michael Harmel, the party's key theorist and also resident in Johannesburg, remained wary of any 'transformationist' approaches to the ANC. In Johannesburg, incidentally, the spatial features of racial segregation ensured that most party base units, the groups, were uni-racial, whereas in Durban and Cape Town groups were more racially mixed. African members on the Witwatersrand were especially likely to be fully absorbed in ANC-related activity.[55] In Durban, the SACP began with comparatively few African members, for locally they had been in a minority in the old CPSA, a residual consequence of concentrated police action against the party after the 1930 anti-pass campaign. The most assertive African communists were trade unionists and Durban would emerge in the late 1950s with the strongest group of affiliates in the ANC-allied SACTU. The dominant personality intellectually in the Durban SACP, Rowley Arenstein, would argue that the chief task for the party should be building factory based organisation.[56] These differences would affect the ways in which SACP members in each centre would understand the overall purpose of their activities and it is to strategic and ideological concerns that I will now turn.

Towards national democracy

At its formation, the SACP decided that its members should involve themselves in legal mass work, in effect working within the ANC or allied organisations. The doctrinal justification for such a move drew on two arguments. The first of these was that South Africa was a 'colony of a special type'. The second proposition was that, given this characteristic, communists should embrace a programme of 'national democratic' aims as a stage that would precede the full development of a socialist society.

A version of colonialism of a special type was spelled out in the CPSA's Central Committee report of 1950, in which South Africa was depicted as containing 'the characteristics of both an imperialist state and a colony'. In this setting, the 'determining' economic sectors, mining and agriculture, depended upon a colonial exploitation of rightless black workers by a white 'imperialist' state, a racial form of exploitation that inhibited workers' development of class consciousness. The local presence of settlers from the 'dominant imperialist

---

52. *Ibid.*, 59.
53. Wits, Historical Papers, Sylvia Neame Papers, A2729, Folder F2, Denis Goldberg, interviewed by Sylvia Neame, London, 1 October 1987. Transcript, 13.
54. Bunting, *Moses Kotane*, 193.
55. Suttner, 'The reconstitution of the SACP', 53.
56. Rowley Arenstein interviewed by Iain Edwards, Durban 1986.

nationality' resulted in the exclusion of black people from the commercial opportunities normally available to privileged groups within the indigenous groups in other colonies. As the
Congress movement developed a mass orientation, workers would increasingly constitute
its leadership.[57]

As the party's theorists argued, because the ANC's leadership was not constituted by an
aspirant black bourgeoisie, then the national liberation that it would seek would not be bourgeois democracy, but something different. For what that something would be, by the early
1950s fresh perspectives about the kinds of societies that might emerge from anti-colonial
movements were beginning to be available from Soviet authorities. Contrary to Zdhanov's
two-camp theory, anti-colonial 'national bourgeoisies' did not necessarily defer to imperialist
interests, Soviet theorists were concluding by 1956. In newly independent countries there
might be a 'non-capitalist road' to socialism in which liberal democracy and nationalisation
of foreign monopoly enterprises under state ownership would allow room for domestic
private undertakings. In seeking to achieve this, workers and black property owners had con-
vergent interests.[58]

Analysts of the party's intellectual trajectory disagree about the degree to which its leaders
kept themselves informed about international communist theory. Working from Soviet
sources, Irina Filatova maintains that the really decisive impact in South Africa of Soviet
notions of national democracy followed the first formal contact between the SACP and
the CPSU in 1960, when the Soviet Party formally adopted the idea of a non-capitalist
road.[59] In fact, though, there was plenty of informal contact between South African communists and Soviet and other eastern European countries through the 1950s. Indeed, Rowley
Arenstein believed that, for party ideologues, countries like Poland and Czechoslovakia represented models of national democracy.[60] South Africans who emigrated to London constituted a special branch of the Communist Party of Great Britain (CPGB) in 1953 and indeed
several South African communists joined the British party before their own,[61] some of them
retaining dual membership of both parties. The London group helped to facilitate communications with other communist parties. By the end of the 1950s, a London unit of the SACP
was formally constituted.[62] South African communists who had arrived in London to undertake studies or for other reasons before 1948 were dissuaded from going home by the advent
of National Party rule and particularly the prohibition of mixed marriages. The Immorality
Act affected Vella Pillay, a South African Indian student in the UK, and his English wife
Patsy, who made London their permanent home while remaining active in the South
African party. Leslie Massina, first general secretary of SACTU visited Czechoslovakia

57.   Everatt, *The Origins of Non-Racialism*, 82–96.
58.   Hudson, 'The Freedom Charter', 78–81.
59.   Filatova, 'The Lasting Legacy', 516–518.
60.   Rowley Arenstein, interviewed by Iain Edwards, Durban 1986.
61.   See Turok who belonged to this group in 1953. For South Africans who joined the SACP through the London
       group see P. O'Malley, *Shades of Difference: Mac Maharaj and the Struggle for South Africa* (New York:
       Viking, 2007), 82–83.
62.   Wits, Historical Papers, Sylvia Neame Papers, A2729, Folder F2, Barry Feinberg, interviewed by Sylvia
       Neame, London, 1 October 1987, Transcript 5. For a fuller account of the London group's development
       see A. Lissoni, 'The South African Liberation Movement in Exile, c.1945–1970' (PhD thesis, School of
       Oriental and African Studies, London, 2008), 49–58.

for a short training course on trade unionism in 1954.[63] Lionel Forman joined the SACP after returning from Czechoslovakia where he had been working for the International Union of Students between 1951 and 1953. After his return to South Africa, Forman maintained a vigorous correspondence 'on the national question' with the Russian Africanist, I.I. Potekhin, posting his letters to Vella Pillay for forwarding from London.[64] Moses Kotane spent nearly a year outside South Africa in 1955 during which time he was hosted by members of the British Communist Party and attended an international youth festival in Warsaw. He also visited East Germany in 1956, apparently. The SACP sponsored a visit by six South Africans, mostly its own members, to the Soviet Union in 1956. A report written by Moses Kotane in 1961 suggests that on several occasions, 'in the past', the party despatched several people 'to the GDR for technical training'.[65] Newspapers and journals edited by party members through the 1950s paid plenty of attention to international communist developments.

Contemporary evidence suggests that South African communists were well aware of the underpinning rationale for national democracy through the 1950s. For example, in 1956 the barrister and journalist Lionel Forman was making the case for non-revolutionary roads to socialism in an issue of *Fighting Talk*, the former journal of the Springbok Legion, now edited by Ruth First.[66] Two years earlier, in an article in the party-controlled weekly newspaper, *Advance*, Forman had addressed what nationhood could be in South Africa, urging his readers to 'get over this weird idea that all national liberatory groups are "bourgeois national"'.[67] At a subsequent public symposium prompted by his article, Forman proposed that the national liberation movement had the potential to become a true people's movement, 'one that will not allow a mere transfer from national oppression [...] but will push forward to people's democracy'.[68] And just what a people's democracy might embody was spelled out in the same year by Moses Kotane, in a pamphlet, *South Africa's Way Forward*. A people's democracy, Kotane explained, would have all the civic freedoms conventionally associated with democracy but it would be more egalitarian. Land would be shared 'among its rightful owners', big mining and other monopoly concerns would become public property, there would be good wages, social security and housing for the homeless.[69] Progression to national democracy was not taken as a predetermined given or an inevitable prospect, though, it would require conscious effort to bring it about.

With respect to their 'legal' activism, the SACP's members' engagement with national liberation between 1953 and 1960 had three particular emphases. First, and most obviously, there were the party's efforts to shape the ANC's ideological predisposition. In 1954, after

---

63. H.R. Pike, *A History of Communism in South Africa* (Germiston: Christian Mission International of South Africa, 1988), 303.

64. Wits, Historical Papers, Sylvia Neame Papers, A2729, F2, Sadie Forman, interviewed by Sylvia Neame, Transcript, 14. For a selection of this correspondence see S. Forman and A. Odendaal, eds, *A Trumpet from the Housetops: The Selected Writings of Lionel Forman* (London: Zed Books, 1992), 190–201.

65. Wits, Historical Papers, Ronald Kasrils Papers, A6.1.4.2, Moses Kotane, Notes on some aspects of the political situation in the Republic of South Africa, 9 November 1961.

66. Forman and Odendaal, *A Trumpet from the Housetops*, 154–156.

67. *Ibid.*, 179.

68. *Ibid*, 182.

69. Reprinted in Bunting, *South African Communists Speak*, 231–241.

the ANC leadership decided to collect popular demands for a Freedom Charter, a National Working Committee assembled composed of representatives from the ANC itself and its allies. Lionel Bernstein joined this committee whose other members included Walter Sisulu for the ANC and Piet Beyleveld from South SACTU, both of whom were shortly to join the Party after a recruiting process that probably preceded their invitations onto the committee. Bernstein drafted the preliminary 'Call' for demands to be submitted for consideration at a Congress of the People one year later and a nationwide process of canvassing steered by provincial committees started. In his autobiography Bernstein describes in some detail the process through which demands were elicited. The committee decided that distilling from these demands a draft Charter was 'just a writing job' and entrusted this task to Bernstein. Working his way through thousands of scraps of paper, Bernstein 'cobbled together a synthesis'. In doing this, he recalled, he 'had no more idea of where to start than anyone else' and he read through the materials 'to get the general flavour' and to identify general thematic categories, doing his best to 'read into' their contents a coherent 'compromise or a consensus'. As he admitted '[the] most difficult part of the exercise was to keep my own opinions from influencing the draft' and he insisted that even those clauses he wrote that prompted most contention, on land reform, nationalisation, and non-racialism were 'everyday stuff' among Congress activists.[70]

This was probably true, but even so Bernstein's understanding of political common sense may well have been affected by the programmatic concepts that he had helped to develop within the SACP. Certainly the Charter conformed closely with Kotane's notion of a people's democracy that he had outlined in his pamphlet in May 1954. On nationalisation, Bernstein suggests that what he had drafted was not intended as 'a gateway to socialism' but simply a means through which racial inequality could be addressed. Writing in 1960, Michael Harmel observed that the Freedom Charter was 'identical in all its main provisions to the demands set forth in the immediate programme of the SACP adopted in 1953'.[71] Moses Kotane, writing one year later, noted that 'all major policy decisions' undertaken by the liberation movement 'either emanate from or have the approval of our C[entral] C[ommittee]'.[72] Bernstein's insistence that he did not intend the Charter's provisions to be socialist is quite reconcilable with the way the Johannesburg communists understood national democracy. At the time, Moses Kotane also argued that the nationalisation advocated by the Charter was not a socialist measure.

From the more 'leftist' ethos of Cape Town, Ben Turok perceived things differently. Cape Town-based communists were determined that the Charter should be a reflection of the Party's minimum programme, whereas Transvaal communists believed 'the Party should lead but not drive'.[73] Turok was invited to attend the Congress as one of 10 keynote speakers with the brief of introducing the economic clause. While staying with the Harmels, on the night before the Congress, he was shown a draft of the charter. He claimed that he redrafted the clause, amending it to stress 'that the commanding heights should be in public

70. Bernstein, *Memory against Forgetting*, 149–155. Slovo confirmed Bernstein's authorship of the first draft in an interview with Sylvia Neame in August 1986 (Wits, Historical Papers, Sylvia Neame Papers, A2729, Folder E1).
71. Harmel, 'Some Notes on the Communist Party'.
72. Kotane, 'Notes on Aspects of the Political Situation'.
73. Ben Turok, interviewed by Tom Lodge, London 1985.

ownership'.[74] At the Congress itself in his speech Turok supplied a much more radical interpretation of the nationalisation provisions than Bernstein intended, telling his audience that there would be 'a committee of the workers to run the Gold Mines [... and] wherever there is a factory and where there are workers to be exploited, we say that the workers will take over the factories'. 'Let us have a people's committee to run the banks', he added.[75]

Turok's account is at odds with Bernstein's memoir. Bernstein wrote that the draft that Congress Alliance Joint Executive leaders reviewed the day before the Congress had already been printed and there were no changes to his original. Ben Turok, though, has been very insistent he was 'the author of the economic clause in the Freedom Charter'.[76] In 1985 he told me that the original version did not refer to the question of industrial ownership but just used vague language about sharing of material resources. Bernstein himself and other senior communists could not attend this meeting because they were banned. When Turok told Harmel about his speech, his host was a 'little appalled', for in calling for a 'people's democracy', 'we'd gone some way beyond where the movement wanted to be'.[77] Nelson Mandela's gloss on the Charter's provisions, published in *Liberation*, the journal edited by Michael Harmel, in 1956, was more likely to be in tune with party orthodoxy when he suggested the 'breakup' and 'democratisation' of monopolies would 'open fresh fields for the development of a non-European bourgeois class'. After this, 'private enterprise' would 'flourish as never before'.[78] In 1959, the Party itself in an editorial (written by Harmel) in the first issue of its own journal, the *African Communist*, declared its maintained adherence to a 'United Front of National Liberation' composed of all classes, 'workers, peasants, intellectuals *and* businessmen' (my italics).[79]

The second way in which the Party would shape the ANC during the 1950s was through its contributions to the ANC's organisational structure. In an organisation in which after the Defiance Campaign membership would reach around 100,000, a few hundred communists would constitute a tiny minority. But they wielded significant influence. In Port Elizabeth, party activists supplied the model for the ANC's ambitious scheme to establish a cell based local organisation, drawing upon their own experiences of establishing party groups in New Brighton, and it was they who explained and proposed the scheme to Mandela during a visit he made to the Eastern Cape in 1953.[80] It was in Port Elizabeth, 'like nowhere else' that the M-Plan was implemented.[81] During the preparations for the Congress of the People, in several regions, it was SACP members working within SACTU structures who, according to oral testimony collected in the 1980s, 'performed the lions' share of the

---

74. Turok, *Nothing but the Truth*, 59.

75. Police record of the Congress of the People, Kliptown, Johannesburg, 25–26 June 1955, extracts reproduced in T. Karis and G.M. Gerhart, *From Protest to Challenge, Volume 3: Challenge and Violence, 1953–1964* (Stanford: Hoover Institution, 1977), 184–204.

76. Turok, *Nothing but the Truth*, 262.

77. Ben Turok, interviewed by Tom Lodge, London, 1985.

78. N. Mandela, 'In Our Lifetime', *Liberation*, June 1956.

79. Editorial, *African Communist*, October 1959.

80. Wits, Historical Papers, A3301, B8–9, Wilton Mkwayi and Raymond Mhlaba interviewed by Barbara Harmel and Philip Bonner, 18 and 27 October 1993.

81. R. Suttner and J. Cronin, *30 Years of the Freedom Charter* (Johannesburg: Ravan Press, 1986), 109.

work', particularly in organising the house to house collection of demands.[82] So communists played an important role in helping to mobilise and train the ANC's base level activists through the 1950s, introducing to them, as Bernstein noted, their own particular style of work and, at least in Port Elizabeth, where the ANC maintained local 'political study groups' using a syllabus drafted by Govan Mbeki,[83] their own view of the world. And in one area at least, organising independently they brought a key new following into the ANC, when the hostel-based communists in Johannesburg, with Flag Boshielo and John Nkadimeng, created a body of migrant workers from Sekhukhuneland, Sebatakgomo, which they decided to 'locate within the ANC'.[84] The communist-managed press also supplied a key organisational resource for the ANC. This included a weekly newspaper, *New Age*, as well as the more occasional journals, *Liberation* and *Fighting Talk*. Aside from their propaganda functions, the newspapers and journals, particularly *New Age*, through its network of street sellers and corresponding reporters, supplied a national system of communication, linking party leadership with key local organisers.

Finally, and most importantly, with respect to organisation, the party provided a group of leaders, disciplined and trained, and despite internal disagreements, united by their vision of overall purpose. Kotane asserted in 1961 that communists effectively led the national liberation movement.[85] As he noted, from their inception, communists were in the majority in SACTU's executive as well as in the top echelons of the (white) Congress of Democrats. Within the ANC, SACP members held key positions. In the leadership elected in 1958, a communist, Duma Nokwe, became secretary general, in place of then banned Walter Sisulu, also a party member, and of the 10 other executive members, at least four others (Alfred Nzo, Leslie Massina, Gladstone Tshume, and Caleb Mayekiso) belonged to the Party.[86]

An especially decisive effect of the party's committed embrace of the national movement was the extent to which it directed the African trade union movement into a supportive role as an auxiliary formation. This was in direct contrast to the situation in the 1940s when many communist trade unionists maintained 'slender contact with the party itself' and held back from wider political commitments.[87] In contrast, in certain regions, according to the Natal trade unionist and SACP member Billy Nair, 'SACTU cadres were actually politicised, educated, in fact trained to staff Congress branches in the first place',[88] though, in this respect, Natal might have been rather exceptional. Rowley Arenstein also suggested that SACTU's role was crucial in ensuring the Party's influence over the ANC in Durban: between the two there was 'an easy relationship', he thought, though this would change after 1960.[89] Oddly enough, the party did not enjoy the same favour with the Natal Indian Congress

82. Reggie Vandeyar, Liz Abrahams and Billy Nair, quoted in Suttner and Cronin, *30 Years of the Freedom Charter*, 39–41.
83. Bundy, *Govan Mbeki*, 82.
84. Delius, 'Sebatakgomo', 312.
85. Wits, Historical Papers, Ronald Kasrils papers, A6.1.4.2, Moses Kotane, 'Notes on Aspects of the Political Situation'.
86. Identified as party members in Mufamadi, *Raymond Mhlaba's Personal Memoirs*, 41.
87. D. Fortescue, 'The Communist Party of South Africa and the African Working Class in the 1940s', *International Journal of African Political Studies*, 24, 3 (1991), 481–512.
88. Nair quoted in Suttner and Cronin, *30 Years of the Freedom Charter*, 146.
89. Rowley Arenstein, interviewed by Iain Edwards, 1986

(NIC) in which there was through the 1950s, according to one Indian activist, 'virulent antagonism towards Communists'.[90]

In which respects did Party influence make a difference with respect to the ANC leadership's decision-making? To what extent did the party determine the choice of campaigning and the tactics that were employed? Tellingly, Brian Bunting, when interviewed by Sylvia Neame in 1986 and at that time not speaking for quotation, maintained that

> in the 50's [...] practically every initiative came from the Party ... practically all the drive came from the Party. I can't think of one basic decision taken from 1950 until Rivonia or even beyond that didn't derive its authority from the party.[91]

Writing in the 1990s, Joe Slovo maintained that 'long before any of the campaigns waned, the question of "what next" had already been the subject matter for many [central committee] agendas'.[92] Moses Kotane's assertions in Moscow in 1961 suggest that essentially the party was in a commanding position, but it would be a simplification from this to conclude that ANC mass actions followed a preconceived party agenda. After all, in the document cited here, Kotane was seeking help from fraternal parties and he obviously needed to emphasise the decisive character of the party's role.

With respect to some of the major set pieces of the period, we can be fairly sure the party did not always make the initial campaigning decision. In the case of the Defiance Campaign, the SACP was still in the process of being constituted. In Cape Town a very similar programme to the Defiance Campaign was conceived by the ex-CPSA dominated Franchise Action Committee in January 1951, but subsequent divisions within the Committee forestalled whole-hearted local communist commitment to the Defiance Campaign.[93] The Congress of the People was originally proposed by Z.K. Matthews, provincial president of the ANC in the Cape; Joe Matthews' father it is true, but not a communist. When, in 1959, the ANC decided to plan an anti-pass campaign, according to Lionel Bernstein, he and other Johannesburg-based party members had strong reservations, as they doubted that large masses of people would be willing to risk the penalties that the state would inflict on campaigners. The 'decision [was] not ours but that of the ANC'.[94] Ben Turok noted that party members were 'not allowed to form caucuses within committees of the mass movement' and they were able to disagree with each other at any debates within the Congresses. However the Johannesburg District Committee 'met at least monthly to discuss various campaigns of the movement' and in any case party members including Turok and Sisulu predominated within the Congress Alliance secretariat, 'a kind of steering committee for the movement'.[95] And 'on difficult questions, Chief Lutuli bypassed his officials and sent for Moses' Kotane.[96] The ANC's choice of campaigning issues was often reactive and opportunist rather than carefully

90. Babenia, *Memoirs of a Saboteur*, 50.
91. Wits, Historical Papers, Sylvia Neame Papers, A2729, Folder E1, Brian Bunting, interviewed by Sylvia Neame, London 14 May 1986.
92. Slovo, *Unfinished Autobiography*, 107
93. D. Musson, *Johnny Gomas: Voice of the Working Class* (Cape Town: Buchu Books, 1989), 108–109.
94. Bernstein, *Memory against Forgetting*, 190.
95. Turok, *Nothing but the Truth*, 90–91.
96. Bunting, *Moses Kotane*, 230

premeditated. What does seem to be the case is that once decided upon, communists both collectively and individually impacted tactically on the ways in which campaigns were conducted.

In particular, it is possible to trace a consistent adherence to united front politics in the kinds of influence that the party exerted over ANC campaigning. Two key examples help to underline this point. According to Bunting, Moses Kotane, himself a resident in Alexandra, played an influential behind-the-scenes role in the Alexandra Bus Boycott, advising the local ANC leadership to include standholders, that is the local landlords, in their committee, and even to back the standholders' association's leader, Mr Mahlangu, as chairman of the committee. It was a decision that helped the local ANC to lose control on the boycott in its final stages as the stand-holders favoured a an unpopular compromise settlement with the bus owners and ANC leaders in Alexandra, who included two new SACP recruits, Thomas Nkobi and Alfred Nzo, who earned a rare rebuke from Michael Harmel for their 'failure [...] to give positive leadership' in *New Age*.[97] Another communist, Moroka (Soweto) resident John Pule Motshabi, was the main organiser of a series of solidarity boycotts across the Witwatersrand.[98]

Moses Kotane may also have been decisive in urging the ANC to merge SACTU's minimum wage campaigning with broader concerns. In a pamphlet published in 1957, shortly after the Congress Alliance organised a well-supported 'stay at home' for a £1 a day minimum wage, Kotane argued the case for drawing 'into the movement' the widest array of groups possible, including the parliamentary opposition. All the signals were present, Kotane maintained, 'of an ever-widening repudiation by Europeans of the Government's terror policy and Apartheid'.[99] Accordingly, in 1958, the ANC called for a three-day stoppage which combined the objectives of discouraging whites from voting for the National Party as well as maintaining the pressure for a minimum wage. A weak response, a consequence of the neglect of any factory-based preparation, convinced ANC leaders to call off the protest at the end of the first day.

Contemporary left-wing critics of both the ANC and the party excoriated the ANC leadership for 'transform[ing] an essentially working class campaign into a broad political front' and for substituting 'a false slogan [...] "The Nats must go"' for the original minimum wage demand. They were critical not only of ANC leaders but also of a 'group inside Congress who professed to be Marxists' for 'surrender[ing] the working class to the mercy of a middle class leadership'.[100] More recent recollections by party members do suggest that these criticisms had a degree of validity. When the tactic was first conceived within the Communist Party, it divided opinion, with those members whose main organisational experience was in the union movement particularly arguing 'that strikes had to be organised at the place of work', not in townships.[101] Communists in Durban, who even in their ANC activities

97. *New Age*, 4 April 1957.
98. O.T. Motshabi, 'Obituary: John Pule Motshabi', *Sechaba*, May 1989.
99. M. Kotane, *The Great Crisis Ahead: A Call to Unity* (Woodstock: A New Age Publication, Pioneer Press, 1957).
100. Socialist League of Africa (Baruch Hirson), 'A Critical Discussion: South Africa: Ten Years of the Stay at Home', *International Socialism* (London), 5 (Summer 1961). https://www.marxists.org/archive/hirson/1961/stay-at-home.htm. Accessed 29 August 2014.
101. Bernstein, *Memory against Forgetting*, 15.

emphasised factory-based mobilisation,[102] disliked the tactic; as Rowley Arenstein put it, it was 'Johannesburg's theory, not ours'.[103]

From the vantage point of the party's leadership, Ben Turok conceded that 'SACTU was often dissatisfied with the way worker issues were handled by us'. Trade unionists often felt that workers' interests were given insufficient recognition and that there was even a bias against trade unionists. Turok himself drafted one of the 1958 stay-away exhortations and he remembers 'Sisulu standing over my shoulder, monitoring the choice of language used'. Even SACP members, Turok recalled, were 'restrained in their choice of language [...] about the political role of workers and the special class interests of workers'.[104] Turok thinks that in Johannesburg SACTU officials were 'economistic and workerist', and this may have been true. In 1958, Betty du Toit, an influential organiser among textile workers, was herself heavily critical of what she termed 'irresponsible strike actions' arguing that workers would be less vulnerable to sanctions as well as police action if they used 'alternative tactics, such as a go slow campaign at the workbench'.[105] On the whole, through the 1950s and early 1960s, the key decisions that resulted with regard to the mobilisation of organised labour for political purposes were made by party leaders such as Moses Kotane and Walter Sisulu, who themselves were fairly disengaged from the trade unions. There were indications of continuing divisions within even the Johannesburg-based African party membership on how and when organised workers should be mobilised[106] but top leaders' commitment to united front strategies did not waver.

Illegal work up to 1960

Running parallel to its Congress Alliance directed activities, the party maintained its own separate undertakings. These included 'regular and formal meetings' by its Central and District Committees[107] and, between 1953 and 1962, six national delegate congresses. Indeed, as Turok wryly conceded in one interview, through the 1950s and up to 1960, the party 'didn't do anything in its own right apart from having meetings'.[108] Congresses initially were attended by around 20 delegates but they became larger and more representative subsequently.[109] Turok attended a Congress in 1954 in a deserted factory outside Johannesburg: it 'came to life when Harmel, the undoubted brain of the movement, took over'.[110] During the 1956–1961 Treason Trial proceedings, Moses Kotane was attending Central Committee meetings three times a week, apparently; those charged in the trial included a large

102. See Billy Nair on holding 'mass meetings directly in the factories' in Suttner and Cronin, *30 Years of the Freedom Charter*, 41–42.
103. Rowley Arenstein interviewed by Iain Edwards, Durban 1986.
104. Turok, *Nothing but the Truth*, 90.
105. B. Hirson, *Revolutions in My Life* (Johannesburg: Wits University Press, 1995), 283. For Du Toit's argument see her *Ukubamba Amadolo*, 126–127.
106. See, e.g., D. Thloome, 'Lessons of the Stay-Away', *Liberation* (Johannesburg) 32 (August 1958), 10–13.
107. Bunting, *Moses Kotane*, 198.
108. Wits, Historical Papers, David Everatt Papers, A2521, Ben Turok, interviewed by David Everatt, 1990, Transcript, p. 21.
109. Bernstein, *Memory against Forgetting*, 131.
110. Turok, *Nothing but the Truth*, 48.

proportion of the party's leadership and their enforced assembly in court facilitated such meetings. Groups also maintained a regular schedule of at least monthly meetings, sometimes holding them in cars if they included African and white members.

Until 1959, aside from evaluating and planning the party's contributions to Congress campaigning, the main purposes of these meetings were to exercise oversight over recruitment and to discuss internal documents generated by the Central Committee. As noted above, recruitment was initially very cautious. There was a special 'D' category of members of people who had not been CPSA members, who had not been jailed for political offences and who did not engage with Congress bodies but whose function was to perform 'deep cover' tasks, including, later, the purchase of property for the party.[111] Training and education of new members was a priority assigned to the groups. Ben Turok ran a study class with new Alexandra members, and he recollected coaching Thomas Nkobi and Alfred Nzo in dialectical materialism in his car.[112] Fundraising was another task. No communists themselves had easy access to private fortunes, though a few came from quite wealthy families.[113] Those with incomes paid a tithe. In practice the main external source of party funding were contributions from sympathetic Indian traders.[114] Yusuf Dadoo's eminent social status within the Indian community as 'Gandhi's favourite son', with his picture in every Indian home,[115] was particularly helpful in eliciting these donations.[116] Party members reciprocated this generosity as several of them for the first time became business proprietors, lending their names to serve as 'fronts' for Indian run businesses threatened with closure under the Group Areas Act.[117] Indians in Natal also contributed most of the donations that helped to pay for printing New Age, a reward for the newspaper's defence of rights threatened by Group Areas.[118] In Johannesburg, the newspaper also supported its costs through a Christmas Hamper savings club, itself providing a modest livelihood for party activists.[119]

No copies of the internal confidential documents circulated through the party's clandestine organisation for this period are available yet in any archive except for those that eventually became public statements published through the legal newspapers and journals or by other organisations. These included Kotane's South Africa's Way Forward and Michael Harmel's cautious assessment of Kruschev's revelations at the Soviet Party's twentieth

111. On D category members: Norma Kitson, Where Sixpence Lives (London: Hogarth Press, 1987), 131. See also S. Clingman, Bram Fischer: Afrikaner Revolutionary (Cape Town: David Philip, 1998), 294.
112. Turok, Nothing but the Truth, 92.
113. Julius First, Ruth First's father, owned a furniture factory outside Johannesburg, the venue for the SACP's second congress (see below). His share portfolio helped him and his daughter re-establish a joint family household in London in exile in 1963. See A. Wieder, Ruth First and Joe Slovo in the War Against Apartheid (New York: Monthly Review Press, 2013), 145.
114. Wits, Historical papers, Ronald Kasrils Papers. A3345, A6.1.4.2, Vella Pillay and Yusuf Dadoo, The Political Situation in the Union of South Africa.
115. P. Raman, 'Yusuf Dadoo: a Son of South Africa', in S. Dubow and A. Jeeves, eds, South Africa's 1940s: Worlds of Possibilities (Cape Town: Double Storey, 2005), 237.
116. For detailed description of political fundraising among Indians and reference to Dadoo's role as a 'referee' see Hodgson, Foot Soldier for Freedom, 77–82.
117. Ibid., 64–65.
1187. Brian Bunting, interviewed by Tom Lodge, London, 27 February 1985.
119. 'Arnold's Christmas Hampers' employed both Arnold Selby and Wolfie Kodesh on £8 a week plus commission and 'virtually financed the paper'. Wits, Historical Papers, Sylvia Neame Papers, A2729, Arnold Selby, interviewed by Sylvia Neame, Transcript, 59–60

congress. Apparently the Central Committee devoted 'several meetings' to a consideration of the congress's proceedings,[120] before concluding that despite the 'great accomplishments and achievements of Stalin, whose place in history is secure', communists needed to acknowledge 'mistakes', including 'violations of collective leadership', and the framing of innocent people. 'Violations of socialist law' were at least partly attributable to the 'incorrect theory of the intensification of class struggle after the defeat of capitalism'.[121] On the whole, this kind of rationalisation sufficed for most South African communists, though Hilda Bernstein much later told one researcher that '1956 was a key year for me [...] because of the revelations of Kruschev'.[122] That year, the Soviet invasion of Hungary prompted 'another crisis of belief'.[123] In Johannesburg Monty and Myrtle Berman protested against the invasion and were expelled, though this was after a history of disaffection with the party line: they refused to join the Congress of Democrats, for example, because it was a whites-only organisation.[124] More typical among Johannesburg-based communists was Bram Fischer's reaction to Kruschev's revelations. He once asked Bob Hepple if there was any authority that refuted the reports about Stalin's crimes. Hepple told him the case against Stalin was unchallengeable. On hearing this Bram Fischer shrugged his shoulders and said, 'Well, we now know what to avoid when we establish communism here'.[125]

In Cape Town, there was sufficient disquiet over the Hungarian events for Fred Carneson to summon a meeting of group leaders at which he explained that country had been a home of reaction for decades,[126] an argument that was subsequently reproduced in *New Age*. Lionel Forman was 'more or less a lone voice' in maintaining his objections to the Soviet invasion.[127] According to his wife, Lionel Forman was troubled by some of the developments in Czechoslovakia during his time there including the Slansky trial.[128] Hilda Bernstein when interviewed in 1984 suggested that the invasion of Hungary did not really disturb the party's composure, though 'there were a few people [...] white intellectuals, who were very upset'.[129] These intellectuals may have included Bernstein herself as well as Ruth First, whose political differences over Communist orthodoxy were a continual source of domestic tension with Joe Slovo.[130]

Aside from such external sources of dissension, the issue that party members most frequently mention as a matter over which they disagreed was secrecy. Clandestine operational rules were not the problem and the use of false names, coded communications, discreet venues, and an organisational structure that kept the identity of party membership even

120. Harmel, 'Some notes on the Communist Party'.
121. Michael Harmel, 'Collective Leadership in the Soviet Union', *New Age*, 5 April 1956. Reprinted in Bunting, ed., *South African Communists Speak*, 244.
122. Wits, Historical Papers, Bernstein Papers, B8.1, Hilda Bernstein interviewed by Padraig O'Malley.
123. Turok, *Nothing but the Truth*, 50.
124. Hirson, *Revolutions in My Life*, 225; see also Clingman, *Bram Fischer*, 213.
125. Hepple, *Young Man with a Red Tie*, 63–64.
126. Turok, *Nothing but the Truth*, 50.
127. Wits, Historical Papers, Sylvia Neame Papers, A2729, F2, Sadie Forman, interviewed by Sylvia Neame, 19 June 1988, Transcript, 24.
128. idem
129. Hilda and Lionel Bernstein, interviewed by Stephen Clingman, 4 September 1984.
130. AnnMarie Wolpe, *The Long Way Home* (Claremont: David Philip, 1994), 64; Alan Weider, *Ruth First and Joe Slovo*, 86 and 92.

internally hidden were accepted as common sense, even within families. But there were arguments at all the early congresses over whether the party should publicise its existence. At the end of 1955 there seems to have been an early decision to do so because Bob Hepple was given a party 'manifesto' to take with him on a trip to London for printing but then the operation was halted because Moses Kotane had received advice against it while visiting East Germany.[131] Generally Moses Kotane and other party leaders who worked most closely with non-communist ANC principals in any case favoured silence fearing that an open announcement would alienate tacit allies as did trade unionists. In October 1959, after the fourth Congress held on the premises of a furniture factory owned by Julius First (Ruth First's father), the launch of *African Communist* (though not initially identified as the party's journal) was the consequence of a compromise suggested by Bernstein after a debate in which Joe Slovo had proposed the party's 'emergence'.[132] The first issue was cyclostyled in a thousand copies and from then onwards the distribution of party propaganda would become a main function of the groups. The CPGB arranged and paid for the printing of the next few editions of the journal after being asked to by South Africans living in London.[133] Secrecy about the party's existence was an issue connected to the way its leaders understood their relationship with the ANC, and there is at least one significant indication that this too remained contentious. John Pule Motshabi much later suggested that the admission into the party's top leadership of African 'intellectuals' from the ANC's leadership was opposed by African workers in the party including himself, David Bopape and J.B. Marks.[134] As already noted, Ben Turok's autobiography recalls from his own experience of working with J.B. Marks that he and other trade union leaders felt that, within the Congress Alliance, 'working class interests were not given sufficient recognition'.[135]

Emergency and after

After the ANC's banning at the outset of the state of emergency on 31 March 1960, the distinction for party activists between 'legal' undertakings conducted within the Congress Alliance and illegal party work disappeared. In contrast to its development in the 1950s, this phase of the SACP's history has been the focus of recent scholarship, centred particularly on its role in the decisions which led to the ANC's embrace of armed struggle. In particular Stephen Ellis's work has offered major revisions in what had been the general understanding of how this happened. Our narrative will take the Party's development up to the end of 1960. Its public announcement of existence during this year and its tentative embrace of armed tactics represent the closure of this phase of its development. The decision to abandon complete secrecy was followed by an expansion in recruitment and other changes: 1960 does represent the final year in a distinct phase in the party's history.

131. Hepple, *Young Man with a Red Tie*, 30.
132. Wieder, *Ruth First and Joe Slovo*, 110
133. For detail see O'Malley, *Shades of Difference*, 85.
134. UCT, Manuscripts and Archives, Simons Papers, 08.1, 'Minutes of Africa Group meeting, 13 May 1982'. There is an oblique reference to the differences between Kotane and Marks in the Sylvia Neame Papers, A2729, Folder E1 Brian Bunting's interview with Sylvia Neame, London, 14 May 1986, Transcript, 6–7.
135. Turok, *Nothing but the Truth*, 90.

The party's own historians and older scholarship projected the adoption of violence as a consequence of the banning of mass campaigning and a process in which during 1961 non-communist ANC leaders and Communist Party strategists simultaneously started questioning the utility of the tactics they had employed through the 1950s. South African researchers assembled in the SADET project and drawing upon oral testimonies from MK veterans they collected in the late 1990s and early 2000s were the first to encounter evidence that the Communist Party had made a collective decision to take up arms before the end of 1960, though individuals in both organisations had begun to consider the use of violence much earlier.[136] Ellis's research exploits fresh testimony and draws upon additional archival sources to confirm that both among Communist Party and ANC rank and file, well before 1960, some people had already been considering the use of use armed action, especially in the Eastern Cape. When it came to systematic organisation of urban guerrilla warfare, though, the party made the key decisions well before the ANC was able to and it was to predominate within MK's command structure, particularly as a consequence of Nelson Mandela's joining the party at some point in 1960. Claims about Mandela's membership had already appeared in certain memoirs but for Stephen Ellis confirmation of this was offered by John Pule Motshabi's assertions recorded in party documentation filed in the Simons' papers.[137] As will become clear, the records used in this research for this paper add both detail and complexity to Ellis's narrative, qualifying some of his findings.

In the standard historiography about this period, the period between the Sharpeville massacre and the stay at home called in May 1961 in protest against South Africa's declaration of a Republic, is presented as the time when it became clear to 'the leaders of the Liberation movement and the Communist Party', in Michael Harmel's words, that '[i]t was necessary to abandon "non violence"' as impractical, a recognition that was 'strengthened by the temper of the masses'.[138] In reality, though, the party's own expansion of organised activity during the emergency as well as the survival of ANC activist networks in certain areas suggests that there remained scope for non-violent kinds of militant opposition.

Johannesburg-based party leaders heard rumours that the police were about to arrest Congress supporters en masse just before the emergency came into force. Even so most of the party's leadership in its main centres were detained and 150 or so communists were arrested altogether. Moses Kotane and Michael Harmel were among those who evaded arrest to live in nine 'safe houses', some of them supplied by 'D category' party adherents. Ben Turok shared various cramped quarters with them for several months and Turok claims that these refuges became hubs 'of campaigning and planning'.[139] On several occasions Kotane travelled around Johannesburg in a car driven by Wolfie Kodesh, making contact with any party and ANC networks whose members remained at liberty.[140] Re-establishing the party's networks was made more difficult apparently, because Michael Harmel had

136. B. Magubane *et al.*, 'The Turn to Armed Struggle', in SADET, ed., *The Road to Democracy in South Africa, Volume 1, 1960–1970* (Cape Town: Zebra Press, 2004), 60–63, 80–91.
137. S. Ellis, *External Mission: The ANC in Exile, 1960–1990* (London: Hurst, 2012), 9–28.
138. Lerumo, *Fifty Fighting Years*, 95.
139. Turok, *Nothing but the Truth*, 104.
140. Bernstein, *Memory against Forgetting*, 196

mislaid a secret list of contacts, one in a series of breaches of security procedures for which he would acquire a reputation.[141]

Late in the emergency, Ben Turok was able to visit Port Elizabeth to discuss the 'rebuilding' of organisation with Raymond Mhlaba. In June, what Harmel termed an 'enlarged Central Committee meeting', and what Bernstein suggests was a 'rump' of the Central Committee, decided, despite objections from Kotane, that the party should announce its existence, a decision that was publicised by a leaflet. Bunting notes that ANC people in townships helped to distribute this leaflet and that by the end of the emergency 'the party had a team of several hundred activists at its disposal in the Johannesburg townships'.[142] Distributing and posting subsequent leaflet issues in the party's name now became a key activity undertaken by its local units. In Cape Town, at least, mailing lists were compiled from telephone directories and hence were mainly of white people.[143] A visitor from the CPGB brought £1000 in response to an appeal sent by the South Africans in April[144] and this helped to pay for printing and costs of renting flats for hide-outs. Harmel's memo, written at the end of 1960,[145] suggested that the party became stronger during the emergency, and in Johannesburg at least, Bernstein thinks, the emergency made relations with the ANC easier. The party recruited more members from among the detainees, which helped to expand its reach amongst ANC followers who remained committed to activism. At the same time, because of the end of open Congress Alliance campaigning, it became possible 'to allocate more cadres to purely party work'.[146]

Such claims about organisational resilience need to be treated with circumspection. But it does seem quite plausible that a body that over the preceding decade had made a point of recruiting people who were already leaders of other groups might well have expanded its influence within the wider movement. And where non-banned Alliance partners had a well-organised local presence, activist campaigning remained possible. In Durban, the NIC supplied offices and networks through which it was still possible to mobilise mass protest during the emergency: Babenia, who worked as the NIC's district organiser, supplies examples of such protests. He also shows how leaders and members of ANC branches were in certain areas able to regroup around the residents' associations that in any case were often led by Congress activists: the Kwa Mashu residents' association was a case in point led by Curnick Ndhlovu, a party member. Here, partly because of the survival of active ANC networks with a popular following, the party's influence came under stronger challenge: Babenia identifies a group of vigorous ANC leaders who were to become increasing hostile to the party in Durban.[147]

During the emergency, the party's organisational structure became more elaborate. A sub-group of the Central Committee, a working committee, was assembling for weekly meetings by the end of the emergency. There are references in memoirs of this period to

141. Hepple, *Young Man with a Red Tie*, 99.
142. Bunting, *Moses Kotane*, 255.
143. Wits, Historical Papers, Sylvia Neame Papers, Sadie Forman, interviewed by Sylvia Neame, transcript, 29.
144. Wits, Historical Papers, Ronald Kasrils Papers, A3345, A6.1.4.2, Y. Dadoo and V. Pillay, 'The Political Situation in the Union of South Africa'.
145. Harmel, 'Some notes on the Communist Party'.
146. *Ibid.*
147. Babenia, *Memoirs of a Saboteur*, 53

the functioning of party Area Committees which may have been a consequence of the growth in the number of groups, though it would have also helped to increase security as groups would cease having direct representation on the district bodies. Several sources indicate that the pace of recruitment increased and that it became less selective. Jean Middleton joined in late 1960 after becoming friends with Hilda Bernstein whom she knew from their shared activities on the Peace Council. She had 'heard of only two potential recruits who refused to join, and both promised to keep the secret'.[148] In the 1950s, the party would only recruit people after its leaders were quite certain about their motivations. Her all-white unit or group 'focused on contact with young people'[149] concentrating on recent entrants to the Congress of Democrats, whom they mentored through a series of activities that tested commitment and courage, night-time spray-painting ANC slogans, for example.[150] More than a decade later it was still possible to make out the text of one of their exhortations in a rundown park on Yeoville's Rockey Street: 'An attack on communism is an attack on you.'[151]

In general, in the cases of Jean Middleton and her closest comrades, their work emphasised propaganda circulation and one of their tasks was the compilation of mailing lists for Hilda Bernstein. As the vetting and criteria for selection of new members loosened, the party became more vulnerable and one of Jean Middleton's group's recruits in late 1962 was Gerard Ludi, the first policeman to infiltrate the party.[152] He would later complain that following his entry into the party, 'in reality there was little action beyond manufacturing and distributing vast quantities of posters and leaflets', some of them reproduced with a child's toy printing set.[153] In general, party leaders now favoured evidence of commitment over doctrinal preparedness: recruiters were encouraged to 'discard the conservative approach[es]' that had prevailed earlier.[154] Jean Middleton later joined an Area Committee, also all white, and here she became more familiar with the party's overall structure. Habitually, Area Committee members used code names in speaking with and about each other, as had been the case with the group with individuals using different names in the different organisational echelons.[155]

---

148. J Middleton, *Convictions: A Woman Political Prisoner Remembers*, (Randburg:Ravan Press, 1998), 12.
149. *Ibid*.16.
150. Another account by a member of this group confirms that one of its assigned functions was 'to infiltrate and control leftist youth organisations operating on the Reef' (Ludi and Grobbelaar, *The Amazing Mr Fischer*, 31.
151. Personal memory and see Ronnie Kasrils, *Armed and Dangerous: From Undercover Struggle to Freedom*, 2nd ed. (Jeppestown: Jonathan Ball, 1998), 5.
152. Ludi had been involved in Congress of Democrat activities for at least two years, joining the Congress after his recruitment into the police's Special Branch in April 1960. In his most recent memoir he claims that he was able to infiltrate a police colleague 'into the movement' who would visit the party's headquarters, supplying the police with the information that led to the arrests at Rivonia in July 1963. G. Ludi, The *Communisation* of the ANC (Alberton: Galago, 2011), 126–127. Joe Slovo maintained that Ludi was not originally an infiltrator but had been blackmailed into playing such a role to avoid a charge under the Immorality Act after being arrested with a black prostitute. Slovo, *Unfinished Autobiography*, 157.
153. Gerard Ludi, The *Communisation* of the ANC, 18.
154. SACP CC, The Revolutionary Way Out, February 1962, text in Lerumo, *Fifty Fighting Years*, 154.
155. Middleton, *Convictions*.

The party's decision to organise armed groups was probably influenced by the reports it was receiving of rural rebellion. Moses Kotane, writing in 1961, claimed the 'Party could report successes of the peasants in Pondoland, Sekhukhuniland, Zululand and Western Transvaal'.[156] Ben Turok visited the leaders of the Mpondo mountain committee in November 1960 on behalf of the ANC and was asked when Congress was going to supply them with weapons. There were earlier contacts, before the emergency between the Mpondos and the Port Elizabeth SACP/ANC principals after requests 'for assistance against government troops'.[157] The Port Elizabeth leaders were divided with Govan Mbeki favouring helping the Mpondos and Raymond Mhlaba against this because he was convinced the revolt would fail.[158] Mhlaba himself had no objections to using violence; indeed, he recalls he had suggested that 'we should fight the Boers' several times at SACP meetings and discussed the issue in some depth with Rusty Bernstein in 1959.[159] Certain narratives emphasise discussions among the emergency detainees as the main generator of the party's policy turn on violence,[160] though interestingly, Bernstein, who with Slovo was the last of the detainees to be released, tells that on the last few days of their detention 'we [had] run out of things to talk about'.[161] Ben Turok maintains that the key agency was supplied by Michael Harmel who wrote a strategic reassessment during the emergency that he presented to Kotane.

According to his biographer, Yusuf Dadoo when he left South Africa at the beginning of the emergency had become an advocate of 'a radical departure in tactics and strategy [...] for a turn to armed struggle'. While visiting Peking in October 1960, Dadoo explained to Mao Tse Tung that 'South Africa's armed struggle could not follow China's strategy of a long march', an argument that implies that he too, as in the case of Raymond Mhlaba, had reservations about an initially peasant-based insurgency. Mao listened politely but was non-committal apparently, though the Chinese did provide military training the following year. For the Chinese, their priority in receiving their South African visitors was to lecture them about the pitfalls of Soviet revisionism.[162] In the 1990s Joe Matthews told researchers that he and Michael Harmel discussed the proposed policy switch with Soviet officials in November 1960 as members of a delegation the SACP sent to attend an international conference of communist parties[163] but Russian sources working with archival materials believe that this happened later, in 1961. This seems more likely as the documents that survive from 1960 in which party leaders are obviously describing their organisation to close 'fraternal' allies do not refer to violence. Soviet officials did agree to provide money, USD30,000,[164] which

---

156. Moses Kotane, 'Notes on some aspects of the political situation in the Republic of South Africa, 9 November 1961'.

157. Mufamadi, *Raymond Mhlaba's Personal Memoirs*, 111; Bundy, *Govan Mbeki*, 99.

158. Govan Mbeki discusses the influence of peasant 'thinking on military lines' upon the decision to set up Umkhonto in *The Struggle for Liberation in South Africa* (Cape Town: David Philip, 1992), 88–93.

159. *Ibid.*, 107.

160. Magubane, 'The Turn to Armed Struggle', 70–72.

161. Bernstein, *Memory against Forgetting*, 217

162. University of the Western Cape, Mayibuye Centre, Essop Pahad, 'A People's Leader: A Political Biography of Dr YM Dadoo', unpublished manuscript, 167, 205–206.

163. Magubane, 'The Turn to Armed Struggle', 81.

164. V. Shubin, *ANC: A View from Moscow* (Belville: Mayibuye Books, 1999).

probably explains how the Party was able to buy a farm in Rivonia, on the outskirts of Johannesburg, in mid-1961 to serve as its headquarters as well as another rural property.[165]

Formal acceptance of violent tactics was at a conference held on 16 December 1960. Before this meeting, a version of Harmel's paper evocatively entitled 'What is to be done' was circulated to party groups as a 'study document'.[166] In Bernstein's memoir the resolution on violence was 'squeezed into the agenda at the tail end of the conference' and was discussed cursorily. Over a three-day meeting most of the time was taken up by Michael Harmel's report on the events at the international communist meeting he had recently returned from, which itself had been pre-occupied with the Sino-Soviet dispute. His description of this part of the proceedings was a revelation for his listeners because until then 'we did not appreciate the depth of bitterness'.[167] Indeed, the year before, a *New Age* report had quoted Chou en Lai reassuring the Soviet party that 'Bonds between China and the USSR [were] unbreakable'.[168] All accounts of the meeting concur that the discussion of the resolution was abrupt and there was no real disagreement. Turok has Bernstein reading the resolution and after its adoption burning the document but in fact a text has survived. The wording of the resolution is reproduced in a typed internal memorandum probably written in late 1962 or early 1963. The resolution first acknowledged that 'the people's movement could no longer' maintain 'exclusively non-violent forms of political struggle' given 'new government tactics' and the risks of 'disillusionment and spread of defeatism'. Therefore, it urged, activists should undertake 'a campaign of education and explanation be carried out within the movement to prepare for forcible forms of struggle when these became necessary or desirable'. In the meantime:

> the Party CC should take steps to initiate the training and equipping of selected personnel in new methods of struggle, and thus prepare the nucleus of an adequate apparatus to lead struggles of a more forcible and violent character.[169]

This wording stops short of an immediate and unequivocal commitment to armed action. Bernstein's memory was that 'we took what was no more than an interim decision. The Central Committee would consider the matter further', though in the meantime small units would be established 'to familiarise themselves with the practice and techniques of forms of armed struggle'.[170]

Reporting in Moscow in November 1961, Moses Kotane told Soviet party officials that at the conference they had agreed that in future they would 'employ some elements of violence during our mass struggles, such as picketing and disruption of communications', and a sub-committee of the Central Committee would consider any further steps 'to be taken in anticipation of armed struggle'. This sub-committee would obtain small arms and organise training in the use of home-made explosives.[171] Bob Hepple, who helped organise the conference

---

165. Rivonia cost R25,000. Julius First helped to finance the purchase from his own savings. For more detail on how the purchase was organised see Clingman, *Bram Fischer*, 293–294.
166. Hepple, *Young Man with a Red Tie*, 104.
167. Bernstein, *Memory against Forgetting*, 225.
168. *New Age*, 5 February 1959.
169. Wits, Historical Papers, Ronald Kasrils Papers, A3345, A6.4.4.1, 'MEMORANDUM'.
170. Bernstein, *Memory against Forgetting*, 227.
171. Kotane: 'Notes on Some Aspects of the Political Situation in the RSA, 9 November 1961'.

and attended it as a member of the Johannesburg District Committee, has been emphatic that there was 'no suggestion at this time of full-scale guerrilla war'.[172] According to Turok, Kotane remained critical of the decision to use violence for the next couple of years at least, though he later told Bunting that he had thought 'the resort to violence was unavoidable'.[173] At the time, though, Hepple recalls Kotane as arguing that 'there [was] still room for then old methods if we are imaginative and determined enough'.[174] Perhaps reluctantly, Kotane nevertheless played a crucial intermediary role in persuading Chief Luthuli to accede in June 1961 to the establishment of MK, though Mandela's voice was also very important in this. In fact, Luthuli remained apprehensive about the embrace of even limited violence and was explicitly critical of the ANC's apparent abandonment of 'the militant non violent techniques' of its former mass campaigning.[175] More widely within the Natal provincial ANC leadership there was unease about Umkhonto's activities, if Bruno Mtolo's account is to be trusted.[176] While African communists remained deferential to the Chief, their comrades were less polite. When Mandela announced his intention to visit Luthuli after returning from Ethiopia, Joe Slovo's reaction was derisive: 'Why report to that old buffer?' he was reported to have said.[177]

The December 1960 decision was opposed in Durban by at least one locally-influential personality who had not attended the meeting. Rowley Arenstein felt that the move was premature and unnecessary and that the party should instead 'emphasise building organisation in the factories'. In Durban SACTU was still capable of maintaining robust industrial militancy, Arenstein believed. He was also critical of what he perceived to be 'the undermining [of] the ANC leadership with [the] establishment of ad hoc committees that left out the leaders of the ANC'.[178] Arenstein was also predisposed to side with China in the Sino-Soviet rift at a time when the party was still undecided on the issue and was called to a meeting in Johannesburg and reproved sharply by Kotane. Every time the party made a decision Arenstein was in opposition, Kotane scolded; 'You are standing alone. Why is this?'[179] Arenstein recalled that after the December conference the Central Committee had circulated a statement condemning Mao's position as un-Marxist, but no such attack appeared in *African Communist* during 1961 and, in October 1961, after receiving an unsolicited invitation from the Chinese, the party would send six of its members including Raymond Mhlaba to China for military training. However, how much influence Arenstein's views had – even among SACP members who were close friends of his such as the trade unionists George and Vera Ponnen and Ronnie Kasrils, a cousin of his wife – is questionable. Kasrils joined the Party in 1961

172. Hepple, *Young Man with a Red Tie*, 106.
173. Turok, *Nothing but the Truth*, 137, 199; Bunting, *Moses Kotane*, 269.
174. Hepple, *Young Man with a Red Tie*, 104.
175. Luthuli writing in the *Golden City Post*, 25 March 1962. Scott Couper, *Albert Luthuli: Bound by Faith* (Durban: University of KwaZulu Natal Press, 2010), 161.
176. On this issue he was probably truthful for other memoirs, Babenia's for example, offers corroboration. See also Mtolo, *Umkhonto we Sizwe*, 23.
177. Rowley Arenstein, quoted in *The Star*, 6 July 1990.
178. Arenstein, interviewed by Iain Edwards, Durban 1986.
179. Babenia, *Memoirs*, 63.

and was inducted into Arenstein's group; shortly afterwards he became a resourceful regional commander for Umkhonto in Durban.[180]

No time was lost in recruiting 'proto armed units' in each of the party's districts. Bernstein noted that by June 1961 these had 'been running for some time'.[181] The party's small group of ex-servicemen were conspicuous in the leadership of the earliest units: Wolfie Kodesh remembered former soldiers were given area command roles.[182] Bernstein also referred to a separate force into which Mandela was enrolling ANC volunteers, 'outside ANC structures'.[183] Hepple remembers that Mandela was present at the meeting on 16 December 1960 sitting next to Sisulu in a back seat and saying little: Joe Slovo told him then that Mandela was attending as an observer.[184] Other people who were present that day have told researchers that Mandela had joined the party by then[185] and John Pule Motshabi's observations about Mandela's recruitment into the party seem to have gone unchallenged when he made them in 1982.[186] Brian Bunting told Sylvia Neame in 1986 that Mandela was at the meeting 'as a member of the CC [...] the only time I met him in that capacity'.[187] Interviewed in 1986, Piet Beyleveld remembered Mandela's recruitment into the party, though he supplied no details and by his own admission in court he only joined the party's leadership structures after the Rivonia arrests so it is unlikely that he had encountered Mandela at a party meeting.[188] More recently, Russian researchers have found a reference to Mandela attending a conference in Cairo during his 1962 visit as a SACP member in a funding request made to the Communist Party of the Soviet Union by the Afro-Asian Solidarity Committee.[189]

Despite all these reports, given the secrecy even among members about who belonged to the party and its committees the evidence for Mandela's membership is not quite definite. Motshabi's testimony is the most detailed evidence available. It appears in two documents,

180. See Kasrils, *Armed and Dangerous*, 144–45 for his recollection of Rowley's Arenstein's views on the sabotage campaign and the Ponens' response. For an irreverent description of Ronnie Kasrils's first bomb-making lesson see H. Strachan, *Make a Skyf Man* (Cape Town: David Philip, 2004), 72.

181. Bernstein, Memory against Forgetting, 230.

182. Wolfie Kodesh, radio interview by John Carlin, 1995, 8, transcript: http://www.pbs.org/wgbh/frontline/shows/mandela/interviews/kodesh.htmlhttp://www.pbs.org/wgbh/frontline/shows/mandela/interviews/kodesh.html, accessed 19 October 2015. Govan Mbeki also referred to the Party establishing its own units, separate from those constituted by ANC leaders in *The Struggle for Liberation in South Africa* (Cape Town: David Philip, 1992), 90.

183. Bernstein, Memory against Forgetting, 230.

184. Hepple, *Young Man with a Red Tie*, p. 106.

185. Padraig O'Malley obtained confirmation of Mandela's membership from Brian Bunting as well as '[o]ther sources embargoed until 2030'. He also quotes from his interview with Hilda Bernstein who may have been present at the meeting as a member of the Johannesburg District Committee: see O'Malley, *Shades of Difference*, 63.

186. UCT, Manuscripts and Archives, Simons Papers, 08.1, Minutes of Africa Group meeting, 13 May 1982.

187. Wits, Historical Papers, Sylvia Neame Papers, A2729, Folder E1, Brian Bunting interviewed by Sylvia Neame, London, 14 May 1986.

188. Wits, Historical Papers, Everatt Papers, Wits, A2521, Piet Beyleveld, interviewed by David Everatt, April 1986.

189. V.G. Shubin cited in I. Filatova, 'Mandela and the SACP: Time to Close the Debate', *Politicsweb*, 24 June 2015, http://www.politicsweb.co.za/news-and-analysis/mandela-and-the-sacp-time-to-close-the-debatehttp://www.politicsweb.co.za/news-and-analysis/mandela-and-the-sacp-time-to-close-the-debate, accessed 19 October 2015.

preserved by Ray Simons from the meetings she attended of the SACP's 'Africa Group' convened in Lusaka. In March 1982 Motshabi recalled that

> in 1953 when people like Nelson and Walter were brought into the family without me and others knowing, and without having taken some of us in confidence, he [Moses Kotane] came to me and asked me to accept their presence within our midst and mentioned that they are in the higher echelons of the movement as members of the CC. I asked him why they do not begin [by] being ordinary members before they are elevated to such high positions'.[190]

And then two months later, Motshabi spoke about his longstanding grievances with the party leadership that dated from when in around 1958 or 1959 the party started bringing in 'new people' with a 'new look'. This caused 'a wrangle in the family' in which 'some people were isolated' and '[t]here was an accusation that we opposed allowing Nelson and Walter into the family, I, J.B. [Marks] and Bopape were opposed'.[191] It is unclear from the document whether Motshabi felt that the accusation was true or not. Aside from the ambiguity over dates, Motshabi's recollections do leave some room for questions about Mandela's membership. If the normal quite lengthy procedures of candidature were short-circuited, it is conceivable that Mandela himself may not have considered himself to be a full member when attending party meetings even if other people present thought of him as 'family', the code term South African communists used to refer to their party. In 1967, in litigation to get his name removed from the liquidator's list of party members, Mandela insisted he had never been a member of either the CPSA or 'of its successor, the South African Communist Party'.[192] Bram Fischer in his court statement at his trial in 1966 noted that sometimes non-members attended Central Committee meetings, senior people from the liberation movement whom 'we wanted to consult'.[193] The memorandum cited above containing the 1960 resolution and written probably at the end of 1962 refers to Umkhonto we Sizwe's command as constituted by six men, five of whom were communists and one other a person 'who we regard as a close party supporter on the verge of party membership'.[194] By that stage Mandela was in prison but there is no record of Umkhonto's

190. UCT, Manuscripts and Archives, Simons Papers, 08.1, John Pule Motshabi, 'On the party Bulletin for Internal Circulation only', ts. 31 March 1980. I am grateful to Hugh Macmillan for finding this document in the Simons Papers and showing it to me.
191. UCT, Manuscripts and Archives, Simons Papers, 09.1, Minutes of Africa Group meeting, 13 May 1982.
192. Nelson Mandela Centre of Memory and Dialogue, Himie Bernard Collection of the Legal papers of Nelson Mandela, NMAP, 2009/13, Nelson Mandela, Letter to the Liquidator, Department of Justice, Re: The Communist Party of South Africa, 23 October 1967.
193. Wits, Historical Papers, Bram Fischer trial transcript, *State vs Abram Fischer*, 238.
194. Wits, Historical Papers, Ronald Kasrils Papers, A3345, A6.4.4.1, MEMORANDUM. The sixth person referred to may have been Joe Modise. The ANC's obituary of Modise released as a press statement (26 November 2001) stated that he had been a member of Umkhonto's High Command 'since its inception', though this is at odds with other equally authoritative sources. In any case, it is most unlikely that a SACP official would have thought that Modise was about the join the party and he never did. Joe Slovo, though, mentions Joe Modise as one of the co-opted High Command members before 1963: Slovo, *Unfinished Autobiography*, 148. Bruno Mtolo also refers to Modise as a High Command member when he visited Natal regional commanders in September 1962, shortly after Mandela's arrest: Mtolo, *Umkhonto we Sizwe*, 48.

command having been reconstituted at that time and it is possible that this sixth person might have been Mandela.

Whatever Mandela's ideological political convictions may have been then, Hepple's impression was that he was certainly one of the keener supporters of the policy shift, prepared to take violence much further towards a fully militarised conflict than is suggested in the qualified wording of the resolution on 'forcible' methods the party adopted in December 1960.

There is another way of thinking about Mandela's SACP membership. If we accept that the larger proportion of evidence suggests that he was a member or at least looked upon by other party supporters as someone who was in the process of becoming a member, questions can still be asked about his loyalties and commitments. For white SACP members and, probably, the older African SACP members of Kotane's generation, the party or 'family', as they called it, was their deepest political affiliation. For Mandela – and possibly Sisulu – joining the party may have been an engagement they welcomed but their first emotional and moral affiliation may have remained with the ANC, their 'primary loyalty', as Sisulu's biographer puts it.[195] And even after joining the party – and if he did, the most likely date for this was at some point in 1960 – Mandela may have still been quite capable of undertaking actions independently of it, as in setting up under his own command a separate armed force, as Bernstein observed. Paul Landau's very thorough exploration of Mandela's thinking at this time does suggest that he had a very different view from his comrades of how the party's long-term relationship with the national movement might evolve. He was ready, for example, in a reflective commentary he wrote at the time, to consider the possibility that the 'working cooperation between a non-Marxist political organisation and the CP ceases because policy differences emerge'.[196]

Conclusion

I will end this narrative with the party poised for its engagement with a new chapter in its history. As this article has shown, the sources that are now available enable a detailed reconstruction of a history that used to be particularly well hidden, when the party was in its most secretive phase. But why does this story matter? Through this period the Communist Party remained a very small organisation. Did it have a wider importance?

This question has divided historians and political scientists who have addressed the development of anti-apartheid resistance in South Africa. The most authoritative early treatments of the ANC during the 1950s and 1960s were by the team originally led by Gwendolen Carter and Thomas Karis. Their six-volume documentary survey of black resistance tended to discount Communist influence within African nationalist organisations. The omission of references to Communist Party activism was especially noticeable in their fourth volume, constituted by biographies. Writing in 1986, Thomas Karis conceded that the

195. Sisulu, *Walter and Albertina Sisulu*, 123.
196. Wits, Historical Papers, Sylvia Neame Papers, A2729, Folder F, Nelson Mandela's letter to Sylvia Neame in 1964 reviewing her manuscript history of the ICU. See P. Landau, 'The ANC, MK and "the turn to violence"', *South African Historical Journal*, 64, 3 (2012), 561.

influence of communists within the wider movement in which they worked in the 1950s was 'to an extent greater than their numbers', but, he insisted, they were never in a position to dominate or control. More specifically he noted the absence of communists among the ANC's top office holders during the 1950s.[197] To an extent Karis's observations were guided by the limitations of reliable information available at the time, but they also reflected the predispositions of liberal sympathisers of the ANC who maintained that the 'independently minded African patriots' who led the ANC were more than capable of prevailing in any collaboration they might undertake with communists.[198]

To a degree, the localised and bottom-up analyses of township-based resistance in the 1950s that the Wits social history school published through the 1980s represented a revision of this view. For example, my own investigation of the local activist trajectories that helped to explain the level of participation in the Defiance Campaign in Port Elizabeth stressed the role CPSA branches played in the preceding decade in creating the networks that sustained the ANC's following there in the 1950s.[199] On the whole, though, because of the emphasis in this kind of work on local settings, it did not directly challenge the earlier contention that when it came to leadership, communists played a subsidiary role. Communist influence at leadership level during the 1950 did receive more attention from historians of trade unionism who were arguing 30 years later that the subordination of SACTU's class preoccupations to the imperatives of national liberation was indeed a consequence of union leaders' embrace of the SACP's notion of a revolution in two stages.[200] But the real challenge to the argument that communists were just one contending influence amongst many came much later. For Stephen Ellis, the ANC's prohibition and its turn to armed struggle were the key developments through which the Communist Party arrived at the point at which it could exercise real authority over the ANC.[201]

Ostensibly, the history surveyed in this article would appear to offer confirmation of Stephen Ellis's depiction of communists as holding command positions in the ANC. If anything, the developments recounted above might suggest this development happened earlier than in Ellis's account and that the movement's organisational changes that accompanied the transition to guerrilla warfare were less decisive. After all, from the mid-1950s onwards, SACP members were already well established in the ANC's top echelon, and indeed held several of the important offices. In certain locations, the party's earlier activist traditions shaped the ANC transformation into a mass movement. During the 1950s, the party's influence within the ANC was consolidated through a vanguardist recruitment strategy that emphasised in local settings the enlistment of community leaders and at the level of its national leadership the drawing into the party's embrace members of the university-educated African 'intelligentsia'. SACP ideologues succeeded in shaping the ANC's programmatic orientation, especially in the central role they played in projecting their vision of a people's democracy into the Freedom

197. T.G. Karis, 'South African Liberation: The Communist Factor', *Foreign Affairs*, 65, 2 (Winter 1986), 267–287.
198. Karis and Gerhart, *Challenge and Violence*, 680.
199. T. Lodge, *Black Politics in South Africa* (London: Longman, 1983).
200. P. Bonner, 'Black Trade Unions in South Africa since World War II', in R.M. Price and C.G. Rosberg, eds, *The Apartheid Regime: Political Power and Racial Domination* (Cape Town: David Philip, 1980), 183.
201. See Ellis, *External Mission*, 76.

Charter, which was adopted by the ANC in the year after the Congress of the People. The party added critically useful techniques, resources and skills to the ANC's organisational capacity.

Contemporary archival materials – documents written by party members at the time – indicate that they understood their role as much more than just influence. In describing the party's relationship with the ANC, Moses Kotane and Michael Harmel used the language of direction and control, not merely prompting and persuasion. But this picture of the party in command is too simple. Firstly, the ANC's organisational structure during the 1950s did not lend itself to centralised leadership and certain important campaigning developments happened autonomously. Opposition to women's passes was a case in point and significantly the SACP's influence over women's organisations was limited. Moreover not all strong local centres of ANC activity were animated by communists. Second, the party was internally divided over strategic issues and even over the meaning of key ideological concepts. For instance there were wide differences over what a national democracy might look like. Party principals who were closest to the ANC favoured the establishment of the kind of post-apartheid social order which many non-communists within the ANC might also have welcomed and it is arguable that without the party the ANC might have adopted a very similar set of aims and objectives. Third, certainly the party's progress towards embracing violent tactics was quicker than the ANC's for after all it was a much smaller and more disciplined formation, but was it really so decisive? There was plenty of evidence of willingness to use violence within the ANC during the 1950s campaigns and this was not confined to ANC members who were also communists. As we have seen, within the party an important section of its leadership retained reservations about the strategic emphasis on guerrilla warfare and right until the SACP's final suppression in 1965, communists remaining inside South Africa remained committed to building political, that is non-military, organisation. Even so, despite these qualifications, the secret history reviewed in this paper is not the story of a sideshow. It played a central role in the unfolding of popular opposition to apartheid between 1950 and 1960.

Acknowledgements

I would like to express particular thanks to Michele Pickover and her colleagues at the Wits Historical Papers collection for all their help in identifying and locating relevant materials. I am also very grateful to the two referees who reviewed this submission to the SAHJ and who provided carefully argued critical commentary. Hugh Macmillan supplied additional documentation which had helped me to modify my argument towards the end of this paper.

The ANC, MK, and 'The Turn to Violence' (1960–1962)

PAUL S. LANDAU

University of Maryland and University of Johannesburg

Abstract

Why did the African National Congress (ANC) appear to embrace violence in 1961? Can one say it did so? Was the Communist Party responsible behind the scenes? What did the 'turn to violence' mean? With a plethora of new sources and reminiscences emerging, one can begin to craft a set of answers. Communists as Communists did not determine the timing of the ANC's embrace of MK (*Umkhonto we-Sizwe*, 'Spear of the Nation'). The ANC was a large member-based organisation which could not nimbly shift in any direction. During the state's repressive and punitive measures in 1960–1962, however, a group of Communist African men from within the ANC hierarchy made use of the unsettled nature of political life to commit the ANC to a new path. They interacted intensively, together with non-African Communists, in the Treason Trial (1956–1961), and then in jail during the 1960 'State of Emergency'. Their aim was revolution. Preeminent among them was Nelson Mandela.

In history some moments are more important than others. In the history of the struggle against colonialism and apartheid in South Africa, the 'turn to violence', or toward 'armed struggle', was a very important moment. The ANC (the African National Congress) is and was the oldest continually existing nationalist political movement in Africa, and it had a long, respected history of non-violent, militant mobilisation against the injustices of the state. Illuminating the particular tipping point past which the ANC espoused violence cannot help but shine a broader light on the struggle against apartheid as a whole. To begin with a preliminary question: Why did the leadership of the law-abiding African National Congress alter nearly 50 years' of its bedrock non-violent policy and initiate a program of (at least condoning) blowing things up?

Several factors weigh in favour of attempting a revised narrative of this juncture. Several young historians are beginning to publish work that will underline the difficulties and indeed catastrophic failures experienced in MK and ANC communities *outside* South Africa in the mid-1960s up through the 1980s. This article is about the initiation of the exile period inside South Africa just before then. Many sources about the early 1960s have also only recently come to light.[1] Published reminiscences now include those in the South African Development and Educational Trust (SADET) project's available material, and there are scarcely known interviews and reports and other material in archives at the Cullen Library and the Mandela Foundation in Johannesburg, the Mayibuye Center at the University of the Western Cape, and the Simons Papers at the University of Cape Town. There is even new source material for understanding Nelson Mandela's thinking in 1960–1962.[2]

Finally there is a sense, among some historians, that a standard narrative has congealed, and that it might best be shaken up. As many South Africans feel they know, in 1960 the ANC 'was banned', and the next year, the leadership of the illegal ANC, the so-called 'National Executive' or NEC or (the C is for Committee), embraced 'armed struggle'. Nelson Mandela led MK, or *Umkhonto we Sizwe,* the 'Spear of the Nation', which became the military arm of the Congress. The standard account marks the 16th of December, an Afrikaner settler-nationalist holiday, as the date MK launched its first attacks in several cities and suburbs, and thereby opened the next phase of the struggle.[3]

Below, we will see that this is a deeply flawed account. The 'turn to violence' began with a crisis and involved others in the struggle besides the ANC. In 1960 the National Party (NP) government shot and killed activists and declared a 'state of emergency' to provide

1. S. Couper, *Albert Luthuli, Bound by Faith* (Scotsville: University of Kwazulu-Natal Press, 2010); P. O'Malley, *Shades of Difference: Mac Maharaj and the Struggle for South Africa* (New York: Viking, 2007); D.J. Smith, *Young Mandela: The Revolutionary Years* (New York: Little Brown, 2010); L. (Rusty) Bernstein, *Memory Against Forgetting: Memoirs From a Life in South African Politics, 1938–1964* (New York: Viking, 1999), A. (Kathy) Kathrada, *Memoirs* (Cape Town: Zebra, 2004), and D. Goldberg, *The Mission: A Life For Freedom in South Africa* (Johannesburg: STE, 2010); R. Mhlaba, *Raymond Mhlaba's Personal Memoirs: Reminiscing from Rwanda and Uganda, as narrated to Thembeka Mufamadi* (Johannesburg: HSRC Press, 2001); and other taped interviews.

2. In 2007, Garth Benneyworth discovered parts of Mandela's diary in the court records of the so-called 'Litte Rivonia' trial (the State v. Wilton Mkwayi and others, 1963); see his 'Armed and Trained: Nelson Mandela's 1962 Military Mission as Commander in Chief of Umkhonto we Sizwe and Provenance for his Buried Makarov Pistol', *South African Historical Journal*, 63, 1 (March 2011), 78–101. The defence records of the Rivonia Trial (1963–1964) are now online courtesy of the Cullen Library, University of Witwatersrand. The prosecution's case was passed from the estate of Percy Yutar (the prosecutor, who had taken it), to the Oppenheimer private library, to the SANA (South African National Archives). Mandela's travel notebook, calendar, and much of his 'diary' from his two 1962 tours of Africa were made available to me at the Nelson Mandela Foundation (hereafter, NMF) in Houghton, Johannesburg. There is Mandela's own autobiography, N. Mandela, *Long Walk to Freedom: The Autobiography of Nelson Mandela* (New York: Little, Brown, 1994), and the raw transcriptions of the interviews (at the NMF) it was based on, made with Richard Stengel of *Newsweek* magazine; but here I am also referring to the Ben Turok interviews cited below. In addition there is uncatalogued material from the exhibits in the Treason Trial (1956–1961) at SANA; and lastly, I conducted a few interviews myself.

3. The standard account is T. Karis and G. Gerhard, 'The Turn to Violence Since May 31, 1961', in Karis and Gerhard, eds., *Challenge and Violence, 1953–1964* (New York: Hoover Institution Press, 1977), Vol. 3 of T. Karis and G. Carter, eds., *From Protest to Challenge: A Documentary History of South African Politics in South Africa, 1882–1964* (New York: Hoover Institution Press, 1971–2010), excellent in many ways, and by (among others) Y.G. Muthien, *State and Resistance in South Africa, 1939–1965* (Brookfield, VT: Ashgate, 1994), 161, and *The Reader's Digest Illustrated History of South Africa, The Real Story, Expanded Third Edition* (assisted by historians including C. Bundy) (New York: Reader's Digest, 1994), 408–411.

scope for similarly open acts of sovereignty. The state then criminalised the ANC, which was about as old as it was, and other opposition groups. Amid a general increase in public acts of political violence, the state in effect behaved lawlessly, and yet relied on the persistent belief in the rule of law among even ANC and Communist Party (SACP) leaders, so as to catch them unawares at home and imprison them. For many South Africans, the government fully delegitimised itself in this process. At the very least, the subsequent transformation of the ANC at the leadership level must be reimagined within this other, encompassing transformation.

At the same time, the effort to forge an interracial, non-racial, military liberationist-interventionist structure capable of surviving the onslaught was audacious. The question went beyond what could be salvaged operationally out of the old ANC membership. The decision to use sabotage in cities, suburbs, and train-yards initiated the first phase of a planned, wider campaign which was to involve the taking of lives, and which had as its *telos* a general insurrection against the state.[4] Nelson Mandela assumed the lead in the effort not because he above others wished move toward violence – there were men in the ANC who had argued in favour of violence for longer and with greater fervency – but because he grasped the need for directing, controlling, and monopolising violence. His models for doing so were Israel, Algeria, Cuba, and China, as well as France, 1789: anti-colonial and revolutionary situations.

The president of the ANC in this period was Chief Albert Lutuli. While the transition to the new modality unfolded, the Nobel committee awarded its Peace Prize to Lutuli as president of the non-violent ANC. The very evening of his return to South Africa, the first MK sabotage attacks began. Who was behind this move? The historian Scott Couper has recently argued that Lutuli neither knew about nor planned the launch of MK, and that his presidential authority had been trampled.[5] Stephen Ellis has recently produced evidence to reinforce that argument and to show, moreover, that the Communist Party international hierarchy lay behind the decision to embrace armed struggle. A set of meetings between top South African Communists and Chinese and Soviet Communists in 1960 preceded (Ellis says, necessarily so) the decision of the South African Communist Party (SACP) Central Committee (CC) to get behind 'armed struggle'. Then came the formation of MK.[6]

The argument that follows holds that neither international Communism nor President Lutuli determined the timing of the ANC's seeming embrace of violent tactics. Nor did the Central Committee (CC) of the SACP with Moses Kotane (of the ANC National Executive) at the gavel pursue that aim. Whatever the president felt, the ANC required open leadership, branch meetings, and votes to change course, but the state's repressive and punitive measures in the late 1950s and especially in 1960–1962 put a stop to that. The narrative below is about how a relatively small group of men and women of different backgrounds, with Mandela and a few ANC-tied Communist allies at its core, acted to reconfigure the struggle as a military one, in a race against time they soon lost.

First, some necessary background, focusing especially on the role of Communists in the struggle. The shift toward violence can be said to have begun with the post-War Youth

4.   As the Rivonia court essentially charged.
5.   Couper, *Albert Luthuli*.
6.   Stephen Ellis, 'The Genesis of the ANC's Armed Struggle in South Africa 1948–1961', *Journal of Southern African Studies* 37, 4 (2011), 657–676.

League, which radicalised the ANC in 1949, committing it to militant action; several activists then went to the Soviet Union and China on student visas, before the state criminalised the Communist Party of South Africa in 1950. The Party was reconstituted a year later, bolstered by World War II veterans, as the underground South African Communist Party or SACP, but could no longer work above ground with the ANC. According to Fred Carneson, when a rump group of Central Committee members met in an open 'brickfields' in 1951, they decided then and there to move toward violent action. But afterwards nothing was done.[7]

The state adopted unusual emergency powers in 1952, with its 'bannings' (often for six months) of many urban African leaders, and the erasure of their public speech. These fundamentally extralegal measures confined people to their districts and villages and eventually even their homes without due process. The various levels of policed enclosure, renewed, and then overtaken with five-year term orders, derailed many career paths for men who would have become leaders in the national ANC; at the same time, they opened quick avenues of advance for others, among them (for instance) Govan Mbeki, a key champion of MK.

In the Eastern Cape, whence Mbeki hailed, and only there, *all* public meetings attended by more than ten people of colour were already prohibited, and so the ANC was forced to operate as a cell-based organisation from 1952 or 1953.[8] The Communists presented an attractive model of coherence without a public face. When the ANC reorganised in the Eastern Cape, under the M-Plan or 'Mandela Plan', organisers drew on the Communist Party's underground form, which entailed the abolition of branch meetings and their replacement with small units not allowed to interact laterally. When the Communists cooperated with the ANC at a middle level, they did so through the incipient labour movement, as well as in Indian, 'Coloured', and White (Congress of Democrats, or 'COD')-coded organisations. This Alliance was public face of the struggle in the 1950s until the M-Plan was introduced everywhere, starting in 1962. At that point, MK began its first recruitment also into cells (or 'groups'); unlike the M-Plan, MK drew not only on the ANC, but also on the other organisations in the Congress Alliance and on the Communist Party for its personnel, and with a clearly defined mission.[9] In a sense, MK was a second attempt to reorganise, under great stress, encroaching on the first attempt.

7.   Wits, Cullen Library, Sylvia Neame Papers (hereafter Neame Papers), A2729, Fred Carneson interview with Neame; Jack Hodgson interview with Neame; and University of the Western Cape, Mayibuye Center, Robben Island Memorial Museum Oral History Collection interviews, [hereafter simply] MCA 6, Fred Carneson interview with Wulfie Kodesh, 1993; and N. Roos, *Ordinary Springboks: White Servicemen and Social Justice in South Africa, 1939–1961* (London: Ashgate, 2005), ch. 9. Thanks to Neil Roos.

8.   This point was made to me both by Ahmed Kathrada (interviewed 7 October 2011) and Denis Goldberg (interviewed 12 October 2011). Dan Tloome, George Mayeka, Oscar Mpeta, David Bopape, and very many other postwar leaders were politically wounded by bannings and loss of employment. The Eastern Cape enforced what had been a countrywide provision passed in 1927.

9.   Bernard Magubane, Phil Bonner, Jabulane Sithole, Peter Delius, Janet Cherry, Pat Gibbs, and Thozana April (hereafter Magubane *et al.*), 'The Turn to Armed Struggle', *South African Development Educational Trust, Vol. 1* (Pretoria: SADET, 2008), especially pp. 80–82 provides an excellent summary with varying tones and positions. M-Plan: R. Suttner, *The ANC Underground in South Africa, 1950–1976* (Cape Town: Jacana, 2008); Mhlaba, *Raymond Mhlaba's Personal Memoirs*; and Mhlaba interrogation in Yutar Papers, 385/8, Ray Mlhaba. Conditions in the Eastern Cape were especially 'tense' and liable to violence.

Particularly on the Rand, African Communists had long played a direct part in the affairs of the Communist Party, back to the days of the International Socialist League and T.W. Thibedi.[10] Famous Africans of the Communist past include Joseph Jack, Johnny Gomas, and Edwin Mofutsanyana; in more recent days there was 'Uncle' J.B. Marks and tough-minded Moses Kotane, the General Secretary of the Party from the late 1930s on. But it was after the War that the Communist Party most centrally brought Africans' concerns into its purview.[11] Communists thereafter took a new interest in African nationalism. Still, in the SACP, it was not Moses Kotane or David Bobape or John Nkadimeng who rang in the big changes in the struggle in 1960–1962. It was not the older Communists of working class origins from the 1930s and 1940s. Instead, it was an incoming group of ANC men, Mandela, Nokwe, Sisulu, men with a broad range of urban connections to money and white Left intellectuals.

In 1953, Walter Sisulu visited the World Democratic Youth meeting, in Bucharest, as a guest of honour along with Duma Nokwe, Henry 'Squire' Makgothi, and several others. From Bucharest, this group went to Warsaw, and then to China for six weeks, quite a long time. Mandela had asked Sisulu to ask the Chinese if they would fund an armed guerrilla conflict: 'When you reach the People's Republic of China you must tell them, ask them, that we want to start an armed struggle and get arms'. Mandela linked this request to his own public espousal of violence in his famous speech in Sophiatown's Freedom Square, in June of 1953. Sisulu recalls that he spoke with the Chinese leadership about controlling overeager youth, who engaged in 'wrong slogans' and wanted armed actions. The Chinese advised extreme caution, saying the road would be 'difficult'.[12]

After China, Sisulu's delegation visited the Soviet Union for an even longer stretch of time, and then returned through the UK, in London, finally spending 'a few months in Israel'.[13] According to Sisulu, back in South Africa, Joe Modise had to travel through the townships in 1954 to calm the young men down because nothing immediately was being planned.

The *Bafabegiya* and the Mandela faction

The origins of the coherence of the group of men who steered the ANC in 1960–1962 lies partly in the relationship between the Transvaal National Congress, the increasingly nonracial Left, and 'Africanist' activists in Johannesburg. Their history emerged through

10. University of Cape Town, Oppenheimer Manuscripts Collection, Upper Campus, Simons Papers (hereafter Simons Papers); family photographs. Cf. C. Rassool, 'From Collective Leadership to Presidentialism: I.B. Tabata, Authorship and the Biographic Threshold', *Afrika Zamani*, 13/14 (2005–6), 23–67.

11. Neil Roos argues that the CPSA freshly turned its attention to *white* labor after the War: Roos, *Springboks*, 75; in the ANC, there had long been Communists and nonCommunists, and people of many other views.

12. MCA 6, Albie Sachs, interview (359), 1,5, 13 December 1992; MCA 6, Walter Sisulu interviewed by Wolfie Kodesh, 6 February 1995, Side B.

13. Thanks to Chris Lee; E. Sisulu, *Walter & Albertina Sisulu: In Our Lifetime* (London: New Africa Books, 2003), 167–171, deviates from the chronology and does not show their return through Israel, 179–181; and MCA, Walter Sisulu, 6 February 1995, 'Side B', on Israel. Also on the trip were Alfred Huchinson, Minding Akane, Arthur Goldreich, and Harold and Ann-Marie Wolpe. I am quite interested to find a recollection of this trip.

the only partially understood mechanics of Mandela's retention of the Transvaal ANC presidency in 1952 and 1955.

In 1955, the ANC and its allies united behind the nonracial Freedom Charter, which spelled out the struggle's basic political demands. For the first half of the weekend meetings, before the Freedom Charter was adopted, however, according to Joe Matthews, a debate played out between Mandela's Transvaal ANC presidency and a group of persistent Africanist dissenters called the *Bafabegiya*, whose leader Mandela had defeated in 1952.[14] The *Bafabegiya* group vented an 'Africanist' plaint that Communists had too much influence on the Transvaal ANC.[15] The *Bafabegiya* were outmanoeuvred and outvoted, however, and the Mandela and Mandela-allied ascendancy was again confirmed. The assembled groups, acting as The Congress of the People, next adopted the Charter on 26 June, with (at least by that point) Mandela, Sisulu, and Ahmad Kathrada watching from a nearby rooftop because they were 'banned'.[16]

Key allies and members of the Mandela Transvaal group, if not most or even all of them, entered the Communist Party formally in this same period. John Nkadimeng recalls he began 'classes' (with Ruth First and Joe Slovo and Rusty Bernstein) along with other parolees after the Defiance Campaign incarcerations.[17] Walter Sisulu became active in the SACP by the mid-1950s. In 1957, Kotane recruited Joe Matthews (son of the legendary Z.K. Matthews of the early ANC) into the SACP and the CC. Duma Nokwe, who was in the Communist Youth League in the 1940s, probably joined the Party around the same time. Ahmed Kathrada addressed Rand Indian-classified youth in the name of Communism in the 1950s; never a higher-up, he usually nonetheless found himself among the leadership. Albie Sachs joined the Party in 1955, and in 1956 he left the country for Youth Meetings in China and the Soviet Union.[18] On 17 August 1957, for the Party-sponsored concert program at Gandhi Hall in Cape Town, Ben Turok and Joe Matthews played an instrumental duet together.[19] A new network of post-war, educated, radicalised men could work together, and they sought each other out in the ANC and the incipient nonwhite trade unions.

The question before these South African Communists in general was whether the conditions were right in South Africa for a revolution. For many of them the answer was

---

14. According to both Mandela, *Long Walk*, and D.J. Smith, *Young Mandela*, and my conversations with Phil Bonner about interviews with struggle veterans, 18 November 2011.

15. 'The Road to Democracy: South Africans Telling Their Stories', Joe Gaobakwe Matthews, http://www.sadet.co.za/docs/RTD/stories/Stories%20-%20Joe%20Matthews.pdf, accessed October 10th, 2010; this is also: Joe Gaobakwe Matthews, interviewed by Sifiso Ndlovu and Bernard Magubane, 18 July 2001, ed. Mbulelo V. Mzamane, chapter one of South African Educational Trust (SADET), *The Road to Democracy: South Africans telling their stories, Vol. 1, 1950–1970* (Pretoria: SADET, 2008). Matthews relates that a Mrs Molapo, a woman opponent of Mandela in the Transvaal ANC (not further identified in any SADET book), protested that she had nothing against Mandela personally, and exclaimed, 'he once left his hat in my house', perhaps implying something more between them. See also David Bobape, 'The Bafagiya', *Liberation*, No. 1 (1954), 17–19, image seen through DISA (Digital Innovation South Africa), http://www.disa.ukzn.ac.za, accessed 4 February 2012.

16. MCA 6, Wulfie Kodesh interview with Walter Sisulu (1995).

17. MCA 6, Wulfie Kodesh interview with John Nkadimeng (1995).

18. C. Glaser, *Botsotsi: The Youth Gangs of Soweto, 1935–1976* (Portsmouth: Heinemann, 2000); Neame Papers, A2729, Interview with Albie Sachs, London, 22 June 1990.

19. University of the Western Cape, Mayibuye Center, Mayibuye Centre Historical papers (MCH) 07, 114, Brian Bunting Papers (hereafter, Bunting Papers), 3.2.1.1–.6.7, programme.

obvious: no. Certainly Jack Simons and Moses Kotane said no. The level of popular participation even in the midst of the famous Defiance Campaign did not augur well for a mass uprising.[20] Did this mean the Party or the ANC would innovate and act further, anyway? Should the CP expend all its energies liaising with workers while the state picked nationalists off? What would become of its post-war Africanisation? These questions hung in the air as the five year terms of 'bannings' were renewed in 1959, against even more people. Certainly *something* had to be done.

The famous Treason Trial against the leadership of the ANC meandered throughout the end of the 1950s over a period of five years (1956–1961) coincident with this heightened display of state force. As several score of them sat together in the 'cage' in 1959 and 1960, as the trial dragged on, seemingly without end, they found time to talk to one another surreptitiously. The old Communist guard in the ANC, as represented by J.B. Marks and Moses Kotane, saw eye to eye with ANC President Chief Albert Lutuli, who (like Oliver Tambo, M.B. Yengwa, Alfred Nzo, and many others in the ANC) was not Communist; but among the younger interlocutors were most of the principals behind the later turn to violence, who were.[21]

In their conversations in and out of the justice system they found themselves allied to white Communists and veterans, often Jews whose parents had earlier been radicalised by persecution. They backed national liberation in and for South Africa (before a workers' uprising) because it was a 'special case', that of colonialism in a single country, which meant that collaborating with the ANC was warranted. Nonetheless sometimes SACP people contemplated other paths. According to Sylvia Neame's interviews, Albie Sachs' SACP cell, including 'Bubbles' Thorn, Denis Goldberg, and Amy Rietstein, reporting to Brian Bunting, drove out to Natal during the violence there over cattle-culling and dipping tanks in 1959. Having seen schools and churches reduced to cinders, they drafted a letter to *The African Communist,* the journal, to the effect that such violence must be guided not by the ANC, but by the Party. The ANC was seen to be 'inadequate to lead such an issue'.[22]

Mandela sat in Communist and ANC meetings both, even while continuing as one of the interminable Treason Trial's defendants. He was already the person the ANC went to for 'implementation' according to Wulfie Kodesh: the can-do, operational leader.[23] According to Ben Turok, in a remarkable set of interviews (given in 1973/4), the year 1959–1960 was a very active one for the SACP, and the Party found itself with

20. Certainly not meeting even the criteria of the recent wave of mass protests in Tunisia, Egypt, Libya, and Syria, for example.

21. Mandela and Slovo, both lawyers, worked together well: Lionel (Rusty) Bernstein, as quoted in Magubane, *et al.*, 'The Turn to Armed Struggle', 65; Smith, *Young Mandela*, 198.

22. Neame Papers, Interview with Denis Goldberg, 28 September 87, 1 October 87, p. 22. Goldberg was a member of the Modern Youth (from Modern World) Society, on Loop St, Cape Town, which tried to liaise with and educate workers. Lionel Foreman, George Peake, Turok, Amy Rietstein, and Albie Sachs and perhaps Albie's brother were in the same milieu. 'Natal' could not have been Cato Manor for Denis Goldberg, because Denis has told me he has never been there, and has no recollection of the event in the late 1950s. In the interview, he says: 'I remember the interest in the unit concerning this'.

23. Wulfie (here spelt Wolfie) Kodesh, interviewed by John Carlin, no date (ca. 2000?), available on PBS: with no spaces: http://www.pbs.org/wgbh/pages/frontline/ shows/mandela/interviews/kodesh.html, accessed 5 January 2012.

unprecedented authority. Turok recalled speaking with Nelson Mandela, who 'was on the District Committee [of the Communist Party] with us and as far as Congress was concerned', was quite useful as a sounding board.[24] Although 'officially' [we] were all 'non violent', 'in private we knew' which direction things were heading, Turok recalled of that time.[25]

Meanwhile conflicts similar to those that involved the *Bafabegiya*, the 'Africanist' faction in the Transvaal, counterposed Mandela's faction freshly against Africanists in the Congress in 1958–1959. This conflict most likely involved the deployment of violent youths on both sides. The Pan Africanist Congress or PAC emerged as a result in April of 1959, with a strong presence in Langa, Cape Town, and on parts of the Rand. On 18 March 1960, the PAC ran an anti-pass protest, called to pre-empt another one ten days later, planned by the ANC. During the PAC-called protest, the state shot seven persons in Langa township, and extraordinarily, killed 69 people in Sharpeville, south of Johannesburg.

As Bernard Magubane suggests, the Sharpeville massacres against the PAC-motivated crowd were 'a decisive turning point in our history'.[26] Many faced the true nature of the state for the first time. The National Party government would shoot people to stop a peaceful action, and then lock in extraordinary powers for itself afterwards. Over the next weeks, PAC sympathisers set fire to government buildings, arguably the first acts of sabotage in the new era. Soon enough they would take up personal violence themselves, in return.[27]

In his famous speech given in lieu of direct testimony at the Rivonia Trial (1963–1964), Mandela plainly said MK was formed to *take charge* of the violence that was already transpiring. Violent conflict broke out all around in 1960–1961, at Zeerust,[28] Sekhukhuni-land,[29] Pondoland, and the cane fields of big sugar estates in Natal. But the biggest

24. Turok said he was involved in top SACP organising meetings three or four times a day 'in different capacities', Mayibuye Center, Brian Bunting papers, Box 131, 8.4.5, interview of Ben Turok by Bunting, October 1973 through May, 1974, for B.P. Bunting, *Moses Kotane, South African Revolutionary: A Political Biography* (Johannesburg: Inkululeko, 1975); hereafter Bunting/Turok. Turok offers a frank assessment of decisions and personalities. This material is not restricted in its quotation, unlike a separate, Wulfie Kodesh interview with Turok, also at the Mayibuye Center, which is. I took extensive notes on the material and thank the South African government for their openness to historical research.

25. Bunting/Turok, Tape 1, October 1973.

26. Bernard Magubane, 'Introduction', SADET, *The Road to Democracy in South Africa, Vol. 1*, 1.

27. Tom Lodge, *Sharpeville, an Apartheid Massacre and its Consequences* (Oxford: Oxford University Press, 2011), 48, 162. Possibly 'Russians' or Lesotho-origin gangster-beaters, by 'Africanists', and gangsters or *tsotsis* from Sophiatown, by Mandela's Transvaal Provincial ANC people; Philip Bonner, personal communication, 18 November 2011. The latter violence is a reference to the Paarl violence in 1963.

28. Ellis, 'The Genesis'; Tom Lodge, *Black Politics in South Africa Since 1945* (London: Longman, 1983), 283. See Siphamandla Zondi's excellent account of the violence in gaMatlala, in Zondi, 'Peasant Struggles in the 1950s: gaMatlala and Zeerust', SADET, *The Road to Democracy in South Africa, Vol. 1*, chapter three, esp. 154–157. In gaMatlala, the chiefship remained close to an underground Congress, and national and local struggles were interleaved up to ca. 1963. Arianna Lissoni's PhD research is illuminating the fascinating conjuncture of Dinokana chiefly authority, circumcision regiments, and the Botswana pipeline for fighters (leading to Communist Party funding and training).

29. P. Delius, 'Sebatakgomo and the Zoutpansberg Balemi Association: The ANC, the Communist Party and Rural Organization, 1939–55', *Journal of African History*, 34, 2 (1993), 293–313, shows the prior involvement of the ANC in Sekhukhuneland.

explosion of violence was Sharpeville, and Mandela and Slovo planned a coordinated response to those killings.[30] As part of it, Mandela and President Lutuli publically burnt their pass books, opening themselves to immediate arrest, and declared a mass stay-at-home. The government began arresting people, and entering African people's homes and beating them in Langa and in other townships, and on 30 March 1960, it declared a 'State of Emergency'.[31] Philip Kgosana, a 23-year-old PAC leader, then led more than 30,000 people in an unprecedented mass assembly, spontaneous in nature, walking through the streets of Cape Town. Mandela, Duma Nokwe, and many other Transvaalers were picked up and put in jail again, temporarily inaccessible to their lawyers. At the same time the government (on 8 April) banned the ANC and the PAC entirely, declaring them illegal.

It was then, most likely in April or May of 1960, that an informal poll, favouring violence, was first taken among the jailed activists.[32] On 19 April 1960, Duma Nokwe remarked to Helen Joseph during *the still in-session* Treason Trial (which dealt exclusively with non-violent activity constituted as treason) that the proceedings were 'out of date' – implying the inevitability of violence in the struggle and, perhaps, direct knowledge of that direction.[33]

With the detention of nearly the whole of the SACP CC and the NEC of the ANC in April and May of 1960, however, the lone survivors on the 'outside' (who held positions of authority already) for at least five months coordinated both the ANC and the SACP together. Bennie Turok (CC), Moses Kotane (CC and NEC), and Mick Harmel (CC), having dispatched Yusuf Dadoo (CC) abroad (in large part because he was past his prime, according to Turok), acted as a triumvirate in directing the struggle: on the run, sleeping in different houses every few nights, keeping in contact with Ruth Matsoane and Bartholomew Hlapane in Soweto and Johannesburg, for instance, and with Rowley Arenstein (despite his eccentricity) in Natal and Archie Sebeko in Cape Town.[34] Mandela was monitored by a policeman, but managed to arrange to spend whole weekends in his office in Johannesburg, and was somehow able to 'report' regularly to Helen Joseph the proceedings of the trial.[35]

When the State of Emergency was partly lifted, in July of 1960, Harmel was with a second group of CC members, led by Yusuf Dadoo, who visited Moscow and China to discuss the situation. They returned with a head-nod for future violent activity.[36] Mandela

---

30. Magubane, 'Introduction', SADET, *The Road to Democracy in South Africa, Vol. 1*, 1.

31. MCA 6, Wulfie Kodesh interview with Fred Carneson (1993).

32. Sisulu, as well as Wilton Mkwayi, and Henry Fazzie, all in separate interviews, appear to agree: Magubane *et al.*, 'The Turn to Armed Struggle', 71. Nkadimeng would have been part of it.

33. Walter Sisulu, as interviewed by Phil Bonner in 1997, cited in Magubane *et al.*, 'The Turn to Armed Struggle', 71.

34. Yet they did quite effective underground organising work, according to Turok. Bunting Papers, Turok, Tape 3 (1974); and see Ben Turok's published views, 'South Africa: The Search for a Strategy', *Socialist Register*, 10 (1973), 341–376, via http://socialistregister.com/index.php/srv/search/titles?searchPage=9, accessed 9 December, 2011.

35. Mandela, *Long Walk*, 216; Helen Joseph who appears to have been given a Communist code name, as she is thus listed in the Simons Papers (UCT) miscellany.

36. Yusuf Dadoo, Mick Harmel, and Joe Matthews were met directly by Mao. Ellis found a report that Mao told the South African delegation that perhaps warfare-wise 'Algeria' was a better model for them than China, which might have given them pause; Ellis, 'The Genesis'; and Magubane *et al.*, 'The Turn to Armed Struggle', 72–73.

and many others were allowed to sleep in their own beds regularly again by 1 September 1960. It was perhaps only then, in his friendship with the Slovos and Joseph and others, that Mandela began attending any Party meetings, around the same time the SACP announced its own existence (against Kotane's strong advice). Meanwhile the arrests began again, and some comrades scattered to Lesotho or Swaziland, such as Ruth First. A first wave of African emigrants (of 27 persons), including Wilton Mkwayi, and Patrick Mthembu, Ambrose Makiwane, and Moses Mabhida, flew to Lagos and Accra in September, and some of them went on later to China for military training.[37] Mick Harmel, the leading intellectual in the SACP along with First and Jack Simons, wrote and circulated a pamphlet called 'South Africa, What Next?', which basically argued for the inevitability of armed struggle.[38]

Still, for a year more, the ANC took no action.

During that year the ANC, underground and abroad, repeatedly called for a national convention. This was the focus while the Treason Trial sputtered to an end. And all the way until the grand acquittal at the close of the Treason Trial, Mandela oversaw the transformation of the ANC by way of the M-Plan.[39] The fact that Turok felt the ANC's connections were open to him, and that the struggle operated efficiently when they were pressed by their persecutors, no doubt came to Mandela's attention. Still, outside the Eastern Cape, the M-Plan was effectively deployed only in a few isolated cases. At one point Joe Slovo, Bram Fischer and a couple of other white comrades tried to join the ANC, as if hoping to exert leadership and create consensus from within, but they were rebuffed.[40] The ANC remained the ANC. In addition, Albie Sachs' cell's letter to the *African Communist* received no response, reinforcing the sense that the SACP's white personnel had less power to set policy than they might have thought. When Sachs, Denis Goldberg, and other Communists finally began supplying Marxist Leninist lectures and practical field training to *young African military recruits*, it would only be under ANC auspices. The struggle awaited the end of the silence on the violence question from the ANC.

The Sophiatown group

So far we have remained within a fairly precise chronology. We must now voyage forward in time, briefly, to Zambia in 1982. There is a strange document in a legacy of papers in Cape Town (as Stephen Ellis discovered): a record of an exiled CC SACP interaction, in which John 'Pule' Motshabi spoke to Moses Mabhida and the rest of the CC, in an almost self-immolating manner. Mabhida in 1982 was both Commander of MK and an ANC officer

---

37. Save one early group of nurses, these men were the first to visit the east and China, and Mkwayi later went with Ray Mhlaba, Joe Gqabi and others to train militarily in China (in October 1961). That caused a small crisis with O.R. Tambo, who was based in London when the banning of the ANC was first bruited in government. OR knew nothing about the shift in progress: Wilton Mkwayi, chapter 24, SADET, *The Road to Democracy: South Africans Telling Their Stories*, 268–9, 289; Mhlaba, *Raymond Mhlaba's Personal Memoirs;* and Sifiso Ndlovu, personal communication, 26 October 2011.

38. Magubane *et al.*, 'The Turn to Armed Struggle', and Denis Goldberg, my interview, 12 October 2011.

39. Mandela, *Long Walk*, 221.

40. Isaac Makopo, chapter 19, SADET, *The Road to Democracy: South Africans Telling Their Stories*, 213 (interviewed by Sifiso Ndlovu, 24 November 2000).

with responsibilities over young recruits clamouring for action. Seated in what was likely a private Lusaka home or office, J.P. Motshabi contextualised his statements by referencing an (unanswered) criticism that the Party was not engaged with the working class. He then mentioned the recruitment into the Family (the Party) of 'Nelson and Walter', and others, in around 1960, calling them the 'Sophiatown group'.

This is important evidence that Nelson Mandela joined the party in or before 1960. But it also reveals the shifting dynamics within the ANC and the SACP at the time. John 'Pule' Motshabi, haranguing the CC, denied the accusation that he (John), his brother Obad Motshabi, and David Bobape had tried to block the entrance of the 'Sophiatown group' when they joined 'the Family' back in 1959–1960. Nor, Motshabi declared, had he, Motshabi, engineered Robert Resha's defeat for the presidency of the ANC as some charged! He denied he was suspicious of white intellectuals, and allowed only that he favoured a worker-based party generally.[41] Motshabi felt slighted himself as a working man and a representative of workers when it came to consulting over policy; he implied Mandela had come in as a bit of an interloper, certainly without having to hawk copies of *New Age* on the street, and was an intellectual and therefore similar to many of the post-war white recruits. The 1982 CC meeting as a whole appears to have accepted the factual basis of Motshabi's unwonted remarks.[42]

In sum – moving back to 1960 – the Sophiatown group had antagonists; some African Communist members opposed them, some who were ANC (like Motshabi) and some who were not; and some of their allies, such as Rowley Arenstein, an influential working class Communist, thought the shift to violence was a terrible idea. Mandela and Sisulu may well have attended several SACP meetings, formally and informally, as Ben Turok recalls at least for Mandela, and it was by no means certain that the SACP would simply back an armed struggle with the ANC at the helm. Robert Hepple, briefly drafted into the CC in 1960, further supplies a text (in the form of an electronic file) about a meeting in December, 1960, which he says he copied from notes he took in 1964. He lists as attending, and therefore as CC members, Mandela, Sisulu, and Govan Mbeki, along with Turok, Mick Harmel, Fred Carneson, Ray Mhlaba, Dan Tloome, John Nkadimeng, and others. The meeting announced the new Communist Party support for the use of force.[43]

Ben Turok (in a 1973 interview with Brian Bunting) recalled a subsequent meeting in preparation for a Party Congress in mid-1961, in which Rusty Bernstein presented the

41. Simons Papers, O8.1, Minutes of Group Meeting, 13/May/82, with GS (Gen. Sec.), JG, JPM, RS, MM in attendance, discovered by Stephen Ellis. Motshabi felt that intellectuals, and especially white ones, in the Party, needed to be overmatched by workers and unionisers (of African origin especially), like him. Moses Mabhida rebuked him, calling him 'a frightened man', but did not contradict him. And see Simons Papers, P1, Motshabi, unpublished ms. autobiography, pointed out by Ellis, 'The Genesis' and by private communication during the month of November, 2011.

42. In fact Motshabi had not been a CC member in South Africa, and had worked for Mandela's Transvaal ANC presidency. In 1960 he briefly fell afoul of the ANC in some way. Ahmed (Kathy) Kathrada does not recall Mandela being at any DC SACP Transvaal meeting and says he does not know if Mandela was a Party member. Pule Motshabi was suspended from the CC from 1982 onwards.

43. Hepple, 'Notes', privately supplied. According to John Nkadimeng's memory, however, he was incarcerated from April 1960 all the way to March 1961, being among the last released, and so could not have attended; MCA-6, Kodesh interview with Nkadimeng (1995).

follow-up report on 'armed force' that Turok and others had participated in drafting. Turok says Mandela protested aloud that it would be difficult convince the ANC to abandon non-violence – 'to sell this to the ANC, particularly to Lutuli', were words he recalled.[44] Hence Mandela as a Communist was already considering his future role as the man who would have to do exactly that, according to Turok.

At the same meeting, according to Hepple, the question was raised as to the perpetuation of the ANC, and an argument had to be made in favour of its survival after its criminalisation, 'underground'. The motion to create another, separate, legal, front organisation, was after discussion, abandoned. Apparently Kotane spoke against the sacrifice of the ANC name, and probably also rallied the votes against the idea that the SACP should expand in place of the ANC. But Mandela's attendance was not missed, either.[45] The result of this ANC presence inside the CP was the perpetuation of the ANC in the vanguard of the struggle. Thus the Sophiatown group husbanded the ANC's hegemony.

An 'All-In African Conference' (24–25 March), originally planned to present a united front (SAUF) out of the ANC and PAC, in the end simply reinforced Mandela's stature as rising ANC leader. The Treason Trial verdict on 29 March then completely acquitted him along with the other accused. Mandela, briefly unbanned and free, now the future military commander of MK, immediately went into hiding, rightly fearing re-arrest. Yet others in the ANC moved within their accustomed orbits, demanding a national constitutional conference, uniting voices of protest. The ANC planned a three-day stay-at-home strike, the last day to fall on 1 June 1961, and the atmosphere in East London (with the 'abeTembes' opposing Chief Matanzima) was precarious, threatening imminent violence.[46] On 28 and 29 May, camouflaged ANC Youth Leaguers including Looksmart Ngudle attacked commuter buses with Molotov cocktails in Nyanga, Cape Town.[47] Yet still there was no official shift in ANC policy and no espousal by any leader of revolutionary violence. Printers and writers and unionisers, Communist and non-, all remained at work and 'above ground'.

For ANC President Lutuli, the stay-at-home represented the highest form of popular political action.[48] When there is less than full compliance in a general strike, however, the police can attack strike-enforcers such as Looksmart and the YL group above, and demand workers board buses – which they did with brutality that May. Mandela oversaw the strike and registered the second day as less than successful, and called the whole action off, perhaps prematurely. He then gave an interview to the *Rand Daily Mail*, in which he suggested that 'the people might be forced to use other methods of struggle'.[49]

---

44. Bunting/Turok, tape 2.
45. Hepple, 'Notes'. Hepple was subject to what amounted to torture and was convinced he would be hanged; and Turok, Bunting Interviews (1973/4), Tape 1 and Tape 3.
46. This emerges from a close reading of the SANA, URU 1964 2266 (DEEL V) 4820, the State vs. Washington Pumulelo Bongco.
47. SANA, Yutar Papers, Police witness reports, 385/24, Vol. 3, Zollie Malindi.
48. Couper, *Albert Luthuli*, 111.
49. Karis and Gerhard, 'The Turn to Violence Since May 31, 1961'; Mandela, *Long Walk*, 270; Mandela supposedly criticised the Party for its internal racial hierarchy in this period, in a way suggesting that he knew the Party from the inside out. Smith, *Young Mandela*, 213, citing O'Malley, *Shades of Difference;* Ellis, 'TheGenesis'.

In some sense perhaps the 'turn' to violence had happened already, as the *International Bulletin* of the SACP from April, 1961, embraced the Pondoland uprising as revolutionary, and hinted at military actions to follow against the state.[50] On the other hand, the ANC only released a list of demands, *inter alia* for an end to the State of Emergency, for wage-hikes, and for a repeal of 'Nazi laws', that was ordinary and expected in its form.[51] In fact, and this must be stressed, the NEC and the ANC's president had not been convinced of the wisdom of a campaign of sabotage.

What was sabotage to do?

Before moving further into the relationship between *the ANC* and 'armed struggle',[52] we must consider what armed struggle was to mean, which was really far from resolved in 1961. Indeed it is not apparent how sabotage was to challenge the state.[53] In a later interview, Rusty Bernstein recalled the sense at the time that the move toward sabotage was made off the back foot, as it were: that they had not thought the thing through.[54] By some partisans, sabotage was lauded as 'striking a blow' and 'heroic', but it was also explained as an act of desperation, understandable, perhaps, but greatly regretted; it was a harbinger of anger liable to burst out in uglier ways. Many comrades in their recollections distinguish sabotage from terrorism (which targeted human beings), but in its SACP CC adoption in December, 1960, the term apparently used was 'armed propaganda', not 'armed struggle'.[55] Even as the rationale was to bring the state to change policies, most informed people doubted it would work. The SACP's public stance in 1962 was opaque: 'Why do people resort to violent acts like sabotage? They only do so when there is no other way of expressing their aspirations for freedom ... So Vorster's Nazi law means more violence, more sabotage in South Africa'.[56] Here sabotage was a negative, like terrorism; and to stop it, apartheid had to be ended.

50. The SACP gave no hint of the new policy in its May Day message for 1961: Cullen Library, Simons Papers, 'May Day, 1961' flyer; Cullen Library, Sylvia Neame Papers, A2729, B13, *International Bulletin*, SACP, April 1961; also with a copy of H. Barrell,'The Historian and Conspirator: The ANC of South Africa and the Political-Military Relationship in Revolutionary Struggle', St Antony's College, Oxford University South African History and Politics Seminar, 20 May 1990.

51. Wits, Cullen Library, ANC, AD 2186 fa23, 'Statement of the Emergency Committee of the ANC', 1 April 1960; in contrast, by 1962 'courage, loyalty and devotion' are asked of the people by the ANC, AD 2186 F-G Box 5 Fa44, 'War Provocation', 26 March 1962.

52. Karis and Gerhart, 'The Turn to Violence', and Document 66, in Karis and Gerhard, eds., *Challenge and Violence, 1953–1964*, 716.

53. E.g. Lodge, *Black Politics*, ch. 10, conclusion. Drab books like R. Borum, *The Psychology of Terrorism* (Tampa: University of South Florida, 2004), are no longer of any use; J. Goodwin, 'A Theory of Categorical Terrorism', *Social Forces*, 84, 4 (June 200), 2027–2046.

54. Wits, Cullen Library, A3299E1 ANC, University of Cape Town Oral History Project, Hilda and Lionel (Rusty) Bernstein, interview with Terry Barnes, 28 February 2001: MK developed in a time in which 'we are not any longer in command of the situation – they are'.

55. Bob Hepple, who attended the meeting; personal communication, October 2011.

56. Cullen Library, Simons Papers (copy), Reel 8, 6.14.1, Flyer, 'Vorster's Nazi Law Can Never Destroy Communism'. Similarly, the 16 December flyer 'warned' that MK was trying to prevent civil (i.e. race) war.

But as we will see, this is not the way sabotage was understood by the leaders of MK.

Traces of internal debates

In 1961 apparently several relevant ANC-NEC 'Working Group' (Rand) and Congress Alliance meetings were arranged. According to one interrogated witness, one of them was attended by Mandela, Sisulu, Nokwe, Govan Mbeki, Moses Kotane, Dan Tloome, George Mbele, Stephen Dhlamini, Dr. G.M. Naicker, and five or six others.[57] The overlap in personnel with the command of the Communist Party was strong, although not all Communists supported sabotage.[58] According to this Rivonia witness, Gopallal Hurbans, who catered two days of Alliance meetings, Mbeki gave a short speech introducing the idea of violence, but then Lutuli opposed the idea, pointedly speaking about 'fighting ... in a peaceful manner'. This was echoed by G.M. Naicker and then by Kotane, and the meetings concluded.[59] In Mandela's account, this meeting took place in June 1961, and he recalls his arguments in favour of armed struggle were dismissed peremptorily and 'cheaply' by Kotane.[60]

We must note that Kotane as General Secretary of the SACP along with several others had been present at the CC *yet did not favour* the ANC's involvement in violence. Some time later, and here it is hard to be precise, Mandela spoke at length with Kotane, and prevailed upon him to allow him to bring the issue up once more before the NEC. This apparently transpired in a marathon discussion in Durban, Natal, either in July or possibly August of 1961. The crucial meeting ran late because they could not adjourn without coming to a decision, as a Joint Congress Alliance meeting, with a fresh group of people, had been scheduled for the following evening.

Kotane, a leader in the ANC's NEC and the CC of the Party, exerted great influence in the struggle, more than even Mandela or Sisulu. Chief Lutuli began the meetings (according to Mandela), along with his aide and top Natal ANC official M.B. Yengwa, as 'opposed [to] this very strongly'.[61] The case made for continuing non-violence was carefully laid out. For one thing, armed acts would subject all of them immediately to arrest! In favour of violence, the case was made was that the ANC must not be left behind by other people, that it must remain at the vanguard of the struggle. When the formation of MK was belatedly but finally approved, because of this argument, we may take it that MK was distinctly to be connected with the ANC, but officially to be kept at arm's length. Crucially Kotane was somehow carried along with Mandela's argument in this vein. Next came the 'Joint' meeting with the Congress Alliance partners. Here Lutuli, according to Mandela,

---

57.   Note addendum to Sources, this article. Yutar Papers, Police Interrogation Reports, 385/23, Vol. 2, Gopallal Hurbans, pp. 293–296. Hurbans recalled more meetings on these matters than Mandela.

58.   Not only Arenstein, but Jack Simons disparaged the 1960 'turn', University of Cape Town, Simons Papers, BC 1081, A1.6 and O16.5, 'Draft Outline Guerilla Warfare' (by Martin Legassick), critiqued by Jack Simons.

59.   Yutar Papers, Police Interrogation Reports, 385/23, Vol. 2, Gopallal Hurbans.

60.   Stephen Ellis suggests that Kotane was insubordinate to Moscow and the Party at this point, because he did not immediately accede to Mandela's requests for armed struggle.

61.   Mandela, *Conversations with Myself*, 76.

said, 'even though we the ANC has decided this, let us present it as undecided to everyone else',[62] allowing him to offer his arguments again before a larger group of sympathetic participants. Kotane's implicit acceptance of the inevitability of Mandela's logic apparently emerged, however, and Mandela's arguments again prevailed.[63]

Yet it was a thorough discussion. We know enough about Nelson Mandela from his prison years and after[64] to accept that much, and Mandela recalls the meetings both as lasting nearly all night. While Mandela could be ruthless as a lawyer, it does not follow that Lutuli was shabbily treated. Rather, Lutuli was brought to a point where he could not creditably argue against others any longer. Nor does this mean however that Lutuli's consent to MK embraced violence for the ANC as an organisation. What took a great deal of convincing was only after all that he and the Alliance (J.N. Singh, M.D. Naicker, the Cachalias, other doubters) *not publically condemn* a newly invented MK. Relinquishing their opposition was the extent of Lutuli's, and so 'the ANC's', and Kotane's, change of mind. Mandela recalled that Moses Kotane summarised the final verdict thus:

> you can go on and start this organization, but ... we as the ANC we are formed to prosecute a non-violent policy, this decision can only be changed by a national conference. We are going to *stick* to the old policy of the ANC.

This was Lutuli's position and the Indian Congress activists' in the Durban meetings, according to Mandela.[65] The non-violent ANC would tolerate the new violent organisation, at least until a 'national conference' changed the ANC itself. (This conference was about as likely to happen inside South Africa as the national convention the ANC demanded to draft a new South African state constitution.[66]) While MK would operate, in Rusty Bernstein's recollection, as 'a separate, independent' body, it would keep the ANC's NEC 'informed'. The SACP's CC did *not* in fact keep the ANC's NEC informed about everything (secrecy was intrinsic to it), so this was an important proviso. While they were having these discussions in

---

62. In this meeting Kotane supposedly told Rowley Arenstein to be quiet in his particular opposition to violence because 'you are a white man', in Magubane *et al.*, 'The Turn to Armed Struggle'. In Mandela, *Conversations with Myself* (New York: FSG, 2010), 80, Lutuli is recollected to Stengel as having fully assented to the ANC's starting 'an army'. According to Ben Turok, Kotane in the mid-1960s was angry with the white Communists who backed the sabotage campaign, blaming them for the destruction of the internal South African ANC. Bunting/Turok, tape 1 (1973).

63. NMF, Stengel interviews with Mandela, 15 April 1993. Mandel, *Long Walk to Freedom*, errantly presents Lutuli's manoeuvre (that of refraining from telling Alliance of the NEC's fresh decision to establish MK) as if it occurred twice, once in a positive light, once in a negative light. This is an editorial error, an artifact of Stengel's assemblage of the interviews to form *Long Walk*; the story of Lutuli's ruse came up in two different interviews, 'Dec. 1992' and '9 Ap. 1993' (the second one is reproduced in Mandela, *Conversations with Myself*, 80). See Mandela, *Long Walk*, 237–238 (of the 1994 hardcover, equivalent to 272–273 of the 1995 paperback edition).

64. This is also Tom Lodge's larger point in *Mandela, A Critical Life* (Oxford: Oxford University Press, 2006).

65. NMF, Stengel interview with Nelson Mandela, 5 April 1993, and 15 April 1993. Also in Mandela, *Conversations with Myself*, 78.

66. Wilton Mkwayi understood even sabotage as being about getting a national convention Cullen Library, State v. Wilton Mkwayi and others, 18 November 1964 to 15 December 1964 ('Little Rivonia Trial').

the winter of 1961, small SACP 'special units', including Ahmed Kathrada and Jack Hodgson, were already cutting phone lines.[67] This would now be MK activity.

The ANC go-ahead for MK was a huge victory for Mandela, achieved through politics and persuasion. Mandela had associated with Communists from the mid-1950s on, and he had managed to field the Communist Party's espousal of sabotage and make it the ANC's own. In the past with the ANC, in ordinary times, such a momentous shift would surely have involved all the branches voting for the new policy, and mostly likely voting in a new president. But these were not ordinary times.

MK, the SACP, and the Alliance

This is not the place to investigate the *implementation* of MK's program, nor how the transition to the M-Plan and the growth of MK groups unfolded on the level of neighbourhoods and branches. But the outline of the story in Natal, as divulged by Rivonia witnesses, suggests that the transition did not always go smoothly. The problem in Natal was not only within the ANC ranks, but with the trade unions and the Natal Indian Congress. Comparatively, such alliances on the Rand were easier, as the Fordsburg-based Transvaal Indian Congress (a much smaller political body) was quite ready for action and its Youth Congress's newsletter was called '*combat*'.[68] In practice, MK recruited from the ANC and the African trade unionists. However, some ANC branches did not just vote themselves out of existence, but clung on. In Durban, the ANC opted to commence violent actions themselves, or barring that, tried to insert themselves in the MK chain of command. As a result, MK appointed the Communist and ANC 'residents' association' president Curnick Ndlovu directly to the Regional Command of MK to coordinate the relationship.[69]

At the top and bottom MK was multi-ethnic and class-varied. MK's 'High Command' was distinctly multi-racial and overwhelmingly Communist, directly influenced by whites such as Harmel, Slovo, Turok, and by military men such as Jack Hodgson and Harold Strachan, and by others like Bernstein and Fischer who had no MK command. At the same time, with MK much of the action of the struggle went into the hands of activists from non-ANC groups in the Congress Alliance; in this sense MK was constructed on the

---

67. Bernstein, *Memory Against Forgetting*, 23; see Goldberg, *The Mission*, and Andrew Mlangeni, in Magubane, *et al.*, 'The Turn to Armed Struggle', 71; and au. interview with Ahmed Kathrada, 7 October 2011.

68. With Wulfie Kodesh; Ahmed Kathrada, Indres Naidoo, and Mac Maharaj came from Fordsburg. R. Sedat and R. Saleh, eds., *Men of Dynamite: Pen Portraits of MK Pioneers* (Johannesburg: Ahmed Kathrada Foundation, 2009), *passim*. The relevant newsletter *combat* I found in SANA, one of the unnumbered, un-indexed 'Treason Trial exhibits' (150 boxes).

69. Yutar papers, 385/308/1 'Essentials of the M Plan', and 385/4/4 'Organization Plan' which projected 550 Zones in South Africa by the end of June 1961; Yutar papers, 385/26, Vol. 4, 722: Bruno Mtolo; identified by Mtolo in his book, *The Road to the Left* (Natal: Drakensberg Press, 1966), 18; SANA, Yutar papers, 385/25, Vol. 3, E. S. (Selbourne) J. Maponya, 495. Stephen Dlhamini, George Poonan (a close friend of Billy Nair), Curnick Ndlovu, and Solomon Mbanjwa were all apparently Communists. Yutar Papers, 385/26, Vol 4, Abel Mthembu, and Vol. 4, Bruno Mtolo (722 ff.) Greater Durban included Hammersmith, Chesterville, Cleremont, Kwa Mashu, Cato Manor and other areas.

ground by the Alliance, even if made by men in the ANC. Furthermore, Richard Stengel, Mandela's ghost writer, recorded the following on tape:

> Mandela: So then now having got that decision at the ANC, we brought in Joe Slovo, Jack Hodgson and Jack Hodgson [Mandela is thinking out loud] and Rusty Bernstein, we brought them in and formed a committee, a High Command [along with Walter Sisulu] and I was Commander of Umkhonto and the chairman of the High Command.

A confusion follows in the transcript, as Stengel does not understand whites as MK leaders. Mandela says, 'Haven't I not mentioned the names there?' and Stengel says, 'No', so Mandela says, 'I forget now, you know? But then the two[,] the Communist Party and the ANC met from time to time, to give us, the High Command to listen to a report ... and give us instructions'.[70] Mandela could have hardly been clearer.

Preparations for the first *actions* drew heavily on World War II veterans, Springbok Legionnaires, and involved a great deal of homemade ordnance. The official MK launch came on 16 December 1961, except for Durban, which went ahead a day early; there was some damage to electrical conduits, and while one man died in an accident, some fuses did not go off, and the flyers that were posted were mostly torn down before dawn. The flyers announced the emergence of *Umkhonto we Sizwe*, Spear of the Nation; the Congress itself had been called *Umbutho we Sizwe* on letterhead for decades, 'Congress of the Nation', so the association was clear. The flyers also declared that non-violence was dead, and that the new strategy had replaced it.[71] Lutuli and Kotane almost certainly differed with the particulars of the message on the flyers.[72]

But violence was not just about tactics. The readings and lectures that Mandela scrupulously took handwritten notes on suggest that for Mandela, Nokwe, Sisulu, Slovo and their allies, sabotage was not just a nudge to the state, not just 'armed propaganda', but was a prelude to, or a part of, *guerrilla war*. Mandela's own words suggest this, and his actions in Algeria, Ethiopia, and at the Pan-African Freedom Movement of Eastern and Central Africa (PAFMECA) in 1962, before his final arrest, make this trajectory even more apparent. He also recollected as much 30 years later.

70.   NMF, Stengel interview with Mandela, interviews on 4, 5, and 15 April, 1993.
71.   SANA, Yutar Papers, 385/32/2/7, 'Umkhonto we Sizwe', 16/12/61, and see Karis and Gerhard, 'The Turn to Violence Since May 31, 1961.'
72.   Ellis, 'The Genesis'; Couper, *Albert Luthuli*. The debate about Lutuli's position on MK's 'launch' is unresolved. One notes the ferocity of his Oslo acceptance speech (pointed out to me by Sifiso Ndlovu), but also that Rusty Bernstein's (requested) speech-writer's draft for the speech included a more direct mention of the 'paradox' given the shift in the struggle which Lutuli disregarded (Bernstein, *Memory Against Forgetting,* 233). There was also a long tradition of generational divergence in the ANC, in which the leadership (here 'the chief' in fact) was greatly respected but beheld almost as a symbol. Arguably this was an even older, African, political-organizational trait, as I elaborate in P. Landau, *Popular Politics in the History of South Africa, 1400 to 1948* (New York: Cambridge University Press, 2010), chs. 1, 2. An alternative account appears in Magubane *et al.*, 'The Turn to Armed Struggle', in which Curnick Ndlovu (from an interview done in ca. 2000 or 2001) refers to his visiting Lutuli in the aftermath of the 16 December 1961 initiation of the sabotage campaign: 'only thing he [Lutuli] raised was that he was not aware that the leaflet [*sic*] was coming out that day', at his return from the Nobel ceremony; 90, n135; 92.

In the last part of this paper, I will re-establish Mandela's own intentions for the struggle in 1961–1962, and connect those intentions to his visit to the PAFMECA conference in February of 1962 and its aftermath. As we will see, Mandela organised the renunciation of the (non-African) Communist alliance, if not formally (yet) the Congress Alliance. This evidence is deployed in favour of my overall interpretation, that it was Mandela's 'Sophiatown group' who saw the shift to violent opposition as inevitable, who tried to take control of it, in the name of the ANC, and who therefore made MK possible.

Nelson Mandela's political notes

In 1961 and early 1962, as the leader of MK, Mandela read several books on revolution and peasant uprisings, among them works on the Malay conflict, the Irgun in Paletstine/Israel, the war in Algeria, the Chinese and the Cuban Revolutions, even the US and Vietnam (and Sun Tzu and Frederick the Great). He may have read much more, but on these books he took meticulous, thorough notes.[73]

In his notes on Che Guevara, *Guerilla Warfare* (Rivonia Exhibit R 25), a book published the year he read it, Mandela stresses two key elements of the Cuban revolutionary's thinking. First, there is no need to wait for all the conditions for revolution to arrive before launching a guerrilla struggle. 'The insurrection can create' these conditions. The conservative peasantry, however, has to see clearly that it is no longer possible 'to fight for social goals within the framework of civil debate ... peace is already considered broken'. The people will get behind reclaiming the land.[74] In his interviews with Stengel, Mandela recalled using these same ideas in conversation with Moses Kotane in 1961. Mandela had argued to Kotane that Kotane was

> doing precisely what the Communist Party in Cuba did; they said the conditions for a revolution had not yet arrived. Following the old methods, you see, which were advocated by Stalin[; while here] we have to decide from our own situation. The situation in this country is that it is time to consider a revolution, armed struggle.[75]

Secondly Mandela in his notes stresses that sabotage 'is an arm of guerrilla warfare'. Subsequently in writing about Chinese agrarian guerrilla war, Mandela noted that specific conditions must come to the attention of 'anyone directing a war', and that grasping practical and historical circumstances was critically important (R 24, 'Strategic Problems of China's Revolutionary War'). It must be up to the educated central command as to how and where to wage war. Control was key.

73. I have compared his handwritten notes adduced by the Rivonia prosecutors to the typescripts they prepared, and they are accurate to the point of being identical. There was no handwritten version for one or two surviving 'exhibits' and one suspects they have been stolen and sold.

74. *Guerilla Warfare* (New York: Monthly Review Press, 1961), also available at http://mecanopolis.org/wp-content/uploads/2007/08/guwar.pdf (approx. 127 pp.), last accessed 5 January 2012.

75. NMF, Stengel interviews with Mandela, 5 April, 1993. A concern with the land runs right through South African political mobilizations of the twentieth century; see my 'Johannesburg in Flames: The 1918 Almost-Was Shilling Strike, *Abantu-Batho,* and the African National Congress', in P. Limb, ed., *Abantu-Batho: A People's Newspaper in South Africa* (Wits Press, forthcoming).

Mandela put South African historical battles in the trans-historical framework of warfare outlined in his notes on the Chinese Communist revolution, writing 'Battle of Blood River 1838' and 'Battle of Isandlhwana 1879' in the margins. He read about the failed Malay uprising, a 4,000-man guerrilla army of whom many were World War II veterans.[76] In part because there was 'not enough bush' in South Africa to allow the kind of guerrilla war he would like optimally to wage, Mandela was particularly attracted to the Israelis' struggle against the British, and to *The Revolt,* Menachem Begin's book about the Irgun.[77] We might recall here that Sisulu and other Communists spent some months in Israel in 1953. We might also note a regional-level meeting (in Zulu and English) of the ANC, Natal, in which a long passage from *The Revolt* appears to have been read into the record:

> And we shall be accompanied by the spirit of millions of our matyrs [*sic*], our ancestors tortured and burned for their faith, our murdered fathers and butchered mothers, our murdered brothers and strangled children. And in this battle we shall break the enemy and bring salvation to our people, tried in the furnace of persecution, thirsting only for freedom, for righteousness and for Justice ...[78]

In fact Mandela was moved by the book and patterned MK's aims on the Irgun's. He summarised: 'A new generation arose. It began to fight instead of pleading'. But Mandela was also most impressed by the Irgun's discipline, and as with Cuba and China, his notes emphasise discussion but then centralisation:

> The High Command controlled all the activities of the Irgun, both military and political. It considered general principles, strategy and tactics, information and training, relations with other bodies and negotiations with their representatives. It took decisions, and orders were given as in all military organizations; but there were never any decisions by an individual. There was always discussion.[79]

After discussion, and once a decision was reached, there had to be absolute obedience. Mandela took the terms 'Regional Command' and 'High Command' into the MK from Irgun terminology.[80]

Many of the leaders in the struggle read books, and sought out information about other anticolonial struggles. Mandela wrote dozens of pages of notes on Chinese guerrilla war, and wrote scores of pages of notes on a work called 'How to be a good Communist', as the Rivonia court was told. Famously 'Operation Mayibuye', a typed document which looked

76. L. Taruq, *Born of the People* (London: Greenwood, 1973 [1953]).
77. Echoed in Mandela, *Long Walk,* 275.
78. Simons Papers, microfilmed facsimiles, Cullen Library, Reel 6, 5.7.1.5. Inthetho ka Mongameli kwi Ngqungquthela Inkomfa Yombutho weSizwe Upondo Lwase Koloni, 1953. This derived from a radio speech given by Begin in 1948, reconciling the Irgun with the State of Israel at its birth in 1948; other parts of *The Revolt* are about how the regular Israeli army had wanted to kill or disgrace the Irgun as terrorists, as Mandela highlighted in his notes. (c.f. M. Begin, The Revolt: The Story of the Irgun (Tel Aviv: Steimatsky Agency [revised edition], 1977).
79. SANA, Yutar Papers, 385, R 18; 'Irg Z. L. Nat M. Organization', Para 13, and p. 4.
80. As Mandela said in his Rivonia valediction: Simons Papers, P1.1, Nelson Mandela 1957–89, Statement at Rivonia (1963).

a lot like a plan for Communist-sponsored invasions, was found with these papers in the July, 1963 police raid on the Liliesleaf Farm at Rivonia, the SACP-provided temporary headquarters for MK. A lesser known typed document was titled 'Organization Plan for the Preparation of Armed Revolution'. This was an SACP outline for 'the second phase' of struggle, with a plan to headquarter a Supreme Revolutionary Council in Johannesburg and based guerrilla armies in rural areas. The document stressed the achievement of a 'concrete understanding of the real situation' on the ground (quoting Kim Il Sung), social layer by social layer, in order succeed.[81] A separate document called 'The Speaker's Notes – a Brief Course on the Training of Organisers' (also secured, like so much else, in the 1963 police raid), is particularly illuminating. It begins, 'You have been appointed to perform the important task of organising the units of Umkonto Wesizwe ... by the high command'. Why did MK start with sabotage? The trainer is advised:

> Sabotage is an invaluable arm of people who fight a guerrilla war. In the initial stages it fulfils the strategic task of creating the conditions necessary for the formation of guerrilla units from among the people.

What follows this are directives and assertions very close to Mandela's own notes on Che Guevara and other guerrilla movements from the literature he perused. Sabotage must be rigorously directed from a central command, or, it must happen in wartime where local actions against the enemy lines are permitted.[82] Sabotage is not a freelance method, but part of something larger. The scenario as some of the MK high command envisioned it involved police converging on increasingly frequent scenes of destruction and then coming under deadly sniper fire. This would draw further policemen in, and create areas of no policing, where others could train their focus. A different debate revolved around 'Operation Mayibuye' and the possibly grand scale of the operation on the ground. Denis Goldberg, on behalf of the high command, priced out the industrial production of several tens of thousands of grenade casings and antipersonnel mines under its rubric. While he never submitted such an order, there were further discussions afoot at Liliesleaf to disaggregate production and reach the same volume piecemeal.[83]

Chinese and African sensibilities

Mandela both toured South Africa and visited other African states and sites of insurgency in 1961–1962. This trip was delegated to him by a 'Working Group' at the NEC level. In

81. Yutar Papers, 385/32/4/4.
82. Literature ordered through the ANC's overseas representatives. Yutar Papers, 385/33/33 (R 54), 'The Speaker's Notes'.
83. Goldberg discusses this in *The Mission*; and, SANA, Yutar Papers, 385/32/3/16, 'Organisation of Local Production', T 125 or T 39, 'Report to Logistics Committee of the [MK] High Command'. Mandela in his Rivonia Trial statement makes both true and untrue assertions in the interest of avoiding a mandatory death penalty. Hence 'I have never been a member of the Communist Party', and Mandela's courtroom argument for sabotage: it would put 'a heavy strain' on the economy 'compelling the voters' (white people) to 'reconsider their position': Simons Papers, P1.1, Nelson Mandela 1957–89, Statement at Rivonia (1963), paras. 59, 27 (and Yutar Papers, 385, courtroom interrogations). As for the actual prospect of guerrilla war: the 'for instance' was from Denis Goldberg, Interview, 12 October 2011; and Goldberg, *Mission*, 92 ff.

fact, in 1960, the ANC and PAC together (with a few ancillary groups), as the South African United Front, had established contact with Ghana. The SAUF had also convened in Addis on 19 June 1960. The following year, shorn of Dr Dadoo and Oliver Tambo, the PAC dispatched Peter Molotsi and Nana Mahomo to Africa again.[84] Now, after another year, Mandela and Oliver Tambo (soon joined by Robert Resha) would tour Africa in their trail, looking for material support, training, camps, and funds, for MK and the ANC, not the PAC. In the course of their travels they went through Nigeria, Ethiopia, Cairo, Morocco, and visited Algeria, spending time with the FLN (the National Liberation Front), where Mandela befriended Ben Bella, and then Cameroon, Mali, and Sierra Leone, Accra, Lagos, Monrovia, Senegal, Khartoum, and back to Addis for some weeks training in soldiery. As he wrote in his 'Notebook' in Algeria, back home, the 'Masses must be made to understand that political action, of the nature of strikes, boycotts and similar demonstrations, has become ineffective standing by themselves [sic]'.[85]

Close to the start of his Africa trip, in early February 1962, in Addis, Mandela attended the 'PAFMECA' conference, which included delegates from all over Africa. PAFMECA brought together African heads of state in a liberatory context. Mandela delivered a planned address and narrativised the history of South Africa as a long history of struggle against oppression, and he announced the birth of Umkhonto we Sizwe (MK) by name, without mentioning that he was its operating commander.[86]

Mandela looked for angles in this context. He noted that both the Egyptian and Ghanaian delegations were unpopular. Ghana's pan-Africanism had already alienated many states. Aloysius Barden, a white, mercenary ex-policeman, bizarrely appointed to run Ghana's Bureau of African Affairs by Kwame Nkrumah, withheld other movements' monies.[87] Mandela also perceived that 'Communists' were disparaged by many new African states, perhaps surprisingly in Zambia and Tanganyika especially, less surprisingly in Addis, where Soviet-backed Ethiopian Communists would soon overthrow Haile Selassie's regime. And not only Egypt, but 'Arabs' in general were distrusted, and indeed two years hence, so-labelled 'Arabs' would be murdered by the Afro-Shirazi party in a mass pogrom in Zanzibar. Africa was not united, as Duma Nokwe later pointedly noted.[88]

The Chinese revolutionary model would be especially favoured by Eastern Cape comrades and by those trained militarily in China. The Chinese strategy for maintaining their popularity from the time of the 1955 Bandung Conference was promulgated in the notion of the 'Third World'. Discussed at the Pan-African Freedom Movement of Eastern

84. Mayibuye Center (MCH) 02, Box 1, ANC London, 1960–72, incl. Jan. 7, 1960 'Constitution', and Interview with Peter Molotsi, SADET, The Road to Democracy: South Africans Telling Their Stories, Vol. 1, 1950–1970 (SADET, 2008).

85. Benneyworth, 'Armed', and Nelson Mandela Foundation, Nelson Mandela Papers, (Rivonia) R 16, Notebook. Mandela wrote 'AFL', Algerian Liberation Front.

86. Briefly 'PAFMECSA' after South Africa was added, the members ultimately became part of the Liberation Committee of the Organization of African Unity, at the urging of Algeria's Ahmed Ben Bello: A. Biney, 'Ghana's Contribution to the Anti-Apartheid Struggle, 1958–94', ch. 2 in SADET, The Road to Democracy in South Africa, Volume 5, African Solidarity, forthcoming, thanks to Sifiso Ndlovu; see also Magubane et al., 'The Turn to Armed Struggle', 673.

87. Biney, 'Ghana's Contribution'.

88. In the document cited in n95, i.e. 'Maloone??'.

and Central Africa conference, the Afro-Asian People's Solidarity Organization, or AAPSO, had voted against seating the COD, the white South African 'Liberal', i.e. mostly Communist organisation allied to the ANC. In late 1961, when the Sino-Soviet split became public, and Kotane, Harmel and the other Communists were in contact with both Moscow and with Peking, the Chinese introduced the resolution and secured a unanimous 'no' vote, in an attempt to separate their Communism (rooted in anti-colonialism) from the Communism of white Europeans and therefore the Soviets. The Chinese hoped thereby to deflect PAFMECA anti-Communism away from them.[89]

At PAFMECA in 1962 several new African nations were leaning toward recognising the PAC alone, not the ANC, as the legitimate representative of the South African struggle. The issue crystallised for Mandela when he met with Zambia's Kenneth Kaunda in private, most likely on 6 February 1962.[90] Kaunda, who would soon liaise with the Chinese, with other Zambians, conveyed that he, Kaunda, was struggling to influence his country's representatives not to abandon the ANC, as they were bucking for the PAC.[91] Mandela learned that the Freedom Charter had much impressed everyone, but when the delegations learned that it was a product of ANC collaboration with whites (Rusty Bernstein in fact had drafted it), they 'were repulsed', or had 'torn it' up.[92] Here was the *Bafabegiya* and PAC issue all over again if in new guise. Now, however, Tambo was with Mandela, and in the company of men from emerging Tanzania, Zambia, and China, the basic demand was for South Africa to join the post-colonial club, which (in turn) required anti-colonialism, not proletarianism. At least for *armed* struggle, 'the four-pronged wheel' model, in which the COD and Indian Congress held nominally equal status with the ANC in the Congress Alliance, was obsolete.

Mandela then decided on the need for a new strategy. In the public record already is the idea that he conveyed to Alliance allies that the ANC's 'tactics' but not its 'policy' would have to change. The argument was already a serious one both with Yusuf Dadoo and with Monty (M.D.) Naicker.[93] But in the end this decision was taken, apparently Mandela again succeeding by his powers of persuasion and leadership. Recently a further document has come to light, a schematic record of a quorum or 'working group' of the ANC National Executive Committee deciding exactly this. There are four men in conversation, sometime

89.   Other factors at work at PAFMECA we can only note in passing. China had already partially defaulted on a promise to fund a Chinese-African People Friendship Association scholarships for South Africans, and other projects. UWC, Mayibuye Center, MCH 02-1 London, 1960–72, South African United Front to China, 5 June, 1962. C.J. Lee, ed., *Making a World After Empire: The Bandung Moment and Its Political Afterlives* (Ohio: Ohio University Press, 2010), Introduction; G.T. Burgess, 'Mao in Zanzibar,' in Lee, ed., *Making a World*, 205; and B.D. Larkin, *China and Africa, 1949–70: The Foreign Policy of the People's Republic of China* (Berkeley: University of California Press, 1971), 59. Kaunda also had dealings apparently with the Yugoslavs.

90.   Nelson Mandela Foundation (NMF), Nelson Mandela Papers, Diary, 1 February 1962, 6 February 1962.

91.   See D. Gordon, *Invisible Agents*, forthcoming.

92.   Yutar Papers, Police Witness reports, Vol. 3, 489–521. Ephraim Selbourne John Maponya, a secretary of Lutuli's in 1962 ('repulsed') and SANA TAB WLD CC1964 578 State vs. Wilton Mkwayi, R-13, Mandela's 'diary.' Mandela in *Long Walk* recalls then a long conversation with Simon Kapwepwe, whom he also swayed, 258.

93.   Mandela, *Long Walk*, 264, 272.

in 1962, in London either before or after Mandela's aborted 'military training' (which ended in mid-July 1962). Excerpted:

> 'Xamela' (i.e. Qamela, Walter Sisulu): [']Tactics can be adjusted[.] We must bear in mind the sensitivity with other minority groups ...
> 'Madiba' (Nelson Mandela): [']What we lack is initiative. We should change our attitude and exert ourselves. Our friends must understand that it is the ANC that is to pilot the struggle. Something bigger should be arranged in Tanganyika.['][94]
> 'Bokwe' (Joe Matthews): [']We are prisoners of our own sins [.] We allowed ourselves to drift. I think cooperation has been carried too far. I think we should expand our offices ... like Zapu and Unip ... [and] make the necessary preparations in Bechuanaland... [']
> 'Gowanini' (Duma Nokwe): ... [']We must take the situation in Africa realistically. If the cause of the struggle in SA can only be put forward through the ANC then we must do so. I do not think it is any step backward. We must explain to our colle[a]gue[s] the step[s] that we feel are appropriate. The policy is decide, there is no question of deviation['].[95]

This articulation of the Africanist course-correction thus deprecated the Alliance. These words constitute the decision to redirect the armed struggle toward a more African-nationalist line, starting immediately, creating the MK of the next 30 years. The Chinese and African nations (Nigeria donated thousands) would fund this ANC, along with the Soviets, and African commanders could train scores and perhaps ultimately thousands of African MK conscripts on African soil. To that end, African leadership, ANC leadership, would come to the fore, and white (and Indian and Coloured) fighters would retreat into a supporting role. This was potentially an explosive idea, because, as we have seen, these allies had been elevated in the middle ranks within the structure of MK (which drew heavily on Communists and Congress-affiliated union men for 'volunteers'), but perhaps that is why the decision had to be made with finality: 'there is no question of deviation', as Nokwe put it.

Most importantly here, this NEC-working group in 1962 shows again that the core subjective agency behind MK was an emergent group of revolutionary ANC leaders. This 'Sophiatown group' and its close allies, if they deemed it necessary, would get rid of their Communist (mostly white) allies and act only in the name of the ANC: that is seen here. Any full account of MK must take the measure of (what was to be) a major, coming change.

A further clue to Mandela's probable forward-oriented thinking (from 1963), should one be needed, can be seen in a commentary he offered the young activist Sylvia Neame during the Rivonia trial, about a paper she was writing about the Communist Party. Bear in mind Mandela was both ANC (MK) and a Communist Party member at the moment he wrote:

94. This constituted the first step in building toward the creation of Morogoro.
95. It was seen by David Smith in Harry Oppenheimer's private library, when Smith was researching his book *Young Mandela,* but Smith does not discuss it and did not fully realize its significance. I found it independently and I've yet found no other notation of it. Yutar Papers, 385/33/13, R 14 (K.R. 17), headed 'Maloone?? 1. Policy of the U.A.R.' It is not clear if 'decided' should be read here, or 'to decide', but at the least, the implication is 'we decide, others follow our decision'. Thanks to Hugh Macmillan for information on Nokwe.

> On several occasions in history, it has happened that the working cooperation between a non-marxist political organization and the C.P. ceases because policy differences emerged, as they have for example in India between the Congress and the C.P., and in several Middle Eastern Countries.[96]

Perhaps just this was in the cards. The trajectory of the struggle as the government's brutality moved toward its final phases described an MK that would hew closely to the ANC. The leadership of the struggle remained Communist in orientation at that moment, because Mandela, Nokwe, Sisulu, Mbeki, Robert Resha, Dan Tloome, Ray Mhlaba, and many others in the leadership were Communists, interested in finding ways to move South Africa toward guerrilla war against the state. The sense above that 'they'd let things slip', that (as Mandela put it) 'our friends must understand' and take a back seat in the effort, made linking MK and the ANC even more important. In 1962, the last big ANC conference for many years took place in Lobatse, Botswana, cementing the shift; and by early 1963, MK agents were informing rank and file ANC members (who had not in some cases associated MK with the ANC and knew little about it), that MK was a 'child' of the ANC and that the struggle had simply entered a 'second phase', much as the December 16th, 1961 flyer announced.[97]

At the end of June in 1962, Mandela and his allies briefly stood at the top of struggle's pyramid. Travelling out to see Lutuli in his Groutville home-arrest, to apprise him of this new policy (again!), Mandela paid a visit to the Durban Regional Command of the Natal corps of MK, where he spoke to a group of MK as their national commander in chief. Mandela said he was 'glad to see' they were all 'young men, not old men', a line elsewhere echoed by Sisulu and Mbeki; he reported that other African countries saluted them; he suggested that one fighter, Eric Mtshali, had offended his Tanzanian hosts by announcing he was a Communist, and that this was a 'dangerous' thing to do (this in continuation of his conversations above); he reported that the Algerian Ben Bella was sympathetic to Communists but not Haile Selassie, and not the Egyptians, who noticed in the pages of *New Age* that they had been criticised 'whenever they did anything against Communism'. Mandela reported that he had brought back £30,000 Sterling from his travels. They needed Party literature and works of history; they had to teach the rural people; they had to be ready to 'fight' the Bantu Authorities. Lastly, that sabotage would not 'end with Sabotage only. After that we will go into guerilla warfare'.[98]

Mandela was captured by the police on the drive home the next day, Sunday, 4 August 1962.[99]

---

96. Cullen Library, A 2729, Neame papers, 1968. Also, in Mandela's valediction at the Rivonia Trial, he says, 'I believe that it is open to debate whether the Communist party has any specific role to play at this particular stage of our political struggle'. (But if in support of the Freedom Charter, we 'welcome' the Party's 'assistance'.)

97. SANA, Yutar Papers, Police Interrogations, 385/25 (Vol. 2), E.S. (Selbourne) J. Maponya, 508-12.

98. Cullen Library, Rivonia, AD 1844 A15: Private Machine, 'Our Copy', Bruno Mtolo with Zulu interpreter.

99. NMF, Stengel interviews with Mandela, 16 April 1993. And in July 1963 came the massive raid on Liliesleaf farm, Rivonia, outside Johannesburg, a hide-out financed through Bram Fischer and offered to ANC and MK leaders, which led to the arrest of so many of them.

Conclusion: MK/ANC as phoenix

Who knows what might have been, but we can summarise what was: a coalescence of authority around *command structures* and secret cells, undertaken by a 1950s-era cache of ANC men in the SACP, under great pressure. These men along with white Communist allies began the first attempt to overthrow the South African government only after that government undertook to destroy them. The principle effect of 1960–1 repression, State of Emergency, and the ANC's 'turn', on the struggle as a whole, was the creation of further institutions favouring the 'abolition of election … and leadership by appointment',[100] in other words, a new kind of organisation, albeit also called the ANC.[101] That transformation has not proved entirely easy to undo.

Amidst the state's brutal repression of dissent, and given the increased attention of the Communist Party to Africans' concerns after World War II, there arose the conditions in which an organised violent response to the violent state could emerge. Soviet and Chinese Communist did not give the go-ahead for violence until key African leaders (who were Communists) also backed it. When they did, change waited for them to persuade the other nationalist and unionist leaders in the struggle; the SACP General Secretary, a commanding figure in the ANC; and finally the rump NEC, and from there, the leaders of the Alliance, to give the okay. Facilitated willy-nilly by the state's neutralisation of so many colleagues, Mandela and a group of 1950s' Communist African nationalists, the Sophiatown group, did this. Emerging in the politics of resistance on the Rand in the 1950s, and cohering during the trials of the 1950s–1960s, they sought to refashion themselves as nationalist revolutionaries, and redeploy the name of the ANC in the process.

Might-have-beens are anti-historical, and the reasoning of the Sophiatown group was eminently defensible and arguably correct in 1961 and in 1962. They did not, however, succeed in the aims they cherished, before they went to jail or left the country for years or decades or were killed. The M-Plan failed to protect or sustain an underground ANC organisation. There was no guerrilla movement to stimulate a mass uprising against the state. The founders of MK defended the ANC's continued relevance, beginning inside the SACP in 1960–1961, a policy that developed along the same vector, from 1963 to 1965, such that the ANC and MK controlled and contained the SACP, and for many years strategically silenced it altogether in Zambia.[102] What larger conclusion, then, can be drawn from the developments outlined here? Clearly that shifts such as 'the turn to violence' can easily be mythologised. The real story of that 'moment' is a messy and heavily contingent one. But nonetheless policymakers may ask: what form of mass politics last escapes the progressive brutalization, with 'state of emergency' powers, of a previously unjust but (largely) rule-following regime? The answer: an external, militarised

---

100. Yutar Papers, 385/25 (Vol. 2), Maponya, 508–513.
101. One thinks of Nietzsche's warning about becoming the monster. Yutar Papers, 385/28 (Vol. 5), Gabriel S. Nyembe, 898 ff., quotes Govan Mbeki's words excluding him from a (Working Group) NEC meeting in Transkei: 'Don't you know that the matters of the African National Congress are handled by only a few people now?'; in this my argument concurs with Couper, *Albert Luthuli*, 91; 102, and work he draws on. Rusty Bernstein in a letter to John Saul, printed in *Liberation Lite: The Roots of Recolonization in Southern Africa* (AWP: 2010), written in 2001, rues this shift in retrospect.
102. The subject of a future essay.

command-and-control operation, funded by foreign donors, immobile, and soon consumed by ancillary turmoil – yet still dedicated to basic virtues and human rights.

Acknowledgements

I would like to thank the University of Maryland and the American Philosophical Society of Philadelphia for financial support, John Soske and the organizers of the 'One Hundred Years of the ANC' conference in September, 2011, in Johannesburg; Denis Goldberg, Raymond Suttner, Hugh Macmillan, and my colleague Arthur Eckstein for read-throughs; and Hylton White and Natasha Erlank for support.

Appendix A: *Note on sources*

The defence's records of the Rivonia Trial held at the Cullen Library, and the Prosecution Records, including exhibits, as held by the South African National Archives in Pretoria (as the Yutar Papers), are used in this article. These include state witnesses' depositions recorded by the South African Police. Especially for the larger project of which this article is part, these texts, the testimony that the state elicited from witnesses at the Rivonia trial, supplies important source material. But under the 'Sabotage Act' of 27 June, 1962, witnesses were held in prison in *90-day periods of isolation*, confined to a small room with minimal human contact, and this three month period could simply be re-imposed. This material therefore consists of coerced confessions or statements made under duress, making the transcripts difficult and problematic as sources: only their most sceptical use is warranted. (Normally, these reports were destroyed by the police, but Yutar preserved his bounded editions of the original police reports with these witnesses' depositions. Denis Goldberg also comments on the problem of torture in an addendum to his book, *The Mission*.) There are times when accounts emerge which Yutar's prosecutorial team did not desire, such that with care the Rivonia trial transcripts can help determine what evidence can and can't be trusted (Wits, Cullen Library, Defence papers of the Rivonia Trial, AD 1844 Box 3 A12–A16, A 12.1, Bennet Nvuya Mashiyana's testimony; Berrange Cross notes; SANA, Yutar Papers, 385/26 (Vol 4); Sikumbuzo Njikelana, 797–799). One must be a better judge of testimony than the Rivonia magistrate, Q. de Wet, who turned a blind eye to torture. But if this material is read carefully, it can provide evidence about the struggle in the years covered here.

Armed and Trained: Nelson Mandela's 1962 Military Mission as Commander in Chief of Umkhonto we Sizwe and Provenance for his Buried Makarov Pistol

GARTH BENNEY WORTH

Sydney, Australia

Abstract

Firearms are inextricably linked to the history of South Africa's liberation struggle and experiences of decolonisation, liberation, and independence for many African countries. Firearms are often perceived as symbols of emancipation from colonial rule, and military leaders, such as Nelson Mandela, who commanded Umkhonto we Sizwe, are no exception, for he is associated with numerous handguns, military weapons and military ordnance during 1962, in particular to a Makarov pistol, originating from Ethiopia. This heritage item holding symbolic and historical value, Mandela claimed he buried at Liliesleaf farm in Johannesburg shortly before being captured in 1962. Although mentioned fleetingly in Nelson Mandela's autobiography Long Walk to Freedom, the provenance of and knowledge about his pistol and the circumstances under which he received it and how he subsequently buried it, together with ammunition and possibly an Ethiopian army uniform, are not widely known. This article details the process by which I established this provenance during 2004 to 2010, and contextualises Nelson Mandela's broader military activities in Africa, discussions he held with freedom fighters and military personnel in Ethiopia and Morocco, the type of military training he underwent, weapons he handled, and activities in South Africa upon his return, once armed and trained.

Introduction

Knowledge about Nelson Mandela burying his handgun at Liliesleaf farm, Rivonia, Johannesburg, emerged during December 1991, when Mandela revisited Liliesleaf, accompanied by Allister Sparks. Mandela enquired who lived on an adjacent property, 'I buried something there,' and then gestured with his trigger finger to indicate an arms cache.[1] Mandela subsequently revisited Liliesleaf in 2003 and asked Nicholas Wolpe, CEO of the Liliesleaf Trust, if he had found his 'gun'. When Wolpe enquired where this was buried, Mandela pointed towards some neighbouring residential properties, as before during 1991.[2]

In March 2004, Wolpe enquired if I had information about Mandela burying a 'gun' at Liliesleaf.[3] I did not and reread Mandela's memoir and biography to identify potential references to firearms and their burial at Liliesleaf. Mandela's memoir contains four references to possessing firearms. An 'old revolver' inherited from his father,[4] an air rifle at Liliesleaf in 1961;[5] an 'automatic pistol' with 200 rounds of ammunition given to him by Colonel Tadesse of the Ethiopian Army prior to returning to South Africa in July 1962;[6] and concealing a 'loaded revolver' in a car on 5 August 1962, when South Africa's Security Police Branch captured him.[7]

The three different weapon types were, an air-operated pellet gun, a magazine-fed semi-automatic pistol, and two cylinder loaded revolvers. My interim conclusion – Mandela would have known these weapon types, having undergone military training; hence he differentiated them.[8] His memoir relates returning to Liliesleaf in July 1962, wearing an Ethiopian army uniform.[9] As verbally claimed, he then buried his Ethiopian pistol and presumably the ammunition and possibly a uniform and later, when captured, possessed a revolver of unknown origin.

In 2005, during an informal discussion I had with Nelson Mandela at Liliesleaf, Mandela confirmed the provenance of his pistol, relating that he buried something important to him and the 'Ethiopians'. Mandela described his cache as, 'very valuable but dangerous,' squeezed his trigger finger with his arm outstretched to emulate firing a handgun and concluded that he hoped his cache is found, 'otherwise the Ethiopians will be disappointed.' Our discussion confirmed that his buried pistol is of Ethiopian provenance.[10]

This has historical significance – the information was not publicly known, yet offers historical understanding about Mandela's actions and activities during a key period in

1. As told to the author by Allister Sparks, November 2004 during which discussion Sparks related that Mandela said that he buried his cache about 50 paces from the Liliesleaf household kitchen. The initial report by Sparks of this discussion was released by Sparks to FORNEWS on 1 January 1992, a copy of which he gave me in November 2004.
2. As related to the author by the CEO of the Liliesleaf Trust, March 2004.
3. At that time I served on the Council of the Nelson Mandela National Museum, appointed by South Africa's national Minister of Arts, Culture, Science and Technology in April 2003. My consultancy Site Solutions ™ was about to undertake a research audit for the Liliesleaf Trust which commenced in 2004 and concluded in 2007. Various searches for the 'gun' ensued in 2004 and 2005, with an additional search in 2006 which was reported in the media.
4. NR. Mandela, *Long Walk to Freedom* (London: Abacus, 1994), 77.
5. *Ibid*, 335.
6. *Ibid*, 363.
7. *Ibid*, 373.
8. Or that Richard Stengel, Mandela's 'ghost writer' erred in describing the pistol as a revolver.
9. Mandela, *Long Walk to Freedom*, 369.
10. Discussion between the author and Nelson Mandela, 6 June 2005. I arranged this discussion with the Nelson Mandela Foundation with the aim of identifying any information about this firearm buried at Liliesleaf.

South Africa's history. With respect to Liliesleaf, his pistol forms a link between the farm and Mandela's role as Commander in Chief of Umkhonto we Sizwe, his African military mission, and the symbolic linkage of firearms to South Africa's liberation struggle and associated heritage of Liliesleaf.[11]

A literature review of Nelson Mandela's 1962 activities as Commander in Chief identified information gaps and inconsistencies while recent publications perpetuate myth and factual distortions. For example, a 2010 publication disregards Mandela's consistent oral history about burying a pistol at Liliesleaf, declaring this a 'puzzling claim for Mandela to make', while continuing popular notions that Mandela concealed his Ethiopian pistol while being captured that the police never found.[12] Mandela's memoir and Anthony Sampson's biography briefly mention certain military specifics, yet provide no detail of him burying a pistol and the weapons with which he trained, and little detail about the content of his discussions with military personnel in Ethiopia and Morocco.[13] However, Mandela's unpublished 1962 diary, journals and military notes offer insight into these intricacies, as does his oral history, which this article details.[14]

Other publications refer to road, rail and safe-house networks operated by the liberation movements in Bechuanaland.[15] Yet they do not integrate the role of Britain's Security Services into Mandela's Bechuanaland airlifts and additional assistance provided to Mandela in Bechuanaland, particularly on his return in July 1962, by a British aligned magistrate and security official, information alluded to in Mandela's memoir. In spaces of public culture, such as the Liliesleaf Museum, Mandela's Makarov pistol is described as Bulgarian made – incorrect, given that Bulgaria started manufacturing Makarov's around 1970.[16] Yet Mandela's buried weapon is currently sought. During August 2010, a South African media report relates that the search at Liliesleaf continues amid tight security.[17]

Consequently, this article offers provenance for Mandela's Makarov pistol which he claims he buried at Liliesleaf, his military experiences in Morocco and training by Ethiopian forces during 1962, while Commander in Chief. Included is a backdrop of certain activities by Britain's Security Service in Bechuanaland in relation to Mandela and other activities by South African intelligence during Mandela's 1962 Africa mission, together with additional information about his capture.

11. Following from my initial discussions with Wolpe in 2004, he then initiated a multi-disciplinary search for Mandela's pistol and ammunition at Liliesleaf from 2004 to 2006. Together with archaeologists and other specialists, we surveyed and excavated various areas, yet no weapons nor ammunition were found.

12. D.J. Smith, *Young Mandela* (London: Weidenfeld & Nicolson, 2010), 276.

13. Mandela, *Long Walk to Freedom*, and Sampson, A., *Mandela The Authorized Biography* (Jeppestown: Jonathan Ball, 1999).

14. I located copies of Mandela's 1962 writings, which include his diary and journal in a declassified file in South Africa's National Archives, Pretoria in 2007 and have used these as part of my source material for this article. Although some of this material is identical to that held in other archival collections, this material represents a separate collection. These works are typed transcripts of Mandela's original handwritten works, presumably made by the police after being seized at Liliesleaf in 1963. See National Archives of South Africa (hereafter NASA), TAB, WLD, CC 578, Trial of Mkwai, Kitson, Chiba, Mathews and Maharaj, 1964.

15. South African Democracy Education Trust, *The Road to Democracy in South Africa, vol. 1* (1960–1970) (Cape Town: Zebra, 2004).

16. Liliesleaf Museum exhibit, as viewed and photographed by the author on 21 March 2010.

17. Noseweek, *The Mystery of the Missing Mandela Makarov* (South Africa, August 2010), 18–21.

Nelson Mandela's Military Mission

In December 1961, the Pan-African Freedom Movement for East Central Africa (PAFMECA) invited the ANC to their 1962 Addis Ababa conference. On 3 January 1962, the ANC National Executive delegated Mandela and instructed him to discuss this with Chief Luthuli. His mission also required arranging political and economic support and military training for MK in recently independent African states. Mandela would link up with Oliver Tambo, who headed the ANC external mission, and explain the strategic shift of the ANC. Mandela was determined to boost the ANC's position to counteract Pan African Congress (PAC) 'propaganda'. His only reservation – a prior promise to remain in South Africa, yet his colleagues persuaded him to go.[18] On 8 January 1962, Mandela met Luthuli in Natal, who approved his mission. Returning to Johannesburg Mandela received his travel credentials from Duma Nokwe, Walter Sisulu, and Ahmed Kathrada.[19]

British-controlled Bechuanaland would form Mandela's exit from and re-entry point into South Africa.[20] Crossing over under his legend as David Motsamayi, Mandela would rendezvous with Joe Matthews, before flying to Tanganyika. A logistics committee finalised his transport, safe houses, and flight.[21] An intermediary chartered Captain Herbert Bartaune's aircraft based in Lobatse, for the airlift. Paid for with a bank draft from Dar es Salaam, Britain's Secret Intelligence Service (SIS) monitored this transaction.[22] British and South African intelligence activities provide a backdrop to Mandela's military mission and contextualise his activities; hence some detail about this is provided.

South Africa's declaration as a Republic justified to Britain a need for a parallel security structure in Bechuanaland.[23] Strategically, this formed part of Britain's 'double game' of balancing immediate interests, such as economic and military investments with the Republic, the economic dependence of the High Commission Territories on South Africa; and increasing risk exposure to negative reaction from newly independent former colonies due to Britain's South African policy (thus coming increasingly 'under fire') – versus longer term trends of changing political realities in Africa and southern Africa.[24] Sir John Maude, High Commissioner to South Africa, described this policy of 'reinsurance' as discreetly building contacts with liberation movement leaders, while not antagonising South Africa's ruling nationalists.[25] Operationally and tactically, this enabled closer observance of potential security issues within Bechuanaland, while simultaneously assisting organisations that would one day gain political power.

---

18. Mandela, *Long Walk to Freedom*, 342.
19. NASA, TAB, WLD, CC 578, Trial of Mkwai, Kitson, Chiba, Mathews and Maharaj, 1964, Exhibit R17.
20. Bechuanaland, Basutoland and Swaziland were then High Commission Territories.
21. Discussions between the author and Ahmed Kathrada, 2004. Kathrada related that with him on this committee were Joe Modise, Harold Wolpe, and possibly Wolfie Kodesh.
22. National Archives of United Kingdom (hereafter NAUK), DO 119/1478, Resident Commissioner to Secretary of State for the Colonies, London.
23. http://dx.doi.org/10.1080/02533950802078897 [accessed 23 January 2010], N. Parsons, 'The Pipeline: *Botswana's Reception of Refugees, 1956–68, Social Dynamics*, 34, 1, (2008), 17–32.
24. NAUK, CAB 114/119, Sir J. Maud to Lord Home, 14 May 1963. Britain was increasingly 'under fire' for its support of white minority states.
25. NAUK, FO 371/161886, Sir John Maude, Note for the Record, 23 October 1962.

British documents refer to setting up 'the pipeline' to enable prominent refugees to move through the Protectorate as fast as possible. The pipeline's operators included a handful of key colonial officers and one police officer reporting directly to Peter Fawcus, the Resident Commissioner. Fawcus in turn reported to Britain's Secret Intelligence Service (also known as MI6). This arrangement sidestepped the Protectorate's Special Branch who, linked to Britain's MI5, were seen as compromised, due to MI5's connections to Southern Rhodesia and South Africa's security establishment.[26] For example, after the Union's 1960 emergency declaration, the South African Police (SAP) Security Branch sought information through police channels about refugees and their activities in Bechuanaland. This was denied, so the SAP pursued steps for clandestine enquiries.[27] To circumvent them, SIS enabled their pipeline.[28]

This aerial pipeline supplemented road, rail, and safe-house networks established by Fish Keitseng and Joe Modise.[29] Operated by the liberation movements, they were also known as the 'road to freedom'.[30] The pipeline ran from Lobatse, via refuelling at Kasane, over-flew Northern Rhodesia to Mbeya, then to Dar es Salaam. It operated as a mini-airline called Bechuanaland Air Safari's, later Bechuanaland Air Services, which Bartaune set up as a Charter Company and, in 1966, was acquired by Botswana National Airways.[31] Financed by Bechuanaland's government (possibly with SIS funds) and Lobatse meat millionaire Cyril Hurwitz, Bartaune (a former Luftwaffe pilot) based himself as resident director at Lobatse.[32]

That the liberation movement's refugee route formed a key SAP intelligence need is supported by a prior Bechuanaland Central Intelligence Committee (CIC) report dated September 1960. This records Bartaune as a SAP Security Branch target. Logical – Bartaune was a key pipeline operator.[33] For example, in February 1961, the SAP Mafeking Security Branch officer visited Lobatse and questioned Bartaune about his recent airlift of F Duncan, VJG Matthews and others. Bartaune gave an affidavit and was warned that he may be summonsed for court proceedings.[34] Continued monitoring of Bartaune may have ramified on Mandela – as Bartaune later airlifted him.

Security Branch inroads continued. 'On 11 October 1961 Sgt PIO, Security Branch Mafeking visited Andrew Rybicki, a pilot employed by Bartaune in Lobatse. It is firmly

26. http://dx.doi.org/10.1080/02533950802078897 [accessed 23 January 2010], Parsons, 'The Pipeline'. One of MI5's key roles during this period was that, 'The Service also kept a close watch on the activities of the Communist Party of Great Britain (CPGB). Various individuals associated with the Communist movement were monitored in the hope of uncovering any connections with espionage or subversive activity;' See https://www.mi5.gov.uk/output/late-1940s-and-1950s.html [accessed 20 January 2010].
27. NAUK, DO 157/9, Bechuanaland Central Intelligence Committee Reports, July 1960–October 1961.
28. http://dx.doi.org/10.1080/02533950802078897 [accessed 23 January 2010], Parsons, 'The Pipeline'.
29. S.M. Ndlovu, 'Heritage Routes for the Liberated South Africans: Using Oral History to Reconstruct Unsung Heroes and Heroines' Routes into Exile in the 1960s', Historia, 47, 2 (2002), 485–489.
30. South African Democracy Education Trust., The Road to Democracy, 413.
31. http://books.google.com.au/books?id = KBmGpaD36cMC [accessed 30 January 2010], B.R. Guttery, Encyclopaedia of African Airlines (Jefferson, NC: McFarland, 1998).
32. http://dx.doi.org/10.1080/02533950802078897 [accessed 23 January 2010]; Parsons, 'The Pipeline'.
33. NAUK, DO 157/9, Bechuanaland Central Intelligence Committee Reports, July 1960–October 1961.
34. Ibid.

believed that PIO recruited Rybicki as an informer.'[35] Shortly thereafter, Colonel Steytler and Major Buys entered Bechuanaland from South Africa under false names. They met Rybicki, whose role (the documents suggest) was to forward information about refugee airlifts that he flew, some of which Joe Matthews organised.[36]

Bechuanaland's CIC key intelligence needs were: the activities of internal political parties, communism, and the recruiting of students by so-called 'iron curtain' countries, labour and union activities, tribal affairs, race relations, political and subversive activities in schools, the activities of the South African Police, political refugees from South Africa and South West Africa, and any subversive activities by individuals.[37]

Joe Matthews was monitored by British Intelligence and the SAP. In 1962, British Intelligence opened a file on Matthews who resided in Basutoland (Lesotho). Classified Top Secret, its documents are marked UK Eyes Only, meaning that Britain did not share this information with strategic allies such as the United States and Canada.[38] Mandela's 1962 file, on the other hand, was classified Secret, one security grading lower than Matthews.[39] None of Mandela's file contents is marked UK Eyes Only, meaning information was possibly shared with Britain's strategic allies, which included the CIA.[40] This may have influenced Mandela's subsequent capture, for the CIA regularly shared information with South Africa's security establishment and are suggested in the literature as role players in his capture.[41]

British Intelligence tracked some of Matthews's prior overseas trips and attempted to ascertain his source of funds and payments made for air charter travel, within South Africa and Swaziland. In November 1960, they monitored him in Moscow, Prague, Tanganyika, and the United Kingdom, among other states.[42]

A January 1961, CIC report records,

> The interest shown by VJG Matthews in this territory is viewed with grave concern The planning and financial assistance behind his recent visit to London, Moscow, the East

35. NAUK, DO 157/9, Bechuanaland Central Intelligence Committee Reports, July 1960–Oct 1961. PIO is an acronym used in the original report to refer to the SAP Security Branch Sgt, presumably used to protect the Sgt's identity, which remains unidentified.
36. NAUK, DO 157/9, Bechuanaland Central Intelligence Committee Reports, July 1960–Oct 1961. Sifiso Mxolisi Ndlovu describes a similar incident that occurred at the same time in 1961 which Ndlovu cites from the Botswana archives and which records that 'information from three different sources in Bechuanaland reported that between the 8 and 11 December 1961 two South African Police Special Branch agents were operating in the areas of Palapye and Serowe. When one of them was asked what the SAP special branch were doing in the protectorate, they replied that they "were going to arrest refugees". They were traveling in a Johannesburg registered car'. See Ndlovu, 'Heritage routes for the liberated Africa', 502.
37. NAUK, DO 157/9, Bechuanaland Central Intelligence Committee Reports, July 1960–October 1961.
38. NAUK, DO 119/1229, Vincent Joe Matthews (VJ), 4 July 1962–4 October 1962.
39. NAUK, DO 119/1478, Nelson Mandela, 1962.
40. Central Intelligence Agency.
41. J. Sanders, *Apartheid's Friends. The Rise and Fall of South Africa's Secret Service* (London: John Murray (Publishers), 2006), 17–20. The information about the CIA's role in Mandela's capture is inconclusive, based on media reports many years after the event and attributed to revelations by American diplomats working in the Republic at that time and which could be disinformation.
42. NAUK, DO 119/1229, Vincent Joe Matthews (VJ), 4 July 1962–4 October 1962.

African territories and Ghana show that he is a force to be reckoned with and those who have met him have been greatly impressed by his personal confidence and political knowledge.[43]

On 11 January 1962, at 15h00, Mandela arrived in Lobatse.[44] As his flight was delayed, he stayed with Fish Keitseng in Peleng village.[45] The next day the local Immigration Officer arrived to inform Mandela that his flight was cancelled and enquired about his plans. Mandela had the 'shock of his life' when told that apart from handling issues of immigration, the agent headed Bechuanaland's Special Branch. He offered Mandela a government house to prevent South African agents abducting him but Mandela politely declined. He preferred 'the warm affection' of his hosts and later met with Mr Motsete, president of the Bechuanaland People's Party (BPP), and Gaboesele.[46]

On 13 January 1962, Mandela held discussions with Motsete, Gaboesele and Keitseng. They decided to hide their movements from the Immigration Officer and received reports that SAP Security Branch 'were around'. On 17 January 1962, the Immigration Officer revisited and appealed that on no account should Mandela venture about, due to abduction risks – no idle threat. In 1960, when Oliver Tambo stayed in Lobatse he narrowly escaped two South African agents intent on chloroforming him before smuggling him back to South Africa.[47] However, Mandela's impression was that the British agent was attempting to prevent him meeting members of the BPP, which he had done.[48]

On 19 January 1962 at 3pm, Bartaune airlifted Mandela into the pipeline.[49] Signals traffic from Britain's Cape Town High Commissioner reveals that British intelligence identified Mandela's Bechuanaland arrival on 13 January 1962, with £600 – the day of his first official visit in Peleng. They correctly reported Mandela and Matthews's departure and, that although South Africa's Security Branch (SB) was unaware of Mandela's presence in Peleng, an informant reported to SB on Mandela's flight details.[50]

On 21 January 1962, Mandela reached Dar es Salaam.[51] He met with Julius Nyerere, who agreed to facilitate a meeting with Emperor Haile Selassie and suggested Ethiopia as an option for MK military training,[52] yet also suggested that the ANC suspend armed

---

43. NAUK, DO 157/9, Bechuanaland Central Intelligence Committee Reports, July 1960–October 1961.
44. NASA, TAB, WLD, CC 578. Trial of Mkwai, Kitson, Chiba, Mathews and Maharaj, 1964, Exhibit R17.
45. NAUK, DO 119/1478, High Commissioner Cape Town to Secretary of State for the Colonies, London.
46. Gaboesele is Mandela's original spelling, See NASA, TAB, WLD, CC 578, Trial of Mkwai, Kitson, Chiba, Mathews and Maharaj, 1964, Exhibit R17. Mandela's autobiography refers to Professor K.T. Motsete, see Mandela, *Long Walk to Freedom*, 343.
47. L. Callinicos, *Oliver Tambo Beyond the Engeli Mountains* (Southern Africa: David Phillips Publishers, 2004) 258–259.
48. NASA, TAB, WLD, CC 578, Trial of Mkwai, Kitson, Chiba, Mathews and Maharaj, 1964, Exhibit R17.
49. Joe Matthews arrived the day before and flew out with Mandela.
50. NAUK, DO 119/1478, Nelson Mandela, 1962. High Commissioner to the Secretary of State for Colonies and the Resident Commissioner Bechuanaland.
51. NASA, TAB, WLD, CC 578, Trial of Mkwai, Kitson, Chiba, Mathews and Maharaj, 1964, Exhibit R17. See also, Mandela, *Long Walk to Freedom*, 345–346.
52. NASA, TAB, WLD, CC 578, Trial of Mkwai, Kitson, Chiba, Mathews and Maharaj, 1964, Exhibit R13.

struggle until Robert Sobukwe's release from prison.[53] Mandela and Matthews then flew to Accra. Mandela received his Ethiopian visa on 29 January 1962, and flew with Tambo to Addis Ababa.[54] The Ethiopian's anti-fascist campaign always inspired Mandela who studied the terrain below, thinking about guerrilla forces resisting Mussolini's army from the forests.[55]

In Addis Ababa they met ambassadors and leaders of political parties.[56] On 3 February 1962, Mandela addressed the conference,[57] his speech, carefully prepared with advice from both Tambo and Robert Resha, outlined the history of South Africa's freedom struggle. He thanked the delegates for their pressure against the apartheid regime and contextualised the birth of MK.[58] Further meetings and support pledges for the ANC followed.[59]

However, Mandela learnt that the ANC alliance with South Africa's Communist Party and Indian political parties unsynchronised them with mainstream African nationalism. Two perceptions prevailed – the PAC represented African interests while the ANC, excessively influenced by white communists was essentially their stooge. To worsen matters, some viewed Chief Luthuli's recent Nobel Peace Prize as the West having bought the Chief. This theme – being out of step – was a matter that Mandela believed he had to address.[60]

On 4 February 1962, Mandela visited the Debra Zain Air Force Training Centre and met with the Ethiopian military. Three days later he visited a camp outside Addis Ababa and witnessed a 'most exciting' military parade with Emperor Selassie taking the salute. Connections with Ethiopia's political and military establishment quickly formed. On 8 February 1962, the conference closed. Emperor Selassie received the ANC delegation. The next day unfolded discussing the SA situation with Ali Ketema Yifru, Ethiopia's Minister of Foreign Affairs. On 10 February 1962, a final meeting followed with Lt. General Kebbede Guebre, Chief of Staff for the Imperial Forces of Ethiopia.[61] Guebre indicated

---

53. Frene Ginwala received a telephone message from the Commissioner at Mbeya – could she authenticate two ANC people just in from South Africa? Matthews identified himself – Ginwala gave the commissioner the go ahead. Shortly afterwards, on 21 January, Mandela arrived at Ginwala's office. See Callinicos, L., *Oliver Tambo Beyond the Engeli Mountains,* 283.

54. NASA, TAB, CC 578, Trial of Mkwai, Kitson, Chiba, Mathews and Maharaj, 1964, Exhibit R17.

55. Mandela, *Long Walk to Freedom,* 348.

56. Foreign representatives included the Ambassador for Guinea and Algerian representatives. This is the first recorded instance of Mandela meeting with the Algerian's who would soon play a key role in his mission, see NASA, TAB, WLD, CC 578, Trial of Mkwai, Kitson, Chiba, Mathews and Maharaj, 1964, Exhibit R17.

57. NASA, TAB, WLD, CC 578, Trial of Mkwai, Kitson, Chiba, Mathews and Maharaj, 1964, Exhibit R17.

58. An excerpt of Mandela's speech with an overview of the PAFMECA proceedings was included in a report to the British cabinet on 20 February 1962 by Britain's Joint Intelligence Committee, see NAUK, CAB 179. 8.

59. With respect to military assistance, the following pledges were received: Egypt agreed to train seven MK members, Algeria and Morocco any number, and Ethiopia 20 and perhaps more. The matter was also raised with Mali, Guinea and Ghana, see NASA, TAB, WLD, CC 578, Trial of Mkwai, Kitson, Chiba, Mathews and Maharaj, 1964, Exhibit R13.

60. NASA, TAB, WLD, CC 578, Trial of Mkwai, Kitson, Chiba, Mathews and Maharaj, 1964, Exhibit R13, see also, Mandela, *Long Walk to Freedom,* 352.

61. NASA, TAB, WLD, CC 578, Trial of Mkwai, Kitson, Chiba, Mathews and Maharaj, 1964, Exhibit R17.

that Ethiopia could take 20 recruits and perhaps more, train them at Kolfe (Colifi) and arrange for a plane to collect them.[62] The Ethiopian's also gave £5,000 to the ANC.[63]

On 12 February 1962, Mandela flew to Cairo with Tambo and Robert Resha.[64] They met ambassadors from Cuba, Czechoslovakia, China, the German Democratic Republic, Indonesia, and Egyptian government representatives. Cuba and Egypt pledged full support.[65] Tambo flew to London, Mandela and Resha to Tunisia where President Bourguiba offered military training and £5,000 for weapons.[66]

Mandela's mission was not just about fund-raising and securing support. As MK's Commander-in-Chief he needed to learn from people who had fought a colonial power for independence, using political struggle and military action. As, 'the situation in Algeria was the closest model to our own in that the rebels faced a large white settler community that ruled the indigenous majority',[67] Mandela and Resha landed in Casablanca on 6 March 1962. They met Dr Abdelkrim Khatib, Morocco's Minister of African Affairs,[68] Jacques Verges, Khatib's personal adviser, who played a role in providing Moroccan financial and military support,[69] and freedom fighters from Angola, Mozambique, Algeria, and Cape Verde.[70]

Discussions on 14 March 1962, with Mario Andrade and Emmanuel Lima about Angola's NLA proved 'fascinating'.[71] Dr Mustafa, head of the Algerian mission in

62. NASA, TAB, WLD, CC 578, Trial of Mkwai, Kitson, Chiba, Mathews and Maharaj, 1964, Exhibit R13. As a prior Colonel, Guebre served as Chief Commander of the Ethiopian Army Contingent to the United Nations Mission during the Korean War: see http://www.tigrai.org/News/Articles1/Major-Nega.html [accessed 30 January 2010]. Two months after meeting with Mandela, Guebre led the Ethiopian Army contingent in the Congo, until 1964, as part of the United Nations intervention: see http://www.un.org/Depts/DPKO/Missions/onucF.html [accessed 30 January 2010].

63. Donated during Mandela's first or second trip to Ethiopia, see NASA, TAB, WLD, CC 578, Trial of Mkwai, Kitson, Chiba, Mathews and Maharaj, 1964, Exhibit R13.

64. NASA, TAB, WLD, CC 578, Trial of Mkwai, Kitson, Chiba, Mathews and Maharaj, 1964, Exhibit R17. See also, Mandela, *Long Walk to Freedom*, 353.

65. NASA, TAB, WLD, CC 578, Trial of Mkwai, Kitson, Chiba, Mathews and Maharaj, 1964, Exhibit R17.

66. Mandela, *Long Walk to Freedom*, 354.

67. *Ibid.*, 354–355.

68. Dr Khatib was the former head of Morocco's Army of Liberation before Moroccan independence in 1956. See C.M. Henry, 'The Dialectics of Political Islam in North Africa', *Middle East Policy*, 14, 4 (2007), 91.

69. NASA, TAB, WLD, CC 578, Trial of Mkwai, Kitson, Chiba, Mathews and Maharaj, 1964, Exhibit R17. According to various sources, Jacques Vergès was born 1925 in Thailand and raised in Réunion. He joined the Reunionese Communist Party and in 1942, the Free French Forces under de Gaulle, and participated in anti-Nazi resistance. After the Second World War, Vergès studied law at the University of Paris. In 1949, Vergès became president of the AEC (Association for Colonial Students) and in the 1950s worked for a while in Prague in a Soviet-led international student union movement under Victor Shelepin (later KGB head under Nikita Khrushchev). During Algeria's freedom struggle, Vergès defended many accused of terrorism by the French government. To limit Vergès's success at defending Algerian clients, he was sentenced to two months in jail in 1960 and temporary lost his license to officially practise law for anti-state activities. He apparently disappeared in the 1970s – some accounts have him working with Pol Pot in Cambodia – after the Khmer Rouge takeover in 1975. In 1979, he returned to practise law as a member of the Paris bar. His clients included various figures such as Holocaust denier Roger Garaudy, Nazi war criminal Klaus Barbie (1987), and international terrorist Ilich Ramírez Sánchez (aka Carlos the Jackal) (1994) If indeed the same person, Jacques Vergès is reported in 2002 to have offered to represent former Serbian President Slobodan Milošević, although Milošević declined any legal advice and in 2003 offered to defend Saddam Hussein. Tariq Aziz assembled a team that included Jacques Vergès; however, the

Morocco, briefed Mandela on Algeria's struggle against the French.[72] Mustafa explained that the original objective was defeating the French through military action, as in Indo-China, and that settlement by negotiation was not visualised.[73] They then realised that a purely military victory was impossible and resorted to guerrilla warfare, designed not for military victory but to unleash political and economic forces.[74] Mustafa stressed that the, 'conception of the struggle when you begin will determine failure or success of the revolution'.

Mustafa outlined that a key part of the general plan is military action, followed by the political objective and then psychological warfare. Tactics are governed by strategy and cover the political consciousness of the masses of the people and mobilisation of international allies – the aim being to destroy the legality of the government to institute that of the people. The political organisation must be in total control of the people while the soldiers, 'must live among the people like fish in the water'. The aim – the ANC's forces should develop and grow while, 'those of the enemy should disintegrate'.[75] International opinion, Mustafa said, 'is sometimes worth more than a fleet of jet fighters'.[76] Mandela described Mustafa's advice as 'brilliant'.[77]

Then it was the turn of Algeria's National Liberation Front (Front de Libération Nationale – FLN), to give Mandela a taste of their front line. On 18 March 1962, Mustafa sent Mandela and Resha to Oujda, the Moroccan headquarters for the National Liberation Army (Armée de Libération Nationale – ALN), the FLN's military arm.[78] They met with Si Abdelhanna, ALN head of the political section. Also present were Si Jamal, Captain Mohammed Smain Lamari, Noereddine Djoudi and Aberraahman.[79]

Hussein family declined his services. In 2008, he represented former Khmer Rouge head of state Khieu Samphan at Cambodia's genocide tribunal. The media have sensationalised him with the sobriquet, 'the Devil's advocate'. See http://www.netglimse.com/celebs/pages/jacques_verges/index.shtml [accessed 21 January 2010] and http://www.independent.co.uk/news/world/europe/stasi-files-say-verges-worked-with-carlos-1384202.html [accessed 21 January 2010].

70.   NASA, TAB, WLD, CC 578, Trial of Mkwai, Kitson, Chiba, Mathews and Maharaj, 1964, Exhibit R17. Angolan leaders included MPLA President Mario de Andrade and José Eduardo dos Santos, President of Angola. The NLA, presumably refers to the National Liberation Army, subsequently called *Exército Popular de Libertação de Angola* – EPLA and in 1974 was renamed FAPLA.

71.   NASA, TAB, WLD, CC 578, Trial of Mkwai, Kitson, Chiba, Mathews and Maharaj, 1964, Exhibit R17.

72.   Mandela, *Long Walk to Freedom*, 355. Mandela spells Dr Mustafa's name in his journal and diary as Dr Mustafai, see NASA, TAB, WLD, CC 578, Trial of Mkwai, Kitson, Chiba, Mathews and Maharaj, 1964, Exhibits R16 and R17.

73.   NASA, TAB, WLD, CC 578, Trial of Mkwai, Kitson, Chiba, Mathews and Maharaj, 1964, Exhibit R16.

74.   Mandela, *Long Walk to Freedom*, 355.

75.   NASA, TAB, WLD, CC 578, Trial of Mkwai, Kitson, Chiba, Mathews and Maharaj, 1964, Exhibit R16.

76.   Mandela, *Long Walk to Freedom,* 355.

77.   NASA, TAB, WLD, CC 578, Trial of Mkwai, Kitson, Chiba, Mathews and Maharaj, 1964, Exhibit R17.

78.   Mandela, *Long Walk to Freedom*, 355.

79.   NASA, TAB, WLD, CC 578, Trial of Mkwai, Kitson, Chiba, Mathews and Maharaj, 1964, Exhibit R17. Noereddine Djoudi later served as Algeria's ambassador to post apartheid South Africa. Mandela refers to Captain Larbi, when in fact his name was Mohammed Lamari, see http://www.timesonline.co.uk/tol/comment/obituaries/article2538907.ece [accessed 21 January 2010]. Major-General Smain Lamari, Algeria's former intelligence chief, was born June 1941 and died 28 August 2007. Lamari reportedly joined the rebel National Liberation Army (ALN) in 1961. By the end of the 1960s he entered Algeria's intelligence services, rose to take charge of internal security, and as counter-espionage specialist became

A general discussion on South Africa ensued. At 4 p.m., accompanied by Djoudi and another officer, Mandela and Resha were driven to the Zegangan training base, situated in former Spanish Morocco, where they toured an Armaments Museum.[80] After dinner they visited the soldier's theatre, listened to music, and watched two sketches depicting propaganda against French rule. The next morning, discussions continued. After lunch, the first recorded instance of Mandela using military firearms occurred. He fired a German Mauser rifle and machine gun, being 'warmly complimented on accuracy'.[81]

The 21 March 1962 started with a visit to the ALN printing works and transmission headquarters in Oujda. Accompanied by two officers they drove to Boubker, visiting the heavily guarded HQ of the Northern Division battalion. After lunch, they proceeded to a battalion forward HQ position on the Algerian border, and entered their dugouts.[82] Using field glasses, Mandela watched some French troops across the border and imagined looking at uniformed South African Defence Force (SADF) soldiers.[83] Mandela was also moved by the visible distress of the numerous refugees around their military position.[84]

After returning to Oujda, a discussion commenced inside Headquarters at 6.30 p.m. around four topics:[85]

(a) the relationship between the ALN inside and outside of Algeria;
(b) the structure of the ALN inside Algeria;
(c) French tactics to destroy the ALN;
(d) the relationship between Sabot and G Operations.[86]

Capain Lamari flagged three additional key points initially not included for discussion:

1. The question of political control of the organisation now preparing for activities (presumably MK). Lamari stressed that in their experience they, 'did not start their own revolution before they had achieved unity of intent – the establishment of the front of national liberation which was a front of individuals not organisations. Organisations were called upon to announce publicly that they had dissolved (but) the Algerian Communist Party refused to do so. Thorough preparation and unity is required before starting a revolution – timing is critical – events must link and create psychological impact and propaganda capital'.[87] Lamari continued that Fidel

---

one of the most influential figures in the 'regime'. He was part of the tight-knit group of senior generals, known collectively as 'le pouvoir', who have been the main source of power in Algeria since independence in 1962. He played a lead role in combating an Islamist insurgency by 'hijacking power', and later was instrumental in negotiations which brought an end to fierce fighting in 2000, while also backing Abdelaziz Bouteflika's rise to the presidency.

80. A collection of ALN armaments including weapons used during the 1 November 1954 uprising and the latest equipment.
81. NASA, TAB, WLD, CC 578, Trial of Mkwai, Kitson, Chiba, Mathews and Maharaj, 1964, Exhibit R16.
82. *Ibid.*
83. Mandela, *Long Walk to Freedom*, 355.
84. NASA, TAB, WLD, CC 578, Trial of Mkwai, Kitson, Chiba, Mathews and Maharaj, 1964, Exhibit R16.
85. *Ibid.*
86. *Ibid.*, as described in Exhibit R16 – this refers to sabotage and guerilla operations.
87. NASA, TAB, WLD, CC 578, Trial of Mkwai, Kitson, Chiba, Mathews and Maharaj, 1964, Exhibit R16.

Castro had apparently stated that Cuba's revolution lost tremendously in terms of time and manpower because of its failure to achieve unity of all parties before the start was made. The initiative must be seized at the beginning which then forces the enemy to adjust their tactics and not pursue their own.

2. The country's elite must be made to realise that the masses of the people, however poor and illiterate, are the country's most important investment. In all activities and operations there should be a thorough fusion of the intelligentsia and the masses of the people – peasants and labourers, workers in the city and so forth. Some of the ALN's best strategists had no prior military experience, so, 'we must seek the support of the entire population with a perfect balance of social classes'.[88]

3. In relation to military action,

the masses of the people must be made to realise that political action such as strikes, boycotts and similar demonstrations are ineffective as solitary tactics. Actions must be accepted as the primary and most essential form of political activity.[89]

Sabotage seeks to destroy the enemy's economy whilst guerrilla operations are intended to sap the strength of the enemies troops... Whilst it is important to have your people trained by friendly countries, this should only be part of the plan. The essential point to grasp is to produce your own experts who will establish training centres either inside or on the borders of the country.[90]

The discussions continued until 2 a.m. the following day.[91]

On 23 March 1962, they met Jacques Verges, 'our friend' in Rabat, who hinted, 'that all our demands will be met, even if NOT fully'.[92] At 8 p.m. they returned to Oujda, accompanied by Verges and Nicanor from Cameroon.[93] The next day Colonel Sieman showed them around. Group photographs were taken.[94] That evening they met Ben Bella at a banquet. On 25 March 1962, they attended, with the Niger and Cameroonian delegates, Ben Bella's inspection of a Guard of Honour.

On 26 March 1962, discussions ensued with the heads of the ALN and officers of the political department.[95] However, Mandela remained influenced long afterwards by advice from Algeria's military commander Houari Boumedienne, who later seized power from Ben Bella. He advised that the purpose of armed struggle should not be to overthrow the apartheid government by force. Rather, the ANC should use this tactic to unleash broader

---

88. *Ibid.*
89. *Ibid.*
90. *Ibid.*
91. NASA, TAB, WLD, CC 578, Trial of Mkwai, Kitson, Chiba, Mathews and Maharaj, 1964, Exhibit R17.
92. *Ibid.* These demands were financial and military support. £3,000 was given to the ANC while Mandela was in Morocco and another £7,000 on 1 May 1962 in Accra on 29 April 1962, when Mandela met with the head of the Algerian Mission, Mr Tewfrik Bouattoura. See NASA, TAB, WLD, CC 578, Trial of Mkwai, Kitson, Chiba, Mathews and Maharaj, 1964, Exhibits R13 and R17.
93. A second car travelling behind contained Andrade and Djibo Bakary of the Sewabe Party Niger, see TAB, WLD, CC 578, Trial of Mkwai, Kitson, Chiba, Mathews and Maharaj, 1964, Exhibit R17.
94. Mandela's diary reference to Colonel Sieman in his diary may be a typing error made by the police who transcribed in his writings that Captain Lamari was also known as Smain Lamari: see http://www.timesonline.co.uk/tol/comment/obituaries/article2538907.ece [accessed 21 January 2010].
95. NASA, TAB, WLD, CC 578, Trial of Mkwai, Kitson, Chiba, Mathews and Maharaj, 1964, Exhibit R17.

political forces which would force the government to the negotiating table.[96] That night they returned to Rabat, met with Dr Khatib, and finalised their mission.[97]

However, the South African Police knew of Mandela's activities in Morocco, particularly the content of some of his discussions in Rabat with Dr Khatib, Jacques Verges, and others during 6–13 March 1962. The South African Brussels based ambassador ran a secret yet reliable source, a former SS officer living in Spain, who in turn handled a Moroccan-based agent.[98] In a Top Secret dispatch to the Secretary of Foreign Affairs the Ambassador, while acknowledging the unsavoury past of this SS officer, guaranteed the integrity of his information and that of his Moroccan-based agent. These two spies reported that the Algerians would dispatch a number of highly trained saboteurs to Dar es Salaam to train locals in sabotage skills for operations in Mozambique and possibly South Africa.[99] While in Rabat, Mandela did discuss Dar es Salaam. When a Moroccan official promised facilities for military training, offered to airlift recruits from Dar es Salaam and asked Mandela, 'where do you want us to send the weapons?' Mandela replied, 'Dar es Salaam'.[100]

On the 28 March 1962, Mandela flew to Mali, then through various states such as, Sierra Leone, Liberia, Ghana and Nigeria. Varying offers of support were pledged, the largest from Nigeria.[101] On 7 May 1962, Oliver Tambo joined Mandela in Accra. In Senegal President Senghor provided Mandela with a diplomatic passport and paid their airfares from Dakar to Britain for a 10-day visit.

British immigration officers were initially hostile, unconvinced by Mandela's legend of David Motsamayi visiting Britain to write a book on the evolution of political thought in Africa, then allowed him through. Mandela later met Yusuf Dadoo and Vella Pillay and informed them that the ANC had to project itself as an independent force, represented by Africans at international conferences.[102] Firmly, he told Dadoo, this was not a departure from ANC policy, rather, an unbundling of being stuck in a nebulous image that appeared to represent everyone, in effect a break with recent ANC policy – and cross Congress cooperation. He visited the Tambo family and met with friends, editors, and leaders of the labour and liberal parties.[103]

96. Sampson, *Mandela The Authorized Biography*, 166.
97. NASA, TAB, WLD, CC 578, Trial of Mkwai, Kitson, Chiba, Mathews and Maharaj, 1964, Exhibit R13.
98. NASA, BTS, 109/7, Training of Saboteurs, Top Secret dispatch, Brussels Ambassador to Secretary of Foreign Affairs, 13 March 1962.
99. *Ibid.*
100. Smith, *Young Mandela*, 257.
101. Liberia gave Mandela $5,000, with an additional $400 for personal travel expenses, see Mandela, *Long Walk to Freedom*, 357 (Mandela's notes in Exhibit R13 state that Liberia gave £2,000). Guinea gave an unrecorded amount, see Mandela, *Long Walk to Freedom*, 358. Nigeria gave £10,000, see NASA, TAB, WLD, CC 578, Trial of Mkwai, Kitson, Chiba, Mathews and Maharaj, 1964, Exhibit R13.
102. British intelligence knew that David Motsamayi was Mandela's pseudonym and legend before he arrived in the UK; see NAUK, DO 119. 1478, Nelson Mandela, 1962.
103. Mandela, *Long Walk to Freedom*, 360. He also sought out literature on guerrilla warfare, which was available in London.

Ethiopia – Armed and Trained

On 26 June 1962, Tambo and Mandela arrived in Addis Ababa. Two days later Mandela became the guest of the Presidential Emergency Force[104] to undergo six months military training.[105] At Kolfe[106] Mandela met his instructors, Colonel Biru Tadesse, Colonel G.E. Bekele, and Lieutenant Befikadu Wondomu.[107] Tadesse and Befikadu played key roles in training Mandela and given their military ranks and Mandela's descriptions as to their instruction, an analysis of his training is possible.

Lieutenant Befikadu, 'an experienced soldier had fought with the underground against the Italians', and focused on Mandela's practical/tactical training.[108] The regimen was strenuous: 'we trained from 8 a.m. until 1 p.m. broke for a shower and lunch, and then again from 2 to 4 p.m. From 4 p.m. into the evening I was lectured on military science by Colonel Tadesse.'[109] On 29 June 1962, Befikadu, started with demolitions training, differentiating between hot and cold demolition.[110] For example, hot demolition explodes and transforms into fire (TNT), as opposed to cold demolition methods, such as:[111]

- throwing oil on roads and felling trees to hinder vehicles;
- cutting telephone wires and communication networks;
- severing electricity lines by throwing wire over and pulling them down;
- inserting sugar or water into fuel tanks and puncturing tyres;
- breaking bridges, burning houses and stations;
- stabbing the enemy and using judo.

Befikadu outlined two demolition systems – a detonating system good for attack and pursuit, versus an electrical system ideal for defence, while detonating chains included TNT mines. Four types of detonators were available – regular, electric, electrical delayed, and chemical. Regarding igniters, Befikadu detailed six types: matches followed by friction, pull, side pull, pressure, and pressure release igniters. As for fuse types, these included, safety, instantaneous, and detonating cord.

Tadesse lectured Mandela on how to create a guerilla force, command an army, and enforce discipline.[112] Tadesse detailed the four-tiered organisational structure of an Ethiopian infantry battalion, starting with a 10-man section as its tactical core.[113] Building upwards, Tadesse then outlined sections and platoons, then the organisation of an infantry company comprising of three platoons. Instruction about a battalion followed, comprising

104. NASA, TAB, WLD, CC 578, Trial of Mkwai, Kitson, Chiba, Mathews and Maharaj, 1964, Exhibits R11 and Exhibit 17.
105. Mandela, *Long Walk to Freedom*, 362.
106. *Ibid.*
107. NASA, TAB, WLD, CC 578, Trial of Mkwai, Kitson, Chiba, Mathews and Maharaj, 1964, Exhibits R11 and Exhibit 17.
108. Mandela, *Long Walk to Freedom*, 362.
109. *Ibid.*
110. NASA, TAB, WLD, CC 578, Trial of Mkwai, Kitson, Chiba, Mathews and Maharaj, 1964, Exhibit R11.
111. *Ibid.*
112. Mandela, *Long Walk to Freedom*, 363.
113. NASA, TAB, WLD, CC 578, Trial of Mkwai, Kitson, Chiba, Mathews and Maharaj, 1964, Exhibit R11.

three rifle companies and one support company, including all weapons deployed by these four hierarchies – rifles, sub-machine guns, machine guns, mortars, hand grenades, bazookas, anti tank and anti-aircraft weapons; and the supporting provisioning and medical services.

Necessary conventional warfare training, considering that MK would confront the SADF, which after the Second World War was structured along a conventional order of battle hierarchy. A case of dual instruction – learning this organizational structure familiarized Mandela with the SADF, which in 1962, did not field specialist counter insurgency/guerilla warfare capabilities.

Fire and movement in attack, retreat and pursuit modes was discussed along with using landmines to halt enemy forces attacking defensive positions and concentrating fire, versus concentrating force. With options for retreat, Mandela noted that it was 'Good to lose time than life'.[114] Lessons included infantry field craft – tiger crawling, monkey walking, frog walk, night movement, and cat or child crawling.

Mandela learnt 'about demolition and mortar firing... how to make small bombs and mines – and how to avoid them'. His military experience began moulding him into a soldier. He 'began to think as a soldier thinks'.[115] At 9 a.m. on 30 June 1962, he practised live demolitions and being on the range[116] probably fired weapons with which he had trained. His Sunday 1 July 1962, notes include firearm details, the following headings are Mandela's exact words:[117]

- **7.92 m.m. Chechoslovak**
  A five-round magazine-fed bolt action rifle, accurate to 400 metres firing 250 shots per hour. I believe Mandela referred to the Czechoslovakian 7.92 mm Mauser rifle, identical to the German Mauser he fired at Zegangan.
- **American Rifle**
  Mandela described an air-cooled, gas blowback, 8-round magazine-fed infantry rifle, weighing 9.5 lbs without bayonet. Muzzle length 24 inches, caliber 0.30, accurate to 500 yards with a range of 3,500 yards, this is the American M1 Garand rifle.
- **60**
  Mandela's description of this weapon is cryptic.
  60
  960
  4 rounds inside like the rifle (check)
  There are 2 kinds of trigger.
  To pull first trigger you need 4.5 lbs of weight. Second 7.5
  Muzzle – pipe
  Cover smoke
  Tying wood and pipe.
  Pulling bolt. Backward.

114. *Ibid.*
115. Mandela, *Long Walk to Freedom*, 362.
116. NASA, TAB, WLD, CC 578, Trial of Mkwai, Kitson, Chiba, Mathews and Maharaj, 1964, Exhibit R17.
117. *Ibid.*, Exhibit R11.

My analysis – Mandela trained with a trigger operated 60 mm mortar. His descriptor '4 rounds inside like the rifle' refers to four tubes racked together, with a handle attachment for carrying, each tube containing a 60 mm mortar bomb. His muzzle term 'pipe' is a universal military term describing mortar barrels. 'Cover smoke' refers to firing smoke bombs as screening cover. 'Tying wood and pipe' refers to an improvised bipod for the mortar pipe, which is manufactured without bipod. Pulling bolt… backward' refers to operating the safety catch at the pipe base. '2 kinds of trigger' is operating either the manual or automatic fire options whilst, 'to pull first trigger you need 4.5 lbs of weight. Second 7.5', refers to either the weight difference in these fire selections or weight differences between smoke and high explosive bombs.

- Chechoslovak Machine Gun
  A bipod mounted, shoulder anchored, air cooled machine gun. Magazine fed with 20 rounds, ranging 1,500 m; weighing 10.5 kilos, firing bursts of 500–600 rounds per minute; my analysis – a Czechoslovakian Bren machine gun.
  - Mandela noted cleaning and firing procedures, and compensation adjustments for cross wind shooting. Under 200 m he aimed directly on target; between 200 and 400 m a man's width upwind off target and over 400 meters two men's width upwind. He recorded three wind types affecting aim. Low wind traveling from 10–1,500 m per minute, high wind between 15–20,000 m per minute and diagonal wind, which required aiming half a man's width off target up wind.

Mandela's diary and journal contain no entries for the week of 2–7 July 1962, other than Saturday 7 July 1962. Befikadu took him to a restaurant serving traditional dishes. On Sunday he dined with Tadesse and Befikadu and thereafter went to the cinema. Possibilities are that his weeks' training left him with no spare time, hence no diary entry the following day.

On 10 July 1962, Mandela viewed a mortar fire demonstration. Two days later, he spent four hours on a shooting range.[118] He trained with an automatic rifle and pistol during target practice on two separate ranges – at Kolfe with the Emperors Guard and another range about 50 miles away with 'the entire battalion'.[119] He fired a pistol – not a revolver. Given transpiring events, he probably trained with a Makarov.

Two additional diary entries follow. On 12 July 1962, Mandela undertook field craft drills including day movement tactics. The next day – his last entry – a 26 km fatigue march with Befikadu, covering the distance in 3 hours.

Return to South Africa

Mandela's six-month training ended suddenly when, after two weeks, the ANC requested his urgent return to South Africa. Tadesse rapidly arranged Mandela's flight to Khartoum

118. NASA, TAB, WLD, CC 578, Trial of Mkwai, Kitson, Chiba, Mathews and Maharaj, 1964, Exhibit R17.
119. Mandela, *Long Walk to Freedom*, 362. He would have fired weapons which he already made notes about, thus the automatic rifle referred to was the Garand M1. Additionally, he fired the Mauser rifle and Bren machine gun.

and 'presented him with a gift: an automatic pistol and two hundred rounds of ammunition'.[120] Mandela holstered the pistol inside his jacket and bandoliered the ammunition inside his trousers around his waist. Carrying the ammunition was tiring, akin to 'carrying a small child on one's back'.[121] In Dar es Salaam he met an MK group, led by Johnstone Makatini and Joseph Jack from Natal, en route to Morocco for military training.[122] Makatini recalled that he nearly fainted at the sight of the Black Pimpernel, 'wearing a holster with a pistol and looking like an accomplished soldier'.[123]

Sisulu and Kathrada entered Bechuanaland, 'to ensure that everything was in order for his aircraft to land', apparently two weeks before Mandela arrived.[124] Joe Modise, who served on Mandela's logistics team, was tasked to rendezvous. Modise contacted Vivian Ezra – 'Look we've got to go and fetch Nelson Mandela. Do you mind doing it?' Ezra replied, 'OK'.[125] Modise posed as Ezra's chauffeur and drove into Lobatse in Ezra's red sports car. After waiting an hour or two, they learned that Mandela would not arrive that day. Modise stayed, Ezra returned to Johannesburg.

President Nyerere provided a private plane for Mandela's flight to Mbeya.[126] Although not mentioned in the literature, Mandela probably stopped at Kasane before reentering the SIS 'pipeline' for Lobatse. Once airborne the pilot redirected to Kanye, where the local magistrate, Denis Arthur T. Atkins, and a 'security man' intercepted Mandela.[127] Atkins brushed aside his denials, threatening arrest if Mandela incorrectly identified himself. Atkins related his instructions as providing help and transportation. Mandela replied, 'If you insist that I am Nelson Mandela and not David Motsamayi I will not challenge you.' Atkins smiled, 'we expected you yesterday', and with his security man, drove Mandela to Lobatse. They rendezvoused with Modise and Jonas Matlou, Mandela's MK collection team.[128]

Atkins advised that, 'the South African police were aware that I was returning, and he suggested that I leave the next day.'[129] Mandela thanked Atkins, traveled to Matlou's house and then informed his team that he would leave that night. Mandela was handed over to Cecil

120. *Ibid.*, 363.
121. *Ibid.*, 363–364.
122. Mandela had recently secured Moroccan military training facilities for MK during discussions with Dr Khatib and Jacques Verges.
123. www.anc.org.za/ancdocs/history/people/jmmakatini.html [accessed on 21 January 2010], Statement by the National Executive Committee of the African National Congress.
124. Sampson, *Mandela The Authorized Biography*, 170, and: Kathrada, A., *Memoirs* (Cape Town: Zebra Press, 2004), 150.
125. Discussions between the author and Vivien Ezra, 2006. Ezra owned Liliesleaf through Navian Ltd, a front company set up by the South African Communist Party for that purpose.
126. Mandela, *Long Walk to Freedom*, 364.
127. None of the literature names this Kanye Magistrate who in 1962 was Denis Arthur T. Atkins; see N. Parsons and G. Gumbo, *Bechuanaland Colonial Administrators c.1884–c.1965* (University of Botswana History Department 2002), http://www.thuto.org/ubh/bw/colad/coloff.htm#n8 [accessed 29 January 2010]. The flight rerouting by Bechuanaland's authorities to Kanye was to sidestep potential South African agents lurking in Lobatse. It forms another example of British intelligence knowing Mandela's movements and assisting him to evade South Africa's security establishment when travelling within their 'pipeline'.
128. Mandela, *Long Walk to Freedom*, 365, and Parsons and Gumbo, *Bechuanaland Colonial Administrators c.1884–c.1965*, http://www.thuto.org/ubh/bw/colad/coloff.htm#n8 [accessed 29 January 2010].
129. Mandela, *Long Walk to Freedom*, 365.

Williams, an MK member, who drove in to replace Ezra.[130] Williams was chosen as he had recently acquired a new car, an Austin Westminster, apparently unknown to the SAP.[131] Posing as Williams's chauffeur, they left that night. Wearing his Ethiopian Army uniform, Mandela arrived at Liliesleaf, during dawn[132] on approximately 27–28 July 1962.[133]

Nelson Mandela's Last Stay at Liliesleaf

Disinformation had circulated that Mandela changed his politics, switched to an African nationalist paradigm similar to the PAC and abandoned historic policies of non racialism. The PAC claimed that he had joined their organisation. Some of the political people back in South Africa were quite disturbed. Consequently, Mandela saw his first duty to meet the ANC leadership in Johannesburg and thereafter report to Chief Luthuli, and the Natal Indian Congress.[134]

Arthur Goldreich arrived home from work to learn that Mandela was back, went to Mandela's room and welcomed him.[135] It was almost nightfall. They walked away from the outbuildings into a field, beyond sight and earshot. Mandela revealed his pistol, which Goldreich recognised as a Makarov and recalled Mandela being extremely proud of it.[136]

Goldreich was keen to learn about Mandela's mission, which they discussed yet Mandela didn't share much detail, because it wasn't any of Goldreich's business, and the less he knew the better.[137] He responded to some of Goldreich's questions, yet spoke more about going to Natal. Mandela expressed confidence that he could persuade Luthuli and that he could be very persuasive, saying, 'You know, I have discovered that I have that capacity and that ability to persuade people to do things, to see the logic and the benefit of what I'm saying.'[138]

The next day Mandela reunited briefly with his wife and children, smuggled into Liliesleaf.[139] That night the ANC's National Working Committee met inside the thatched cottage to debrief him; Walter Sisulu, Moses Kotane, Govan Mbeki, Dan Tloome, JB Marks and Duma Nokwe, a rare reunion.[140] Mandela overviewed his travels, itemised monies received and offers of training.[141] He reported encountering reservations, 'about the ANC's cooperation with whites, Indians and particularly communists'. This perception of the ANC as a stooge of communists forms a regular theme in Mandela's debriefing notes, another insight into his perceptions and experiences at PAFMECA and in Africa.[142]

130. *Ibid.*
131. Kathrada, *Memoirs,* 150.
132. Mandela, *Long Walk to Freedom*, 365.
133. My assessment of the literature and other sources not quoted in this paper.
134. Discussions between the author and Ahmed Kathrada, 2004.
135. Arthur Goldreich, a member of MK and the SACP fronted Liliesleaf by renting the farm from Vivian Ezra's Navian Ltd, a front company established by the SACP for this purpose.
136. Discussions between the author and Arthur Goldreich, 2004, 2005, and 2006.
137. *Ibid.*
138. *Ibid.*
139. Sampson, *Mandela The Authorized Biography,* 170.
140. Mandela, *Long Walk to Freedom*, 369.
141. Country's confirmed as pledging military training and funding for military purposes were: Ethiopia, Egypt, Tunisia, Morocco, Algeria, Liberia, and Guinea. With respect to Morocco Mandela's notes for this meeting contain an annotation that he 'had previously discussed the matter with Julius' which could refer to Julius Nyerere, or if a typing error by the police transcriber, Julius could refer to Jacques Verge. 'Definite

Mandela related that the Zambian leaders were, 'bewildered by the ANC's non-racialism and communist ties'.[143] Both he and Tambo believed that to reassure the ANC's African allies who would finance and train MK, the ANC had to appear more independent. Mandela proposed reshaping the Congress Alliance to position the ANC as the clear leader, particularly when it came to issues that directly affected Africans.[144] Sisulu agreed – they should adjust tactics, not policy, cautioning that they remember minority group sensitivities. Nokwe's view was that cooperation had carried too far and that the organisation had been allowed to drift. These were serious propositions, requiring consultation with the entire leadership. The Working Committee urged Mandela to brief Luthuli. Mbeki suggested they dispatch someone else; jeopardising Mandela's safety at a time when he should push ahead with MK was too risky. Everyone, including Mandela, overruled Mbeki.[145]

If Mandela buried his Makarov pistol at Liliesleaf, then he did so that night, with assistance from some, or all of these comrades, the 'we' from the meeting. His reasons for burying a firearm at Liliesleaf remain unknown. That he left his journals and writings behind suggests intent to return there. After selecting an appropriate spot in an open plain, next to a tall tree, 'We dug a pit, deep enough so that a plough wouldn't uncover it, then wrapped the stuff in tin alloy and plastic, put a layer of gravel over it and a tin plate so the rain wouldn't get in, and covered it with soil.'[146]

Mandela's logistics committee was concerned, given extra security requirements yet Sisulu told them, 'You arrange for Madiba to go.' The committee was, 'looking around' for options when Cecil Williams drove into Liliesleaf, presenting a dilemma. Having collected Mandela in Bechuanaland, the committee viewed Williams as potentially compromised. They assumed the Protectorate police liaised with the SAP and may have supplied details of Mandela's arrival.[147] However, Mandela and the ANC leadership overruled them.[148] Additional precautions were ignored. Kathrada suggested Mandela shave off his beard, as police photographs depicted him bearded, yet to no avail.[149]

promises' were made by Senegal and the Sudan. Mandela (at times accompanied by Tambo and Resha) raised £25,000 in funds, which have been referred to in this article. All these monies were sent to Tambo in London, of which £2,778 was sent to South Africa, presumably carried back by Mandela and handed over during this meeting, see NASA, TAB, WLD, CC 578, Trial of Mkwai, Kitson, Chiba, Mathews and Maharaj, 1964, Exhibit R13.

142. NASA, TAB, WLD, CC 578, Trial of Mkwai, Kitson, Chiba, Mathews and Maharaj, 1964, Exhibits R13 and R17.

143. Mandela, *Long Walk to Freedom*, 369. Mandela was referring to Kenneth Kaunda and other UNIP members who he met at PAFMECA. On 6 February 1962, he and Tambo had, 'an hours chat with K Kaunda on the SA situation'. See NASA, TAB, WLD, CC 578, Trial of Mkwai, Kitson, Chiba, Mathews and Maharaj, 1964, Exhibit R17.

144. Mandela, *Long Walk to Freedom*, 369–370.

145. *Ibid.* Mandela's journal also refers: 'The ANC Executive has considered the matter and decided that tactics must be modified to accommodate to this climate of opinion in the Pafmecsa area.' See NASA, TAB, WLD, CC 578, Trial of Mkwai, Kitson, Chiba, Mathews and Maharaj, 1964, Exhibit R13.

146. Discussion between Nelson Mandela and the author 6 June 2005 and between Nelson Mandela and Allister Sparks, 1991 as related to the author in 2004 by Sparks.

147. Discussions between the author and Ahmed Kathrada, 2004.

148. *Ibid.*

149. T. Lodge, *Mandela: A Critical Life* (Oxford: Oxford University Press, 2006), 101.

Mandela left Liliesleaf the following night.[150] Posing as Williams's driver, he reached Natal and met Luthuli and other MK comrades. On 5 August 1962, Mandela was captured near Howick, while returning to Johannesburg. Williams was driving.[151] When the lead unmarked police car overtook them, Mandela saw two other cars behind their Austin. He considered jumping out and making an escape into the woods but realised he might be shot. They slowed and came to a stop.[152]

An unshaven policeman, who appeared not to have slept in a while, approached Mandela's window. Mandela assumed that this meant that they had waited for them for several days.

> In a calm voice, he introduced himself as Sergeant Vorster of the Pietermaritzburg police and produced an arrest warrant. He asked me to identify myself. I told him my name was David Motsamayi. He nodded, and then, in a very proper way, he asked me a few questions about where I had been and where I was going. I parried these without giving him much information. He seemed a bit irritated and then he said, 'Ag you're Nelson Mandela, and this is Cecil Williams, and you are under arrest! He informed us that a police major from the other car would accompany us back to Pietermaritzburg. The police were not yet so vigilant in those days, and Sergeant Vorster did not bother searching me.[153]

Armed and trained, Mandela considered shooting his way out. 'I had my loaded revolver, and again I thought of escape, but I would have been greatly outnumbered'. Mandela relates that he then concealed his revolver and notebook containing numerous names and addresses within the upholstery of the front seat.[154]

Detective Sergeant WA Vorster's unpublished account differs. Major Smidt commanded the police team, which included Vorster. Once Vorster's vehicle overtook and forcibly stopped Williams, Smidt exited his vehicle wedged behind William's car, identified Mandela and Williams inside their car and informed them they were arrested on 'suspicion'.[155]

> The White gave his name as Cecil Williams while the Bantu gave his name as David Motsamayi. I searched the Bantu while Staff Sergeant Van Rooyen searched the White man. The relevant two persons involved were taken to the Main Street police offices, where they were detained after Major Smidt had informed them of the charge on which they were being detained, of which they were suspected.[156]

Mandela and Vorster concur that the police identified both occupants in their car. The SAP capture group knew exactly who they were looking for and came prepared with a warrant, issued in Johannesburg in 1961. Mandela was arrested under Section 2 of the Criminal Law Amendment Act No 8 of 1953.[157]

150. Mandela, *Long Walk to Freedom*, 370.
151. *Ibid.*, 371. Mandela wrote that he and Williams, 'often took turns behind the wheel'.
152. *Ibid.*, 372.
153. *Ibid.*, 372.
154. *Ibid.*, 372–373.
155. NASA, NAN 52, Box 12, MS 385.28, Statement by Detective Sergeant W.A. Vorster.
156. *Ibid.*
157. As detailed in Nelson Mandela's Warrant of Arrest.

Mandela later claimed that they never found his revolver and notebook.[158] Subsequent authors continue this thread. A 2010 publication states that, 'There was no examination of the car or frisking the arrested men...The police, witless to the end, never bothered to search the car and those items were never found'. However, this author provides no additional evidence to support his claim, which Vorster's account contradicts.[159]

Vorster records both captives being frisked after Mandela and Williams exited the Austin, as per operational procedure. If Mandela concealed his revolver and notebook, he did so before his vehicle stopped; otherwise Vorster and Van Rooyen would have found them on him. An unlikely scenario is that Mandela later successfully concealed these items during the drive to Pietermaritzburg, with a police major sitting behind his shoulders. The police had captured the 'Black Pimpernel', their most wanted fugitive. They would have later searched Williams's car and retrieved any concealed property.

Conclusion

Mandela's mission succeeded in raising funds, secured support for military training and greater backing for the ANC and MK. During 1962–1963, Morocco, Algeria, Egypt and Ethiopia provided training to 135 MK members. Thereafter, the Soviet Union provided more specialised training.[160] Discussions with Moroccan and Algerian anti-colonial struggle veterans offered Mandela insight into the insufficiencies of solely pursuing military action. Rather, action forms one of many tools used in political struggle, combined with international opinion, mobilisation, and pressure to de-legitimatize the opponent. Tactics later pursued by the ANC and Mandela during the 1980s and 1990s negotiations with the apartheid regime.

Mandela presented the ANC's position to counter PAC 'propaganda' and through his actions (and those of other comrades), 'the ANC emerged strong from PAFMECA,' with greater backing from newly independent African states and North Africa.[161] Mandela noted concerns he encountered about ANC policy and tactics and that, 'the ANC must regard itself as the vanguard in SA of the Pan African movement.'[162] He conveyed this during his Liliesleaf debrief and leveraged support for the tactical readjustments agreed to that night. He then met with Luthuli and presented his findings.[163]

Regarding his pistol, three possibilities exist. The first – he buried pistol and ammunition at Liliesleaf and took his uniform with to Natal. This scenario of the buried pistol concurs with thee discussions with Mandela over a 14-year period at Liliesleaf; where

158. Mandela, *Long Walk to Freedom*, 373.
159. Smith, *Young Mandela*, 276.
160. South African Democracy Education Trust, *The Road to Democracy*, 454–459.
161. NASA, TAB, WLD, CC 578, Trial of Mkwai, Kitson, Chiba, Mathews and Maharaj, 1964, Exhibit R.13.
162. *Ibid.*
163. Mandela, *Long Walk to Freedom*, 370–371.

he both recollected and described burying a handgun on the farm, the third discussion during which he told me that his weapon was of Ethiopian provenance.[164]

The second was that he rolled up his pistol and ammunition inside his uniform and buried the bundle. He then wore a second uniform in Natal; possible as it is standard practice for soldiers undergoing training to be issued more than one uniform.

Ronnie Kasrils who attended the 4 August 1962, meeting in Natal described Mandela as, 'bearded and in khaki trousers and shirt, he towered above us as he shook each one by the hand. Wearing a solemn expression, he looked every inch a commander'.[165] Later that night Mandela attended a social gathering in Durban, where a 2006 publication, has him wearing a uniform.[166] Other accounts recollect the uniform yet no account has emerged recalling Mandela with a pistol in Natal.

The third possibility – the Makarov was with him when captured, which Mandela's memoir describes as a revolver.[167] Smith's 2010 publication states that Mandela, 'only ever referred to one gun, the gift from the Colonel in Ethiopia, and it was with him when he was arrested'. Smith provides no substantiating evidence and is inaccurate, given the two revolvers and one pistol which Mandela's memoir relates he possessed, and he consigns Mandela's consistent oral history of burying a handgun at Liliesleaf to the realm of the 'puzzling'.[168] Nor is any explanation offered by Smith for the disappearance of the ammunition, which was not with Mandela when he was captured. None of the other literature consulted offers any explanation as to the disappearance of pistol and ammunition.

Upon review, the evidence suggests that Mandela buried his Makarov (or another unidentified firearm) at Liliesleaf. Carrying bundle and spade, he walked away from the household and outbuildings, with their occupants, dogs, and geese, followed a footpath downhill towards the river and fields, where in pitch darkness he was concealed. Selecting the silhouette of the tallest tree in fields with which he was familiar, he dug deep into the softer soil of the ploughed and broken lands, deep enough so that no plough might uncover it, he placed his cache into the hole, covered it with tin plate corrugated iron, salvaged from farm scrap heaps while en route, and filled in the hole. After brushing away his tracks, Mandela walked uphill back to his room.

Immediately after the 1963 raid, the police brought in the SADF's Engineer Corps. They swept the grounds with landmine detectors.[169] If they located the cache then the security establishment kept this quiet, similar to Mandela's revolver and notebook, for the media reports nothing found.[170] If not unearthed, perhaps the cache was inadvertently uncovered during 1970s farm subdivisions and housing developments, yet no record has emerged.

---

164. Discussion between the author and Nelson Mandela, 6 June 2005 during which Mandela described his cache as 'important' to him, and the 'Ethiopians' and 'very valuable but dangerous'. He squeezed his trigger finger and stretched out his arm as if holding a handgun to reiterate his narrative. Mandela said that he hoped his cache could be found, 'otherwise the Ethiopians will be disappointed'.
165. Kasrils, R., *Armed and Dangerous: From Undercover Struggle to Freedom* (Jeppestown: Jonathan Ball, 1998), 39.
166. Lodge, *Mandela: A Critical Life*, 102.
167. Mandela, *Long Walk to Freedom*, 373.
168. Smith, *Young Mandela*, 276.
169. His cache would have created a prominent electronic signature if a detector was swept over it, obvious to any military engineer that this was a site worth excavating.
170. *Sunday Times* press clipping, 14 July 1963, author's collection.

Consequently, if not uncovered, Mandela's cache lays buried beneath suburbia, where the tree once stood. Concealed by Nelson Mandela – armed and trained.

References

Publications

Callinicos, L., *Oliver Tambo Beyond the Engeli Mountains* (Southern Africa: David Phillips Publishers, 2004).
Guttery, B.R., *Encyclopaedia of African Airlines* (Jefferson, NC: McFarland, 1998).
Henry, C.M., 'The Dialectics of Political Islam in North Africa', *Middle East Policy*, 14, 4 (2007), 84–98.
Kasrils, R., *Armed and Dangerous: From Undercover Struggle to Freedom* (Jeppestown: Jonathan Ball, 1998).
Kathrada, A., *Memoirs* (Cape Town: Zebra Press, 2004).
Lodge, T., *Mandela: A Critical Life* (Oxford: Oxford University Press, 2006).
Mandela, N.R., *Long Walk to Freedom* (London: Abacus, 1994).
Ndlovu, S.M., 'Heritage Routes for the Liberated South Africans: Using Oral History to Reconstruct Unsung Heroes and Heroines' Routes into Exile in the 1960s', *Historia*, 47, 2 (2002).
Parsons, N., 'The Pipeline: Botswana's Reception of Refugees, 1956–68', *Social Dynamics*, 34, 1 (2008), 17–32.
Parsons, N. and Gumbo, G., *Bechuanaland Colonial Administrators c.1884–c.1965* (Botswana: University of Botswana History Department, 2002).
South African Democracy Education Trust, *The Road to Democracy in South Africa, vol. 1*, (1960–1970) (Cape Town: Zebra, 2004).
Sampson, A., *Mandela The Authorized Biography* (Jeppestown: Jonathan Ball, 1999).
Sanders, J., *Apartheid's Friends The Rise and Fall of South Africa's Secret Service* (London: John Murray Publishers, 2006).
Smith, D.J., *Young Mandela* (London: Weidenfeld & Nicolson, 2010).

National Archives of South Africa

BTS, 109/7, Training of Saboteurs, Brussels Ambassador to Secretary of Foreign Affairs.
NAN 52, Box 12, MS 385.28, Statement by Detective Sergeant WA Vorster.
TAB, WLD, CC 578, Trial of Mkwai, Kitson, Chiba, Mathews & Maharaj, 1964.

National Archives of the United Kingdom

CAB 114/119.
CAB 179/8, Joint Intelligence Committee Reports.
DO 119/1229, Vincent Joe Matthews (VJ).
DO 119/1478, Nelson Mandela, 1962.
DO 157/9, Bechuanaland Central Intelligence Committee Reports.
FO 371 161886.

Surveyor General Cape Town

Aerial photograph of Liliesleaf, 1961.

Discussions

Ezra, Vivian, 2006.
Goldreich, Arthur, 2004, 2005, 2006.
Kathrada, Ahmed, 2004, 2005.
Mandela, Nelson, 2005.
Sparks, Allister, 2004.
Wolpe, Nicholas, 2004.

Internet Sources

www.anc.org.za/ancdocs/history/people/jmmakatini.html, Statement by the National Executive
    Committee of the African National Congress [accessed 21 January 2010].
http://www.independent.co.uk/news/world/europe/stasi-files-say-verges-worked-with-carlos-1384202.
    html [accessed 21 January 2010].
www.mi5.gov.uk [accessed 20 January 2010].
http://www.netglimse.com/celebs/pages/jacques_verges/index.shtml [accessed 21 January 2010].
http://www.thuto.org/ubh/bw/colad/coloff.htm#n8 [accessed 29 January 2010].
http://www.tigrai.org/News/Articles1/Major-Nega.html [accessed 30 January 2010].
http://www.timesonline.co.uk/tol/comment/obituaries/article2538907.ece [accessed 21 January 2010].
http://www.un.org/Depts/DPKO/Missions/onucF.html [accessed 30 January 2010].
www.mi5.gov.uk [accessed 20 January 2010].

Transformations in the ANC External Mission and Umkhonto we Sizwe, c. 1960–1969

ARIANNA LISSONI

(University of the Witwatersrand)*

This article focuses on key policy, strategic and ideological developments in the ANC external mission and its army, Umkhonto we Sizwe (MK), during their first decade of exile. It seeks to illustrate that the ANC's transformation into a liberation movement in exile during this period and its continued survival were not a matter of unproblematic progression. Rather, this process entailed a series of re-negotiations and re-adjustments, which were triggered by changes in the material conditions of struggle as they unfolded after Sharpeville. The difficulty experienced by the ANC leadership in exile in grappling with these changes produced potentially disintegrative internal strains in the second half of the decade, which can be viewed as the main catalysts behind the call for a Consultative Conference in Morogoro in 1969. At a leadership level, these tensions concerned issues of representation, organisational structure and, ultimately, political strategy. At the heart of the debate between the ANC and its allies was the full incorporation of all South African exiles previously associated with the Congress Movement into the external mission, signalling a gradual transition from the multi-racialism of the 1950s to the creation of a unitary, non-racial liberation front. Closely related to the issue of non-racialism was the progressive adjustment of the ANC to the armed struggle, which was made especially difficult by the continued separation of military from political structures. Hence the concern of this article with the state of affairs within MK, in particular with pressures from below, matters of military strategy, and the relationship between the military and the political movement.

This article focuses on key developments in the African National Congress (ANC) and its army, Umkhonto we Sizwe (MK), during the 1960s. Because of the clampdown on both above-ground and underground resistance in the early 1960s, this decade has tended to be viewed as period of relative quiescence in the history of the liberation struggle and has received little attention by historians of South Africa.[1]

Only in recent years has this gap in the literature begun to be bridged and the full complexity of this decade begun to be understood[2] – thanks to new oral history and

---

* This article is based on my PhD thesis, 'The South African Liberation Movements in Exile, c. 1945–50', SOAS, May 2008. It was first presented at a joint SOAS-Birkbeck workshop on 'Liberation Struggles in Southern Africa, International Solidarity and the Anti-Apartheid Movement: New Perspectives' in January 2006. I would like to thank Wayne Dooling (my PhD supervisor), and Hilary Sapire for organising the workshop and Saul Dubow for providing initial comments.

1 Most accounts of the liberation struggle either end with the banning of the ANC and the Pan-Africanist Congress (PAC) in 1960 and the subsequent turn to armed struggle, or they almost literally 'jump' from the early 1960s to the Durban strikes of 1973. Until recently, Tom Lodge's chapter on 'Revolutionary Exile Politics, 1960–1975' provided the only overview of the period stretching from the early 1960s to the 1976 Soweto uprising. See T. Lodge, *Black Politics in South Africa Since 1945* (London, Longman, 1983), pp. 295–320.

2 See South African Democracy Education Trust (hereafter SADET) (ed.), *The Road to Democracy in South Africa*, Vol. 1, 1960–1970 (Cape Town, Zebra Press, 2004), and *The Road to Democracy: South Africans Telling Their Stories*, Vol. 1, 1950–1970 (Johannesburg, Tsehai Publishers, 2008).

documentary material that became available after 1994, and upon which this study draws. Building on this emergent body of scholarship, this article challenges the characterisation of the 1960s as an interlude of political quiescence. It argues that although the 1960s witnessed the progressive silencing of the internal resistance movement, this was also a difficult time of experimentation and change, during which the exiled ANC had to adjust to the dramatically altered conditions of struggle emerging in the post-Sharpeville context. An in-depth analysis of what happened to the ANC and its allies in the 1960s is important to reaching a greater understanding not just of this decade, but also of the years that followed. In fact, one could argue that it was on the basis of the achievements, as well as of the difficulties, setbacks, disagreements and doubts that appeared at this time, that the ANC was able to reappear as a significant force inside South Africa from the late 1970s and ultimately to emerge victorious in 1994.

Within a few years from its banning and the momentous decision to take up arms, the ANC almost, although never completely, ceased to function in South Africa[3] (where a large portion of its leadership languished in prison) and was effectively transformed into a movement in exile. Forced to operate under conditions of illegality after long years of mass campaigns and extra-parliamentary activity, cut off from its internal support base, separated from South Africa by a physical barrier of countries that were either allies of the apartheid state or too economically dependent on it to be able to oppose its policies, the exiled ANC faced enormous challenges. First, it had to devise a new international structure and an acceptable image in order to establish itself internationally and gather support for the struggle at home in diplomatic, financial and military terms. In the early 1960s, competition over international support with the rival Pan-Africanist Congress (PAC), especially – and crucially – among African states, led the ANC to adopt the decision that its external machinery should be shaped around a little known principle, which came to be internally referred to as the 'African image'. Such a decision was in tune with the strong Pan-African sentiments sweeping over the African continent, where the PAC's Africanism found more resonance than the ANC's multi-racial approach.

By the mid-1960s, the external mission of the ANC had to assume the leadership of the entire movement as a result of the severe hammering received by the underground network at Rivonia. Increasingly, the 'African image' became a source of tension between the ANC and its non-African supporters in exile, as the various parts of the former Congress Alliance now found themselves isolated – and at times in conflict. This development set off a further renegotiation of the relations that had existed between the ANC and its partners in the former Congress Alliance in South Africa, which was ultimately resolved with the opening of ANC membership to non-Africans at the Morogoro Conference. The ultimate catalyst behind the decision to convene a Consultative Conference, however, originated within the ANC itself, and more specifically within its armed wing, Umkhonto we Sizwe, which by the late 1960s was in a deep state of crisis. From 1966 onwards, growing discontent in MK camps erupted in a series of desertions, rebellions or small mutinies. These incidents pointed to a widening gap between the political and military wings of the ANC and by 1969 had come to threaten the organisation's very existence.

---

3 Raymond Suttner's research on the ANC underground between Rivonia and the Soweto uprising has demonstrated that despite the severity of the blows suffered by the ANC in the early 1960s, the ANC never entirely disappeared inside South Africa. In fact, the ANC's continued – albeit little visible – underground presence throughout the 1960s helps explain its subsequent re-emergence after 1976. See R. Suttner, *The ANC in South Africa to 1976* (Johannesburg, Jacana, 2008).

The Politics of Multi-Racialism in the 1950s

In the course of the decade prior to the ANC's banning, African resistance politics had started to shift from a narrow ideology of African nationalism to a 'gentler', all-inclusive type of nationalism, which pointed towards unity with other minority groups and united action.[4] As Saul Dubow has argued, this shift reflected 'a new awareness of South Africa as a multi-racial or multi-ethnic society'.[5]

In the early 1950s, this multi-racial understanding informed the creation of the Coloured People Congress (CPC) and the white Congress of Democrats (COD), which, together with the ANC, the South African Indian Congress (SAIC) and the South African Congress of Trade Unions, came to constitute the broad union of forces known as the Congress Alliance. Despite the fact that many would have preferred to join a unitary organisation open to all, the ANC and its non-African supporters agreed on the need to establish organisations with racially separate identities. Practical concerns influenced this decision. First, the geographical separation of different groups into locations, ghettoes, and homelands posed serious problems of organisation. And second, different issues affected different groups at different times, thus demanding different approaches. As Reg September, former General Secretary of the CPC, has explained:

> We couldn't take the question of limit between the different social groups for granted, it is something that you had to work for. You couldn't for example take it for granted that the CPC would call a meeting against the imposition of pass laws in South Africa and expect the African community to participate in it. It didn't work that way, it couldn't work that way, because it wasn't an issue for the Coloured people.[6]

The multi-racial or multi-national character of the Alliance became embodied in the 1955 Freedom Charter, which stated that 'South Africa belongs to all who live in it, *black and white*' and that 'all national groups shall be protected by law against insults to their race and national pride'.[7]

The principle of multi-racialism was influenced ideologically by the Communist Party's 'two-stage' (or 'Independent Native Republic') theory, which was based in turn on Stalin's ideas on nationality.[8] Following the 1928 Comintern, the Communist Party of South Africa (CPSA) had adopted a resolution which called on its members to work with the nationalist movement for the establishment of an 'Independent Native Republic' – with guarantees for minority groups – as the first of two stages towards the establishment of a socialist order.[9] During the 1950s the South African Communist Party (SACP), which was secretly formed in 1953 following the dissolution of the CPSA in 1950, developed the notion of 'colonialism of a special type', according to which the situation in South Africa was that of a unique type of colonialism, where an independent 'oppressing White nation occupied the same territory

---

4 Lodge, *Black Politics*, p. 68.
5 S. Dubow, 'Thoughts on South Africa: Some Preliminary Ideas', in H.E. Stolten (ed.), *History Making and Present Day Politics: The Meaning of Collective Memory in South Africa* (Uppsala, Nordiska Afrikainstitutet, 2007), p. 67.
6 Interview with Reg September, Cape Town, 15 February 2005.
7 'Freedom Charter', adopted by the Congress of the People, 26 June 1955, Document 11, in T. Karis and G.M. Gerhart, *Challenge and Violence, 1953–1963*, Vol. 3, in T. Karis and G.M. Carter (eds), *From Protest to Challenge: A Documentary History of African Politics in South Africa, 1882–1964* (Stanford, Hoover Institution Press, 1977), pp. 205–8. Emphasis added.
8 According to Stalin's definition, a nation is a 'historically constituted, stable community of people, formed on the basis of a common language, territory, economic life, and psychological make-up manifested in a common culture'. J.V. Stalin, 'Marxism and the National Question', *Prosveshcheniye*, 3–5, March–May 1913, available at: http://www.marxists.org/reference/archive/stalin/works/1913/03.html
9 A. Lerumo, *Fifty Fighting Years: The Communist Party of South Africa* (London, Inkululeko, 1971), pp. 63–6.

as the oppressed people themselves and lived side by side with them'.[10] Through this theory, which became the 'ideological glue' holding the alliance between the SACP and the ANC together over the next 40 years,[11] the SACP aimed to resolve the chronic internal debate on the relationship between the class struggle and the national struggle, and in turn on the relationship between the Party and the national liberation movement. The 'colonialism of a special type' and 'two stage' theories were reaffirmed in *The Road to South African Freedom*, the programme adopted by the Party's Sixth Congress in November 1962. The programme pointed out that:

> It is this combination of the worst features both of imperialism and colonialism within a single national frontier which determines the special nature of the South African system.[12]

Arising from this analysis, the programme established that:

> As its immediate and foremost task, the SACP works for a united front of national liberation. It strives to unite all sections and classes of oppressed and democratic people for a national democratic revolution to destroy white domination. The main content of this Revolution will be the national liberation of the African people.[13]

By adopting this approach, the SACP was able to bear its mark on the national liberation movement as a whole without, however, counterposing itself to it.

The External Mission of the ANC and 'African Image'

During its last legal conference in South Africa in December 1959, the ANC Executive had made provisions for its newly-elected Deputy President Oliver Tambo to leave the country to 'carry abroad the message of its vision and solicit support for the movement' in the event that the ANC would be banned.[14] At the time this decision was taken, however, there had been 'no anticipation of the PAC arising as a factor outside or for that matter inside the country'.[15] Wide media coverage and international condemnation of the Sharpeville massacre of 21 March 1960 ensured the PAC 'overnight recognition'.[16] Following Sharpeville, the problems presented by the PAC's newly gained notoriety were temporarily overcome through the setting up of the South African United Front (SAUF).[17] The creation of the SAUF was greatly encouraged by independent African states, where the liberation of southern Africa was understood within a framework of African unity. The rift between the ANC and the PAC troubled leaders like Nkrumah, who argued that 'a union of the two liberation movements [...] was both necessary to achieve success at home and appropriate for Pan-Africanism

---

10 South African Communist Party (SACP), *The Road to South African Freedom: The Programme of the South African Communist Party* (London, Bowles, 1964), p. 27.
11 D. Everatt, 'Alliance Politics of a Special Type: The Roots of the ANC/SACP Alliance, 1950–1954', *Journal of Southern African Studies* (hereafter *JSAS*), 18 (1992), p. 19.
12 SACP, *Road to South African Freedom*, p. 29.
13 *Ibid.*, p. 4.
14 L. Callinicos, *Oliver Tambo: Beyond the Engeli Mountains* (Cape Town, David Philip, 2005), p. 253.
15 University of the Western Cape (hereafter UWC), Mayibuye Centre Historical papers (hereafter MCH) 70, Survey of the External Mission of the African National Congress of South Africa, February 1965.
16 Karis and Gerhart, *Challenge and Violence*, p. 332.
17 The SAUF was created by a small group of ANC, PAC, SAIC, SWANU and SWAPO leaders in exile. Its formation was announced at the second Conference of Independent African States in Addis Ababa in June 1960. The SAUF's aim was to mobilise world opinion and to draw governments into active participation in the application of various pressures (economic and political) on South Africa. The PAC's boycott of the May 1961 stay-away can be viewed as the main, although not the only, factor for the Front's final dissolution in March 1962. See Y. Dadoo, 'Why the United Front Failed', *New Age*, 29 March 1962.

in the region'.[18] However, as the crisis in the SAUF developed, the ANC and partner organisations in the Congress Alliance in South Africa 'engaged in a very thorough discussion as to what was required to replace the SAUF'.[19]

By the late 1950s, the ANC's collaboration with its non-African allies had given rise to allegations within Africanist circles that the ANC 'danced to the tune of the Communists'.[20] Moreover, the ANC's multi-racialism appeared out of step with developments on the rest of the continent, where African leaders were not accustomed to the ANC's approach on race and distrusted its relationship with the SAIC and the Communist Party. During the 1958 All African Peoples' Conference in Accra, the ANC struggled to reconcile its ideology of non-racialism and its policy of co-operation based on the Freedom Charter with ideas such as the 'African Personality' and 'Pan-African Socialism' contained in the Conference's 'Call to Independence'. The ANC submitted a memorandum to the Conference in which it outlined the vision of 'a democratic South Africa embracing all, regardless of colour or race who pay undivided allegiance to South Africa and mother Africa'. Although its ideology implied 'a recognition of the concept of African Nationalism', because of the unique economic, social, and political history and racial set-up in South Africa, the ANC explained that it had had been 'progressively developing the concept of an all embracing "Africanism"'. For this reason, the ANC argued, the 'liberatory organisations and movements which hold diverse political and social theories and principles', although united in the common anti-imperialist and anti-colonial struggle, should not be forced 'to adopt a common ideology and philosophy'.[21]

The PAC, on the other hand, had recognised the appeal of Pan-Africanism from the very beginning and 'Africanist leaders put heavy emphasis on what they conceived to be the identity of interests of Africans in South Africa and Africans in the rest of the continent'.[22] The PAC contested the notion of South Africa's 'exceptionalism' (which the ANC subscribed to, and in which the SACP's 'colonialism of a special type' theory was rooted) and argued instead 'that South Africa is an integral part of the indivisible whole that is Afrika'. Rejecting multi-racialism as 'a pandering of European bigotry and arrogance' and 'a method of safeguarding white interests', the PAC aimed at a 'government of the Africans by the Africans, for the Africans', which would not guarantee minority rights.[23] The PAC had adopted the target date for African freedom in 1963 set by the All African People's Conference. It also shared the Conference's vision of a continental government and of a union of African states, based on an 'Africanistic Socialist democratic order' which in turn would favour the development of the 'African personality'.[24] In South Africa, Pan-Africanism had thus come to be equated with the PAC.

Mandela was taken aback on discovering how much support the PAC had gained abroad when he toured the African continent in early 1962 to assess the disposition of African states

---

18 Callinicos, *Oliver Tambo*, p. 264. The idea that the ANC and the PAC should unite in a common front was one that outlived the SAUF. For the rest of the decade and beyond, pressure for the formation of a united front was exerted by African leaders through the Organisation of African Unity (OAU), established in 1963. The OAU's African Liberation Committee, the sub-committee in charge of channelling financial, military and logistical aid to liberation organisations, laid it down as a condition for recognition and support that different liberation parties in each given African country must come together in a common liberation front to direct political activities.

19 University of Fort Hare (hereafter UFH), Liberation Archives, Oliver Tambo Papers, Box 81, File B.2.3.1, Political Report of the NEC to the Consultative Conference of the ANC, Morogoro, April 1969.

20 B. Bunting, *Moses Kotane, South African Revolutionary: A Political Biography* (Bellville, Mayibuye Books, 1998, 3rd edn), p. 244.

21 Notes for Delegates to the All African People's Conference to be held in Accra, Ghana, December 1958, Issued by the ANC. Available at: http://www.anc.org.za/ancdocs/history/boycotts/accra58.html

22 Karis and Gerhart, *Challenge and Violence*, p. 321.

23 R.M. Sobukwe, Opening Address, Inaugural Conference of the PAC, April 4–6, 1959, document 39a in Karis and Gehart, *Challenge and Violence*, p. 516.

24 See Manifesto of the Africanist Movement, document 39b, in *ibid.*, pp. 517–24.

towards the armed struggle. Once back in South Africa, Mandela informed his colleagues that 'the ANC had to appear more independent to reassure our new allies on the continent', and proposed 'reshaping the Congress Alliance so that the ANC would be clearly seen as the leader, especially on issues directly affecting Africans'. When ANC President Chief Albert Luthuli replied that 'he did not like the idea of foreign politicians dictating policy to the ANC', Mandela countered by saying that his plan 'was simply to effect cosmetic changes in order to make the ANC more intelligible – and more palatable – to our allies'.[25] In other words, the ANC had to appear more genuinely 'African'. After Mandela's return to South Africa, 'the phrase "the image" which the ANC presents to the outside world became a nucleus of wide ranging discussions',[26] which led to the formulation of a policy internally known as the 'African image'.

The possibility of reproducing outside the country the same Congress Alliance machinery that existed inside the country[27] (in which certain sections were now legal and others illegal) was discarded, and so was the idea that each organisation in the Alliance should set up its own external mission (which would have resulted in a counterproductive dispersion of energies and resources). Instead, it was agreed that the external mission should reflect the fundamental fact that the essence of the struggle at home was the liberation of the African people, which would in turn introduce democratic rights for all. In view of the fact that central to the external mission's work would be 'obtaining the assistance and alliance of the African states', this type of machinery was thought to be the most suitable one to facilitating the achievement of the movement's aims without having 'to win converts in the African states to our concept of non-racial unity'.[28] In the end, it was unanimously decided by the leadership of the entire Congress Alliance that an ANC external mission should be set up 'to serve as representative not only of the ANC but the whole progressive movement in South Africa'.[29]

Despite being the subject of 'comprehensive and at times acrimonious' debate, these decisions were reconfirmed at the Lobatse Consultative Conference of October 1962,[30] the first ANC conference since its banning. The Conference acknowledged the growing importance of the external mission, whose role would be to arrange for military training and support, and to carry out international solidarity work.[31] At this stage, a relatively strong leadership was still active inside South Africa which could issue directives for the external mission to carry out.

The guidelines concerning the external organisational apparatus of the ANC and its partners were also approved by the SACP at its 1962 Conference. Like Mandela, the SACP had also become concerned that a 'distorted presentation of our image abroad' had created a situation in which:

> It is the alliance which has been seen abroad, increasingly as the Congress movement, and not the real national organisations, vastly unequal in size and in importance which make it up. The effect has been, in propaganda abroad, to eclipse the leading role and nature of the ANC; and to mute the leading aim which is the liberation of the African majority.[32]

---

25 N. Mandela, *Long Walk to Freedom: The Autobiography of Nelson Mandela* (London, Abacus, 1995), pp. 369–71.
26 UWC, MCH70, Survey of the External Mission of the African National Congress of South Africa, February 1965.
27 Prior to March 1960, the Congress Alliance had functioned through the Joint Congress Executives, the formal head of the Alliance, and through the National Action Council, a consultative, non-policy making body with delegates from each of the sponsoring organisations.
28 UWC, MCH70, Survey of the External Mission of the African National Congress of South Africa, February 1965.
29 UFH, Liberation Archives, Oliver Tambo Papers, Box 81, File B.2.3.1, Political report of the NEC to the Consultative Conference of the ANC, Morogoro, April 1969.
30 UWC, MCH70, Survey of the External Mission of the African National Congress of South Africa, February 1965.
31 UFH, Liberation Archives, Oliver Tambo Papers, Box 81, File B.2.3.1, Political Report of the NEC to the Consultative Conference of the ANC, Morogoro, April 1969.
32 'A Landmark in South Africa's History: The Sixth National Conference of the South African Communist Party', *International Bulletin*, 4, December 1962, in A. Drew (ed.), *South Africa's Radical Tradition: A Documentary History*, Vol. 2, 1943–1964 (Cape Town, Buchu Books, 1997), pp. 358–64.

The SACP argued that this 'false' image needed correction in order to make it clear that 'the leader of this movement is and has always been the African National Congress'.[33]

All of this, however, was to change dramatically soon. The Rivonia raid of 11 July 1963 and the trial that followed led to the smashing of virtually the whole of the underground network. The ANC, however, was trying to minimise the seriousness of the arrests by claiming that they would only 'lead to a redoubling of efforts to bring down the Verwoerd regime of repression, plunder and tyranny'.[34] Rivonia was a major setback for the movement, which in effect transformed the ANC into an organisation in exile. Anthony Sampson reported at the time, 'The ANC is certainly not dead [...]. But the individual African leadership which has been prominent for the past ten years is now effectively incapacitated inside the Republic.'[35] The external mission now found itself in charge of leading the whole movement, including 'organising for internal work, which had never been its job when established'.[36]

Rivonia gave way to a major wave of political exile, which further transformed the initial conditions under which the ANC had been given a mandate to represent the movement internationally. In keeping with the idea of the 'African image' and in trying to dispel the perception amongst African leaders that the ANC was an organisation controlled by white and Indian communists, ANC members going into exile, including well-known communist leaders such as Moses Kotane and J.B. Marks (the SACP General Secretary and Chairman), settled in those African capitals that hosted ANC offices. On the other hand, the United Kingdom, and London in particular, became the principal destination of the majority of white, Coloured, and Indian exiles. These individuals found themselves in 'organisational limbo'[37] as a result of the decision that only the ANC should open offices abroad.

Criticism of the 'African Image'

By February 1965, ANC offices had been established in London, Algiers, Cairo, Lusaka, and Dar es Salaam, where the organisation's provisional headquarters were stationed. These were in fact and in practice ANC offices, led by ANC personnel, responsible to the ANC executive. After three years of existence, the ANC external mission could proudly boast that a tremendous amount of work had been carried out, 'in particular in relation to the new phase of the struggle', with numerous freedom fighters being sent for training overseas, including to socialist countries. Most importantly, close working contact had been established with African states, especially Tanzania, thanks to the effective projection of the 'African image', which had been so successful that 'the PAC's attempt to portray itself as the only African organisation in South Africa has hopelessly failed and in fact politically and ideologically the PAC has suffered complete rout in Africa'.[38]

Although the ANC felt it was finally on the ascendancy in the battle for legitimacy vis-à-vis the PAC as the vanguard party in the struggle for national liberation in South Africa, for some, the 'African image' had been *too* effective. According to its critics, the

---

33 *Ibid.*

34 *South African Freedom News*, Dar es Salaam, African National Congress of South Africa, 12 July 1963.

35 *The Observer*, London, 1 March 1964.

36 UFH, Liberation Archives, Oliver Tambo Papers, Box 81, File B.2.3.1, Political report of the NEC to the Consultative Conference of the ANC, Morogoro, April 1969.

37 T.G. Karis and G.M. Gerhart, *Nadir and Resurgence, 1964–1979*, Vol. 5, in Karis and Carter (eds), *From Protest to Challenge* (Pretoria, UNISA Press, 1997), p. 36.

38 UWC, MCH70, Survey of the External Mission of the African National Congress of South Africa, February 1965.

external mission only reflected 'the majority, and not the minorities who are subject to oppression in South Africa'. Secondly, they were concerned that the notion of the 'African image' entailed an implicit 'danger that in deference of the views of certain reactionary states in Africa [...] the present machinery might make concessions on matters of principle on the question of non-racial democracy'. Thirdly, the current external setting did not accord room at the policy-making and decision-making levels to 'certain persons who are very important in their political organisations at home', as well as inhibiting full use of all available manpower resources.[39] This was particularly true of London, where the bulk of South African exiles worked on the fringes of the ANC office, mainly through the British Anti-Apartheid Movement, the World Campaign for the Release of South African Political Prisoners and the International Defence and Aid Fund.

The first indication of these problems of international representation (or rather what was perceived as lack of representation) was a dispute between the President of the CPC Barney Desai and the ANC external mission, which started to brew as early as August 1963. As he arrived in exile, Desai noticed that the ANC external mission 'was neglecting to mention the position and role of minority groups in South Africa'.[40] Moreover, he became concerned that because of the 'African image' policy, the Coloured community in exile in the UK was being excluded from the work of the external mission. He argued that both the internal and the external conditions of the struggle had changed to such an extent that they now called for revision. In accordance with the CPC policy to pursue the ideal of a non-racial democracy, Desai proposed that the CPC 'sink its identity in the ANC and disappear as a separate organisation'.[41] Desai's overtures, however, were rejected by the ANC on the grounds of African nationalism and as contrary to the 'African image'. Relations between Desai and the ANC progressively deteriorated until they reached breaking point in March 1966, when Desai unilaterally dissolved the CPC to join the PAC with a few other CPC men 'as Africans and equals'.[42] The merger with the PAC was publicly announced as 'the final nail in the coffin of the Congress Alliance' which, it was claimed, 'had failed because it led to a sectional and racialistic approach to South African politics'.[43]

Although it did not represent a significant threat to the ANC, Barney Desai's clash with the ANC is nevertheless indicative of the seriousness of the discontent among South African exiles in the UK. In fact, the issue of external representation was not settled with Desai's defection to the PAC and the problem of fully incorporating all exiles into the structures of the ANC external mission continued to raise its head throughout the rest of the decade. In the second half of the decade, London emerged as the key centre in a process of discussions, which have also been referred to as the 'London debates'.[44]

The 'London Debates'

Some steps towards strengthening the ties between the ANC external mission and partner organisations in the Congress Alliance started to be attempted from 1965 onwards on Tambo's initiative. Despite these efforts, 'a genuine problem' was still being reported by ANC supporters in London:

---

39 *Ibid.*
40 UWC, Mayibuye Archives, MCH70, Memo on Coloured People Congress External Representation [n.d.].
41 UWC, MCH70, Barney Desai and Cardiff Marney, Memorandum to the External Mission of the African National Congress – External Representation, London, 18 June 1964.
42 UWC, MCH70, *CPC International Bulletin*, 19 March 1966, London.
43 UWC, MCH70, SACPC External Representation, Press Release, London, 19 March 1966.
44 See J. Frederikse, *The Unbreakable Thread: Non-racialism in South Africa* (London, Zed Books, 1990), p. 99.

For these supporters it is not enough to call on them to work in the various solidarity movements abroad. They also feel the need to work actively in the building of support for the organisations of which they are members at home.[45]

At the ANC's request, a London Congress Committee headed by Yusuf Dadoo was set up to handle the matter of effective participation of non-African exiles in London. In its submissions, the London Committee argued that the Congress Alliance had fulfilled its historic role, and that it was time for new forms of alliance to be created. In the present conditions of illegality or semi-legality, where no formal delegates could be elected or given mandate to a conference, 'constitutional niceties' could not longer be adhered to.[46] The Committee also spoke of the liberation forces as engaged in a struggle for power by revolutionary means against the apartheid forces in all fields: political, economic, social and military. Such was the emergency situation that:

> A nation at war requires a Council of War. [. . .] The leaders outside the country have to do what can no longer be done at home – to formulate policy and take practical steps to give leadership to our respective communities and the South African people as a whole. It is in the spirit and tradition of our movement that all the various groups and organisations that constitute the forces of revolution in our country must do this work together and not in isolation from one another.[47]

The proposal of a Council of War (which can be viewed as a forerunner of the Revolutionary Council established by the Morogoro Conference in 1969) implied the recognition by the London Committee that armed activity was the most important means by which the struggle could now be advanced. Howard Barrell has established that the armed struggle emerged as the central feature of MK's operational strategy at a very early stage, and that in fact the sabotage campaign was always intended as a transitional phase towards the development of the armed struggle proper.[48] This view is supported by Vladimir Shubin, according to whom 'by the beginning of 1963 the Umkhonto High Command was not merely planning isolated acts of sabotage, but was working on strategies and tactics for a revolutionary war, an armed uprising in reply to armed repression by the government. The overthrow of the government by armed struggle [in other words, armed revolution] was the stated goal.'[49] After the arrest of the second National High Command (NHC) in late 1964, MK's leadership had passed to the ANC external mission in its entirety. Yet, the military and political aspects of the struggle continued to be kept as separate units which still operated, in many respects, independently from one another. A Planning Council was set up by the ANC external mission to replace the old NHC. However, unlike the old NHC whose composition was non-racial, the Planning Council was an exclusively ANC body. This meant that non-African SACP leaders who had played a prominent role in MK's formation and early sabotage operations now found themselves almost completely cut off from its direction.

The ANC's failure to fully gear itself towards the armed struggle also had a theoretical dimension. In fact, the changeover from legitimate, extra-parliamentary struggle to violent revolutionary struggle had not been accompanied by a similar qualitative change in the movement's programme, 'attitude and state of mind to correspond to the new phase'.[50]

---

45 UWC, MCH70, Proposals for strengthening liaison between the External Mission of the ANC and other organisations in the Congress Alliance, November 1965.

46 The bulk of the ANC executive had been elected in 1959 in conditions of legality and under a general policy of non-violence. Although the liberation struggle had undergone a radical transformation since then, the same leadership continued to function.

47 UFH, Liberation Archives, ANC Morogoro Papers, Box 6, File 53, Problems of the Congress Movement.

48 H. Barrell, 'Conscripts to their Age: African National Congress Operational Strategy, 1976–1986', D.Phil thesis, St Anthony's College, University of Oxford, 1993, available at: http://www.sahistory.org.za/pages/library-resources/thesis/barrel_thesis/CHAPT1.htm

49 V. Shubin, *ANC: A View from Moscow* (Cape Town, Mayibuye Books, 1999), p. 51.

50 University of Cape Town (hereafter UCT), Manuscripts and Archives, Simons Collection, P8, Internal Position.

The Freedom Charter had been drawn up during the days of legitimate, extra-parliamentary struggle and 'drafted with a view to providing the broadest possible basis for a meeting point – a meeting between the White minority and the disenfranchised majority'. The document, which had been written 'without a revolutionary mind', had nevertheless remained at the basis of the movement's political objectives even after the turn to armed resistance. In other words, the ANC had been 'conducting a revolutionary War without a revolutionary theory'.[51]

An ANC Sub-Committee consisting of Moses Kotane, J.B. Marks and Duma Nokwe was put in charge of responding to the suggestions made by the London Committee. The group of ANC leaders questioned the formation of a new body, or a Council of War, on the grounds that not all organisations formerly associated with the Congress Alliance had formally taken up the armed struggle. They also lamented that the problems raised by their colleagues in London implied doubt in the leadership of the ANC.[52]

Both the London Committee and the ANC Sub-Committee in Tanzania were composed of leading SACP members who, however, found themselves on opposing sides over the issue of external representation. These differences manifested themselves along geographical and racial lines, partly as a result of the pattern of political exile that has been described earlier. The divide was perhaps deepened by the SACP's decision to abstain from establishing formal structures in Africa, including in MK camps. When Ben Turok raised the question of the SACP's absence from Africa in a letter to Kotane in 1966, he was told that 'there was no role for the party in the present circumstances and that any attempt to recreate the party would lead to the expulsion of the ANC from the region by governments which were hostile to communism'.[53] Moreover, as Ndebele and Nieftagodien have pointed out, 'those communists who were based in Africa, such as Robert Resha and Tennyson Makiwane, had come under the influence of the very strong Africanist currents sweeping through the liberation movements in the 1960s'.[54]

A meeting of a top-level selection of Congress Movement leaders in exile was finally convened by the ANC in Morogoro in November 1966. This was the first official meeting of the Congress Alliance partners in exile. The debate at the meeting essentially centred on the nature of the organisational structure at home and abroad on the basis of the exchanges of opinion which had taken place thus far.[55] Whereas the London-based, non-African leaders pleaded for greater participation in the ANC external mission, either through the opening of membership or the creation of suitable structures, their Africa-based, African colleagues continued to resist such proposals.[56]

Although no final solution to the problem of full participation was agreed on, one concrete step towards the inclusion of non-African minorities in the work of the ANC in exile was the creation of a Co-operation and Co-ordination Committee after the meeting. This was an internal, non-public sub-committee whose members were appointed by the ANC from non-African organisations in the Congress Alliance to facilitate co-ordination. According

---

51 *Ibid.*
52 UFH, Liberation Archives, ANC Morogoro Papers, Box 6, File 53, Report of the Sub-Committee on Problems of the Congress Movement.
53 B. Turok, *Nothing but the Truth: Behind the ANC's Struggle Politics* (Johannesburg, Jonathan Ball Publishers, 2003), p. 211.
54 N. Ndebele and N. Nieftagodien, 'The Morogoro Conference: A Moment of Self-Reflection', in SADET (ed.), *The Road to Democracy*, Vol. 1, p. 584.
55 Present at the meeting, which was chaired by Oliver Tambo, were: Ray Simons, Moses Kotane, Robert Resha, William Marula (aka Flag Boshielo), M.P. Naicker, Joe Slovo, Moses Mabhida, Joe Matlou, Alfred Kgokong, J.B. Marks, Johnny Makatini, John Pule, Reg September, Michael Harmel, Joe Matthews, Ruth Mompati, Duma Nokwe, Mandy Msimang, James Hadebe, Yusuf Dadoo, and Mzwai Piliso.
56 See UFH, Liberation Archives, ANC Morogoro Papers, Box 8, File 68, 'Notes on a meeting of the joint Congress Executives', Morogoro, 26–28 November 1966.

to Joe Slovo, 'for the first time members of the SACP were included officially in such apparatus' by virtue of their connection with the Party.[57] The Committee also began to work with the ANC's Planning Council on military and other sensitive matters.

Unrest and Crisis in MK

The Morogoro Conference of 1969 can be viewed as the climax of the discussions that had been taking place between the ANC external mission and members of other Congress organisations based in London throughout the second half of the 1960s. The demands of non-African exiles were in fact fulfilled at Morogoro through the opening of ANC membership to all exiles regardless of race and through the creation of a new non-racial body, the Revolutionary Council. The ultimate catalyst for the conference was, however, the challenge faced by the ANC leadership in the aftermath of the Wankie and Sipolilo campaigns, which had thrown the ANC into crisis.[58]

Possibly the greatest military problem faced by the ANC in the 1960s (a problem that persisted well into the next decade and beyond) was a geographical or physical one: the lack of friendly border countries in which MK could establish rear bases. Until the collapse of the Portuguese colonial empire cracked open South Africa's strategic invulnerability, there were no contingent borders from which MK could launch its operations, nor were there any established routes through which trained guerrillas could be infiltrated in large numbers. After completing their military training in African and socialist countries, MK fighters were being sent back to the camps in Tanzania, where they were growing more and more impatient.

Available evidence suggests that by 1966 the ANC 'faced tremendous resentment from people in the camps'[59] resulting in a series of rebellions, desertions, or what could be interpreted as small mutinies, knowledge of which has since been buried by the ANC. The exact date and number of these incidents is uncertain. One of the first of such episodes seems to have occurred in early 1966 at Kongwa (Tanzania), which had been established in mid-1964 as a transit camp. By 1965, however, between four-and five hundred cadres were stationed there indefinitely.[60] As it gradually became clear that they 'were in for a long wait' before they could return to South Africa, the guerrillas' morale started to flag. Frustration over returning 'home' eventually led a small group of cadres from Natal to steal some trucks and drive off. Whether their aim had been 'to make their own way home',[61] or 'to discuss their grievances with the leadership' in Morogoro,[62] they were intercepted by the Tanzanian authorities within 80 kilometres from Kongwa and taken back to the camp. Joe Modise, MK's Commander-in-Chief, set up a formal commission of enquiry with charges of desertion and theft. Moses Mabhida, MK's National Commissar, disagreed with Modise, arguing that since they were trying to reach South Africa the cadres were not deserters.[63] According to one of the survivors, 'nothing happened about the incident' in the end and after being reprimanded by the leadership, the rebel men were relocated to Zambia to be redeployed in Rhodesia.[64]

The truck incident was symptomatic of the degree of ferment in MK camps, and may have been a factor in the ANC's decision to form an alliance with the Zimbabwe African People's

---

57 UWC, MCH02, J. Slovo, 'Thoughts on the Future of the Alliance', April 1969.
58 See also Ndebele and Nieftagodien, 'The Morogoro Conference', pp. 586–7.
59 Interview with Terry Bell, Muizenberg, 19 February 2005.
60 A. Sibeko (with J. Leeson), *Freedom in Our Lifetime* (Durban, Indicator Press, 1996), p. 82.
61 *Ibid.*, pp. 84–5.
62 R.M. Ralinala, J. Sithole, G. Houston and B. Magubane, 'The Wankie and Sipolilo Campaigns', in SADET (ed.), *The Road to Democracy*, Vol. 1, p. 483.
63 Sibeko, *Freedom in Our Lifetime*, p. 85.
64 'Gizenga' Mpanza, quoted in Ralinala *et al.*, 'The Wankie and Sipolilo Campaigns', p. 483.

Union (ZAPU) in 1967. In 1967–8, ANC–ZAPU combined forces embarked on a series of military incursions, known as the Wankie and Sipolilo campaigns, into Southern Rhodesia. The ANC's aim was to establish a secure base in Rhodesia and to create a route into South Africa through which MK cadres could be infiltrated back. However, these attempts failed in both their aims, and resulted in several losses and the imprisonment of many guerrillas – including MK's political commissar Chris Hani, who was jailed in Gaborone for approximately 16 months. The Wankie and Sipolilo debacles led to further demoralisation, not only within MK, but also in the movement as a whole. In his autobiography, Sibeko wrote that in the period following Wankie 'the armed struggle seemed to be in a lull, trained MK people were being neglected and a gulf seemed to have developed between most of the leadership and the rank and file. Even Kaunda noticed something was wrong and referred publicly to ANC leaders, who were usually seen in hotel restaurants, as "chicken-in-the-basket freedom fighters".'[65]

During this period, a spate of desertions took place, with small groups of MK cadres escaping from the camps in Tanzania and Zambia as they learned that their names were on the list for Rhodesia. Among these MK guerrillas was Gerald Sisulu, Walter and Albertina Sisulu's nephew, who claimed that the operation in Rhodesia 'was never properly explained to us. We just got everything through the grapevine. We were told that all the guys who were fighting there had been wiped out.' For this reason Sisulu decided he 'wanted no part' in the plan and went AWOL in Dar es Salaam where he was picked up by the police and jailed alongside other deserters.[66] Some of those who managed to escape arrest sought asylum in Kenya, where in early 1969 the number of refugees could have been as high as 80.[67] Amien Cajee, Maurice Mthombeni, Omar Bamjee, and Hoosain Jacobs, who had fled to Kenya in 1967–8, vented their grievances in a public statement in 1969.[68] They complained of shortages of essential commodities (such as food and clothing) and war material in the camps, as well as neglect by the leadership, problems of corruption, tribalism, preferential treatment and unjust punishment.[69] Furthermore, they criticised Wankie as an operation staged 'to get rid of unwanted dissenters' and claimed that dedicated men had been deliberately sent down for the ANC's leadership 'own prestige and material benefit'.[70]

On their return to Zambia in late 1968, Hani and six other MK commissars and commanders discovered that 'there was a widespread feeling of dissatisfaction in the movement and that there was an urgent desire for radical changes in organisation, policy and strategy'. Driven by 'the sole intention of invigorating the movement with a new spirit' and the desire 'to return to our country in order to confront the enemy,' they requested a meeting with the ANC leadership.[71] At the meeting, chaired by the ANC General Secretary Duma Nokwe, they were asked to put their case in writing. They drew up a memorandum – better

---

65 Sibeko, *Freedom in Our Lifetime*, p. 95.

66 Quoted in E. Sisulu, *Walter and Albertina Sisulu: In Our Lifetime* (Cape Town, David Philip, 2002), p. 221.

67 *Sunday Times*, Johannesburg, 27 January 1969.

68 Excerpts of their statement (which was sent to several Western organisations) appeared in the Johannesburg *Sunday Times* on 6 July 1969.

69 Some of these problems were not unique to MK but troubled other national liberation armies in the region as well. See for example Luise White's account of the mutinies surrounding the assassination of ZANU's National Chairman Herbert Chipeto. L. White, *The Assassination of Herbert Chipeto: Texts and Politics in Zimbabwe* (Bloomington, IN, Indiana University Press, 2003).

70 *Sunday Times*, Johannesburg, 6 July 1969.

71 UCT, Manuscripts and Archives, Simons Collection, P7, 'Grounds of appeal and addendum thereto in the matter of expulsion from the African National Congress of Jeqa Buthelezi, Wilmot Bempe, Alfred Khombisa, Wilson Mbali, Jackson Mlenze, Chris Nkosana, Bruce Pitso, March 1969'.

known as the 'Hani memorandum'[72] – which they hoped would 'create a feeling of urgency that would lead to a renewal of the offensive against the enemy'.[73] The authors of the memorandum spoke of a 'deep crisis' in the ANC in exile, 'as a result of which rot has set in'.[74] They criticised the ANC leadership for having 'created a machinery which has become an end unto itself' and expressed their concern about 'the careerism of the ANC leadership abroad who have, in every sense, become professional politicians rather than professional revolutionaries'.[75] They were equally disturbed by the complete lack of co-ordination between the ANC and MK, which they felt was 'being run independently of the organisation' to the point that 'the ANC has lost control over MK'. An example of this was the inability of MK's security department 'to furnish the organisation with the fate of our dedicated comrades in Zimbabwe' and 'the criminal neglect' of MK guerrillas 'fallen in battle, sentenced to death or serving long term imprisonment'.[76]

The 'Hani Memorandum' can be viewed as an expression of the malaise that had been growing for some time within the ANC in exile; the grievances it raised 'went much further than the outburst of the seven rebels emerging from Botswana's prisons. Underlying the anger was the deep unease that the struggle, after almost a decade in exile, had failed.'[77] Joe Matthews later claimed that the ANC leadership did not officially discuss the 'Hani memorandum', and that rather than responding specifically to the document, Tambo proposed that a consultative conference be convened instead.[78] This, however, does not seem to be entirely accurate. The memorandum was in fact initially dealt with severely as a matter of military discipline, rather than of political nature. Its signatories were expelled from the ANC by a military tribunal in Lusaka first,[79] and the decision was confirmed by headquarters in Morogoro on 28 March 1969.[80] Some within the leadership, who had been infuriated by the criticism levelled against certain individuals, even demanded that the authors of the memorandum be executed. It was only thanks to what Hani described in retrospect as Tambo's 'intelligent leadership' and inclusive approach that the death sentences were overruled.[81]

However, it was due to the actions of Hani and his comrades that the ANC leadership finally woke up to the dangerous crisis that had been developing within the ranks of the organisation in exile. Whereas until this moment the ANC external mission had maintained that it had no mandate to hold new elections, Tambo now realised that 'a consultative, decision-making event was not only vital but overdue'.[82] In February 1969,

---

72 See the article by Hugh Macmillan in this issue, 'The African National Congress of South Africa in Zambia: The Culture of Exile and the Changing Relationship with Home, 1964–90', which also discusses the 'Hani Memorandum'.

73 UCT, Manuscripts and Archives, Simons Collection, P7, 'Grounds of appeal and addendum thereto in the matter of expulsion from the African National Congress of Jeqa Buthelezi, Wilmot Bempe, Alfred Khombisa, Wilson Mbali, Jackson Mlenze, Chris Nkosana, Bruce Pitso, March 1969'.

74 Quoted in T.X. Makiwane, *Against the Manipulation of the South African Revolution* (Dar es Salaam, October 1975), p. 10. Long extracts from the memorandum are reproduced in this pamphlet. However, there appear to be no copies of the memorandum in any public archive. A complete copy of the document is forthcoming in *Transformations* as 'The "Hani Memorandum"': introduced and annotated by Hugh Macmillan'.

75 *Ibid.*, pp. 11–12.

76 *Ibid.*, p. 13.

77 Callinicos, *Oliver Tambo*, p. 322.

78 Karis and Gerhart, *Nadir and Resurgence*, p. 34.

79 The tribunal was composed of two members of the executive, Mzwai Piliso and Joe Matlou, and three of the military command. See H. Macmillan, 'The African National Congress of South Africa in Zambia' in this issue.

80 UCT, Manuscripts and Archives, Simons Collection, P7, Grounds of appeal and Addendum Thereto in the Matter of Expulsion from the African National Congress of Jeqa Buthelezi, Wilmot Bempe, Alfred Khombisa, Wilson Mbali, Jackson Mlenze, Chris Nkosana, Bruce Pitso, March 1969.

81 Quoted in Callinicos, *Oliver Tambo*, pp. 325–26.

82 *Ibid.*, p. 330.

the ANC issued directives concerning preparations for a conference, which was envisaged as 'the climax of a campaign of discussion, criticism and proposals covering all aspects of our work'.[83] Everyone who wished to was invited to prepare a submission expressing views and criticism. In other words, the Conference represented an important exercise in democratic participation, the idea being of bringing into the discussion process the political and military movement, including external offices, publicity and research sections, members and supporters of the ANC and the Congress Alliance, individual experts and, perhaps most significantly, MK units. Among the central issues to be discussed were 'the consolidation of the various national groups and progressive organisations in the revolution', 'the structure of our movement', and 'the relationship between the political movement and the national liberation army – Umkhonto we Sizwe'.[84]

Conclusion

In the early 1960s, the ANC adopted the decision that it should present an 'African image' to the outside world. This would serve the purpose of presenting an image that was both acceptable and appealing to the ANC's potential supporters on the continent. However, from the mid-1960s the 'African image' policy had also become a source of strain between the ANC and its non-African supporters. The debates of this period can be viewed as evidence of the difficult transition from the multi-racial approach of the Congress Alliance of the 1950s to the creation of a unitary, non-racial liberation front under the leadership of the ANC. Far from being linear, this transformation was complicated by the adoption of the 'African image' policy in the early part of the decade. Underlying the 'African image' problem was an enduring ideological tension between non-racialism and African nationalism within the ANC, which both preceded the history of the organisation in exile, and was not fully resolved with the opening of ANC membership to non-Africans at the Morogoro Conference in 1969.[85]

Prior to Morogoro, the non-racial substance of the liberation struggle had in part been given form through MK. Since its birth in 1961, MK had accepted in its ranks people of all origins and functioned as a single non-racial organisation. On the other hand, the development of armed struggle during the 1960s was one of the very reasons why, by the latter part of the decade, the ANC in exile was faced with the urgent necessity to reconsider and revise its structure, strategy, programme and aims. The decision to embark on guerrilla warfare, with the ultimate aim of overthrowing the South African government by armed revolution, from around 1963 made the continued separation of political and military structures increasingly problematic.

The problems of representation that had emerged in London in the second half of the 1960s came to converge with pressures from the military camps, where MK cadres were growing increasingly disaffected with the ANC leadership. The discontent within MK pointed to a widening gap between the political and military wings of the organisation. This situation had led to an *impasse*, which could only be overcome by working out of new strategies, objectives and structures. In other words, by the time the Morogoro Conference was called, the ANC leadership was lagging behind in creative ideas, and vitally needed to put itself back in pace with both its rank and file and its non-African allies. The significance of this process of self-renewal and change is that the ANC and its allies were able to stay together by working out effective and acceptable strategies and structures thanks to the

---

83 UWC, MCH70, Duma Nokwe, Directive concerning preparation for Conference, Morogoro, 18 February 1969.
84 *Ibid.*
85 In fact, the conflict was to erupt again in the 1970s and lead to the expulsion of the Group of Eight in 1975.

commitment to unity of all the dominant strands in the Congress Alliance. In spite of the disagreements, the issues and arguments that emerged in this period were ultimately about not whether, but *how*, this could best be achieved. Given the huge rifts in South African society, this was quite a remarkable achievement.

Healthcare in Exile: ANC Health Policy and Health Care Provision in MK Camps, 1964 to 1989

MELISSA ARMSTRONG

Carleton University, Canada

Abstract

The ANC's early health provisions that in 1977 culminated in a bureaucratised Department of Health were critical for the survival of Umkhonto weSizwe (MK) cadres and the ANC's exile movement more generally. This article examines how the relationship between the medical sector and the military changed throughout the time that the ANC and MK were in exile while indicating instances where they influenced each other. While the Health Department's relationship with the military was never severed, the strength of the relationship fluctuated considerably from the early formation of the medical sector to the greater establishment of an institutionalised Health Department.

> As is well known, our earliest Health Team developed out of the needs of Umkhonto We Sizwe in the camps [...] Let it be clearly understood: WE NEED YOU AS MUCH AS WE NEED FOOD, WATER, OR AN AK![1]

The African National Congress' (ANC's) Department of Health (DoH) played a critical, though inconspicuous role in the liberation movement. Health and disease form some of the most intimate and important aspects of social experience, and indeed, accounts of illness, injury and the immediate role of doctors appear in memoires of exile.[2] Similarly, in 1997, the ANC's second submission to the Truth and Reconciliation Commission recognised the impact that the medical sector had on Umkhonto weSizwe (MK) camp life:

---

1.   University of Fort Hare Archive-ANC Mozambique Mission (hereafter UFH-AMM) 17, 6, 'Opening of the Consultative Committee Meeting by the Secretary General- Comrade Alfred Nzo...' [24 November 1982].
2.   See e.g., B. Gilder, *Songs and Secrets* (South Africa: Jacana Media, 2012), 63, 87; W. Welile Bottoman, *The Making of an MK Cadre* (Pretoria: LiNc, 2010), 84.

general conditions in the [MK] camps were at times difficult [...] Medical supplies and other essential items were not always readily available. Tropical diseases, particularly malaria, were rife, and there were too few doctors in Angola to adequately service all those in the camps, cadres and prisoners alike.

However, the medical sector, in both exile memoires and the ANC's submission, is mentioned only briefly and thus far, encounters with the medical sector only make up a few of the small contextual details within the larger liberation struggle story.

The story of the ANC's DoH in exile is an important one. The DoH was established to meet the fluctuating needs of the military effort. The DoH was not under military command but its intimate relationship with MK helped to shape the character of the Department; the medical institutions that were designed to serve the effort felt the pressurised situation of fighting a prolonged 30-year liberation struggle. The Department was formed under pressure, fragmented across Southern Africa and thrust into a tenuous working environment and could therefore not always deliver an effective and transparent medical effort, and its relationship with the military was not static. As the struggle wore on, the Department developed additional focuses and responsibilities while maintaining its commitment to serve military interests.

I seek to illuminate the relationship between the ANC's DoH and MK between 1964 and 1984 (just after the Angolan camp mutinies, discussed below). This paper aims to develop a deeper understanding of the character of the DoH and the decisions made by the Department while in exile, and is based mainly on analyses of archived DoH correspondence, minutes of health meetings and international donor reports. It has two parts: the first part examines the early formation of the medical sector in 1964 and develops a chronological history of its institutional and infrastructural development up to the early 1980s. The second part spotlights the relationship between MK and DoH before and after the Angolan mutinies in 1984. The behaviour of the DoH in Angola at this time exemplified the changing relationship between the military and the medical sector. While the DoH's relationship with the military was never severed, the strength of the relationship fluctuated considerably from the early formation of the medical sector to the greater establishment of an institutionalised DoH.

Formation and development of the ANC Department of Health

The development of a health plan for the treatment of the ANC and MK against injury, illness and disease was a continual negotiation and renegotiation of priorities and possibilities from the beginning until the end of the exile period. This first half of the exile period, between 1964 and mid-1976 witnessed a relatively low profile, neglected medical sector.[3] The medical sector was not well developed partly because the military

---

3.   This is made evident by a number of documents that describe the problems facing the department. See e.g., HP-JHB-KGC, Part 3 Folder 23 'Interim Report of the Commission of the RC Secretariat on the State of Affairs in MK in East Africa', 1 April 1975; HP-JHB-KGC, Part 3 Folder 20 'Report on Youth & Students section to the National Executive Meeting held in East Africa in December 1972', December 1972.

force was small and possibilities for development few.[4] The ANC responded to health crises in an ad hoc, reactive fashion in order to maintain the health of the cadres and the ANC's leadership. It drew heavily on the resources of host countries while also trying to find internal solutions for non-acute illnesses and injuries.[5]

In 1964, the Tanzanian government gave the ANC a large section of land located 250 km West of Dar es Salaam where the ANC established Kongwa camp. According to Issac Makopo, the chief logistics officer stationed in Kongwa from 1964 to 1967, the disease burden (especially foot fungus and eye diseases) in Kongwa made medical provision a necessity.[6] Consequently, it was the medical needs of MK cadres that gave rise to an ANC medical provision. Leslie Sondezi was appointed as the first medical officer in the camp and Jackson Mbali soon supplemented his efforts. They quickly converted one of the camp buildings into a clinic with a four- to five-bed inpatient capacity utilised by MK cadres as well as local Tanzanian residents. Neither Sondezi nor Mbali were doctors (they were medical orderlies), but the ANC had already sent four inadequately trained medical personnel abroad for further medical training.[7]

The medical needs of the cadres could not be completely serviced at the small camp clinic, especially as it lacked a doctor. Healthcare in Tanzania was augmented by local Tanzania government medical facilities and assistance from the international community. Kholeka Thunyiswa, a South African nurse who went into exile in 1962 and settled in a Dar es Salaam hospital, stated that South African nurses in Tanzanian government hospitals treated ANC cadres who needed further provision than could be granted by the small clinic operating at Kongwa.[8] The medical facilities provided by the Tanzanian government were in Dodoma or, for more serious cases, Dar es Salaam.[9] These scant medical provisions were designed to service an estimated 400 to 500 MK cadres in Tanzania during this time.[10] Due to the relatively small size of the contingent, it was also possible to send severe cases abroad

4.   Many scholars show that after the Wankie Campaign (the attempt to move cadres into South Africa through Zimbabwe in 1967) the military effort was not actively engaging the South African Defence Force (SADF): C. Bundy, 'Cooking the Rice outside the Pot? The ANC and SACP in Exile, 1960–1990', in K. Kondlo, C. Saunders and S. Zondi, *Perspectives on the ANC Centenary* (forthcoming); T. Karis, G.M. Carter and G.M. Gerhart, eds, *From Protest to Challenge: Nadir and Resurgence, 1964–1979*, vol. 5 (Standford: Hoover Institution Press, 1972). By the 1970s, Political Military Council was making recommendations to train medical staff that could accompany guerrilla forces on missions but it is unclear from the records whether this was acted upon: HP-JHB-KGC Part 3 Folder 23 'Interim Report of the Commission of the RC Secretariat on the State of Affairs in MK in East Africa', 21 April 1975.

5.   For example, the ANC's annual budget gives some indication of the number of cadres using local services. HP-JHB-KGC Part 3 Folder 20 'Rough estimates of annual expenditure', 5 January 1972.

6.   SADET, *The Road to Democracy: South Africans Telling their Stories: Volume 1, 1950–1970* (South Africa: Tsehai, 2008), 210–211.

7.   *Ibid.*

8.   *Ibid.*, 461–463.

9.   *The Fourth Dimension – The Untold Story of Military Health in South Africa*, ed. Col Ricky Naidoo (Editor-in-Chief) (Pretoria: South African Military Health Service: Department of Defence, 2009).

10.   Population estimates for the ANC and MK throughout the exile period are not established. ANC and MK personnel were widespread and liberation fronts necessarily have a secretive nature. The estimation of 400–500 cadres was given by C. Williams, 'Living in Exile: Daily Life and International Relations at SWAPO's Kongwa Camp', *Kronos*, 37, 1 (2011), 65. This number also aligns with Maurice Mthombeni's estimate quote later in this article: HP-JHB-KGC Part 3 Folder 16, 'Southern Africa: A Betrayal', *The Black Dwarf*, 26 November 1969.

to militarily allied countries such as the Soviet Union or the German Democratic Republic.[11]

During these years, when the health infrastructure was first being established, MK cadres criticised the ANC leadership's efforts to provide for their daily needs and deliver healthcare. In the main, these voices raise the issue of two-tiered health care and neglect. Perhaps the most damning of accusations was levelled by one of the early ANC defectors, Maurice Mthombeni, in 1969. While his complaints were by no means limited to health, health care was clearly featured in an article appearing in *The Black Dwarf*:[12]

> [M]edical facilities were very poor. There was a small camp clinic of 12 feet by 14 feet, which housed five patients of varying diseases at a time. The 'Medical Officer' wasn't very well acquainted with his medical supplies which consisted largely of pain killers, mercurochrome, purgatives and suchlike. All bodily pains were treated alike, and a neurotic case was treated in the same way as a case with a simple headache. The medical supplies in the clinic were insufficient for the four hundred freedom fighters in the camp.[13]

The bulk of the accusations from Mthombeni were rebutted in a response by the ANC Youth and Student's Section in London in '"Black Dwarf" Talks White Trash'; the rebuttal focused on discrediting Mthombeni as a reliable source but does not address his complaints regarding the medical facilities and personnel.[14] Another instance of cadres taking issue with the medical facilities can be found in the 'Hani Memorandum', drafted in 1969, following the Wankie Campaign (the attempt to move cadres into South Africa through Zimbabwe in 1967). Item 14 of the Memorandum states:

> It is very alarming that double standards as regards to health of the members of the Organisation are maintained. Whenever leaders are sick arrangements are made for them to receive excellent medical attention without delay but this sort of concern is hardly shown to the rank and file of the movement. We maintain that all of us are important in so far as the Revolution is concerned and should thus be accorded the same treatment.[15]

Despite the leftist leanings of the armed movement, it should come as no surprise that the medical services were neither adequate nor equally provided. The medical sector was an unofficial provision system; its lack of formal existence made it difficult to hold anyone accountable for poorly run services. Further, while the ANC and MK were mainly based in Tanzania, the exiled movement was at a fledgling stage and medical services were not a primary concern.

The early 1970s has been called the 'nadir in exile'[16] and was characterised by internal leadership battles and a frustrating inability to send cadres home to fight. As Davis

11. See e.g., HP-JHB-KGC Part 3 Folder 24, 'Circular to all our offices', 12 Februrary 1976; UFHA-ALM, Box 31 (Folder 11): 'ANC department of Health: Report on Personnel and Training', 2 April 1987.
12. *The Black Dwarf* was a socialist newspaper published in the United Kingdom between 1968 and 1972.
13. HP-JHB-KGC Part 3 Folder 16, 'Southern Africa: A Betrayal', *The Black Dwarf*, 26 November 1969.
14. HP-JHB-KGC Part 3 Folder 16, 'Black Dwarf Talks White Trash', 26 November 1969.
15. H. Macmillan, 'The "Hani Memorandum" – introduced and annotated', *Transformation*, 69 (2009), 106–129.
16. C. Bundy, 'Cooking the Rice outside the Pot? The ANC and SACP in Exile, 1960–1990', in Kondlo, Saunders and Zondi, *Perspectives on the ANC Centenary*.

explains, 'ten years into exile, the core of the ANC/SACP alliance remained a relatively small, increasingly aged group, beleaguered by their precarious foothold in Africa, preoccupied with internecine disputes'.[17] Despite the relative stagnation in the early 1970s, the ANC's bureaucratic apparatus spread further across the region, which had an impact on health infrastructure. The ANC officially established its new headquarters in Lusaka, Zambia while most of the MK cadres remained in Tanzania. Further, new locations with an ANC presence developed. For instance, in the early 1970s in Dar es Salaam the ANC developed Kurasini Camp, which was designed to accommodate ANC traffic to and from the city.[18] The camp housed a small clinic, used mostly by psychiatric patients being treated at a Muhimbili Medical Centre (also in Dar es Salaam). Muhimbili now had a handful of ANC doctors whose priority was to treat ANC and MK patients.[19] A second transit camp in Tanzania (near Morogoro) called Magadu, established in the early 1970s, ran a small clinic called Moretsele with a single medical officer and was able to deal with minor illnesses and injuries.[20] Having just formed its headquarters in Zambia, the ANC also used the existing medical facilities there, mainly the University Teaching Hospital (UTH) in Lusaka.[21] While new healthcare services arose in this period, the unofficial medical sector remained regionally divided (it was not linked by a centralised medical department) and responsive on a case-by-case basis.

While the ANC was clinging to survival through this period of stasis, the dynamics of the region were rapidly changing. In 1975, Mozambique and Angola gained independence from Portugal and the ANC and MK benefited significantly from this turn of events. Not only did the South African Defence Force lose territory from its buffer zone (the area north of South Africa that remained under the control of South Africa's allies) but the governments led by the People's Movement for the Liberation of Angola (MPLA) and the Mozambique Liberation Front (FRELIMO) granted the ANC permission to create military camps in Angola and Mozambique, allowing for new strategic military possibilities. Those possibilities were further realised after the Soweto school uprisings occurred in June 1976, which sent a wave of students into exile, eager to enlist in MK and fight against the apartheid government. Students could either finish their education[22] or join MK; over the next five years, many students opted to join MK.[23] In 1976, MK established four camps in newly liberated Angola to accommodate the new trainees. Most

---

17. S. Davis, 'Cosmopolitans in Close Quarters: Everyday Life in the Ranks of Umkhonto we Sizwe (1961–Present)' (PhD dissertation, University of Florida, 2010), 44.
18. *The Fourth Dimension.*
19. *The Fourth Dimension*; corroborated by University of Fort Hare Archive-ANC Lusaka Mission (UFHA-ALM), Box127 (Folder236): 'The Structure of the Department of Health and its Function', 3 October 1986.
20. *Ibid.*
21. HP-JHB-KGC Part 3 Folder 20 'Rough estimates of annual expenditure', 5 January 1972.
22. The plans for the Solomon Mahlangu Freedom College (SOMAFCO) in Mazimbu, Tanzania, began in 1977 in response to the need to provide a basic education for school age children and young adults. Secondary schooling began in 1978 with an estimate of 50 students, and by 1984, that number is estimated to have increased to 202 (about 450 including primary students): S. Morrow et al., *Education in Exile: SOMAFCO, the ANC school in Tanzania, 1978 to 1992* (Cape Town: HSRC Press, 2004), 20; HP-JHB-KGC, P3(56): 'Report of the Commission of the NEC appointed to investigate the allocation and utilization of the financial resources of the organization in regions of the Front Line States and Forward Areas, March 1984-July 1984', 31 July 1984.
23. S. Ellis, 'Mbokodo: Security in ANC Camps, 1961–1990', *African Affairs*, 93, 371 (1994), 279–298.

were sent to the largest of these four camps, Novo Catengue, situated in central Angola. Estimates vary dramatically on the numerical strength of MK throughout the 1970s and 1980s. However, based on the combined capacity of the camps operating in 1976, it appears that just fewer than 1000 cadres were in Angola by the end of 1976[24] and probably just over 2000 by 1988.[25] Due to events in 1975 and 1976, the medical sector's relationship to MK changed. Rather than attempting to deal with health crises on a case-by-case basis, the neglected and poorly developed medical sector was required to transform into a more formal bureaucratic institution able to communicate with the growing MK force across a much larger territory in exile.

On 27 August 1977, an official ANC DoH was inaugurated.[26] The DoH's mandate was to evaluate the existing situation and begin to build a foundation for a competent DoH. By 1979, the department comprised Chairperson Peter Mfelang and Secretary Manto Tshabalala, as well as elected medical representatives from each region with an established ANC presence. Angola, Tanzania and Zambia had 'health teams' due to the already existing medical structures in these regions. The health teams were, at least initially, headed by doctors.[27] Based on the rudimentary capacity for health provision inherited from the previous decade, coupled with the rapidly expanding exile population, the DoH was poorly equipped at this early stage to deal with the health situation. A number of medical personnel were affiliated with the ANC DoH but on permanent staff, the Department could only claim three doctors, two nurses and 10 to 15 medical auxiliaries.[28]

The institutional relationship between the DoH and the military can be understood by the ANC command structure (Figure 1). The National Executive Council (NEC) was superior to the Political Military Command (PMC) and the External Coordinating Committee (ECC). These were the most authoritative bodies for MK and the ANC respectively, and both reported to the NEC. The ECC secretariat was responsible for overseeing the Office of the President, the Secretary General (SG) and the Treasurer General (TG). The DoH was one of several departments reporting to the office of the SG.[29] This placement of the DoH on the ECC branch of authority separated it from the military command structure. Therefore, the DoH had a dual relationship with the military; on the one hand, the department had a formal, institutional relationship with the PMC- mediated by the NEC. On the other hand, the relationship was built on the ground on a case-by-case, region-by-region basis in much the same way that it had been previously.

The DoH's own internal structure was formalised in 1979 (Figure 2). At the most basic level, medical clinics and dispensaries reported to the Regional Health Teams (RHTs). These RHTs had Regional Health Committees (RMCs) that were made up of a chairperson, a secretary, and two-to-five additional members.[30] They were responsible for coordinating the health activities in the regions as well as submitting quarterly reports to

24. HP-JHB-KGC, P3(100): 'Appendices to the Second Submission by the ANC to the TRC', 12 May 1997.
25. These estimates will be expanded upon in text below.
26. UFHA-ALM, 112(96): 'Report of the East Africa Health Team Meeting', 10 May 1981.
27. Mozambique had a less established team headed initially by nurse Florence Maleka in Maputo.
28. UFHA-ALM, 112(96): 'Report of the East Africa Health Team Meeting', 10 May 1981.
29. UFHA-ALM, 127(236): 'Structure March 1983'. Some individuals occupy multiple offices.
30. Between 1977 and 1989 some of the titles of the positions changed. For clarity, the 1983 structure and models are used.

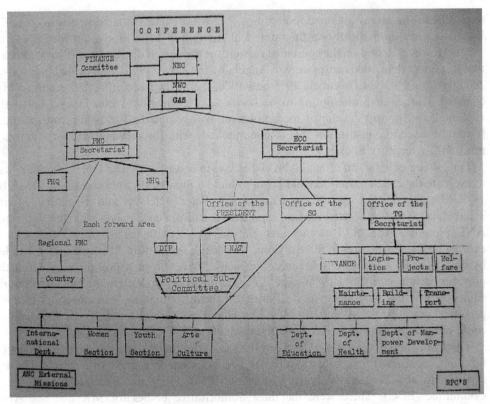

Figure 1. The African National Congress' Organisational Structure. UFHA-ALM, 127(236): 'Structure March 1983'.

the Health Chairperson in Lusaka.[31] In 1983, a new body, the Health Secretariat, was constituted.[32] Headquartered in Lusaka, the Secretariat was a sizeable bureaucracy with more extensive oversight and coordinating functions. The Secretariat had six portfolios in 1983: the Secretary, who headed the DoH and was responsible for the reports to be sent to the SG (Dr Peter Mfelang); the Deputy Secretary who acted in the place of the Secretary where needed but also corresponded with the regional departments (Dr Manto Tshabalala); the Administrative Secretary, who kept the minutes of meetings and the health records (Mrs Edna Miya); the Information and Publicity Officer who was in charge of correspondence with health personnel in South Africa and with the creation and distribution of a health bulletin (Dr Haggar Macberry); Personnel Officer who kept a record of those who were health personnel across the regions (Dr Ike Nzo); and finally the Health Education Programme Officer who planned and evaluated programmes to educate

31.   The Health Secretariat was elected by a summit of health personnel called the Health Council. The Health Council held meetings to discuss the progress of the department.
32.   UFHA-ALM, 31(11): 'Preamble', 26 March 1985.

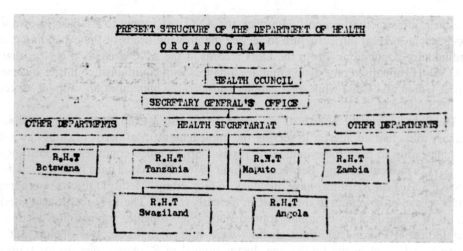

Figure 2.   Health Department Structure, 1983. UFHA-ALM, 127(236): 'The Structure of the Department of Health and its Function', 3 October 1986.

ANC personnel on health related material (Mrs Khulukazi Mzamo).[33] An additional five portfolios were added in 1986.[34] On paper, the most powerful organ of the DoH was the Health Council,[35] made up of health personnel from each of the RHTs and DoH officials in Lusaka. It convened every three years to discuss health policy.[36]

The creation of a health bureaucracy did not strengthen the medical sector's relationship with the military. Rather, the creation of a bureaucracy enabled the health sector to divide its attention between taking care of cadres' illnesses and injuries and looking to future medical developments in exile and at home in South Africa. As shown below in part 2, the new avenues of attention were not completely separate from one another. The DoH's outward focus was coloured by its military foundation and its obligations to the liberation movement; likewise, the institutional response to the military became increasingly focused on the future. The following section establishes the DoH's new focus on future development in exile, which is followed by analysis of the DoH's immediate interests in responding to the needs of MK cadres.

One of the first avenues exploited by the newly-established DoH was the supportive international community. Up until the late 1970s, the DoH was reliant on host countries

33.   UFH-AA, ALM, 127, 236, 'Secretariat Job Description'; 1983 names taken from UFH-AA, ALM, 31, 11, 'Report of the National Preparatory Committee (NPC) [Lusaka. November 1986]; In 1986 Dr Haggar Macberry, Dr Manto Tshabalala, Dr Ralph Mgijima, Dr Pren Naicker, Dr Zakes Mokoena, Dr Bob Mayekiso, Mr Mkhulu Radebe, Mrs Winnie Nkobi, Mrs Edna Miya, Mrs Florence Maleka and Mrs Regina Nzo were elected to become the new health secretariat. The secretariat therefore expanded to include a number of extra portfolios, one of which was someone to keep inventory of drugs in all regions. However, the new positions are not clearly allotted in the attainable record.

34.   UFHA-ALM, 127(236): 'Secretariat Job Description' [1986]. For details of office-holders see UFHA-ALM, 31(11): 'Report of the National Preparatory Committee', November 1986.

35.   UFHA-ALM, 160(1a): 'Objective and Critical Analysis of the Present State of Affairs in the Health Department', 24 November 1982.

36.   The Council convened for the first time in 1980: UFHA-ALM, 112(95): 'Minutes of the special Health Council Meeting held in Lusaka January 24–25, 1982.'

and their infrastructural support. However, the ANC now sought to establish its own semi-independent medical infrastructure to service the growing needs of the expanding civilian and military populations. From the DoH records at the ANC archive, it is clear that the ANC DoH capitalised on existing military alliances with communist countries such as the Soviet Union and Cuba while also gaining considerable humanitarian support, especially from Scandinavia.

The fight against the apartheid government was also a Cold War struggle and so the military allies had an interest in serving the immediate medical needs of cadres as well as training cadres to meet these immediate needs.[37] Soviet-allied countries provided most of the ANC's medical training. Between 1968 and 1986, '21 doctors have been trained [in the USSR]; 3 Medical Assistants have qualified. In fact, many "Medical Officers" were trained under special programmes in the USSR in the early 60's'.[38] The 1987 report also provided details of 22 medical professionals trained since 1985: Bulgaria trained nine doctors and one Industrial Pharmacist; three doctors were trained in Cuba; two doctors and one pharmacist trained in the GDR; one doctor trained in Romania; one doctor trained in Zambia; two doctors trained in Britain; and two doctors trained in Tanzania.[39] In 1988, there were seven ANC graduates of medicine from Cuba alone.[40] Not only were the military alliances interested in training ANC personal, they were also an important supplier of reliable medical personal on the military front. One commander noted:

> [...] our organization become [sic] impressed by the attitude and medical work of the Cubans in Angola. From their own experience they know that it is impossible to develop the revolution in one day. As doctors they are more adapted to the African situation, more modest in their technical and political attitude. In fact they know better what is the attitude of international solidarity, because they were trained under their difficult circumstances of socialism.[41]

The military's relationship with the DoH enabled the latter to better utilise the international resources available from the Soviet-allied countries.

The humanitarian international support took on a markedly different form and flavour. Rather than focusing on the military effort, humanitarian aid was geared towards providing medical equipment and supplies, medical infrastructure and providing extended care to an exiled (rather than explicitly military) community.[42] Additionally, humanitarian aid was responsible for the bulk of the monetary donations. Backed by humanitarian aid, the ANC's DoH was able to open two major health centres.[43] In 1978 the Medisch Komitee Angola (MKA), a Netherland-based donor, agreed to fund a new hospital in

---

37. V.G. Shubin, *ANC: A View from Moscow* (Cape Town: Mayibuye, 1999).
38. UFHA-ALM, 31(11): 'Report on Personnel and Training', 2 April 1987.
39. UFHA-ALM, 31(11): 'Report on Personnel and Training', 2 April 1987.
40. HP-JHB-KGC, P3(88): Raymond Nkuku to Alfred Nzo.
41. UFH-AA, ALM, 112, 94, Letter to Comrade Nzo signed Henk Odink [31 January 1984].
42. Throughout the 1960s, 1970s and 1980s, South Africans moved into exile without intention to join the military. Some aid organisations called these people 'refugees' rather than exiles and humanitarian aid was funnelled through liberation movements to target these people: E.H. Østbye, 'The South African Liberation Struggle: Official Norwegian Support', in T.L. Erikson, ed, *Norway and National Liberation in Southern Africa* (Stockholm: Elanders Gotab, 2000), 131–176.
43. From internal funds, the ANC was able to construct a third major health centre in 1984: Emmasdale clinic near the Headquarters in Lusaka.

Mazimbu for the SOMAFCO[44] community.[45] The hospital was called the ANC-Holland Solidarity Hospital. (The hospital building process did not begin until 1982 and the hospital did not open until 1 May 1984).[46] The Norwegian People's Aid (NPA) funded the second facility: a clinic and training centre in Viana, a site near Luanda, Angola.[47] The centre was opened in stages between 1985 and 1986.[48]

This division in the nature of the funding impacted the character of the DoH and subtly changed the relationship between the DoH and MK. As the bulk of the monetary funding was aimed at providing for an exiled community rather than a military movement, the Department increasingly saw itself as more than simply a service for the military.[49] This changing self-image impacted the service provided, the uses of resources as well as medical staff's opinion of their relationship with military, as shown below.

Backed by international support, the DoH attempted to provide medical services across Southern Africa to its military and non-military populations. An assessment of the DoH in the mid-1980s must necessarily be ambivalent. On the one hand, the ANC's health infrastructure was impressive. The movement could boast of three major medical sites – the main site being the ANC-Holland Solidarity Hospital – as well as a number of supporting medical posts throughout each of its occupied regions. Yet despite the efforts of the DoH, the ANC never saw any of their medical facilities used to full capacity. As one report concerning the ANC-Holland Solidarity Hospital stated:

> The hospital was planned as a fully fledged hospital offering the following services: diagnostic services – facilitated by laboratory techniques and x-ray, in-and out-patient treatment including medical and surgical treatment, MCH [mother and child health]-services incl[uding] deliveries and immunization, dental services, health education, preventive health. Despite the fact that the buildings have been ready for two years, only part of the specialized physical facilities are in operations, and the hospital is only able to offer a limited range of services.[50]

For a variety of reasons, even with international support, the ANC suffered from a chronic shortage of medical personnel to staff their facilities.[51] The DoH also battled to maintain a

44. SOMAFCO (Solomon Mahlangu Freedom College) was a school developed for school-aged exile community members in Mazimbu, Tanzania. Soloman Mahlangu was an MK cadre and deployed in South Africa. At age 23 (in 1979) he was executed for his involvement in clandestine actions against the government.

45. UFHA-ALM, 112(94): 'Tshabalala to Comrade Thomas', 26 December 1981.

46. UFHA-ALM, 31(8): 'Health Supply in the Tanzanian Region', n.d. [1987?].

47. *Ibid.*

48. The DoH never opened a major health centre in Mozambique. The Mozambican RHT only ever operated out of local infrastructure in Nampula and Maputo and referred patients to Tanzania and Harare as required. This was onerous as the Mozambican RHT was additionally responsible for medical provisions in Swaziland and Lesotho.

49. While the military was without question an important source of support to the ANCs DoH, the archival documents do not show large amounts of monetary support given. Instead, the military support was oriented towards training medical personal and sending medical reinforcements to serve the military effort. The monetary support was given by humanitarian aid and helped to fund infrastructure projects, purchase supplies and pay medical bills as mentioned above.

50. UFHA-ALM, 31(8): 'Health Supply in the Tanzanian Region', n.d. [1987?].

51. The issue of medical staff is an item in many health reports. See e.g., UFHA-ALM, P2 33(1): 'Report and Minutes of the Meeting of the Health Secretariat', 3 August 1984.

consistent supply of equipment, drugs and transportation,[52] and when drugs and equipment were sent, the departmental disorganisation led to delays in processing the supplies and sometimes resulted in spoilt or expired drugs.[53] Transportation was especially inadequate. The ANC needed vehicles that would not break down on the rough terrain and abuse of these vehicles occurred in the initial period. Making matters worse, an intoxicated driver damaged an ambulance in Tanzania and there were complaints that others made personal rather than medical use of the vehicles.[54] Therefore, even with the new medical facilities, patients with acute injuries or illnesses were most often sent to Harare, UTH, Morogoro, Dar es Salaam or further abroad.

The DoH attempted to arrange for educational clinics and programmes to make ANC and MK comrades aware of health-related issues. Indeed, as previously mentioned, one of the Secretariat portfolios in 1983 was the Health Education Programme Officer whose sole purpose was to plan programmes to educate ANC personnel on health related material.[55] The bulk of this education was delivered in Mazimbu, Tanzania, where, especially in the mid-1980s, the social worker, Sherry MacLean,[56] was able to lead many of these educational sessions.[57] These awareness clinics focused on sex education,[58] mental health, and later, HIV/AIDS, and the DoH produced pamphlets and other educational materials to distribute to ANC and MK comrades.[59] The Department also produced resources for the medical personnel: 'The Health Secretariat acquired and distributed books to all health teams. These were reference books for health workers to facilitate diagnosis and treatment...'[60] Staff were also encouraged to attend medical educational workshops on various topics such as malaria, dental care, mental health, and nutrition.[61] These efforts, however, fell short of what the Department felt was necessary for the movement. Many of the regional reports or minutes of Secretariat meetings outline the desperate need for greater health-related education.[62]

Not only did the Department have to deal with the infrastructural and educational shortcomings, but its ability to manage its own affairs suffered from a number of interpersonal conflicts and organisational setbacks. In 1982, Secretary General Alfred Nzo

---

52. The shortage in supplies is also an item in many health reports. See e.g., UFHA-ALM, 31(11): 'Preamble' 26 March 1985.
53. UFHA-ALM, 111(89): 'A brief Report on the medical situation in Dar es Salaam and Morogoro areas', 8 March 1979.
54. UFHA-ALM, 112(96): 'Confidential Report on Comrade Joe Mosupye', 30 December 1981.
55. UFHA-ALM, 31(11): 'Report of the National Preparatory Committee', November 1986.
56. Sherry MacLean was not an ANC member but rather an international volunteer working with the exiled community in Mazimbu and Dakawa, Tanzania.
57. FHA-ALM, 31(8): 'Health Supply in the Tanzanian Region', n.d. [1987?].
58. By the mid-1980s, there is an emphasis to provide sex education to female cadres in Angola. See for example: UFHA-ALM, 106(53): 'Report on Work Done in Caculama', 8 March, 1985.
59. C. Tsampiras, 'Politics, Polemics, and Practice: A History of Narratives about and Responses to AIDS in South Africa' (PhD dissertation, Rhodes University, 2013); C. Tsampiras, 'Sex in a Time of Exile: An Examination of Sexual Health, AIDS, Gender, and the ANC, 1980–1990', *South African Historical Journal* 63 (2012), 3.
60. UFHA-ALM, 127(236): Draft: Health Secretariat Report to the 3rd Health Council Meeting', 29 July 1986.
61. *Ibid.*
62. See e.g., FHA-ALM, 31(8): 'Health Supply in the Tanzanian Region', n.d. [1987?].

wrote to Tshabalala stating that it was natural and expected for any new department to experience 'teething problems' but that he was confident that this would sort itself out.[63] These interpersonal and group conflicts persisted and the regional reports and correspondence often contain vehement complaints or accusations against other DoH members. In 1982 Dr Sipho Mthembu, stationed in Tanzania as an ANC doctor stated:

> [T]he only thing [Tshabalala] contributed to the struggle is confusion [...] To date, despite repeated verbal accusations against her behaviors and attitude, she still believes in doing things single-handed [...] To her, other members of the Medical Team are pawns in a one-man-on-the-stage [sic] chess game.[64]

Mthembu was not alone in his frustration with the leadership;[65] throughout the 1980s, a number of prominent medical personnel resigned. And while Tshabalala is not overtly named in all cases, it is apparent that she was a key factor in the widespread staff dissatisfaction and for these reasons, she was suspended in 1987.[66]

Alongside interpersonal issues, the DoH struggled to communicate efficiently and to coordinate its projects and reports across the regions. The RHTs were asked to send quarterly reports to the Secretariat.[67] However, this was rarely done in the early period of the DoH. To a great extent this was due to medical staff shortages and lack of clinic administration.[68] Patients were often sent from one region to another without accompanying documentation,[69] and some cadres were sent to the wrong region.[70] It was difficult for health teams to keep a detailed inventory; as a result, clinics were often inadequately stocked. Furthermore, the lack of transportation made it difficult to coordinate between medical facilities within the same region. A 1986 report stated:

> The functions of the Health Secretariat have been undermined because of a variety of reason viz: [sic] Secretariat members are seattered, [sic] they have less time to devote to Secretariat work due to their regular employment locally, there exist [sic] poor cooordination [sic] and communication with certain sectors of the movement, strained interpersonal relationships etc. Council must seek ways to strengthen the health Secretariat with the aim of improving efficiency, coordination and communication, particularly with regional structures.[71]

This call for reform might have been the cause of electing an additional five members to the Secretariat that year.[72]

---

63. UFHA-ALM, 160(1a): 'Consultative Committee Meeting Between the Working Committee and Health Department Held from 30 November to 2nd December 1982 in Lusaka- Zambia.'
64. UFHA-ALM, 160(1a): Sipho Mthembu to Chief Representative, Secretary General, 31 May 1982.
65. See e.g., UFHA-ALM, 160(1c): Dr Mthembu to the Medical Department, 12 March 1984.
66. Supported by Ralph Mgijima, Tshabalala was reinstated in 1989.
67. UFHA-ALM, 31(8): 'Health Supply in the Tanzanian Region', n.d. [1987?].
68. See e.g., UFHA-ALM, 160(1a): 'Report on Trip to Maputo', 5 July 1982.
69. UFHA-ALM, 112(96): 'Report of the East Africa Health Team Meeting', 10 April 1981.
70. UFHA-ALM, 160(1c): 'Medical Report', October 1983.
71. UFHA-ALM, 127(236): 'The Structure of the Department of Health and its Function', 3 October 1986.
72. Ibid.

The Department of Health in Angola before and after the 1984 mutinies

By the early 1980s, the medical sector had moved a long way from its starting place as a small clinic in the military camp at Kongwa. Not only had the sector developed a formal structure, it was no longer literally or figuratively centred within the military camp. The Department had its headquarters in Zambia and its main referral hospital in Tanzania, both at a distance from the main sites of military camps. However, this shift away from the military did not sever the DoH's relationship with the military or remove it from its obligations to MK cadres. Much of the medical infrastructure in place across Southern Africa was designed to address the needs of cadres that had been medically referred away from military zones and the level of medical provision in the military zones fluctuated throughout the 1980s. Yet there were inconsistent levels of attention and care paid to the military in that region.[73]

The ANC listed 12 camps used by MK in Angola (Figure 3). These camps operated between six months and 12 years. Camps included: Gabela Training Camp (1976–1977) that accommodated about 40 cadres; Engineering Luanda Transit Camp (1976–1977) that accommodated approximately 200 cadres; Nova Catengue Training Camp (1976–1979) that accommodated about 500 cadres; Funda Training Camp (1976–1988) that accommodated around 100 cadres; Benguela Transit Camp (1977–1982) that accommodated about 300 cadres; Quibaxe Training Camp (1977–1989) that accommodated about 200 cadres; Fazenda Military Camp (1978–1980) that accommodated about 200 cadres; Pango Camp (1979–1989) that accommodated about 400 cadres; Viana Transit Camp (1979–1989) that accommodated about 400 cadres; Caxito Training Camp (1979–1984) that accommodated about 100 cadres; Camalundi Camp (1980–1981) that accommodated about 350 cadres; and Caculama Camp (1981–1989) that accommodated about 400 cadres.[74] (Recently, there has also been discussion about Camp 13 and Camp 32 (Quatro)[75] but this paper will not be analysing the health situation in these prison camps.) According to the dates given, there were between four and eight camps operating at one time. According to the estimated camp capacity, there would have been almost 1000 cadres in 1976 when only four camps were open. In the 1980s, the number would have risen to around 2000 cadres. However, from estimates made by other scholars of MK, it would appear that MK had a more significant presence in Angola.[76]

73. MK was also operating from other regions across Southern Africa. I choose to concentrate on Angola because it is the focal point of the military effort and the primary cite of military camps for MK in the 1980s. Further, Angola had a regional health team and the DoH-military relationship is most clearly visible in this region.

74. HP-JHB-KGC, P3(100): 'Appendices to the Second Submission by the ANC to the TRC', 12 May 1997.

75. For a more detailed discussion of the prison camps, see S. Ellis, *External Mission: The ANC in Exile 1960–1990* (London: Hurst & Co., 2012); P. Trewhela, *Inside Quatro: Uncovering the Exile History of the ANC and SWAPO* (South Africa: Jacana Media, 2009). Also see: HP-JHB-KGC, P3(100): 'Further Submissions and Responses by the ANC to Questions Raised by the Commission for Truth and Reconciliation', 12 May 1997.

76. The secretive nature of MK makes the population records and camp locations inconsistent between archive records and scholarly estimates. Scholarly estimates have been outlined in T. Lodge, 'State of Exile: The African National Congress of South Africa, 1976–86', *Third World Quarterly*, 9, 1 (1987), 1–27. Lodge shows that as of 1987 estimates of MK numbers ranged from 10,000 (Howard Barrell) to 5,400 (Stephen Davis). More recently, Hugh Macmillan has put forward a more conservative estimate of MK's numerical

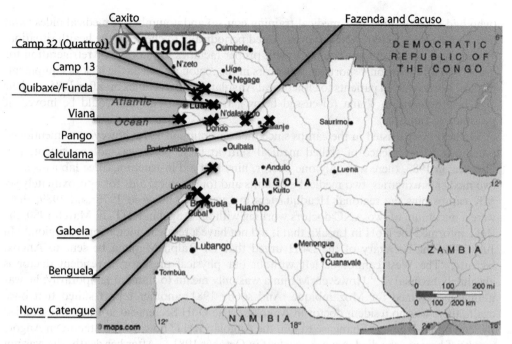

Figure 3. Umkhonto weSizwe camps in Angola. Note: Camp locations are approximate, but as accurate as possible; camps were placed, by the author over political map of Angola. Maps.com, 'Angola Political Map', http://www.maps.com/ref_map.aspx?pid=11884 accessed February 19, 2014.

Angola was not an easy place to establish an ANC RHT. Despite Angola's formal independence, it was engaged in a bloody civil war throughout MK's time in the region. The ANC was able to draw on local services but the Angolan Government's health infrastructure was weak, understaffed and overburdened.[77] In most cases, due to the inability to treat patients in Angola, attempts were made to send cadres experiencing acute illnesses or injuries to Tanzania.[78] Nevertheless, the department worked to provide some level of basic care to cadres in each of the military camps. One report stated that each camp was equipped with a small medical post that included a reception area, treatment room and small dispensary.[79] Designed to supply primary care, the posts were typically staffed by one medical assistant

strength; he estimates that by 1988, there were just over 2000 cadres in Angola: H. Macmillan, *The Lusaka Years: The ANC in exile in Zambia, 1963 to 1994* (South Africa: Jacana Media, 2013).

77. The weakness of local services was highlighted by a report done on an existing hospital in Cacuso (in the North West region of Angola). The evaluation of the hospital was done by the DoH in order to assess whether the Department would invest into the hospital and use it to serve MK cadres as well as Angolan residents. FHA-ALM 160(1b): 'Initial Report on Cacuso Hospital Prepared by Manto Tshabalala', 17 October 1983.

78. Correspondence and reports mention the need to transfer patients. See for example: FHA-ALM 161(3d): 'African National Congress Department of Health Report- Health Department January 1983-December 1983', December 1983; FHA-ALM 160(1c): 'Dr S.P. Mthembu to Dar es Salaam Medical Department', 12 February 1984.

79. J. Hippe and A. Pedersen, *Health Care in an Exile Community: Report on Health Planning in the ANC* (The Norwegian Trade Union Research Centre, 1987).

(who had taken a three-year medical training course) and a number of medical aides (who had been trained *in situ*). ANC doctors visited periodically to check on the health situation. The medical posts were not equipped with proper facilities for storage or refrigeration for drugs.[80] With the chronic shortage of doctors in the region as well as the lack of equipment, medical posts referred patients to either local Angolan health facilities or, after 1985, to their own health centre in Viana (discussed below); from there, patients would be moved, if possible, to Tanzania.

Medical posts existed in the camps since their inception in 1976; however, as mentioned previously, the presence of skilled medical staff at these posts was not consistent. For instance, in 1983, there was only one doctor, nine first aid instructors, three lab assistants, two medical auxiliaries, two medical assistants and four medical aids for approximately six MK camps plus the regional Headquarters in Luanda.[81] Between 1976 and 1989, there were a maximum of two ANC doctors working with the Angolan RHT. In March 1980, the RHT informed the DoH in Lusaka that it did not have a resident doctor for the region.[82] In July 1980, the Secretary of the DoH urged that Dr Ralph Mgijima be sent to Angola because, 'The West cannot be left without our physical presence; a resident doctor is absolutely necessary'.[83] However, Mgijima was only meant to stand in temporarily; he was ultimately destined for Mozambique. And so by 1981, another report stated that once again, there was no resident doctor in Angola.[84] The DoH Secretariat in Lusaka responded by sending Dr Nomava Shangase to join the Angolan RHT; however, her tenure in Angola was brief because she died in a car accident in October 1981.[85] After her death, she was not replaced until 1983 when Dr Sipho Mthembu agreed to go to Angola.

In 1984, the Norwegian People's Association (NPA) with secondary support from the Medishe Komittee Angola (MKA), provided funds and materials for the construction of a clinic in Viana, 20 km east of Luanda. The clinic in Viana was finished in 1985 and staffed by Scandinavian solidarity workers and ANC health personnel. Also in 1984, the NPA, the United Nations High Commissioner for Refugees (UNHCR), and the Finnish Africa Committee supplied funds and materials to erect a 3951 m^2 training centre that was handed over to the ANC in December 1985[86] and officially opened in September 1986. The first one-year ANC/South West Africa People's Organisation (SWAPO) medical training course began that month, with 20 students. The training centre was aimed at South African refugees, and members of the ANC and MK. The training centre was set up to offer many courses in medical aid, mechanics and other vocational occupations in order to create self-sustainability.[87] It was also designed to train health professionals for a new South Africa: 'the DoH must be highly organized and be ready to meet the ever growing needs in the period of our struggle and in the period of reconstruction and development of our

80. *Ibid.*, 56–57.
81. UFHA-ALM, 161(3d): 'Report: Health Department January 1983–December 1983.'
82. UFHA-ALM, 112(96): 'The Health Department Report', 18 March 1981.
83. UFHA-ALM, P3A2, 6(7): 'Memorandum to the Secretary-General from the Health Department', 21 July 1980.
84. UFHA-ALM, 112(96): 'Report of the East Africa Health Team Meeting', 10 May 1981.
85. UFHA-ALM, 132(271): 'Telex Message Received from Luanda', 21 October 1981.
86. UFHA-ALM, P3A2, 39(39): 'Finnsolidarity: ANC Viana Centre', 25 September 1986; Finnsolidarity oversaw the implementation of the whole project.
87. UFHA-ALM, P3A2, 39(39): 'Finnsolidarity: ANC Viana Centre', 25 September 1986.

country.'[88] In 1987, the clinic and training centre was named the Moses Kotane Health Centre.[89] It had a six-bed in-patient capacity, and was staffed by two doctors, two nurses, one medical assistant, and three medical aides. On a monthly basis between 200 and 300 patients were treated, half of whom were local Angolans. It was not equipped for most intensive procedures or for maternal and child health issues and so patients needing extra care would be referred to Luanda, Lusaka, Harare or Mazimbu.[90]

Throughout the period that MK was in Angola, the DoH struggled to appropriately equip each medical post with health supplies. Some of the camps were a three- or four-day journey from Luanda. In 1979, the Angolan RHT ordered gynaecological equipment for the region; the equipment was sent to Lusaka but took a further six months to reach Luanda.[91] Once supplies arrived in Angola, the dispersal to medical posts was difficult and unreliable. The roads were poor and rain-washed, Angola was engaged in civil war and transport had to avoid South African Defense Force (SADF) detection. Adding to these difficulties was the fact that the RHT suffered a chronic shortage of medical transport.[92] Indicative of desperation, in 1981, the RHT asked the DoH if it could appeal to the Angolan DoH for an ambulance. However, for reasons that are not completely clear,[93] the RHT was sternly warned against asking the Angolan DoH;[94] by 1983, they were given two 4x4 Landrovers that were donated by Norway.[95] Unfortunately, these vehicles were sorely insufficient to cover all Angolan camps. Consequently, communication between the camps and the regional headquarters in Luanda was not reliable and it was therefore difficult to transfer acutely ill cadres.

The feelings of cadres towards Angolan camps were varied. On the one hand, cadres entered Angola already eagerly anticipating their departure to fight in South Africa. Barry Gilder wrote of his observations while entering into Quibaxe camp:

> There is an air of expectation, excitement even. (Later I would come to know that this feeling of anticipation accompanied the arrival of any transport from outside the isolation of the camp. These trucks brought [...] comrades who came now and again to the camps to select people for the front – to go to fight at home, which is what we all came here for in the first place...).[96]

Camp memoirs demonstrate the camaraderie in camps, and the united purpose to fight the enemy. However, cadres were not deployed in South Africa as they had expected but

88. UFHA-ALM, 127(236): 'Role of Students during training and after training', November 1986.
89. Moses Kotane was a political leader in both the South African Communist Party and the ANC. In the mid-1960s, Kotane became the Treasurer-General for the ANC in exile. Following a stroke, Kotane was sent to Moscow where he died in 1978 at age 73.
90. Hippe and Pederson, *Health Care in an Exile Community*, 56–66.
91. UFHA-ALM, 112(95): 'Minutes of the ANC(SA) Medical and Health Committee', 21–26 January 1979.
92. *Ibid.*
93. The relationship between the Angolan Health Department and the ANC DoH operated on relatively good terms. In my opinion, the warning against asking the Angolan Health Department for an ambulance had something to do with the DoH wanting to remain semi-autonomous.
94. UFHA-ALM, 111(89): 'Health Department', 30 July 1981.
95. The report states that the ambulances were given by Norway. Presumably, they were donated by the Norwegian People's Association (NPA) but it is conceivable that the Norwegian Government itself may have donated them. UFHA-ALM, 161(3d): 'Report- Health Department January 1983–December 1983.'
96. B. Gilder, *Songs and Secrets: South Africa from Liberation to Governance* (South Africa: Jacana Press, 2012), 53.

instead were trained and held in Angola for indefinite periods of time. Camp dynamics contained a tension between anticipation and frustration; between military preparedness and prolonged periods of inactivity.

The 1984 mutinies became a symbol of the tension and unrest in the camps.[97] In December 1983, MK cadres joined People's Armed Forces for the Liberation of Angola (FAPLA) against South Africa-backed National Union for the Total Independence of Angola (UNITA). One MK unit[98] accompanied FAPLA forces to fight UNITA while a second unit of 104 cadres was sent to guard Cangandala, a FAPLA position. Many cadres were keen to put their military training into action. However, ill-disciplined behaviour in Cangandala caused commanders to move MK out of the area. Additionally, a badly planned military operation resulted in five MK casualties. Cadres resented fighting in Angola instead of within South Africa. Drawn from both units, two groups of cadres travelled to Viana in protest, wishing to speak to the leadership. In February, a 'Committee of Ten' was formed by the cadres to discuss their collective grievances with the leadership. Instead, FAPLA troops arrived in Viana and attempted to disarm the group. Violence broke out, and between four and ten cadres were killed and 31 were captured and imprisoned.[99]

In order to assess the situation in 1984, the NEC established a Special Commission headed by James Stuart to investigate the situation in Angola.[100] The Commission, known as the Stuart Commission stated: 'It is clear that since 1979 there has been a gradual development of an explosive situation which finally erupted in December 1983.'[101] It commented on unfavourable aspects of camp life including but not limited to poor administration and leadership, unfair and often extreme disciplinary measures, unacceptable camp conditions, and an unfavourably long stay in camps. The Commission also explicitly mentioned the deteriorating health conditions in the camps citing the lack of medical personnel and the high rate of illness.

There is enough evidence to show that the DoH was well aware that the health situation was deteriorating in the camps in the early 1980s and it responded to the situation with a distinct lack of conviction and urgency. On the one hand, the camps in Angola were in need of stable, long-term medical attention. On the other hand, Angola was a tense military zone and was known to be an undesirable work environment. Additionally, as previously stated, those with acute injuries or illnesses were not even treated by doctors in Angola but were referred away from the military front.[102] In 1982, the Angolan RHT sent a report to the

---

97. For a more detailed account of these events, see S. Ellis, *External Mission: The ANC in Exile 1960–1990* (London: Hurst & Company, 2012); P. Trewhela, *Inside Quatro: Uncovering the Exile History of the ANC and SWAPO* (South Africa, Jacana Media, 2009). Also see: HP-JHB-KGC, P3(100): 'Further Submissions and Responses by the ANC to Questions Raised by the Commission for Truth and Reconciliation', 12 May 1997.

98. The size of this unit is not specified but cadres were taken from four MK camps and some of the camps were virtually emptied. This suggests that several hundred to 1000 cadres went to FAPLA's aid.

99. HP-JHB-KGC, P3(55): 'Report: Commission of Inquiry into Recent Developments in the People's Republic of Angola, March 14, 1984, Lusaka', 14 March 1984.

100. James Stuart's MK name was Hermanus Loots.

101. HP-JHB-KGC, P3(55): 'Report: Commission of Inquiry into Recent Developments in the People's Republic of Angola, March 14, 1984, Lusaka.', 14 March 1984.

102. UFHA-ALM, 161(3a): Tshabalala to Chief of Staff, 21 August 1984.

Secretariat stating that health conditions in the camps were unacceptable.[103] There were sanitation issues due to the poor water supply and the diet of the cadres was inadequate. Further, no doctor had been sent to replace the late Dr Nomava Shangase. In the second half of 1982 (and fully acknowledged in 1983), a Chloroquine-resistant strain of malaria made the malaria epidemic in the camps an even more pressing problem and new treatment, proper facilities and a doctor were desperately needed in the camps. A 1983 report later showed that the malaria prevalence rate, infections in ear, nose and throat, and the rate of unwanted pregnancy were increasing.[104]

In 1983, the DoH recognised the urgency of sending a resident ANC doctor to Angola but it is also clear that Angola was an opportunity to exile dissident medical personnel from the main department. In October 1983, three medically trained personnel, Dr Shangase[105] (not Nomava Shangase), Dr Sipho Mlambo[106] and Gwendoline Sello[107] received an order from Joe Modise to relocate to Angola. They each wrote to the Secretary General protesting this order. Dr Shangase wrote:

> Its [sic] very clear to me that this order comes from Dr Shabalala using Cde. Modise. All this kind of victimization comes of the friction between Dr Manto and Dar team [...] The most bitter part of this order is that Angola is a war zone and I am not trained but told to go there, is it possible realy? [sic].[108]

Dr Shangase's letter was the most assertive but generally reflected the frustration of the other two letters. They were not forced to move to Angola. Instead, the DoH requested that Mthembu go to Angola, a move that is further understood when recalling the letter criticising Tshabalala's leadership in the DoH, quoted above. The offer was strengthened by a 10,000 shilling incentive from the treasury. He arrived in Angola in October 1983.[109]

Mthembu's nomination for the position in Angola was indicative of the DoH's relationship with the military in Angola at that time. In October, Mthembu began trying to restore the relatively poor health situation in the region. He recommended that Caxito be closed down. He also referred a number of patients to be sent to Lusaka for treatment and rehabilitation. However, by March of 1984 (following the Stuart Commission) Mthembu writes:

> To cut a long story short, this forces me to conclude that I am a TIMELY BUT UNCELEBRATED FOOL of the Medical Department. A timely fool because I agreed to go to Luanda at the time when the situation was very bad. Uncelebrated fool because by going to Luanda I was in fact being EXILED but I did not know this. Comrade Chairman [sic] if my going to Luanda was to serve a sentence, then let me be properly charged and the sentence specified – otherwise I am not going to serve this Department any-more [sic].[110]

103. UFHA-ALM, 112(95): 'Minutes of the special Health Council Meeting held in Lusaka: January 24–25, 1982.'
104. UFHA-ALM, 161(3d): 'Report- Health Department January 1983–December 1983.'
105. UFHA-ALM, 160(1b): Dr Shangase to Secretary General, 5 October 1983.
106. UFHA-ALM, 160(1b): Sipho Mlambo to Secretary General, 5 October 1983.
107. UFHA-ALM, 160(1b): Gwendoline Sello to Secretary General, 5 October 1983.
108. UFHA-ALM, 160(1b): Dr Shangase to Secretary General, 5 October 1983.
109. UFHA-ALM, 161(3d): 'Report: Health Department January 1983–December 1983.'
110. UFHA-ALM, 160(1c): Dr Mthembu to the Medical Department, 12 March 1984.

Mthembu's recommendations were not followed and he felt that his authority was being usurped while in Angola. His perception was not unfounded. As noted previously, a year prior to taking up his post in Angola, Mthembu wrote to the Secretary General expressing disapproval of Tshabalala. The Stuart Commission confirmed Mthembu's perception when it stated: 'Despite the fact that Angola is generally regarded as reliable rear base of our struggle [sic], it has been used as a dumping ground for enemy agents, suspects, malcontents and undisciplined elements.'[111] A doctor was urgently needed in a very undesirable medical work environment, and it was convenient to have a dissident doctor placed in Angola.

The tension in the camps did not lead to the complete abandonment of healthcare in Angola, because they remained the military front and were thus important to the liberation movement. In October 1983, Tshabalala, Oliver Tambo (the President of the ANC) and members from the Angolan RHT visited the Angolan hospital in Cacuso,[112] evaluating it as a potential site for a hospital that could be renovated and better equipped to serve as an ANC DoH-operated hospital. Since the Cuban doctors had departed, the hospital was left without a doctor and staffed by nine Angolan medical personnel – these nine medical staff served a local population of 90,000 Angolans.[113] The hospital needed a water supply, equipment and medical staff, but the ANC considered this location as a potential medical site to be used by its military and the Angolan government was in full support of ANC-Angolan cooperation at the hospital. It is unclear as to the extent of the support given to the hospital, if any, as follow-up to these initial evaluations does not appear in the archives. However, it is significant that the President of the ANC travelled to Angola in an attempt to improve inadequate health conditions in the camps.

During the last quarter of 1983, tensions continued to rise. In January 1984, before the mutinies occurred, a security department report stated:

> A number of cdes [comrades] are suffering from kidney ailment in Caculama, none has [sic] been taken to Luanda for proper treatment. This unhealthy state of affairs has resulted in some comrades coming up with a slogan 'Get out of Angola to avoid death'.[114]

This slogan marked the height of camp unrest as well as the height of health shortcomings.

The Stuart Commission made a number of recommendations to the NEC. Among those, was the need for generators, water pumps, recreational material, improved cadre training and development, a just system of determining enemy agents, the closure of Caxito and improvements to the health services.[115] In essence, the Commission sought to increase the presence of logistical support and administrative capacity in the camps. The NEC took

---

111. HP-JHB-KGC, P3(55): 'Report: Commission of Inquiry into Recent Developments in the People's Republic of Angola, March 14, 1984, Lusaka', 14 March 1984.

112. UFHA-ALM,160(1c): 'Medical Report', October 1983; UFHA-ALM 160(1b): 'Initial Report on Cacuso Hospital Prepared by Manto Tshabalala', 17 October 1983.

113. UFHA-ALM,160(1c): 'Medical Report', October 1983; UFHA-ALM 160(1b): 'Initial Report on Cacuso Hospital Prepared by Manto Tshabalala', 17 October 1983.

114. UFHA-ALM, 132(272): 'The following is an extract of a report from the Security Dept. dated 3rd. January 1984.'

115. HP-JHB-KGC, P3(55): 'Report: Commission of inquiry into Recent Developments in the People's Republic of Angola, March 14, 1984, Lusaka', 14 March 1984.

the commission's recommendations seriously and attempted to regain control over the situation in Angola.[116] Corresponding with the NEC efforts, the DoH's relationship to the military in Angola was strengthened and reemphasised.

Dr Haggar Macberry was sent to head the Angolan RHT.[117] Macberry was the Information and Publicity officer of the Health Secretariat. He provided consistency in Angola by remaining the head of the region's RHT until 1989. In 1987, Macberry was joined by Florence Maleka and Dr Bob Mayekiso, both elected members of the Health Secretariat in 1986. The shift from Mthembu to Macberry represents a renewed attempt to strengthen the DoH's direct administrative capacity in the context of the military camp.

In May 1984, Macberry conducted camp-by-camp health evaluations. He reported: 'Health services everywhere play an important role in the life of every individual, so it should be in our organization, but that seems non-existent especially in the camps...'[118] The ANC had to improve its Angolan health infrastructure and building started on the Viana clinic and training centre in 1984. In May, Tshabalala requested that Dr Mogale, the only ANC dentist, be seconded from Lusaka to Angola for a month to perform dental examinations on the cadres in Angola.[119] In July and August 1984, the DoH redoubled its efforts on the war against malaria. It proposed joint programmes of malaria control with the Angolan DoH[120] and also appealed to World Health Organisation (WHO) for funding and support for a malaria treatment program.[121] By the end of 1984, WHO sponsored 10 ANC students to attend medical school in Angola.[122] Additionally, a more comprehensive report compiled by Dr Macberry on disease prevalence in the camps was done, providing data on incidence rates for malaria, asthma, bronchitis, diseases of ear, nose and throat, and tuberculosis.[123] It was possible to make referrals for sick cadres to receive proper treatment in Angola or in other ANC regions.[124] Finally, by the end of the year, camp Caxito was officially phased out due to the high prevalence of malaria.

The change in the medical attention paid to military camps before and after the mutinies shows that the DoH had developed a prudent relationship with the military. The DoH was operating in Angola because serving the military was at the foundation of its *raison d'être*. But the DoH carried out its obligations with an agenda and weighed its other priorities against the attention paid to the military camps. The events in 1983 and 1984 in Angola highlight this calculated relationship.

Conclusion

In this article, I sought to examine how the relationship between the medical sector and the military changed throughout the time that the ANC and MK were in exile while indicating

116. L. Callinicos, 'Oliver Tambo and the Dilemma of the Camp Mutinies in Angola in the Eighties', *South African Historical Journal*, 64, 3 (2012), 587–621.
117. UFHA-ALM, 132(272): 'Angola Report', 2 May 1984.
118. *Ibid.*
119. UFHA-ALM, 161(3a): Tshabalala to Rachel Mogale, 24 May 1984.
120. UFHA-ALM, 161(3a): Tshabalala to the Secretary, July 1984.
121. UFHA-ALM, 161(3a): Tshabalala to Dr Quenum, 8 August 1984.
122. UFHA-ALM, 160(4): 'Department of Health: Circular to all Departments', 1984[?].
123. UFHA-ALM, 132(272): 'Angola Report', 2 May 1984.
124. UFHA-ALM, 31(11): 'Preamble', 26 March 1985.

instances where they influenced each other's development. The needs of the military at Kongwa camp in 1964 provided the impetus for the rudimentary beginnings of the medical sector. Over the next decade, new clinics were established and the medical sector grew but it remained informal and provided reactive case-by-case medical attention to cadres. In 1977 the medical sector was formalised into a Health Department but this new establishment did not strengthen the military-medical relationship. The Department had the opportunity to both look for support among the international community and plan for the future development of health care in exile while also dealing with the immediate needs of military cadres. As a result of the mutinies, the DoH was able to shift its relationship with the military to a calculated position; while still supplying medical care in Angola, the Department prioritised its obligations to the military camps according to the political situation on the ground. Just prior to the mutinies, the Health Secretariat sent an unfavourable staff member to work in Angola; after the mutinies when the ANC wanted to make a more concerted effort to improve the conditions in Angola, the Department sought to establish a firmer, more effective presence.

The DoH's part in the South African liberation struggle story has not yet been fully explained. Cadres have recorded memories of being sick or injured in exile but these short descriptions are just snapshots of the contact that occurred between individuals and this Department. However, these brief encounters were shaped by a much broader process, namely the shifting relationship between the medical sector and the military.

Author Note

Since this article was originally published, the dynamics between Department of Health staff members has been more clearly illuminated. Dr. Manto Tshabalala often was able to eloquently and convincingly refute the allegations leveled against her by the staff. Despite being pushed out of office by fellow Department and staff members, Tshabalala was reinstated by Ralph Mgijima in 1989. At the time Sipho Mthembu's letter was written (1982), he and Tshabalala were disputing the mishandling of Tsh 10,000 (approximately $900 USD) and his accusations were a reflection of their ongoing quarrel. Therefore, the Tsh 10,000 mentioned in the article was not an incentive offered by the Department of Health but rather money it was thought that Mthembu owed the Department. See UFHA-ALM, 160(1): "Manto Tshabalala to Doodles Gaboo re Account Tsh 10,000.00", 23 March, 1983. Mthembu was not only sent to Angola for his criticisms of Tshabalala, he was also accused by members of the East Africa Health Team of being unstable, anti-social and unfit to work at the Mazimbu clinic. University of Fort Hare Archive-ANC SOMAFCO Health Department, 8(20): 'Meeting of the Regional Health Team with the National' 15 August 1983. These accusations further support the argument that Angola was neglected by the Health Department prior to the mutinies in 1984.

Main Machinery: The ANC's Armed Underground in Johannesburg During the 1976 Soweto Uprising

Thula Simpson

University of Pretoria

Having completed their training in Military Combat Work (MCW) in the Eastern Bloc by the early months of 1976, the first of the new generation of Umkhonto we Sizwe (MK) recruits were prepared for infiltration into South Africa by the mid-year. This article tells the story of the first unit to be deployed into South Africa in the new phase of the African National Congress's (ANC) armed struggle. It details some of the challenges they faced implementing the lessons of MCW in the practical circumstances faced in South Africa. The years preceding 1976 had seen the ANC unable to prosecute military operations within South Africa owing to the logistical challenges of launching incursions to South Africa from their bases in Zambia and Tanzania. Independence for Angola and Mozambique had made such incursions possible, but only just, as this article shows. It explains how issues of command and control in a theatre of war spread over the whole southern African region remained formidable problems for the movement. This was the major factor that stalled the endeavours of this unit in reaching the state where it could begin operating militarily. It was a mix-up that occurred during an attempt that was made to establish contact between the ANC's internal and external structures to discuss these issues, which led to the collapse of the mission. Finally, the article will consider the lessons learned by the ANC from the mission, and explain the significance of the experience within the entire context of the history of the armed struggle.

This article revisits the 1976 Soweto Uprising – a major watershed in South African history – with specific focus on a theme receiving increased attention in the historiographical literature on the South African liberation struggle, namely the precise nature of the African National Congress's (ANC) involvement in the event. For whether it be the extent of ANC participation in the regrouping of underground forces within South Africa in the mid-to-late 1960s (Suttner 2008), or its contribution to the revival of the trade union movement early the following decade (Legassick 2008; Sithole 2009), or its comparative popularity vis-à-vis its nationalist rivals by the end of the 1970s (Jeffery 2009), the questions of how closely the histories of the South African nation and its leading nationalist movement ought to be identified with each other, and, if so, how far into the past that identification ought to be claimed, are ones that have over recent years drawn the attention of historians to a growing extent.

This article follows on from one published previously in the pages of *African Studies* (Simpson 2011), in which I engaged with these questions as they related to the period spanning from the late 1960s to the mid-1970s. In that article, the questions featured as part of a broader discussion of the links the ANC was able to establish from Swaziland into South Africa in the early 1970s. That article described how such clandestine networks were able to connect with the underground within South Africa, which then spirited recruits abroad to receive military training courses that were designed to respond to the peculiar challenges the guerrillas would face when they returned to wage armed struggle inside South Africa.

This article deals with the return. It provides a case study of some of the practical problems guerrillas faced in implementing the lessons of the training in Military Combat Work (MCW) that they had received abroad. But it also engages the larger questions about the degree of ANC hegemony over political developments within South Africa during the liberation struggle era. The debate over these questions has suffered, in my view, by not being informed by in-depth case studies analysing directly and in detail the extent of the ANC's physical capacity to exercise its influence over the development of mass protest at ground level during the struggle.

This article provides such a study. Considered together with its predecessor, it shows that any claim that the ANC was absent during the growth of mass resistance activity from the late 1960s onwards, is simply untenable. However, it also shows that to claim that the growth of mass opposition was *instigated* and *directed* by the movement from abroad is to greatly exaggerate matters. It does so by highlighting the objective limitations the ANC faced in its ability to control protest activity within the country. As I have discussed elsewhere (Simpson 2009a), these limitations owed to the strength of the South African state, manifested in the regime's ability to deploy force far beyond its borders. In turn, the state's reach forced the ANC to operate across overextended logistical lines, thereby undermining the liberation movement's ability to exercise adequate command over political and military developments inside the country.

Crucially, the resulting checks on the ANC's coercive power required that relations between the movement and the existing opposition groups it encountered inside the country had to be cooperative rather than dominative. This article provides evidence indicating how this process unfolded. The most important of the internal opposition groups were those belonging to the Black Consciousness (BC) movement. The article describes how relations between the ANC and BC organisations were extended during the uprising, as the former sought to create a base amongst the latter from which its military wing *Umkhonto we Sizwe* (MK) could generate armed struggle. In the earlier article it was described how BC influenced students like Mosima Sexwale, Naledi Tsiki and Selaelo Ramusi were recruited into MK by the ANC prior to 1976; this article relates how their activities dovetailed with that of the popular resistance movement they encountered upon their infiltration of South Africa during the events of 1976.

The first of the new generation of MK members recruited in the mid-1970s to complete their military training were Naledi Tsiki and Selaelo Ramusi. After the conclusion of their courses in East Germany at the end of April 1976, they were flown in mid-May to Tanzania, where they were accommodated in flats on the University of Dar es Salaam campus. Their arrival coincided with a meeting in the Tanzanian capital of the Revolutionary Council (RC) – the body created by the ANC to oversee the development of political and military struggle within South Africa – which had convened to discuss the formation of a new command structure for MK. The pair was visited at their university lodgings by ANC leaders such as Joe Modise and Joe Slovo (who were MK's two commanding generals), Eric Mtshali (who was the ANC's chief representative in Tanzania), and Thomas Nkobi, the ANC treasurer.

The duo were asked what their training had entailed, and it transpired that Slovo, who Ramusi and Tsiki had met on their way to and from Berlin airport, had received the same course in East Germany. They were then told that their presence was unexpected. The fact that even Modise and Slovo were in the dark concerning their movements indicates the difficulties of maintaining up-to-date communications in a struggle spanning continents. The leaders promised to bring the combatants' return on to the agenda of the forthcoming meeting, but the notice proved to be too short for the conference to be able to decide where to deploy the guerrillas. Modise informed the two of this when he came to brief them a couple of days later. He nevertheless promised that the matter remained under consideration and a decision would be reached soon on where they would be sent.[1]

Until February 1976 the ANC had a fairly dynamic structure in Swaziland, but this was destroyed by the arrest of its leaders Thabo Mbeki and Albert Dhlomo by the kingdom's police force (Simpson 2009b:101–2). The closure of this channel compelled the organisation to look for alternative corridors of infiltration. They initially focused their planning on Botswana, where they devised a scheme for Ramusi and Tsiki to register as university students in the country. This institutional affiliation would provide the two with cover stories as they embarked on building an MK 'machinery' (i.e. command structure) in Botswana that would oversee the commencement of armed struggle in the adjacent South African province of the Transvaal. After completing this task, the duo would be withdrawn to work as political commissars in MK camps in other African countries. Slovo and Modise returned to Dar es Salaam early in June 1976 to discuss the proposal, but Ramusi and Tsiki objected that they would have no business lecturing cadres in the camps about what it was like operating in South Africa when they themselves had no experience of the same. They requested that the plan be amended accordingly to remedy this shortcoming, and Modise and Slovo relented by deciding to allow for a period in which the combatants would enter South Africa to conduct an operation before withdrawing to build the machinery. For the time being however, this was all to no effect because Ramusi and Tsiki were unable to register as students in Botswana.[2]

This impasse was resolved by the impressive renaissance of the ANC's structures in Swaziland in mid-1976. This rebirth was led by Moses Mabhida, the ANC's chief representative in the country, his deputy Stanley Mabizela, his chief assistant Henry Chiliza, as well as other colleagues such as Ablon Duma and Joe Mkhwanazi.[3]

From August 1976 this group was joined by John Nkadimeng, who till then had been chairman of the ANC underground in Johannesburg, known to its members as the Main Machinery. After Nkadimeng's departure from South Africa, the Main Machinery passed into the hands of Joe Gqabi and Martin Ramokgadi, and from this point onwards, the clandestine nexus between Johannesburg and Manzini was re-established with remarkable speed.

Couriers such as Joe Tseto, an old, close friend of Ramokgadi's, provided the glue between the two structures. The Ramokgadi and Tseto families had actually lived together for a number of years at 57, 11th Avenue in Alexandra (which along with Soweto was one of the two main black townships that serviced white Johannesburg). After moving diagonally across the street to number 62 in 1975, Tseto established a successful 'combi-for-hire' business, involving him using a Volkswagen minibus (of the kind that became the backbone of the privately-owned public transport system in much of sub-Saharan Africa in the late 20th century) as a taxi or rentable vehicle. Soon after Ramokgadi's wife died in July 1976, he approached Tseto about entering the business. He said that he was prevented from buying a vehicle in his own name due to his unemployed status, and suggested jointly purchasing a combi, with him paying for his half from the proceeds of the life insurance on his wife. Tseto agreed and the pair bought a minibus on 27 July 1976; Tseto was then persuaded to use the vehicle to drive to Swaziland on ANC underground work. Between August and December 1976, he made at least three trips to Swaziland transporting letters to Nkadimeng, and returning with brown envelopes stuffed with money – either R1,000 or R2,000 – that kept the Main Machinery afloat and probably paid for, amongst other things, a second combi that he and Ramokgadi bought on 23 September 1976.[4]

Another courier was Ramokgadi's cousin, Alpheus Ramokgadi. He would collect recruits, whom the Main Machinery wanted to go abroad and receive military training with MK, from the corner of Louis Botha Avenue and Corlett Drive on the outskirts of Alexandra. He would drive them to a village near Malelane in the eastern Transvaal, south of Kruger National Park, in an area that was a hive of ANC activity. The recruits he delivered would then be transported to Swaziland by other couriers, whilst he would collect cadres recently arrived from the kingdom and escort them to Johannesburg.[5]

But the most active of the couriers was Ian Deway Rwaxa. Between April and December 1976 he made 52 documented trips to Swaziland (a figure that does not include the many undocumented crossings he made in which he either jumped the border fences surrounding the checkpoints or bribed officials not to stamp his passport so as to avoid arousing the suspicions of the police over the number of times he was traversing the borders), in which he escorted over 260 recruits, up to 80 of whom he had enlisted himself. Rwaxa also became extensively networked within ANC structures in both Johannesburg and Swaziland. In the latter he became Chiliza's deputy, whilst in Johannesburg, after having initially been recruited in September 1975 by Christopher Manye, the leader of an underground structure that was conducting recruitment work in the Johannesburg area on the ANC's behalf but independently of the Main Machinery, he was recruited into the Main Machinery in the early months of 1976. Through Rwaxa, these two structures, which were conducting similar work in overlapping areas but had hitherto not been acquainted, became aware of each other and started working together.[6]

Such were the positive aspects of Rwaxa's omnipresence. However, there was a negative side to his ubiquity. This was that he knew so much about the workings of the underground as a whole that if for any reason he was captured and decided to talk – which was a possibility given the sheer volume of the work he was conducting, and the South African security branch's propensity for torture – he was in a position to cause the collapse of the ANC's entire clandestine network.

This was a potential danger for the future, but in the meantime, owing to the work of these and other couriers, the ANC was not only able to transport a large number of recruits out of South Africa to receive military training, but was also able to establish substantial stores of firearms, grenades and dynamite in the Johannesburg area, all smuggled in from Swaziland.[7]

II

This revival of the links between the ANC's Johannesburg and Swaziland structures solved MK's problem regarding the deployment of Ramusi and Tsiki. The two MK guerrillas had grown impatient at being marooned in Tanzania, especially after news filtered through to them of the uprising in Soweto, which was their home township. They protested that they ought to have already been home, partaking in the fighting. In mid-August 1976 Modise and Slovo reported to them the welcome news that the logjam had at last been cleared and their infiltration could commence. They told Ramusi and Tsiki to prepare for imminent deployment to Mozambique, where Moses Mabhida would give them further instruction. They said that the RC was delighted that the training they had received in the Eastern Bloc had featured a strong focus on sabotage, because, they said, the ANC had identified a sabotage campaign designed to cripple the government and cut off supplies as being its preferred method of advancing the armed struggle.

Finally, the two were ordered not to contact friends and family whilst on the South African leg of their mission: the ANC had put in place plans, they were told, to ensure that representatives of the movement's internal underground would be able to receive them when they arrived.[8]

Ramusi and Tsiki flew to Maputo late in August 1976. A week later they were met by Mabhida, who told them that the task the RC had set them was to sabotage the railway lines connecting South Africa with either Rhodesia or Mozambique. Mabhida then gave them a stern lecture on ANC guidelines regarding military attacks. It was contrary to movement policy, he said, to 'shed innocent blood'. He added that the ANC was distinguished in this respect from the nationalist guerrillas in Rhodesia, who, he asserted, had conducted operations in which civilians had been targeted. Mabhida voiced his own strong approbation of the ANC's stance, voicing his abhorrence of acts such as throwing grenades into restaurants. He then discussed the phase of the two combatants' mission that would follow the act of sabotage. As mentioned earlier, this next stage was envisaged to involve the two building a military command in one of the countries neighbouring South Africa, but Mabhida now stated that this part of the mission would be conducted in Swaziland rather than Botswana. Mabhida added that, once established, the machinery would be responsible for servicing underground units in Natal and the Transvaal. Before departing, Mabhida gave Ramusi and Tsiki a timetable of all the trains running in the Transvaal, and told them to begin planning the sabotage operation. They did so after he left, with Ramusi proposing targeting the railway lines to the east of Pietersburg (now Polokwane) in the northern Transvaal. He knew the area well, being an alumnus of the nearby University of the North.[9]

Ramusi and Tsiki's forward march continued to proceed in agonisingly slow instalments, however. When they left South Africa to receive their training in December 1975, they had hoped to return between three and six months later.[10] However, the difficulties of organising transport, couriers and communications over the distances involved, limited what was achievable. Only in early October 1976 did Ramusi and Tsiki advance to Swaziland. Within Swaziland they were stationed in a hut on the eastern outskirts of Manzini that the ANC used for its underground work. There the duo conducted further planning for their sabotage operation. On the basis of their discussions over the matter, the two decided to conduct an initial trip to South Africa in which they would conduct reconnaissance and identify a target. They would then withdraw to Swaziland, and on D-Day return and steal a car to get to the scene of the attack. After having conducted the operation they would withdraw to Johannesburg and dump the car on the outskirts of Alexandra, before being ferried by the underground to Swaziland. When Mabhida visited them at the hut on 15 October, they briefed him on their plans, including their desire to conduct the reconnaissance on 17 October. Mabhida accepted the proposal and returned a couple of days later with Chiliza, Rwaxa and an individual named Simon Mohlanyaneng, who would spearhead the illegal crossing into South Africa.[11]

Ramusi and Tsiki's reconnaissance mission within South Africa involved them boarding a train to the northern Transvaal, and then reconnoitring the tracks leading to the village of Dikgale. They observed all the trains passing through Dikgale station, and after realising that none arrived in the hours immediately following midnight, they decided to lay their explosives during that time interval when they returned a few days later. Ramusi and Tsiki returned to Swaziland on 18 October, and on the following morning briefed Mabhida on how the reconnaissance had gone. They agreed with him that they would depart to launch the mission proper on 21 October.[12]

III

Mabhida returned a couple of days later with four tins containing explosives, R120 in cash, and two Scorpion pistols. The latter were for use if apprehended by the South African police and searched in a way that risked having their explosives uncovered. MK cadres were given orders to offer resistance if ever in danger of being arrested by the South African Police.[13]

In the early hours of Friday 22 October, Mohlanyaneng again marched Ramusi and Tsiki across the border fence. The trio walked on the other side until they reached a car in which they found Alois Manci of the Main Machinery, and a driver known as 'Mandla', who escorted them to their accommodation at 124, 7th Avenue in Alexandra.

Ramusi and Tsiki decided to rest in the township over the weekend, and the ease with which they did so led them to start considering a change to their future plans. Specifically they discussed the feasibility of establishing their command machinery *within* Alexandra itself. That very weekend had seen political violence spike in Johannesburg's black townships: in Soweto, the police opened fire on two funeral processions held for victims of earlier state violence. These incidents particularly incensed Ramusi, who wanted to take retaliatory action against passing security force vehicles. Tsiki tried to dissuade him, but the possibility exists that he did not succeed, because on the Sunday, Jabulani Police Station in Soweto was bombed, and though in a later trial the state tried to pin responsibility for the attack on a group called the 'Soweto Suicide Squad', Ramusi later confided to a colleague, Mosima Sexwale, that he (Ramusi) had conducted the assault himself (Brooks and Brickhill 1980:254; Hirson 1979:252; Kane-Berman 1981:147).[14]

During final preparations before departing for the train sabotage operation in Dikgale, Ramusi and Tsiki drew a picture of a grenade onto a poster, which they hoped to attach to a tree near the scene of the operation. On the Monday they were driven by the underground to the town of Springs, where they stole a vehicle, which they used to drive to Dikgale. They waited there until around midnight, when Ramusi departed to lay two explosives on the railway line. However, he was forced to flee before he had placed the main charge firmly on the tracks, when he heard a train approaching. Then, as he and Tsiki escaped from the scene of the attack, a torrential downpour ensued, which, unbeknownst to them, forced the charge to slip off the line completely. The charge was later recovered unexploded beside the railway line, and the incident only succeeded in delaying a few trains rather than derailing the network as had been hoped. They fled southwards, stopping about three kilometres from Dikgale where they planted another explosive, but this one was later defused by the police before it exploded, and a tin containing Tsiki's fingerprints was later recovered from the scene. The duo completed their return to Johannesburg, where they dumped the stolen car in an industrial area surrounding Alexandra, before being escorted to Swaziland by Manci and Mohlanyaneng.[15] In the haste of their departure they proved unable to pin their poster near the scene of either of their attacks.

It was only when Tsiki was brought to trial in 1977 that the ANC fully found out what had gone wrong with the explosions. On 27 October 1976, however, as the disappointing results trickled in, Tsiki and Ramusi briefed Mabhida on what they knew about the operation. At that time they also discussed the next stage of their mission, and said they felt they could build the machinery within South Africa. Mabhida initially hesitated, but after persistent persuasion from the two he relented and said he would arrange for the Main Machinery to provide them accommodation and transport, with Manci serving as liaison between two structures. He added that their task would be to build an MK military machinery that could service underground units in Natal, the Transvaal and the Orange Free State. This suggestion was met with some disquiet by Ramusi and Tsiki, because at every stage in which they had been briefed about the mission its scope had increased: initially in Tanzania with Slovo and Modise it was for the Transvaal; in Mozambique with Mabhida it grew to include Natal; and now, in Swaziland, to include the Orange Free State as well. They emphasised that this was now a tall order that would require the construction of a very extensive underground to service their needs, and that they would need substantial support from the movement if they were to succeed. They mentioned two essential forms of assistance: the first was not to be pressured to undertake operations before the underground was strong enough to allow them to evade police scrutiny, whilst the second concerned reinforcements, with them specifically asking for Mosima Sexwale to be recalled from the Soviet Union to join them. Mabhida agreed to issue the call for Sexwale, but in the meantime offered them the services of Lele Motaung, another cadre who had been trained in the Soviet Union and was presently idle in Maputo.

Over the next few days, Mabhida opened consultations with the Main Machinery over the change of plans. In these talks, Mabhida agreed with the Johannesburg-based underground structure, that for security reasons they would not be fused with the MK cell into a joint unit, though, as we will see shortly, there was apparently not enough time to clarify exactly what the working arrangement between the two structures would be. Six days later, Mabhida returned to the wooden hut in

Manzini accompanied by Mohlanyaneng and Motaung, and said that the infiltration into South Africa would proceed that night. Prior to the departure, Mabhida suggested that Mohlanyaneng be added to the MK structure in order to augment its numbers, and ordered the others to begin apportioning posts in the command structure. This they did, making Tsiki commander, Ramusi commissar, and Motaung logistics chief. Mohlanyaneng led these three through the bush surrounding Mananga/Bordergate, and they were met on the other side of the border by Manci, a member of the Main Machinery named Jacob Seatholo, and a third individual called Amos Lubisi, before being driven to Alexandra.[16]

Their arrival in Alexandra provided further illustration of the complexities of ensuring proper coordination in a struggle conducted in such a large theatre. Firstly, it transpired that one of the group was not expected, so the Johannesburg underground had to spend a good deal of time travelling back and forth to Swaziland trying to verify his credentials and clarify the role he was to play in the underground.[17]

But this was not the only surprise the Main Machinery had in store for it. A couple of days after the arrival of the MK cell, Manci and Norman Tshabalala of the Main Machinery attended an introductory meeting with the military unit. Ramusi opened proceedings by communicating Mabhida's orders: Mohlanyaneng was to be transferred from the political to the military underground, and the Main Machinery's principal function henceforth would be to render the MK men assistance with housing, transport and recruits. This came as a surprise to the two representatives of the Main Machinery because their understanding, based on consultations with Mabhida over the previous days, was that the military unit would be answerable to them. Though Tshabalala helpfully offered to accommodate two of the guerrillas at the house in Brakpan that he shared with his disabled brother, Manci demurred, saying he would have to discuss the demands with his colleagues. The underlying misunderstanding was not articulated openly until a meeting a couple of days later between Tsiki and Ramokgadi, which began cordially enough when the former asked for assistance with housing, to which the latter said there was a half constructed shack in the garden of his house at 57, 11th Avenue in Alexandra, which the military structure could use if they could repair it. However when Tsiki tried to move the discussion to transport, Ramokgadi asserted the Main Machinery's claim to pre-eminence. Tsiki countered that his understanding, obtained from Mabhida, was that the Main Machinery's function was to render the MK unit 'support services'. A further meeting was called a couple of days later to discuss the issue, and a tentative agreement was reached there that the Main Machinery would render the MK group assistance with housing and recruits, with Ramusi acting as the liaison between them.[18]

Tsiki missed this last meeting because he was fulfilling a commitment to train an individual recruited by Mohlanyaneng named Samson Ndaba, who became the first local inhabitant to be put through his military paces by the MK cell. At an initial meeting held at Ndaba's house, Tsiki was sufficiently impressed by Ndaba's performance in the political discussion they held to invite him to join MK, though he was less enamoured when Ndaba arrived at the first training session the following day and said he had divulged the contents of their conversation to his brother Victor, who also wanted to join MK, and would be arriving soon. Nevertheless Tsiki agreed to train both Ndaba brothers and began by outlining the ANC's history, political programme and structures, before explaining the importance of MCW to what he and his colleagues were trying to achieve in Alexandra. Next he discussed how the cell system worked, along with methods of operating in the underground such as utilising camouflage and writing letters, as well as military techniques such as how to assemble, dismantle, load and aim the Scorpion and Tokarev pistols, and how to use defensive and offensive grenades. The course lasted six days, and when it concluded Tsiki told the brothers to each recruit three persons and train them in the politico-military arts that they had learned, and thereby get an underground cell structure up and running, in keeping with the tenets of MCW training.[19]

By this time, however, the deal patched together by the MK cell and the Main Machinery a few days previously was already fraying at the seams. There were two basic reasons for this: the first was that the political structure's resources were soon stretched trying to cater for the military cell's needs, and quite quickly most of Gqabi, Ramokgadi and Manci's time was being spent arranging meetings, accommodation and transport for the trained men and their recruits.[20]

Some progress was made in terms of finding accommodation early in November when Mohlanyaneng found vacant properties at a plot in a village called Jonathan in the Winterveld area north of Pretoria. Then about ten days later, Jacob Seathlolo suggested contacting a friend of his named Roger Makao, a trade unionist who lived alone at 48, 8th Avenue in Alexandra. This proved a good lead: Tsiki was able to stay there every two or three nights, and was eventually able to recruit Makao into the ANC underground, whilst he used the house to militarily train Makao and another recruit whom Makao managed to find in Soweto. Though these additions helped somewhat, they did not provide the MK unit with nearly enough in terms of safe houses to enable them to be sufficiently mobile to run and hide and elude the enemy in the event of a keen police hunt.

However, despite this, the Main Machinery already felt it was pushed to the limit in terms of the support it was able to provide. This was announced by Ramokgadi in a meeting that he called with Ramusi in mid-November. He said that the military cadres would need to make alternative transport arrangements as the Main Machinery was running out of money, and also intimated that members of the political structure were becoming uneasy at being seen in the company of the MK cell, owing to concerns about security. The two decided to send Tshabalala to Swaziland to discuss these problems with Mabhida.[21]

The second problem was that the deal reached did not broach the larger controversy regarding the issue of the chain of command between the political and military structures. The Main Machinery continued to insist that as the MK cell had entered 'their' area, it should operate under their instructions – including them having veto power over armed operations – whilst the guerrillas held their ground, countering that they *were* acting under political authority, namely that of the RC, adding that if the Main Machinery wanted to change these arrangements they would have to raise the matter with the external ANC because, as soldiers, they could not countermand their commanders without receiving authorisation from their superiors. In all probability the matter would have easily been solved if the internal structures had been able to discuss it with the RC, because the military underground was not opposed in principle to accepting leadership from the Main Machinery. On the contrary, in Joe Gqabi, an MK veteran from the 1960s, there was an individual on hand who commanded their respect and would have been ideally placed to exercise overall control. But this is where the problem lay, because, once again, communication out of the country was a protracted and laborious process, and so the matter festered.[22]

The absence of regular communications between the front and the rear had a further negative consequence in that it created something of a leadership vacuum as the externally-based commanders were unable to exercise adequate supervision and guidance over the MK unit's work. The result was that much of the daily activity of the trained men took on an aimless aspect with them spending much of their time driving from place to place, to no apparent purpose.[23]

It must nevertheless be emphasised that there were no pitched battles and that it was rather a case of the members of the two structures grappling with the complex tasks of building a functional underground. Throughout the process they continued to work closely and cooperatively together, for example at finding recruits, with the Main Machinery helping to put the MK cell in touch with members of the student movement in the Johannesburg area who, since the Soweto Uprising, had been trying to organise military training from the ANC.

At the beginning of July 1976, the national executive of the South African Students' Movement (SASM), which was the organisation whose call for a protest march had sparked the insurrection the previous month, mandated one of its members, Elias Masinga, to travel to Mozambique to contact the ANC. When he departed in mid-July, he left a colleague Cleophas Kehla Shubane in charge of heading SASM's underground cells and maintaining contacts with ANC leaders in the Johannesburg area.[24] Before Masinga left, SASM's regional committee in Soweto renamed itself the Soweto Students' Representative Committee (SSRC), and a radical section of this new structure's leadership, including figures such as Murphy Morobe, Billy Masethla, Super Moloi, TT Mtinjane and Paul Langa, formed a sub-committee that they named the 'Soweto Suicide Squad', which they gave the task of providing greater force to mass demonstrations called by the SSRC by engaging in acts of violence such as sabotaging communication lines, firebombing buildings, and assaulting individuals who failed to adhere to the organisation's orders (Brooks and Brickhill 1980:160–1; Moss 1982:155).[25]

In Mozambique and Swaziland, between July and mid-November 1976, Masinga received training in underground political work. When he completed his course he was told by Mabhida to return to South Africa.[26] In Soweto he was reacquainted with Masethla and Morobe, who said they wanted to join MK. The trio consulted Joe Gqabi on the matter, and he arranged for Rwaxa to transport them to Swaziland at the end of the month to discuss it further with the ANC's external leadership. This was done, and at a meeting that took place in Manzini in late November 1976, Masethla and Morobe provided an outline of the SSRC's activities. On the basis of the discussions that followed, two important decisions were reached. The first was that the objectives of the SSRC and the ANC were consistent with each other, and that the underground structures of the two organisations within South Africa should be fused into one.[27] The second related to the issue of military training, which the SSRC members had come to Swaziland to discuss. Mabizela and Mabhida told the students that if they wished they could proceed to Mozambique to receive the training there, but informed them that the ANC leadership had recently made a decision to focus on mobilising its armed forces within South Africa, based on its concerns about the rapidity with which its external military camps were filling up as a result of an exodus of youths seeking to join MK after the Soweto Uprising. The movement would therefore prefer them to return and contact the MK structure that had been established in the Johannesburg area. The SSRC members agreed to exercise this latter option, and before departing were told that upon their return to Soweto they should contact Manci and Gqabi, who would be able to put them in touch with the MK unit. Manci successfully managed to provide the link by arranging a meeting on 27 November between Tsiki and a taxi driver named Obed Tshabango, who was able to arrange contact with the SSRC members (Hirson 1979:251–2).[28]

Likewise the Main Machinery facilitated the extension of the military cell's work into the northern Transvaal. This time the key man was Martin Ramokgadi, whose family hailed from the area. At his suggestion, safe houses were established in the Batlokwa area near Pietersburg, whilst Ramokgadi also persuaded his friend and fellow ex-Robben Island prisoner, Peter Nchabaleng, to engage in recruiting work in the area of the village of Apel in the district of Sekhukhuneland where he lived. Ramokgadi and Tsiki travelled to Sekhukhuneland in late November to receive a progress report on how this recruitment work was progressing, but Nchabaleng was not present.[29]

IV

Upon their arrival back in Johannesburg from Apel, Ramokgadi and Tsiki received word that Sexwale was waiting in Swaziland, and they immediately assembled a team to collect him from Manzini. Sexwale had arrived in Maputo earlier in the month and, as with Ramusi and Tsiki in Dar es Salaam, his presence caught the ANC's structures in Mozambique unawares. These Maputo structures then had to spend some time finding out what to do with him. The matter was finally resolved when Mabhida arrived to escort Sexwale to Swaziland where he stayed in the same hut that had earlier accommodated Ramusi and Tsiki. Whilst there, Sexwale was told by Mabhida that he would take over from Tsiki as commander of the MK unit, but that the military underground's overall task remained the same, namely to recruit and train as many people as possible. After about three weeks in the hut, a team including Manci, Ramusi, Norman Tshabalala and Amos Lubisi arrived in Manzini to collect Sexwale on 29 November. Between them this group agreed an infiltration plan involving Tshabalala driving Lubisi, Manci, Ramusi and Sexwale to within two kilometres of the Mananga/Bordergate checkpoint, whereupon the latter four would disembark, with Lubisi leading the team on foot into South Africa across the border fence. They would then march to a prearranged point where they would reunite with Tshabalala, who would have passed through the border post 'legally' with the vehicle, and would then drive them to Alexandra. Before departing Mabhida and Chiliza handed the group a suitcase containing an AK-47 machine gun, a paper bag containing four Scorpion pistols, and 12 tins filled with grenades, explosives and cartridges.[30]

This time the crossing failed. The first part went well as in the early hours of 30 November, Lubisi led Manci, Ramusi and Sexwale across the border fence and into South Africa. However, as the group marched by the side of the road towards their rendezvous with Tshabalala, they were approached by a police vehicle. This prompted them to all look away simultaneously, thus arousing the suspicions of the driver, a Sergeant Makushi, who reported the incident at the border post. Two colleagues, Constable Brits and Sergeant Khoza, set out to investigate and caught up with the ANC group further down the road. Khoza inquired where they were from and Lubisi said 'Magudu', which was the name of a nearby village. Khoza then asked them to open their luggage, and Manci replied that there was no key. Certain that this was nothing more than one of the many cases the police had to deal with of locals crossing the border illegally, Khoza told them to board the police Land Rover, and kept an eye on them through the window behind the passenger seat, as Brits drove towards Bordergate. Faced with the prospect of being disarmed without resistance – a fate that we must recall they were told not to submit to under any circumstances – the group made a plan whilst huddled together at the back of the vehicle. Ramusi announced that he had a grenade in his pocket and handed it to Sexwale, and the group dispersed with Sexwale moving to the front of the vehicle behind the driver. He removed the grenade from the wrapping paper it was contained in and found that it was primed. As the vehicle neared Bordergate, Sexwale leaned over the window on the driver's side. Khoza thought Sexwale wanted to say something to Brits and so tried to alert his colleague, but gave up, concluding he could not be heard over the din of the engine. Sexwale then threw the weapon – a defensive grenade nick-named the 'pineapple' because of its shape – into the driver's cabin. The grenade had a four second delay, during which it emitted a foul smell that caused Brits to apply the brakes. It then exploded, enabling the ANC men to escape. As they did so they shed most of their supplies: in the police van they abandoned the paper bag containing the explosives and the suitcase carrying the AK-47, and Ramusi dropped his Scorpion pistol and fake ID book. Their retreat assumed some order in the bush where Sexwale organised them into column file and Lubisi led them into Swaziland.

Meanwhile, back in South Africa, Khoza took charge of the police van from Brits (who was seriously wounded with injuries that would leave him crippled for life), and continued towards Bordergate. On the way he saw approaching none other than Norman Tshabalala, who had passed through the checkpoint and was on his way to collect his colleagues. The policemen flagged Tshabalala down and compelled him to take them to the nearest police station. There the officers on duty made him transport Brits and Khoza to Komatipoort Hospital. Only then was Tshabalala allowed to return to Alexandra and that evening he briefed the Main Machinery of the day's events. By that time Lubisi, Manci, Ramusi and Sexwale were also in safety in Swaziland; they had marched for five hours in the kingdom until they reached a village from where they negotiated a lift to Manzini. When they tried to brief Chiliza, he told them he had heard all about the events on the news.[31]

V

Unbowed, the ANC tried again on 6 December. Manci and Ramusi were again involved, but were accompanied this time by Bonny Sikhakhane, one of the cour-iers in the underground. The plan devised involved Manci and Ramusi accompa-nying Sexwale into South Africa via the bush surrounding the Sandlane/Nerston, rather than Mananga/Bordergate checkpoint, with Sikhakhane travelling legally through the Oshoek/Ngwenya border post with his vehicle and then circling southwards to meet the others at the town of Amsterdam, near Nerston. This time the plan proceeded without hitches and Sexwale was transported to Alexan-dra, where he called a meeting of the entire MK cell. This took place in Jonathan in the Winterveld.

Three issues needed to be addressed by the MK unit at the time. The first issue was its own restructuring: Ramusi communicated Mabhida's instruction that Sexwale be made commander. Then, after discussions amongst themselves, the group decided to keep Ramusi commissar and Motaung logistics chief, whilst putting Mohlanyaneng in charge of transport, and reassigning Tsiki to serve as treasurer.

The second issue was the unresolved matter of the precise relationship between the MK cell and the Main Machinery. Tsiki suggested sending a joint political and military structure delegation to Swaziland to resolve the issue with Mabhida. His colleagues seconded this.

Finally, the third issue the unit had to grapple with was a demand they had received from Mabhida that they undertake a military operation on the upcoming symbolic date of 16 December. This suggestion was not received favourably. For the cell, it was just the kind of pressure to engage in military action before the underground possessed the capacity to withstand the inevitable police follow-up that Ramusi and Tsiki had asked to be exempted from when infiltrated to build the machinery. The group decided to report back to Swaziland saying that, whilst they were not refusing the order, they nevertheless thought it ill-advised.[32]

The unit's immediate priority was to extend its existing military training programmes. Tsiki only just returned from the Winterveld meeting in time to fulfil a scheduled follow-up meeting with Obed Tshabango, at which 8 December was set as the date to begin training the SSRC members. On that day, Tsiki inducted Masethla, Masinga, Morobe and Super Moloi into MK and began familiarising them with the Tokarev and Scorpion pistols. Training was to have resumed the following day, but on the morning of 9 December Ramusi and Sexwale were arrested at Roger Makao's house. Though this proved a case of mistaken identity, by the time they were released in the afternoon it was too late for Tsiki to make the appointment.

On 10 December, Sexwale joined Ramusi and Ramokgadi in travelling to Sekhukhuneland where they met Nchabaleng and received a report from him on how recruitment in the area was going. When Nchabaleng said that he and his son Elleck had recruited three locals, Sexwale offered to begin training immediately, but Nchabaleng refused, saying he first wanted to consult with another ex-Robben Island prisoner living in the area. An alternative arrangement was made whereby Sexwale would return a week later to begin the training. He headed back to Alexandra with Ramusi and Ramokgadi, and that evening he told Tsiki to leave the township and 'lie-low' in one of the ANC's hideouts in the northern Transvaal because of the volatile security situation in light of the previous day's arrests.[33]

As Tsiki had suggested, a joint political and military structure delegation was sent to Swaziland shortly afterwards. It consisted of Ramusi and Gqabi, but they were unable to meet Mabhida as he was out of the country, so the long-awaited discussion to resolve the issue of how to organise the internal command remained unresolved. Gqabi returned to Johannesburg but Ramusi stayed behind and Rwaxa was sent to collect him. However, when Rwaxa arrived in Manzini he was told to return to Alexandra immediately and tell the underground there to reorganise itself because Tshabalala had absconded from a hideout in the Winterveld where he had been since the Bordergate incident. Since the explosion on 30 November, the police had been scouring Johannesburg's black townships looking for leads, and they had specifically inquired about Tshabalala, though they claimed that this was because they wanted to give him a medal. The ANC feared that Tshabalala had buckled under the pressure and would report to the police. Though this proved to be a false alarm as Tshabalala resurfaced a few days later, the very confusion accompanying his absence enabled the police to obtain the lead they required to crack the case. On 15 December, whilst on his way back to Alexandra to fulfil the order given him, Rwaxa was arrested at immigration at the Oshoek border post after producing a Lesotho passport. He had received this document from Peter Sexwale, Mosima's brother, who was also an MK operative, on a recent visit to Lesotho. Previously Rwaxa had always used a South African passport to cross to and from Swaziland, and an alert official noted the discrepancy, leading to his arrest. At some time during interrogations held over the next few days at Ermelo and Krugersdorp police stations, and at security branch headquarters in John Vorster Square in Johannesburg, Rwaxa succumbed to the torture he was subjected to, and revealed his role in the ANC underground.[34]

Oblivious to the fact of its fate having been sealed, the MK cell forged ahead with its training work. More correctly, Sexwale did, because with Tsiki in hiding, Ramusi in Swaziland, and Motaung and Mohlanyaneng possessing useful cover stories that the underground did not want to jeopardise, he was saddled with the responsibility. After a couple of abortive attempts, he was able, through Gqabi, to arrange a meeting with the SSRC recruits on 17 December. He agreed to resume their training when he returned from his commitments in Sekhukhuneland, where from 18 to 20 December he not only instructed Motale Mantati, Aron Debeila and Stephen Lekgoro, the three local recruits the Nchabalengs had found, but also Peter and Elleck Nchabaleng themselves. When this was done, he returned to Soweto, and between 22 and 23 December, picked up the training of Masethla, Masinga, Moloi and Morobe from where Tsiki had left off. The content of the course was the same he had provided in Sekhukhuneland: political lessons expounding the basic programme of the ANC (with him noting having a particularly hard time winning the SSRC members from what he described as the 'SASO mentality' of black exclusiveness to the ANC's position that it was not 'down with the white man', but rather 'joining hands with the white man to bring a defeat of the present government' – all evidence of the kind of encounters that the ANC had with rival political tendencies whilst operating on the ground in South Africa, rival tendencies against whom the movement could only hope to prevail by persuasion rather than force), along with military training involving lessons in the use of hand grenades and the Tokarev and Scorpion pistols.[35]

Christmas 1976 came and went without any sign of Rwaxa, which alerted the Johannesburg underground to the fact that something was awry. They arranged for Bonny Sikhakhane and Carl Rabotho, two of their couriers, to travel to Swaziland on 28 December to investigate. On the day they departed, Ramokgadi informed Sexwale that Nchabaleng had found further recruits in Sekhukhuneland. Sexwale arranged to travel to Apel the following day to train them, but changed his plans after the township police arrested Sammy Seathlolo overnight.

Sexwale wanted to be on hand both to discover the younger Seathlolo's fate (remember his older brother Jacob was a part of the Main Machinery) and to be around for Rabotho and Sikhakhane's scheduled return on 2 January 1977. He therefore ordered Tsiki and Mohlanyaneng to be sent to Apel instead, and on 29 December the latter accompanied Ramokgadi to look for Tsiki at the hideout in the northern Transvaal where he was based. Sexwale meanwhile decamped to 124, 7th Avenue in Alexandra, where he stayed with Motaung.[36]

Sexwale and Motaung were therefore sitting ducks on 31 December 1976, when the police launched a massive coordinated raid on ANC underground properties in Soweto, Alexandra and the West Rand, based on information provided by Rwaxa. When the Police asked Sexwale who he was, he replied 'Solly Khumalo', which corresponded with the name in the fake reference book he had in his possession, which had been given him by Chiliza in Swaziland. The police arrested him regardless, and took him outside where they flashed a torch in his face before asking an individual in a waiting car to identify him. A voice, which Sexwale recognised as Joe Tseto's, replied 'that's him', though there remained some confusion over precisely who 'he' was, because in the subsequent interrogation at John Vorster Square the police kept asking questions like 'Where's Mosima? Where's Naledi Tsiki? Where are the guns? Were you ever trained?' – they evidently thought they had in their custody 'Solomon Khumalo' who had been trained by Mosima Sexwale and/or Naledi Tsiki. By the evening of 1 January 1977 a clearer picture had emerged, but for positive identification purposes the police called in Rwaxa, who entered the cell wearing a mask, but one in which the eyeholes were sufficiently large for Sexwale to recognise him immediately. Rwaxa then departed and the police returned, announcing that they knew they had in their custody the 'terrorist' Mosima Sexwale. Realising the game was up Sexwale confessed his role in the Bordergate incident and led the police to weapons he and Motaung had stored at 124, 7th Avenue in Alexandra.

On 31 December the police also raided Manci's house in Jabulani, Soweto; he was not home, but the SSRC recruits Masinga, Masethla, Morobe and Moloi, who were using the property as an underground hideout that night, were arrested and taken to Protea Police Station – where they saw Gqabi – and then to John Vorster Square, where they were positively identified, also by a man in a hood (but not Rwaxa). Further information from Rwaxa then enabled the police to extend their raids to Jonathan, and the operation culminated in Sekhukhuneland, where, between 2 and 3 January 1977, Peter and Elleck Nchabaleng, Simon Mohlanyaneng and Naledi Tsiki were arrested.[37]

VI

The abovementioned events have never been recounted in the detail offered in this article. For earlier accounts, see Barrell (1993:144-151), and Houston and Magubane (SADET 2006:383-9). The reason for such close scrutiny is in order to make a larger point, which I fear cannot prevail in the historiography unless made comprehensively. In this article, I have argued that the extant evidence relating to the period in question shows clearly that the size of the ANC's internal underground was not sufficient to serve as a base for armed struggle, and more importantly, I illustrate the reasons why.

What comes out clearly in this particular episode are the problems posed to MK by having to operate over as large a geographical area as it did. The reason why the distances were so great was because the South African state effectively denied MK safe sanctuaries anywhere near the territory in which it sought to operate. The consequence was that it was difficult for the movement to communicate messages, transport men, and offer guerrillas safe places to retreat after operations – in other words to exercise all the multifarious functions provided by 'bases' in war. A close consideration of the story of this group of MK cadres, who later became known as the 'Pretoria Twelve' after the case in the Supreme Court of South Africa where much of the information discussed in this article was divulged, highlights how problems created by having to operate over great distances arose time and again whilst they were active in the underground, and how, for the soldiers among them, the lack of close support in terms of communications, supply and places to retreat, were the principal obstacles that they encountered.

From Ramusi and Tsiki's arrival in Tanzania without the foreknowledge of their commanding officers, to their subsequent slow advance towards South Africa, to the confusion regarding Mabhida's message over how the military cell was to coordinate with the existing core of ANC personnel in Alexandra, and then to the inability to contact the movement's external leadership to resolve this issue, most of the problems discussed in the period covered by this article were reducible to the question of the large theatre across which MK was compelled to operate.

The result of MK having to operate across overextended logistical lines at the end of which the ANC lacked infrastructure such as safe houses that could accommodate the guerrillas within South Africa, meant that contact, and hence effective command and control between the rear and the front, was extremely difficult to establish. Besides serving to limit MK's ability to coordinate its armed actions within South Africa and mount effective operations against the state, this factor also meant that relations between the ANC and groupings within South Africa that the liberation movement relied on to advance its struggle, such as the BC movement, had, of necessity to be cooperative rather than dominative.

This article has demonstrated the status quo that existed in the mid-1970s as far as the abovementioned issues are concerned. Whilst it may be argued that the scenario outlined in this article changed and that the ANC was able to impose its hegemony over black communities in the following decade, my research on the armed underground in the 1980s (Simpson 2009c; Simpson 2010) suggests strongly that this was not the case. What my research instead indicates is that relations between the external liberation movement and the mass-based internal resistance were far more complex during the struggle than much of the existing literature maintains. Accordingly, I predict that close examination of processes occurring on the ground will reveal that claims that the ANC was either nothing, or, alternatively, that it was everything in the unfolding of popular resistance will prove unfounded, and that the documentary record will instead reveal the unfolding of complex patterns of cross-fertilisation between the ANC and the popular resistance movements inside South Africa, as members and ideas flowed between these two pillars of the freedom struggle who increasingly came to feel that they needed each other: the former could provide the guns, and the latter the mass manpower on which the achievement of liberation was considered to depend.

Notes

1. University of the Witwatersrand Historical Papers (hereafter UWHP); Karis-Gerhart Collection A2675 (hereafter KGC) folder 26/part III (hereafter 26/III) Naledi Tsiki, deposition to the SA Police, 3 Feb 1977 (hereafter 'Tsiki deposition'):12, 19–21; UWHP, KGC, 39/ I Howard Barrell interview with Naledi Tsiki, 26 Nov 1990 (hereafter 'Barrell interview with Tsiki, 26 Nov'):1253, 1256–7.
2. UWHP, KGC, 39/I 'Barrell interview with Tsiki, 26 Nov':1257–8.
3. UWHP, AD1901 Political Trials (hereafter PT), box 62, *S v MG Sexwale & others*, court record vol 25, testimony of Ian Deway Rwaxa, 9 Feb 1978 (hereafter 'Rwaxa testimony, 9 Feb'):1166–7; UWHP, PT, box 65, folder 019 (hereafter 65/19), *S v MG Sexwale & others*, judgement by Myburgh, J 5 April 1978 (hereafter '*S v Sexwale* judgement'):2271.
4. UWHP, PT, 65/1, *S v MG Sexwale & others*, testimony of Martha Tseto, 19 Jan 1978 (hereafter 'Martha Tseto testimony'):150–1, 164–6; UWHP, PT, 65/13, *S v MG Sexwale & others*, testimony of Joseph Tseto, 27–28 Feb 1978 (hereafter 'Joseph Tseto testimony'):1801–3, 1833–35, 1840–2; UWHP, PT, 65/14, *S v MG Sexwale & others*, 'Joseph Tseto testimony':1843–47, 1852–6, 1871, 1877–8; UWHP, PT, 65/19, '*S v Sexwale* judgement':2318; UWHP, KGC, 39/ I, 'Barrell interview with Tsiki, 26 Nov':1261.
5. UWHP, PT, 65/2, *S v MG Sexwale & others*, testimony of Alpheus Ramokgadi, 20 Jan 1978:192–6.
6. UWHP, PT, 62, *S v MG Sexwale & others*, court record vol 25, 'Rwaxa testimony, 9 Feb':1165, and court record vol 28, testimony of Ian Deway Rwaxa, 13 Feb 1978:1287–8; UWHP, KGC, 26/III, 'Tsiki deposition':51; UWHP, KGC, 39/I, 'Barrell interview with Tsiki, 26 Nov':1248, 1260; UWHP, PT, 65/19, '*S v Sexwale* judgement':2270, 2272.
7. UWHP, PT, 65/13, *S v MG Sexwale & others*, 'Joseph Tseto testimony':1819–21.

8. UWHP, KGC, 26/III, 'Tsiki deposition':20–1; UWHP, KGC, 39/I, 'Barrell interview with Tsiki, 26 Nov':1256-8.

9. UWHP, KGC, 26/III, 'Tsiki deposition':22–3; UWHP, KGC, 39/I, 'Barrell interview with Tsiki, 26 Nov':1257.

10. UWHP, KGC, 39/I, 'Barrell interview with Tsiki, 26 Nov':1251.

11. UWHP, PT, 62, *S v MG Sexwale & others*, court record vol 25, 'Rwaxa testimony, 9 Feb':1186; UWHP, KGC, 26/III, 'Tsiki deposition':23–5.

12. UWHP, KGC, 26/III, 'Tsiki deposition':25–6.

13. Ibid:27; UWHP, PT, 62, *S v MG Sexwale & others*, court record vol 26, 'Rwaxa testimony, 10 Feb':1210-12; UWHP, PT, 65/19, '*S v Sexwale*' judgement':2261, 2273; UWHP, KGC, 39/I, 'Barrell interview with Tsiki, 26 Nov':1260.

14. UWHP, KGC, 26/III, 'Tsiki deposition':27–8; UWHP, KGC, 25/III, 'Mosima Sexwale, deposition to the SA Police, 4 Feb 1977' (hereafter 'Sexwale deposition'):55; UWHP, PT, 65/15, *S v MG Sexwale & others*, 'testimony of Jacob Seathlolo, 3 Mar 1978':2124; UWHP, PT, 65/17, *S v MG Sexwale & others*, testimony of Jacob Seathlolo, 6 Mar 1978:2178-9; UWHP, KGC, 39/I, Howard Barrell interview with Naledi Tsiki, 5 Dec 1990 (hereafter 'Barrell interview with Tsiki, 5 Dec'):1276–7.

15. UWHP, PT, 65/19, '*S v Sexwale* judgement':2293–4; UWHP, KGC, 39/I, 'Barrell interview with Tsiki, 26 Nov':1258; UWHP, KGC, 26/III, 'Tsiki deposition':28–9; UWHP, KGC, 25/III, 'Sexwale deposition':55.

16. UWHP, KGC, 26/III, 'Tsiki deposition':31–3; UWHP, KGC, 28/III 'A Report on the South African situation, prepared by Marius and Jeanette Schoon, c1977' (hereafter 'Schoon report'):18; UWHP, KGC, 39/I, 'Barrell interview with Tsiki, 26 Nov':1260, 1262; UWHP, KGC, 39/I, 'Barrell interview with Tsiki, 5 Dec':1271, 1276; UWHP, PT, 62, *S v MG Sexwale & others*, court record vol 26, testimony of Ian Deway Rwaxa, 10 Feb 1978 (hereafter 'Rwaxa testimony, 10 Feb):1228-9.

17. UWHP, KGC, 28/III 'Schoon report':18.

18. UWHP, KGC, 26/III, 'Tsiki deposition':33–5; UWHP, KGC, 39/I, 'Barrell interview with Tsiki, 26 Nov':1261, 1263.

19. UWHP, KGC, 26/III, 'Tsiki deposition':35–6; UWHP, PT, 65/5, *S v MG Sexwale & others*, testimony of Samson Ndaba, 27 Jan 1978 (hereafter 'Ndaba testimony'):546–7; UWHP, PT, 65/6, *S v MG Sexwale & others*, 'Ndaba testimony':548–52, 563.

20. UWHP, KGC, 28/III 'Schoon report':18.

21. UWHP, KGC, 26/III, 'Tsiki deposition':37–40; UWHP, KGC, 25/III, 'Sexwale deposition':55, 57, 70; UWHP, KGC, 39/ I, 'Barrell interview with Tsiki, 26 Nov':1263–4.

22. UWHP, KGC, 39/I, 'Barrell interview with Tsiki, 26 Nov':1261-3, and 5 Dec 1990:1277.

23. UWHP, KGC, 28/III 'Schoon report':18.

24. UWHP, KGC, 28/III, statement of Elias Tieho Masinga, accused no 5, prepared for defence in *S v MG Sexwale & others*, 1977/8 (hereafter 'Masinga statement'):1-3; UWHP, KGC, 28/III, 'Masinga statement re the making of the police statement':4.

25. Raymond Suttner interview with Murphy Morobe, 26 Aug 2003 (hereafter 'Suttner interview with Morobe'):20.

26. UWHP, KGC, 28/III, 'Masinga statement':2.

27. UWHP, PT, 62, *S v MG Sexwale & others*, court record vol 26 'Rwaxa testimony, 10 Feb':1200-1; UWHP, KGC, 28/III, 'Masinga statement':3-4.

28. UWHP, KGC, 25/III, 'Sexwale deposition':64, 67; UWHP, KGC, 26/III, 'Tsiki deposition':41.

29. UWHP, KGC, 39/I, 'Barrell interview with Tsiki, 26 Nov':26:1264–5; UWHP, PT, 65/1, *S v MG Sexwale & others*, 'Martha Tseto testimony':155; UWHP, KGC, 25/III, 'Sexwale deposition':62–3.

30. UWHP, KGC, 25/III, 'Sexwale deposition':47–50; UWHP, KGC, 28/III 'Schoon report':18.

31. 'Grenade attack – alert on border', *Rand Daily Mail*, 1 Dec 1976; UWHP, KGC, 25/III, 'Sexwale, deposition':50–4, 59; UWHP, KGC, 26/III, 'Tsiki deposition':41; UWHP, PT, 65/19, 'S v Sexwale judgement':2257, 2278-84; Charles Alfred Zeelie, amnesty application to the Truth and Reconciliation Commission (TRC) for the assaults on T Sexwale, JB Sibanyoni and G Martins, 11 October 2000 (hereafter 'Zeelie, TRC').

32. UWHP, KGC, 39/I, 'Barrell interview with Tsiki, 26 Nov':1266; UWHP, KGC, 28/III 'Schoon report':19.

33. UWHP, KGC, 39/I, 'Barrell interview with Tsiki, 5 Dec':1275; UWHP, KGC, 25/III, 'Sexwale deposition':62–3; UWHP, KGC, 26/III, 'Tsiki deposition':43–5. 'S v Sexwale judgement':2295–6.

34. UWHP, PT, 62, *S v MG Sexwale & others*, court record vol 26, 'Rwaxa testimony, 10 Feb':1224, 1226-7, 1231; UWHP, KGC, 39/I, 'Barrell interview with Tsiki, 26 Nov':1262, 1266; UWHP, KGC, 25/III, 'Sexwale deposition':64; 'S v Sexwale judgement':2276-7; 'Zeelie, TRC'.

35. UWHP, KGC, 25/III, 'Sexwale deposition':58, 64–75; UWHP, PT, 65/7, *S v MG Sexwale & others*, testimony of Stephen Morepi Lekgoro, 2 Feb 1978:797–807, 812, 814–6, 824–5; UWHP, PT, 65/8, *S v MG Sexwale & others*, testimony of Abinar Mathabe, 3 Feb 1978:901–3; UWHP, PT, 65/19, 'S v Sexwale judgement':2288.

36. UWHP, KGC, 26/III, 'Tsiki deposition':46; UWHP, KGC, 39/I, 'Barrell interview with Tsiki, 26 Nov:1266; UWHP, KGC, 25/III, 'Sexwale deposition':76–7, 80–1.

37. UWHP, PT, 62, *S v MG Sexwale & others*, court record vol 27, 'Rwaxa testimony':1249; UWHP, KGC, 25/III, 'Sexwale deposition':81–2; UWHP, KGC, 25/III, 'Sexwale deposition':82; UWHP, KGC, 26/III, 'Tsiki deposition':46–7; UWHP, KGC, 28/III, 'Masinga statement re the making of the police statement':1; UWHP, PT, 65/19, 'S v Sexwale judgement':2259; testimony by Charles Zeelie and Tokyo Sexwale, 'Zeelie, TRC'; 'Suttner interview with Morobe':15, 20–1.

References

Barrell, H. 1993. 'Conscripts to their Age: African National Congress Operational Strategy, 1976 – 1986'. DPhil thesis, Oxford'.

Brooks, A. and Brickhill, J. 1980. *Whirlwind Before the Storm: The Origins and Development of the Uprising in Soweto and the Rest of South Africa from June to December 1976*. London: International Defence and Aid Fund.

Hirson, B. 1979. *Year of Fire, Year of Ash. The Soweto Revolt: Roots of a Revolution?* London: Zed Press.

Jeffery, A. 2009. *People's War: New Light on the Struggle for South Africa*. Johannesburg: Jonathan Ball.

Kane-Berman, J. 1981. *Soweto: Black Revolt: White Reaction*. Johannesburg: Ravan Press.

Legassick, M. 2008. 'Debating the Revival of the Workers' Movement in the 1970s: The South African Democracy Education Trust and Post-Apartheid Patriotic History'. *Kronos* 34(1):240–66.

Moss, G. 1982. 'Crisis and Conflict: Soweto 1976 – 1977'. MA thesis. University of the Witwatersrand.

SADET (South African Democracy Education Trust). 2006. *The Road to Democracy in South Africa*, (Vol. vol 2). Pretoria: Unisa Press.

Simpson, T. 2009a. ''The Making (and Remaking) of a Revolutionary Plan: Strategic Dilemmas of the ANC's Armed Struggle, 1974 – 1978''. *Social Dynamics* 35(2):312–29.

Simpson, T. 2009b. 'The Bay and the Ocean: A History of the ANC in Swaziland, 1960 – 1979'. *African Historical Review* 41(1):90–117.

Simpson, T. 2009c. 'Umkhonto we Sizwe, We are Waiting for You': The ANC and the Township Rebellion, September 1984 – September 1985'. *South African Historical Journal* 61(1):158–77.

Simpson, T. 2010. 'The Role of the African National Congress in Popular Protest During the Township Uprisings, 1984 – 1989', in W. Beinart and M.C. Dawson (eds), *Popular Politics and Resistance Movements in South Africa*. Johannesburg: Wits University Press.

Simpson, T. 2011. 'Military Combat Work: The Reconstitution of the ANC's Armed Underground, 1971 – 1976'. *African Studies* 70(1):103–22.

Sithole, J. 2009. 'Contestations over Knowledge Production or Ideological Bullying?: A Response to Legassick on the Workers' Movement'. *Kronos* 35(1):222–41.

Suttner, R. 2008. *The ANC Underground in South Africa to 1976: A Social and Historical Study*. Johannesburg: Jacana.

'Umkhonto we Sizwe, We are Waiting for You': The ANC and the Township Uprising, September 1984 – September 1985

THULA SIMPSON

University of Pretoria

Abstract

This article discusses the ANC's relationship with the youth-led township rebellion of the mid 1980s which has not received adequate attention in the existing literature on South African resistance politics. The argument made is that while the ANC lacked a physical presence in the townships and was thus unable to organise the uprisings, the appeal of its confrontational policies – and above all its armed struggle – meant it was accorded the mantle of symbolic leadership by the youths spearheading the fighting. The intangibility of mass consciousness and the difficulty of gauging it though conventional archival sources means the article relies heavily on the testimony of contemporary witnesses, and particularly journalists. The origins and dynamics of the uprising are investigated in the article and the gestation of the insurrection within the townships for almost a year before its eventual eruption is discussed, as is the manner in which the rebellion's lack of formal leadership proved to be its greatest strength by making it difficult to quell. The timeframe covered spans the first year of the uprising because it witnessed in microcosm the basic themes which dominated mass politics in South Africa for most of the following decade.

Prior to 1984 acts of political violence within South Africa were committed overwhelmingly by established political organisations, and of those engaged in violence against the apartheid state, the African National Congress (ANC) was the most prominent. Nonetheless, the scope of the armed struggle waged by the ANC through its military wing Umkhonto we Sizwe (MK) remained at the level of sporadic attacks, and the movement's initiatives to escalate its military effort were repeatedly frustrated by police countermeasures. The pattern of political violence within South Africa shifted following the government's introduction of a new constitutional dispensation late in 1983, and opposition within African communities to the new political structures rapidly assumed a violent dimension. The resistance was spearheaded by that stratum of the urban black population most commonly referred to by political commentators as 'youths', or, within activist circles as 'comrades', '*amabutho*' (warriors), or 'young lions'. The youth-led violence presented both opportunities and challenges to the ANC, for although its randomness conflicted with the controls the movement had always imposed in the prosecution of its own armed struggle, it also simultaneously appeared to offer an answer to the question that had long bedevilled the movement, namely of how to intensify military pressure on the state. This article discusses how the ANC sought to resolve the dilemmas created by the emergence of these new patterns of violence.

I

In a referendum on 2 November 1983, South Africa's white electorate approved a bill first introduced to parliament by the ruling National Party (NP) in May 1983. The legislation proposed establishing a tricameral parliament that would give white, coloured and Asian communities separate racially-exclusive chambers granting each group control over their 'own affairs', with 'general affairs' affecting all racial groups becoming the responsibility of a multi-racial presidential cabinet. Black Africans were excluded from these provisions. Government spokesmen argued that adequate provision for their political representation existed in three legislative measures known as the 'Koornhof bills', named after the minister of Cooperation and Development, Piet Koornhof. These allowed for granting a select few Africans the right to reside permanently in white areas, and provided blacks in urban areas with an upgraded system of local government.

One of these bills was the Black Local Authorities Act, originally introduced in 1982, which granted increased autonomy to community councils in African townships, including greater responsibility for financing their own affairs. Elections for the first 26 councils converted under the new legislation took place in November and December 1983. However the turnout was only 21 per cent, down from 30 per cent in community council elections in 1978.[1] Furthermore, the balloting was accompanied by sporadic outbreaks of violence. Some voters complained that certain candidates threatened to evict them if they voted for the opposition, while there were attacks on the homes of five election candidates in townships around Port Elizabeth and a petrol bomb attack on the home of the former deputy mayor of Soweto on the eve of the opening of the polls.[2]

These developments aroused considerable interest in ANC ranks. Some within the organisation began trying to track down members of the groups involved in the internal violence with the aim of inducing them to leave the country to be trained in the use of hand grenades; when they returned they could use these skills in the townships. The desire to establish links was mutual, for many of those involved in the internal violence were simultaneously looking to contact the

---

1. J. Grest, 'The Crisis of Local Government in South Africa', in P. Frankel, N. Pines and M. Swilling, eds, *State, Resistance and Change in South Africa* (London, New York and Sydney: Croom Helm, 1988), 94–7.
2. C. Cooper, S. Motala, J. Shindler, C. McCaul, and T. Ratsomo, eds, *Survey of Race Relations in South Africa in 1983* (Johannesburg: South African Institute of Race Relations, 1984), 258–9; J. Kane-Berman, *Political Violence in South Africa* (Johannesburg: South African Institute of Race Relations, 1993), 38.

ANC in order to receive military training. Additionally, many senior ANC members who had MK guerrillas under their responsibility volunteered that their charges be trained as prospective members of similar groups. Consequently, there was a steady flow of recruits into Botswana, both from South Africa and from the ANC's military bases in central Africa, all looking for military training in the proposed units. By the beginning of 1984, training facilities for this purpose were established in Botswana and five units were established within South Africa. However, the South African security forces kept close tabs on these developments. By the reckoning of Cal Saloojee, one of those responsible for overseeing the military training in Botswana, spies had infiltrated the first group that he trained, while Mac Maharaj, a senior ANC member, estimated that perhaps one in 10 of those trained in Botswana in 1984 were double agents. By mid 1984 the ANC's training structures in Botswana were thoroughly penetrated by enemy operatives.[3]

II

In Soweto, where there had only been a 10.7 per cent turnout in the council elections, a new wave of attacks on councillors began on 16 January 1985 when the home of the new mayor of the township, E.T. Tshabalala was petrol bombed. The next day, the home of the former mayor of Dobsonville, Soweto, was also attacked. In the following month, a group calling itself the South African Suicide Squad (SASS) emerged to claim responsibility for these attacks in pamphlets distributed in Naledi, Soweto. The group listed its reasons for employing violence as that 90 per cent of Sowetans rejected the councils; that the councils entrenched the apartheid system; and that councillors had failed to deliver on their promises to reduce rents. Each SASS bombing was followed by a call to a local newspaper claiming responsibility for the attack. The SASS also frequently left pamphlets at railway stations after such operations, warning remaining councillors to 'expect the worst' if they failed to resign their posts within a month. The role of the suicide squads has been overlooked in most historical sources, but their effectiveness quickly became apparent. As early as February 1984 the security situation had deteriorated to the point where the Soweto Community Council felt compelled to issue a plea to the national government for a pay increase due to the fact that their 'high-risk' jobs exposed them to 'dangers unheard of in white areas'.[4]

Attacks in the townships soon spread beyond councillors to include individuals of any description considered to be working within 'the system'. Often the victims were merely persons against whom the attackers held a grudge, and trade unionists, policemen, school principals and religious figures numbered among those targeted. As the August 1984 elections for the coloured and Indian chambers of the tricameral parliament drew near, petrol bomb attacks spread beyond

3. H. Barrell, 'Conscripts to their Age: African National Congress Operational Strategy, 1976–1986' (DPhil thesis, University of Oxford, 1993), 326–30.
4. P. Younghusband, 'South Africa Faces Stormy Election Campaign', *The Globe and Mail* (Canada), 28 July 1984; R. Wicksteed, 'South Africa: Government Sponsored Councils under Attack', *IPS Inter-Press Service*, 20 December 1984; C. Cooper, J. Shindler, C. McCaul, F. Potter, and M. Cullum, eds, *Survey of Race Relations in South Africa 1984* (Johannesburg: South African Institute of Race Relations, 1985), 82–3.

African townships to other communities, beginning on the morning of 20 July when the homes of four election candidates, three Indians and one coloured person, were targeted.[5]

In a striking contrast to their success in penetrating the ANC's Botswana structures, the police made little headway in their struggle against the suicide squads. They admitted this publicly in statements made in July 1984, when they openly confessed their failure to have unearthed much information about the origins, composition and structure of such groups.[6]

At the same time, however, the actions of the suicide squads posed a challenge to the ANC, because the violence they perpetrated blurred the boundaries that the external movement had hitherto always tried to maintain between 'soft' and 'hard' targets in its own armed struggle. As Tom Lodge noted, since 1976 when MK attacks within South Africa resumed after a decade of absence, operations launched were characterised by the manner in which their timing and target selection demonstrated a concern to avoid civilian deaths. The attacks undertaken focused on infrastructure associated with the state such as railway lines, administrative buildings, and police stations, and were conducted in such a way as to identify the ANC with concerns and issues pertinent to township residents.[7] By contrast, most petrol bomb attacks by suicide squads involved throwing 'Molotov cocktails' through the bedroom windows of the intended victims in the still of night.[8]

Consequently, the ANC leadership hesitated to publicly associate itself with such groups until it received feedback about how the wider ANC membership, the state, and the population in the townships responded to their activities. The ANC was also uncomfortable that many of the groups insisted on referring to themselves as 'suicide squads', preferring the moniker 'grenade squads' instead. Eventually, the ANC backed down, and again the issue was one of how this might be received in the country at large. Some ANC members thought that the title suicide squad might inspire the black population and make whites apprehensive. For the time being, then, the ANC's response was one of 'wait and see'.[9]

This caution was displayed on 10 August 1984, when the president of the ANC, Oliver Tambo, first commented publicly on the SASS. At a press conference called to admit MK's responsibility for a car bomb that had killed five black civilians in Durban on 12 July 1984, he denied any dealings with the SASS. Tambo used the occasion to berate the MK guerrillas responsible for the attack in Natal as having been 'inexcusably careless', saying: 'we have made it clear that this is becoming intolerable – this failure to take precautions to avoid hitting people you are not intending to hit', before reassuring observers that although increased civilian casualties would regrettably become unavoidable within the context of an escalating war, the ANC remained staunch in its policy of attacking only strategic military targets.[10]

5.   Cooper *et al.*, *Survey of Race Relations 1984*, 84; P. Laurence, 'Political Bombings Hit Four Homes: Coloured Candidates Standing for Election to South Africa's Tri-racial Parliament', *The Guardian* (London), 21 July 1984.
6.   P. van Slambrouck, 'Bombs Hit Homes of South African Blacks', *Christian Science Monitor* (Boston,,MA), 24 July 1984; Younghusband, 'South Africa Faces Stormy Election Campaign'.
7.   T. Lodge, *The ANC After Nkomati* (Johannesburg: South African Institute of Race Relations, 1985), 5.
8.   Cooper *et al.*, *Survey of Race Relations 1984*, 82.
9.   Barrell, 'Conscripts to their Age', 329–30.
10.   A. Meldrum, 'ANC Leader Says his Bomb Squad "Inexcusably Careless": Car Bomb Attack in South African City of Durban', *The Guardian* (London), 11 August 1984.

III

From 3 September 1984, the underground war in the townships was subsumed within a larger, open mass revolt. The uprising began in the Vaal Triangle, a cluster of townships 45 miles south of Johannesburg, and the impetus came from the issue of rents, which were higher in this area than anywhere else in the country. For example in Sebokeng, the Vaal township with the lowest rents at R50 per month, rates were higher than the highest charged in Soweto which stood at R48 per month. Beginning in August, protest meetings organised by the Vaal Civic Association and local shop stewards were held in all Vaal Triangle townships, culminating on Sunday 2 September where a decision was made that residents should refuse to pay their rents.[11]

At one of these meetings in the township of Sharpeville, calls were made for stayaways from work and schools, to begin on 3 September. However in Sharpeville, Sebokeng and Evaton, the demonstrations turned violent when protesters hurled petrol bombs and bricks at police, barricaded roads and set fire to buildings, beginning on the Sunday and continuing throughout the following day. Police fired rubber bullets to drive off looters and arsonists, but this did not contain the rebellion and by the end of the week more than 40 people were dead, including the black deputy mayors of Evaton and Sharpeville.[12]

For the government, the Vaal uprising was less a spontaneous outbreak than an event planned and orchestrated by organisations with ulterior political motives. Whilst driving through the Vaal townships on 6 September 1984 with three other cabinet members in two armoured personnel carriers brimful with police, Law and Order minister, Louis Le Grange, rejected claims that grievances over rent hikes had caused the violence, saying: 'There are individuals and other forces and organisations very clearly behind what is happening in the Vaal Triangle', although he declined to comment any further at that stage.[13]

He was more forthcoming a month later when addressing the Transvaal Province Congress of the NP on 5 October 1984. There he declared that the illegal ANC and South African Communist Party (SACP) were orchestrating events through the medium of the United Democratic Front (UDF), a mass coalition formed in August 1983 to oppose the constitution. Le Grange charged:

> When the [UDF's] actions in the republic are judged against its objectives, affiliations, public actions, pronouncements ... one can reach no other conclusion but that [it] is pursuing the same revolutionary goals as the banned ANC and South African Communist Party, and is actively promoting a climate of revolution.[14]

To buttress his argument, he pointed to the fact that over 90 per cent of UDF officials were former ANC members and quoted from banned ANC and SACP publications which praised the UDF and declared it worthy of support.[15]

---

11. Labour Monitoring Group, 'The November 1984 Stayaway', in J. Maree, ed., *The Independent Trade Unions, 1974–1984: Ten Years of the South African Labour Bulletin* (Johannesburg: Ravan Press, 1987), 260.
12. J. Kane-Berman, 'Third World Review: How Black Anger has Backfired: Political Frustration of Blacks in South Africa', *The Guardian* (London), 7 December 1984.
13. T. Baldwin, 'Cabinet Ministers Tour Riot Areas, Doubt Rent Hikes Caused Violence', *The Associated Press*, 6 September 1984.
14. T. Baldwin, 'Government Accuses Anti-Apartheid Group of Promoting Revolution', *The Associated Press*, 5 October 1984; *United Press International*, 5 October 1984.
15. *Ibid.*

As the violence spiralled in following months, this was a theme government spokesmen returned to repeatedly. The essence of the charge was as follows: an 'ANC/SACP/UDF alliance' was working in cahoots to generate a 'revolutionary climate' in South Africa, with the latter serving as an internal front for the others. The UDF's tasks in the alliance's political division of labour were to propagate the ideology of the external organisations, promote the ANC as a suitable alternative to the existing authorities, and generate a political mood amongst blacks in which they would not only come to view revolutionary violence as being morally justified, but would also be inspired to actively partake in it. This campaign of mass radicalisation was implemented in three stages – the 'organising phase', the 'politicising phase', and the 'mobilising phase' – and was undertaken at UDF rallies and meetings where the speeches delivered, songs sung, poems recited, as well as placards, banners and symbols displayed, were all allegedly subtly crafted by the alliance to indoctrinate those present by means of discrediting the government, promoting the ANC as its alternative, and glorifying revolutionary violence.[16]

For its part, the UDF rejected the charge from the outset. At a press conference called on 10 October to refute Le Grange's speech, UDF spokesmen condemned the minister's 'mischievous' allegations and reiterated the front's commitment to achieving democratic change through exclusively lawful and peaceful means. They added that while the UDF may have received endorsements from the external organisations, it remained powerless to 'influence the content of the publications of the ANC and SACP, as we have no access to these publications'.[17]

At the time, such protests were no more than the truth. As Jeremy Seekings has written, the focus of the UDF's work before the Vaal uprising centred on mobilising opposition to the constitution rather than engaging with civic struggles in the townships. Consequently, the UDF's attention was focused on coloured and Indian rather than African communities. Although the UDF had commenced with establishing affiliate structures in African townships in the months before the Vaal uprising, there was ultimately no correlation between areas where UDF organisation was strongest and those where insurrectionary activity was at its most intense, for, as Seekings states, it so happened that 'the major township struggles of 1984 on the Rand occurred in areas where the UDF was weak, and the townships where the UDF's affiliates were stronger were relatively quiescent'.[18]

The views of the UDF's national leadership about the front's political role only began to change slowly in response to the upsurge of resistance in the townships in late 1984. However, not until around mid 1985 was a majority within the front's leadership converted to the view that the UDF's role was to function as a permanent entity committed to fight the apartheid system in its entirety, rather than to operate as an ad-hoc formation devoted to engaging on the single issue of the constitution.[19]

---

16. University of the Witwatersrand Historical Papers (hereafter UWHP), Joint Management Centres (hereafter JMC) A266F, Captain Fouché, 'The UDF. Transkei Course', c. September 1985, 2–14.

17. J.F. Smith, 'Opposition Group Says Ban would Exacerbate Crisis', *The Associated Press*, 10 October 1984; see also the *Financial Times* (London), 11 October 1984; P. Laurence, 'United Democratic Front Defends its Opposition Record', *The Guardian* (London), 11 October 1984.

18. J. Seekings, '"Trailing behind the Masses": The United Democratic Front and Township Politics in the Pretoria-Witwatersrand-Vaal Region, 1983–84', *Journal of Southern African Studies*, 18, 1 (March 1992), 94–6, 108.

19. *Ibid.*, 96.

This conversion came too late to reverse a trend of disillusionment among many activists within UDF affiliates in the townships who sought a more confrontational approach. According to Seekings, as early as September 1984 these activists had become 'indifferent or even hostile towards the UDF' and began operating independently of its national and regional structures. These militants viewed themselves as being under the jurisdiction of the ANC rather than the UDF, and justified their activities accordingly as being responses to calls from the former to intensify confrontations with the state. Meanwhile other members of UDF affiliates in the townships remained closer to the front's national leadership and prioritised establishing new political branches over advancing confrontational policies.[20]

In short, there was no uniform approach and no collusive conspiracy to foment violence. It is true that the ANC sought to use the UDF as a conduit for its political strategies in the manner charged by the government. However it was repeatedly frustrated in its attempts to do so. As late as March 1986 Oliver Tambo was still calling for the ANC to build its own 'underground structures within the UDF' so as to provide it with 'the correct guidance'.[21]

However, though innocent of charges of being involved in a formal conspiracy orchestrated by the ANC and SACP to foment violence, there was nevertheless a direct link between the UDF's calls for ostensibly non-violent forms of protest such as work stayaways and consumer, rent and school boycotts, and instances of political violence in the townships.

In the month following the Vaal uprisings a stream of anecdotal reports emerged from the townships about gangs of youths claiming to be UDF 'comrades' or Congress of South African Students (COSAS – a UDF affiliate) militants, erecting barricades to prevent residents from going to work; attacking those who tried to do so; moving from school to school ordering students out of class; hurling stones and petrol bombs at policemen; attacking buses and taxis; digging trenches in the streets; destroying buildings; and assaulting members of rival organisations – all in order to enforce boycott and stayaway calls.[22]

Such charges were particularly widespread following a work stayaway called by the Release Mandela Committee, a UDF affiliate, on 17 September 1984, which was held to protest the presence of the security forces in the townships. The protest met with mixed success, but it was followed by a number of anti-apartheid organisations, such as the Azanian People's Organisation (AZAPO), coming forward to protest both that not only were they not consulted about the stayaway, but that many blacks were subjected to coercion to get them to support the protest.[23]

It soon became clear that most of the youths partaking in the violence were autonomous agents not under the control of any particular organisation. This was manifested by the events that emerged in the weeks following September 1984, with groups of youths undertaking actions such as disrupting school assemblies in the name of an organisation, only for the organisation concerned to repudiate their actions. The disruption caused by such acts, and the inability of the

20. J. Seekings, *The UDF: A History of the United Democratic Front in South Africa, 1983–1991* (Cape Town: David Philip, 2000), 125.
21. Kane-Berman, *Political Violence*, 42.
22. *Ibid.*, 33; J. Wentzel, *The Liberal Slideaway* (Johannesburg: South African Institute of Race Relations, 1995), 45.
23. Kane-Berman, 'Third World Review'.

student groups to control the violence conducted in their name, led them to lose a great deal of the support of the wider population in the townships.[24]

IV

In the meantime, unrest quickly grew beyond the capacity of the South African Police to contain, and therefore beginning on 6 October 1984 in Joza Township on the outskirts of Grahamstown, and then in Soweto the following morning, the South African Defence Force (SADF) was brought in to support police operations.[25]

The ANC's response to this turn of developments was euphoric. On 18 October 1984, a commentary on the organisation's broadcasting station Radio Freedom declared jubilantly: 'There is no way out for the Botha regime ... Botha's guns and batons are failing. This is being demonstrated every day in the streets of Soweto, Sharpeville, Sebokeng, [King] Williamstown and other areas'.[26]

However, the notion that children armed at best with rags stuffed into bottles filled with petrol – and more often merely with stones – could resist the might of the security forces was put into perspective five days later when in the early hours of 23 October 1984, a combined police-military force including some 7 000 SADF troops surrounded Sebokeng, cordoned off the sections of the township most affected by unrest, inundated the streets with troops standing 15 metres apart, and conducted a house-to-house search of about 19 500 residences in a hunt for 'instigators' and 'revolutionaries'. Those not detained in the sweep were forced to wear orange armbands, green stickers or coloured ink on their fingers to prove that they had been interrogated and screened. Meanwhile, people's hands were stamped with the message 'friendly forces', and the security forces distributed badges reading 'I am your friend, trust me' and 'Cooperation for peace and security'. Leaflets were distributed declaring 'We are your friends – we are here to help you', and handbills urged students to return to class. From Sebokeng the security forces proceeded to give Sharpeville, Boipatong and Evaton the same treatment. This operation was codenamed 'Palmiet' in Afrikaans, meaning bullrush in English. A sober Radio Freedom commentary spoke that night of 'stunned black people' in Sebokeng looking on from their front doors 'wearing bright orange or green stickers to show that they had been cleared by the security forces'.[27]

24. Wentzel, *The Liberal Slideaway*, 47.

25. M. Evans and M. Phillips, 'Intensifying Civil War: The Role of the South African Defence Force', in Frankel, *et al.*, *State, Resistance*, 117.

26. 'ANC Calls for a Determined Offensive Against Apartheid', *BBC Summary of World Broadcasts*, 22 October 1984, based on text of commentary entitled, 'The Way Forward to Victory', broadcast on Radio Freedom, Addis Ababa, 18 October 1984.

27. 'ANC Comment on Black Township "Siege" Operations', *BBC Summary of World Reports*, 26 October 1984, based on text of commentary entitled 'The Township of Sebokeng Falls into an Operational Area', Radio Freedom, Addis Ababa, 23 October 1984; G. Cawthra, 'South Africa at War', in J. Lonsdale, ed., *South Africa In Question* (London and Portsmouth: James Currey and Heinemann, 1988), 74; M. Murray, *South Africa, Time of Agony, Time of Destiny: The Upsurge of Popular Protest* (London: Verso, 1987), 254–5.

In all, 358 people were arrested during Palmiet, and the following day, Brigadier Bert Wandrag, the commander of the joint police-military task force, described the enterprise as a sparkling success, boasting that people long sought by the police had been arrested and that arms and ammunition had been found and confiscated. However, the accomplishments of the operation were in fact quite modest, and this provided another important indicator of the unstructured nature of the uprising. As Lieutenant Henry Beck of the South African Police commented on the same day, none of those arrested were charged with violations of security laws, with most having been apprehended for minor statutory crimes such as possession of dagga, pornography and stolen goods, while others were hapless victims of the pass laws. Meanwhile, in terms of captured arms and ammunition, only a few unlicensed guns were found. Quite simply, the evidence of formal planning and organisation such as underground cells of revolutionaries or concealed caches of weapons that the security forces evidently envisaged unearthing when they launched this hunt for 'instigators', 'revolutionaries', 'arms' and 'ammunition', had not materialised.[28]

Their failure was dramatised on 24 October, when almost immediately after the troops completed their phased withdrawal from the four townships they had occupied, a crowd of 2000 formed in Sebokeng to confront the remaining police contingents, thereby starting a fresh round of street fighting. On the same day, more than 70 000 children launched an impromptu school boycott in the four townships occupied during the operation. These events, combined with outbreaks of rioting in townships to the east and west of Johannesburg, and others around Grahamstown and Port Elizabeth in the Eastern Cape during the course of Palmiet, caused many journalists to begin dismissing the whole enterprise as a fiasco. A spokesperson for the ministry of Law and Order, Leon Mellet counselled them against this on 24 October, saying: 'Can it be expected that immediately, the following morning, everything returns to normal? Let's give it a couple days'. However, a couple of days later the situation had not improved, and on 31 October the police and army were back in Sebokeng, Sharpeville, Boipatong and Bophelong (the township neighbouring Sharpeville), setting up road blocks and patrols to break up crowds of student school boycotters.[29]

In the following months this pattern was witnessed repeatedly: as the security forces deployed into a particular township, violent protest flared elsewhere; as they withdrew, unrest resumed where they had been. The floundering response of the security forces, resembling a fire engine racing repeatedly to the wrong fire, only fanned the flames of insurrection. Furthermore, these events, transmitted worldwide by an international press corps that had virtually unfettered access to the country at the time, communicated the message that the government's writ in black areas only ran because of the huge military superiority the security forces enjoyed over virtually defenceless township inhabitants. In 1985, daily television images of confrontations between gun-wielding policemen and rock-throwing youths fuelled the debate in international circles over whether or not to impose sanctions on South Africa.

28. T. Baldwin, 'Students Continue Boycott after Massive Raid', *The Associated Press*, 24 October 1984; P. Laurence, 'Anger at Role of Troops in Township Raid: South African Military Operation in Black Townships', *The Guardian* (London), 25 October 1984.
29. P. Laurence, 'Black Youths Riot in Cape Province', *The Associated Press*, 31 October 1984; see also *The Associated Press*, 1 November 1984; Evans and Phillips, 'Intensifying Civil War', 117; and Murray, *South Africa: Time of Agony*, 255.

V

While the rioting continued unabated, student groups felt that organised political protests among youths were running out of steam. By the beginning of October, COSAS leaders believed that the student protests they had been responsible for organising were losing momentum. They put his down to a combination of the failure of the state to respond to its demands, the detention of large numbers of activists, and a campaign by councillors and school principals to entice pupils back to class in time to sit end of year exams. This led them to seek a new departure, and they called for an emergency meeting of UDF affiliates for 10 October 1984 to discuss the way forward. Having used the meeting to persuade the community organisations to join them, COSAS then called on the labour movement for assistance. Hitherto the major labour union, the Federation of South African Trade Unions (FOSATU), had remained aloof from political protest and had confined its activity to shop floor organisation. There had been much debate within the union movement over the issue of political engagement, and while FOSATU had decided to remain politically non-aligned, others such as the South African Allied Workers' Union (SAAWU) did not take long to throw themselves into confrontational politics. COSAS's direct call for worker support placed FOSATU on the spot and forced it to give a definitive answer on its position regarding political involvement. In response, FOSATU held a central committee meeting on 19–21 October where delegates from the Transvaal called for the federation to embrace the principle of participating in political struggles. The meeting authorised the formation of a sub-committee made up of FOSATU members from the Transvaal that was given the authority to undertake whatever actions it deemed necessary.[30]

On 27 October 1984, FOSATU representatives were among 37 organisations present at a meeting in Johannesburg where COSAS repeated its call for worker support for student demands. It was decided at the meeting to call a two-day stayaway in early November that would be co-directed by an ad-hoc structure named the Transvaal Regional Stay-away Committee, made up of the organisations represented at the meeting – including the unions. It was also decided to broaden the political demands of the stayaway beyond student demands to encompass wider union and community issues.

In the event, the November stayaway proved to be the most successful yet, with the Johannesburg Chamber of Commerce estimating that at least 50 per cent of the black work force in the Johannesburg industrial region had failed to show up for work. However, once again a supposedly voluntary withdrawal of labour was accompanied by attacks on government buses, trains and administration buildings, arson on the homes of local black officials, and the stoning of black policemen.[31] There was also coercion directed at members of rival political groups. Soon after the stayaway, 16 Black Consciousness organisations met to discuss the problem, with speakers claiming that most people had participated in the stayaway more out of fear than solidarity with the cause. Others asserted that the intimidation that accompanied the protest had alienated a sizeable proportion of workers. Meanwhile, Mangosuthu Buthelezi, the leader of the Inkatha movement made a speech in which he recommended that in future members of his organisation should retaliate against forced mobilisation, saying:

30. Labour Monitoring Group, 'The November 1984 Stayaway', 264–7.

if they burn your house you should burn their houses too ... COSAS works among your children exhorting them to lose their lives on township streets. COSAS will fail and in failing they will drag our children down with them'.[32]

The seeds of future internecine conflict between various black opposition groups were thus sown, but for the time being, the ANC and UDF chose instead to avert their gaze to the bright vision they imagined the November stayaway had opened up, in which the politically engaged trade union movement would combine its efforts with those of organisations from the wider community, thereby creating realistic prospects for an all-round popular insurrection.

The vision ultimately proved to be a mirage, because the divergence of economic, rather than political interests between the various sections of the black community were too great. Africans in general were determined to be rid of apartheid, but by no means all students (or their parents) were enthusiastic about sacrificing their education and hence their economic future in school boycotts without end. Nor, in a time of recession, was the average black consumer happy to spend as much as double the usual amount for staple goods at local stores during extended consumer boycotts that exploited their control of a captive market to inflate prices. Although there was a general commitment to liberation among blacks, there was no agreement on the methods of struggle being employed, and there was also widespread resentment towards the forced mobilisation that had become characteristic of the mass boycotts.

The months following the November stayaway highlighted perhaps the most fundamental schism within the black community: the class contradiction between unionised workers anxious to preserve economic gains accrued through collective bargaining, and unemployed township youths committed to confrontational policies.[33] The precariousness of organised labour's position was highlighted on 8 November 1984, the day after the conclusion of the November stayaway, when SASOL, the state owned oil-from-coal conversion plant, fired 6 000 of its black workers who participated in the stayaway and 'deported' them to the Bantustans.[34] Unlike the workers, the unemployed had nothing to lose in lengthy work stayaways. In fact, if such protest action led to mass redundancies that would create job openings in an otherwise forbiddingly tight labour market, they actually had a great deal to gain.

VI

Though no match for the SADF, by mid 1985 township militants had succeeded in achieving the collapse of local authorities through ceaseless attacks on any persons or property associated with councils in the black townships. Between 1 September 1984 and 28 May 1985, no fewer than 257 black councillors had resigned, and by the end of June 1985 it was estimated that fewer than

31. P. van Slambrouck, 'Black Workers Join Wave of Protest in South Africa', *Christian Science Monitor* (Boston, MA), 7 November 1984; A. Cowell, 'Toll Rises to 16 in South African Rioting', *The New York Times*, 7 November 1984.
32. Kane-Berman, *Political Violence*, 33; Wentzel, *The Liberal Slideaway*, 50–1, 230.
33. R. Lambert and E. Webster, 'The Re-emergence of Political Unionism in Contemporary South Africa?', in W. Cobbett and R. Cohen, eds, *Popular Struggles in South Africa* (London: James Currey, 1988), 31, 34–5.
34. 'South Africa: U.S. "Concerned" About Detention of Union Leaders', *IPS-Inter Press Service*, 9 November 1984.

six local councils remained operative in the entire country. So few blacks were willing to serve in these structures by mid 1985 that Chris Heunis, the minister of Constitutional Development, was forced to begin appointing white civil servants to manage township affairs.[35]

The ANC was largely a spectator in this process. Its ability to guide and influence events on the ground was crippled by the inadequacy of its organised presence within the country. A confidential document produced in May 1985 by the ANC's political headquarters emphasised how little progress had been made towards delivering on a commitment made in September 1980 to establish leadership structures within South Africa. Whereas in 1980 the numerical strength of the ANC's political network inside the country was numbered at 200, by May 1985, according to the document, this number had risen to 'just above 500 cadres spread over 110 units with an average of 3 members per unit and 178 individual operatives'. Furthermore, most members of such networks were youths or students and thus not senior figures with the credentials to occupy positions of leadership.[36]

The ANC's military strategy at the time concentrated on infiltrating insurgents armed with hand grenades into South Africa's townships in order to reinforce the uprising. This strategy received two major setbacks in June 1985. Firstly, on 14 June 1985, two days after a group calling itself the Western Cape Suicide Squad launched petrol bomb attacks on the homes of two coloured parliamentarians, South African soldiers launched a pre-dawn raid on ten ANC targets in Gaborone, Botswana, in which at least 15 people were killed. At a press conference in Pretoria on the day of the raid, Constand Viljoen, who headed the SADF, displayed documents and weapons which he claimed had been seized, including an RPG rocket launcher and a silencer for an AK-47 rifle, which, he said, security police had discovered the ANC was planning to use in attacks on black and coloured politicians in South Africa later in the month. He added that the properties attacked were used by the ANC to train and accommodate its members sent from Angola via Zambia en route to South Africa. Meanwhile, Brigadier Herman Stadler of the police claimed that a number of the houses attacked were also used as centres for the 'crash course' training of members of 'the Transvaal and Western Cape Suicide Squad', who, after leaving South Africa, were sent into Botswana for a few days training and then posted back into the country on missions.[37]

As these events unfolded, in Duduza Township on the East Rand, a police double-agent named Joe Mamasela was in the process of implementing a mission named 'Operation Zero Zero'. According to later testimony from the head of the Security Branch, General Johan van der

35. A. Cowell, 'South Africa's New Mood', *The New York Times*, 27 March 1985; B. Streek, 'Black Anger Makes Botha's Councils Melt Away', *The New York Times*, 14 April 1985; P. Laurence, 'Violence in South Africa Causing Collapse of Black Township Governments', *Christian Science Monitor* (Boston), 19 July 1985; M. Hornsby, 'Emergency as Before – and Why it Will Continue', *The Times* (London), 25 July 1985; R.B. Cullen and R. Wilkinson, 'The Young Lions', *Newsweek*, 16 September 1985; A. Cowell, 'Generation Gap Adds Tension among South African Blacks', *The New York Times*, 18 September 1985; J. Herbst, 'Prospects For Revolution in South Africa', *Political Science Quarterly*, 103, 4 (Winter, 1988–1989), 668–9; Wentzel, *The Liberal Slideaway*, 43.

36. UWHP, Karis Gerhart Collection: A2675, Part III, Folder 61, 'Organisational Report From PHQ', Lusaka, 21 May 1985, 3–5.

37. 'Further Reports on SADF Chief's 14th June Statements on Gaborone Raid', *BBC Summary of World Broadcasts*, 18 June 1985, based on excerpts from report by SAPA in English, Pretoria, 14 June 1985.

Merwe, the police were worried about their inability to protect black policemen and councillors, particularly those in the Vaal Triangle and the East Rand. They had received news that a group of activists was planning a series of attacks on black policemen in the East Rand and they tasked Mamasela with infiltrating the group. He successfully managed to do this early in June when he arrived in Duduza, saying he was 'from Lusaka' and was seeking to arm senior COSAS members.[38]

On 24 June, Mamasela and another police agent collected a group of recruits and drove them in a minibus to a derelict mine in the bush. There he produced two Russian RGD5 hand grenades packed with TNT and possessing a fragmentation radius of 15 to 20 metres. He explained the firing mechanism and the recruits then conducted a successful trial run. Duly satisfied, they returned home. As they had agreed, they met again the following night at three collection points. Among the operations were to be grenade attacks on the homes of two security policemen in Tsakane and Kwathema, grenade attacks in Duduza, and a limpet mine attack on a power sub-station in Kwathema. Mamasela appeared that night with the weapons and told the youths to strike at midnight. However the grenades he provided them were modified with a zero-timed delay mechanism, meaning they would detonate immediately upon use. Meanwhile, another student by the name of 'Congress' was given the modified limpet mine rather than a hand grenade due to Mamasela's fear that the recruit would later be able to identify him.[39]

In KwaThema the three students headed for the policeman's house but when the first pulled his grenade's pin it exploded in his hand, killing him instantly. In Tsakane, two others died the same way. Meanwhile, the limpet mine for the attack in Kwathema also exploded prematurely. In Duduza itself, the planned attack was broken up by the sudden arrival of police. An explosion killed one youth as he ran, while three others fled. According to a forensic specialist hired by the families of those who had been killed, they were blown up when they attempted to use their grenades against the police. The police then withdrew, leaving the three dismembered bodies in a dirt alley for the local community to discover. When police returned after dawn to collect the corpses, they had to use tear gas and rubber bullets to disperse an irate crowd of about 2 000 that had gathered.[40] The incident complicated the ANC's task of complementing the efforts of fighting forces in the townships, because it meant that in the future anybody claiming to be from MK was under suspicion. Nevertheless the activities of such groups continued throughout the country – largely without ANC coordination and control.

VII

Since 1976, when the state outlawed outdoor gatherings for reasons other than sport or religion, the principal forums available to Africans for open political expression shifted to court trials, indoor meetings, and above all, funerals of political activists. At these funerals, the symbols, songs, slogans and salutes of banned organisations were openly displayed in calculated defiance

38. G. Frankel, 'A Woman Lost to Mob Justice; South African's Uncle: "We Feel For the People Who Did This"', *The Washington Post*, 29 July 1985; D. Beresford, 'The Killing of Maki Skosana: Background Report on Violence in South Africa Following Suspicious Deaths of Black Activists', *The Guardian* (London) 26 July 1985; *Truth and Reconciliation Commission of South Africa Report, Volume 2, The State inside South Africa between 1960 and 1990* (Cape Town: Juta, 1998), 259–61.

of the security forces that were always present in force observing events from the periphery of proceedings. Typically, the coffins of the dead would be draped in ANC colours and lowered to songs saluting MK, while dances would be performed imitating MK guerrillas in action, whether firing assault rifles from the hip or doing the 'toyi-toyi', i.e. the jog-trotting march performed by MK in ANC military camps. Furthermore, the speeches delivered at the gatherings were usually interspersed with chants paying tribute to the ANC's imprisoned or exiled leadership. In effect the funerals became sites of mass political rallies for banned organisations. Before the Vaal uprising, the state acted to limit attendance at funerals to between 15 000 and 20 000, and sought to denude the gatherings of their political significance by making the families of the bereaved sign authorisation forms that no political speeches or songs would be delivered during proceedings. However, these methods proved ineffective and during the insurrection funerals played a crucial role in sustaining levels of political mobilisation among the masses. As the journalist Allister Sparks observed, during the uprising there was a funeral almost every weekend for people who had been killed in clashes with the authorities. At those funerals, police would open fire on demonstrators, thus creating the next week's funeral – feeding an unending cycle of rage and mourning.[41]

The funeral of the four COSAS members involved in the abortive attack in Duduza was typical of the genre. At the ceremony, which was held on 10 July 1985, as nine police armoured personnel carriers stood watching from a nearby ridge and a spotter plane circled overhead, Bishop Desmond Tutu, a patron of the UDF who had been awarded the Nobel peace prize in October the previous year, used the opportunity to implore those gathered to desist from employing violence as a method of struggle. However, the younger generation of COSAS activists paid no heed; instead they called for action against the police and informers. 'We say no to the South African Defence Force and yes to Umkhonto we Sizwe' declared one, while another implored: 'We are unarmed. Umkhonto we Sizwe, we are waiting for you'.

As Tutu stepped out of the cemetery, the crowd suddenly turned on a black onlooker who had been identified as a policeman. The suspect was prevented from leaving the area and was dragged from his car, which was overturned and set alight. Enraged youths assaulted the man with clubs and whips before dousing him with gasoline and dragging him toward the flames. With Tutu declaiming, 'This undermines the struggle!', Simeon Nkoane and Kenneth Oram, two other bishops, jumped into the melee, creating enough of a diversion for the man to escape. Tutu then dragged him into a car driven by Nkoane and he was sped away to safety. Afterwards, hundreds of youths took to the streets, taunting the police who roamed the periphery of the township in

39. *Ibid.*
40. *Ibid.*
41. T.G. Karis, 'Revolution in the Making: Black Politics In South Africa', *Foreign Affairs* (Winter 1983/4), 387; 'South Africa: Controversy Postpones Funeral of Black Killed During Protests', *IPS-Inter Press Service*, 4 March 1985; A. Robinson, 'United against Apartheid', *Financial Times* (London), 10 May 1985; E. Rieder, 'Crucibles of the Black Rebellion: South Africa's Townships', *The Nation* (7 September 1985); Cowell, 'Generation Gap Adds Tension'; Allister Sparks quoted in Episode 5 '1980–1990' of 'The History of the African National Congress', Video series directed and produced by Dali Tambo.

their armoured personnel carriers. After several feints, the police entered the township firing tear-gas canisters and rubber bullets into groups of rock-throwing youths.[42]

The anger in Duduza had still not subsided 10 days later when another political funeral for a local activist was held in the township. One of the attendees was a young woman named Maki Skosana. She was well known to local COSAS members, but since the abortive grenade attacks, stories had been circulated in the township that she was a police agent. The basis of the claim was a rumour that Mamasela had a girlfriend by the name of 'Maki' who had originally introduced him to the students who died in the attacks. Some of the survivors of Operation Zero Zero also claimed that they had seen her with him. Skosana knew of the rumours and had even gone to a local priest to tell him about them, but she maintained that she was innocent and refused to flee. She tried to carry on as normal, and was present at the funeral on 10 July. However, at the funeral of 20 July accusations surfaced that she was an informer and a hastily formed mob caught her as she fled across a field. With a television crew filming the events, her attackers beat her with sticks, kicked her, tore her clothes off and poured gasoline over her while she was pinned to the ground by a large rock. They then set her ablaze while one of the youths rammed a bottle into her vagina. The mob chanted and danced in celebration of their triumph as she died before them.[43]

Skosana's death made the national television news that night. Footage of her burning was broadcast after an announcement by President P.W. Botha that an indefinite state of emergency was to be introduced in 36 townships around Johannesburg and the Eastern Cape with effect from midnight. The scenes of the killing in Duduza were juxtaposed with footage from another funeral held on the same day in Cradock in the Eastern Cape for Matthew Goniwe, Sparrow Mkhonto, Fort Calata and Sicelo Mhlawuli, four activists who had been murdered on 27 June 1985. In Cradock, SACP flags and imitation AK-47 assault rifles were brandished by mourners chanting 'Umkhonto we Sizwe', while others carried placards demanding that the ANC's exiled leadership begin supplying them with weapons such as bazookas and AK-47s.[44]

These events highlighted the extent to which the political culture among the black youth in the townships had become infected by the symbols and slogans of the armed struggle waged by the external movement. This militarisation was marked by an especially close identification by the youths with MK. Ari Sitas notes in an article about youth activists in Natal, that the common

42. P. Laurence, 'Tutu Intervenes to Save Life of Beaten Black: South African Bishop Acts to Prevent Death', *The Guardian* (London), 11 July 1985; Laurence, 'Violence in South Africa'; H. Anderson, P. Younghusband, J. Whitmore, 'A Test for Bishop Tutu', *Newsweek*, 22 July 1985; G. Frankel, 'Tutu Rescues Man from Mob: Suspected Policeman Attacked in S. Africa', *The Washington Post*, 11 July 1985.

43. Cullen and Wilkinson, 'The Young Lions'; Cowell, 'Generation Gap Adds Tension'; Frankel, 'A Woman Lost To Mob Justice'; Beresford, 'The Killing of Maki Skosana'; *TRC, State inside South Africa*, 261.

44. A. Cowell, 'Emergency Power Granted to Police by South Africa', *The New York Times*, 21 July 1985; M. Hornsby, '50 000 Chant Defiance at Sombre Funeral Rally: South African Protest', *The Times* (London), 22 July 1985; Hornsby, 'Emergency as Before'; 'ANC's Call to Seize Weapons: Eliminate Collaborators', *BBC Summary of World Broadcasts*, 25 July 1985, based on excerpts from a commentary broadcast by Radio Freedom, Addis Ababa, 22 July 1985; R. Miller, A. Sparks and W. Lowther, 'South Africa Under Siege', *Maclean's*, 5 August 1985; A. Robinson, 'Like a Dream that Never Happened', *Financial Times* (London), 27 March 1987.

themes in the lyrics of the songs sung by the crowds at mass gatherings were of 'the self as hero, as liberator, as an MK cadre, crossing the border and back, shooting and fighting'.[45]

This identification was fuelled by contact between internal activists and MK cadres infiltrated from abroad, a tendency that was becoming increasingly prevalent during the mid 1980s. Evidence of this was provided in court trials that indicated a fluid relationship between the above-ground youth movement and the ANC's political and military underground. It became clear that the ANC underground was indeed drawing recruits from the ranks of the young activists and was providing training for them.[46] These ties increased after the declaration of the state of emergency, due to the fact that growing repression made engagement in open political activity in the townships more difficult. It also contributed to a sharp increase in the number of young people who joined the MK underground. This meant that the discourses, debates and experiences of the external movement percolated through into the townships.[47] Funerals provided the most visible manifestation of this cultural penetration.

One of the government's first measures after the declaration of the state of emergency was to clamp down on funerals. They stipulated that people attending funerals would be restricted to travelling along predetermined routes between the service and the ceremony and that no flags, banners, placards or pamphlets would be permitted during any procession. It was decreed further that funerals could only be held for one person on any one occasion.[48]

VII

In the first week of the emergency, the security forces swept through 36 townships in the Eastern Cape and Johannesburg regions, rounding up more than 1 000 opponents of the regime. Altogether, 16 died during that week, with most being killed by police.

Security force counter-insurgency methods remained modelled on the pattern seen during Operation Palmiet in October 1984, with armed motorised patrols sent into the townships to conduct hunts for so-called ringleaders and instigators, before departing. These methods again failed. A conversation between a black reporter and his white colleague driving through Soweto sometime in September 1985 that was later recounted by Alan Cowell of *The New York Times* gave an indication of why this was so. The black journalist explained how violence in the townships usually unfolded, saying:

> If there are just one or two kids on a corner they'll probably do nothing. If there are 20 or 30 of them, the chances are you'll be stoned, at least. If there are 200 or 300 who think you are the system, or, if you are the police, then it's real trouble.[49]

45. A. Sitas, 'The Making of the "Comrades" Movement in Natal', 1985–1991', *Journal of Southern African Studies*, 18, 3 (September 1992), 635.
46. Lodge, *The ANC after Nkomati*, 6.
47. K. Naidoo, 'The Politics of Youth Resistance in the 1980s: The Dilemmas of a Differentiated Durban', *Journal of Southern African Studies*, 18, 1 (March 1992), 161–2.
48. J.A. du Pisani, M. Broodryk, and P.W. Coetzer, 'Protest Marches in South Africa', *The Journal of Modern African Studies*, 28, 4 (December 1990), 585–6.
49. Cowell, 'Generation Gap Adds Tension'.

Police tactics proved wholly ineffective in countering this opportunistic violence. Indeed, by removing alleged 'ringleaders' and 'agitators' – who in most cases were simply the most articulate and experienced activists in the community – their methods were actually counterproductive because they created a political vacuum into which unruly, undisciplined elements surged, making the rising more ferocious. As Desmond Tutu lamented: 'They have arrested the very people they should be talking to …What you are left with is a faceless mob, which is much harder to control'.[50]

As had happened previously, when townships in the Transvaal and the Eastern Cape were placed under martial law during the emergency, unrest boiled up elsewhere – in this case in Natal and the Western Cape. In Natal, widespread looting and rioting broke out in townships to the north of Durban following the 1 August 1985 funeral of the lawyer Victoria Mxenge, when the police tried (for the first time) to enforce the new measures on the conduct of funerals.[51] Meanwhile, in the Western Cape, violence began on 29 August after authorities cancelled a march to Pollsmoor prison that was organised to demand the release of Nelson Mandela who was being held in custody there. School boycotts were called in response, and the ensuing confrontations in the streets between youths and the police turned violent. Declaring that the situation in the region had reached a 'state of pre-insurrection', the government extended the state of emergency to the Western Cape on 26 October 1985.[52]

Localised, informal, spontaneous resistance conducted with rudimentary weapons continued to characterise the insurrection. According to estimates made by the security forces in September 1985, there had thus far been 9 951 incidents of stone throwing; 1 525 petrol bomb incidents, but only 43 hand grenade attacks.[53] These figures indicated the disparity between organised violence with sophisticated weapons and local, outbursts of unplanned rioting conducted with rudimentary arms.

The figures also emphasised the failure of the ANC's attempts to supplement the uprising by providing youths in the townships with access to modern weapons and training in their use. In an interview in September 1985 on the occasion of the first anniversary of the Vaal uprising, MK's chief political commissar, Chris Hani, voiced the frustration within the movement on this state of affairs when he said that ANC leaders were 'not satisfied' with Umkhonto's contribution to the uprising and were 'working for a situation [in which] our people, everyone, would have an AK[-47]'. He went on to say:

> If our people had AKs, the situation would be radically changed in a few months. If all those people going out challenging the Casspirs [South African armoured personnel carriers] had some rocket launchers and AKs, then those soldiers and police would not be patrolling those streets.

50. Cullen and Wilkinson, 'The Young Lions'; Cowell, 'Generation Gap Adds Tension'; D. Beresford, 'Comrades of the Burning Spear: The Path to Civil War in South Africa', *The Guardian* (London), 27 May 1986.
51. Murray, *South Africa: Time of Agony*, 316.
52. Cheryl Carolus and Johnny Issel in 'Episode Five: Not the Kings and Generals 1983–1990' of 'Ulibambe Lingashoni – Hold Up the Sun: The ANC and Popular Power in the Making', Video series, directed by L. Dworkin; L. Staniland, 'Struggling for Community: Civic Activism in Greater Cape Town 1980–1986', Occasional Paper no. 100 (Edinburgh: Centre of African Studies, University of Edinburgh, 2005), 33–4.
53. UWHP, JMC: A266F, Captain Fouché, 'The UDF. Transkei Course', c. September 1985, 23.

He also confirmed that MK was receiving a new flow of military aid from the Soviet Union, including AK-47s, land mines, explosives and uniforms that it was hoping to use in furthering the struggle.[54]

Conclusion

According to the minister of Law and Order, in the nine years to 31 December 1985 there were 398 insurgent attacks in South Africa. During this period 79 insurgents and 85 civilians and/or security personnel were killed. As John Kane-Berman notes, the resulting average of 18 people killed per annum paled into insignificance compared with the death toll from political violence in the nine years after January 1985, in which the annual average of fatalities exceeded 1 850 – over 100 times the 1976–1985 rate.[55] These figures indicate the dramatic increase in the scope of political violence in South Africa occasioned by the township uprising.

Although the uprising took place independently of the ANC, the external movement was nonetheless able to profit from it, as it found that the youths spearheading the fighting identified with the organisation and viewed themselves as responding to its calls for confrontation. When the ANC called for the townships to be made ungovernable, the youths in black areas took it upon themselves to serve as the shock-troops. Furthermore, when the (pro-ANC) UDF called for boycotts or stayaways, the youths again appointed themselves as agents to enforce these calls. The action undertaken by the youth was indeed the spur of the liberation movement's calls for violent confrontation and 'non-violent' protest alike.

However the unrestrained nature of this violence and intimidation imposed a severe strain on the black African community. By September 1985, the end of the period under discussion, there was widespread feeling within black communities that the disruption caused by the youth had gone too far. Accordingly, by that time, initiatives had commenced to persuade pupils to go back to school and to pass authority back to the communities. Another development that was also in evidence by this time was a degree of conflict between black groups. In the end, youth-led violence, which had once seemed to be so advantageous for the ANC in advancing its objectives, proved to be a double-edged sword.

54.   J. Albright, 'Blacks Armed Soon, Predict ANC Chiefs', *Courier Mail*, 3 September 1985.
55.   Kane-Berman, *Political Violence*, 45, 98.

References

Albright, J., 'Blacks Armed soon, Predict ANC Chiefs', *Courier Mail*, 3 September 1985.

Anderson, H., Younghusband, P. and Whitmore, J., 'A Test for Bishop Tutu', *Newsweek*, 22 July 1985, 32.

Baldwin, T., 'Cabinet Ministers Tour Riot Areas, Doubt Rent Hikes Caused Violence', *The Associated Press*, 6 September 1984.

Baldwin, T., 'Government Accuses Anti-Apartheid Group of Promoting Revolution', *The Associated Press*, 5 October 1984.

Baldwin, T., 'Students Continue Boycott after Massive Raid', *The Associated Press*, 24 October 1984.

Barrell, H., 'Conscripts to their Age: African National Congress Operational Strategy, 1976–1986' (DPhil, University of Oxford, 1993).

Beresford, D., 'Comrades of the Burning Spear: The Path to Civil War in South Africa', *The Guardian* (London), 27 May 1986.

Beresford, D., 'The Killing of Maki Skosana: Background Report on Violence in South Africa Following Suspicious Deaths of Black Activists', *The Guardian* (London) 26 July 1985.

Cawthra, G., 'South Africa at War', in Lonsdale, J., ed., *South Africa in Question* (London and Portsmouth: James Currey and Heinemann, 1988), 64–77.

Cooper, C., Motala, S., Shindler, J., McCaul, C. and Ratsomo, T., eds, *Survey of Race Relations in South Africa in 1983* (Johannesburg: South African Institute of Race Relations, 1984).

Cooper, C., Shindler J., McCaul C., Potter F., and Cullum, M., eds, *Survey of Race Relations in South Africa 1984* (Johannesburg: South African Institute of Race Relations, 1985).

Cowell, A., 'Emergency Power Granted to Police by South Africa', *The New York Times*, 21 July 1985.

Cowell, A., 'Generation Gap Adds Tension among South African Blacks', *The New York Times*, 18 September 1985.

Cowell, A., 'Toll Rises to 16 in South African Rioting', *The New York Times*, 7 November 1984.

Cowell, A., 'South Africa's New Mood', *The New York Times*, 27 March 1985.

Cullen, R.B. and Wilkinson, R., 'The Young Lions', *Newsweek*, 16 September 1985, 21.

Du Pisani, J.A., Broodryk, M. and Coetzer, P.W., 'Protest Marches in South Africa', *The Journal of Modern African Studies*, 28, 4 (December 1990), 573–602.

Evans, M. and Phillips, M., 'Intensifying Civil War: The Role of the South African Defence Force', in P. Frankel, P., Pines, N. and Swilling, M., eds, *State, Resistance and Change in South Africa* (London, New York and Sydney: Croom Helm, 1988), 117–46.

Frankel, G., 'A Woman Lost to Mob Justice; South African's Uncle: "We Feel for the People Who Did This"', *The Washington Post*, 29 July 1985.

Frankel, G., 'Tutu Rescues Man from Mob: Suspected Policeman Attacked in S. Africa', *The Washington Post*, 11 July 1985.

Grest, J., 'The Crisis of Local Government in South Africa', in Frankel, P., Pines, N. and Swilling, M., eds, *State, Resistance and Change in South Africa* (London, New York and Sydney: Croom Helm, 1988), 87–116.

Herbst, J., 'Prospects For Revolution in South Africa', *Political Science Quarterly*, 103, 4 (Winter 1988/9), 665–85.

Hornsby, M., '50 000 Chant Defiance at Sombre Funeral Rally: South African Protest', *The Times* (London), 22 July 1985.

Hornsby, M., 'Emergency as Before – and Why it will Continue', *The Times* (London), 25 July 1985.

Kane-Berman, J., *Political Violence in South Africa* (Johannesburg: South African Institute of Race Relations, 1993).

Kane-Berman, J., 'Third World Review: How Black Anger has Backfired: Political Frustration of Blacks in South Africa', *The Guardian* (London), 7 December 1984.

Karis, T.G., 'Revolution in the Making: Black Politics In South Africa', *Foreign Affairs* (Winter 1983/4), 378–406.

Miller, R., Sparks, A. and Lowther, W., 'South Africa under Siege', *Maclean's*, 5 August 1985.

Labour Monitoring Group, 'The November 1984 Stayaway', in Maree, J., ed., *The Independent Trade Unions, 1974–1984: Ten Years of the South African Labour Bulletin* (Johannesburg: Ravan Press, 1987), 259–80.

Lambert, R. and Webster, E., 'The Re-emergence of Political Unionism in Contemporary South Africa?', in Cobbett, W. and Cohen, R., eds, *Popular Struggles in South Africa* (London: James Currey, 1988), 20–42.

Laurence, P., 'Anger at Role of Troops in Township Raid: South African Military Operation in Black Townships', *The Guardian* (London), 25 October 1984.

Laurence, P., 'Black Youths Riot in Cape Province', *The Associated Press*, 31 October 1984.

Laurence, P., 'Political Bombings Hit Four Homes: Coloured Candidates Standing for Election to South Africa's Tri-Racial Parliament', *The Guardian* (London), 21 July 1984.

Laurence, P., 'Tutu Intervenes to Save Life of Beaten Black: South African Bishop Acts to Prevent Death', *The Guardian* (London), 11 July 1985.

Laurence, P., 'United Democratic Front Defends its Opposition Record', *The Guardian* (London), 11 October 1984.

Laurence, P., 'Violence in South Africa Causing Collapse of Black Township Governments', *Christian Science Monitor* (Boston), 19 July 1985.

Lodge, T., *The ANC after Nkomati* (Johannesburg: South African Institute of Race Relations, 1985).

Meldrum, A., 'ANC Leader Says his Bomb Squad "Inexcusably Careless": Car Bomb Attack in South African City of Durban', *The Guardian* (London), 11 August 1984.

Murray, M., *South Africa, Time of Agony, Time of Destiny: The Upsurge of Popular Protest* (London: Verso, 1987).

Naidoo, K., 'The Politics of Youth Resistance in the 1980s: The Dilemmas of a Differentiated Durban', *Journal of Southern African Studies*, 18, 1 (March 1992), 143–65.

Rieder, E., 'Crucibles of the Black Rebellion: South Africa's Townships', *The Nation*, 7 September 1985, 169–73.

Robinson, A., 'Like a Dream that Never Happened', *Financial Times* (London), 27 March 1987.

Robinson, A., 'United against Apartheid', *Financial Times* (London), 10 May 1985.

Seekings, J., '"Trailing behind the Masses": The United Democratic Front and Township Politics in the Pretoria-Witwatersrand-Vaal Region, 1983–84', *Journal of Southern African Studies*, 18, 1 (March 1992), 93–114.

Seekings, J., *The UDF: A History of the United Democratic Front in South Africa, 1983–1991* (Cape Town: David Philip, 2000).

Sitas, A., 'The Making of the "Comrades" Movement in Natal', 1985–1991', *Journal of Southern African Studies*, 18, 3 (September 1992), 629–41.

Smith, J.F., 'Opposition Group Says Ban would Exacerbate Crisis', *The Associated Press*, 10 October 1984.

Staniland, L., 'Struggling for Community: Civic Activism in Greater Cape Town 1980–1986', Occasional Paper no. 100 (Edinburgh: Centre of African Studies, University of Edinburgh, 2005).

Streek,, B., 'Black Anger Makes Botha's Councils Melt Away', *The New York Times*, 14 April 1985.

Truth and Reconciliation Commission of South Africa Report, Volume 2, The State inside South Africa between 1960 and 1990 (Cape Town: Juta, 1998).

Van Slambrouck, P., 'Black Workers Join Wave of Protest in South Africa', *Christian Science Monitor* (Boston), 7 November 1984.

Van Slambrouck, P., 'Bombs Hit Homes of South African Blacks', *Christian Science Monitor* (Boston), 24 July 1984.

Wentzel, J., *The Liberal Slideaway* (Johannesburg: South African Institute of Race Relations, 1995).

Wicksteed, R., 'South Africa: Government Sponsored Councils under Attack', *IPS Inter-Press Service*, 20 December 1984.

Younghusband, P., 'South Africa Faces Stormy Election Campaign', *The Globe and Mail* (Canada), 28 July 1984.

Sex in a Time of Exile: An Examination of Sexual Health, AIDS, Gender, and the ANC, 1980–1990

CARLA TSAMPIRAS

History Department, Rhodes University

Abstract

By the start of the 1980s, the African National Congress (ANC) had been banned for 20 years and members of the organisation were either working 'underground' or in exile communities, offices, or missions around the globe. By the mid-1980s AIDS was becoming an increasing concern for both the ANC and the countries that hosted its major settlements. Drawing on AIDS education material and other archival sources relating to the ANC Department of Health, this article asks questions about sex in exile communities. Focussing initially on AIDS education material and then on two interconnected topics – namely pregnancies and STIs (with a particular focus on AIDS) – it explores these aspects of the sexual landscape of exile communities for insights into sexual practices and sexual health needs. It also asks if there are any gendered assumptions, by individual ANC members or organisational structures, evident in the discussions about, understandings of, or responses to, these topics.

A pamphlet, a three-part video, and a poster

Figure 1.   ANC AIDS education pamphlet (SAHA, NAMDA Collection).

Figure 2.   Still from AIDS education video 'As Surely as an AK' (IISH).

Figure 3.   Eastern Cape Department of Health AIDS education poster (UFH Library bookshelf).

This is an article about how a pamphlet, a video, and a poster dealing with AIDS provided the impetus for questions about the ANC, sex in exile, and gender, and helped shape the answers to these questions (see Figures 1–3). The pamphlet, entitled 'Meeting the Challenge of AIDS', was found while searching for something completely different in an archive.[1] It was a bad photocopy of a bad photocopy of a typed two-page document that was 'Issued by the ANC Health Department, Lusaka'. This assertion showed that the pamphlet belonged to a time of armed struggle before the ban on the ANC was lifted in 1990 and when it still had its HQ (headquarters) in Lusaka. The copy of a significant, and elusive, AIDS education video entitled *'As Surely as an A.K.'* was discovered in an archive

1.   The South African History Archive NAMDA Collection, AL3182.

in another country.[2] This 25 minute video was made in 1989 by Solidarity Films and was commissioned by the ANC Health Department. Finally, a bright poster designed and funded by the 'Eastern Cape Department of Health – HIV/AIDS Unit' which boldly states 'Men Make A Positive Difference' was stuck to the end of a bookshelf in an archive in the Eastern Cape. The geographical marker and toll free AIDS helpline number on the poster suggests that it dates from after 1994.

On closer inspection the pamphlet, video and poster each employed symbols or scenarios that were meant to appeal to the audience viewing them and relied, in part, on an evocation or representation of gender identities to communicate their messages. Each of the sources illustrate what images and evocations of gender were deemed appropriate for their respective audiences, while also demonstrating idealised, inspirational gender roles that the producers of the sources, and by extension, sectors of the ANC, were interested in promoting.

The 'Meeting the Challenge of AIDS' pamphlet shows a line drawing of a womyn[3] and man, both in uniform and both carrying AK47s and draws not only on ideas of struggle and armed resistance in the image, but also actively invokes it in the text (Figure 4).[4] The image represents men and womyn as armed fighters and in so doing, draws on identities of masculinities and femininities mediated through service to 'the struggle'.[5] The image

2.   International Institute of Social History (IISH), Amsterdam, the Netherlands, Anti-Apartheid and Southern Africa Collection, BG V8/226, *As Surely as an A.K.* (video, Solidarity Films, c.1989; 25 minutes). The IISH catalogue listed the film as being scripted by Carolyn Roth and Vic Finkelstein and originating from the London-based UK RHT.

3.   The author asserts her preference for the spelling of 'womyn' with a 'y' as an ideological and political action marking the importance of language and feminisms in research. In this article the conventional spelling of women/women is only used when quoting directly from sources. The challenge to the binary notions of sex and the associated binary notions of 'gender' offered by Judith Butler and others are also acknowledged in this spelling. Using this spelling allows these complexities of identity performativities to be recognised while also dealing with the practicalities of writing about sources that often reflect a way of ordering the world that includes ideas, actions, relations and structures that primarily divide people into 'women' and 'men'. These ideas, actions, relations and structures also proscribe and prescribe particular, though not static, (gender) roles to these categories of people. The use of 'womyn' within this text is an effort to allude to these constructions visually and subvert them in the printed text.

4.   The text of the pamphlet notes for example, that the HI virus 'invades and immobilises their immune system, and stops it from doing its job of protecting the person against infections – in the same way as an enemy agent might infiltrate an army and prevent it from acting against attack' and that '[I]t is essential that we protect our movement, our comrades and ourselves from further spread of this serious and deadly infection' and '[I]f we fail to respond effectively and immediately to the challenge of Aids (sic) we risk the extensive spread of infection in our ranks which will have disastrous and irreversible consequences for our Movement and our future'.

5.   Works by Cocks and Suttner, for example, reflect on the multiple understandings and challenges to notions of 'masculinities' and 'femininities' that being part of MK or the ANC underground evoked. In these discussions informants also articulate a variety of performative responses to being 'a man' or 'a womyn' in the underground movement and show that these notions were continuously contested. See J. Cock, *Colonels & Cadres War and Gender in South Africa* (Oxford: Oxford University Press, 1991), 150–186, and R. Suttner, 'Women in the ANC-led Underground' in N. Gasa (ed), *Women in South African History* (Cape Town: HSRC, 2007), 233–256, and R. Suttner, 'Masculinities in the African National Congress-led Liberation movement', Kleio, 37, 1 (2005), 71–106. For the purposes of this article definitions of 'masculinities' and 'femininities' are drawn from work by Morrell and work by Lindsay and Miescher. Morrell notes that 'Masculinity [and femininity are] ... collective gender [identities] and not ... natural

MEETING THE CHALLENGE OF AIDS

What is AIDS?
Aids is an illness for which there is no cure and which is usually fatal.
It is caused by a virus — the Human Immunodeficiency Virus, or HIV. This virus does two thing, to an infected person:

1. It invades and immobilises their immune system, and stops it from doing its job of protecting the person against infections — in the same way as an enemy agent might infiltrate an army and prevent it from acting against attack.
2. The virus can also cause damage to the brain affecting the person's ability to think and act clearly.

Once someone is infected with this virus they will remain infected for life. However, there may be a long period of time when they are unaware of having a serious infection, because at first there are no signs or symptoms of illness. But, from the time someone is first infected and for the rest of their life, they will be able to pass the virus on to other people.

How is the virus passed from one person to another?
There are only a few ways that this infection can be spread.
1. By sexual intercourse.
2. By injection of blood from an infected person or an injection through a needle which has been used on an infected person and not properly sterilised.
3. From an infected mother to her baby before birth.

It is important to realise that any of us — man or woman — may become infected with this virus and may pass it on to other people, in the ways mentioned above,
It only takes one exposure, through sex for example, to be infected by the virus.
It is essential that we protect our movement, our comrades and ourselves from further spread of this serious and deadly infection.

What is to be done about HIV infection and AIDS?
Health workers and health facilities must, of course, do everything they can to eliminate the risk of infection spreading in blood and injection needles.
In our sex lives, though, the responsibility to prevent the spread of HIV infection and Aids can only rest with us.

1. The more sexual partners someone has the more likely he/she is to become infected with the Aids virus. Therefore it is important to stick to one partner.
2. The way the virus enters the body during sex is in the fluids of the man and woman. Using a condom (sheath) during intercourse is absolutely essential to protect you and your partner from getting or passing on this infection. Condoms also reduce the risk of other sexually transmitted diseases like gonorrhea, and will prevent unwanted pregnancies.
3. We must rely on each other to act according to these guidelines. If our attitudes and behaviour make this difficult, these must be discussed and debated like other political issues and in this way we will be able to challenge the obstacles in our way.

If we fail to respond effectively and immediately to the challenge of Aids we risk the extensive spread of infection in our ranks which will have disastrous and irreversible consequences for our Movement and our future.
The only way we can stop the spread of HIV infection and Aids is to protect our comrades and ourselves by putting into practice the guidelines outlined above, and making sure all our comrades do the same.

Avoid having many sexual partners.
Always use a condom when having sex.
Be aware of the problem of Aids and educate yourself and others about it!

ISSUED BY THE ANC HEALTH DEPARTMENT, LUSAKA

Figure 4. AIDS education pamphlet evoking 'the struggle' in both text and imagery.

specifically demarcates 'a male' and 'a female' soldier – arguably presented as a pair rather than as part of a larger unit – and so acknowledges the role of womyn and men in the armed struggle, despite the ratio of womyn to men soldiers being fairly small.

attribute[s]. [They are] socially constructed and fluid. There is not one universal masculinity, but many masculinities [and similarly not one universal femininity, but many femininities]. These are 'not fixed character types but configurations of practice generated in particular situations in a changing structure of relationships' (R. Morrell, 'Of Boys and Men: Masculinity and Gender in Southern African Studies', *Journal of Southern African Studies*, 24, 4, Special Issue on Masculinities in Southern Africa [December 1998], 605). Lindsay and Miescher (quoted in Suttner, 'Masculinities in the African National Congress', 74) note that masculinities and femininities are a 'cluster of norms, values and behavioural patterns expressing explicit and implicit expectations of how men [and womyn] should act and represent themselves to others. Ideologies of masculinity like those of femininity are culturally and historically constructed, their meanings continually contested and always in the process of being renegotiated in the context of existing power relations'. In short masculinities and femininities are a collection of variable constructed behaviours associated with correctly 'performing' as 'a man' or 'a woman' in contexts which can be mediated by any number of factors including historical, temporal, cultural, political, social, economic, generational, linguistic, sexual, intellectual and physical. Hegemonic 'masculine' and 'feminine' characteristics, although also constructed and mediated, can also be ascribed to 'men' and 'women' inter-changeably as either positive or negative characteristics i.e. a sensitive man or an 'unfeminine' woman.

The text emphasises shared risk of infection and responsibility for stopping infection by noting that 'it is important to realise that any of us – man or woman – may become infected with the virus and may pass it on to other people' and arguing that 'in our sex lives... the responsibility to prevent the spread of HIV infection and Aids [sic] can only rest with us.' In terms of prevention, readers were asked to avoid having multiple partners, use condoms during intercourse and 'rely on each other to act according to these guidelines'. Readers were also informed that condoms reduced the risk of other STIs and would 'prevent unwanted pregnancies'. In relation to relying on each other, the pamphlet noted '[I]f our attitudes and behaviour make this difficult, these must be discussed and debated like any other political issues and in this way we will be able to challenge the obstacles in our way'.

The film *As Surely As an A.K.* opens with scenes of comrades in military fatigues undergoing training, interspersed with scenes of protest, and day-to-day activities in what are presumably exile settlements. After the title credit the film shows three men in an ANC office having a conversation that includes a discussion about sex and sexual partners (Figures 5 and 6). The three characters are a proudly (hetero)sexually active man who maintains multiple sexual relationships simultaneously; a younger man interested in hearing about and learning from the sexual prowess of the 'Casanova' character; and a man who questions the appropriateness of the sexual behaviours taking place especially in light of the condition of a young comrade 'Luke' who is visited by various characters while he is in hospital. The first part of the film thus revolves around men discussing sexual performance and appropriate 'moves' to attract womyn, and challenges to those representations of masculinity by a male character who raises questions about safe sex and AIDS.

The second part of the film also takes place in an office, but in this scenario the two characters are an older womyn who has been in exile for a long time and a younger womyn,

Figure 5.   Title shot from 'As Surely as an AK'.

Figure 6.   Male characters discuss dating and sexual partners in part 1 of the video.

newly arrived and still adjusting to being in exile. The younger womyn, while looking for teabags, discovers condoms in the handbag of the older womyn and immediately judges her as immoral. The older womyn challenges the younger womyn on her misguided, judgemental and naive attitude about sex, and highlights the importance of womyn taking responsibility for their sexual health (Figures 7 and 8).

This scene creates an opportunity for a discussion about womyn's (hetero)sexual practices and about maintaining sexual health. The older womyn is the focal point of

Figure 7.   Female characters discuss sexual partners and condom use in part 2 of the video.

Figure 8.   Female characters challenge stereotypes about womyn insisting on condom use.

information about AIDS in this scene and not only highlights the seriousness of AIDS but also provides basic AIDS education. The title of the film derives from a scene in the video where the older womyn comrade informs the younger womyn that 'AIDS will kill you as surely as an A.K.47' and that the future of the movement depends on addressing AIDS and preventing its spread.

   The scenarios that are presented are interspersed with 'hospital scenes' where various characters visit 'Luke' – a once healthy, brave MK soldier who now lies in the hospital dying of AIDS (Figures 9 and 10). Although Luke is given chances to speak and raises concerns about being stigmatised and ignored by his friends, he serves chiefly as a warning and is clear about his impending death declaring 'I've got AIDS man, I'm not going to get

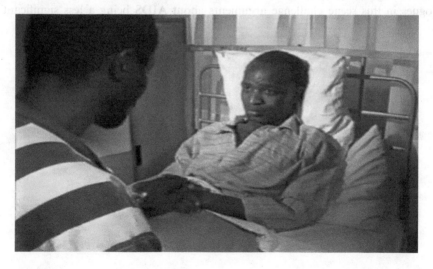

Figure 9.   Characters visit 'Comrade Luke' in hospital.

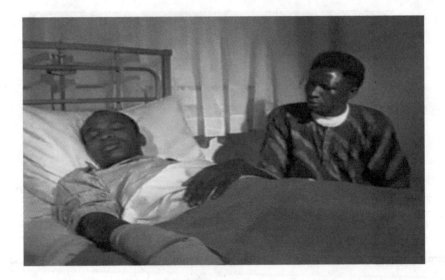

Figure 10. Comrade Luke has AIDS and gets increasingly ill throughout the video.

better!' Luke's accusations of being isolated and ignored by the other 'guys' from his unit create the opportunity to discuss stigma in relation to comrades with AIDS and complements the other scenes which dispel myths on the means of transmission and infection, highlight the importance of taking responsibility for sexual encounters, address the judgements attached to womyn carrying condoms, and emphasis that womyn should insist on their use.

The final part of the video takes place around a kitchen table and brings the principle characters together (Figures 11 and 12). All the characters have now visited Luke and the dialogues in this scene challenge arguments about AIDS being a less significant danger

Figure 11.   In the third part of the video discussions about responsibility and blame become heated.

Figure 12.   Myths about AIDS are challenged and discussed.

than being in exile or being part of the liberation movement, declare the inappropriateness of laying blame and seeking vengeance, and argue for greater mutual respect between men and womyn that should extend to respecting each other enough to practice safer sex. The video thus deliberately evokes gendered engagements with sex and sexual practices to provide food for thought and discussion.

The poster 'Men Make a Positive Difference' has on its right-hand side a vertical line of black and white head-and-shoulder pictures of 'struggle heroes' (Figure 13).[6] The main text on the poster (aside from the obligatory ABC message) notes that: 'What these men had in common was the passion to fight against all forms of human suffering and [sic] of which HIV/AIDS is one' and 'These men made the difference, where are you? Take care my man.' The poster's audience is clearly identified as 'men' and draws on other men as male role models who, arguably, are meant to typify the kind of men that the audience should aspire to. As such, the men being called to action are asked to make a positive difference in fighting against HIV by emulating a number of exemplary men who come to symbolically represent (at least in this poster) an idealised 'manhood'.

The poster is from a time after exile and banning, and was created in a new political dispensation, but it draws on, and grew out of, a time of struggle. The poster is included in this article because it is an important reminder of how historical contexts shape ideas (and the messages and images on educational posters), and acts as a marker of the continuity and resonance of these ideas, messages and images.

While separated by time, place and political dispensation, the pamphlet, video and poster are linked in a number of ways. For one thing, they all draw on struggle or military

6.   The men depicted are Oliver Tambo, Sabelo Phama, Robert Sobukwe, Chris Hani, Lionel Forman and Steve Biko.

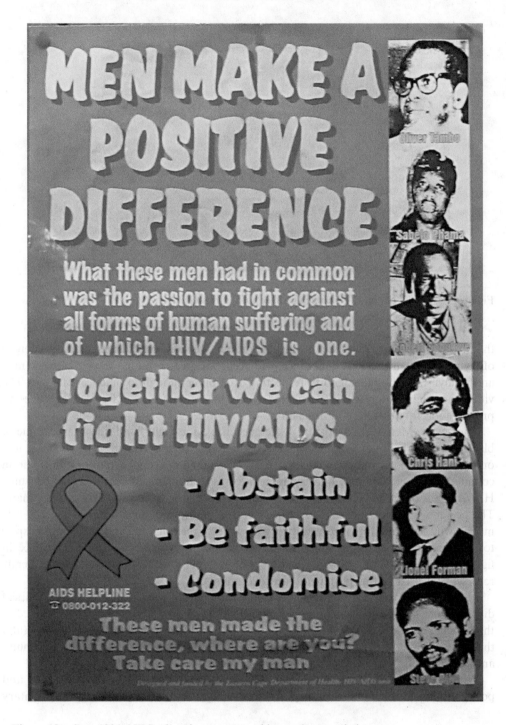

Figure 13.   Post-1994 AIDS education poster evoking male struggle heroes.

metaphors, symbols, and language when examining AIDS or responses to AIDS.[7] The examples are also linked as media because they all reflect existing gendered identities even while suggesting new ones. Furthermore, they are linked by their primary purpose and subject matter, namely providing an audience with information about AIDS.[8] AIDS, however, is intimately linked to sexual practices, and sexual practices are linked to individuals, and individuals are linked to communities, and individuals and communities, in exile or anywhere else, are linked to gender roles and gendered realities, both internally- and externally-constructed.

The reflections and recreations of womyn and men and their relationships as featured in the pamphlet, video and poster presumably had some relationship to real-life strategies or policies designed to open up spaces and opportunities in which 'attitudes and behaviours' about sexual practices, sexual health and gender could indeed be 'discussed and debated like any other political issues'? If so, where might these 'real-life' examples be found, how might they be understood, and would they be able to provide any insight into sexual practices, sexual health, or individual or institutional gender constructs within the ANC during a specific period of exile?

The growing body of academic work on the ANC that has begun the process of using gendered analysis to examine the gendered nature of exile or 'underground' experiences provided insights into what was possible and how gender constructs could be explored.[9] These works have analysed the impact of feminisms and non-feminisms on the functioning and ideological shaping of the organisation and shown how gender, gender roles, and

7.　The evocation of military metaphors in relation to diseases is not an unfamiliar practice, particularly in relation to AIDS. While it was arguably appropriate for a banned movement engaged in an armed liberation struggle, it is still a gendered evocation most frequently associated with 'the masculine' For more on AIDS and military metaphors see for example P. Treichler, 'AIDS, Homophobia and Biomedical Discourse: An Epidemic of Signification', Cultural Studies, 1, 3 (October 1987), 31–70, M. Connelly, 'Rumours of War: De-constructing Media Discourses of HIV/AIDS in South Africa', (MA thesis, Rhodes University, 2002) and M. Connelly and C. Macleod, 'Waging War: Discourses of HIV/AIDS in South African Media', African Journal of Aids Research, 2, 1, (2003), 1–11.

8.　The film especially is an interesting example of AIDS education media and deserves in-depth analysis in its own right – not least of all because of the, for the time, progressive approach that it took. While it is difficult to gauge how much impact the film had, how successfully it was distributed amongst ANC communities, or even how many people saw it the film did seem to have a lasting impact on those who saw it. The film was frequently mentioned during interviews for the thesis from which this work is drawn and features similarly in Mbali's oral interviews for her thesis (see M. Mbali, "The New Struggle": A History of AIDS Activism in South Africa, 1982 – 2003' [PhD thesis, University of Oxford, 2009], 125–126), indicating that the memory of the film certainly stayed with those who saw it. For more on AIDS in films see R. Hodes, 'HIV/AIDS in South African Documentary Film, c. 1990–2000', Journal of Southern African Studies, 33, 1, (March 2007), 153–171.

9.　In this context, a gendered analysis is one which uses 'gender', in the words of Fox-Genovese, 'as a primary category of historical analysis' and recognises that it is 'as deeply ingrained in social and economic formations and the political institutions to which they give rise as class relations' (E. Fox-Genovese, 'Placing Women's History in History', New Left Review, I/133 [May–June 1982], 15–16). Gender, for the purposes of this article is, as per Morgan: 'an analytical category that locates [the category man and womyn] within a broader framework of their social, cultural and political relationships' (S. Morgan, ed., 'Introduction' in The Feminist History Reader [Abingdon: Routledge, 2006], 9). While recognising the contested and structured nature of gender, the definition employed here also acknowledges that these relational engagements are mediated by inherent power dynamics and other constructed identifiers of difference.

challenges to 'conventional' gender roles mediated the lived experiences of people in a variety of contexts within the ANC. The works have fulfilled a multitude of functions, from recording experiences, to revising and challenging 'hegemonic' narratives about 'the struggle', and have revealed contested and complex engagements with notions of gender, 'masculinities' and 'femininities', and the respective roles of groups of people defined as men and womyn. These developments and discussions (often spanning disciplines) are the result of works by, amongst others, Cock, Erlank, Hassim, Meintjes, Suttner, Unterhalter and Walker.[10]

In attempting to answer the questions raised by the pamphlet, the video and the poster, and contribute to the growing body of work mentioned above, this article now undertakes a gendered analysis of recommendations, reports, papers, project proposals, correspondence and other archival sources from, or relating to, the ANC Department of Health.[11] Focussing on two different but interconnected topics – namely pregnancies and STIs (with a particular focus on AIDS) – it explores these aspects of the sexual landscape of exile communities for insights into sexual practices or sexual health needs. It also asks if there are any gendered assumptions, by individual ANC members or organisational structures, evident in the discussions about, understandings of, or responses to, these topics.

This article is drawn from a thesis chapter that discusses the response of the ANC in exile to AIDS more broadly.[12] The larger piece of work examines the discussions and developments around AIDS programmes by the ANC Department of Health. In addition, the chapter refers to the international presence of the ANC Department of Health and its relationship with international health organisations and international departments of health and governments. Both national, regional and international relationships and realities influenced how AIDS was addressed and understood by ANC members at a variety of levels. While AIDS programmes, AIDS education and workshops were discussed and implemented, there is insufficient information to determine the reach or effectiveness of such interventions. Similarly, while it is not currently possible to determine the reach of

10. See J. Cock, *Colonels & Cadres*; N. Erlank, 'Gender and Masculinity in South African Nationalist Discourse, 1912–1950', *Feminist Studies*, 29, 3 (2003), 195–215; F. Ginwala, 'Women and the African National Congress 1912–1943', *Agenda*, 8 (1990), 77–93; S. Hassim, 'Nationalism, Feminism and Autonomy: The ANC in Exile and the Question of Women', *Journal of Southern African Studies*, 30, 3 (September 2004), 433–455; T. Lyons and M. Israel, 'Women, Resistance and the Armed Struggle in Southern Africa', *African Studies Association of Australasia and the Pacific: Review and Newsletter*, 21 (1999), 5–11; S. Meintjes, 'The Women's Struggle for Equality During South Africa's Transition to Democracy', *Transformation*, 30 (1996), 47–64; A. Sitas, 'The Making of the "Comrades" Movement in Natal, 1985–1991', *Journal of Southern African Studies*, 18, 3 (September 1992), 629–641; R. Suttner, 'Masculinities'; R.Suttner, 'Women in the ANC-led Underground'; E. Unterhalter, 'The Work of the Nation: Heroic Masculinity in South African Autobiographical Writing of the Anti-Apartheid Struggle', *The European Journal of Development Research*, 12, 2 (2000), 157–178; C. Walker, *Women and Resistance in South Africa* (Cape Town: David Philip, 1991) and J. Wells, *We Have Done with Pleading: The Women's 1913 Anti-Pass Campaign* (Johannesburg: Raven Press, 1991).
11. The article draws primarily on written and visual texts as the first steps in undertaking research in this area, and acknowledges that oral and other sources should form the basis of future complementary research.
12. See C. Tsampiras, 'Politics, Polemics and Practice: Narratives about, and Responses to, AIDS in South Africa, 1980–1990' (PhD Thesis, Rhodes University, forthcoming).

the pamphlet, video and poster, they do, provide interesting insights into some of the (gendered) ideological frameworks present within the ANC.

Health care, health concerns, and health provision in exile

As Surely as an A.K showed urban-based comrades working in an office and visiting a friend in hospital, while the pamphlet depicted soldiers in 'the bush' prepared for combat. So how was health care provided in different exile contexts, who provided it, and what were some of the major health concerns?[13] The ANC's Department of Health was officially established in 1977 to systematically address the complex health needs of ANC exile communities. The Department comprised of a Health Secretariat that directed and monitored the work of five 'Regional Health Teams' (RHTs) namely Angola, East Africa, UK, Zambia and Zimbabwe. In turn, each RHT had Regional Health Committees made up of staff from the ANC health establishments.

The Department identified its key functions as providing basic curative services, dental services, mental health services, preventative and health education services, and maternal and child health services.[14] The Department was also responsible for referring patients to hospitals if further treatment was required.[15] For ANC members in exile (by the ANC's own reckoning about 20,000 in 1990), particularly those living in 'rural' settlements or undergoing training as MK soldiers, health care was often solely provided by individual ANC health care workers or through the hospitals and clinics established by the ANC's Department of Health.[16] For those living in cities in host countries, health care could sometimes be accessed through existing public health facilities.[17]

The largest ANC settlements were in Tanzania, and the East Africa RHT was responsible for the day-to-day running and management of the hospital and health centres that served the exile communities, particularly those at the Mazimbu and Dakawa settlements with the associated Solomon Mahlangu Freedom College (SOMAFCO) and

13. It is important to note that being in exile (or underground) was an experience mediated by time, duration of time in exile, physical location, gender, roles and positions held within the organisation and any other combination of factors. Living in Berlin and studying was, for example, a very different experience from helping to build and sustain a settlement, or moving constantly between South Africa and frontline states. The notion of being in 'exile' and 'exile communities' are therefore concepts that carry multiple meanings mediated by context-specific factors, see Tsampiras, 'Politics, Polemics and Practice'.
14. These were further divided into antenatal, deliveries, under 5 clinic, family planning and immunization.
15. The University of Fort Hare - ANC Archives (hereafter UFH-AA), ANC Lusaka Mission (hereafter ALM) records, p2a, 41, 63, ANC Department of Health Project Proposal n.d. [c. 1987], 1–2.
16. In the 'Declaration on Health and Welfare in Southern Africa' issued at the Maputo Health Conference on 15 April 1990 there is a section dealing specifically with returning exiles that reads:

> To address the urgent problem of the return to South Africa of more than 20 000 exiles, the conference endorses the formation of a National Reception Committee, through which the ANC together with other progressive mass-based organisations, can work out concrete measures for the rapid and effective integration of returnees into South African social, political and economic life.

The declaration was printed in *Critical Health,* no. 31/32 (August 1990), 5.
17. For an overview of the formation, functioning, challenges and concerns of the ANC Department of Health see Tsampiras, 'Politics, Polemics and Practice'.

Dakawa Development Centre, respectively. The Angolan RHT's remit included the health needs of the various *Umkhonto we Sizwe* (MK) training camps predominantly located in Angola, while the Zambian RHT was responsible, amongst other things, for a clinic and, what were referred to by the Department as, 'three outlying health posts'.[18] The role and functioning of the Zimbabwe RHT appears to have been fairly minimal and was predominantly occupied with facilitating patient transfers from other areas to Zimbabwe health centres for treatment.[19] The London-based UK RHT did not provide health care directly, but played a unique role centred on its capacity to access health information and expertise, and to facilitate meetings and discussions with a variety of important health care professionals and organisations.

Archival documents show that the experiences, responsibilities, and resources available to each of the RHTs varied considerably, and regional differences had an impact on the capacity and ability of RHTs to provide health care generally. These regional factors were complicated by the fact that the health needs of the entire organisation were provided by just over '50 health personnel on a free and voluntary basis'.[20] In addition to the general stresses of living in exile, ANC health care workers had to provide medical care for a variety of health concerns ranging from malaria, TB, hypertension, addictions, child malnutrition, unwanted pregnancies and STIs, to mental health issues resulting from the trauma caused by the violence, torture and warfare associated with the struggle against apartheid.

Amongst the myriad of emotional, mental and physical health needs mentioned above are those that directly relate to sex – namely pregnancies, contraception, and STIs (particularly AIDS). These aspects of life (and health) in exile were important enough to regularly feature in reports, correspondence, minutes and other documents generated at all levels of the organisation from health care workers staffing clinics, to regional health team members, to members of the Health Secretariat and members of the ANC's National Executive Committee (NEC). Examining how pregnancies and STIs (and by extension contraceptives) were discussed throughout these levels of the organisation allows us to explore aspects of the complexities of sex in exile, and acknowledge the multiple links that join AIDS to sexual practices and gendered realities.

Pregnancies, parenting, and responsibilities for prevention

In the 'Meeting the Challenge' pamphlet reference is made to infected mothers being able to pass HIV on to their babies, while the dual functions of condoms as preventing STIs and 'unwanted pregnancies' are highlighted. In the video, reference is also made to the multifunctional role of condoms, but little attention is given to mother-to-child transmission (MTCT). The references to pregnancies in the sources clearly indicate that there were womyn in the movement who fell pregnant. In addition, the fact that one of the key functions of the Health Department of an armed resistance movement was maternal and child health services, speaks to the reality of child-birth amongst members of the

18. ANC Department of Health Project Proposal, c. 1987, 3.
19. UFH-AA, ALM p2a, 42, 89, 'Reorganising for a Healthier Revolutionary Movement', Report of ANC Health Department Seminar, 1987, 5.
20. UFH-AA, p2a, 41, 63, ANC Department of Health Project Proposal, c.1987, 3.

organisation, and the familial contexts of comrades who sometimes left children when they went into exile, or brought children into exile with them.

While more focussed research on children, childbirth and childcare in the ANC camps and settlements needs to be undertaken, what is important here is whether or not there is evidence that shows that responsibilities for conception, contraception, termination and childcare were linked to ideas about gender. A series of recommendations on 'The Crèche and Parental Care' by the ANC Department of Education and Culture made in 1980, reveal very clear gendered notions about parental care.[21] Under the heading 'Medical Opinion' the report noted that:

> All children up to school-going age not only need parental care but, for normal psychological development, need mother-love which can only be provided by the mother or a mother substitute. Absence of such mother-love relationship at that tender age invariably results in psychological inbalances (sic) and such children grow up with a variety of neurotic "Hang-Ups".[22]

Under a section entitled 'General Consensus' the report stated that

> it is the opinion of the participants that abandoning children at a tender age to communal care without the mothers or mother-substitutes would be nothing short of a criminal exercise endangering the very formative and future development of a normal child.[23]

In light of this, the meeting 'strongly recommended' that until the ANC, particularly the Women's Section, could find ways of implementing a programme to provide suitable mother-substitutes, young mothers should be tasked with assisting the organisation to arrange proper mother-substitutes before they could serve the movement. In terms of childcare, the 'strong recommendation' was that:

> ... the decision for young mothers to personally take care of their children... until weaning, should be maintained. This is very important for the good of the child and also brings home to the understanding of the mother the seriousness and complexity of child upbringing.[24]

The 1983 progress report for SOMAFCO in Mazimbu and the ANC Dakawa Development Centre provides some insights into what programmes had been implemented for mothers. In addition to providing insights into the situation on the ground in Tanzanian settlements, it includes sections on the nursery and primary schools on site, and the Charlotte Maxeke Day Care Centre (see Figure 14).[25] The report explained that the day care centre catered 'for children of working mothers on the Complex and for those children whose mothers are away on scholarships or other ANC missions'.[26]

21. UFH-AA, ALM p2a, 6, 9, Recommendations of the 3rd Council Meeting of the ANC Department of Education and Culture on 'The Crèche and Prenatal Care', 14–18 August 1980.
22. Ibid., 1.
23. Ibid., 2.
24. Ibid., 2–3.
25. IISH, BRO 833/10 Fol, ANC Progress Report, Solomon Mahlangu Freedom College Mazimbu: ANC Development Centre Dakawa, 1983. According to the report the nursery school was attended by 'over 80 children between the ages of 3–6 years'.
26. Ibid., 6–7.

Figure 14.   Children at the Charlotte Maxeke Day Care Centre, SOMAFCO Progress Report 1983 (IISH).

Until December 1982, 'young mothers and babies were scattered in various far flung residences in Morogoro' but were thereafter housed in 'new hostels in Mazimbu' named the 'Charlotte Maxeke Hostels for Expectant and Young Mothers'. The 'expectant mothers' had to assist with cooking and caring for the children, cleaning communal areas, and 'organising the general activities of the Day Care Centre' and were expected to partake in all aspects of community life, which included being encouraged to join adult education classes. In 1982 the hostel housed '32 mothers and 32 children plus 18 children without parents who are resident'.[27] The mothers were 'expected to care for their own babies for at least one and possibly two years after birth' after which they could 'continue with their fulltime studies or return to other missions, while their children remain in our care'.[28]

27.   IISH, BRO 833/10 Fol, ANC Progress Report, 7.
28.   *Ibid.*

While the SOFAMCO report highlights positive responses to providing care for pregnant womyn and children, other documents voice concerns about the 'problem' of unplanned pregnancies and the availability (or otherwise) of contraceptives. In the official correspondence unplanned pregnancies are, perhaps understandably in the context of exile communities, an armed struggle, and inadequate maternal and childcare facilities, often raised as a point of concern.

A 1987 report from the Health Secretariat about a meeting with the NEC regarding the state of the Health Department, noted that: '[T]here is a need to bring under control the growing number of unplanned pregnancies in the settlements. Since August 1986, there were 5 unplanned pregnancies in the settlements'.[29] That the NEC would raise the issue of unplanned pregnancies shows that it was of concern at the highest level of the organisation.

Contraceptives and unplanned pregnancies also featured as topics of discussion in all the RHT reports.[30] Thus, in 1987, Dr Bob Mayekiso, the Secretary of the Angolan RHT, noted, 'we must prevent these unplanned pregnancies in the army' and that there was 'an urgent need for a contraceptive programme in the region'.[31] A month later, in response to letters received from the Health Secretariat, Mayekiso noted:

> We agree with the need to set up an efficient contraceptive service for our women comrades in the region and that the loop is preferred to the pill. We are awaiting the minutes of your meeting with the Women's Secretariat. We will try to give at least two weeks' notice to the Women's Secretariat of any women comrades who are pregnant and to be transferred to Mazimbu.[32]

Mayekiso's tone is not condemnatory of those who fall pregnant, but it is clear that the focus on contraceptives to prevent pregnancies and on assisting womyn who are pregnant is the responsibility of the womyn concerned and organisationally directly linked to the Women's Secretariat.

The concern about unplanned pregnancies in Angola was reinforced in the formal regional report for 1987, which noted that there were 'a high number of *unplanned pregnancies* in the region' and observed that the supply of contraceptives needed to improve 'soon' and that a health education programme 'must get off the ground'. It also noted that

29. UFH-AA, ALM, p2a, 41, 69, ANC Department of Health – Report on the Meeting of the NEC on the State of Organisation of the Department, Health Secretariat, 19 February 1987.
30. These topics continue to appear in regional health reports for East Africa until 1990 and appear sporadically in the other RHT reports until 1990. I did not always find complete sequences of RHT reports in the archive, but subsequent discussions indicated that they may be found in Health Department (rather than regional) files, so future researchers may wish to revisit this conclusion.
31. UFH-AA, ALM p2ad, 6, 6, correspondence, Bob Mayekiso, Angola RHT to The Secretary, ANC Department of Health, Lusaka, 21 January 1987.
32. UFH-AA, ALM p2ad, 6, 6, correspondence, Bob Mayekiso, Angola RHT to Winnie Nkobi, ANC Health Secretariat, 25 February 1987. While additional corroborating evidence is needed, my reading of the preference for IUDs rather than contraceptive pills is that IUDs were more 'practical' in that, although they required medical intervention for insertion or removal, once successfully inserted they would last for several years. By contrast, the logistics and cost of continually sourcing and distributing contraceptive pills would have been more arduous and efficacy would have been influenced by the ability to ensure continuous supplies of contraceptives.

the region had agreed that 'the decision to proceed with a *social abortion* must be left to the woman herself – she should not be pressurised either way'.[33]

In contrast to the Angolan report, East Africa recorded a good supply of contraception and offered to come to Angola's aid. The East African RHT agreed that 'in general *all* women of reproductive age should be offered contraceptive measures' and '[C]ondoms should be generally promoted as a contraceptive measure'.[34] The Zambian RHT report also referred to condoms and pregnancies and noted that:

> To avoid the problem of pregnancies in Zambian women we need to carry out health education, provide contraceptives (including condoms) to our comrades and their Zambian partners. The children in these circumstances must be supported by the organisation. AIDS, STD and contraceptive preventive functions of condoms should be emphasised in our health education programmes.[35]

In these statements, pregnancies are identified as unwanted and a 'problem' – although it is unclear if this is only for the movement's goals, the womyn and men who may not have wanted children, the children born from these relationships, or the health care workers who had to provide support for the parents and children. What these records do reveal is that programmes and decisions relating to pregnancies and parenting were gendered, as were the ideas about who had primary responsibility for preventing pregnancies.

The importance placed on addressing pregnancies through all levels of the organisation reveal two rather obvious points; firstly, vaginally receptive (hetero)sex between fertile people was occurring without contraception and resulting in conception and childbirth. The undeniable evidence of unprotected sex means that sexual practices amongst some members in exile provided opportunities for HIV infection and MTCT.

Secondly, as the recommendations made by the Department of Education and Culture as well as the structure of the programme at SOMAFCO show, the models of childcare and early childhood education were centred on biological mothers or other womyn as primary carers, either out of practical considerations or out of gendered notions of childcare being the sole responsibility of womyn. The roles or expectations of men as fathers, partners, carers or progenitors are invisible and the 'seriousness and complexity of child upbringing' does not appear to be seen as equally relevant to the men who 'fathered' the children, as it was to the womyn who 'mothered' them.

The records also reveal more complex factors about pregnancies mediated by gender but also by physical location and association with the ANC. The responsibilities for childcare are exclusively linked to womyn and the responsibility for preventing pregnancies are primarily linked to womyn, but the ability to take responsibility could be affected by the region a person was based in. The availability of, or access too, contraceptives differed

33. UFH-AA, ALM p2a, 42, 89, 'Reorganising for a Healthier Revolutionary Movement', Report of ANC Health Department Seminar, 1987, pp. 5 and 9, emphasis in the original. The issue of 'social abortions' was also raised in the East Africa report which noted that Tanzanian law prohibited social abortions (p. 5). 'Social abortion' refers to the use of prostaglandin agents, usually in the form of pills, to induce a termination. Terminations requiring procedures performed by health care workers have been referred to as 'surgical', 'medical' or 'clinical' abortions depending on the procedures used.
34. *Ibid.*
35. UFH-AA, ALM p2a, 42, 89, 'Reorganising for a Healthier Revolutionary Movement', Report..., 7.

from region to region. Similarly, the ability to make a choice about terminating a pregnancy would have depended on the legal status of terminations in each region and, in those regions where they were available, being able to access appropriate clinics and trained health care staff.[36]

While the sources reveal little about the womyn who became pregnant, what is evident is that location and age markers were used to categorise some of the womyn. The use of the term 'young mothers' for example indicates an age-related or possibly generational understanding of the womyn who were pregnant without indicating how 'young' one had to be to be defined as a 'young mother' rather than 'a mother'.[37] While the regional report from Zambia indicates that it was not only womyn MK soldiers or ANC members who were conceiving children, but also 'Zambian women'.

The reference in the Zambia RHT report to 'our comrades and their Zambian partners' suggests that in this region male ANC members were involved in sexual relationships with Zambian womyn. The records do not however provide insight into the 'nationality' of female ANC member's sexual partners in this or any other regions. The concerns about AIDS, STIs, pregnancies and managing the (sexual) relationships between ANC members and 'local' Zambian communities does however reveal the links between comrades and host populations through intimate relationships, parenthood, familial obligations, and sexual health and ill-health concerns. What is also interesting about the Zambia RHT is that male ANC members in the region are particularly targeted to receive condoms, whereas in most other sources the primary focus is on providing womyn with contraceptives.

The focus on providing womyn with contraceptives and the commentary on the availability of terminations of pregnancy, can be read as a deliberate gender strategy by the ANC to acknowledge the bodily integrity of womyn and empower womyn to take control of their bodies and reproductive choices. The obvious absence in the discussion however, is the responsibility inherent in the male body for reproductive choices and in male partners respecting the bodily integrity of their heterosexual womyn partners.

36. In reality, access to legal terminations of pregnancy was complicated and womyn were seldom allowed to request terminations. The archive does not always specify the legal status of terminations in each region, although there is reference to 'social abortions' being forbidden under Tanzanian law (see UFH-AA, ALM p2a, 42, 89, 'Reorganising for a Healthier Revolutionary Movement', 5). However a report by the United Nations Population Division, Department of Economic and Social Affairs entitled *Abortion Policies: A Global Review* published in 2002 provides an overview of abortion policies by country and includes some historical context on abortion laws. The report indicates that Angola, Tanzania and Zimbabwe had (and still have) conservative abortion laws, while abortion laws have been 'more liberal' in the United Kingdom and Zambia. While the ANC reports support womyn comrades' right to choose whether or not to terminate a pregnancy, and womyn comrades were having terminations, the ability to actually obtain a termination may have made the discussions a moot point. For individual country profiles see *Abortion Policies: A Global Review* available on the United Nations website at http://www.un.org/esa/population/publications/abortion/, accessed October 2011.

37. Some insight into how 'young' young mothers may have been is provided in handwritten notes documenting the main points raised in RHT report backs at a meeting in 1987. Referring to the East Africa report back in relation to contraceptives, the notes indicate that in the East Africa region 'women of the reproductive age group are generally given (contraceptives), and actually it has been specifically decided to be given after even young 13/14 year olds fell pregnant'. See UFH-AA, ALM p2a, 42, 103, Notes of RHT Reports, 10 October 1987, n.p.

The discussions about contraception and pregnancy might indicate the influence of feminist and human rights discourses in the movement at this time. However, as Meintjies and Hassim have shown, the fight to acknowledge womyn's roles and rights within the organisation, and the gendered nature of their experiences in exile, were complex, so additional research would be needed to ascertain if this was the case. It is also possible that ideas of appropriate interactions and bodily integrity were influenced by other cultural, religious, political, or spiritual ideologies.

In exploring pregnancy as one feature of the sexual landscape of exile communities it is evident that there were particularly gendered understandings of, and engagements with, notions of responsibilities for the reproductive results of sexual activity (children).[38] There is also evidence that male involvement in sexual practices and relationships did not come with the same sets of responsibilities as it did for womyn. While the physical results of womyn's sexual practice in terms of pregnancy often required the ANC to address the consequences of those sexual practices directly, there is little evidence to suggest that men's sexual practices were similarly addressed.

STIs and the advent of AIDS

The pamphlet, video and poster are all AIDS education materials and they are all meant to transmit information about this particular subject of sexual (ill)health to their respective audiences. It is that respective audience too, that the media are meant to reflect (and sometimes challenge) in terms of sexual practices and behaviours. The pamphlet represents soldiers in the armed struggle, the video was clearly scripted to present characters and situations that comrades in exile could identify with (as opposed to what generic, imported AIDS education videos would have presented), and the poster recalled a sense of belonging to a community struggling for change. So what do the 'real-life' archives reveal about STIs and AIDS in an exile context?

STIs, and concerns about how to prevent them, featured frequently in health documents from all levels of the movement and from international supporters who worked with the movement. By the mid-1980s, general discussions about STIs began to specifically identify AIDS and the HI virus associated with it. At the 3rd ANC Health Council in July 1986, for example, a report from the Health Secretariat provided an overview of the achievements,

---

38. A project proposal for a 'Contraceptive Programme for the ANC' noted that there was an increase in the number of young people coming into exile and that 'unplanned pregnancies in a young refugee population [could] have potentially serious health and social implications, especially for the younger members of the community'. As such the ANC sought contraceptives in order 'to provide a regular and suitable supply of contraceptives to both women and men in the refugee settlements'. In terms of the actual types and amount of contraceptives required, the proposal asked for 35,000 condoms and 7,000 packets of oral contraceptives to be supplied annually, and 1,050 IUDs to be supplied every two to three years. It is unclear how many condoms would be distributed per person, but the oral contraceptives would be sufficient to supply 538 womyn a year, with another 1,050 womyn being fitted with IUDs. Based on these figures 1,588 womyn would receive contraceptives. There is no indication of whether the proposal was successful or whether the programme was implemented. See UFH-AA, ALM, p2a, 41, 63, African National Congress, Contraceptive Programme for ANC, August 1987.

failures and concerns of the Health Secretariat between 1983 and 1986.[39] In a section of this report on disease prevalence, malaria was identified as the primary disease concern but the report went on to note that 'sexually transmitted diseases, others complicating [sic] in pelvic infections and infertility continue to pose a big problem also. Lately there have been reported cases of AIDS'.[40] Also presented to the Health Council was a paper by Dr H. Macberry that identified areas of concern in connection with the transmission of STIs generally, and provides insights into factors that would have facilitated the spread of HIV specifically at this time.[41]

Macberry's overview of treatment and prevention strategies relating to STIs included the observation that social stigma and shame about STIs was prevalent and prevented comrades from seeking treatment. This in turn resulted in greater opportunities for complications and, because of the frequency of STIs, 'constitute[d] a very serious public health problem'.[42] The paper reported a rise in gonorrhoea in some of the ANC 'establishments' and noted the importance of tracing sexual contacts as a means of preventing new infections, or diagnosing and treating new cases. Rather than apportioning blame or accusing any particular settlement or group of people for transmitting gonorrhoea, the paper practically addressed an issue that was presented as a shared 'public health concern' for all ANC comrades.[43]

The paper noted that for each index case presenting for treatment there were usually two more people affected, but observed that

> it is usually more complicated than this, so that by the time the index patient has sought medical care he or she may have had intercourse with a further individual. Mark you the ratio of male to female in some of our establishments is 15:1 or even 20.[44]

The specific reference to sex ratios in settlements opens up a number of areas of speculation. Taken in conjunction with the statement about the more 'complicated nature' of infection rates it could indicate that, for 'heterosexual intercourse', womyn had a large pool of men to choose from as monogamous partners; that sexually active heterosexual womyn would have been 'in high-demand' and, depending on the sexual pressures and inequalities prevalent at the time, could have chosen or been coerced or forced into having numerous male partners. It could also indicate that sexually active men may have been engaging in sexual relationships (where possible) with non-ANC womyn[45] or there may have been male 'homosexual' or male-to-male sexual activity.

39. The report on the work done by the Health Secretariat was presented to the meeting by Peter Mfelang, then Secretary for Health of the ANC (SA).
40. UFH-AA, ALM 127, 236, Draft Health Secretariat Report to the 3rd Health Council Meeting, 29 July 1986, 4.
41. H. Macberry, 'The Spread of Communicable Diseases Amongst Our Communities in Exile, in Particular TB and STDs', UFH-AA, ALM 127, 236, Paper to the 3rd Health Council Meeting, 29 July 1986.
42. Ibid.
43. This is in stark contrast to the hegemonic narratives of AIDS evident in, for example, the medical community in South Africa, or in official political discourse. See Tsampiras, 'Politics, Polemics and Practice'.
44. Ibid.
45. In other words womyn resident in the area or surrounding area but not necessarily members of the ANC.

In addressing STIs, the paper's tone is frank but not condemnatory and reflects more honestly the complexity of sexual activity. Similarly the processes identified for case management, treatment, prevention of re-infection, and control of new infections was in line with international protocols and still forms the basis of more contemporary STI management.[46] The paper also identified reasons why STI management was difficult.

Apart from the aforementioned feelings of shame preventing people from coming forward for diagnosis, the paper observed that lack of knowledge was a problem and that 'despite sexual freedom there [was] still a great (deal) of ignorance and misunderstanding of the possible health sequelae' of STIs.[47] The difficulty of ensuring patients followed lifestyle changes (such as refraining from sexual intercourse or drinking) while undergoing treatment is commented on, as is male opposition to safer sex options like condom use. The paper notes: 'preventive measures such as the use of condoms etc. as partial barriers to infection are advised (although we do get a bit of resistance from the male comrades – because according to them there is no proper contact)....'.[48] Speculating on an effective way forward, the paper notes:

> In the end, successful control of this group of infectious diseases will depend as much on advances in the clinical field as on an increased sense of responsibility amongst our community ... There is no complacency and there can be no truce with ... STDs.[49]

The belief that education and knowledge would provide the foundation of STI transmission prevention echoes much of the early thinking about HIV programmes. Similarly, references to individual responsibility remained a consistent aspect of AIDS prevention programmes and were reflected in similar language and sentiments in both the pamphlet and the video. Both these assumptions appeared to assume that agency and choice were equitably accessible to all members of a 'community' and not influenced by gender, sexual orientation, class (or economic means) or 'race'. They also assume a particularly empowered position from which responsibility for sexual health and practice can be taken that does not always reflect the realities of how sexual relations are constituted. The role of a particular type of male sexuality, or at least the type of sex practices that certain men considered appropriate (flesh-on-flesh, unprotected, penetrative sex), in STI transmission was mentioned, but unfortunately not fully explored or engaged with.

The aforementioned 1987 report from the Health Secretariat regarding a meeting with the NEC about the Health Department, that had included points about unplanned pregnancies and contraceptives, noted 'the rate of incidence of affected comrades with AIDS in our communities is alarming'.[50] The report indicated that the NEC had tasked the

---

46. See for example *The Public Health Approach to STD Control*, UNAIDS Technical Update, May 1998, athttp://whqlibdoc.who.int/unaids/1998/a62393_eng.pdf and UNAIDS; *Sexually Transmitted Diseases: Policies and Principles for Prevention and Care*, UNAIDS Best Practice Collection, 1999, World Health Organisation (WHO) website http://whqlibdoc.who.int/unaids/1997/UNAIDS_97.6.pdf , accessed 18 May 2010.

47. Macberry, 'The Spread of Communicable Diseases', 1.

48. *Ibid.*, 2.

49. *Ibid.*, 2–3.

50. UFH-AA, ALM, p2a, 41, 69, ANC Department of Health – Report on the Meeting of the NEC on the State of Organisation of the Department, Health Secretariat, 19 February 1987.

Health Secretariat with 'screening our communities in exile, carrying out a massive education campaign [and] discussing the future of identified cases'.[51] The sequential but separate engagements in this report with two of the possible results of unprotected sex – children and STIs – reminds us of the complexities of the sexual landscapes that people inhabited. It also reminds us that contraceptives, pregnancies, and STIs cannot be neatly disaggregated into separate areas of intellectual concern, but need to be viewed as forming connected parts of the sexual landscape.

A report by J. Hippe and A. Pedersen of the Norwegian Trade Union Research Centre, undertaken for the ANC to assist in health planning and delivery, also provided an overview of the situation in regard to STIs by 1987.[52] The report focused on the Angolan, East African and Zambian RHTs noting that they were in the 'three most important regions' and observed that 'there are severe problems of malaria and sexually transferred diseases in all the regions'.[53]

For the Angolan region the report indicated that the 'incidence of sexually transmitted diseases is reported to be alarmingly high' and, while gonorrhoea was the main problem, 'the risk of spreading the HIV-virus [added] a further dimension to the need for prevention of venereal diseases'.[54] The health team indicated 'a general lack of contraceptives in the settlements' and noted that although 'some education material on AIDS [had] been circulated in the region' there had been 'no systematic effort to spread information on the disease'.[55]

When discussing the situation in Zambia, the report noted that although the ANC HQ was in Lusaka and Lusaka therefore played a central role as a transit area for new ANC exiles, there were no fully developed settlements in Zambia. Instead, the permanent ANC community in Zambia lived in and around Lusaka, unlike other ANC exile communities that were relatively isolated from host communities. The situation in Zambia thus allowed for 'deeper integration' into Zambian society, which Hippe and Pedersen cautioned could influence the rate of HIV infections. They noted that:

> Integration does, however, increase the risk of large scale spreading of the HIV virus [sic] to the ANC members. It is estimated that 40% of the educated elite in Zambia is infected by the HIV virus. A random test among blood donors in Lusaka showed that 30% of the males in the sexually active age group carried the virus.[56]

Referring to the disease patterns identified in the Zambian region they continued:

> We don't know if cases of AIDS or HIV positive persons in the ANC population have been registered. The very high incidence of gonorrhoea and other venereal diseases indicates that the conditions for also spreading the HIV virus [sic] among the membership could be alarmingly

51. UFH-AA, ALM, p2a, 41, 69, ANC Department of Health – Report on the Meeting of the NEC on the State of Organisation of the Department, Health Secretariat, 19 February 1987.
52. J.M. Hippe. and A.W. Pedersen, *Health Care in an Exile Community – Report on health planning in the ANC*, The Norwegian Trade Union Research Centre, 1987.
53. *Ibid.,* 4.
54. *Ibid.,* 52.
55. Hippe and Pedersen, *Health Care in an Exile Community*, 52.
56. *Ibid.,* 69.

favourable. The prevalence of the virus among the local population is so high that AIDS must be regarded a very serious threat to the ANC-community. According to members of the regional health team there have been negotiations with the local authorities to establish an AIDS screening program for the exiled community. [57]

This analysis shows the intimate relationship between the health status of host communities and the ANC exile communities, and speaks too of the Zambian authorities' engagement with, and recognition of, the need for epidemiological information and formalised responses to HIV and AIDS. It was also in Zambia that specific emphasis had been placed on providing contraceptives to ANC members and their partners. Exile communities 'stepped-into' and were part of the disease and health patterns of the communities they lived in, especially in situations where integration, intimacy, and mobility was easier.

The information provided about AIDS and the attention it received in regional health team reports again varied. The Annual Regional Health Report from East Africa (covering the period January 1986 to March 1987) for example listed malaria, gastrointestinal disorders and respiratory infections as the major problematic diseases. In terms of AIDS, it mentioned only that '[T]here is a high demand for devices for contraception – particularly condoms as this is … [a] … safety measure against the spread of AIDS'.[58] The report notes that STDs 'are rare among the South African community in the region'[59] and later noted that the arrival of a gynaecologist had 'relieved the community of a great gynaecological burden, particularly among the younger lady comrades' and that the new doctor was 'working on a sex education course and family planning in Somafco and the rest of the community'.[60]

The comment about STDs being rare among 'the South African community' stands counter to the arguments made at the National Health Conference and seems to suggest that STIs were less rare among the 'non-South African' (i.e. local Tanzanian) community. This, read in conjunction with the sex education and family planning priorities identified by the new gynaecologist, would suggest a complex set of sexual health relations and needs being met by health care workers. It also reinforces the intimate relationship between the sexual health of 'South Africans' and 'non-South Africans' or exile and host communities living together. The use of the term 'South African community' is problematic as it removes any differences relating to length of time in the region, length of time to get to the region, and original places of origin within South Africa. All these factors would have influenced people's health status and their impact on the health of their host communities.

The East Africa report included a section on health issues raised at the National Youth Conference (NYC) and observed that 'the Youth' were concerned that 'ANC health workers should meet the challenge posed by the struggle'.[61] The East Africa RHT 'noted with concern that AIDS was not discussed at all at the NYC' and agreed 'to use Youth

---

57. *Ibid.,* 70.
58. UFH-AA, ALM, p2a, 41, 64, Annual Regional Health Report East Africa from 1 January 1986 to 27 March 1987, p.2a.
59. *Ibid.,* 2c.
60. *Ibid.,* 3.
61. UFH-AA, ALM p2a, 42, 89, 'Reorganising for a Healthier Revolutionary Movement', Report, 5.

structures to disseminate AIDS educational material'.[62] These statements reveal that the concerns of the 'younger' ANC comrades represented by the Youth League were focussed primarily on meeting health demands more obviously linked to the struggle, such as mental health problems because of torture and detentions, and those perhaps more visible and with more immediate affects than AIDS, such as gunshot wounds. By contrast, the 'older' members of the RHT were concerned about the lack of attention given to AIDS by 'the Youth', indicating a number of possibilities. The RHT members may have been seeing the effects of AIDS first-hand or were just more aware of the potential problems posed by the pandemic, or the RHT members were particularly concerned about the sexual health of younger comrades either because younger comrades were dying of AIDS or because of the ongoing concerns with unplanned pregnancies and STIs amongst a younger sector of the exile community. Finding sufficient personal files or medical records in the archives to be able to undertake a 'generational' analysis of illnesses or health concerns would prove difficult, but this certainly opens an interesting avenue for further research.

The health report from Zambia for July to September 1987 reported that 1,274 cases had been treated at the ANC clinic, 76 of which were STDs (71 males and 5 females). The report notes that five of the STD cases were 'referred to UTH [University Teaching Hospital] for HIV' but 'there had been no follow up as yet'.[63] UTH was presumably able to test for HIV antibodies and would have been better equipped than the clinic to provide pain relief or other medication to alleviate opportunistic infections. The details of Joe Ethwell's case provides one of the most detailed accounts of the experience of a comrade with AIDS and speaks to the complexity of decision making by sexually active people. The report notes:

> *Joe Ethwell*: Died at the UTH on the 5th October 1987. Cde Joe was 23 yrs old and he first attended our clinic on 2/6/87, and diagnosis was STD. According to his case notes he stated that he had the same problem in 1985. Anti-biotics were administered and condoms were given. The patient never reported back for review.
>
> He then reappeared on 28/7/87 with multiple body abscesses – for which he was treated with Ampiciliin caps. Again he didn't come for review. The patient reappeared on the 11/8/87, c/o chest pain on breathing, rashes all over the body – with a temperature of 37.3 degrees... we reached a diagnosis of 1. Flu; 2. Fungal infection. He was treated and appeared to be responding to treatment.
> On the 22/9/87, the patient reported back with the same occipital headache and a backache – his condition had deteriorated. He was referred to the UTH for admission. At the UTH the patients' condition was deteriorating very fast, he was unable to feed himself or sit up in bed. We were feeding him each time we took food to the hospital.
>
> He passed away in the early hours at 00h01 on Monday 5/10/87. The doctors suspected AIDS? (HIV)[64]

The support of health care workers in providing food and physical support evident in this account reminds us of the individual people behind the general discussions of sexual

---

62. *Ibid.*
63. UFH-AA, ALM, p2a, 42, 89, Zambia Health Report – Period July – August – September, 2.
64. *Ibid.*, 3–4.

practices and general health. The case notes detail the AIDS related illnesses that were already part of the global litany of opportunistic infections, and reveal repeated STIs. They do not reveal what motivated the behaviours of a sexually active young man, explain the complex interplay of emotional, physical and mental factors that shape sexual expression, or give any indication of why he did not complete his treatment regimen or return for a check-up. Ethwell reminds us that between proposals, programmes, and practicalities are, of course, people.

Another rare insights into what was of concern to ANC comrades staffing and using the health care facilities comes from correspondence between Dr Ralph Mgijima, ANC Secretary for Health, and Mirjam Dahlgren of ARO (the Africa Groups of Sweden Recruitment Organization).[65] Dahlgren and Mgijima maintained a regular and friendly correspondence and in one of the letters, Dahlgren provided Mgijima with some informal feedback that echoed concerns about levels of knowledge about STIs that RHT members had raised in other fora and were reflected in dialogue scripted for the video. Dahlgren had sent an ARO member, Gunilla, to facilitate the training of ANC health personnel to run STI workshops. In addition to the necessary official reports Gunilla had also shared her experiences with Dahlgren who, in turn, shared them unofficially with Mgijima. Dahlgren recounted some of Gunilla's major concerns as follows:

> It seems that your health personnel need some more education to be able to start up the information campaigne [sic]. They didn't have sufficient basic knowledge about STDs and the prevention or about pedagogy – how to inform. Also, it seems that many leaders are not aware of the serious situation with the very dangerous complications of the STDs and therefore not motivated enough to start up with information campaigne about the prevention of the STDs. And if the health educators don't feel that the leaders are with them they will never have the courage to start up and the communities will suffer too much with the complications of these diseases.

> ...Gunilla received many inofficial [sic] visits from various people in Tanzania, mostly men, which asked about "when will the campaigne start, we need it very much etc". Gunilla really wanted to assist, but the local representative (who also participated in the workshop in Lusaka) didn't wanted [sic] for various reasons. I didn't say that she didn't have reasons, but I wanted to point out that it seems to be big needs [sic] of information about STDs. People want to know so they may protect themselves from transmission and also from no-planned [sic] and no-wanted [sic] pregnancies.[66]

Dahlgren's mention of the efforts made by comrades to seek out advice and information about STIs, STI prevention and contraception, reinforces RHT observations and concerns around these matters. The reference to the hesitancy of the local representative to engage with the concerns of comrades (justified or otherwise) also reveals the human complexities inevitably inherent in such campaigns and in negotiating complex sexual landscapes.

Realities and representations – a conclusion

As with all history, there are of course, missing, invisible, or unseen people and intimacies in this account, and in the heteronormative documents and official responses. Those who

---

65. ARO was one of the international solidarity organisations that the ANC worked with.
66. *Ibid.,* 2.

planned pregnancies are not easily identifiable, neither are those who maintained sexual health by always using condoms, nor those who took mutual responsibility for contraception to prevent pregnancies, nor those who did not partake in heterosex. The men who wanted to act as primary carers, and the womyn who did not, are also absent. The nature of sexual relationships is not immediately evident and would undoubtedly reflect the normal complexities of sex and intimacy. Similarly, the range and types of sexual practices and performances of sexuality are not obvious and have to be inferred.

The RHTs and the Health Secretariat had already highlighted unplanned pregnancies and sexually transmitted infections as problems for the organisation, and the official documents and responses reveal the importance of employing a gendered analysis to structures within an organisation. In the already complex realm of sex, HIV complicated the issues further. While the physical end results of sexual activity were being highlighted as problematic, there was little engagement with the socio-political and personal ideologies that influenced sexual behaviour. As a result, there was insufficient engagement with the multiple masculinities and femininities – and the complex relational aspects of a multitude of gender dynamics – within the movement to help address HIV transmission. As the pamphlet, video, poster, and official archive remind us, AIDS is intimately linked to sexual practices, and sexual practices are linked to individuals, and individuals are linked to communities, and individuals and communities – in exile or anywhere else – are linked to gender roles and gendered realities, both internally- and externally-constructed.

From the concerns of officials responsible for addressing sexual health, to those raised by health care workers 'on the ground', or revealed by comrades seeking advice, glimpses can be caught of the concerns, practices, and ideas that mediated awareness of sexual health, sexual practices, and sexual performance. What can also be seen is how gender roles mediated many of these aspects of sex in exile. Relying on a gendered analysis of the sexual landscape of an exile community does provide insights into the complex sexual practices and sexual health needs of individuals. It also allows us to identify gendered assumptions at personal and individual levels, and at regional and organisational levels.

Acknowledgements

I would like to acknowledge the Research Office at Rhodes University and the National Research Foundation (NRF) of South Africa for the financial assistance (through internal funding and via the Thuthuka programme, respectively) that allowed me to undertake this research. I would also like to thank Mr Mosoabuli Maamoe, the archivist at the University of Fort Hare, South Africa, and the archivists at the International Institute of Social History (IISH), Amsterdam, for their help and assistance in my quest for sources. A special debt of gratitude to Sandra Swart for her patience, and to Neil Overy for his comments and suggestions. Thanks also to the reviewers for their insightful comments and thought-provoking questions.

Index